CYBERIDENTITIES AT WAR

EASA Series

Published in association with the European Association of Social Anthropologists (EASA)
Series Editor: James G. Carrier, Senior Research Associate, Oxford Brookes University

Social anthropology in Europe is growing, and the variety of work being done is expanding. This series is intended to present the best of the work produced by members of the EASA, both in monographs and in edited collections. The studies in this series describe societies, processes, and institutions around the world and are intended for both scholarly and student readership.

CYBERIDENTITIES AT WAR

THE MOLUCCAN CONFLICT ON THE INTERNET

Birgit Bräuchler

Translated from the German
by Jeremy Gaines

berghahn
NEW YORK · OXFORD
www.berghahnbooks.com

Published in 2013 by
Berghahn Books
www.berghahnbooks.com

English-language edition
©2013 Berghahn Books

German-language edition
©2005 Birgit Bräuchler
Published by transcript Verlag, Bielefeld
Cyberidentities at War: Der Molukkenkonflikt im Internet
By Birgit Bräuchler

Library of Congress Cataloging-in-Publication Data

Bräuchler, Birgit.
[Cyberidentities at war. English]
Cyberidentities at war : the Moluccan conflict on the Internet / Birgit Bräuchler ;
translated from the German by Jeremy Gaines. — English-language ed.
 p. cm. — (EASA series ; v. 20)
 Includes bibliographical references.
 ISBN 978-0-85745-854-4 (hardback : alk. paper) — ISBN 978-0-85745-897-1
(institutional ebook)
 1. Ethnic conflict—Indonesia—Maluku—Computer network resources.
2. Social conflict—Indonesia—Maluku—Computer network resources.
3. Online social networks—Indonesia—Maluku. 4. Ethnology—Indonesia—
Maluku—Computer network resources. 5. Maluku (Indonesia)—Religion—
Computer network resources. I. Title. II. Series: EASA series ; v. 20.
 DS646.67.B73 2013
 959.804'1—dc23

2012032939

British Library Cataloguing in Publication Data

A catalogue record for this book is available from the British Library

Printed in the United States on acid-free paper

This translation was generously funded by the Wenner Gren Foundation.

ISBN: 978-0-85745-854-4 (hardback)
E-ISBN: 978-0-85745-897-1 (e-book)

For my mother

Everyone has the right to freedom of opinion and expression; this right includes freedom to hold opinions without interference and to seek, receive and impart information and ideas through any media and regardless of frontiers

The United Nations' Universal Declaration of Human Rights, Article 19, 10 December 1948

(1) Any propaganda for war shall be prohibited by law. (2) Any advocacy of national, racial or religious hatred that constitutes incitement to discrimination, hostility or violence shall be prohibited by law

The United Nations' International Covenant on Civil and Political Rights, Article 20, 16 December 1966

Contents

List of Illustrations and Tables

Illustrations

Tables

Acknowledgements

Cyberidenties at War is finally available in English! This book is a product of its time, given the rapidly developing Internet technologies and communication modes, but has lost nothing of its relevance, as I explain in the newly added epilogue. The epilogue outlines in which directions the situation in the Moluccas and the theoretical and methodological matters discussed in this book have developed since the German edition of the book went to press in 2005. I would like to thank all those who helped to make this translation project happen, including the European Association of Social Anthropologists (EASA) and the Wenner Gren Foundation, who provided the funds, Berghahn Books, who accepted the book manuscript for publication, and the Asia Research Institute at the National University of Singapore, who provided me the space and time to initiate the project. I am grateful to the people in charge of the EASA series, who led and accompanied the selection, translation and publication process, which extended over more than five years due to various (unfortunate) circumstances and delays: Eleni Papagaroufali, Benoît de L'Estoile and James Carrier. I would also like to thank Marion Berghahn for her interest in the book project and her enthusiasm to get it published and Ann Przyzycki DeVita from Berghahn for her continuous support during the translation and publication process. Thanks Ann, Marion and James for your stamina and support! My thanks also go to various members of the EASA committee who supported this translation project in one way or another: Dorle Dracklé, Shalini Randeria and David Shankland. Several people engaged in new media research provided me with suggestions for further references and feedback on drafts of the epilogue for the English edition of *Cyberidenties at War*. I would like to thank John Postill, Tim Stevens, Jonathan Marshall, Heidi Campbell and Christopher Helland for their valuable input.

I would also like to use this opportunity to again thank all those who helped me to complete this study. My thanks go to my former advisors at the Institute of Social and Cultural Anthropology, Ludwig-Maximilians-University Munich: Prof. Frank Heidemann, Prof. Matthias S. Laubscher and Prof. Kurt Beck. They have accompanied me in this innovative field of research, encouraged me in my work and given me opportunity to present and discuss my theories and results in their colloquiums. The research project was made possible by a scholarship from Ludwig-Maximilians-University in Munich and by the German Academic Exchange Service (DAAD). I am grateful for their financial assistance.

In the Netherlands my thanks go to the Moluks Historisch Museum (MHM) and the Information and Documentation Centre for the Moluccas in Utrecht – in particular Wim Manuhutu and Ron Habiboe – and to Victor Joseph. Not only did they give me access to their archives and up-to-date information; in our numerous conversations I was gradually able to gain a sense of the complexity of the Moluccan conflict. They also provided me with valuable contacts in the Moluccan community in the Netherlands and the Moluccas. I would generally like to thank the entire MHM team, which, during the many hours and days I spent there, always ensured there was a very pleasant and friendly atmosphere. Even if they are not mentioned by name here, I thank all the other people with whom I engaged in discussion, who shared their knowledge and views of the Moluccan conflict with me, whether they were Dutch Moluccans or academics and organizations.

Particular thanks go, of course, to the main characters in this book, the Moluccan cyberactors, even if, at their own request, I am unable to name most of them here. Without them and their Internet presence this project would not have come about. I thank the webmaster of the Forum Komunikasi Ahlus Sunnah wal Jama'ah, who always endeavoured to answer my questions. I thank the Masariku network, its founders and its active members for including me on their list and readily discussing and answering my many questions, online and offline, on the Internet, in Jakarta and in Ambon. They gave me an insight into their work and made additional information and material available. And I thank Kees Böhm, who regularly sent me the newsletter of the Crisis Centre of the Diocese of Ambon. He never tired of addressing my enquiries and his door and ear were always open when I finally arrived in Ambon. I would like to take this opportunity to emphasize that for the most part all these people, in the Netherlands and in the Moluccas, engaged in these activities on top of their actual jobs, so as to provide the outside world with information about the Moluccan conflict and strive for a solution to it, which at times took up a considerable amount of time. They have my utmost respect!

Even though it is not possible for me to name them all here, I am most grateful to all those in Ambon and surroundings who shared their views of, and experiences in, the conflict with me, and those who, in one way or another, helped me. I would also like to thank those friends who, despite the conflict situation, made my stay in the Moluccas so pleasant, first and foremost Om Boy and Tini, who welcomed me in such a loving, friendly way into their home, Merry, Magdalena and Kiev.

In Jakarta I would like to thank my partner institute at Universitas Indonesia, and in particular Yunita T. Winarto and A. Fedyani Saifuddin, the head of the Anthropological Institute. I would also like to thank my friend Faizah Nur and her family, who looked after me so well in Jakarta, and Ziza and Olly (thanks Tiwi, for introducing me to your friends!).

My thanks also go to Dieter Bartels, who kept a critical eye on my project from afar, so to speak, and always helped me with tips and suggestions. I would also like to thank Keebet and Franz von Benda-Beckmann, who always had an open ear for my questions. I thank Karl Bräuchler, Jörg Kern, Klaus Hahne and Dieter Bartels for their efforts in the busy final stage of the German edition of this book.

By no means least of all my hearty thanks go to my parents, Karl and Renate Bräuchler, and to my partner, Jörg Kern, for their untiring confidence in me and my work. They survived good and bad phases during this project, accompanied me through highs and lows, and always encouraged me in my project.

This book is dedicated to my mother, who was unfortunately unable to witness the completion of this work.

List of Abbreviations

ABO	Ambon Berdarah Online (Bloody Ambon Online, website)
AJI	Aliansi Jurnalis Independen (Alliance of Independent Journalists)
AMNM3	Satgas Amar Ma'ruf Nahi Munkar Muslim Maluku (Task Force for the Enforcement of Divine Commandments and Prohibitions among Moluccan Muslims)
APJII	Asosiasi Penyelenggara Jasa Internet Indonesia (Indonesian Internet Service Provider Association)
BANKOM	Bantuan Komunikasi Radio Kemanusiaan (Radio Communication Support for Humanity, Protestant radio station in Ambon)
BBM	Buton, Bugis, Makassar (Muslim migrants on Ambon)
BBS	Bulletin Board System
BIMM	Badan Immarat Muslim Maluku (Association for the Coordination of Muslims in the Moluccas)
CCDA	Crisis Centre of the Diocese of Ambon
CMC	Computer-mediated communication
DDII	Dewan Dakwah Islamiyah Indonesia (Islamic Propagation Council of Indonesia)
FKAWJ	Forum Komunikasi Ahlus Sunnah wal Jama'ah (Communication Forum of the Followers of the Sunnah and the Community of the Prophet)
FKKI	Forum Komunikasi Kristen Indonesia (Communication Forum of Indonesian Christians, ICCF)
FKKM	Forum Komunikasi Kristen Maluku (Communication Forum of Moluccan Christians)

FKM	Front Kedaulatan Maluku (Moluccan Sovereignty Front)
FPI	Front Pembela Islam (Islamic Defenders Front)
FPIM	Front Pembela Islam Maluku (Islamic Defenders Front of the Moluccas)
FPKM	Forum Pembela Keadilan Maluku (Forum of the Defenders of Justice in the Moluccas)
FSUIM	Forum Silaturahmi Umat Islam Maluku (Friendship Forum of the Islamic Community in the Moluccas)
GBI	Gereja Bethel Indonesia (Bethel Church of Indonesia)
GPM	Gereja Protestan Maluku (Protestant Church of the Moluccas)
GPPM	Gerakan Perempuan Peduli Maluku (Movement of Concerned Moluccan Women)
GSM	Gema Suara Muslim (Echo of the Muslim Voice, radio station in Ambon)
HAIN	Help Ambon in Nood (Moluccan organization in the Netherlands)
IAIN	Institut Agama Negeri Islam (State Islamic Institute)
ICC	International Christian Concern
ICCF	Indonesian Christian Communication Forum (Forum Komunikasi Kristen Indonesia, FKKI)
ICG	International Crisis Group
ICMI	Ikatan Cendekiawan Muslim Indonesia (Association of Indonesian Muslim Intellectuals)
IFC	International Friends of Compassion
IHRC	Indonesian Human Rights Committee
IRC	Internet Relay Chat
ISP	Internet service provider
KISDI	Komite Indonesia untuk Solidaritas Dunia Islam (Indonesian Commitee for Solidarity with the Islamic World)
KOPASSUS	Komando Pasukan Khusus (Special Forces Command)
LJAWJ	Laskar Jihad Ahlus Sunnah wal Jama'ah (Jihad Warriors of the Followers of the Sunnah and the Community of the Prophet)
MHI	'Maluku Hari Ini' ('Maluku today', Laskar Jihad news service)
MMC	Maluku Media Centre

MMI	Majelis Mujahidin Indonesia (Indonesian Mujahidin Council)
MML	Masariku mailing list
MOF	Maluku Outreach Foundation (Moluccan organization in the United States)
MSC	Missionaires du Sacré Coeur (Missionaries of the Sacred Heart)
MUD	Multi-User Domain or Multi-User Dungeon
MUI	Majelis Ulama Indonesia (Indonesian Council of Islamic Religious Scholars)
MWN	Maluku Watch Network (Moluccan organization in the United States)
NU	Nahdlatul Ulama (largest Muslim organization in Indonesia)
OCHA	UN Office for the Coordination of Humanitarian Affairs
PCC	Persecuted Christian Concern
PDI	Partai Demokrasi Indonesia (Indonesian Democratic Party)
PDI-P	Partai Demokrasi Indonesia-Perjuangan (Indonesian Democratic Party – Struggle)
PDS	Pemerintah Darurat Sipil (civil state of emergency)
PGI	Persekutuan Gereja Indonesia (Indonesian Association of Protestant Churches)
PPK PGI	Pusat Penanggulangan Krisis Persekutuan Gereja Indonesia (Crisis Management Center of the Indonesian Association of Protestant Churches)
RMS	Republik Maluku Selatan (South Moluccan Republic)
RRI	Radio Republik Indonesia
SAGU	Solidaritas Anak Negeri Maluku (Moluccan Solidarity Foundation)
SARA	Suku, Agama, Ras dan Antargolongan (ethnicity, religion, race and class)
SIL	Summer Institute of Linguistics
SPMM	Suara Perjuangan Muslimin Maluku (Voice of the Moluccan Muslims' Struggle, Laskar Jihad radio station in Ambon)
TAPAK Ambon	Team Advokasi Penyelesaian Kasus Ambon (Advocacy Team for the Resolution of the Ambon Case)

TNI	Tentara Nasional Indonesia (Indonesian Army)
TPG	Tim Pengacara Gereja (Church Lawyers' Team, Ambon)
TPM	Tim Pengacara Muslim (Muslim Lawyers' Team, Ambon)
TVRI	TV Republik Indonesia
UIM	Umat Islam Maluku (Islamic Community of the Moluccas)
UKIM	Universitas Kristen Indonesia Maluku (Christian University of the Moluccas)
Unpatti	Universitas Pattimura (Pattimura University, Ambon)
UNRC	UN Resource Center
VOC	Dutch East India Company
Warnet	*Warung Internet* (Internet kiosk)
WWW	World Wide Web
Yongab	Batalyon Gabungan (United Battalion)

Introduction

News coverage of both the 1991 Gulf War and the 2003 Iraq War represented the zenith of the medialization of conflict. Media presentation decides whether and how conflicts and wars – often fought far away from viewers – are made accessible to a global audience. American journalists were intentionally placed amongst rows of U.S. troops (embedded journalism) during the Iraq War to give the public the feeling they were receiving information directly from the battlefield or that they themselves were eyewitnesses. And yet this was not so very different from the usual approach, the predominantly indirect representation of both combatants and victims of non-Western countries. That is, the people affected rarely spread their own news or produce their own images (Shaw 1998: 237). Traditionally, Western mass media have afforded massive coverage to the wars and conflicts fought in states and territories in which the so-called West takes a particular interest – an interest that evidently stems primarily from the type and quantity of the respective countries' raw material reserves. Conflicts in other regions – for example, in the Moluccas – would scarcely be noticed; for many, they would simply not exist, and even interested parties would only be able to obtain information at great effort were it not for the Internet.

The Internet has heralded a new epoch not just in terms of conflict representation, but also in the way conflicts are waged. As a result, those affected can now themselves put local information directly on a global platform, acquaint a global audience with their perspective on the respective conflict, and use various strategies to extend the conflict into cyberspace, the social space constituted by the Internet. Because this information is firsthand, the perception of the conflict in the outside world and reactions to it are influenced more enduringly by such representations than if the events were represented in the traditional mass media. To date, studies focusing on the topic of conflict and the Internet have largely restricted their scope to so-called cyberwars, generally meaning attacks on computers and websites by means of viruses, mail bombs or hackers (see Arquilla and Ronfeldt 1993; Campen and Dearth 2000). 'Cyberwar', 'cyberterrorism', 'cyberattacks', 'cybervandalism' and 'Web war' have become popular headlines across the international press in the context of conflicting parties' or terrorist groups' instrumentalization of the Internet (see, e.g., BBC World News 1999a; Fischermann 2001; Hashim 2001; Onggo 2001). Here, the technological aspect of the Internet comes to the fore, not cyberspace as a social platform. A detailed anthropological or sociological study on the important topical nexus 'conflict and the Internet' is still yet to be published. Cyberspace as a social sphere in which conflicts can be both presented and waged forms the central tenet of *Cyberidentities at War*, which aspires to fill this research vacuum. Anthropology can make a particularly valuable contribution here, especially with its approaches in conflict and identity research.

All kinds of groups, among them numerous religious groups, utilize the Internet as a means of self-representation. It is interesting that even radical Islamist groups make use of the Internet, given their advocacy of a return to the traditional Islamic society of Medina during the age of the Prophet Mohammed and subsequent opposition to modernity. Jihad is thus being transferred to the online arena, where not just physical attacks are executed on computers, but where the Internet is also used as a vehicle for propaganda, as an effective medium for communication and for the exchange of encrypted messages (see Bölsche 2001; Robbins 2002). The fundamentalist Muslims involved in the Moluccan conflict, the Laskar Jihad, also exploited the Internet's potential as a vehicle for self-representation and propaganda to the full. In this way the Laskar Jihad and their philosophy became known throughout the world, although radical Muslims are just a small minority in Indonesia. This work analyses the Laskar Jihad's cyberpresence in order to create a benchmark for the study of similar kinds of online projects.

The medium's communication characteristics are of paramount importance for the success of such Internet campaigns. What people refer to as 'new media' – amongst which the Internet assumes a prominent position – are distinguished from traditional forms of (mass) media by criteria such as interaction, interconnectedness, multimediality and independence from a fixed physical location.[1] Transmitted messages and presentations can virtually no longer be seen as separate to the medium. McLuhan's (1964, 2001) assessment that 'the medium is the message' is more appropriate now than ever. Never before has one and the same medium offered such diverse channels of communication; never before have people had so much information at their disposal. It is now possible to integrate words, images and sound, video, print media, TV and radio and to combine these with Internet-specific unilateral, bilateral and multilateral modes of communication. Private spheres can be created on the Internet, only accessible to a certain group of people, or conversely, spaces intended for the public to access. The exchange of information is either entirely free or subject to the 'censorship' of a moderator.

A unique and multifaceted communication potential is thus emerging, with the ability to contribute decisively to the formation of identities and to assume a key role in conflict situations. The significance of traditional media in the processes of constructing and mobilizing ethnic identities and for the creation of an ethnic consciousness has already been highlighted a number of times (see, e.g., Goonasekera and Ito 1999; Ginsburg 1995: 265). Yet with the Internet, a medium is now available through which identity projects can be constructed in a far more convincing and appealing manner, with the additional advantage that they have a far wider reach, and, owing to the interactive potential, through which the 'public' can actively participate in the negotiating process of collective identities. Although there is plentiful evidence of the significance of the Internet for social movements and ethnic groups, Internet researchers have to date paid precious little attention to the interesting construction and negotiating processes of collective identities. In Moluccan cyberspace we are dealing with precisely this presentation and construction of collective identities. Here the Internet serves to establish imagined online communities, commensurate with Benedict Anderson's 'imagined communities' (1998) and Arjun Appadurai's 'imagined worlds' (1996).

Since the proliferation of the Internet, we have had to separate ourselves from traditional notions of communities. The principle of locality has been rescinded; interaction, however, is still possible. The Internet can connect people and groups living on opposite sides of the globe, allowing them to form social structures and create new communities or change and extend existing ones, both of which exist in the imagination of the often locally disconnected community members and can be expressed via the Internet (Mitra 1997: 58). This trend – rooted in the nature of the Internet – ultimately represents the continuation of a line that was previously exhibited in anthropology as a result of increasing globalization and migration. In 1991 Arjun Appadurai called for a new form of ethnography to encompass 'the impact of deterritorialization on the imaginative resources of lived, local experiences' and in doing so highlighted the role of imagination in future social life (196). In the age of the Internet, integrating this imagination into the local experience of each individual is of even greater importance.

The Moluccan conflict, which broke out in Eastern Indonesia in January 1999, and its presentation and delivery on the Internet will serve as a case study, making clear the role the Internet can play in a conflict as well as the significance of the construction of collective identities and the development of imagined communities. Originally I did not intend to approach the Moluccan conflict via the Internet, but rather conduct extended field research on location. However, I was forced to abandon this plan, as there were no reliable indications in 1999–2000 that the unbelievable atrocities being carried out in the conflict would end in the near future. A safe trip seemed impossible.[2] Nonetheless, my interest in the conflict on the Moluccan Islands – long praised as a shining example of the harmonious relationship between Christians and Muslims, precisely the groups now fighting – did not wane. The Internet was the only medium providing detailed information on the conflict, supplied not just by Moluccans abroad and aid and human rights organizations worldwide, but also by people and groups on the islands and directly involved in the conflict. After having followed these depictions for a considerable period it soon became clear that not just an exchange of information was taking place, but also that much farther-reaching social processes were playing out and that a broad field for anthropological research was emerging.

More and more websites emerged dedicated to the Moluccan Islands tragedy over the course of the conflict, in line with the typical excess of information provided on the Internet.[3] I had to make a logical selection as to what would form the concrete focus of my research. What I found most interesting was the presentation on the Internet of people, institutions or organizations stationed in Ambon; that is, people directly involved in the conflict who were continually represented on the Web over an extended period of time. Such groups evinced a direct connection between the offline space on the Moluccan Islands and online spheres where the conflict, or rather information on it, was conveyed directly from the battlefield to the wider world. They claimed to provide firsthand information that would subsequently be consumed by an enthusiastic audience on both a national and international level. Furthermore, many other national and international websites, as well as the press as a whole, referred to the contributions of these 'pioneers'; they partly translated them, forwarded them and used them as part of their broader information policy, so that firsthand news played a key role in determining the image of the Moluccan conflict emerging outside the Moluccas themselves.

Presentations of this sort are rare on the Internet, and all the more interesting for precisely that reason. Only three groups were directly involved in the conflict at the same time and all maintained a constant presence on the Web. They are *the* Moluccan cyberactors,[4] even if they did not all originally stem from the Moluccan Islands themselves, and they constituted Moluccan cyberspace. On the one hand, the percentage of the Indonesian population with access to the Internet is still very low, despite significant increases; on the other hand, the Internet seemed to be of paramount importance to the aims of those actors who, in addition, happened to live in a very remote part of Indonesia. This apparent contradiction renders the topic all the more interesting. As the presentations of the Moluccan cyberactors ran along religious lines, differences within the Christian and Islamic blocks were blurred for the audience not directly involved in the local situation. On this stage, dozens, if not hundreds, of small, locally contested points of contention and battles that were largely, but not exclusively, fought between Christians and Muslims became part of a broader single conflict between Islam and Christianity. The Christians were represented by the Catholic Crisis Centre of the Diocese of Ambon (CCDA) and the Protestant Masariku Network, while Muslims were represented by the Communication Forum of the Followers of the Sunnah and the Community of the Prophet (Forum Komunikasi Ahlus Sunnah wal Jama'ah, FKAWJ). The information provided by these three groups was – to a more or less obvious degree – influenced by their respective religious leanings, even if this did not manifest itself in intentionally biased representations in every case.[5] The impression that this was a religious conflict is exacerbated by such online representation.

The question that arises concerns the connection between the Internet, religion and identity in the Moluccan conflict and the significance of the Internet for the conflict as a whole. Over the course of the online projects initiated by Masariku, the CCDA and the FKAWJ, imagined communities developed that defined themselves according to a respective common identity, but that only existed on and through the Internet per se. The depiction and description of these groups are the result of my lengthy observations and interpretations of the respective list discussions or websites. At the same time, I am also concerned with the interpretations of the groups themselves. In order to analyse the identity politics of such online actors, we need to both understand the construction process of online identities and consider the essentialist rationales (Calhoun 1995: 204). In our case, that is the connection between religion and identity. Moreover, the means these groups utilized online, the goals they thus pursued and the relationship between online portrayals and the offline sphere must also be fathomed. The results of this research will offer answers to the question of the significance of the Internet in conflict situations.

Here the Internet serves as a medium for providing news and interpretations that can not only be qualitatively differentiated from those of the Indonesian national media (Hill and Sen 1997), but can also impact on the conflict itself as a result of the strategies implemented by the actors, the scope of the Internet and the consequent influence exerted on a global audience. For the Moluccan cyberactors it was possible via the Internet to circumvent established authorities such as the Indonesian government and national press, which largely ignore local voices (Hill and Sen 2002: 210), and globalize locally driven discourse, knowledge and perspectives. Only via the Internet were the groups behind the Moluccan cyberactors able to reach a wide audience, enabling their local communities to expand and become imagined communities with members worldwide. This represents a fundamental development in the waging of local conflicts, which have thus been suddenly transmitted to the outside world on a massive scale and generate an entirely different conflict audience than would have been possible without the Internet. As a result of the Internet's interactive character, this audience also has the opportunity to participate in the projects, and thus exert at least an indirect influence on the conflict.

Yet my research projects and analyses are not exclusively dedicated to the Internet as a medium and its possibilities, but also its content, that is, the conflict discourse in the online sphere and the lines of argument adopted by cyberactors, which formed a fundamental component of the identity politics they pursued online. I analyse the respective online performance of Moluccan cyberactors, as well as the content they convey and the integration of online projects in an offline context. The results thus aim to offer Internet and conflict researchers without a specific local interest new insights, as well as those with an interest in the events of the Moluccan conflict and the conflict perspectives of the parties involved. In doing so I am not just interested in a causal analysis (much was published on this in the course of the over three-year conflict) or indeed the actual events of the conflict itself, but rather the dynamics of the conflict and the factors that fostered its continuation independent of the original causes.[6] The use of media and the instrumentalization of religion are of great significance here. The local conflict's dynamics were not simply transferred to its depictions on the Internet; instead, the conflict developed a dynamic of its own in cyberspace.

Anthropological Internet research, like the methodological tools that underpin it, is still very much in its infancy.[7] The few approaches that already exist have been adopted here and further developed during the research process. My research demonstrates how anthropological research can be carried out in cyberspace by means of a concrete example, and the sort of contributions anthropological approaches and methods are able to produce in general for Internet research. In contrast to previous research projects focusing on the Internet conducted in the social sciences, my methodological approach is characterized by three points, which can be viewed as attributes of traditional anthropological field research, yet which have been paid little respect in the field of Internet research to date. These three points were taking the research subject's context into account, participant observation and the length of the research.[8] I spent over two years following the projects of the respective cyberactors in the Moluccan conflict as a member of or subscriber to their mailing lists and newsletters, reconstructing preceding periods (before December 2000) with the aid of their online archives. At the time of my research there was no other study that had researched events in a certain social space on the Internet over a similarly long period of time. Only an extended period of research enabled me to follow the list discourse beyond various phases of the conflict and to grasp the dynamics of the lists and the sites themselves, a prerequisite of being able to trace the community and identity creation processes that occur online. This online research was supplemented by participant observation in the Moluccan crisis area. Although the state of affairs had quietened down to some extent by the beginning of my stay, the research conditions were understandably not ideal. However, since the conflict was the subject of my research, these difficult conditions also enabled me to obtain greater insights. The aim of my offline research and a supplementary private email exchange was to grasp the Moluccan cyberactors' offline context, which is just as important to anthropological field research as the subject of the research itself. The aim was not to verify or disprove the course or the events of the conflict depicted online as a result of on-site observations. Instead, I was interested in gaining insights into the sociocultural context and the motives of the groups and individuals who presented the conflict on the Internet, and demonstrating what significance they attached to use of this medium. Though several Internet researchers in the social sciences advocate a contextual approach, they rarely address the sociocultural offline context of Internet users in a concrete manner.

The theoretical basis of my research and a corresponding set of conceptual instruments are developed in Chapter 1. I make both indirect and direct reference to these repeatedly throughout the text. As Internet research represents a relatively new field for anthropology, themes that are of particular interest to my work (social formations and identity on the Internet) are explored in more detail. As a result, the position of the research within existing discourse should become clear. Chapter 2 is concerned specifically with anthropological Internet research, the research tools developed and the work's methodology. Chapter 3 provides an overview of the Moluccan conflict as a background for the Moluccan cyberprojects and explores the correlation between religion, identity and conflict that features so prominently in both the offline and online spheres in question. Chapter 4 offers a brief overview of the Internet in Indonesia and the Moluccan Islands and presents the Masariku mailing list as an online community. The CCDA's and FKAWJ's online projects are described and analysed in Chapters 5 and 6. Online connection to the international community was of particular importance for the CCDA, as was an expansion of jihad into cyberspace for the FKAWJ.

The remaining chapters refer to all three Moluccan cyberprojects. In Chapter 7 the characteristic attributes of the discourses in Moluccan cyberspace are defined. Using key conflict themes, the various structures of cyberactors' textual and visual arguments are depicted. Chapter 8 deals with the implementation of Internet-specific strategies such as flame wars and cross-posting. Moreover, here the difference between communities' self-representation and their perception by others becomes clear, and it is evident that individual projects do not exist in isolation in cyberspace, but rather refer to one another extensively. After previously – with the exception of Chapter 3 – having dealt exclusively with representation and phenomena in the online sphere, Chapter 9 establishes a direct connection with the offline sphere, which always has a presence in the online space. At its core is the offline milieu of the Moluccan cyberactors, their embedding in the local context and their offline activities, as well as their motives and the ideas of individual members vis-à-vis their online mission. Consequently, the close connection and interplay between the online and the offline becomes clear. Chapter 10 provides a summary of Moluccan cyberprojects, addressing the problem of their representativeness and authenticity. The Internet is subsequently described as a factor in the conflict, likewise being able to play a role in other local conflicts in which individual actors make use of its potential. Finally, additional insights for conflict, identity and Internet research are highlighted – and prospects for future research outlined.

English quotations have been transferred directly from the original (including grammatical and spelling errors) in order to maintain their authenticity. This does not affect their intelligibility. I have translated all Indonesian quotations. Version 5.5 of Microsoft Internet Explorer has been used for the screenshots pictured. Page references for cited or paraphrased Internet documents should be understood as a guide, since pagination can differ depending on the browser, editor or printer used to view them. The date references following Internet addresses refer to the day I visited the site, and do not necessarily correspond to the date on which the documents were created. I cannot rule out the possibility that websites, links or passages cited in this work may not exist at the time it goes to press. Those pages may still be available via the Internet archive at http://www.archive.org/.

Notes

1. Patrick Stähler's definition of new media (http://www.business-model-innovation.com/definitionen/neuemedien.htm, 30 July 2002, 13 January 2012).
2. I only know of one anthropologist, Dieter Bartels, who risked visiting the Moluccan Islands in mid-2000 and who had to find refuge when it was raining bullets. I personally visited the Moluccan Islands for two months in early 2002 when the situation had considerably improved.
3. For more on the so-called data smog, see Jordan (1999: 117–27) and Shenk (1997).
4. Cyberactors are people or groups active in the social spaces created on the Internet.
5. This is almost inevitable, especially when the respective groups have no access to information 'from the other side'. In general there can never actually be neutral information in a given conflict, according to Susan L. Carruthers (2000: 17), even if the respective parties claim or at least try to be neutral and impartial, and to reflect this in their reporting.
6. On the (internal) dynamics of violence, see Trutz von Trotha (1997) and Peter Waldmann (1995).
7. For a brief update on anthropological Internet research, see the book's epilogue.
8. Traditionally, anthropological field research is scheduled to last one year, in order to cover the various stages of an annual cycle in the society under observation.

1

Cybertheoretical Foundations

On the one hand, the Internet opens up a plethora of possibilities that, on the other hand, have clear limits. Both elements exert a crucial influence on the virtuality debate, as well as on social formations and identities on the Internet.

The Internet – opportunities and limits

Given the exponentially increasing contingent of Internet users worldwide, the number of studies by sociologists, communication scientists and, to a lesser extent, anthropologists on the formative opportunities presented by this medium and its influence on the coexistence of its users has also risen substantially.[1] In recent years this has resulted in a veritable boom in publishing. Typical of such euphoric publication surges are a great many superficial studies, which appropriate without reflection concepts from other areas of sociocultural research or keywords that appeared with the first social science publications on the topic of the Internet. Furthermore, many of these publications view the Internet's role primarily as that of information provider; many sociological and psychological research projects target the user as an individual and the interplay between the medium and its user's personality and identity structure (see Reid 1991; Turkle 1995). There are numerous studies of the Internet on topics such as globalization, society, identity or the formation of groups and organizations (see Castells 2000, 2001b, 2001c; Chandler 1998; J. van Dijk 1999; H. Miller 1995; Slevin 2000). However, cyberanthropology, which should explore both online phenomena and their offline context, is still in its infancy. In terms of virtual computer games, discussion forums and chat rooms, as well as research projects, for example, on the much-cited Zapatista movement on the Internet, users' cultural environment has barely been taken into account by Internet researchers in the social sciences to date. Stefan Schwara (1999) has criticized the fact that the majority of publications on cyberspace are concerned with economic and technical aspects, while they neglect social and cultural components or construct utopian scenarios that bear no relation to substantive contemporary analysis. So-called new technologies[2] would, however, lead to the fundamental transformation of the structure and meaning of modern society and culture that would require a realignment of academic concepts and theories (Schwara 1999: 260). Aside from descriptions of physical Web-based attacks on computer systems (so-called cyberwars) and verbal flame wars contested via the Internet, there are likewise no in-depth studies on the role the Internet can play in a conflict originally waged offline.

Boom to doom scenarios

Speculations and sociopolitical narratives in the context of the explosive expansion of Internet access as a result of the development of the user-friendly, graphically elaborate World Wide Web (WWW) in the early 1990s ranged from hope-filled visions of a just information society[3] to the nightmare of the dissolution of all value systems and total rejection (Zurawski 2000: 136): the 'boom' to 'doom' scenario (Hamelink 2000: 1). Critical voices feared increasing controls, the strengthening of existing power relationships, a growing concentration of media and power in the hands of just a few oligopolies and the exclusion of disadvantaged people from cultural and political transformation processes (Castells 2001b, 2001c; J. van Dijk 1999: 2, 101; Hamelink 2000: 19, 22; Hartmann 1998: 11; Interrogate the Internet 1996: 127; Kollock and Smith 1999: 4; Kress, Leite-García and Leeuwen 1997: 270; Norris 2000b: 1; Poster 2001: 615; Wellman and Gulia 1999: 168–69; Zurawski 2000: 148). Additionally, unequally divided access to the Internet as a global network for information and communication opened into a global *digital divide* that reared its head both between industrialized and developing nations (*global divide*) as well as within individual nations (*social divide*), as Norris (2000a: 1) notes (see also J. van Dijk 1999: 142; Norris 2000b: 4; Warf and Grimes 1997: 262). NUA data prove that the number of Internet users exploded from 16 million in 1995 to 254 million in January 2000 and 606 million in September 2002, so that around 10 per cent of the world's population were online, compared to around 4 per cent in 2000.[4] Nearly 90 per cent of Internet users are white and paid more than the average, in their early to mid-thirties and resident in the 'developed world' (see Graphics & Visualization & Usability Center 1998; Jordan 1999: 49–55, 2001: 3). The International Telecommunications Union's (ITU) Internet indicator in Geneva provides information on the state of affairs vis-à-vis the Internet in various countries. The statistics for Indonesia and Germany in the years 1999 and 2001 are juxtaposed in Table 1.

According to NUA statistics, in January 2002 the number of Internet users in Indonesia reached 4.4 million (around 2 per cent of the country's entire population), while in February 2002 the corresponding figure for

Table 1. Internet survey – Germany and Indonesia

Country	Population (millions)	Hosts (total)	Hosts (per 10,000 persons)	Users (thousands)	Users (per 10,000 persons)	Est. no. of computers (thousands)	Est. no. of computers per 100 persons
1999[5] Indonesia	approx. 203.0	21,052	1.01	900	43.01	1,900	0.91
Germany	approx. 81.8	1,635,067	199.00	14,400	1,752.60	24,400	29.70
2001[6] Indonesia	approx. 220.0	45,660	2.13	4,000	186.19	2,300	1.07
Germany	approx. 82.4	2,426,202	294.58	30,000	3,642.54	27,640	33.60

Germany was 30 million (around 38 per cent) (http://www.nua.com, 12 November 2002). All of these figures, according to Pipa Norris, should not tempt us to neglect other factors that exert an influence on Internet usage. Norris has devised an 'Internet Engagement Model', which views the implementation of new technologies as a product of individual resources (time, money, computer literacy, language skills, social networks, individual motivation) as well as the structural opportunities of the respective countries (Norris 2000a: 2–3; see also J. van Dijk 1999: 148–52; Elkins 1997: 147). We must also assume that some people consciously reject the Internet (see Hamelink 2000: 89; Warf and Grimes 1997). This part of the equation becomes important in research on the Internet's role and influence in so-called disadvantaged regions, amongst which Indonesia numbers.

Positive voices in the Internet debate emphasize its potential to facilitate equality and mobilize people, which, however, not only promotes democratization, but can also constitute a mouthpiece for 'undesired' minorities (such as, for example, radical political groups) (see, e.g., Hamelink 2000: ix; K. Thompson 2001; Zickmund 1997: 185). According to James Slevin (2000: 9–10, 177), Internet technology enables the individual to participate in events and exert an influence in political decision-making processes that would normally be beyond his or her scope, and thus at the same time ensures that distant events, which would previously not have attracted our attention, can now exert an influence on us. Jan van Dijk (1999) is concerned with a balanced representation of the transformative process of our modern society into a networked society. Like Slevin (2000: 169), van Dijk asks us to come to terms with the ambivalent nature of the Internet:

> The network structure is a dual structure. A combination of scale extension and scale reduction marks all applications of the new media in the economy, politics, culture and personal experience … A dual structure results in several opportunities explained in the previous chapters: centralization and decentralization, central control and local autonomy, unity and fragmentation, socialization and individualization. (J. van Dijk 1999: 221)

Such a dualistic nature does not imply a splitting of society, but rather an expansion and an increase in the complexity of the spectrum of social positions (J. van Dijk 1999: 235). Additionally, the Internet is just as much a local phenomenon as a global network,[7] which contributes to its ambivalence.

Visionaries of our Western societies, which have been conquered by technologies such as the Internet and the accompanying floods of information, talk about the advent of a new epoch – of a 'network society' or 'knowledge age' (see Castells 2001c; J. van Dijk 1999; Progress and Freedom Foundation 1994) – whilst others reference the Internet as 'alter deus' and 'anti-leviathan' (Bredekamp 2001). I would like to distance myself from the visionary models of Manuel Castells (2001c), who propagates the notion of a networked society dominated exclusively by networks (including media communication networks) and the people who have access to them.[8] Nonetheless, it behoves us to reconsider concepts such as community, identity and conflict, especially in the context of the Internet. There is an incredibly large potential for research in this area. The challenge for anthropologists lies in comprehending the qualitative transformation of the aforementioned concepts and in fructifying the corresponding anthropological theories and methods for the nonlocalizable social space that is the Internet, meaning transferring, adapting, expanding and ultimately applying them.

Internet, cyberspace and virtuality

The Internet numbers amongst the so-called new media, characterized by their interactive functionality and participatory character (see J. van Dijk 1999: 11; Eickelman and Anderson 1999a: vii), features that are conspicuously absent in traditional mass media such as television, press and radio. Exceptions are possible, but according to Luhmann (1996: 11), these seem staged and are also treated as such by broadcasters. The Internet is able to pry open this 'operatively closed system' (Luhmann 1996) of traditional mass media. It facilitates unidirectional, bidirectional and, indeed, multidirectional modes of communication. Information and messages posted on the Net are directed at individuals, selected members or to everyone who has access to it. Those communicating can be separated in spatial terms, and the exchange of information takes place simultaneously (synchronous) or staggered in time (asynchronous). For Mark Poster (2001: 613), the Internet is the only technology that imitates the democratic structure of the telephone and yet also supersedes it: 'The shift of a decentralized network of communications makes senders receivers, producers consumers, rulers ruled, upsetting the logic of the understanding of the first media age' (Poster 2001: 618). The Internet constitutes a platform on which both static and moving images, text and sound, can be united in a way never before possible, and can thus cater for several senses at the same time. This has created an entirely new, powerful potential for communication. McLuhan's (1964) famous sentence 'Media are the extension of man' is especially applicable to the Internet, because it helps us, at least partly, to overcome limitations vis-à-vis time, space, information and our own body.⁹ The space constituted by the Internet figures as a horizon of experiences mediated by the media and establishes an expansion or a new level of the already multifaceted reality inhabited by humans, which, however, experiences a qualitative alteration and expansion, in particular with reference to concepts such as identity, locality and community.

The term 'cyberspace' crops up repeatedly over the course of this work. The number of times this concept has been defined is probably commensurate with the number of treatises on the topic of the Internet or other electronic networks.¹⁰ Initially, it was coined in the early 1980s by science fiction writer William Gibson, who used it to describe a new virtual world in the form of a 'consensual hallucination' (1984: 5) experienced by people who live or work in the abstract space constructed by computer networks. In general, the concept is used as a metaphor for the unavailable physical space in electronic communication networks. It is thus becoming possible to relocate deterritorialized and delocalized events and movements, that is, in cyberspace. In this work I would like cyberspace to be understood as the social space constituted by the Internet, meaning the online surroundings where everyone who has Internet access can meet, interact, communicate, form groups and negotiate identities, discuss, talk, exchange information and play – either simultaneously or with a time lag, unidirectionally, bidirectionally or multidirectionally. Websites, chat rooms, news groups, mailing lists, multi-user domains (MUDs) and avatar worlds can be regarded as 'locations' in Internet cyberspace, according to Stegbauer (2001: 140). A broad selection of various modes of communication is available, ranging from websites, mailing lists, news groups, bulletin board systems (BBSs), newsletters and chat forums to MUDs, fantastical role playing, the subject of research by Sherry Turkle (1995), amongst others. Significant modes for this sort of work will be treated in more detail later on. Depending on the form of communication in question, we can differentiate between a private sphere in cyberspace (email, mailing lists with limited access, etc.) and a public sphere (websites, open news groups etc.) (see Piliang 2000: 105; Slevin 2000: 83; Zurawski 2000: 179). The separation between the public and the private is blurred in a corresponding combination (see J. van Dijk 1999: 126; Fernback 1997: 50).

All debates revolving around the connection between the Internet and society, virtual communities and identities are rooted in the significant discussion on the apparent contradiction of a virtuality constituted by the Internet or comparable media, and the reality experienced by people rooted in their locality: the dichotomy between virtuality and reality or virtual and real reality. I am consciously talking about an apparent contra-

diction, as I would like to propound the dissolution of precisely this dichotomy. Social scientists researching the Internet would be well advised
to distance themselves from the concept 'virtual', as it is correspondingly
tainted, or to eliminate its connotations. Indeed, nonexistent worlds initially branded as 'virtual' are simulated in computer games with the aid of
technical means (helmets, suits, glasses, gloves, etc.) directly linked to the
human sensory system (Turkle 1995: 181). Yet such games only cover a
small section of all computer-mediated phenomena, which many people
now unthinkingly place in the 'virtual reality' sphere.

It would be more logical to revert to a concept established as part of a
debate on national identities (B. Anderson 1998) and the worldwide process of globalization (Appadurai 1996), and instead of talking about 'virtual' to refer to the 'imaginary' – which is an integral component of the
'real' human world, but can still differ qualitatively.[11] If the term 'virtual' is
nevertheless used in this work, especially in reference to existing debates,
in no way do I wish to advocate the real-virtual dualism. And like Mike
Sandbothe (1996), I do not wish to connect any normative associations of
any sort to this. The two concepts serve only to enable us to differentiate
between different constructional levels of reality on a descriptive level. It
is far more logical to differentiate between online and offline experiences,
as has Lori Kendall (1999: 61), as an indicator for the respective level of
reality researched, whose relationships to one another are both highly
complex and multifaceted. The term 'real life' ('RL') as an expression of
the offline space should be used in quotation marks, as interaction via the
Internet is just as real as all other forms of interaction (Wellman and Gulia
1999: 168n2).

People often talk enthusiastically of the abolition of temporal and spatial constraints in the context of the Internet, as well as the transcendence
of time and space – of borderless freedom. Castells (2000: 381) refers to
'the timeless landscape of computer networks', a new culture that has resulted from a dissolution of location and the abolition of time (the unification of time, past and future) through the 'space of flows' (informational
paradigm) and 'timeless time'. Critics argue on the one hand that we have
to move away from conventional notions of spatiality, and on the other
that the time-space patterns are most likely mutually dependent in both
the offline and online spheres. Christine Hine fundamentally criticizes the
view of the dissolution of space in so far as it is premised upon too limited
an understanding of our notions of spatiality:

> Spatiality, in a sociological sense, refers to more than physical proximity and
> distance. Spatiality ... becomes a way of thinking through the mutual avail-
> ability and shared coherence of situated practices, interpretations and accounts.
> (Hine 2000: 104)

According to this view, spatiality on the Net is defined less in terms of
distance and more in terms of connections. In contrast to the aforemen-

tioned vision of the transcendence of time and space, it emerges that the Internet has multiple temporal and spatial arrangements (Hine 2000: 106, 114). Rheingold (2000: 51) also advocates the view that a place is cognitive and social, but not geographical.[12]

According to Slevin (2000: 71), the time-space pattern of information and other symbolic content available on the Internet is always in some way an expression of activities of real people or real organizations. Of course, it is undeniable that people living far away from one another can talk to each other simultaneously via the Internet, that people can participate in discussions through asynchronous modes of communication such as mailing lists and news groups pursued on a global basis without the need to adhere to any sort of temporal or spatial guidelines, and that all sorts of information is available around the clock and can be linked almost without restriction, endlessly rearranged and safely stored for posterity.[13] All of this may well entice us to talk about the dissolution of time and space in cyberspace. As I will illustrate using the Moluccan conflict, cyberspace cannot be seen disassociated from the local level, 'real' reality, and thus no disassociation from time and space can occur either. Rather, temporal sequences in cyberspace and in the local context are mutually dependent, and events in the offline sphere that are bound by space and time as well as historical events are reflected in cyberspace. The specific location/space/region remains as a point of reference – at least in real political cases of Internet usage – not to be confused with the aforementioned MUDs. Yet, that does not necessarily mean that territorial borders – such as those of the nation-state, for example – cannot be undermined with the help of the Internet (Poster 2001: 615) and the area of influence and entry decisively extended. As a result of its potentially vast reach, clear statements on the influence individual campaigns, statements, discussion contributions, etc., can exert in cyberspace are practically impossible. To a certain extent, transience is curbed in cyberspace by the capacity for archiving and data storage, which are available in a variety of applications. Under certain circumstances they contribute to the establishment of a cultural memory, which can be of decisive significance to identity projects.

Social formations on the Internet

In previous research into the Internet, the question of whether stable social formations are possible in cyberspace has been much discussed. The debate was decisively influenced by Howard Rheingold, the father of 'virtual communities' (VCs). Published in 1993, his book *The Virtual Community: Homesteading on the Electronic Frontier* is predominantly based on his own experiences as a member of the computer-mediated network The WELL (Whole Earth 'Lectronic Link).[14]

From virtual to personal communities

In terms of the relationship between society and the Internet and the debate on VCs, I would like to differentiate between three positions that
have arisen particularly as a result of the different assessment of the relationship between virtuality and reality: the parallel, simulation and
contextual approaches. The parallel approach assumes that both levels
exist parallel to one another and form respective separate communities.
David Porter (1997) argues that two parallel worlds are developing as a
result of the Internet – virtuality and reality – that exist independently
of each other. He is criticized for ignoring social and cultural context, in
which online information and other symbolic content is produced and
received.[15] Classic examples of such parallel worlds are the MUDs described by Sherry Turkle (1995) and Elizabeth Reid's (1991) Internet relay
chats (IRCs), from which the famous dicta 'Real life [is] just one more
window' and '[I]t is possible to appear to be, quite literally, whoever you
wish' come. Regardless of the backgrounds and individual psychological
approach adopted in these studies, the results are often applied to other
modes of communication. Spanish sociologist Manuel Castells does not
just address the Internet, but electronic networks in general. In his trilogy
on the emergence of the 'network society' (1996, 1997 and 1998), Castells
presents the societal change that accompanies new media and network
technologies.[16] According to Castells, the network society, whose cultural
forms of expression are, in the sociologist's opinion, disassociated from
history and geography, splits from the rest of society, the 'fourth world',
which has no access to the network society (Castells 2000: 368, 2001c:
507). This has led to the emergence of parallel worlds 'whose times cannot
meet' (2001c: 459).

Two theoretical perspectives are subsumed under the second aforementioned position, simulation. The first concerns the virtual level overriding
reality and ultimately remaining, as a simulation of it, the only 'reality',[17]
and the second the fact that in principle communities cannot develop online, and are at the most pseudocommunities.[18]

The contextual approach emphasizes that the virtual level needs to
be considered within its 'real' sociohistorical context at all times. Many
sociologists and anthropologists are advocates of this approach, which
sees the Internet and other networks as part of existing social structures
and disassociate themselves from the notion of a total 'computer revolution' (see, e.g., Hakken 1999; Wilson and Peterson 2002). Networks'
technological infrastructure always influence a society's social structure,
in much the same way as a certain social structure, conversely, also influences design and the use of the technological infrastructure (J. van Dijk
1999: 142). In *The Internet and Society* (2000), sociologist James Slevin
describes how users' local cultural, social and historical context influences
the Internet and vice versa, and therefore decisively shapes their online

experiences and the use and influence of the medium (see also Hamelink 2000; S. G. Jones 1999; Kendall 1999). This approach assumes that media networks constitute social environments, which supplement normal social networks and face-to-face communication, yet do not replace them or even stir such social systems' foundations, as Castells propagates (J. van Dijk 1999: 222–23). Slevin (2000) concludes that virtual and real, that is, online and offline communities, are closely intertwined and cannot be separated from one another. The Internet is, according to Slevin, like other media, an expansion of man (see also J. van Dijk 1999: 190, 208; Marshall 2001: 90). Technology in itself, in Nessim Watson's (1997: 108) view, does not suffice to expunge the differences that people in the offline world have created amongst themselves. In general, only a handful of authors have really systematically considered the transferability of offline concepts such as community, groups or networks in the online sphere; an example is Christian Stegbauer (2001) in his book *Grenzen virtueller Gemeinschaft: Strukturen internetbasierter Kommunikationsforen* (Boundaries of virtual communities: Structures of Internet-based communication fora).

This study can initially be said to ascribe to the contextual approach, but I would like to develop this approach further, highlighting the qualitative change of existing social and cultural forms. Unfortunately Slevin does not go far enough in his book. He presents a plethora of interesting questions on the potential of the Internet in the context of relationship patterns, the activism of organizations, groups and individuals, new forms of solidarity and interactivity between groups that were previously separated by geographical and social factors, as well as the mediation of network-based violence and conflicts (Slevin 2000: 5–6). He offers optimistic answers that both elucidate and continue his approach and fundamental position, yet ultimately provide the reader with no advice on how these conceptions and ideas can be implemented in reality. Advocates of this contextual approach include Daniel Miller and Don Slater (2000). The two anthropologists describe the Internet as an ideal means of cultural expression for the population of Trinidad and Tobago, the subject of their research, which is thus also a component of one, inseparable reality:

> Our presentation should convince you that 'being Trini' is integral to understanding what the Internet is in this particular place … [The Internet] provided a natural platform for enacting, on a global stage, core values and components of Trinidadian identity such as national pride, cosmopolitanism, freedom, entrepreneurialism. (Miller and Slater 2000: 1–2)

For this reason the authors resist the concept of virtuality, since this signifies the constitution of a space separate from normal social life, while in their case the Internet is directly embedded (ibid.: 4–5). In my opinion, however, online spheres do not only constitute a reproduction of offline reality. Both are closely intertwined but can yield new or expanded social formations or identity projects online in the expansion of the offline context. Correspondingly, according to Helen Morton (1999: 243–44), for instance, the Kava Bowl (an online forum created by descendants of the Tonga Islands worldwide) does not represent an entirely new or isolated community. Rather, it is an expansion of the existing Tongan community and is beginning to transform it.

More recent studies have shown that the much-heralded great revolution in everyday communication, and particularly in the social lives of Internet users, has not occurred. Online practices have not initiated any radical changes, but rather embedded themselves within existing practices and everyday power relationships (Wilson and Peterson 2002: 449). Important insights in this direction have been provided by studies in various U.S. and Canadian suburbs and communities conducted by research groups led by Canadian sociologist Barry Wellman.[19] The findings show that the Internet constitutes an expansion of existing communication options and, in contrast to the once-predicted increasing social isolation of Internet surfers (Breslow 1997: 254–55), in some cases even contributes to the intensification of local relationships as well as long-distance relationships, and, additionally, to an increased number of connections based on so-called weak ties. Willingness is increasing to extend contacts beyond social and cultural borders (Wellman and Gulia 1999). A new understanding of communities is crucial here, which, according to Wellman (1999: xiii), must no longer be understood in the sense of neighbouring communities as 'tightly bounded, densely knit groups of broadly based ties', but in the sense of social networks, 'usually loosely bounded, sparsely knit networks of specialized ties'. Particularly on the Internet we often deal with so-called communities of interest or interest groups (see also J. van Dijk 1999: 160; Mizrach 1995; Nelson 1996: 296; Rheingold 2000: 9; Schwara 1999: 271).

Initial enthusiasm was thus short-lived, and people's worst fears allayed. Rheingold's *virtual communities* have been largely demystified. A third phase now needs to follow in which the Internet's potential should be researched in a far more discriminating manner. At the Association of Internet Researchers' (AoIR) third International Internet Conference in October 2002, it was striking that a large majority of all social science–based Internet studies were highly Western-centric (that is, American and European) in terms of both their approach and research subject. Particular importance is attributed to individualism. Interest centred on communities relating to the individual, so-called personal communities (Wellman and Potter 1999), as well as studies and projects on the implementation of Western notions of democracy in the course of increasing interconnection and the accompanying propagated growing influence of the grassroots on political decision-making processes. With the exception of China, which seems to have drawn numerous researchers' attention as a result of its highly comprehensive state regulation of access to the Internet, countries in the non-Western world were hardly considered. Many of the findings of such Western-centric studies cannot be applied to countries and societies more geared towards collectivism or where access to the Internet must be organized in a collective manner owing to insufficient infrastructure and funds. There is a distinct lack of studies on Internet projects catering for a collective from the outset, a communal issue that is not oriented first and foremost to the interests of an individual. Moreover, research projects on the Internet as a mobilizing factor in social movements or in instances of conflict need to be pushed forward. Precisely because it is often the case that cultural, ethnic or religious campaigns for mobilization and community formation seek to network people and groups strewn across the globe, I would like to take this opportunity to present a notion of community, that of 'imagined communities', that is also particularly important for a better understanding of the processes in Moluccan cyberspace, the subject of my research.

Imagined communities

In order to better acquaint ourselves with the concept of communities and social groups on the Internet, we need to distance ourselves from traditional notions of community. The real-virtual dichotomy can also be nullified by an imagination principle promoting the formation of community and identity. Close ties based on locality, neighbourhood, common responsibilities, etc., and forming corresponding communities may well not be a thing of the past, but being present in the same physical space as someone else is no longer a prerequisite for the formation of a group (see Giddens 1991: 2, 146–47; Meyrowitz 1998; Slevin 2000: 93; Watson 1997: 120; Wellman and Gulia 1999: 169–71). New, mediatized locations of presence have developed with the ability to take over this function (WZB – Projektgruppe Kulturraum Internet 1996: 8).

In 1983, Benedict Anderson published his book *Imagined Communities: Reflections on the Origin and Spread of Nationalism* as a contribution to the debate on nationality and identity (the German edition cited throughout this text was published in 1998). In his work Anderson makes clear how, despite a lack of local simultaneity, something approaching a national consciousness can emerge amongst the inhabitants of a nation and indeed through imagination – people's imaginative ability, primarily fed by national print media.[20] Print media are widely dispersed, reaching broad sections of a population, and can thus function as mediators and messengers of national and shared notions, ideas and values.[21] Nations thus become imagined communities. According to Anderson, the concept of synchronicity plays a significant role in the imagination of communities, be they national, religious or otherwise. To substantiate this he provides the example of newspapers as fiction, the practically simultaneous consumption of which evokes an extraordinary mass ceremony (Anderson 1998: 30, 37, 60). This standard is more than met by the Internet, owing to the speed of information exchange and accompanying efficiency of communication it provides. In his *Long-Distance Nationalism,* Anderson (1992) goes a step further, extending his concept of imagined communities to a connection that exists between communities living in the diaspora and their country of origin. In Anderson's view, the concept of nationality could be absolved of its territorial connections through media-supported imagination.

> They can find ways to speak to the relatives on the telephone, communicate by fax, send money by telex, and receive photos and videos, all in the twinkling of an electronic eye. The mediated imagery of 'home' is always with them. (Anderson 1992: 8)

Internet communities are also often composed of conglomerates of users spread widely across the globe. As with national consciousness, in these cases a feeling of community and identity is conveyed and imagined in cyberspace via the media. Yet in contrast to print media, the Internet also offers interactive modes of communication that appeal to the individual's power of imagination in a far more direct and memorable manner. As an identity-forming force, imagination can be of particular significance in times of disorientation, in which many social identities are in a state of crisis. According to Kremser (1999: 283), the survival of both economic networks and territorial powers is now dependant on whether local populations are capable of swiftly acquiring new knowledge and developing a collective imagination. In times of crisis, the symbolic dimension of 'virtual' communities can have far more weight than the material one. They are either purely instrumental or manifest themselves in real political action, as Jan Fernback (1997: 39–41) argues. The Internet can be a community- and identity-promoting factor, particularly in the case of the diasporic communities Anderson speaks of. It provides these people with the opportunity to maintain contact with their home community and the respective local context, as well as potentially even play a role in influencing developments there.[22] Furthermore, online diasporic communities are in a position to function as multipliers and convey the interests of their national or ethnic brothers to a broader public. In general, according to Watson (1997: 124), online communities have an advantage over their purely offline counterparts in terms of the forms and content of their representation in the public sphere.

Stefan Schwara (1999: 263) views Benedict Anderson's imagined communities and Hobsbawm and Ranger's *The Invention of Traditions* (also published in 1983) as evidence that globalization has led to the restoration and, from a certain viewpoint, also to the production of 'homeland', 'community' and 'locality' and not, as many have assumed, to the destruction of the once so secure and collective 'homelands'. Here Schwara refers to Arjun Appadurai, who broached the role of the imagination for the significance of location as a lived experience within a globalized, despatialized world. In this new global order, imagination is simultaneously both a social practice and a central element for all forms of action (Appadurai 1996: 31). Appadurai takes Benedict Anderson's thoughts a step further and talks about imagined worlds, that is, 'the multiple worlds that are constituted by the historically situated imaginations of persons and groups spread around the globe' (ibid.: 33). According to Appadurai, more and more people now live in imaginary worlds, which, as such, could come into conflict with one another (ibid.).[23] The power of imagination is especially crucial for the interconnection and communitization of people in the diaspora with their homeland through the media (ibid.: 4). Ethnic elements, such as language, skin colour or kinship, are undergoing increasing globalization, which is the content of so-called ethnoscapes or 'landscapes of group identity' (ibid.: 49). Yet imagination does not mean that the social structures studied do not have any social reality independent of their images and representations, as Anthony D. Smith (1998: 137–41) argues, criticizing Benedict Anderson's ideas. In Smith's opinion, these ideas undermine the sociological reality of nations and the collective feeling of so many people. Imagination is not commensurate with 'unreal', 'imaginary', or 'nonexistent', but should rather be understood in the sense of 'imagined' – linked to real people, places and events and building upon them. Imagined communities are not unreal, but simply imply that the creation of communities is taking place in a different way or on a different level – yet predominantly with reference to a concrete local level.

Appadurai accords the Internet as a social space just as little attention in his considerations as Benedict Anderson, despite the fact that it plays a crucial role in the processes he describes. Correspondingly, both authors' concepts can be transferred to this sphere. The concept of imagined worlds, in which the territoriality and visuality principle is transcended, must be a central element of all social science–based Internet research. There are already several approaches that point in this direction. David Hakken (1999: 176) underlines the significance of cyberspace imaginations for the development of social groups such as friendships, location-independent communities and spontaneous political networks. Contemporary anthropologists are, in Hakken's view, thoroughly conscious of the extent to which cultures are 'invented' and the significance of the active imagination that accompanies this. Yet Hakken (1999: 227) qualifies his vision of a 'really new way of being', as he is of the opinion that 'cyber-imaginings' have previously been neither sufficiently conscious nor collective. This restriction is primarily a result of the one-sided focus of Hakken's research, which is limited to the computer networks of Western technology-based companies. It is mainly individual identities that play a role in this case. However, we can reach completely different conclusions depending on the context. This study makes it clear – and indeed proves – that collective identities and conscious identity projects assume an important position in cyberspace as representations or as an expansion of offline projects.

According to Fernback (1999), communities should be studied more as communities of meaning and significance than units arrested in terms of territory, which is why communities can indeed also form in cyberspace. Shawn Wilbur (1997: 8) argues that in such cases common qualities, intellectual property, identities or ideas are the outstanding community-forming elements, whereby the roots of community have inevitably drifted into a very abstract field. We must not let ourselves be tempted by seemingly elegant and coherent definitions of community such as, for example, Rheingold's, and impose old concepts upon the new phenomena of decentralized, computer-mediated multitasking networks (Wilbur 1997: 15). Imagination, into which spatiality is projected in the form of collective ideas, goals and memberships, is an equivalent basis for the formation of communities, as Benedict Anderson (1998) and Appadurai (1996) convincingly demonstrate. Communities or groups that form in cyberspace take as their basis the imagination of these concepts, which is fed in various ways.

'Collective imagination' (Jordan 1999: 179) is the basis for people who do not know each other or have not met, yet who have committed themselves to a common concern by formulating a vision that everyone understands and supports. A notion of their own community exists in everyone's head, in Benedict Anderson's case (1998: 14) of the national community, and on the Internet, of the online community. The power of imagination ensures that a group of people views itself as a community, and not as a set of individuals (Jordan 1999: 206). What is important here is that sufficient 'us-related' information is circulated (Foster 1997: 25). Communities should not be differentiated according to their 'realness', but instead by the way in which they are imagined (B. Anderson 1998: 15). Nancy Baym (1998: 40–47), a supporter of the contextual approach, believes that the way in which communities are imagined is influenced by a raft of existing structures, such as external context (country, language, Internet environment, etc.), temporal structures (synchronous or asynchronous, regularity of meetings, working hours of participants, etc.), the system's infrastructure and the group's intentions and characteristics of members (number, makeup, hierarchies, skills). In the course of communicative interaction, participants appropriate and utilize the resources and rules that these structures offer:

> The result is a dynamic set of systemic social meanings that enables participants to imagine themselves as a community. Most significant are the emergence of group-specific forms of expression, identities, relationships, and normative conventions. (Baym 1998: 38)

Both McLaughlin, Osborne and Ellison (1997: 166) and Thiedeke (2000: 47) highlight the significance of the time factor in such an online community-building process, for a Web-based 'telerobotic art installation' and for MUDs and IRCs, respectively. However, in Thiedeke's view (2000: 59–60), the prerequisite for this is that so-called '[i]magoidentities are known, participants regularly appear by way of contributions and reference is also made to posts and identities reciprocally and repeatedly'. In my view, it is not necessary for every participant to disclose their real identity if the imagoidentities are stable, and thus a stable set of orientation parameters is created for all members within which positions and identities are defined. In addition to the abovementioned time factor, the reference to a certain political situation that is of interest to all participants can also play a crucial role in the formation of a group, and thus, under certain circumstances, compensate for a lack of direct online interaction. Baym (1998: 59, 62) has accurately remarked that offline relationships between participants and a consensus in ongoing discourses are community-forming factors. Yet if no corresponding patterns of interaction and meaning are formed and no group-specific community feeling is conveyed, we cannot talk of community (ibid.: 63).

Removing virtuality

Howard Rheingold (2000) argues that the porous nature of the border between the real and the virtual is essential in enabling the transfer of concepts of community to virtual social worlds. In order for a community to function as such, it is necessary for at least a section of its members to also construct a relationship to one another in 'real' life. Nonetheless, Rheingold (2000: 22) regards the contrast between 'real' and 'virtual' as essential: 'Nobody mistakes virtual life for real life, even though it has an emotional reality to many of us.' Udo Thiedeke (2000) also sticks rigidly to this notion. In his research on 'virtual groups', he differentiates these from 'everyday' and 'usual' communicative relationships, as the former create no face-to-face contacts and take place in a 'highly artificial communicative environment' constructed and altered by the communicating participants themselves (ibid.: 24). Ute Hoffmann (1998) talks of the 'artificiality of the conditions of communication'. Some people may wonder which consciously induced communicative situation,[24] be it a university seminar, a company workshop or a gathering of friends at home or the pub, is not constructed and thus artificial. Thiedeke's line of argument for the continuance of the real-virtual dichotomy is therefore incorrect. In this case I agree with Nessim Watson (1997: 129) that the distinction between 'virtual' and 'real' communities is unjustified. 'Virtual' communities would already be pigeonholed as 'unreal' owing to the meaning of the word alone, which promotes the idea that what occurs online may well be *like* a community, but not *really* a community. This would contradict the feeling and perception of many people who participate in online communities.

By accepting the distinction between real and virtual communities, we will blind ourselves to recognizing that these online collectives may be the new form which representative democracy is taking ... This complex process of re-thinking, 'community' may thus be the key to representation in the public sphere. (Watson 1997: 130)

Moreover, as a result of the virtualization of online communities, people often fail to pay enough heed to the fact that such communities are closely linked to local situations and can also have a corresponding influence on them. Appadurai describes this using the example of Indians living both in India and abroad and their role in fundamentalist and moderate movements in their homeland: through the process of deterritorialization and the corresponding webs of financial transactions and religious identifications, the cultural identity of Hindus abroad is closely connected to fundamentalist Hindu politics in their homeland (Appadurai 1998: 14). In analogy to our imagined communities, Appadurai talks of 'virtual neighborhoods':

Virtual neighborhoods, no longer bounded by territory, passports, taxes, elections, and other conventional political diacritics, but by access to both the software and hardware that are required to connect to these large international computer networks ... Information and opinion flow concurrently through these circuits, and while the social morphology of these electronic neighborhoods is hard to classify and their longevity difficult to predict, clearly they are communities of some sort, trading information and building links that affect many areas of life, from philanthropy to marriage. These virtual neighborhoods seem on the face of it to represent just that absence of face-to-face links, spatial contiguity, and multiplex social interaction that the idea of a neighborhood seems centrally to imply. Yet we must not be too quick to oppose highly spatialized neighborhoods to these virtual neighborhoods of international electronic communication. The relationship between these two forms of neighborhood is considerably more complex. In the first instance, these virtual neighborhoods are able to mobilize ideas, opinions, moneys, and social linkages that often directly flow back into lived neighborhoods in the form of currency flows, arms for local nationalisms, and support for various positions in highly localized public spheres. Thus, in the context of destruction of the Babri Masjid in Ayodhya by Hindu extremists on 6 December 1992, there was an intense mobilization of computer, fax, and related electronic networks, which created very rapid loops of debate and information exchange between interested persons in the United States, Canada, England, and various parts of India. These electronic loops have been exploited equally by Indians in the United States standing on both sides of the great debate over fundamentalism and communal harmony in contemporary India. (Appadurai 1996: 195–96)

As Slevin (2000: 107) explains, we are not concerned with demonstrating that people who use the Internet are linked by a mysterious biological force of attraction, but rather by reasons connected with their active participation in certain projects and their intentions in the specific social and historical context in which they find themselves. Whether online or offline, a community is necessary when the communication that takes place within its parameters is viewed as meaningful and important by its members (Poster 2001: 621). Yet Internet communities are not just reproductions or extensions of offline communities; their structures and form of communication can differ substantially as a result of the various modes of communication offered by computer-mediated channels (anonymity, hierarchies, etc.) (see Jordan 1999: 103; Morton 2001b: 68, 2001c: 5; Wellman and Gulia 1999: 186). These new forms of interaction and identity creation in the online sphere need to be researched (Poster 2001: 620).

Watson's and Appadurai's arguments are of crucial relevance for my work's own concerns, which deals with the significance of the Internet presentation of a conflict by groups involved in it. These groups attempt to achieve certain goals with their cyberpresentations, as well as construct a broad network around their core community – closely linked networks of offline relationships, anchored locally both on the Moluccan Islands themselves and on Java. They form communities of interest with members affected by the conflict to varying degrees, where information is exchanged and emotional support is provided, campaigns are invoked and connections to similar cases and contacts are created. Owing to the local separation, since not all members know one another and interaction does not occur between all members of the group, I am concerned with communities imagined by a majority of the members. Without this community feeling, a common goal, reciprocal acceptance, common values and ideas, lent expression through a collective identity, the online contributions and commitment shown by individuals would be pointless.

Identity on the Internet

In the context of online community projects, the Internet becomes a venue for collective identity projects, through which the respective communities define themselves, retain their members, market themselves to prospective new members and project their image to the outside world. Referring to Benedict Anderson's notion (amongst others) of imagined communities, Jan Assmann (1999: 133) categorizes collective identities as social imagination, thus creating the connection between the two concepts.

Identity crises and the politics of representation

Identity crises and multiple identities are key terms in the debate on postmodernity, intended to give pointers on the increasingly deterritorialized character of contemporary cultural identities:

> [They] cannot be defined according to national origin or other types of inherent belonging, but rather by the intricate and extensive web of relationships

that different individuals and groups establish in their daily practice and in their imaginary enactments. (Olalquiaga 2001: 591)

The Internet has evolved into a significant laboratory to enable experimentation with the construction and reconstruction of a decentralized and multiple self that characterizes postmodern life (Turkle 1995: 49, 180), 'a technology that is bringing postmodernism down to earth' (Turkle 1997: 81). Yet Craig Calhoun's study *Critical Social Theory and the Politics of Identity* (1995), as well as Stuart Hall's article 'Our Mongrel Selves' (1992), demonstrate that we cannot start talking of 'multiple' identities only in the context of the Internet, cyberspace or postmodernity. According to Calhoun (1995: xv), the phenomenon of simultaneously inhabiting diverse worlds that can all be unified in one person has repeatedly surfaced throughout human history. However, we can assume that in the age of globalization and growing interconnectedness, the number of identity crises rises. According to Castells (2001c: 3), global flows of capital, power and images and at the same time an uncontrolled and confusing transformation determine the world in which the search for identity, collectively or individually, ascribed or constructed, becomes a fundamental source of social significance. In his view, people searching for identity would primarily form groups based on religious (partly in the form of religious fundamentalism), ethnic or national identities.

> This is why identities are so important, and ultimately, so powerful in this ever-changing power structure – because they build interests, values, and projects, around experience, and refuse to dissolve by establishing a specific connection between nature, history, geography, and culture. Identities anchor power in some areas of the social structure, and build from there their resistance or their offensives in the informational struggle about the cultural codes constructing behavior and, thus new institutions. (Castells 2001b: 360)

Yet Castells (2001c: 3) separates this sphere pertaining to the renaissance of identities from the world of the Internet. He talks of a 'bipolar opposition between the net and the self', a state of structural schizophrenia. Yet it is often precisely the opposite that is the case: both spheres cannot be separated in this way. Instead, they exert an increasing reciprocal influence on each other, which has been proven in numerous examples of ethnic or religious Internet communities and social movements that unify precisely this 'network' and the elements Castells categorizes as primary identity markers (religion, ethnicity or nation). We certainly cannot talk of an 'opposition' when these groups make use of the Internet to present themselves, their identities and their aims. Sociologist and anthropologist Nils Zurawski (2000: 175) also emphasizes in his critique of Castells the possibilities and significance of the Internet for the dynamic relationship between forms of exploration of familiar and unfamiliar identities.

Identity projects are increasingly conducted in the media, and in particular on the Internet. John Thompson's (1995) views on the individual can be applied to group identity projects. Thompson argues that as a result of the increase in media-related experiences, the self has become a symbolic project that actively constructs the individual. In doing so, it utilizes symbolic materials it has at its disposal, which it assembles to create a coherent narrative of its self-identity. Such narratives are, Thompson continues, flexible and can change over the course of time as a result of the addition of new symbols, fresh experiences, etc. (J. Thompson 1995: 210). Communication media enable a representation of this constructed 'reality' (Slevin 2000: 93–94n15). Media, identity and culture are fixed components of the ongoing debate on the politics of representation as well as the question of how offensive images of disadvantaged groups can be analysed and criticized:

> Culture was now conceived as a field of representation, as a producer of meaning that provided negative and positive depictions of gender, class, race, sexuality, religion, and further key constituents of identity. The media were thus seen as potent creators of role models, gender identity, norms, values, and appropriate and inappropriate behavior, positioning audiences to behave in diverging ways. Audiences, however, were eventually able to perceive themselves as active and creative, able to construct meanings and identities out of the materials of their culture. Culture and identity were thus regarded as constructed, as artificial, malleable, and contestable artefacts and not as natural givens. Representations in turn were interpreted not just as replications of the real, reproductions of natural objects, but as constructions of complex technical, narrative, and ideological apparatuses. The emphasis on the politics of representation called attention to media technologies, as well as narrative forms, conventions, and codes. It was determined that formal aspects of media texts, such as framing, editing, or special effects could help construct specific representations and that various technologies produced different products and effects. (Kellner and Durham 2001: 25)

Using the example of the significance of print media for national identity, Benedict Anderson (1998) demonstrated that media can play a crucial role in the construction and presentation of identities. Sofos (1999: 168) emphasizes the role of television in preserving nationalist geography: it enables more people to participate in public rituals, etc., whose local character is thereby transcended.

The characteristics of identity constructions on the Internet

Internet research to date has related primarily to the presentation of individual identities.[25] Far too little attention has hitherto been devoted to collective identity projects, the object of this study. Exceptions are sociological research works on social movements and studies of movements of minorities and people in the diaspora (see, e.g., Diani 2000; Nip 2002; Cisler 1998) that are often highly superficial. However, the findings of individual-oriented studies can provide pointers for collective identity research.

Playing with identities

'You are what you pretend to be' (Turkle 1997: 73), 'you can be whoever you want to be' (Turkle 1995: 184) and 'it is possible to appear to be … whoever you wish' (Reid 1991). In other words, playing with identities is at the centre of the numerous studies on MUDs and IRCs, such as those by Sherry Turkle (1995, 1997) and Elizabeth Reid (1991). Yet given the scope and applicability of the findings of her sociopsychological studies (which in her view also apply to, e.g., BBSs and news groups), Turkle (1997: 72) is too euphoric. Naturally the offer of anonymity and pseudonyms is also acknowledged here and strategically implemented. Nevertheless, users' offline identity and their sociocultural background – which has led them to become involved in current discussions on the Internet – are of far greater importance than in MUDs, with their almost limitless freedom vis-à-vis identity formation and game design. Yet even if the performance of identity is a fixed component of any interaction and this is also strongly promoted on the Internet, an explicit playing with identities is rather a component of the peripheral zones of cyberspace, in particular MUDs and chat groups, where boundaries between online and offline spheres are deliberately fabricated (see also Castells 2001a: 118; Dahlberg 2001; Hine 2000: 120). Even if studies such as Sherry Turkle's suggest a general change in our understanding of (individual) identity processes and content and in the emergence of new forms of social formation, according to David Hakken the design and content of identities in cyberspace are just as culturally anchored as in earlier social design types: 'Individuality is not invented out of nothing; it means distinctive selection from among the conflicting, increasingly incoherent, identity options made available through the often ambiguous options offered by culture' (Hakken 1999: 90). Offline identity and offline context condition, so to speak, online identity (see J. van Dijk 1999; S. G. Jones 1999; Slevin 2000).

Collective identities on the Internet

In cases of political action and collective identity projects, too, the Internet is an ideal tool for creating 'new' identities from a pool of existing materials and symbols, for continually altering them and presenting them to a wide audience. However, with regard to collective identity projects in which, on the one hand, several people participate and, on the other, which seek to address and under certain circumstances integrate a broader public, we have much less freedom in our choice of identity elements than for individual presentations. We are bound by common goals, values and ideas, a certain symbolism, existing notions of friends and enemies, a common history, events in certain offline contexts, etc. Without such points to latch on to, these projects remain without collective acceptance. According to Castells (2001b: 7), the building blocks for identity construction processes come from different areas, 'from history, from geography, from biology, from productive and reproductive institutions, from collective memory and from personal fantasies, from power apparatuses and religious revelations'. Who uses what means and materials in order to design specific formations of identity in cyberspace in the case of the Moluccan conflict will be examined in later chapters. It becomes clear that the people and groups behind these presentations are anchored in a social and cultural context that also lies latent in cyberspace and determines Internet users' actions. The processes in Moluccan cyberspace can only be understood and meaningfully classified in relation to users' offline contexts, which of course does not mean that new phenomena will not arise. For this reason, the study of identity projects with an impact in real political actions is usually far more complex than that of MUDs, whose players are also rooted in offline contexts, but whose effect on the online sphere normally remains limited. In the case of MUDs, people seek to create parallel identities; in that of mailing lists and forums on current topics that directly affect many of their members, people seek to expand identity projects in the offline domain into cyberspace, thereby initiating qualitative change and ultimately integrating cyberspace into users' offline projects, in turn having an impact on them. The expansion or relocation of some project areas into cyberspace provide, according to Ute Hoffmann (1998), space for new kinds of actions and interactions, through which social relationships can be established, shared worlds constructed and alternative identities tried out. This space is available twenty-four hours a day, and information flows have a global reach, operate in real time and never end (Jordan 1999: 168).

One of the few detailed anthropological works on collective identities on the Internet is Nils Zurawski's book *Virtuelle Ethnizität* (2000), in which he describes the relationship between the Internet and ethnicity:

> [Both] constitute ... a resource, with which to organize oneself without a central authority. And ultimately, if ethnicity consists of symbols and narratives, these can be transported via the Internet. Or, in other words, the Internet can act as a medium which offers – on the basis of egalitarian communication – a technological resource for the self-organization of ethnic groups. (Zurawski 2000: 6)

The Internet provides an ideal framework for the decentralized and transnational self-organization of groups (ibid.: 151), which Zurawski demonstrates with reference to the significance of cultural and ethnic identity resources on the Internet (ibid.: 167). The concept of 'virtual ethnicity' targets different levels of the relationship between the Internet and ethnicity, which are of differing complexity 'in terms of the relationship between an "internal world" (Internet, artificial "virtual" worlds) and a "real" external world surrounding it (society, economy, politics, culture)' (ibid.: 168). Zurawski focuses on the mutual influence of ethnicity and globality, that is, local identities and global processes. Accordingly, 'virtual ethnicity' in cyberspace cannot take on any form, but is always historically linked to a previous form of ethnicity, which is located locally (in the cultural and geographical sense) (ibid.: 170). What is especially important here is the representation of ethnic groups and information on the Internet (ibid.: 176). A special issue of *Cultural Survival Quarterly* – 'The Internet and Indigenous Groups' – edited by Steve Cisler (1998) unfortunately provides only very brief examples of how indigenous peoples use the Internet in their constant struggle to preserve their cultures and languages and improve relations with their neighbours. For instance, Albert Gabrial (1998) describes the strengthening or 'reconstruction' of identity and the ethnic community, with the help of the Internet, for expatriate Assyrians. Jean Armour Polly (1998) shows how the Internet is a historical archive of inestimable value for the Oneida Indians. Keola Donaghy (1998) reports on an Internet-based language-learning project for Hawaiian children and adults, which has enabled groups of Hawaiians living abroad to establish contact and form a community. Thus, generally speaking, communication via the Internet can greatly strengthen ethnic groups and their identities (Zurawski 2000: 180; see also Bresler 2001; Elkins 1997; K. Thompson 2001: 32).

The Internet is also suited to constructing networks of local resistance groups fighting oppression, censorship, violence and exploitation as, for instance, in Myanmar, East Timor or Chiapas, and calling certain groups to collective action.[26] Even Castells (2001b: 361) notes the Internet's extensive mobilization potential, be it of environmental activists, feminists, religious fundamentalists, nationalists or 'localists':

> It appears that it is in the realm of symbolic politics, and in the development of issue-oriented mobilization by groups and individuals outside the mainstream political system that new electronic communication may have the most dramatic effects. (ibid.: 352)

Thus the Internet was, for example, an important communications and organizational tool for the Zapatistas in Chiapas, the Chinese Falun Gong sect, the spread of protest against the WTO in Seattle in December 1999, the patriot movement in the United States and the Mayan cultural rights activists in Guatemala (see Castells 2001b: 72–97, 2001c: 7; Jordan 1999: 166; Nelson 1996: 290). Mobilization also took place via the Internet in the East Timor conflict (Hill 2002: 25). The Internet can be used to create a counterpublic sphere (Zurawski 2000: 180–81) or, as Craig Calhoun (1995: 242) would say, an alternative public space. These processes, according to Zurawski (2000: 182), can certainly influence the understanding and perception of ethnicity and lead to a change in the respective cultural discourses. Jon W. Anderson (1996) speaks of a 'creolization', which takes place online when people of the same culture who are living far apart in spatial terms (geographically and socially), such as migrants and 'those who have stayed at home', come together.

Internet-specific trends in identity construction processes

Meanwhile, we have moved on from the much criticized and refuted[27] reduced-social-context-cues model, which social scientists formulated in the 1980s based on their laboratory-like experiments on computer-mediated communication (CMC), and with which they predicted an egalitarian communication and participation on the Internet, in which feelings play no role (see, e.g., Kiesler, Siegel and McGuire 1984; Sproull and Kiesler 1986; Valacich et al. 1993). However, the 'uncertainty factor' in the identity debate remained. Kolko and Reid (1998: 223–26) argue that the Internet is not just an identity-creating medium, but rather can also contribute to a deepening of the identity crisis and a process of dissolution. Personal identities on the Internet are unbinding and static, as they can simply be dissolved or replaced. Thus, they claim, no development of the self can take place, and communities, which moreover are not localizable, and group affiliations remain unbinding and empty, and therefore ineffective. That said, the opposite becomes evident in the analysis of the cyberactors involved in the Moluccan conflict. The groups studied existed on the Internet for several years and during this time constructed stable identities, either by way of membership and various posts to a mailing list or by way of clear presentations on a website. Such identities are in fact also involved in the dynamics of the conflict and adapt to it. Ultimately, however, the Internet remains ambivalent with regard to its ability to create identity. The game of identities, the lack of social context cues, anonymity and a nonbinding character constitute the uncertainty factor still present on the Internet, as here all distinctions perceived as reliable and familiar are lost and familiar features of personal and social identity (at least at first glance) disappear (see Hoffmann 1998; Slevin 2000: 113).

Despite all of this, the Internet is being accorded increasing significance in the identity construction and presentation process. By deliberately withholding or distributing information, identities can be managed and the perception of others influenced (Jaffe et al. 1995). Erickson (1996) therefore sees the predominant function of personal websites and the WWW less in the publication of information and more in the construction of identities. For him, the WWW is a 'social hypertext'. Variations of the verbal language, an electronic 'para-language' (strategic use of uppercase letters, arrangement of characters in so-called emoticons, deliberate misspellings, word choice, writing style and structure, etc.) inform involved affective and socioemotional processes in the online domain (see Jaffe et al. 1995; H. Miller 1995). Studies nowadays tend to term computer-mediated communication a spontaneous and highly emotional mode of communication (see Baym 1995: 22; Lévy 1996; H. Miller 1995; Thiedeke 2000; Walther 1996: 17). Then there is the option of using audiovisual elements to reinforce impressions accordingly. The restriction to text-based communication is in this context another major shortcoming of previous studies on the Internet.

Appearance versus performance

Due to a lack of immediate impressions as regards people engaged in communication, more than ever performance is at the forefront of any identity project; as Joseph Walther (1996: 20) put it, 'performance rather than appearance'. Computer-mediated communication can therefore become the basis of a selective self-representation (ibid.: 19). When presenting themselves in face-to-face situations, people are often hampered by their appearance, their limited audience and their lack of control over spontaneous verbal and nonverbal responses (Goffman 1969). In CMC many of these restrictions are lifted; in particular, websites are suitable for an undisturbed, elaborate, strategic self-portrayal (see, e.g., Chandler 1998; Döring 2002; D. Miller 2000; Miller and Mather 1998). From the sender's perspective there is the option of an optimized self-presentation, and from the recipient's perspective, an idealized perception (Walther 1996: 17, 19). On the one hand this can encourage greater self-disclosure and authenticity, but on the other it can promote conscious masquerade and deception of others (Döring 2002). In the case of collective identity projects, freedoms are limited, however, by their offline context. Self-presentation is linked to motives and aims that have emerged in this context, yet the possibilities for their presentation on the Internet are almost unlimited.

Another important argument against excessive enthusiasm in terms of identity presentation and the control of communication is the problem of controlling perception. Indeed, although we have more control over our communicative behaviour and its effect online, once 'said', comments are immediately beyond our control. This applies to both websites and discussion forums: '[M]essages posted to Usenet groups take on a life of their own, simultaneously representing the poster but out of the poster's control' (S. G. Jones 1997: 27). We then have no control or only a limited influence on the path the information takes, its ultimate effect, and the reactions it provokes. Images we create of ourselves or our group on the Internet also become independent (see also Chandler 1998: 4; D. Miller 2000: 22; Sandbothe 1996). There is the danger that comments have an undesired effect, but also the opportunity to achieve, through the momentum of the Internet, a self-multiplying effect without any additional effort.[28]

Anonymity versus authenticity

On an individual level, anonymity and the use of pseudonyms play an important role in Internet communication. Ananda Mitra (1997) refers to the fact that the sender can hide his identity from the scrutiny of the public as one of the most essential aspects of Internet communication. It is an important strategy for Internet users (see Dery 1993: 560–61; Mitra 1997: 68n10; Turkle 1995) to (seemingly) avoid social exclusion as well as sanctions for their online behaviour (see Jaffe et al. 1995; Thiedeke 2000: 27). However, numerous online observations disprove this assumption of impunity, where 'anonymous' agents were punished where necessary, for example, by being excluded from forums or mailing lists or by means of verbal (such as flame wars) or physical online attacks (such as mail avalanches or virus attacks).[29] A crucial factor in differentiating individual identity projects from collective identity projects is that the latter live precisely off making their identity explicit. Anonymity would spell the end for them. Individual members, in contrast, have the opportunity to remain anonymous or to adopt pseudonyms.

Owing to the (individual) anonymity granted by the Internet under certain circumstances and the manipulability of material sources, an analysis often raises the question of the authenticity and representativeness of subjects present on the Internet and their posts (Schwara 1999: 272). This applies to both individual and collective identity projects, although the verifiability and stringency of collective representations must be much greater to obtain the required acceptance. Even though it has been a long time since the notion of an 'authentic culture as an autonomous internally coherent universe' has been able to be upheld (Rosaldo 1989: 217), in self-representations or reports, authors still claim authenticity and recipients of information question the authenticity, that is, the accuracy and truth of the material. Slevin (2000: 72) considers deterritorialization a reason for the loss of authenticity on the Internet, which Internet users seek to counteract by using a particular rhetoric: 'By stressing the "situatedness" of those using the internet, the "places" in virtual reality – webpages, the IRC channels, the news groups, etc. – are no longer just "out there". They become articulated with reality.' The excessive expression of emotion can be another way to make up for the lack of authenticity. Web authors, according to Christine Hine (2000: 12, 142), make use of the full range of aesthetic and discursive strategies to make their pages convincing. The temporal dimension of the Internet plays a role here, she notes; the immediacy, but also the archiving of information and posts and the reference to firm locations through which we try to closely link online statements and offline events (ibid.: 124). Both the presentation of facts that are assumed to be common contextual knowledge of the targeted community, and the presentation of details of an event and its background and a claim to expert knowledge can also increase the appearance of authenticity (ibid.: 126–27, 131). Topicality, visuality, the naming of sources and inclusion of links are crucial.

Since direct interaction is often omitted from websites, the imagined audience, according to Hine (2000: 136–41), is crucial for said intended authenticity. Web authors thus attempt, for example, to give the impression that not just an individual, but a group, often presented as a 'we' group, is behind a website. It is for this reason that often the specified contact is the anonymous and neutral 'webmaster'. The publication of readers' letters, surveys, forms, etc., must also be seen in this light. Thus, we can certainly combine anonymity and authenticity, namely the effacement of (individual) identities on the one hand, and the performance of (group) identities with a claim to authenticity on the other. With such opportunities, Web authors can go much further in their quest for authenticity than was possible in traditional print media. Authors such as Hugh Miller and Russell Mather (1998) are far too cautious in their statements on this matter and rarely, if at all, discuss the interactive (email contact, readers' letters, surveys and forms) and integrative potential (text, images, sound) of websites. In the empirical section of this study on the Moluccan conflict I will present examples of how we attempt to further increase the degree of authenticity of presentations on the Internet.

Ananda Mitra (1997) sees an authenticity problem of a different kind. The ephemerality and rapid transformation of the nature of the 'Internet beast' enable at best a snapshot at a set time of the image produced and circulated precisely at that time, whereby all claim to authenticity that researchers could lay as regards their interpretation of Internet discourse evaporates (Mitra 1997: 76). Here Mitra addresses the aforementioned problem of the nonbinding nature of the Internet and its affiliations. Admittedly, the fast-paced nature of the Internet is both a methodological as well as an existential problem for Internet research, for example, if the site under investigation disappears from one day to the next.[30] Yet in a way, Mitra's view is based on a long-obsolete, static notion of culture. In my view, this constant change even presents a great opportunity, if not a precondition for being able to research the emergence of social formations and identities in cyberspace. If we follow this change (e.g., as a member of a mailing list or observer of a website) for a longer period, we can observe, for instance, the development of identity projects and community-building processes. That would be impossible if all presentations on the Internet were static.

Status and authority

In particular, the abovementioned earlier experimental studies of CMC (see, e.g., Kiesler, Siegel and McGuire 1984; Sproull and Kiesler 1986) reveal cyberspace as a space in which the existing hierarchies of 'real life' are meaningless and equitable communication takes place. This idea of cyberspace as the ideal public sphere Jürgen Habermas (2001) dreamt of has in part persisted to the present day.[31] Meanwhile, however, numerous studies have demonstrated that, especially if we follow a process of communication and interaction on the Web in its 'natural' environment, new hierarchies may well develop, or old ones may be strengthened; by means of corresponding behaviour, participants can achieve a certain status that sets them apart from other participants in the communication (see, e.g., J. van Dijk 1999: 212; Jaffe et al. 1995; Paccagnella 1997; Walther 1996: 15–16). All kinds of factors can contribute to the increase in status and power of a Web author or member of a mailing list or forum, such as corresponding paraverbal means, flaming, a moderating role, technical expertise and financial means, the quality and quantity of posts, time spent online, claims to real-life skills, the right motivation, answering questions in news groups, dispute settlement, the maintenance of frequently asked questions (FAQs), etc.[32]

Alongside familiar identity patterns, established authority patterns have also started to falter in our networked society. We face a plurality of sources of authority, whose responsibilities are often unclear or are in competition with each other. Now the nation-state is only *one* source of power and authority, as Castells (2001b) argues. It has to share these with a variety of power sources, 'supranational macro-forces' and 'subnational micro-processes' (ibid.: 307):

> These are networks of capital, production, communication, crime, international institutions, supranational military apparatuses, non-governmental organizations, trans-national religions, and public opinion movements. And below the state, there are communities, tribes, localities, cults and gangs. (ibid.: 304)

The Internet, through which groups and communities with corresponding authorities form, can contribute to a further diffusion of the balance of power and claim to authority. Castells (2001b: 69) refers to the abstraction of power in a network of computers, which leads to the disintegration of existing mechanisms of social control and political representation. Yet Lincoln Dahlberg (2001) stresses that differences in power and status in the online sphere are closely linked to social hierarchies and identities in the offline sphere. The ability to obtain authority and achieve success online depends greatly on resources (time, money and skills) possessed offline. In addition, online status is often directly strengthened by the willing disclosure of offline identities in cyberspace. If, however, certain basic conditions are met, the Internet gives individuals and groups alike the opportunity to freely debate topics in expanded time-space dimensions, to present their integrity and elicit trust in others in their actions. According to Slevin (2000: 47), this empowers the user 'to make things happen rather than have things happen to them', enables new forms of solidarity and cooperation and could even contribute to the dismantling of traditional hierarchies (ibid.: 47–49). Slevin is here, as so often, too optimistic and rarely proposes concrete realization options. The Internet's potential should certainly not be underestimated, for it lends a voice to individuals and groups that without it would never have had the opportunity to address the public and such a large audience. Thus the Internet also has considerable potential to exert influence and gain power in both the online and offline spheres. Yet ultimately this depends crucially on the extent to which the voices on the Web are heard and whether they have a lasting impact, and there is no guarantee of this.

Summary

The Internet is an ambivalent medium in terms of its effects on the social, political, economic and cultural environment. On the one hand it enables comprehensive control of its users and contributes to the consolidation of the existing balance of power, leading to a digital divide that separates the people of the world who have access to the Internet from those who do not. On the other hand it can lead to the increased political mobilization of groups of people, as well as the strengthening of cultural identities, and lend all kinds of people and groups previously denied a voice a platform of expression on the global stage. The potential for integrative communication partly raises the restrictions placed on people as regards space, time, information and body, thus decisively extending the Internet user's area of influence. In the social sciences, especially anthropological Internet research, studies must therefore not concentrate solely on the information presented, but should above all also examine the transformation of social structures such as community and identity.

Various positions have been explored in the academic debate on online communities. I have focused on the contextual approach, which assumes that processes in cyberspace are shaped by the specific offline context of its visitors and interact with it. This should also annul the virtuality-reality debate, as the online and offline spaces complement each other and are part of one and the same reality. For a better understanding of community-forming processes on the Internet, we need to distance ourselves from traditional ideas of community and the locality principle and embrace Benedict Anderson's concept of *imagined communities* (1998) and Arjun Appadurai's *imagined worlds* (1996). The Internet provides space and resources for identity construction, in which performance and authenticity play an important role, as do status and authority, which can either be acquired online or taken over from the offline sphere. Collective identities on the Internet are of particular interest for my research. Here, there is less a focus on experimentation and free play, but more on a conscious recourse to identity-defining elements that are generally taken from the offline context of people participating in an online project and that are intended to unite all members in an imagined community. By means of collective identity projects, the Internet can, for example, be used strategically to preserve cultures and languages, to connect a diaspora with its country of origin, or to expand and support resistance networks and social movements.

Notes

1. There is already sufficient written material on the history or development of the Internet by ARPANET, a U.S. computer network developed in 1969 for

military purposes and designed to withstand nuclear attacks, the emergence of electronic mail systems, diverse news groups such as the best-known and most comprehensive 'Usenet' in 1985, MUDs in the 1980s and 1990s, and ultimately the development of the World Wide Web (WWW) in the early 1990s, which was to enable a broad mass of people to have access to the Internet via user-friendly interfaces. For example, see the following authors: Adams and Warf (1997: 140–41); Hicks (1998: 53–55); Steven G. Jones (1998b); Rheingold (2000: Introduction); Rogers and Malhotra (2000); Slevin (2000: 27–54); and Zurawski (2000: 151–59). Christine Hine (2000: 14–27) provides an overview of the various approaches to Internet research from the mid-1980s.

2. Computer and information technology, nanotechnology, and biotechnology continue to be referred to with the term 'new technologies'.

3. On this see John Perry Barlow (1996) in particular, who was criticized by Thomas Barth (1997), Zurawski (2000: 129–35) and Hamelink (2000: 22–23), amongst others, for his naïve optimism and total blindness in the face of social injustice.

4. Nua.com describes itself as an 'authoritative online source for information on Internet demographics and trends' (http://www.nua.com, 12 November 2002).

5. International Telecommunications Union, 2001.

6. International Telecommunications Union, 2002.

7. On the first point, see, e.g., Miller and Slater (2000); on the latter point, see Shields (1996: 3, 6). On the principle of glocalization, which describes the interplay between localization and globalization, see Robertson (1998).

8. For a critique of Castells's model see, amongst others, Jan van Dijk (1999: 24) and Miller and Slater (2000: 8).

9. For more on this, see Jan van Dijk (1999: 190, 197, 208); Marshall (2001: 90); Sobchack (1993: 575–78); and Turkle (1995: 20).

10. Definitions of cyberspace are provided by, among others, Escobar (1994: 216); Fernback (1997: 37, 39); Hakken (1999: 1); Hamelink (2000: ix, 9); Hartmann (1997: 6); Hicks (1998: 55, 66); Steven G. Jones (1997: 22); Jordan (1999: 26, 59); Marshall (2001: 81); Progress and Freedom Foundation (1994); Rheingold (2000: xx); Schwara (1999: 261); and Whittle (1997: 7, 9).

11. In the context of the discussion on so-called *virtual communities,* other authors have already made reference to Benedict Anderson's concept of *imagined communities* (Baym 1998; Nelson 1996; Piliang 2000). Often, however, these are simply comparisons and the idea itself is not pursued consistently enough.

12. On the concept of time, space and locality in a globalized world, see also Appadurai (1996).

13. For more on this, see Castells (2000: 381) and Jan van Dijk (1999: 20, 156–57).

14. According to Rheingold (2000: 25–55), The WELL was initiated to create 'real' connections between people, whereby members' 'real life' (that is, in other words, the offline sphere) takes centre stage in conversations between the users. Rheingold's book should be read with this in mind. In his statements and definitions Rheingold remains contradictory to his concept of community and has also been criticized on several occasions for his overarching optimism, his tendentiousness, his unreliable generalizations, his American leaning and his popular science–like style (see, e.g., Stegbauer 2001: 71; Zurawski 2000:

128–29). In response, in 2000 Rheingold added a chapter to his 1993 book in which he offers more specificity and critical probing of certain statements, provides more precise bibliographic references and offers interested readers an extended bibliography.

15. See Kendall (1999: 67) and Slevin (2000: 55); only at the end of his introduction does Porter (1997: xvi) concede that Internet culture has a certain influence on 'reality'.

16. Although originally published in 1996, 1997 and 1998, throughout this text I refer to the editions published in 2000 and 2001 (cited as 2000, 2001b and 2001c).

17. See Baudrillard (2001); Olalquiaga (2001); and Poster (2001). Jean Baudrillard's ahistorical approach has been criticized on multiple occasions; see Durham and Kellner (2001: 517) and Hamelink (2000), amongst others.

18. See Steven G. Jones (1997: 16, 1998a: 21); Lockard (1997: 224–26); and McLaughlin, Osborne and Ellison (1997: 146). Advocates of this approach mainly refer to James Beniger's (1987) research on the personalization of the mass media by the simulation of interpersonal communication. According to Beniger (1987: 369), a *pseudo community* is the hybrid that results from interpersonal and mass communication.

19. Detailed information on these studies is given on Barry Wellman's website (http://www.chass.utoronto.ca/~wellman/main.html), and in Wellman and Haythornthwaite (2002).

20. For Elwert (1989), too, the attempts to form imagined communities in view of the deficient character of previous definitions of nationalism, nation, ethnicity and similar concepts are very attractive, since an identity that is only tangible in our imagination is not particularly vulnerable, and yet can also be distinguished by features of greatness and authority.

21. Calhoun (1995: 258) is of the opinion that the mass media's role assumes particular importance when it comes to strengthening the notion of social connections amongst the members of a 'large scale category', such as the nation. Calhoun (1995: 266–67) gives the example of Ayatollah Khomeini's speeches, which were widely circulated on cassettes and thus reached an international Islamic audience. For more on the significance of electronic media in the formation of identities and communities, see Morley and Robins (1995).

22. Examples of diasporic communities on the Internet are provided by, e.g., Miller and Slater (2000) for Trinidad, Mitra (1997) for Indians, Jon Anderson (1996) for people of Middle Eastern origin living abroad, Morton (1999) for people from the Tonga Islands and Poster (1998) for Jews.

23. The building blocks for these imaginary worlds constitute, in Appadurai's view, the five dimensions of 'global cultural flows', whose relationship to one another is marked by an increasing level of incoherence, since people, machines, finances, images and ideas pursue less and less unified paths in a world of increasing globalization and networking and are thus increasingly deterritorialized (1996: 37, 53): (1) *ethnoscapes*, (2) *mediascapes*, (3) *technoscapes*, (4) *financescapes* and (5) *ideoscapes*. Here, the suffix *-scape* refers to the unclear, irregular, not clearly localizable forms of these *landscapes* (ibid.: 33).

24. 'Consciously induced' should be highlighted in this context in order to preclude criticism that one could not *not* communicate anyway (Watzlawik, Beavin and Jackson 1969: 50–53).

25. Examples include Bahl (1997); Hakken (1999); Reid (1991); and Turkle (1995).
26. See, e.g., Gurak (1999); Mele (1999: 292); and Uncapher (1999). Such potential lies in telecommunications technology in general, even if thanks to the Internet the possibilities have at the same time increased vastly. Telephone and other information technologies were and are, according to Nguyen and Alexander (1996: 109), important factors in undermining existing categories of political power – e.g., in the Soviet Union – in so far as they enable links between domestic critics of the regime and sympathizers abroad, for instance.
27. For more on this see Jaffe et al. (1995); Paccagnella (1997); and Walther (1996).
28. In fact, the same danger also existed for conventional print media, but the dimensions and scope have expanded with the Internet, and the possible exertion of influence (via space and time) and the feedback on such projects have increased enormously.
29. The means available for sanctioning on the Internet are naturally limited, as with imagined communities more generally. Elwert (1989: 447) lists the nation as an example, establishing that, 'albeit honour and disgrace are explicitly important guarantors of the adherence to the norms of this great companionship, they cannot function at the same level of concentration displayed by groups of acquaintances (face-to-face groups)'.
30. This can be avoided by timely archiving.
31. See Durham and Kellner (2001: 36); Slevin (2000); and Thiedeke (2000: 27–28). Closely linked to this is the debate on so-called cyberdemocracy. At one end of the spectrum of opinion, the Internet is viewed as an acephalous network that facilitates democratization processes (Lévy 1996; Rheingold 1993: Introduction and chap. 4; Zurawski 2000), while at the other end it is seen as a space of unlimited control and *mind management* (Dahlberg 2001; J. van Dijk 1999: 101, 116, 125; Hamelink 2000: 19; Hartmann 1998: 12, 16; Kolko and Reid 1998: 216; Lockard 1997: 220; Nguyen and Alexander 1996: 120; Norris 2000a: 1; Piliang 2000; Poster 1997; Rheingold 2000: chap. 10). See also Castells (2001b: 350–51); Dahlberg (2000); and Kollock and Smith (1999: 4).
32. On this see Donath (1999: 30–31); Jordan (1999); and Mitra (1997: 74).

2

Anthropological Internet Research and Methodology

It was at a relatively late stage that anthropology discovered the Internet as a field of research. Given the above-mentioned, hitherto highly one-sided Internet research, it is high time that more anthropologists faced this challenge. Anthropology, which aims for an emic perspective and attaches just as much importance to the context of a research object as to the latter itself, can make valuable contributions to theoretical and methodological approaches to Internet research, especially with regard to concepts such as identity, community, culture and communication, and their application to cyberspace. We have, in part, already seen this in the chapter on cyber-theory. In this chapter, however, I would also like to address the problems that arise when we apply anthropological methods to cyberspace, discuss the existing approaches for examining mailing lists, news groups and web-sites as research resources, and develop them further. These methodolog-ical tools were used to examine presentations of the Moluccan conflict on the Internet, but can equally be applied to other, comparable research projects. I propose religion and conflict on the Internet as possible top-ics for anthropological Internet research, as both play a role in Moluccan cyberspace.

Cyberanthropology

The possibility of integrating text, images and sound into the same sys-tem, and of interacting irrespective of distance from different locations at a chosen point in time (synchronous or asynchronous) and in a global network, has fundamentally changed the character of communication (Castells 2001c: 356). The integration of tele-, data- and mass communica-tion takes place in a single medium (J. van Dijk 1999: 9). Most previous Internet studies, primarily geared towards text-based CMC, pay far too little attention to this. According to Castells (2001c: 402–3), the Internet has given rise to a new symbolic environment that allows us to integrate information from all kinds of sources into one common cognitive pattern. Here, it becomes ever more important to not only present Internet communication in the form of conveyed information, but also examine and describe the impact of the transformation of social structures, such as types of interaction and social identities, that accompany these new forms of communication (Meyrowitz 1997: 60–61). We must take care not to stop at describing the individual parts of the Internet, as the medium stands for something that is greater than the sum of its parts (Costigan 1999: xviii). Different modes of communication and forms of presenting information can produce different effects (J. van Dijk 1999: 194–95).

In 1980 Philip Schlesinger highlighted the significance of the ethnographic approach for the examination of media in order to obtain fundamental information on the work ideologies and practices of these cultural producers (363). In his 1994 essay 'Welcome to Cyberia: Notes on the Anthropology of Cyberculture,' Arturo Escobar called for an academic anthropological debate on this dynamic research field, including other new technologies besides the Internet. Yet a real debate did not get going for a long time. Anthropologists kept a distance, and mostly considered the Internet a tool for publishing and teaching purposes (Morton 2001c: 3) or a medium for academic exchange (discussions, text, sound and image material, databases, etc.) and for institutes, museums and researchers to present their work (Schwimmer 1996). They did not consider it the generator of a social and cultural space that is a subject of examination itself. Among the small number of anthropological monographs on the Internet available are *Cyborgs@Cyberspace? An Ethnographer Looks to the Future* by David Hakken (1999), *Virtuelle Ethnizität* by Nils Zurawski (2000), *The Internet: An Ethnographic Approach*, an ethnography of the Internet in Trinidad by Daniel Miller and Don Slater (2000), and *Virtual Ethnography* by Christine Hine[1] (2000). In addition, a number of essays that explore both the Internet as a social space and the application of anthropological methods to study it have been published in recent years, for instance, by Daniel Chandler (1998), Stefan Schwara (1999), Manfred Kremser (1999), and Wilson and Peterson (2002), as well as the collection of essays *Computer-Mediated Communication in Australian Anthropology and Sociology*, edited by Helen Morton (2001a). Like other disciplines, cyberanthropology has hitherto primarily focused on Western, and in particular North American, participation in cyberspace (Morton 2001c: 7). However, there are also studies of the Internet as a means for people living in diaspora as well as ethnic minorities to preserve and promote their language and culture and consolidate their cultural community. Furthermore, there are studies on the role of the Internet as a communication channel for sociocultural movements.[2] Johannes Fabian's (2002) essay, which explores the potential of the Internet to change the conditions of ethnographic writing, points in an entirely different direction.

I understand cyberanthropology or the anthropology of cyberspace to be the subdiscipline of anthropology that studies the cultural peculiarities in the social space constituted by the Internet (cyberspace) and its respective sociocultural context. For Mizrach (1995) it is the study of people in 'virtual communities' and networked environments; for Schwara (1999: 267), it is anthropology that considers the virtual space a cultural space. I have deliberately avoided the term 'virtual' in my definition. Moreover, cyberanthropology should not only consider the so-called cyberspace, but also take into account the sociocultural and historical context in which the space itself and its visitors are anchored. We do not enter a virtual world that is detached from the conventional context of reality (see, e.g., Hartmann 1997: 3, 1998: 11; Schwara 1999: 267). According to Helmers, Hoffmann and Hofmann (1996), the Internet is by no means a neutral transport network that can be organized and used arbitrarily, and certainly not a legal black hole. Rather, it is a network that has been developed and shaped by a group of people with particular qualifications, ideas and standards that can be identified and characterized using anthropological methods. In their research, Helmers, Hoffmann and Hofmann observed how a special, Web-compatible form of usage and rules of social interaction – 'netiquette' – have emerged (1996: 16–17), a kind of social contract that in my opinion cannot necessarily be applied to other Internet communities. This example, however, seeks to show that despite a strong contextual orientation and connection, something culturally independent can emerge through the expansion of our conventional 'territory' into cyberspace and its specific communication potential.

Development of methods

Christine Hine (2000: 65) argues that the 'ethnographic object' is also shaped by the technologies used and that all forms of interaction are of ethnographic relevance, which ultimately is ethnography. The organization of interaction with informants through the technology employed is just as relevant as the ethnographer's interactions with the technology, she claims. However, as Escobar (1994: 14) has already pointed out, new technologies will transform our ideas on field research. At the beginning of the cyberanthropology era, Helmers, Hoffmann and Hofmann (1996) assumed that the application of anthropological field research methods to the Web-based world, which at the time had hardly been studied in this way, would present few problems. This is due to the fact that the Internet culture is, firstly, public and therefore accessible to ethnographers for research purposes; secondly, it is possible for ethnographers to participate in the cultural community they wish to study; and thirdly, any expression of culture, including that on the Internet, can equally serve as a source of knowledge. They believed that the Internet afforded numerous sites and opportunities for the observation of social interaction. In addition, it would be possible to interview people and analyse documents. Applying established research methods as briefly described here by Helmers, Hoffmann and Hofmann (1996) is, in principle, possible, but requires more discerning and critical consideration. I would now like to highlight some methodological thoughts that these early cyberanthropologists did not consider or afforded insufficient attention. References to the methods of the design and analysis of Web presentations in the preceding chapter will not be explicitly repeated here, but are placed in this context.

The deterritorialized subject

Arjun Appadurai (1998: 38) advocates substituting terms used in the past for entities such as towns, villages, municipalities and localities with 'ethnoscapes'. These are populated by people who inform the transformation currently taking place, namely tourists, immigrants, refugees, expatriates, guest workers and other mobile groups and individuals (ibid.: 12). Anthropologists can no longer assume that 'when they choose a certain place as their research subject, they will find, compared to a greater perspective, something more fundamental, accidental and therefore more "real"' (ibid.: 23).[3] Rather, it is the complex, partially imagined lives mentioned above that, according to Appadurai, have to form the basis of ethnography today, at least of an ethnography that seeks resonance in a transnational, deterritorialized world. The power of imagination becomes a crucial force in the development of social life and the ideas related to it are often transmitted through the mass media (ibid.: 23). Thus the 'ethno' in ethnography takes on a quality we can hardly identify and no longer place, to which the descriptive practices of anthropology have to adapt (Appadurai 1996: 48).

The Internet is reinforcing these tendencies. We can consider Appadurai's statements a plea to anthropologists to closely study the Internet, even if Appadurai himself does not yet directly address this field. In Internet research, groups and cultural phenomena only become fathomable through the metaphor of cyberspace, or so Schwara claims (1999: 265). According to him, cyberspace is becoming the new international space for anthropology, in which field research is conducted to examine the corresponding interactions, processes and social formations and to present various identity formations. Miller and Slater (2000) propose a different kind of locality principle. They seek to find out how Internet technologies are understood, accepted and used in particular local contexts. For the majority of Appadurai's ethnoscape inhabitants, too, the actual place of origin is of great importance, be it for people living in the diaspora, refugees or tourists. Moreover, in the case of the Moluccan Islands a concrete spatial reference repeatedly becomes very clear in Internet presentations, or rather it supplies the very basis and legitimacy of the Moluccan cyberspace I explore and the related development of deterritorialized, transnational networks and communities.

Field research and participant observation on the Internet

In anthropological Internet research, too, the great importance of participant observation seems undisputed, even if opinions differ regarding its implementation. A participant observation–based approach to the technologies used by a group of people to be examined, argues Schwara (1999: 271), is a prerequisite for making statements on the nature and meaning of the interrelationship between humans and their technological environment. According to Miller and Slater (2000: 21–22), immersion in one particular case, reference to a specific locality and participant observation (e.g., in chat forums), which generate longer-term contacts, are keystones of an ethnographic approach in Internet research. Morton (2001a: 5) argues that the notion of field research has to radically alter, as 'the field' appears as text on a screen, so to speak, and the social group to be observed can include people scattered all over the globe. There are in principle two kinds of online research: distanced or involved (Morton 2001a: 6), or rather distanced or discursive and communicative (Schwara 1999: 271). *Distanced* research includes evaluating material sources (texts, images, nicknames, emoticons, etc.) and observing social interaction. We can analyse mailing list and news group posts and websites as well as the way they present a particular topic, who owns and maintains them, and the target audience, etc. According to Morton (2001a), *involved* research implies participation in chat forums and other synchronous forms of CMC or using email to conduct interviews. The 'subjectivity' and 'self-will of social agents' is revealed, so Schwara (1999: 271) suggests, through the establishment of discursive and communicative relationships. Participant observation enables the researcher to gain a better understanding of the scope of a participant's identity performance and of its significance for him (Kendall 1999: 71).

Christine Hine (2000) has attempted to conceive a methodological framework for anthropological Internet research. She examined various websites and news groups concerning Louise Woodward, a teenage au pair who had been accused of murdering the child in her care. In the course of her research, she developed ten 'principles of virtual ethnography'. These principles do not propagate a concrete methodological approach, but rather are fundamental statements that are a precondition for conducting field research in and on the medium of the Internet. Several of the ten points had already been discussed before Hine or were being addressed by other authors around the same time; others can be seen as a given in the imagined worlds discussed by Appadurai. Hine summarizes the principles on two pages. As they also aid understanding of the work at hand and its field of research of imagined communities and identity projects on the Internet, I would like to quote them in brief:

> 1) The sustained presence of an ethnographer in the field setting, combined with intensive engagement with the everyday life of the inhabitants of the field site, make for the special kind of knowledge we call ethnographic ... The status of the Internet as a way of communicating, as an object within people's lives and as a site for community-like formations is achieved and sustained in the ways in which it is used, interpreted and reinterpreted. 2) ... Interactive media such as the Internet can be understood as both culture and cultural artefact ... 3) ... We can usefully think of the ethnography of mediated interaction as mobile rather than multi-sited. 4) ... The object of ethnographic enquiry can usefully be reshaped by concentrating on flow and connectivity rather than location and boundary as the organizing principle. 5) ... The challenge of virtual ethnography is to explore the making of boundaries and the making of connections, especially between the 'virtual' and the 'real' ... 6) ... Virtual ethnography is interstitial, in that it fits into the other activities of both ethnographer and subjects ... 7) Virtual ethnography is necessarily partial ... 8) Virtual ethnography involves intensive engagement with mediated interaction ... The ethnographer's engagement with the medium is a valuable source of insight. Virtual ethnography can usefully draw on ethnographer as informant and embrace the reflexive dimension ... 9) ... The shaping of the ethnographic object as it is made possible by the available technologies is the ethnography. This is ethnography in, of and through the virtual. 10) ... It is an adaptive ethnography which sets out to suit itself to the conditions in which it finds itself. (Hine 2000: 63–65)

These are very general statements that must be put in more concrete terms in each particular case. Critics accused Hine of not nearly satisfying all the principles in her own empirical study (Zurawski 2001b). Hine responded by saying that she only intended to provide a framework:

> It is true that the principles which I outline are broader than the empirical study which I actually carry out to illustrate them. The whole idea of having 'principles' for ethnography, and the grandiose declaration of 'virtual ethnography', were supposed to be a bit tongue in cheek. Ethnography always has been adaptive, and ethnographers always have explored myriad cultural connections, but sometimes we risk forgetting these facts. The principles are meant to be provocative, and to encourage imaginative thinking about ways of shaping ethnographic projects that address the Internet. By taking on a media event as the theme for an ethnography I was hoping to demonstrate that one could take seriously as ethnographic encounters the many different kinds of interaction and information that the Internet provides, and that one could actually embrace the uncertainty that comes from not having a specific location to study. (Hine 2001)

Thank you, Christine. That does not mean to say that I fundamentally agree with the conclusions she draws from the principles for her specific case study. Hine fittingly regards the Internet as culture (2000: 14–26), but also as a cultural artefact (ibid.: 27–38) that is shaped by its social context (e.g., various interest groups' expectations of the medium, future use, desired audience). Thus, she simultaneously describes the Internet as 'performative spaces' and 'performed spaces' (ibid.: 116). As I have pointed out several times, we must not only consider the Internet a transmitter of information and symbolic content, but also examine the new forms of action, interaction and social relationships (ibid.: 36; see also J. Thompson 1995: 4). With this dual principle, Hine (ibid.: 39) aims to help eliminate the processes responsible for constructing the border between the virtual and the real, but in many passages of her book she herself does not get beyond this dichotomy (see, for example, the fifth of her ten research principles). Zurawski (2001a) criticizes Hine for not abolishing the polarity, for she does not really perceive the Internet as social practice, the extension of existing social relationships.

Furthermore, the question arises as to whether and in what way online field research should be complemented by offline field research (Bell 2001: 194–98). Hine (2000: 44–45) argues that the physical journey to the field will become superfluous for an ethnography of the Internet, as interactions with the research field can now be mediatized through the Internet. Access to the field will be negotiated online from home, interactions between relevant individuals and groups will be observed online and communication with participants will take place online. Yet, as in the case of conventional field research, the relationship between the ethnographer, reader and research subject is still inscribed in the ethnographic text: 'The ethnographer is still uniquely placed to give an account of the field site, based on their experience of it and their interaction with it. … ethnographic authority resides with the ethnographer who was there' (Hine 2000: 46). Other Internet researchers, such as Nancy Baym (1995), complement their online results and experiences with face-to-face contact in order to gain an insight into the sociocultural environment of the people in question. Hine (2000: 48–49) views this inclusion of the offline sphere into the research as an attempt to verify online observations and, thus, to make results seem more authentic, or as a result of the pursuit of ethnographic holism. She argues that ethnographers assume an asymmetrical position by using additional and different means of communication compared to their informants in order to understand the latter and in so doing risk their empirical authenticity. In her view, online field research should therefore remain exclusive. I would like to elaborate on this point.

If anthropologists examine a social space constituted solely on the Internet such as, for example, most MUDs and possibly also some chat forums, I agree with Hine. However, if the social space on the Internet is constituted primarily on the basis of and with reference to offline events (or an event), it is useful, if not necessary, to complement online with offline research. Accordingly, Morton (2001a: 6) argues that knowledge of the cultural background of cyberactors and presentations is important in order to understand much of the news in cyberspace. If possible, according to Kendall (1999: 71), researchers should aim to find access to the offline context. Indeed, how can Hine be sure that members of an online forum do not use additional communication channels offline or are not in contact with other members offline? In my opinion, combining online and offline research is not so much – as Hine believes – about obtaining authentic knowledge, the existence of which I doubt in any case. Rather, it is about investigating the presentation of certain topics, groups and people on the Internet and relating the portrayals and forging links with the sociocultural context of the people involved, as well as with relevant offline events. It is not about validating online content, but about the presentation of these alleged 'truths'. We need to examine – and here I agree with Hine again – what informants consider authentic:

> Assuming a priori that authenticity is a problem for inhabitants of cyberspace is the same kind of ethnographic mistake as assuming that the Azande have a problem in dealing with the contradictions inherent in their beliefs about witchcraft. It should be addressed as an issue for the ethnography as and when it arises during interaction. (Hine 2000: 49)

Precisely to break down the dichotomy between virtuality and reality and to achieve a better understanding of the potential of the online sphere to expand the offline, it is helpful in many cases to get acquainted offline with the context of those who publish these presentations online and with the conditions under which the (media) texts available online are produced, that is, 'the situationality of those texts' (J. Thompson 1995: 84).

Websites as research sources

Websites enable us to pass on information, make connections via links and present topics, projects, movements, people or groups on the Internet. Every site, so Slevin (2000: 143) suggests, reveals a great deal about the cultural context in which it was developed. In contrast to mailing lists, websites focus on the presentation of information rather than communication between individuals and communities. Daniel Chandler (1998) investigates the phenomenological aspect of websites and impressively describes how identities can be constructed online by way of personal websites.[4] Websites are also audiovisual media and far more dynamic than print media, which is why, according to Chandler (1998), the Web is the ideal medium for the dynamic processes of identity construction and preservation. These presentations can expand the author's potential influence in terms of both space and time. They lead to a visible transformation of the relationship between the public and the private sphere, for activating a website is tantamount to a worldwide publication. In his paper Chandler refers to personal websites; however, his findings and methods can, by and large, also be applied to collective identity projects on the Internet.

Critics point out that information on the WWW is hard to verify and therefore could be fictitious (see, e.g., Rubio 1996; Sandbothe 1996), and that the Web tempts people to manipulate their public identities more than was possible with traditional media (see Chandler 1998: 10–11; Jaffe et al. 1995; H. Miller 1995). As my study focuses on the presentation of this information and not its validity, I would like to end this discussion here. I will return to the problem of anonymity and the manipulation of identities later, using specific examples. The conceptual design of a web-site seeks to create identities using existing material by contextualizing websites and lending them meaning by way of content and form. When analysing them, it is therefore insufficient to focus solely on the content of the WWW 'texts', but is particularly important to also take into account both their form of presentation and significance (Mitra and Cohen 1999: 181). Through the specific use of available techniques and paralinguistic means such as linguistic style, structure and vocabulary, websites imply much more information than that which they ostensibly provide (H. Miller 1995). According to Slevin (2000: 65), the integration of all kinds of text, sound and visual elements, which can be distributed at will across several windows, results in a collage effect: 'The screen is thus a patch-work of various information flows, a negotiated dynamic narrative made up of the juxtaposition of what otherwise might be heterogeneous items of knowledge and information.'

By way of the window technique and links, the traditional linearity of a presentation, as found in other media, is eliminated and replaced by com-plex networks of websites and information windows (see, e.g., J. van Dijk 1999: 175–76). Turkle (1995: 258) claims that links are a decisive factor in identity formation: '[O]ne's identity emerges from whom one knows, one's associations and connections.' The links provide references to the website author's (personal) networks and interests (Erickson 1996): 'Show me what your links are, and I'll tell you what kind of person you are' (H. Miller 1995). However, links can be an expression of various relationships, ranging from agreement through neutrality to rejection. The presenta-tional mode of websites can be complemented by interactive components, such as email and chat buttons, forms, guest books and letters to the edi-tor. The visitor can directly contact the website's author, obtain additional information and provide feedback, which, in turn, might influence the further design of the website. By reflecting identities, by attracting visitors with their appeal, whatever its nature, and by actively seeking to have an effect, in Hine's view (2000: 93) websites become acts of communication.

Ultimately, when analysing websites it is important to examine not only the visible elements and details, but also the context in which they were developed and the online environment into which they have been integrated. According to Hine (2000: 26), this is the only way to view them as meaningful social acts that enable the creation of relationships on the Internet. Hine particularly highlights the role of the 'imagined audience' during the creation and development of a site (ibid.: 92–93). As in the Woodward case, she says, this is often about the image of a group exposed to a (global) public whose support, solidarity or even financial aid it wishes to gain. It is therefore important to produce a Web presence that is as appealing and suited to the medium as possible (Zurawski 2000: 185). There is a range of strategies (aside from the manipulation of search engines) that website authors can employ to attract Internet users' attention and construct socially effective websites. Wanting aesthetics, for example, can be a tactic used to create an impression of reliability and accuracy, while an aesthetically highly sophisticated website may function as a trap by virtue of its appearance alone: it draws in passing surfers, so to speak, and at the same time extends the circle within which this fame can spread (D. Miller 2000: 16–17). In addition to the aesthetic component, the extent to which a website is up to date (Hine 2000: 93), the publication of letters to the editor or references from other websites contribute to its prevalence and renown.

The Internet has its very own approach to time. Even if time does not lose its meaning in cyberspace, as is often propagated – Castells (2001c: 491), for example, speaks of 'simultaneity' and 'timelessness' – it still offers the possibility of bringing together present, future and past in a unique way. Besides its topicality, it can offer a look to the future, but above all, it can also take a look back at the past, be it through archives that store the history of a website or mailing list or in the form of a historical online review on a case and its background. This, of course, is also possible using other types of media. Yet the Internet enables us to continuously update an article and to refer to other and new interesting reports via hyperlinks and thus successively write an article's own history without any additional effort. Once-static documents and presentations are now becoming dynamic. References to external offline events and chronologies, according to Hine (2000: 101), enable the visitor to successfully navigate this tangle of time in cyberspace. By making reference to external chronologies, a close link can be established between the online and offline spheres and their respective timescales and events within them. This will become clear in the Moluccan case study.

News groups and mailing lists as research sources[5]

Due to their communicative, interactive nature, news groups and mailing lists are better suited to creating solidary online communities than websites (see McLaughlin, Osborne and Ellison 1997: 149; Rubio 1996). Whereas the identity of individuals can become visible from just a few posts in a news group or mailing list, collective identities only emerge and develop gradually. That said, visitors to certain websites may be confronted with a sophisticated presentation of the identity of the person or group behind it. As a member of news groups or lists, an anthropologist can observe communication and the establishment of relationships on the Internet (Stegbauer 2001: 281). Ultimately, a lot of what has been said about the study of websites can be applied to this field: how time is handled, the possibility of integrating text, image and sound in a single post, the significance of the linguistic style used, the focus on a particular audience (in this case, the topics and goals of an online discussion group) and finally the significance of the context of the post and author for a proper understanding of these events. In addition to the fact that the posts refer to offline events, Hine (2000: 102) says we should also take into account how much time individual members are able to devote to online activities.

According to Hine (2000: 150), we should see online groups as social factors and posts on a mailing list or news group as meaningful social actions. In order to classify them or understand them in the first place, we would need to develop cultural competencies with respect to these groups. In my opinion, following the discourse in these forums for long enough is a prerequisite for this. The necessary length of time depends firstly on when we subscribed to the list, secondly on how short- or long-lived the offline events that the posts relate to are, and thirdly on how group identity is lived out and explicated. A good first step is to trace a discussion back to the very beginning, as that is where the foundations for the social network and a potentially emerging community are laid. Then it makes sense to follow the discussion through a number of different phases of the offline events in order to identify potential effects on the course of the debate. If identities on a list are dealt with very openly, it takes less time to gain an insight into the nature and the composition of a list than when the participants are shy of revealing their true identity. In this I absolutely agree with Lori Kendall (1999: 70–71), who argues that the impression of anonymity in a forum can subside if we follow a list discussion long enough. This presupposes that the mailing lists exist for a lengthier period of time and that memberships are relatively stable. Gradually, the identities and intentions of the different avatars become obvious even if participants do not mention their real name. Moreover, other authors point out that we can sometimes also find references to identities in account names, the reputation of domain names, the content and style of posts, links to a participant's own website or older posts, signatures, etc. At the same time, however, participants may deliberately attempt to deceive others regarding their identity, for instance, by using constructed email addresses, or hide all references to themselves (see, e.g., Donath 1999; Jordan 1999: 68–69). Whichever strategies individual members adopt, they influence the image we get of their group and the presentation of their project.

In news groups, posts are usually archived for a certain period of time, and in mailing lists, even for the entire time the list exists. This changes the usual character of offline communication, as posts cannot be withdrawn and can be accessed at any time by all members. Internet researchers, particularly sociologists, very much like to draw on archives, as they provide a complete database of communicative activity ready to be analysed. This seemingly spares the researcher the tedious job of collecting data in the field and, moreover, enables the examination of debates that have long since been concluded. However, when these databases are used, two factors crucial to the evaluation of these records, namely, the online and offline context of each post and the dynamics of the lists, are lost. Yet both are crucial, at least if we wish to develop an understanding of the online processes in anthropological terms. Accordingly, Hine (2000: 23) writes that the above method fails when we seek to comprehend a participant's experience of being flooded with emails, waiting for messages, receiving them in the wrong order, etc. – 'the experience what it is like to be a user' (see also Korenman and Wyatt 1996: 227).

According to Stegbauer (2001: 278–83), we can observe typical structural patterns in Internet-based communication, in particular mailing lists, when we study Internet forums. The macrostructure of mailing lists is thus shaped by a centre-periphery hierarchy that is primarily characterized by differences with respect to the frequency of posts and differing tasks of participants.[6] With their numerous contacts, key actors dominate the social fabric of the mailing lists. The periphery, so Stegbauer claims, allows for a horizontal differentiation of 'debaters', who mostly give their opinion on certain topics, 'posters', who provide information on events and sources, and 'lurkers'. The latter neither appear in the social space itself, nor do they generally establish any relationships with the other members of the social space, although they make up the majority of the overall communication space. Stegbauer does not specifically address the moderators. In moderated mailing lists, moderators are responsible for the admission of new members and, moreover, a central point of contact for all incoming posts. The moderator decides which posts can be sent to members and which must be censored, leading Kevin C. Thompson (2001: 36) to assign to the moderator the role of the police, while Kollock and Smith (1999: 5) refer to him or her as a benevolent dictator. Stegbauer (2001: 280–81) mentions two further factors that structure Internet-based communication, namely, the point in time when the various members joined the discussion, for it determines whether and to what extent they have the group's contextual knowledge, and the participants' origin, as the actors' central interests have taken shape less on the Internet itself and more in the central areas of life outside the communicative worlds of the Internet.

I would like to address the highly disputed role of the so-called lurkers once again, separately, because they constitute the majority in the mailing lists and news groups I have examined, as well as in, presumably, most others. They are often referred to as free riders.[7] As Stegbauer (2000) states, an observation of communication spaces that does not take into account the majority of participants would inevitably lead to a distorted picture. For the purposes of ethnographic studies on news groups, however, Hine (2000: 25) finds it sufficient to focus on the active participants and not take into consideration the invisible lurkers, for they would prove to be unimportant for the ethnographer in the same way as for the news groups. Katie Argyle (1996), in contrast, is convinced that it suffices simply to know of one's own participation. In her opinion, one can be equally as involved as a silent participant and thus be part of the group; these were her conclusions from her observation of and participation in the news group Cybermind and resulting contacts. Stegbauer (2001: 279) likewise contradicts the view that the position of nonactive participants is irrelevant or that they even freeload. According to him, their role is not unimportant, particularly when it comes to passing on information from the individual forums to other forums and from the Internet to the offline sphere. Lurkers can function as multipliers of mailing lists. Furthermore, a large number of lurkers naturally also tells us something about the appeal and prevalence of a list or news group, about interest in them and, thus, in a subject or debate. This increase in prestige can be of great importance to the initiators or other people involved. Ultimately, Stegbauer (2000: 127–28) also concludes that only those who are perceptible to others as actors with identity form the actual community, even though they form only a small minority among actual participants.

The term 'lurking' is often used to refer to the unannounced observation of online interactions between participants of discussion groups (K. Thompson 2001: 35n10). This offers a number of advantages when examining the social field of news groups and mailing lists. Compared to qualitative interviews and document analyses, Hofmann (1998) considers lurking a more promising method to find out about the emic perspective of the Internet and the laws and rules that constitute this shared social space. In mailing lists, we can directly participate in the negotiation process of these rules and observe patterns of interaction without influencing them (Kollock and Smith 1996: 114). Topics (everyday situations, rituals and traditions, etc.) that are not mentioned in an interview or mentioned only in passing can be followed up close and live. And depending on who speaks, our perspective on the events changes. Thus, Hofmann (1998: 15) terms the mailing list a collective and multivoiced informant. Kollock and Smith (1996: 114–15), however, caution against excessive enthusiasm, for just like all other forms of observation, the observation of Internet forums has its limitations. In the first instance, private references or ambiguities cannot be recognized here, either. Moreover, participants can use other communication channels other than news groups, such as private emails or even the telephone, letter or a personal meeting. In the end, Hofmann (1998: 15–16) likewise does not conclude that mailing lists are per se superior to other research resources and certainly not that they could replace them, but rather that they complement other resources. Parallel to her online investigations, she conducted offline interviews with the Internet authors she had previously observed and came to the conclusion that the results of the two forms of examination differ not in the extent to which they are in touch with reality or authentic, but in the way they represent reality.

Methodology of this study

> The ethnography which is presented in the next ... chapters is nei-
> ther a truth nor a fiction, but an account of an ethnographically
> constructed field of social interactions.
> Christine Hine, *Virtual Ethnography*

The first step in conducting an anthropological field study is selecting and defining a field. By selecting cyberactors and defining Moluccan cyber-space (the selection criteria are stated in the introduction), I constructed the ethnographic field in which I planned to conduct my online field re-search. Prerequisite for a participant observation among the Moluccan cy-beractors were membership of their mailing lists (FKAWJ and Masariku), subscription to their newsletters (CCDA) and regular visits to their web-sites (FKAWJ), which granted me access to the social spaces constituted online. I established contact with the cyberactors in a variety of ways. In the case of FKAWJ I registered impersonally for their mailing list via its Yahoo! online platform. Although Masariku uses the same platform for its mailing list, references must be given before membership is granted. My contacts to Moluccans in the Netherlands who, in turn, were in personal contact with the founders of the list and able to confirm my motives, were very helpful here. I established contact with the CCDA via email and I was subsequently registered as a subscriber to the newsletter. Here again, links to members of the CCDA, which I had established during my stay on the Moluccan Islands in 1996, were beneficial. By the end of 2000 I was a member of all three groups, and from then on received comprehensive and up-to-date information on the Moluccan conflict, most of which was in Indonesian.[8]

Especially in the case of Masariku, following the list discourse turned out to be highly time-consuming, but crucial in order to understand the communitization and identity-finding processes taking place. Whereas in the case of the CCDA and the FKAWJ almost all reports sent were writ-ten by the senders themselves (and all of which I included in my analysis), a great number of external contributions, such as newspaper articles, were forwarded via the Masariku mailing list. This is why the number of emails per month sometimes reached several hundred. Here, I concentrated on posts that list members and founders wrote themselves. I have only taken forwarded newspaper articles into account insofar as they serve the un-derstanding of the list discourse or the above-mentioned processes. Only

in the case of Masariku was active participation in the list discussion possible thanks to the way the list is set up. I limited my activity to an email,
in which I introduced myself as a doctoral candidate of the Faculty of Social and Cultural Anthropology at the University of Munich and openly
explained my motives, plus a few interposed questions that referred to
specific posts by list members. By participating mostly passively (as a
lurker) and staying in the background, I wanted to avoid unnecessarily
influencing the list discourse.[9]

My participation primarily took the form of my being accepted as a
member, admitted and integrated into the dynamics of the lists. I built
up a relationship with individual list members by establishing email contact with them.[10] Thus, I was integrated into the online social fabric. By
combining distanced and involved research methods I was able to get to
know the members of the Masariku list as constituent parts of their online
environment on the one hand, and as individuals who take part in online
projects for individual reasons on the other. For similar reasons, I contacted via email the webmaster and list administrator of the FKAWJ and
the CCDA, in addition to analysing their websites and newsletters. Depending on my counterpart, the email exchange took place in Indonesian
or English. In the case of Masariku I had personal email contact with *all*
fifteen active members at the heart of the list, and with twenty-eight list
members overall, which, with a total membership of two hundred, spells a
relatively high percentage (14 per cent). Only three of my personal queries
remained unanswered in the end, although it was regularly the case that I
did not receive replies to questions I openly addressed to members of the
Masariku list. In personal emails to specific members, I once again introduced myself and explained my intentions.

The research period was a decisive factor in the success of my study.[11]
Only through long-term participant observation of online processes was
it possible to acquire cultural competencies with respect to the groups investigated, enabling a meaningful interpretation of the list discourse and
an understanding of the dynamics and different phases of the discourse,
and allowing me to move on the same level as the other members. This
is the only basis on which I could speak of true participation, develop an
emic perspective and experience what it means to be a member, and, at
especially bad moments in the conflict, be confronted, e.g., with an incredible number of emails and countless documents showing its horrors.
Long-term participation was essential to comprehend the intensity of this
experience, something we do not have if we merely extract all the data
from the list's archive. The seemingly 'regulated conditions', which will be
presented in the following chapters on the cyberactors (the profiles of the
posts, groups and members, their working methods, and the communitization, idealization and identity-shaping processes) were not explained as
topics in the spaces studied (lists as well as websites) and are the result of
this long-term participation and observation, which were accompanied by

continuous analysis and interpretation. That means that anthropological research traditions were being continued on the Internet, yet at the same time had to be adapted as regards establishing contact and actually conducting the research.

Yet a discourse analysis, be it online or offline, should simultaneously document the sociocultural context of the discourse, which is not only influenced by its respective context, according to Teun van Dijk (1997: 19), but can, in turn, have an impact on the latter, too. In order to investigate this interaction between the discourse in Moluccan cyberspace and its context both in the online and offline sphere, I examined the online environment of the cyberactors and also conducted offline research.[12] Through literature research in Germany and the Netherlands as well as establishing contact with Moluccans and Moluccan organizations in the Netherlands, I obtained background information on and ethnographic details relevant to the Moluccan conflict, for example, the *pela* alliance system and traditional feuds between villages. A research trip to Indonesia (Jakarta and Ambon) afforded me insight into the working environment and sociocultural context of the cyberactors. My aim was to get acquainted with the production conditions of Internet posts and the integration of the cyberactors in the local context; it was not about checking or verifying their online presentations. To this end I employed participant observation and conducted numerous interviews with active online members as well as people and organizations that were either in contact with them or the subject of the online posts. Only in the case of FKAWJ members was participant observation in an offline context impossible, as they live very withdrawn lives in the Moluccas, rarely mix with the local population and are not allowed to openly interact with women. However, I was able to conduct interviews with the webmaster in Jakarta and the heads of the public relations (PR) departments in Jakarta and Ambon. Moreover, I successfully established contact with local Laskar Jihad sympathizers in the city of Ambon.

Religion and conflict on the Internet

Miller and Slater (2000: 25) observed that religious communities use the Internet to solve the problem of spatial dispersion and bring together fellow believers from different places – be it in the wider diaspora or within their community. For instance, the Internet enables the people of Trinidad to be a part of global Hinduism despite spatial separation (ibid.: 178). Given that one of the key actors in the cyberspace of the Moluccan conflict is a radical Islamic group, I would first like to take a closer look at the topic of the Internet and Islam, which hitherto has unfortunately received far too little attention (Bunt 2000: 143). In view of the anti-Western attitude of many radical Islamic groups, it is all the more surprising when they use the medium of the Internet, which is clearly dominated by the English language and Western industrialized nations. I will subsequently address the topic of the Internet and conflict.

Islam online

Niklas Luhmann (1996: 153) concludes that the reality of the mass media replaces the knowledge prescriptions that were provided in other social formations by excellent positions of observation: by sages, priests, the no-bility, or the city, by religious, politically or ethically distinguished ways of life. However, Luhmann does not address the question of what would happen if precisely these 'excellent positions of observation', such as re-ligious groupings and authorities, made use of the mass media or, in our case, the Internet. The Internet enables them to present themselves to an international audience and to establish links to widely distributed like-minded people and fellow believers. 'Cyber Islamic Environments', as Gary R. Bunt (2000) calls Islamic Internet presentations, provide primary sources of Islam online – be it the Koran, Hadith or Sunnah – and also enable Muslims to listen to online recitations from the Koran at work, at home or in their academic environment. The Internet offers both original and translated English-language material that is otherwise hard to come by. Digitally, in a multimedia format, texts, speeches, and educational and propaganda material can be disseminated effectively (ibid.: 66). According to Bunt, the use of the Internet as a source of information has been increas-ing rapidly among both Muslims and non-Muslims, meaning that online material also shapes their conception of Islam and of Muslims (ibid.: 3).

Bunt (2000) asks whether a 'digital *umma*', meaning a digital Muslim global community, is emerging or being promoted on the Internet and, if yes, whether this is a 'real' or 'imagined' phenomenon. Moreover, he wants to know to what extent an idealized notion of Muslim identity, compared to reality, is being created in cyberspace, and how this might influence individuals and groups, especially those that find themselves in hostile situations (ibid.: 11–12). In the Moluccan conflict, too, such con-siderations are of interest in terms of the Muslim presence in cyberspace. Many Muslim websites, so Bunt (ibid.: 43) suggests, could be seen as emu-lating the concept of a global (electronic) *umma*, for they enable access to specific ideas and communication without borders. Yet, on the other hand, the Internet is multivoiced – a key characteristic. Different branches of Islam (Sunnis, Shiites or Sufis) with very different interests (i.e. loyal to the government or opposition, paramilitary or representing students) all present themselves on the Internet. This gives the user an impression of great fragmentation rather than that of a global Muslim community (ibid.: 105, 130–31). Yet common to all Muslim participants is that they consider the Internet an integral part of their information strategies. Cyber Islamic Environments are, according to Bunt, a primary medium for religious, political and ideological leadership. Websites, chat forums and emails play a crucial role in the creation of cohesive electronic identities in cyberspace for Islamic political agendas and concerns. Many of these sites are linked with each other; however, the concept of a free dialogue, a shared agenda or even a common cyber-Islamic identity or community has not been realized (ibid.: 102–3, 133).

As with the self-presentation of other groups and individuals, here too the question arises as to who decides what the interpretation should be and thus the authenticity claimed. Decisions on specific questions of faith and law – so-called *fatwas*, expert opinions of Islamic jurists – on the Internet can, on the one hand, contribute to a unification of the global Islamic community in this respect. Yet, on the other hand, they might also undermine the authority of traditional religious leaders (see, e.g., J. Anderson 1997; Bunt 2000: 107). Eickelman and Anderson (1999b: 2) argue that the Internet gives the Muslim community a new feeling of a discursive, performative and participatory public, the emergence of a 'Muslim public sphere', which is characterized by an ever more open, global competition for the authoritative use of the symbolic language of Islam (see also Mandaville 2001: 152–77). Of course, other media also contribute to this. Just as the speeches of Ayatollah Khomeini and others in Iran were spread via cassette tapes in the 1970s, for example, in the late 1990s videotapes circulated of people preaching and demonstrating against the regime in several countries of the Arabian Peninsula. Tapes, flyers and fax machines serve the same purpose in Morocco, Afghanistan and Saudi Arabia (see J. Anderson 1999; Calhoun 1995: 266–67; Eickelman 1999; Eickelman and Anderson 1999b: 3). With the Internet, the scope and degree of influence have entered a new dimension, through which less people might be reached locally, but all the more will be reached worldwide. According to Esad Coşan, the leader of the İskenderpaşa Nakşibendi Order in Turkey, the media represent the new spaces for jihad, the striving for Islamic faith (Yavuz 1999: 183). Bunt (2000: 17) likewise highlights that the Koran in cyberspace is a continuation of the obligation to *da'wa*, the propagation of Islam. Moreover, he notes, the Internet enables the integration of other contemporary *da'wa* media such as online books, newspapers and pamphlets, as well as audiovisual radio and TV material and tape recordings of Islamic messages.

On the one hand, Islamist groups resist the influence and phenomena of modern times, yet on the other they often make use of the technological achievements in order to pursue their goals. They use the freedoms of the Internet and create websites or mailing lists to spread their version of Islam, increase the number of their followers and establish links to like-minded people. The Al-Qaeda network, for example, maintained its own website (http://www.alnaeda.com) until the latter was 'conquered' by American hackers, Palestinian groups have websites (including http://www.palestine-info.co.uk/hamas/), and other websites provide informa-

tion on jihad worldwide (such as http://qital.tripod.com/).[13] Thus, even
these radical groups have moved beyond the offline sphere in their propagation of jihad. The Yahoo! mailing group "uk_muslims: E-group for all
Muslims,"[14] for example, sent the following invitation with the subject
'Join the Cyber Jihad against Israel' in message number 309 (9 November
2000):

> Al Salam Alikom
> Invitation to all muslims online join the cyber jihad against the Israely sites.
> Their loss is our gain. so spread the word
> check this site: http://www.kuds.8m.com/
> if you know any similar activities please inform us so we can join.

However, there are still no systematic investigations of Islamic fundamentalist cyberpresence and its influence on the global interconnectedness of
the respective organizations or the course of local and regional clashes.[15]

Internet and conflict

The style of reporting in local, national and international media has a decisive impact on a conflict and the way in which outsiders perceive and react
to it. This has been proven by numerous analyses and examples (see, e.g.,
Allen and Seaton 1999b; Butler 1995; Hudson and Stanier 1998; Karetzky
and Frankel 1989; Knightley 1975). Media have the power to turn local unrest into a global media event in which people from all over the world can
participate. The media are agents of war and an integral part of the world
they describe. They also provide good insight into the way in which, in
conflict situations, ethnicity is instrumentalized as the allegedly underlying cause in order to divert attention from the real socioeconomic and
political problems (see, e.g., Allen and Seaton 1999a; Seaton 1999; Sofos
1999). The idea is created of fixed and quasi-natural group membership,
such as the 'Serbs', 'Croats' and 'Muslims' in the Yugoslav Wars (Allen
1999: 39). Those involved as well as observers need these simple categories
in order to understand the conflict, to know '[w]ho's it between' (Keen
1999). Depictions of the respective 'others' as usually extremely cruel
and inhumane in contrast to the helpless 'we' group become important in
media representations. Yet, especially in communication mediated by the
media, the key actors or constructers and their audience, that is, potential
members of the 'we' group, are not present in the same place. According
to Bernhard Giesen, this has an impact on the communication and construction process:

> Communication between absent actors therefore requires a functional substi-
> tute for the presence of the audience. One way of meeting this requirement is
> the simulation of personal encounters and the imagination of a strong mutual
> bond between the speaker and his audience. For example, the speaker can ap-

peal to moral or religious convictions, can point to an outside threat or enemy or the risk of the demise of traditions and community. The collective identity of the speaker and audience is thus constructed, staged and imagined by way of references to cultural codes whose validity is considered beyond doubt and a matter of course. (Giesen 1999: 80)

When this process of identity construction is transferred to the medium of the Internet, these simulations and common imagined ideas become very important.

Even more recent studies on the topic of media and conflict, such as those by Allen and Seaton (1999b) or Hudson and Stanier (1998), do not address the role of the Internet in conflicts. Yet groups involved in conflicts worldwide are increasingly using the Internet to spread their views. Like the role of the media in conflicts in general (see Halliday 1999; Seaton 1999), that of the Internet is likewise highly ambivalent. On the one hand, the Internet provides a global audience with an insight into a conflict of which it might otherwise never have known, often even doing so with firsthand information, that is, not mediated by journalists, as in mass media. On the other hand, however, the Internet gives the parties involved the opportunity to present the conflict in a way that serves their purpose and, thus, the opportunity to influence and manipulate their audience and the international community and expand the conflict. Hardly any works on this topic have been published to date. Previous examinations of the interrelationship between the Internet and conflict are essentially limited to cyberwars, generally physical attacks on individual strategic computers via the Internet, and flame wars, verbal battles carried out online.

Computer-mediated communication is much less neutral and dry than was assumed in the 1980s. This is due, among other things, to flame wars – clear, very emotional written conflicts conducted in cyberspace that involve a ruthless exchange of personal insults. In this environment, participants generally use far stronger wording than they would in a face-to-face situation offline (see, e.g., Barry 1991: 243; Faruk 2001: 10; Franco et al. 1995: 14; Hamelink 2000: 42; Kiesler, Siegel and McGuire 1984: 1129–30; Tepper 1997: 41; Turkle 1995: 13n4), possibly because they can hide behind their pseudonyms and, given the physical absence of their opponent, do not have to fear any penalties (see Dery 1993; Jordan 1999: 86). The emotional intensity can be increased still further by means such as the exclusive use of capital letters, which in an offline context corresponds to shouting. It is also possible to deliberately trigger online conflicts by using the technique of cross-posting. Here, a post from a mailing list or news group is extracted from its context and placed in a different one (e.g., another mailing list) in order to provoke heated comments and debates (Mitra 1997: 66–67).

According to Franco et al. (1995), however, in some circumstances flames can also have a positive effect on the community spirit of a group. Flames can help define the common values of an electronic community in contrast to another. Franco et al. (1995: 15) even speak of a rite of passage, which determines who will increasingly commit themselves to the community and who will leave it. According to Slevin (2000: 141–42), conflicts that are carried out on the Web can ultimately help individual people, groups or organizations gain recognition and support for their activities. Unfortunately, Slevin does not explore the topic of the Internet and conflict in greater depth. Somewhat idealistically, he merely points out that the Internet could, for example, reduce the conflict potential of intercultural communication situations, as it promotes dialogue, and that it could in general contribute to a better mutual understanding given the high frequency of communication, the diversity of information and its global reach (ibid.: 179). Yet, conflict and violence are integral parts of our societies, which is one reason why the interaction between the Internet and conflict needs to be examined in detail.

When development of the Internet was in its infancy and particularly after the launch of the WWW, users could easily get the impression that this was an entirely free, almost anarchistic space where state censors had no power. Dissident movements all over the world (e.g., in Cambodia, Indonesia, Mexico, Sri Lanka and Tibet) use the Web to fight for their political freedom, distribute corresponding material and create news groups (Hamelink 2000: 140). I have already provided some examples of sociopolitical movements and politically, culturally or religiously motivated, partially extremist groups that use the Internet to take their cause to an international level and to expand their group of supporters. However, from so-called cookies on individual computers to complex software technology surveillance and filter mechanisms, there is a range of means in cyberspace to monitor users' movements and take appropriate measures where necessary (see, e.g., Hamelink 2000: 125–26; Slevin 2000: 214–15). In China, for instance, the government uses these methods to strictly regulate access to the Internet and the selection of information available on the Web. According to Cees Hamelink (2000: 132–33), protecting personal data, too, is becoming ever more problematic due to the possibilities the Web offers. Yet users themselves also restrict their freedom, for instance, by way of mutual exclusion from news groups or censoring posts in mailing lists. In this way, undesired or differing opinions from specific circles can be blocked out (Hamelink 2000: 45).

Ultimately, the debate on the topic of cyberwar is primarily limited to physical attacks on individual computers via the Web. Hackers seek to penetrate foreign computer systems to obtain certain information or they try to paralyse politically strategic computers belonging to the government or their enemy by overloading the system or transmitting viruses. Hamelink (2000: 114–15) provides several examples of cyberattacks, for instance, on Pentagon and National Aeronautic and Space Administration (NASA) computers, respected search engines and the U.S. Department of Defense. In the context of the Israeli-Palestinian conflict, too, there are regular reports of Web attacks on central computer hubs. According to Hamelink (2000), the so-called cyberwar is an attractive and 'clean' alternative to conventional armed conflict.

Notes

1. Christine Hine actually has a background in the field of the 'sociology of science and technology', which, however, also included ethnographic education (Hine 2001).
2. John B. Thompson (1995: 203) likewise highlights the significance of media coverage and preservation of traditions for diaspora communities and migrants.
3. George E. Marcus (1994: 46–47) also argued that traditional ethnography has to explore new spatial concepts that accompany the idea of a dispersed, multi-local identity.
4. See also Erickson (1996). The application of the term phenomenological to this approach is based on Slevin's (2000: 172–74) criticism that Chandler (1998) does not sufficiently take into account the structured social relationships in which the construction of the site is embedded, instead only examining their phenomenological composition. Chandler (1998: 3), however, is more interested in the construction process of the website authors' identities, which, he claims, is reflected in the construction process of websites.
5. News groups and mailing lists are email-based discussion groups that are organized by a central administrator. Mailing lists distribute incoming posts to all members, whereas in the case of news groups they are filed at a WWW address that is accessible to all members. Selected members, in most cases the initiators, can act as moderators. Access to these groups is restricted or open.
6. Herbert Rauch (1983: 262) divides large groups into the so-called main speakers who make up a very small percentage of the group but have a decisive influence on the formation of milieus within the group. Rauch calls this inner circle of events the 'arena'. All 'passive' members of a large group, who are always in the majority, can be referred to as the 'gallery', merely contributing 'passive response' to the events. In addition, there is an interactive middle class contributing primarily 'active response'.
7. Some mailing lists and unidirectional newsletters represent an extreme case where only one person 'speaks' and everyone else listens.
8. In the case of Masariku and the FKAWJ I was able to reconstruct the discourse that had taken place in their respective online spaces until December 2000 using their online archives (Yahoo!). The CCDA sent me all reports published before that date via email.
9. The online announcement of my research did not trigger any discussion and the discourse was continued as before (I did not officially introduce myself until several weeks after joining the list, enabling me to make this comparison).
10. In classic anthropological research, too, that is, participant observation in the offline sphere, researchers do not establish relationships with all 'members of the field', but have specific informants and friendships.

11. This study takes into account posts made between the time when the individual Moluccan cyberprojects were set up (August 1999 and June 2000) and early 2003. By then I was able to look back upon more than two years of online field research in Moluccan cyberspace.

12. From mid-May to mid-July 2001 I stayed in the Netherlands, mostly at the Royal Netherlands Institute of Southeast Asian and Caribbean Studies (KITLV) in Leiden, and the Moluccan Historical Museum (MHM) and Moluccan Information and Documentation Centre (Infodoc Maluku) in Utrecht. In February and March 2002 I was in Indonesia.

13. No longer available in 2012.

14. http://groups.yahoo.com/group/uk_muslims.

15. The essay by the Anti-Defamation League on the subject *Jihad Online* (2002) provides an initial idea.

3

The Moluccan Conflict

A focus on key stages in the Moluccan conflict and on both local and national factors sheds light on the complex mechanisms involved. Since an identification with religion plays such a prominent role in the conflict at the local and cyberspace levels, it seems meaningful to explore the interrelationships of religion, identity and conflict.

Conflict description and analyses

Following is the description a reporter gave of the state of things in Ambon City in early 2000.

> Ambon is a city divided. Muslims occupy one end of town, Christians the other. Along the middle is a no-man's-land that acts as a line of partition. Armed soldiers keep a tense watch next to the barbed wire and the checkpoints. Around them are the reminders of the religious hatred that has torn Ambon asunder. Most buildings have been razed to the ground; those still standing are little more than burnt-out shells. A graffito on the wall of a rained department store scrawls out a defiant message: 'Muslim power vanquishes the Nazarenes.' Another reads: 'Christians conquer Muslim pigs.' For generations, Ambonese of both faiths practiced pela gandong – peaceful coexistence – under which mosques and churches were built together.[1] But it is clear that the tradition now lies buried underneath the rubble. (McCawley 2000)

As a result of the conflict, Ambon City and all areas of life for its inhabitants were divided along religious lines: Christians and Muslims live in separate areas and go to separate markets, public transport is segregated by religion and children attend separate schools;[2] even public agencies such as the post office had to be duplicated, so that there was a branch in the Muslim quarter and a branch in the Christian quarter. Refugees were housed in separate camps.[3] This segregation of Moluccan society continued into neighbouring villages and islands, and even extended to the Northern and Southeastern Moluccas. Bar a few exceptions,[4] there are no longer any mixed-religion villages. Christian or Muslim minorities in the villages were either driven out or fled. Muslims could no longer meet Christian members of their family or friends, and vice versa. Communication between the two territories became impossible and to cross the demarcation line meant running the risk of death. This physical and psychological division essentialized religious identities. Both sides now fear appropriation and repression by the 'other's' religion.

The beginning of the Moluccan conflict[5]

The date usually used as the official beginning of the Moluccan conflict is 19 January 1999, when the Muslims celebrated the end of Idul Fitri, the month of fasting. The conflict was triggered by a dispute between a Christian bus driver, Yopie Louhery, and a (Bugis) Muslim, Nur Salim, in the bus terminal in the area in between Batumerah and Mardika, two districts of Ambon City.[6] Only shortly thereafter rumours abounded throughout Pulau Ambon[7] that various churches and mosques had been torched, and the personal dispute swiftly escalated into a conflict between the Christian and Muslim religious communities in the Moluccan Islands. Although in the first few days Christian wrath and violence was directed mainly at the property of Muslim immigrants (first and foremost Butonese, Bugis and Macassaris, or BBM), owing to the ostensibly religious character of the conflict the Ambonese Muslims sided with their fellow Muslims and not with the Christian members of their ethnic community.

The incident of 19 January 1999 spread swiftly, although it was not unusual in the city of Ambon, and Christians and Muslims alike took this as proof that it was part of a larger scenario that had long since been planned and to which various occurrences beforehand pointed. The Moluccan Muslims suggest that 19 January 1999 was preceded by so-called test cases, minor incidents between Christians and Muslims in Ambon and finally, on 14 January 1999, in Dobo (Aru, Southeastern Moluccas), during which Christians purportedly practiced and planned their attack strategies, something the Christian side denies. Corresponding rumours must have been in circulation on both sides weeks before 19 January, such that owing to the tension in the air, some Muslim families refrained from paying their Christian friends the customary visit for Christmas in 1998, and the morning of Idul Fitri in 1999 was unusually quiet.[8] Opinions differ greatly between the Christians and the Muslims as to who pulled the strings behind the scenes, causing the unrest.

The spread of the conflict and the arrival of the Laskar Jihad

Since many inhabitants of Ambon City originate from the one or other of the surrounding islands, the conflict very swiftly spread to the neighbouring Lease Islands (Haruku, Saparua and Nusalaut), Seram and Buru

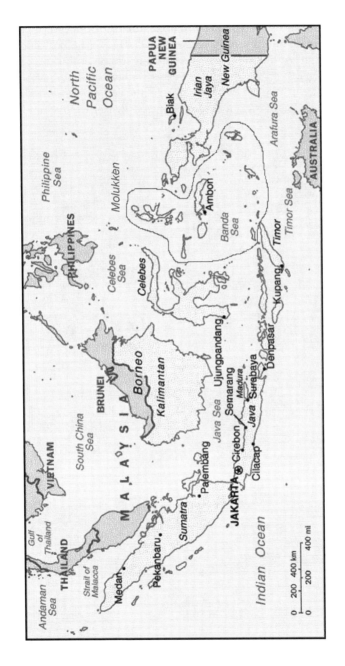

Illustration 1. Map of Indonesia[9]

(Illustration 2). In March 1999, the wave of violence spilled over onto Kei (Southeastern Moluccas). Even the Banda Islands (situated between Ambon and Kei) were not spared, and in August 1999 the conflict spread to the Northern Moluccas. Often only a rumour sufficed to trigger a new trouble spot.[10] To mention only one example, in Tidore (Northern Moluccas), the dissemination of a forged letter in which a priest called for the Christianization of the Moluccan Islands led to massive violence by Muslims against local Christians (Nanere 2000: 63–80). At the end of December 1999 the conflict peaked with the Silo Church, one of the largest Protestant houses

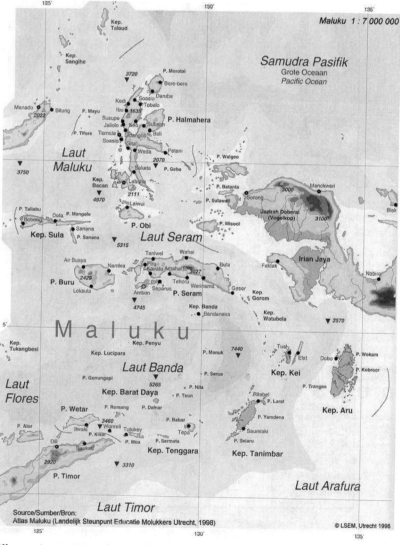

Illustration 2. Map of the Moluccan archipelago

of worship in Ambon City, being burnt down; within the space of only a few days hundreds of people, including women and children, had been massacred in several Muslim villages in North Halmahera.

Each act of violence was met with revenge by the other side, and thus the Moluccan conflict developed, quite independent of its causes, its own dynamics of attack and counterattack that served to widen the gap between the two religious groups. This resulted in a spiral of violence that persisted for more than three years, claimed thousands of lives on both sides and proved to be very difficult to break.

In response to the massacre in the North Moluccas, on 7 January 2000 Al Chaidar, a follower of a movement that champions an Islamic State of Indonesia (Negara Islam Indonesia, NII), organized a major rally at the National Monument in Jakarta, attended, according to George Junus Aditjondro (2001b), by forty thousand to one hundred thousand people, among them Amien Rais, chairman of the People's Consultative Assembly (MPR) and a former head of the Muhammadiyah, Indonesia's second largest Muslim organization, and Hamzah Haz, vice president of Indonesia in 2003, as well as twenty-two militant Muslim organizations. Here, for the first time, a jihad in the Moluccas was proclaimed. In early April 2000, the FKAWJ organized a second major religious meeting *(tabligh akbar)* at the Senayan Stadium in Jakarta, where thousands of jihad warriors, armed with sabres, gathered to demonstrate their readiness to head for the Moluccas. When Indonesian president Abdurrahman Wahid rejected their call to immediately bring the violence in the Moluccas to an end, the FKAWJ dispatched its warriors, the Laskar Jihad (jihad troops) to a military training camp in Bogor, Java, and then, in early May 2000, sent them to the Moluccan Islands (see Detikcom, 10 and 16 April 2000; International Crisis Group 2000a). Despite protests by both Wahid and many Muslim leaders, the security forces responsible in Surabaya Port did nothing to prevent the Laskar Jihad from boarding ship.[11]

The goal of the Laskar Jihad was to assist their fellow Muslims in their struggle against the Christians and protect them from being, so the message was, wiped out. In this way, the relative balance of forces between the local Muslims and Christians was shifted, and not in the Christians' favour. Whereas in the first few months of the conflict, both sides tended to fight with simple weapons (machetes, spears, bows and arrows, and handmade weapons and bombs), modern weaponry was now increasingly deployed (see also Bartels 2000). Although other radical Islamic groups in Indonesia, such as the Islamic Defenders Front (Front Pembela Islam, FPI)[12] and the Indonesian Mujahidin Council (Majelis Mujahidin Indonesia, MMI), had sent warriors to the Moluccas, the FKAWJ's Laskar Jihad are the best known, owing to their performance at the local and national levels and their presence in the national and international media, as well as through their own media, and thus have the greatest influence on the discourse surrounding the Moluccan conflict. According to the International

Crisis Group (2000a: 9), the Laskar Jihad assumed control of the existing militias on the Moluccas. Often during action there was no way of telling whether outside or local jihad warriors were involved, as many local Muslims shrouded themselves in wide white robes when fighting, just as did the Laskar Jihad.

Whereas the conflict had calmed down somewhat during the previous months, the arrival of the Laskar Jihad heated things up and violence ensued on a quite unprecedented scale: on 22–23 June 2000 the Christian University of the Moluccas (Universitas Kristen Indonesia Maluku, UKIM) was destroyed, on 3–4 July, the state Pattimura University was burnt to the ground, and on 6 July the Christian village of Waai, which had more than six thousand inhabitants, was razed to the ground, as was the Christian village of Sirisori and the Muslim village of Iha on Saparua on 22–23 September. On 27 June 2000 the government declared a civil state of emergency (Penguasa Darurat Sipil, PDS), to no avail.[13] Muslim groups within the Moluccas and elsewhere repeatedly claimed from the beginning of the conflict onwards that the Christians had deliberately sparked the unrest in order to take up the cross of the Moluccan independence movement of 1950, which foresaw a South Moluccan Republic (Republik Maluku Selatan, RMS), and secede from the state of Indonesia. Like a self-fulfilling prophecy, on 18 December 2000 a Christian doctor in Ambon City, Alex H. Manuputty, announced the foundation of the Moluccan Sovereignty Front (Front Kedaulatan Maluku, FKM) in order to achieve the goals of the RMS, which was at the time put down by force. Since the Indonesian government was not able to put an end to the conflict and protect human rights, so Manuputty claimed, independence was the only way out. The FKM became a thorny political issue and the decisive factor in the conflict from the viewpoint of the Muslims and the government. As the purported kingpin in the conflict, Manuputty was twice arrested and in early 2003 sentenced to three years in jail. The leader of the FKAWJ, Ja'far Umar Thalib, was likewise twice held on remand during the deployment of the Laskar Jihad in the Moluccas, probably as a result of international pressure. However, in January 2003 he was cleared of all charges, ostensibly owing to a lack of evidence against him.

Organizations in the Moluccan conflict

Unlike the Christians, who are organized through the church, the Muslims in the Moluccas had no central representative organ. The Indonesian Ulema Council (Majelis Ulama Indonesia, MUI), although officially the highest Muslim authority in Indonesia and with branches throughout the country, was unable to assume that function during the conflict in the Central Moluccas, as in Ambon City it lacked both popular support and a strong chairman. The latter had emigrated to the north after the outbreak of hostilities and the temporary chairman, Abdul Wahab Polpoke, was highly controversial, especially among Muslim hardliners. Countless local organizations were founded in an effort to unite the Muslims in the conflict. A small selection is presented here.[14] Jusuf Ely, for example, an influential Muslim in Ambon City, claimed to represent all Muslims on Leihitu, Ambon's northern peninsula. In February 1999 he set up the Bloody Idul Fitri Task Force, which was primarily defensive in function; he was at the time chairman of Yayasan Jaziratul Muluk,[15] which mainly cared for the welfare of refugees. Alongside Ely there were various businessmen, such as Abdullah Tuasikal and Amir Latuconsina, who planned reconstruction projects and also benefited economically from these. The mission of countless jihad positions *(posko-posko jihad)* was to act as command centres and provide protection for the different districts and villages.

Among the newly founded Muslim organizations were a series of extremist Islamic groups such as the Friendship Forum of the Islamic Community in the Moluccas (Forum Silaturahmi Ummat Islam Maluku, FSUIM), run by Rustam Kastor and Husni Putuhena,[16] the Forum of the Defenders of Justice in the Moluccas (Forum Pembela Keadilan Maluku, FPKM), run by Kastor, and the Task Force for the Enforcement of Divine Commandments and Prohibitions among Moluccan Muslims (Satgas Amar Ma'ruf Nahi Mungkar Muslim Maluku, AMNM3), run by Muhammad Attamimi, a lecturer at the State Islamic University in Ambon (Sekolah Tinggi Agama Islam Negeri, STAIN). The AMNM3 became known in particular for its activities countering prostitution, gambling and the consumption of alcohol. In May 2000 the Laskar Jihad arrived and laid claim to representing the local Muslim population. A quite different tack was taken by the Inovasi Group (a nongovernmental organization, or NGO), founded in April 2000 by several Muslim organizations to establish, together with the Christian NGO Hualopu, the Christian-Muslim reconciliation movement BakuBae, of which Jusuf Ely was also a member. In the final instance, none of these organizations succeeded in emerging as the central information conduit and voice representing the interests of all Muslims in the Moluccas. A large assembly of Moluccan Muslims (Musyawarah Besar Muslim Maluku) at the Al-Fatah Mosque in Ambon City in June 2001 therefore resolved that all Muslim groupings and the Muslim community of the Moluccas as such be united in an Association for the Coordination of Muslims in the Moluccas (Badan Immarah Muslim Maluku, BIMM). The foundation of the BIMM received the blessing of the governor of the Moluccas and Ali Fauzi, a former hardliner, was appointed its chairman.

On the Christian side, the Catholic Church set up a crisis centre, and the Catholic and Protestant Churches put a team of lawyers in place (Tim Pengacara Gereja, TPG), later to be replaced by the Protestant Church crisis centre. The three primarily concerned themselves with the aftermath of the conflict (refugees, evacuation, advocacy, etc.) and became the mouthpiece of the Diocese of Ambon and the Protestant Church of the Moluccas (Gereja Protestan Maluku, GPM). At the grassroots level, Berthy Loupatty and Agus Wattimena, both of whom resided in Kudamati, a 'Christian' district of Ambon City, emerged as the leaders when it came to mobilizing combatants, attacks and campaigns of revenge. Since 1984 Berthy had been leader of the Coker (Cowok Keren, 'Pretty Boys'), which was, according to Berthy, a 'band of drinkers, partygoers and gamblers' with eight permanent members and sympathizers all over Ambon and the surrounding islands. Until the outbreak of unrest there are said to have been Muslim Coker supporters, too.[17] Once the conflict started, Berthy had to share ruling the roost with Agus Wattimena, an employee of the Protestant Church who in the course of the conflict gradually gained the status of grassroots leader and became almost better known in that capacity than Berthy, which led on various occasions to disputes within the Christian camp. Christian circles termed Agus's group Black Horse (Kuda Hitam), whereas the Muslims called it Christian Soldiers (Laskar Kristus). On the Christian side there were also numerous command centres inside and outside Ambon City that served to coordinate the defensive and offensive strategies. While Agus is said to have received support from the Netherlands, the assumption is that Berthy collaborated with elements of the Indonesian Army's Special Forces Command (Komando Pasukan Khusus, Kopassus). Agus was shot in March 2001 (or shot himself), and Berthy surrendered to the police in December 2002 after a national search warrant had been issued for his arrest, as he and the Coker were suspected of being involved in various raids and bombings in Ambon and the neighbouring islands.

Both sides founded many NGOs in the course of the unrest. While prior to 1999 there were no more than two dozen in the Moluccas, by early 2002 the figure had leaped to well over three hundred, with many of the NGOs also seeking to profit from the conflict. There were also international NGOs such as Mercy Corps, Action Contre la Faim and various United Nations (UN) aid organizations.

Government measures and peace initiatives

The Jakarta government was maligned by Christians and Muslims alike for its inability to take effective steps to bring the Moluccan conflict to an end. Various members of government, the president and the vice president[18] visited the Moluccas on several occasions, without making any promises and always emphasizing that the Moluccans themselves needed to find a way out of the mess they were in. The findings of a team of investigators the government sent to the Moluccas were never published, nor were they a visible success. Moreover, in September 1999 the province of the Moluccas was divided into two provinces, the predominantly Muslim North Moluccas or Maluku Utara and the Moluccas or Maluku (Central Moluccas and Southeastern Moluccas), in the vain hope that this would enable the conflict to be brought swiftly under control.[19] First and foremost, however, the central government opted for military means. By July 2000 a total of some 14,000 soldiers were stationed on the archipelago, compared with 5,300 one year earlier; however, they evidently did not want to bring things under control, or were not able to (International Crisis Group 2000b: 4).[20] Parts of the Indonesian Army (Tentara Nasional Indonesia, TNI) had clearly taken sides during the armed conflict, which is why on 26 June 2000 the Pattimura forces in Ambon were placed under the command of a Balinese Hindu, I Made Yasa, in the hope that he would guarantee the TNI's greater neutrality.[21] Taken together with the state of civil emergency that had been declared, in the longer view this seems to have reduced the intensity of the conflict.

Of the various peace conferences the government organized, it was the conference in Malino, in South Sulawesi, in February 2002 that first bore fruit. Malino had been preceded by a whole raft of peace efforts at both the local and the national level. Above all, in the first few months after the outbreak of hostilities, *adat* and religious leaders had frequently met to swap ideas on how to stop the violence and to best influence their respective congregations accordingly.[22] During this time, there were many who appealed to people to remember the traditional Muslim-Christian alliance system *(pela)* and use it to bring about peace. There were interreligious initiatives such as the Movement of Concerned Moluccan Women (Gerakan Perempuan Peduli Maluku, GPPM) and the BakuBae movement, which organized interreligious meetings and events both locally and nationally. There were also international efforts to bring about peace, such as the interreligious aid projects launched by international NGOs and UNICEF's joint computer project for Christian and Muslim pupils. One of the largest peace events prior to Malino took place in Langgur, on Kei Kecil, in the Southeastern Moluccas, and was entitled National Dialogue on Revitalizing Local Culture for Rehabilitation and Development in the Moluccas towards a New Indonesia. From 15 to 18 March 2001, more than 1,500 religious, *adat*, government and NGO representatives, intellectuals, students and people from the worlds of business and law from the entire Moluccan Islands convened there. The venue had been carefully selected, as the unrest had been relatively swiftly terminated in the Southeastern Moluccas, above all owing to the fact that the *adat* leaders were still highly influential in that region (see, e.g., Laksono 2002). It was no doubt thanks to these countless peace efforts that between 2001 and 2002 the number of major attacks gradually dwindled. Instead, the number of bombings and attacks by small 'ninja' groups, often clad in black garb, rose. It became apparent that the war-weary Moluccan population could no longer be so easily incited and provoked as had been the case in 1999 and 2000.

The most successful peace negotiations took place in mid-February 2002 in Malino. Since shortly beforehand negotiations had been held at the same place on the conflicts in Central Sulawesi, the event became known as Malino II. Invitations had gone out to thirty-five representatives, respectively, of the Muslim and Christian sides, and the outcome was an eleven-point plan to terminate the conflict and put an end to the violence. Among other things, this included an investigation into the role of the FKM and the Laskar Jihad in the conflict, to be conducted by an independent national team, an endeavour to prevent separatist tendencies, an offensive against illegal possession of arms, the assertion of law and order and the stronger recognition of local traditions by religious figures. Countless socialization events were then held in Ambon City and in villages in the Central Moluccas in an attempt to familiarize the population with the results of Malino II and augment the chances for their implementation. Radical Muslim circles and individuals, including the FKAWJ, the FSUIM, Putuhena, Attamimi and Kastor, refused to recognize the eleven points of the Malino II plan, as they did not regard the thirty-five Muslim delegates as representative of the will of the Moluccan population, and therefore refused to accept the results achieved at the negotiating table. Furthermore, other groups would seem to have had an interest in a continuation of the conflict, be it elements of the military or police, private individuals or local bands that profited from the conflict (International Crisis Group 2002: 19–21).

The sense of euphoria in the city of Ambon following Malino II soon dissipated as in its wake came further bombings, an arson attack on the governor's office and a raid on the Christian village of Soya di Atas that again led to the deaths of several people, including women and children, as well as the destruction of one of the oldest churches in the Moluccas. Although the civil state of emergency was still in place in the Central Moluccas more than one year after Malino II (in the Northern Moluccas it was lifted in mid-2003) and by no means were all eleven points of the plan implemented, for the government Malino II constituted the official end of the conflict, as it were. From Malino II onwards, the attempts at rapprochement on both sides increased, even if it was not until the end of 2002 that violent attacks actually apparently ceased. In October 2002, the Laskar Jihad withdrew from the Moluccas and the FKAWJ was dissolved. The religious dividing lines in everyday life remained in play in the interim and not until early to mid-2003 did they gradually start to fade. One of the major challenges then became enabling the huge number of refugees to return to their homes and to restore everyday Christian-Muslim life.

To this day, there are no exact figures for the Moluccan conflict as regards the death toll, the number of injured persons and refugees or how many churches and mosques were destroyed. Many documents and data were destroyed during the unrest, communication between the parties to the conflict was as good as impossible, there was no central registry for the dead or for refugees and, in particular, many Muslim migrants simply fled the Moluccas. The numbers differ greatly depending on the source. Official figures are, or so the commentators assume, usually below the real figures owing to the difficulties of collecting the data. According to the government in the city of Ambon (*Data Pemerintah Provinsi Maluku*), by December 2001 more than 330,000 persons were officially registered as refugees in the Moluccan Province and about 30,000 residences and 253 places of worship (a roughly equal number of churches and mosques) had been destroyed. The various reports and media coverage speak of a total number of dead for the Moluccas as a whole of between 6,000 and 15,000, with the number of refugees estimated at almost 700,000 – in other words, almost a third of the entire population of the Moluccas had to flee at one point or another during the conflict (International Crisis Group 2002: i).

The Crisis Centre of the Diocese of Ambon (CCDA) estimates the number of Catholic churches destroyed by March 2002 at 77 and puts the figure for Protestant churches at 180; in total, it suggests, some 10,000 to 13,500 people lost their lives (Böhm 2001, 2002b; personal conversation with the head of the CCDA on 15 March 2002). According to I. J. W. Hendriks, the chairman of the GPM, by the end of 2001 a total of 184 Protestant churches had been destroyed in the Moluccan Province and some 1,500 members of the GPM killed.[23] Former chairman Sammy Titaley went on record in March 2001 saying that 2,000 GPM members had been killed, 192 churches had been destroyed, and 190,000 members of the church had fled.[24] According to the Manado Post of 21 August 2000, in the North Moluccas alone 3,931 persons had been killed in the period up to August 2000. According to Jumu Tuani, who continued to compile the MUI statistics after the president left, by the end of 2001 304 mosques had been burnt down in Maluku Province and some 5,000 Muslims killed. He suggested that 623,000 Muslims had by then fled the Moluccas and about 28,000 Muslim refugees were in the city of Ambon (personal conversation, 18 and 22 March 2002). The North Moluccan MUI announced on 16 February 2000 that in its area 3,567 persons had perished, 93 mosques been burnt down and 11,089 homes destroyed, and that in the cities of Ternate and Tidore alone there were 91,505 refugees (http://www.laskajihad.or.id/bantu/mandat.htm, 14 November 2001). Evidently, there was chaos as regards what the real figures were, and this was further complicated by the various press reports.

Local and national factors underlying the conflict

During the more than three years of the conflict, not only Indonesians, but also international NGOs, Christian organizations and academics from various disciplines published countless analyses of the conflict. They studied the cultural and ideological background of the conflict, the role of the political and military elites, the events that preceded 19 January 1999 and the overall Indonesian context.[25] While authors such as Aditjondro and Schulte Nordholt primarily examined the external causes of the conflict and put forward the hypothesis that it was instrumentalized and provoked, Bartels, for example, investigates the local factors that contributed to the outbreak of the conflict. The fierceness and sustained character of the Moluccan conflict can only be explained if we combine both approaches and analyse both the local and national factors that, taken together, turned the Moluccas into a powder keg that exploded on 19 January 1999.

Local factors driving the conflict

Like North Sulawesi, Irian Jaya and the Eastern Lesser Sunda Islands (Nusa Tenggara Timur), the Moluccas are an exception in Indonesia as compared with the rest of the republic, as Christians account for a very high proportion of the population, and in parts are actually in the majority.[26] It is for precisely this reason that the Moluccas were repeatedly praised in Indonesia as a paramount example of peaceful coexistence, given the harmonious relationship between Christians and Muslims there. This was decisively the product of the traditional *pela* alliances that existed between villages in the Central Moluccas irrespective of their religious affiliations, that is, between Christian and Muslim villages, which pledged to provide reciprocal assistance in times of crisis and when building a mosque or church, and mutually celebrated festivities accordingly.[27] Yet what was overlooked in the panegyrics was that in the Moluccas there had always also been violent conflicts between villages, most of which tended not to have anything to do with religion, however. Between villages such as Haria and Porto, Itawaka and Noloth, Ouw and Ullath (all Christian and all on Saparua) or between Waai (Christian), Tial and Liang (Muslim) on Ambon and city districts such as Mardika and Batumerah, there were long-established traditions of feuds.[28] These hinged primarily on economic advantages, disputes over land and borders, and the disagreements never assumed the scale that confronted the Moluccans from January 1999 onwards, but were always swiftly put to rest by traditional intermediaries (see Bartels 2000; F. von Benda-Beckmann 1999; Cooley 1961: 108–10, 234–38; Strijbosch 1992). However, the Muslim and Christian communities never really mixed. People celebrated Christmas and Idul Fitri together, but there were usually no interreligious marriages. Most villages had been either majority or completely Christian or Muslim for centuries,[29] and even in Ambon City many districts had always been considered 'Christian' or 'Muslim', even if the population was essentially mixed. The relationship was more of tolerating coexistence than of harmonious mutual understanding.[30]

A 'traditional' conflict of a different kind is that between local Christians and/or Muslims and Muslim immigrants (primarily BBM). The shared religion, Islam, was for a long time not a sufficiently strong factor to integrate or unite the local Muslims and the BBM (F. von Benda-Beck-mann 1990: 30–31). At times, the local population spoke of the 'BBM danger' *(bahaya BBM)*. Specifically, in recent years, the Butonese and Bugis have increasingly been considered as frequently drunk and prone to violence (Mearns 1996: 102). As regards the relationship between Christians and the BBM, the ethnic differentiation also applied to the business world. While the BBM, for example, controlled the cycle rickshaw business *(becak)* and the markets, the Christians preferred office jobs (see Mearns 1996, 1999).[31] In the course of the economic crisis that commenced in 1997, the Christians needed to reorient themselves, leading to economic envy of the BBM. In the conflict in question, as David Mearns (1999: 32) suggests, the Christians' hatred of the lesser educated and poorly paid Butonese surfaced. Only after many Christians had lost their jobs in the course of the conflict and no Muslim *becak* drivers dared enter Christian territory did the Christians more or less enter this field of business (Nirahua 2003).[32]

In the conflict at hand, religion only became such an identity-defining element because it was accorded ever-greater importance in the Moluccas over the last twenty to thirty years, while the significance of *adat* and the *pela* alliances receded. The reasons for this included the destruction of traditional village administration systems with the Indonesian government's implementation of a uniform village law (Law No. 5/1979) in the 1980s, growing urbanization, and the influx of Muslims from outside the Moluccas in the context of government transmigration programmes and spontaneous migration.[33] The city of Ambon has always been an ethnic patchwork in which ethnicity posed no effective organizational structures.[34] In the course of Suharto's Islamization policy from the beginning of the 1990s onwards, Muslims gradually assumed administrative posts that had hitherto been dominated by Christians.[35] In the course of this gradual Islamization of Moluccan society, the distance between local Christians and Muslims essentially widened, the dissatisfaction among Christians grew and bonds became more closely knit between local Muslims and their brothers in faith, the BBM (see, e.g., Aditjondro 2000e, 2001a).

National factors driving the conflict

The Moluccan conflict cannot be considered independent of the developments in Indonesia where, following Suharto's resignation, ethnic and religious tensions that had long been suppressed everywhere broke out in the so-called SARA conflicts (Suku, Agama, Ras dan Antargolongan = ethnicity, religion, race and class) and often culminated in violent conflict. In the case of the Moluccas, alongside the Indonesian government's transmigration programmes, the decisive factors driving the conflict at the national level were Suharto's Islamization policies, which as of 1995–96 led to increasing anti-Christian upheaval throughout Indonesia, and Suharto's resignation itself, with all its consequences (see, among others, Aspinall, Klinken and Feith 1999; K. van Dijk 2001; Forrester 1999; Hefner 1999; Manning and Diermen 2000; Schwarz 1999; Schwarz and Paris 1999).

Because at the end of the 1980s Suharto felt his power was no longer sufficiently guaranteed by the military, he sought backup from Islam, whose political movements (and the influence thereof) he had until then always suppressed. He seized upon measures that nurtured the hopes of those groups in Indonesia that since the country's independence in 1945 had advocated the introduction of an Islamic state in Indonesia, the world's largest Muslim country, whose constitution had hitherto rested on the so-called five pillars *(Pancasila)*: belief in one God, humanity, Indonesia's unity, democracy based on consensus and social justice (see, among others, Hefner 2000a; Mangkey 2000; Meuleman 2001; Ramage 1995). The foundation in 1991 of the Association of Indonesian Muslim Intellectuals (Ikatan Cendekiawan Muslim Indonesia, ICMI) by B. J. Habibie, at the time minister of research and technology, amounted to sounding the starting gun for Islam's political upturn in Indonesia, instrumentalized by Suharto.[36] Next was the opening of an Islamic bank, the extension of the authority of Muslim courts, the repeal of the prohibition on veils being worn in schools, the foundation of an Islamic daily *(Republika)*, the dissolution of the state lottery, etc. (Hefner 1997, 2000a: 18–19).

Abdurrahman Wahid, elected the first democratic president of Indonesia in 1999, was highly critical of this new development, as it was in this way religion, he said, became politicized and instrumentalized and Islamic fundamentalists were given a boost (Ramage 1995: 70–72). By contrast, for Amien Rais, a prominent ICMI member, the politics of Islamization constituted the only way to avert the threat of the Christianization *(kristenisasi)* of Indonesian society, which, he suggested, was evidenced by the growing number of Christians who were in ministerial positions or high-ranking members of the military during the New Order (Ramage 1995: 99). Irrespective of this, religion has always been a political beast in Indonesia, be it during colonial times, when in the opinion of the Muslims the switch to Christianity signalled loyalty to the colonial overlords, or in independent Indonesia, where Suharto banned atheism for fear of communism and people had to profess to one of five religions (Islam, Protestantism, Catholicism, Hinduism or Buddhism) and religious instruction became mandatory in schools (see, e.g., Feillard 2000a; Laksono 2002). In his effort to divide the opposition along religious and ethnic lines, from 1996 Suharto's strategies became increasingly anti-Christian and anti-Chinese (Hefner 2000a: 19), fully in line with the mind-set of Muslim hardliners such as KISDI,[37] which claimed the Indonesian economic crisis was attributable to a Zionist-Jewish world conspiracy that was planning Suharto's overthrow (Hefner 2000a: 202–3). After Suharto resigned, the last barriers seemed to be gone, and a plethora of Islamic newspapers and parties arose, as well as various Islamic groups, including the above-mentioned

FPI, MMI[38] and FKAWJ. Noorhaidi Hasan suggests these groups were united in their claim to fight for Allah's cause and their anti-Western and anticommunist attitude (http://www.iias.nl/iias/research/dissemination/phd/noorhaidi.html, 9 March 2002).

We should see the sudden surge in anti-Christian upheaval in Indonesia as of the mid-1990s in this context. According to figures from the Indonesian Christian Communication Forum (2001),[39] under Sukarno's 21-year presidency only 2 churches were destroyed, burnt down or closed, while under Suharto the figure was 456 (in 32 years), 275 alone in 1995–98; under Habibie, from May to October 1998, 156 churches were destroyed, burnt down or closed, 232 under Abdurrahman Wahid from November 1998 to July 2001 and 60 under Megawati from August 2001 to January 2003. Given these trends, John A. Titaley (2001) assumes that the Moluccan conflict is part of a far larger plan of Islamization designed to elide any traces of Christianity in the Moluccas and in Indonesia as a whole.

Alongside radical Islamic Muslims, who remain a small minority in Indonesia,[40] many analysts suggest that the military and supporters of the former Suharto regime had an interest in the Moluccan conflict, for which religion was instrumentalized (see, e.g., Aditjondro 2000a, 2000b, 2000d, 2001a, 2001b; Chew 2000; M. Cohen 2000; Hefner 2000b, 2001; Houben 2000a, 2000b; Institut Studi Arus Informasi 2000a; International Crisis Group 2000a, 2000b; Lev 2001; Mangkey 2000; McCawley 2000; Salampessy and Husain 2001; Schulte Nordholt 2000b; Sihbudi et al. 2001; Watch Indonesia 1999). After the fall of the Suharto regime, the new government initiated reforms that were supposed to gradually overcome the Indonesian military's double function *(dwifungsi)* as defence unit and political factor (see, e.g., Anderson, Shiraishi and Siegel 1999: 142–43; Liddle 1999; Liem Soei Liong 2000; Mangkey 2000; Tesoro 1999). Thus, the military, or at least a part of it that was not prepared to accept these developments, says Aditjondro (2001b), had several reasons to actively participate in initiating or prolonging the Moluccan conflict: first, to delay the reforms and maintain their dual role; second, to preserve the integrity of the nation's territories; third, to defend the territorial structure of the TNI; fourth, to defend the military's economic interests; and fifth, to distract attention from human rights violations by the military. The organization TNI Watch, for example, found out that renewed unrest broke out in Ambon while Wiranto, the then commander in chief of the TNI who was accused of human rights violations in East Timor, was being interrogated (SiaR News Service 22 May 2000). Moreover, there are suspicions that Suharto circles were likewise involved in the Moluccan conflict to preserve their business interests there, to damage the government and to divert attention away from the investigations into the assets of various members of the Suharto family.

An incident in Jakarta's Ketapang district and its consequences are seen as a harbinger of, or rather as part of the orchestration of, the Moluccan conflict. On 22 November 1998 an argument arose there between Ambonese Christians, who worked as doormen at a casino, and local Muslims. On the back of a rumour that the Ambonese Christians had trashed a local mosque, trucks of Muslim youths were brought in who destroyed some churches out of revenge and killed several Ambonese. The military used the incident as a reason to round up all Moluccans without papers in Jakarta and send them back to Ambon, and they included many of the Ketapang people who had sworn revenge. According to Aditjondro (2001a: 111), this may have been a stroke of cunning by Suharto supporters in order to stir up unrest in Ambon (see also Jubilee Campaign U.K. 1999). On 30 November, Christians held a demonstration in Kupang, West Timor, protesting the destruction of churches in the Ketapang incident. Suddenly, once again a truckload of young men arrived who within the shortest space of time set fire to a Bugis district and a mosque. According to Human Rights Watch (1999: 6), both acts were instigated by the military, which wished to benefit from the civil unrest and created a highly tense situation in Ambon. This prompted the government in the Moluccas to warn religious leaders not to respond to provocation and rumours given the pending Christmas and Idul Fitri celebrations.

The media in the Moluccan conflict

The media also embodied the religious dichotomization of Moluccan society. First of all, the notion of a religious conflict was gratefully adopted in the media coverage and indeed the media no doubt played a major role in shoring up that image. Secondly, a division occurred in the sense that certain media were categorized as belonging in the Christian camp, others in the Muslim one. Analyses of the conflict to date have paid far too little attention to the possible way this fed back into the conflict. The Indonesian Institute for Studies on the Free Flow of Information (Institut Studi Arus Informasi, ISAI) dedicated an issue of its magazine *PANTAU* (2000b) to the Moluccan tragedy *(Petaka Maluku)* and an analysis of reporting on it in the major national dailies – *Kompas, Suara Pembaruan* and *Republika*. The study suggests that *Republika* evidently championed the Muslim outlook and in its articles on the Moluccan conflict often spoke of a religious conflict, while *Kompas* and *Suara Pembaruan*, which could function as the mouthpiece of the Christians in the Indonesian media world, eschewed any explicit Christian standpoint and shied away from strongly emphasizing the religious aspects. Muhammad Qodari (2000) believes this to be an aftereffect of the *Orde Baru*, the New Order under Suharto.

At the local level, dailies, radio and TV stations can be classified far more accurately in terms of belonging to a specific camp. Owing to the conflict, in 1999 an independent Muslim daily, *Ambon Ekspres*, split off from the *Suara Maluku* daily, which, like *Siwalima*, was regarded by the

Muslims as an organ of the Christians. The offices were in the Christian and Muslim areas respectively, the staff journalists either Christians or Muslims. Since the journalists were denied access to much of the information on the respective other side, reporting was invariably one-sided or incomplete, even if the reporters sought to remain neutral. Thus, in the Muslim districts of Ambon City the newspaper stands sold, for example, *Ambon Ekspres,* the weekly *Suisma* (Suara Umat Islam Maluku, Voice of the Moluccan Islamic Community), *Jurnal Islam,* books by Rustam Kastor and Husni Putuhena, and, however clichéd this may sound and however little it says about actual or merely ideological links, Osama bin Laden posters; while in the Christian districts you could buy *Suara Maluku, Siwalima, Kompas* and posters and calendars of Jesus. The national TV station TV Republik Indonesia (TVRI) and the Radio Republik Indonesia (RRI) broadcasting house in Ambon were often accused by the Muslims of being pro-Christian. In actual fact, both were strongly government-influenced and TVRI had a Muslim and Christian crew, even if the main office was in the Christian section of town, where the RRI studios were also to be found. Contact with the 'other side' was only possible by phone, making any objective and balanced reporting impossible.[41] In the Christian camp it was primarily the FKAWJ media in Ambon that came in for fierce criticism; these included the provocative radio station SPMM (Suara Perjuangan Muslimin Maluku, Voice of the Moluccan Muslims' Struggle).

Not until early 2001 did the person responsible for the civil state of emergency, Saleh Latuconsina, repeatedly warn the Moluccan people that they should not allow themselves to be provoked by the reports in certain local and national papers, TV and radio stations and called on the media to report neutrally, and actually took firm steps in this regard (see, e.g., *The Jakarta Post,* 28 February 2001; satunet.com, 27 March 2001). One was to resolve to close down SPMM, something that never actually happened; another was the 28 August 2001 prohibition on any journalist coverage of FKM activities. This prompted the TNI to attack two journalists from *Siwalima* and *Suara Maluku,* as they wished to take part in the same reconciliation meeting as Alex Manuputty in Waisarissa (Seram). For organizations such as the Indonesian Alliance of Independent Journalists (Aliansi Jurnalis Independen, AJI) and Reporters Without Borders (Reporter sans frontières, RSF), the civil state of emergency posed a major threat to the freedom of the press and was a cause of great concern and protest (Press Freedom Alert 2000). However, to date no one has yet considered that the conflict also continued in the medium of the Internet.

Even if the Moluccan conflict was triggered by something else or was provoked or orchestrated by political or military masterminds, these local and national factors enabled religion to become a factor defining identity in the conflict, and not membership of an ethnic group, for example. Moreover, religion is an ideal means to create identity in times of crisis or conflict. Religion can function for both those involved and outside observers as a means for grasping and explaining a conflict. In the case of the Moluccas this led to the highly complex structures and mechanisms of the conflict being simplified, something decisively fostered by the media coverage. According to Peter Kreuzer (2000: 20), the conflict was thereupon realigned to primordial (religious) identities and its structures dichotomized. Each individual was, he suggests, forced into a collective identity, with neutral or intermediary positions not being possible, as this would have fostered the suspicion that the person was betraying his own side. In fact, in particular on the Muslim side people who sought to act as intermediaries between Christians and Muslims constantly had to fear attacks from among their own ranks.

Excursus: The relationship between religion, identity and conflict

A more in-depth examination of the concept of identity underpinning the cybertheoretical considerations on collective identity provides an additional tool for analysing the Moluccan cyberprojects. I wish to follow Alberto Melucci (1995: 51) and grasp the concept of collective identity not as a fact or essence, but as an analytical instrument through which we view 'reality'. It can help as such to analyse phenomena that cannot be explained using other models. Collective identities may not be a theme per se in Moluccan cyberspace, but they do comprise an effective tool with which to better analyse and understand events and phenomena there. Interestingly enough, established offline identity strategies resurface in the identities constructed in the online world.

Collective identity

Essentially, we can distinguish in research into identity between two positions that differ in terms of what foundations they assume identities rest on. The primordialists suggest that phenomena such as ethnicity and religion are grounded in human nature, as it were, while the constructivists object that identity must be construed as a process of negotiation and construction. Since Fredrik Barth (1969), research into ethnicity and identity has focused less on the context of fixed patterns of identity and more on the dynamic process of negotiating the limits between two social groups that in this way first have an identity ascribed to them or attribute an identity to themselves. Thus, Zdzislaw Mach (1993: 269) defines identity as a dynamic process of reciprocal identification between partners in a social situation; identity, he says, is created symbolically here by constructing boundaries and images that define the groups and their relations to one another. Other commentators consider collective identity an ongoing process of negotiation (Melucci 1995: 44), a 'social construction' (Giesen 1999: 69) or 'social imagination' (Assmann 1999: 133). According to Melucci (1995: 44), the interactive process of construction engenders a framework in which collective actions can then occur. Accordingly, collective identities have to define specific goals, means and fields of action to which the active network of relations between the individual actors is then aligned. An identity project can, however, only be successful, he continues, if a certain degree of emotional effort is brought to bear, by means of which the individual develops a sense of belonging. Moreover, the subject must exist across various phases in time, adapt to its environment, set itself off from others and find its identity recognized (Melucci 1995: 44–45). Jan Assmann (1999: 134) suggests that the process whereby members become aware of this is crucial, as it first generates a 'we' consciousness, a feeling of solidarity and of belonging as well as stimuli that then guide action.

Construction and the politics of identity

Max Weber (1976: 237, 241) already referred to a 'believed community' that facilitates the process of communitization, when describing ethnic groups. The way this (ethnic) common belief arises is artificial, Weber suggests, namely, the result of a construction process, as there are no objective criteria for an ethnic community. Weber (1976: 238) cites linguistic, religious and political communities of fate, aesthetic distinctions and differences in how everyday life is lived as examples of ethnic differences. Research into ethnicity, identity and religion is often very closely interlinked. Depending on the context and interests involved, religion can become an element defining ethnicity, as, for example, is Buddhism for the Singhalese, Hinduism for the Tamils, and Islam for the Malays. In the case of conflict, such as the war in the Balkans, religion is often a key component of the feeling of ethnicity (Appleby 2000: 63–71). In line with Barth's model, Hitchcock (1996: 10–11) affirms that identity is constantly being (re-)created by conscious action, that is, it has to be constructed. Owing to its dynamic nature, ethnicity can be used as a strategic resource in this process of construction. Ethnicity and ethnic solidarity are then created in relation to the elements of a culture (among others a shared history, origin myths, language, descent, territoriality, lived practices) and through this their primordiality simultaneously established (Zurawski 2000: 41).[42] Depending on the situation, the identity-defining elements, namely, the patterns of inclusion and exclusion, change, something that can be decisive in the event of conflict (see Eriksen 1991: 129; Hitchcock 1996: 11; Meyrowitz 1997: 62; Rutledge 1985: 49–50).

Friedrich Heckmann (1997: 46) accuses the constructivists of construing ethnicity as a purely artificial construct that is only imagined but is not real. This criticism is based on a similar fallacy as regards the principle of imagination: that it has no claim to 'reality'. However, it has frequently been demonstrated that construction must not be confused with invention, and that 'identity constructors' have to resort to a repertoire of materials and symbols that depend strongly on a specific cultural and historical context if they are to create effective identity projects.[43] The materials used are, however, filtered and constructed by the memory, imagination, narratives and myths of the respective actors (Hall 1994: 395). In the case of cultural (or collective) identities, Stuart Hall (1994) continues, it is not essences that are entailed, but a positioning that takes its cue from the respective circumstances. Politics of identity is thus always involved, a politics of positioning. Collective identities are defined by the motivation, goals and context of the persons who participate in the construction process (see Baumann 1999: 21; Castells 2001b: 7; Mach 1993: 5). Depending on whom one seeks to set oneself off from, the respectively different elements are taken up and activated (Mach 1993: 7). Moreover, every individual usually inhabits several 'worlds' at once, that is, each is a member of several 'we groups' whose meaning changes for each individual depending on his personal and general situation (Calhoun 1995: xv).

As regards the politics of identity, Calhoun (1995) weighs essentialism (primordialism) up against constructivism, whereby his choice of the term 'politics of identity' already implies that identities, even if they rely on primordial elements, are always constructed. He would thus suggest that simply outlining the construction process is inadequate, as this does not provide an explanation of why people continue to refer to essentialist identities and why these often trigger profound emotions (ibid.: 198–99). In other words, we need to consider both the essentialist justifications and the construction process in order to be able to analyse the politics of identity (ibid.: 204). Since religion is one of the essentialist justifications in the Moluccan conflict and also plays an outstanding role in the construction process in cyberspace, later in this chapter I will address the link between religion, identity and conflict more closely. Politics of identity can, Calhoun (ibid.: 220–21) proposes, occur on different levels and make use of different categories. Many strategies in the politics of identity seek to deploy categories on a larger scale, such as Islam, which can be supplemented to differing degrees by local networks, something that may be decisive for possible mobilization campaigns. The abstract quality of these categories constitutes an outstanding element and thus a kind of trump among the many other identities of the persons involved. The danger is that these powerful categories of identities become an element of oppression and/or essentialism.

The Internet provides an almost ideal framework in which to lock into the larger categories of identities, as it enables the limitations of time and space to be overcome, at least in part. A prime example is the incorporation of local identities into the overarching identity categories of Islam and Christianity, which in the Moluccan case defined the lines of the conflict for a long time, even if the conflict was not essentially religious. In this way, many people were mobilized who found themselves in an iden-

tity crisis owing to the developments of recent decades. Any internal dialogue was extinguished, at least as regards the presentation of identities to
the outside (see also Calhoun 1995: 221). In public space, spokesmen and
representatives often attracted more attention, recognition or influence in
terms of these larger-scale categories (ibid.: 240). Here, identities that have
been essentialized by ethnic and religious elements need not, according
to Zurawski (2000: 75), of necessity correspond to the everyday identities and cultures of the people and groups that were their source, as can
be seen clearly in the Hindu nationalist discourse of the Hindutva. What
is decisive, he proposes, is the effect of identity management, be it on the
part of the state, political elites or social movements that refer to a shared
ethnic identity. In addition to the essentialization of their own identity,
a monolithic 'other opposite' is created that is in strict contrast to one's
'own'. In the case of the Hindutva it is the Muslims, and in the national
narrative of the Singhalese on Sri Lanka the Tamils.

'We' groups and 'the others'

In the construction process of collective identities, both the existence of
and participation in shared knowledge and a common memory (Assmann
1999: 139) play a role – as does the conscious process of demarcation from
those excluded from the 'we' group, in this way offsetting possible weaknesses in self-image and/or distracting from them and strengthening one's
own identity. Communities, Anthony Cohen (1985: 74, 107, 116) claims,
receive their feeling of self by setting themselves off from others, such
that a symbolically simple public face for the community arises that can
on the inside be a symbolically complex private face. As early as Weber
(1976), we find in the discussion on ethnicity references to a subjective
feeling of community and of integrative, shared action versus excluding
and despising others who are different (ibid.: 234) and 'ethnic honour'
versus the inferiority of outside customs (ibid.: 239). Assmann (1999: 153)
differentiates between the integrative and distinctive intensification of cultural formations depending on whether the emphasis is to be integration
or demarcation, whereas Schlee (2002: 19) distinguishes between inclusive
and exclusive identity strategies when analysing 'we' groups.

Demarcation often takes the form of a contrastive model, as Mach
(1993: 7) terms it, in which a few positive and attractive features of one's
own culture are chosen as elements of the self-image, while the image of
'the others' is established on the basis of a few, unappealing characteristics of their culture(s). Assmann (1999: 134) states that antagonism is thus
one of the conditions enabling reflection on and intensification of underlying structures and thus engenders collective identities – us against 'the
others' (Butler 1995: 99–100). Heterogeneity and differences within the
group thus created are ignored (see also Mach 1993: 10–11, 16, 43; Assmann 1999: 157) in order to take a resolute stand against an outside rival
or a certain risk: 'Here, the strength of a collective identity depends on the

perceived outside challenge and not on mutual reciprocity as established by cooperation' (Giesen 1999: 108). In a war there can be no neutrality (see Juergensmeyer 2000: 173–75; Kakar 1997: 54; Tambiah 1996: 269, 278, 280). It is necessary to categorize and stereotype a group of people as collective enemies, to depict them as inhuman and immoral, to depersonalize them and treat them as a unit, as it is easier to attack a dehumanized mass than a person whom one possibly knows and against whom one possibly actually has no antipathy (Giesen 1999: 93).[44] This legitimates the use of violence and justifies killing (Orywal 1996: 35).

Equally as important as self-ascription and demarcation for firming up a collective identity are their confirmation and recognition by outsiders and/or a specific outside ascription (see Elwert 1989: 447–48; Giesen 1999: 123; Jenkins 1994; Melucci 1995: 47). Outside ascriptions, that is, the image attached to a group from the outside, need not be the same as its image of itself. In the extreme case, Calhoun says, those involved do not even consider themselves a 'we' group, or they only came together as a 'community' to set themselves off from another group, without correspondingly close ties or the same values, ideas and objectives. Under certain conditions, such 'pseudo-group formation' can be as effective as a 'real' community and can also possibly evolve into such (Calhoun 1995: chap. 7).

In the process of identity construction and reproduction, the circulation of symbols such as cultural values and elements, religious commonalities, geographical references, normative and formative texts, a shared language and history or the way these are interpreted by the respective parties can be decisive (Assmann 1999: 139–42).[45] In a necessarily selective process, historical events are referenced here, such that each group reconstructs its own particular history, as it were, that then becomes the reference point of political action. In this way, the group seeks to give current events meaning and fit them into that history (Elwert 1989: 441). A history that is created in constant interaction by the actors can substitute for the lack of a shared past that shores up mutual trust and collective identity (Giesen 1999: 105). The history of a group also enables those to participate in the collective identity of the community who were not directly involved in the individual events (Giesen 1999: 120). As we will see later, the list archives that the Moluccan cyberactors created online were able to serve this purpose.

Religion, identity and conflict

The gap between the 'we' group and 'the others' becomes greater if significant themes and interests come into play. The result is antagonism and conflict, dividing the world into two opposing, polarized halves, to each of which contrary values are ascribed: good, civilized, progressive, clean, well-mannered and moral versus bad, primitive, reactionary, dirty, vulgar and immoral. In a conflict, the opposing groups can then only define themselves in terms of the aspect of identity, which marks the greatest difference and the basis for the conflict. As in the Moluccas, in wars and conflicts religion can assume an outstanding role as the identity-forming element. Religion constitutes a major category in that thanks to its abstraction at the one end and its local rootedness at the other it can unify and mobilize people of different persuasions.[46] For believers, religion and related values and duties are God-given and thus beyond the ambit of human influence, which is why people are willing to unconditionally obey that image. Abe Wade Ata (1988) suggests that via religion identities are rendered sacred by 'a projection of order beyond temporal contingencies'. Religion can offer a supernatural justification for secular demands and infuse them with a permanent (and nonnegotiable) aura (Appleby 2000: 61).

Polarization and mobilization through religion

If one concurs with Clifford Geertz (1993: 123), then in everyday life religion constitutes an important point of orientation for the believer, as it conveys to him a sense of the world, his role and his relationships within it, by means of which he can assign meaning to his intellectual, emotional and moral experiences. What is decisive, Geertz suggests, is that religious concepts not only provide an interpretation of social and psychological processes, but also provide the person with actual instructions for behaviour and action, that is, themselves decisively influence the course of these processes. Religion can show its followers what truth is, what is 'really real', what is reasonable, human and moral (ibid.: 124). In particular in times of crisis, this orientational framework can exert an immense influence on how a conflict is structured and on identity politics (see, e.g., Schiller 1997: 182–83). Religion can not only emerge as *the* point of orientation in a conflict, but can also serve to legitimize that conflict. Even if religion is not the actual cause of the conflict, under certain circumstances it steers behaviour in a conflict situation decisively towards escalation or deescalation (Hasenclever and Rittberger 1999: 1). Religion is ideally suited to translating opaque forms of conflict into an absolute form, creating clear conditions and unequivocal lines along which the conflict ensues. Gerd Baumann (1999: 23–24) states, for example, that in complex situations of social conflict dividing lines based on ethnicity, nationality or migration are often transformed into religious ones, as in the former Yugoslavia and in Northern Ireland. As soon as an event is declared a religious conflict, acts of cruelty and killing become acts of reverence for which the respective religion provides the motivation, organization and moral justification (see also Juergensmeyer 2000; Sofsky 1996).

The major religious cultures such as Christianity and Islam embody, so Benedict Anderson (1998: 19) suggests, huge communities that were first conceivable primarily thanks to the medium of a holy language and scriptures that were passed down. The faithful then derived from these the corresponding values and symbols that become the elements defining the community. Muslims from all manner of countries thus depend, for example, not on a commonly spoken language to communicate, but instead the shared symbolism and language of their holy scriptures, classical Arabic. Weber affirms this overarching character of religion as something that creates a sense of community:

> Common language and the ritual regulation of life, as determined by shared religious beliefs, everywhere are conducive to feelings of 'ethnic' affinity, especially since the 'intelligibility' of the behaviour of others is the most fundamental proposition of group formation. (1976: 238)

The symbols and ceremonies that religions make available to us can be used strategically to construct and strengthen identities, to integrate groups and call for action (see Rutledge 1985; Schiller 1997). Religion can be used strategically in all manner of ways in identity politics (Rutledge 1985: 56–67): it can serve to ward off outside influences, for example, Westernization or colonialization (Kartodirdjo 1972), secure material support or form a common identity-fostering basis in the event of ethnic or other social differences. Whatever the regional and local differences, every Muslim can, for instance, cite an (imagined) worldwide Muslim community, the *ummah*,[47] while Christians refer to the Christian world community.

Religious symbolism

Religious symbols play a major role in identity politics for conflict parties that primarily define themselves by membership of a religion: a cross or a crescent moon, sacred places or religious concepts such as the idea of a holy war or a world community of the faithful. Religious symbols are, Geertz (1993: 127) suggests, the expression of a world order, of values and instructions for behaviour and thus especially suited to triggering emotions. Sacred places are of crucial importance to every religious community. They comprise territorial markings that remind us that despite being scattered geographically and geared spiritually to a life in the hereafter are not indifferent to territorial claims (Appleby 2000: 61). Since sacred places are the clearest expression on the surface of the world of a link between cosmology and private experience, the focus of religions is strongly on these holy centres and maintaining control over them (see Das 1990: 11; Veer 1994: 11). A famous example of a never-ending struggle between adherents of two religions over the same parcel of holy land is that of the Babri Mosque in Ayodhya, India, which radical Hindus razed to the ground in December 1992 in the conviction that the location was originally consecrated to their god Rama. Laying siege to and destroying holy places and buildings such as churches, mosques, synagogues and shrines is a fail-safe method of hitting a (religious) opponent hard and where it hurts. Often in conflicts, such places serve one's own group as a safe haven and final bastion. They give the group a sense of security and belonging (Ata 1988: 3).

In the religious world, specific points in time are similar in significance to sacred places, examples being holy days, the times for prayer or religious services and the Muslim month of fasting (Juergensmeyer 2000: 133–39). An attack during one of these periods is automatically perceived on a larger scale as it is not just a matter of a physical offensive against individuals, but an attack on core and sacred values of the entire religious community. Religion provides rituals of provocation that kindle unrest and trigger violence, something that is often far more socially, economically or politically motivated than actually religious in nature. The violation of key religious symbols such as slaughtering a cow in front of Hindus or playing loud music outside a mosque during prayers can become a legitimate trigger for a communal uprising and violence (see, e.g., Jaffrelot 1996: 99–100; Kakar 1997: 57; Singh 1990: 162; Tambiah 1996: 231–36).

Concepts such as a worldwide religious community or the idea of a holy war (jihad in Islam or the crusades in Christianity) serve to deepen or extend so-called religious conflicts. Jihad also became a central symbol for the radical Islamic groups involved in the Moluccan conflict. Given the narrow interpretation of the concept of jihad by these radical minorities, the general purpose of jihad, namely, to make an effort on behalf of the religion, gets confined to the wings, as these groups focus in their struggle with non-Muslims on a bellicose conflict, on gaining say by striking slogans and on one-sided coverage, thus drowning out the voice of the moderate masses.[48] The Laskar Jihad thus inherited a trend that has been visible among certain Islamic groups worldwide since the mid-twentieth century and was above all initiated by Egyptian Sayyid Qutb (1906–65). In his treatise *Milestones* (1960), he developed an interpretation of jihad that was to become the core doctrine of extremist groups. Qutb suggested that it was necessary to return to Islam's true values as they were represented by the original Islamic community in Muhammad's day. Influenced by Maulana Sayyid Abul Ala Maududi (1903–79), Qutb championed a vision of Islam as an all-embracing concept. He considered both the minimalist interpretation of jihad (in other words, the above-mentioned 'general' interpretation) and the Prophet's prohibition on battle as a temporary stage on a long path during the Mecca period. In his opinion, jihad does not involve defending a national homeland but instead an order to expand the borders of Islam to the ends of the world (Appleby 2000: 91–95).

Gosman and Bakker (1991: 14) say that a declaration of a holy war is a propaganda tool in order to better motivate Muslims to do battle.[49] Juergensmeyer (2000: 145) labels battles waged in the name of a religion 'cosmic wars'. Their significance extends beyond the limited lives of the individual combatants by linking up with the great battles of a legendary past and the metaphysical conflict between good and evil. For example, the Muslim who sacrifices his life in the jihad becomes a martyr and achieves personal salvation (Juergensmeyer 2000: 146–47). He acts in the name of God, who guides him. Irrespective of how the battle ends, you cannot lose, as you are either victor or martyr (Gosman and Bakker 1991: 15). This ability of religion to tear the faithful out of their secular environment psychically, as it were, underpins the logic of religious violence (Appleby 2000: 91). The absolute character of a cosmic war makes compromises improbable and those who are prepared to negotiate then become enemies – among both the radical Palestinians and the radical Israelis, for example (Juergensmeyer 2000: 154). Thus, in the Moluccan conflict moderate Muslims who entered into negotiations with the Christians came under pressure from the Laskar Jihad. Religious 'fundamentalists' are, states Appleby (2000: 74), especially skilled at channelling energies and the intensified religious self-confidence that goes hand in hand with a religious revival. They have no scruples in politicizing religious passions, as they consider it their holy duty to prepare religious warriors to do battle on injustice and oppression. Each and every believer must thus of necessity become an activist.

The religious concept of jihad has repeatedly played a role in Indonesia's history, even if the majority of the population advocates a moderate form of Islam. Jihad in its interpretation as a holy war against unbelievers and oppression became a symbol of the uprising and mobilization against Dutch colonial power (see Kartodirdjo 1972; Legge 1964: 52–54). In 1965, after an attempted communist coup, the jihad by Indonesian Muslims was directed against the PKI, the Indonesian Communist Party, and all its members (Hefner 2000a: 16, 108). In 1977, a small group of radical Muslims joined forces to form the Komando Jihad, which fought against the communists and for Indonesia to declare itself an Islamic state, but was brutally suppressed by the government (Bruinessen 1996: 26). In the context of the theory of a world Jewish conspiracy that was widespread in Indonesia (Bruinessen 1994) and the attendant anti-Western stance among Muslims, the jihad became a symbol of resistance to the West. In the course of the conflicts in the Moluccas and Central Sulawesi as of 1999, the Muslim side proclaimed a jihad and Muslim warriors were mobilized and recruited to do battle against the Christians and all enemies of Islam.

Notes

1. Such articles served to glorify the *pela* alliances during the conflict in a one-sided fashion. For detailed studies on *pela* see note 27 in this chapter.
2. Only at the state Pattimura University (Unpatti) was an effort made to maintain interreligious operations. Unpatti, originally located outside Ambon City in Poka, was destroyed in the course of the unrest, and as an interim solution relocated to a school building in the Christian/Muslim border area at the heart of Ambon City.

3. The only exception was the camp at the naval base in Halong, Ambon.

4. A noteworthy exception was Wayame village, located on Ambon Bay across from Ambon City, where Muslim and Christian inhabitants alike stubbornly refused to attack each other.

5. I shall only provide a very cursory account of the course of the conflict, and will supplement it in the following chapters by numerous references and interpretations by the Moluccan cyberactors. Since the background of the conflict and how it took place differed widely from one Moluccan region to the next (the Northern, Central and Southeastern Moluccas), in my remarks I will concentrate on the Central Moluccas and on Ambon City.

6. Very soon after the outbreak of the conflict, the majority Muslim Batumerah became completely Muslim and Mardika purely Christian. The same happened in all the other city districts.

7. Ambon is the name both of the capital city of the Moluccas (Kota Ambon) and of the island (Pulau Ambon) where the eponymous city is located.

8. I would like to thank Zairin Salampessy at TAPAK Ambon (Team Advokasi Penyelesaian Kasus Ambon, Advocacy Team for the Resolution of the Ambon Case) and Dieter Bartels for these references.

9. http://www.laskarjihad.or.id, 5 August 2001 (Gallery section). Frame demarcating the Moluccas added by the author.

10. On the role of rumours in the Moluccan conflict, see also Spyer (2002).

11. The Laskar Jihad themselves were purportedly unarmed, but their weapons arrived shortly thereafter on a separate ship (Aditjondro 2001a: 118; Hefner 2001: 1). The government's problem in dealing with the jihad warriors in the Moluccas was, so Kirsten Schulze (2002: 65) suggests, that Indonesian Muslims rated any attempt to remove them from Ambon or to disarm them as an anti-Muslim act and the promotion of Christian/Muslim peace initiatives was also considered pro-Christian. Consequently, the Laskar Jihad's actions not only met with approval, but measures against them were obstructed and the warriors were thus protected.

12. See, for example, the article by Ron Moreau (2000).

13. The PDS is one level below martial law and places the police directly under the person commanding the PDS. The PDS authorizes houses to be searched, a curfew to be imposed, the freedom of the press to be restricted, telecommunications to be monitored, demonstrations and mass events to be prohibited and spot checks on people. The then governor of the Moluccas, Saleh Latuconsina, was placed in command (International Crisis Group 2002: 8).

14. This information is mainly attributable to interviews I conducted with Muslim representatives in Ambon City in February and March 2002.

15. Foundation of the Peninsula of Kings. Ely himself renders it as Foundation of the Country of Many Kingdoms.

16. Putuhena was also the Moluccas Coordinator of the Muslim Lawyers' Team (Tim Pengacara Muslim, TPM) and a board member of the Islamic Defenders Front of the Moluccas (Front Pembela Islam Maluku, FPIM).

17. Personal conversation with Berthy Loupatty, 7 March 2002. According to Bartels (2000), the gangs of jobless youths from different districts in Ambon City, who had fought one another before the conflict broke out, was another reason the conflict took root so swiftly in the Moluccas: 'These gangs then metamorphosed themselves into freedom fighters defending their neighbor-

hoods against outside attacks and invading those of their enemies to burn them down.' The emergence of youth gangs in Ambon is closely linked to the urbanization process and the related increase in unemployment and youth crime (Klinken 2001; Steijlen 2001).

18. Since the outbreak of the Moluccan conflict in January 1999, the Indonesian president has changed three times: J. B. Habibie until October 1999, Abdurrahman Wahid until July 2001 and then Megawati Sukarnoputri. In 2004, Susilo Bambang Yudhoyono (SBY) took over.

19. The border between the North Moluccan and Moluccan provinces runs north of the islands of Buru and Seram (see Illustration 2).

20. The military constantly complained that it did not have sufficient soldiers and equipment, given the fact that the conflict spread across the widely scattered islands of the Moluccas, and that it was thus unable to bring the conflict under control (International Crisis Group 2002: 4).

21. Owing to the high proportion of Muslims in the TNI, the military is said to have frequently sided with the Muslims, while the local police units, the majority of which were Christians, were accused of supporting the Christians.

22. *Adat* is a term for tradition and customary law in Indonesia.

23. Personal conversation on 21 March 2002. This only covers the dead whose families applied to the church for assistance and financial support.

24. Report by the Catholic Crisis Centre of 6 March 2001. According to the statistics of the Indonesian Christian Communication Forum (2001), in the Moluccas from 19 January 1999 to 31 January 2001 180 churches were partially or completely destroyed or burned down, and purportedly the same happened to only 28 mosques.

25. To name a few examples here (others will be named in the course of the chapter): Aditjondro (2000a, 2000b, 2000d, 2000e, 2001a, 2001b); Al-Jakartaty (2000); Alqadrie (1999); Bartels (2000); K. van Dijk (2001: 379–96); Fellowship of Indonesian Christians in America (1999); Habiboe (2000); Hefner (2000b, 2001); Human Rights Watch (1999); Institut Studi Arus Informasi (2000a); International Christian Concern (2001); International Crisis Group (2000a, 2002); Joseph, Manuhutu and Smeets (2000); Jubilee Campaign U.K. (1999); Klinken (1999, 2001); Lokollo (1999); Mangkey (2000); Mann (2000); Manuhutu et al. (2000); Pelly (1999); Rachmat (2001); Sala Waku Foundation (1999); Salampessy and Husain (2001); Schulte Nordholt (2000a); Sihbudi et al. (2001); Sinansari Ecip (1999); TAPOL (1999); Titaley (2001); and Tomagola (2000, 2001a, 2001b, 2001d, 2001e). Indonesian publications such as Awwas (2000); Husaini (2000: 178–86); Jaiz (1999); Tim Penyusun Al-Mukmin (1999); and Tuasikal (2000) convey a very one-sided (Muslim) angle on the conflict. Even persons who were directly involved in the conflict have published books on it. First and foremost, I should mention two Ambonese Muslims who can be considered to belong more to the radical end of the Islamic scale: Rustam Kastor (2000a, 2000b, 2000c, 2000d) and Husni Putuhena (1999, 2001); see also Putuhena and Tawainella (2001). For an analysis of the factors underlying the conflict and the course it took in the North Moluccas see Aditjondro (2001a: 107–9); Ahmad and Oesman (2000); Alhadar (2000); Bubandt (2001); Nanere (2000); Taylor (2001); and Tomagola (2001c). On the conflict on the Banda Islands see, for example, Tinnemans (2001) and Winn (2000).

26. Of the approximately two million inhabitants in the North Moluccan and Moluccan provinces, some 59 per cent are Muslims, 35.3 per cent are Protestants, 5.2 per cent are Catholics and the rest are Hindus, Buddhists and others. In the North Moluccas, Muslims account for about 70 per cent of the population, as compared with about 50 percent in the Moluccas (Badan Pusat Statistik Propinsi Maluku 2000: 10; Bureau of Statistics 1997, http://www.websitesrcg. com/ambon/Malukupop.htm, 22 July 2002 and 13 January 2012). In Indonesia as a whole, Muslims constitute some 87 per cent of the population.

27. The reasons behind the various *pela* alliances and the exact shape they took differ greatly. For a detailed treatment see Bartels (1977). See also Huwaë (1995, 2001); Lokollo (1997); Pattiselanno (1999); and Strijbosch (1985).

28. During the unrest as of January 1999, too, the fighting was not exclusively between Christians and Muslims; there were repeatedly conflicts within the respective camps or between two Christian or two Muslim villages (see, e.g., Bartels 2000).

29. The reason is that usually an entire village joined a religion. To avoid conflict, villages with populations of mixed religions such as Tial (Pulau Ambon) and Sirisori (Saparua) had been divided back in colonial days into a Christian and a Muslim village that were then called Tial Serani and Tial Islam or Sirisori Kristen and Sirisori Islam (Kraemer 1927: 82).

30. I would like to thank Ron Habiboe, Wim Manuhutu, Fridus Steijlen and Dieter Bartels for their useful comments here.

31. Frank Cooley (1961: 79) remarks that the Christian populations despised physical work that went beyond tending one's own garden and commercial activity, which is why these were dominated by 'more recent' groups of immigrants, in particular the Butonese and the Macassaris.

32. According to Dieter Bartels, in the chaotic conflict situation not all these often unowned *becak*s changed into Christian hands legally. *Becak*s even cropped up in (Christian) villages such as Ullath on Saparua (personal email on 12 September 2003).

33. See, for example, Ajawaila (2000); Bartels (2000); Lee (1997); Manuhutu (2000a); Pattiselanno (1999); and Taylor (2001). On the impact of Muslim immigration on the Christian-Muslim relations in Ambon, see also Mearns (1999). As part of state-supported transmigration programmes, between 1969 and 1999 97,422 people emigrated to the Moluccas, more than half of them to the Central Moluccas. Given a total population of two million, that is almost 5 per cent. The majority came from Buton and Java, meaning they were Muslim. There are no figures on spontaneous transmigration. Estimates range from 50,000 to 200,000 (Regional Office of the Ministry of Transmigration and Forest Settlers Province of Moluccas, http://www.websitesrcg.com/ambon/transmig.htm, 22 July 2002 and 13 January 2012). While in 1930 about 60 per cent of the Moluccan population was Christian, prior to the unrest the proportion had fallen to only 40 per cent. Since in the course of the conflict many non-Moluccan Muslims fled, the ratio of Christians has probably risen again (Manuhutu 2000a: 9–10).

34. Dieter Bartels and Fridus Steijlen (personal conversation 2001) suggest that this was fuelled by the fact that the Ambonese and Central Moluccans are themselves very fragmented and define themselves more by their family, clan or village membership than via a shared Ambonese or even Moluccan iden-

tity. In Ambon City itself, there were not only many non-Moluccans, but also many emigrants from other Moluccan islands.

35. This competition was noticeable years earlier, when Muslims in Indonesia increasingly gained better training opportunities (which, under Dutch rule, often only Christians had access to) and sought higher job positions.

36. The 'cultural' upturn of Islam had already been promoted in prior years by the *Orde Baru,* the so-called New Order under Suharto: thousands of mosques, prayer houses and Koran schools were built, each year tens of thousands of Indonesians received support for their pilgrimage to Mecca, and a great deal of money was invested in all levels of religious education (Hefner 2000a: 17, 120; Ramage 1995: 83).

37. The Indonesian Committee for Solidarity with the Islamic World (Komite Indonesia untuk Solidaritas Dunia Islam, KISDI) was founded in 1987 under the leadership of Ahmad Sumargono and others as an associated member of the Islamic Propagation Council of Indonesia (Dewan Dakwah Islamiyah Indonesia, DDII) in order to express Indonesia's sympathy for the dire straits of the Palestinians (Hefner 2000a: 107–9).

38. Contributions to the MMI's founding congress were published by Irfan Suryahardi Awwas (2001).

39. The ICCF or FKKI (Forum Komunikasi Kristen Indonesia) was founded in the face of increasing acts of violence against Christians in Indonesia on 26 January 1997 in Prigen, East Java (Tahalele 1998).

40. Or in the words of Hefner (2001: 1): 'Let me begin by emphasizing that hard-line, anti-pluralist Muslims are a tiny minority in Indonesia relative to their moderate and democratic Muslim counterparts. This fact has been proved in social research, but was also decisively demonstrated during the free and fair elections of June 1999, when hardline Muslim parties won less than 5% of the vote, versus more than 50% for parties of democratic reform. The jihad fighters are no more representative of the majority of Indonesian Muslims than Maluku Christian fighters are of Indonesia's minority (9%) Christian community.'

41. I would like to thank Victor Joseph, a Moluccan journalist in the Netherlands, for this information. On the media world in the Moluccas during the conflict see also Eriyanto (2003); Joseph (2000); the special edition of *ALERT magazine* (Southeast Asian Press Alliance 2002); and the articles in *Gatra* of 17 March 2001, 'Peaceful Coexistence Among Journalists of Maluku', and *The Straights Times* of 12 November 2000, 'Mirroring Sectarianism in the Streets'.

42. This is also the tack taken by Stanley Tambiah (1989: 336), who suggests ethnicity combines the semantics of primordial and historical claims with the pragmatism of calculating choice and opportunism in the dynamic context of political and economic competition between interest groups.

43. Accordingly, Schlee and Werner (1996: 14) criticize the metaphor of 'invention', as it is currently to be encountered in many book titles (such as *The Invention of Traditions*), as being an unfortunate choice, as what is involved is a construction rather than an invention from nothing.

44. Prime examples are the representations of Muslims by Hindus in India and vice versa (Jürgenmeyer 1998; Kakar 1997; Singh 1990; Tambiah 1996; Veer 1994; Weiss et al. 1996).

45. Symbolism is an elementary component of identity politics. Symbols express values, ideologies and stereotypes that structure the experience of the members of a social group and express the relations between different groups. They play a fundamental role in the identification and demarcation process of a group (Mach 1993: x) and are a suitable means of mobilizing people, kindling emotions and conveying ideas and values (ibid.: 35–37).

46. See also Rutledge (1985: 53–67). Werner Gephart and Hans Waldenfels (1999) have published a collection of essays on the topic of religion and identity.

47. On the history of the *ummah* as a source of identity, Appleby (2000: 61) notes: 'In the final quarter of the twentieth century, Islamists have portrayed membership in the *umma* as the common source of identity binding together believing Arabs, non-Arab Africans, South Asians, Indonesians, and many other peoples from various nations. In practice, however, the universalism of Islam has collided repeatedly with its diverse cultural particularities.'

48. See, for example, HAMKA (1976: 145). On the concept of jihad, see also Leemhuis (1991) and Peters (1991).

49. The research by Gosman and Bakker (1991: 14–15) showed that even nonreligious groupings use the term as a metaphor to express their highest objectives.

4

The Masariku Mailing List

An Example of an Online Community

'Can you imagine what would happen to Ambon if the cyberworld were never invented and the information technology were not existent?' a member of the Masariku mailing list once asked me. And indeed, the use of the Internet in the Moluccan conflict is a prime example of the important role this particular medium plays in a country in which for decades the freedom of the press was a foreign concept to the government. The *Orde Baru* saw the media as a means of creating a national culture throughout the far-flung archipelago that enabled Suharto's development policy and authoritarian leadership to be enforced (Sen and Hill 2000: 11–12). So as to maintain the impression of unity and harmony, all reporting on ethnic-religious tensions (SARA conflicts) was strictly forbidden. It was only in the last decade of the *Orde Baru* that the Indonesian government, on account of the rapid developments in technology, lost control. The state control mechanisms failed to register the Internet technology that was emerging at the end of the Suharto era, and it was to play a decisive role in the transition from the *Orde Baru* to the *Era Reformasi* (Reform Era).

The Internet in Indonesia and the Moluccas

In 1994 one of the first connections to the global Internet was made by the Indonesian Science and Technology Network (IPTEKnet), which from the mid-1980s had been built up by respected Indonesian universities with state funding.[1] In May 1995 the first Internet service provider (ISP) in Indonesia (Radnet) was set up. In 1996 the Indonesian Post Office decided to expand its range of services and in each provincial capital introduced ISPs, which were linked via Wasantara Net. That same year the Indonesian ISP Association (APJII) was founded.[2] Primarily in cities, numerous Internet shops and cafés opened, which activists and students used to exchange information and news that went far beyond that available in the established media in Indonesia. Printed copies of this news were made and distributed, meaning that even those with no access to the Internet were aware of what was happening.[3] As sharing Internet accounts and passwords is commonplace in Indonesia, it is extremely difficult to gauge the actual number of Internet users (Hill and Sen 1997: 74; see also http://apjii.or.id/ind/statistik.html, 28 March 2002). According to an APJII study, in Indonesia 43 per cent of users had access to the Internet via *Warnets* (Internet kiosks), 41 per cent at work, 12 per cent at home and 4 per cent at school. Whereas email was the most frequently used function, news sites such as Detikcom and online daily newspapers were the most-visited websites. Like their average European and U.S. counterparts, Indonesian Internet users were between twenty and forty years old, 70–80 per cent male, the majority with a university education and from a middle- to higher-income background.[4]

Even if in 2002, statistically speaking, no more than 2 per cent of the Indonesian population had access to the Internet, observers maintain that it played a decisive role in the struggle for democracy and stability in Indonesia.[5] By way of example, just a few hours after the attack on the headquarters of the Indonesian Democratic Party (Partai Demokrasi Indonesia, PDI) on 27 July 1996, a detailed chronology of the events was posted on the Internet.[6] According to Basuki (1998: 100), however, the significance of cyberspace as 'a real battleground between the pro-democracy activists and the supporters of the Suharto rule' became evident a year earlier, when, on account of the human rights situation in Indonesia, the Legal Aid Institute (LBH) issued an urgent appeal on the Apakabar or INDONESIA-L mailing list set up by McDougall in 1990. It was concerning a female activist who had led a workers' strike in East Java and, it is assumed, was killed by the military. Basuki maintains that within a few hours of the appeal being posted online, the Indonesian president and the Foreign and Defence Ministries were swamped with protest faxes and an 'NGO-instigated online information war against one of the harshest military regimes in the world' started (ibid.: 100). Other explosive material to be posted online and subsequently distributed offline during the Suharto era included, for example, lists of his family's and friends' assets. In 1996 the Indonesian magazine *Tempo,* which the government had banned in 1994, went online as *Tempo Interaktif.*

According to Basuki (1998: 101), this online information played a decisive role in strengthening public opinion that it was time for the Suharto government to resign: 'The Web began to be transformed into a weapon of dissent in Indonesia' (ibid.: 99). As an alternative source of information, the Internet made people aware of the lies being perpetrated by the other media and the government (see Coronel 1998; Luwarso 1998: 93). There are indications that the government made repeated attempts to sabotage emails and ISPs, though without any significant success. In the months leading up to Suharto's resignation in May 1998, the Internet was used to avoid media such as the press and TV, which were censored by the state. According to David L. Marcus (1999), the Internet played a decisive role in the revolt as a factor in the escalation and acceleration in the speed of events. In the struggle for independence in East Timor the Internet was used to attract international attention and support (Hill 2002). Here, however, the Indonesian government enjoyed more success by attacking a provider in Ireland and destroying the East Timor online domain located there (.tp), which had been initiated, among others, by the Nobel Peace Prize winners Ramos Horta and Bishop Belo (see BBC World News 1999b; Bunt 2000: 136).

Following Suharto's resignation, freedom of the press was introduced in Indonesia and in October 1999 the institute that represented its suppression, the Ministry of Information (established in 1945), closed (Sen and Hill 2008: 8). Nonetheless, even then many journalists were reluctant to write critically about the government and give the minorities in the country a voice. For precisely this reason the Internet also played a decisive role in the Moluccan conflict with regard to the spreading of information that would never have appeared in the national media. On several occasions the use of the Internet for propaganda purposes on the part of the conflicting parties and for provocation was the subject of reports in both the national and international press.[7] The potential of the Internet as a medium for resistance or in a conflict was recognized, but detailed analyses, which take into account the online and offline context of what was posted, were still missing.

As in every other provincial capital, in mid-1996 the Indonesian Post Office installed an Internet server in Ambon City (Wasantara Net) – together with the ISP in Ternate (North Moluccas), the only one in the entire archipelago. In a side room at the post office there were four computers available for Internet users.[8] Otherwise, there was just one other *Warnet* in Ambon, which was likewise operated by Wasantara and had four computers. Both were in the Christian area. In Muslim territory, outside the city and on the other islands there was no public access to the Internet. The Muslim branch of the post office, which had been forced to open on account of the conflict, had no computer equipment whatsoever. Data relating to individual Internet access via the Wasantara server in both Christian and Muslim territory were stored separately in the respective post offices. According to the Internet officer at the main post office in Ambon, the number of Internet users dropped substantially due to the conflict. Many subscribers fled and their data were deleted. Whereas in 1996 there were supposedly around 500 users, in 2000 there were only 300, a year later 290 and in March 2002 only 108 in the Christian area and 23 in the Muslim one.

The one hundred and eight subscribers on the Christian side included nine local NGOs, six foreign NGOs and UN organizations, five institutes of Pattimura University (Unpatti),[9] eleven Church institutions, four local media (*Suara Maluku, Siwalima,* RRI and DMS Radio), fourteen government offices and seventeen banks and companies. The twenty-three registered users on the Muslim side included the magazine *Suisma*, the state electricity company, three companies and otherwise private individuals, some of whom were in journalism, but behind which could have been NGOs or companies.[10] As part of a reconciliation project initiated by UNICEF in October 2001, every day Muslim and Christian schoolchildren were given instruction on twenty computers in the municipal library, located in the border area between the Christian and Muslim parts of the city. Outside tuition time the public could also use the computers to access the Internet.[11]

The situation regarding the Internet in the Moluccas is in stark contrast to the huge presence of the Moluccan conflict on the Internet. In the course of the conflict numerous websites, in some cases online newsletters and mailing lists, emerged that were devoted to the tragedy on the Moluccas, though there were vast differences between the type and the amount of information provided, the structure of the sites and their motives and the way the authors presented themselves. In some cases the sites attempted to present the conflict in a neutral manner, while in others they represented a clear Christian or Muslim perspective. Many of the websites were maintained by Moluccans abroad or Moluccan organizations. Many were devoted exclusively to the conflict, while others, for example, those of international Christian or Indonesian Muslim organizations, devoted a section to it.[12] Christians and Muslims at the local conflict level were also represented on the Internet. On the Muslim side the FKAWJ claimed to represent all Muslims. Moderate Muslims in the Moluccas had no voice in cyberspace. On the one hand, the requisite resources (computers and Internet access) appeared to be even less available among Muslims than among Christians. On the other, some maintain that the Muslims either lacked the requisite computer skills or simply had no interest in portraying their view of the conflict online. It is quite possible that they did not dare spread their own perspective in view of the claim on the part of the Laskar Jihad to be their representative voice.

Masariku, the CCDA and the FKAWJ in Ambon were in the privileged position of having Internet access and being able to use it with their interests in mind. As such, they were able to create a counterforce to other groups' portrayals, as well as to reporting in other media, and, as Zurawski (2000: 187) would conclude, able to exert decisive influence on the gathering and control of information about the Moluccan conflict and the images and representations generated with it. In order to make their own stances clear and record the 'truth', reports on individual events as well as chronologies and analyses of the conflict were provided, letters written to influential people and organizations and posted online together with photographs of victims, captured weapons, religious symbols and rituals, not to mention lists of losses and donations. For the international community, as well as many Moluccans living outside the Moluccas, the Internet was a primary source of information, such that what was portrayed in cyberspace had a decisive influence on the way they perceived the conflict and responded to it. As far as their presence in cyberspace is concerned, the importance of the Moluccan cyberactors is undisputed, as an analysis of the online environment of individual projects in the following chapters reveals.

It is also evident, however, that on account of the infrastructure in the Moluccas alone, Moluccan cyberspace does not correspond with the ideal public described by Habermas, which with the spread of the Internet many people had hoped for. Even if in theory everyone could have access to the Internet, we should not be blind to the fact that discourse on the Internet is dominated by a certain elite, people in leading roles and outstanding speakers (Piliang 2000: 101, 116). Even if these are people at the grassroots level who are affected, Jonathan Benthall (1995: 207) warns, they are possibly pursuing their own interests and not necessarily complying with their claim to be representatives of the population. I, however, am interested less in whom the three groups examined actually represented and more in the images of the Moluccan conflict and the people they claim to represent that they, influenced by their particular perception of the local context, created for a large, widespread audience, and what they aimed to achieve with those images.[13]

In terms of their presentation and performance, how open they were (private or public), their membership, their structures, their strategies and objectives, and their impact and reach, we are dealing with three very different online projects. With all of them, the exchange and provision of information was of immense importance, though the target groups differed. Here religious, national and international communities played just as much a role as diaspora communities. Regardless of the number of people involved, in none of these three cases was there any concern with giving expression to the individual identities of these people, but rather with the creation and portrayal of collective identities, through which in each case one side of the conflict was represented and a specific audience targeted. Whereas it was of no real significance for the projects themselves if individual members remained anonymous or adopted pseudonyms, the project itself lived from making this collective identity explicit, which was essential both for the members and the general public in order to be able to exist as an imagined community. Nevertheless, it was individuals, with their respective backgrounds, who played a dominant role in how the collective was structured and how it was perceived by the public.

In presenting these Moluccan cyberprojects, I will investigate who used which tools, means and material in order to appear authentic, build up communities and establish identities. As was demonstrated in Chapter 2, different group-specific forms of expression, identity, relationships to one another and normative agreement, dependent on a series of existing structures, emerge online. As such, the character of the imagined communities can be very different, in our case from an actual to the presentation of an idealized community. The mode of communication the Moluccan cyberactors chose, in other words, the way they intended to communicate via the Internet and present their point of view, in one, two or several directions (by website, newsletter or mailing list), was responsible for the various 'communitization processes'.

In Moluccan cyberspace, too, the construction of identities has nothing to do with invention. The Moluccan cyberactors availed themselves of what are known as 'cultural codes' (Giesen 1999: 69), that is, materials and elements that emerge as a result of the actors being embedded in a specific sociocultural and historical background. Only in this way can authenticity and a coherent image of a collective identity be created, which is a prerequisite for an effective identity project. Furthermore, according to Giesen (1999: 69), as social constructions collective identities are always also decisively shaped by local circumstances, that is, the situational conditions that are beyond the domain of the actors involved but nonetheless exert a major influence on the communal creation of borders, in our case, the conflict on the Moluccas. Given the conflict situation, an outside threat from the opposing side existed, leading to a demarcation mechanism automatically coming into force. A 'we' group is depicted as opposed to 'the others', both of which predominantly identified themselves by their religious affiliation.

For the most part, previous studies of social online formations and publications of social scientific Internet research do not permit identification of identity construction and communitization processes, as the researchers did not follow the online projects for a sufficient length of time and did not utilize participant observation of the online occurrences. However, long-term participant observation in Moluccan cyberspace, as well as the analysis and interpretation of the resultant ethnographic material, enabled me to identify the social structures of this area, to fathom out the identity politics of Masariku, the CCDA and the FKAWJ, and to portray the above-named processes. Only a detailed exposition of these interpreted online processes enables the reader to get an idea of these communities similar to that in the imagination of their members and initiators.[14]

The MML – its founders, contributions, and members

In the Moluccan conflict, the Masariku mailing list (MML) aimed to represent the Moluccan Christians, and in particular the Protestants. In the social sphere that the MML constituted, a discourse gathered pace that was dominated by the member profile and different categories of articles and culminated in a specific communitization and identity-finding process. In this, inclusion and exclusion mechanisms played an important role, as did the argumentation structure of list members, the symbolism used to create identity and the group dynamics, determined by members' interaction and their networks of solidarity and action.

The beginnings of Masariku online

Masariku was the first Moluccan group to provide online information on a regular basis. Masariku used the free Yahoo! platform, on which so-called electronic groups (egroups) can be set up and built up via mailing lists (http://groups.yahoo.com). There it is possible to store text and image archives, set up a chat forum and link section, conduct polls and maintain a group calendar. Using the Group Settings, the founder of the list determines whether membership in the list is to be open, whether it is to be moderated, who can post news and if the moderator's approval is required to do so, whether the archives can be accessed by the general public or group members only, and whether email attachments are allowed. MML was founded on 17 August 1999; in other words, eight months after the conflict began. The address of its home page is http://groups.yahoo.com/group/masariku. Over the months, the number of members stabilized at approximately 200, peaking in December 2000 (18 December 2000)[15] at 299; membership numbers slightly decreased after mid-2002, when some regarded the conflict as over.[16] Indonesian was defined as the language for communicating. Most of the articles were indeed in Indonesian, in some cases with a touch of Ambonese. Only a small percentage of the articles in Indonesian were translated into English. Articles by international organizations or from the international press were mostly in English and very few of them were translated into Indonesian. The Group Settings were: 'Restricted membership', 'Unmoderated', 'All members may post', 'Archives for members only' and 'Email attachments are permitted', meaning that the parameters for free, open discourse among members accepted by the moderator were in place. The group describes itself as follows:

> The Masariku mailing list distributes information about the Moluccan conflict and the difficulties experienced by the Churches in Indonesia. It is maintained by the Masariku Network, an information and action network for the Moluccans. We hope that the Masariku archive posted on the egroups site becomes a source of material for all manner of campaigns and studies on the Moluccan conflict.[17]

One of the list's major concerns was to redress the imbalance in the reporting on the Moluccan conflict, primarily in the Muslim-dominated national Indonesian press and other Muslim media. Here the Christians were erroneously portrayed as the aggressors in the Moluccan conflict, which in many parts of Indonesia whipped up anti-Christian sentiment (24 January 2000).[18] The intention was to establish an opposite pole with which to deliver, in particular, information from a Christian point of view,

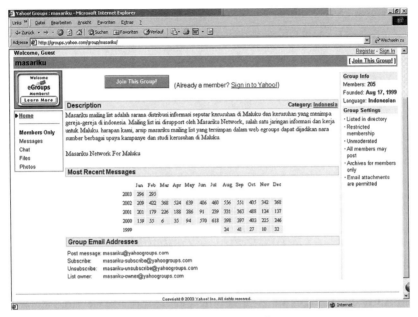

Illustration 3. Masariku – Yahoo! Groups on 28 February 2003

to correct and complement the Muslim-oriented articles, but primarily to counter the Muslim allegations of separatism on the part of the Christians. After all, they wanted to save the Christians in the Moluccas from being wiped out (18 August 2002). Of the Yahoo! features mentioned above, Masariku only used the archiving function, with which text and, from 4 April 2000, also images were archived (6 June 2000). There was no separate website. As the Masariku mailing list was not public, one had to apply informally to be accepted. This took place either through an email to the moderator, in which one outlined in brief one's motives and interests, or on the recommendation of a member one was friends with, acquainted with, or related to. Such letters of recommendation appeared frequently in the list. The applicants were often Moluccans who were living abroad and had family in the Moluccas, and for that reason were looking for detailed, up-to-date information about the conflict in their home country. Furthermore, one could of course become a member through contacts to founding members in the offline sphere. Having successfully registered, new members then received a letter from the list moderator (in English), the subject heading of which read 'Welcome to Masariku', describing once again the aims of Masariku and promising the subscriber firsthand, up-to-date information about the Moluccan conflict. It was expressly emphasized that everyone was invited, in line with his or her abilities and opportunities, to contribute to the discussion and also to take concrete action (email from masariku-owner@egroups.com, 18 December 2000):

Dear All,

You have been subscribed to masariku@egroups.com by masariku Network to provide you recent information about Maluku send from Maluku.

This groups has created primarily to provide exchange information, ideas about recent situation in Maluku, and also to create a forum discussion on how to get work together for Ambon.

The important things is how to contribute our talent and ability to work together for Ambon.

Let make our best to Ambon Manisee!

regards,

Masariku Network Moderator

Paul

Categorization of contributions

Given the heterogeneous membership, the list discourse was extremely diverse and took place on several levels. The contributions ranged from detailed descriptions of local conflict-related occurrences to scholarly analyses of the conflict and letters of petition to the international community. In addition to this formal side, the members gave expression to their feelings in the form of cries for help, avowals of solidarity and energetic calls not to continue idly looking on while their brothers and sisters were slaughtered in the Moluccas. Forwarded and posted were reports by the Masariku Network itself, reports by other, mostly Christian organizations in the Moluccas, articles in the local, national and international press,[19] articles by online news services and other Indonesian news groups such as SiaR, Apakabar, and AmbonNet,[20] and reports, analyses and letters by organizations from outside the Moluccas that were mostly national and international Christian organizations, as well as other European and American organizations. In addition, appeals to the UN and calls to prayer and to take part in corresponding demonstrations worldwide were posted, as well as commentaries and responses to the above contributions.

Whereas in the first few months the information exclusively addressed the situation in the Moluccas, as of 2000 the catchment area was extended and the subject of the information posted included politics, the military, and Islam in Indonesia in general, information about other trouble spots in Indonesia (Aceh, Timor, Kalimantan, Sulawesi, Papua), and other topics worldwide of relevance to members and their interests. One focus was the situation in the Muslim world in the Middle East and a possible link between Al-Qaeda, Osama bin Laden and radical Islamic groups in Indonesia. The reason for this expansion was certainly on the one hand the increasing number of active members able and willing to cover a wider spectrum, and on the other the endeavours of these members to put the

Moluccan conflict in a wider context and put forward a provocation theory that assumed that the actual initiators of the conflict were to be found on Java rather than in the Moluccas, be they individual elements of the military, the government, the former Suharto regime or extremist Muslims. For this reason the Indonesian Association of Protestant Churches (Persekutuan Gereja Indonesia, PGI), whose articles were entered in the MML by its founders, made an appeal to Christians and Muslims alike in Ambon not to let themselves be used for the political and economic interests of the wire-pullers behind the Moluccan conflict, and implored the government and the military to break up this political conspiracy and end the conflict (30 December 1999).

The Masariku founders and members in Ambon divided their posts into different categories. Reports with the subject lines 'Masariku Report', 'Maluku Report', and 'Masariku Update' provided information on events in the conflict in the Moluccas and their background: detailed descriptions of individual attacks and occurrences (when, where, and who was involved), analyses of them, chronologies of the conflict, and lists of victims and destroyed buildings. In the 'Testimony' series, Masariku enabled affected Christians themselves to have a say and relate their traumatic experiences when attacked, when fleeing, as prisoners, or as victims of enforced conversion measures by Muslims. The cruelty of the Muslim attackers, their superiority with regard to weapons, and the involvement of the military and jihad fighters were documented here. These witnesses' statements were an important element in the Masariku Network's argumentation structure. They created a direct link between the members and the experiences of the local population and gave the impression of authentic reporting. The 'Potret Maluku' or 'Photo-Photo' series, which contained photos of victims and the destruction of private and public property, also served this purpose. In 2002 the group launched its 'Masariku Watch' category, documenting its efforts to get to the bottom of individual events in the conflict and, where possible, expose the wire-pullers.

The number of emails sent via Masariku between August 1999 and February 2003 totalled 12,034. The monthly number (see Illustration 3) was heavily influenced by events in the offline sphere. High points in the conflict and waves of violence at the local level caused a corresponding rise in the number of posts. The conflict escalation in December 1999–January 2000 led to a first peak, after which the situation calmed down again, which is evident from the fall in the number of monthly posts. Following the arrival of the Laskar Jihad in the Moluccas in May 2000, the conflict escalated again. It now took on a different dimension and the Christians feared being wiped out. Correspondingly, the number of emails exploded from 94 in May to 570 in June and 618 in July. The rhythm in reporting was thus based on the rhythm of the fighting. Events at the local level, information and momentum were transferred directly into cyberspace. In the case of the Moluccas, cyberspace cannot be considered separately from the local and offline level and its embedment in space and time; temporal sequences in the local context determine those in cyberspace.

Given the intensity of the reporting and the number of news items arriving in the inbox daily, as a Masariku member one had the feeling of being drawn into the course of events, as it were. Through detailed descriptions of the conflict, complemented by maps for orientation, as well as photos of gruesomely disfigured victims and acts of destruction, Masariku members worldwide were confronted on a massive scale in their homes with the local situation in the Moluccas. By being bombarded with these impressive documents, they became involved in the Moluccan conflict on an emotional level. They had the feeling of being directly involved in the conflict and in the suffering of those embroiled in it, and every day waited anxiously for the next reports, the previous ones frequently having ended with 'to be continued' *(bersambung)*. The Masariku members in Ambon felt obliged to the other members to make the latest information available via the mailing list without delay. If a report was not delivered on time, for example, because there was no electricity or because the Internet provider was down, they would apologize for the delay. From around March 2001, the direct link in the MML between waves of violence and news was not so clear. This is because one of the Masariku members, originally from Ambon but living abroad, had, in terms of numbers at least, dominated the list with his posts, which in terms of subject matter went far beyond the local events in the Moluccas.

The list discourse took the form of long and short threads, in which important topics in the conflict and the expansion of the Masariku Network were discussed, though there were also numerous individual posts. According to Stegbauer (2001: 161), long threads are an indication of more contacts and more discussion, whereas a large proportion of individual news items (single threads) points to the list being primarily used to spread information. In the case of the Moluccan conflict, its speed often made it impossible to devote any length of time to any one topic; for this reason we encounter numerous short commentaries and individual posts, which, though they do not directly reference one another, are related on account of a particular offline event.

How the Masariku Network operates

The Masariku maxim was the broadcasting and dissemination of information directly from the field into cyberspace. The reports usually came from active Masariku members in Ambon and its surroundings, and occasionally from normally passive members in Ambon, or from Moluccans and Moluccan organizations abroad, who had been informed of the current situation through a visit to Ambon or by contacts there. In addition to the more detailed Moluccan reports and updates, there were also snippets of information about the condition of the infrastructure in Ambon, the electricity supply, the closing of banks and authorities, etc., as well as short initial information about attacks with the headings 'The latest news from Ambon …' (*Berita terakhir yang diperoleh dari Ambon …*), 'STOP PRESS' or 'BREAKING NEWS'. On 27 June 2000 a list member warned local members about an attack on Christian territory he had been informed of by relatives in Ambon with the headline 'Urgent!'. In her 'Letter from the Killing Field of Maluku' (*Surat dari Killing Field Maluku*), another member, who was visiting her home of Ambon with friends, described how, thanks to a warning from a soldier friend, she had just been able to avoid an attack by the well-armed 'whites', by which she meant the Muslims (1 July 2000).

Masariku saw itself not only as a network that provides information, but primarily as one that takes action. The Masariku team in Ambon journeyed to the Central Moluccas in order to get a picture for itself of the situation in the various regions and to pass on the information to list members. It was only on 20 February 2001[21] that a cofounder of the list outlined more precisely 'How Masariku operates' (*Bagaimana Kerja Masariku*) in the field. Masariku was established in August 1999, initially as a small, dynamic group in Ambon and Jakarta, whose members exchanged information about the conflict so as to be able to analyse the situation in the Moluccas. After a few months, a system was developed for action and more targeted reporting delivered.[22] The main goal was to build up an accurate database on the Moluccan conflict, which at both the national and international level was to be a basis for and provide support for all advocates in the Moluccan conflict. Information was to be made available in the form of written and audiovisual data (photos and videos). For strategic reasons, but primarily on account of the lack of people to compile and upload reports, analyses, opinions and chronologies of the conflict, as well as the time-consuming processes of transcribing witnesses' statements that had been recorded on cassettes and editing videos, not all data was published immediately on the Masariku mailing list. For this reason, but also to maintain witnesses' anonymity, details of sources were often incomplete or missing entirely.

In order to be able to cover as wide a spectrum as possible, and also compile insider knowledge, Masariku attempted to gain access to the citizens, the regional government, the Church, the local media, the military, and the police with a view to mobilizing forces vertically and horizontally. In an effort to balance out the one-sided, Muslim-oriented reporting on the Moluccan conflict, it cooperated with the Ambonese daily newspaper *Siwalima* (1 January 2000) and as of January 2000 *Siwalima* sporadically forwarded its reports to the MML. Furthermore, the MML sometimes integrated news from the Protestant radio station ALPHA OMEGA, which is stationed in Ambon and maintained by BANKOM (Bantuan Komunikasi Radio Kemanusiaan, or Radio Communication Support for Humanity), and reports by local NGOs such as the Christian Yayasan

Hualopu and the Christian-Muslim Yayasan Sala Waku Maluku. In some cases, Masariku staff also worked as volunteers on Masariku actions, such as information gathering in the field and the evacuation of Christians in Seram (25 July 2001).

As the Masariku teams often worked in the heart of the conflict, they were exposed to great danger: cameramen were shot at and beaten up, their cameras destroyed. In attempts to mediate in a dispute, members ended up between the two fronts and were shot at; during an evacuation process a member was injured by a mine, while another was trapped in Muslim territory as conflict broke out there (see, e.g., 1 January, 20 December 2000, 27 February 2001). Furthermore, Masariku initiated evacuations, in particular of Christians forced to convert or flee. As the areas were often very inaccessible (e.g., in Seram, Kesui and Teor), these were very time-consuming and costly. Special investigation teams were recruited to clear up these cases. Working for Masariku was voluntary and unpaid. For this reason the field workers, often students who also had to concentrate on their academic career, could change at any time. Financing the individual projects (material and transport costs, telephone, Internet and other incidental costs) became more and more of a problem, in particular in view of the administration of an ever-increasing amount of data and the coordination of an expanding Masariku Network, as part of which Masariku members in Ambon organized visits by foreign delegations and Moluccan associations. Unpaid bills and a lack of material often meant there was a delay in the delivery of material to the list, on top of which Masariku mostly had just one computer available for uploading information. Even though it was not fundamentally about money, but rather the Moluccas, in the long run the continued work of Masariku was only possible through the support of friends worldwide and donations from Christian aid organizations.

The founders of the list repeatedly emphasized that ideally the MML wanted to be a mouthpiece for all Moluccans, Christians and Muslims alike, as they were all victims of an external conspiracy. If we follow the Masariku explanations thus far and the list discourse in general, it does, however, become clear that Masariku received its information primarily from the Christian side and Christian institutions, and as such automatically almost exclusively reflected the view and the situation of the Christians in the conflict. There can be no mistaking a close link between Masariku and the Church and its networks. For example, in the first few months after Masariku was founded, when the network was still being set up and the sending of reports was not yet either systematized or categorized, press statements by the PGI Crisis Management Centre (Pusat Penanggulangan Krisis PGI, PPK PGI) were forwarded by Masariku members in Jakarta. From the outset Bob, an Ambonese pastor who worked for the PPK PGI, was a member of Masariku and very active in the analysis of conflict situations and backgrounds. Reports by the Church's team of lawyers in

Ambon (TPG)[23] were also included in the list. The Masariku members obviously used the Church network to obtain information directly from the trouble spots. In the reports, pastors and Protestant parishes from various corners of the Moluccas were repeatedly quoted as sources, for example, that of the North Moluccan parish (Sinode Gereja Masehi Injil Halmahera), Saparua (Klasis Gereja Protestan Maluku Saparua) and the Lease Islands (Klasis GPM Pulau-pulau Lease), as well as individual churches and clergymen on the island of Ambon.

Establishing connection and the start

The first emails to be exchanged via the MML were devoted to establishing links between the founding members within and outside the Moluccas. In the very first email dated 17 August 1999, the members were welcomed with the words 'Welcome to the Masariku eGroup', and informed of the email address of the group's manager and its home page.[24] In a second email dated 18 August 1999 the founder requested the other members to register online and confirm the connection. A series of confirmations followed and the 'founding fathers' were linked: Richard, Paul, Franky, Bob, Julius, and Ron. As they obviously knew each other well, there were no individual introductions. For outsiders the 'secret' of the individuals' identities was only revealed if one had followed the list discourse over a long period of time: Paul, Franky, and Bob are pastors of the Protestant Church in Jakarta and Ambon. They are all Christians and all Moluccans like, later on, a large proportion of the members of the list, though at the time it was founded Ron and Franky were living in Ambon, Julius in Australia, and the rest in Jakarta. Also on 18 August 1999, Richard posted a short explanation of the egroup's purpose and objectives, as opposed to the following emails, in English:

> A little explanation of the intention of this egroups.
>
> To link all of us in the link which is need to clarify and verify all the data came from our friend in Ambon. The data which then will be used for several purpose related with each task that should be carry by every part of us, i.e. Julius will need those data for update the home page that was created, also PGI in Jakarta will need for plan and create the appeals to the related committee/organization looking for their concern in situation our brother and sister facing in Ambon.
>
> Mainly it would provide us with the accurate data that can be use by each of us in the link to do some thing for Ambon. Any input to improve this mailing list, please let me or Ron know.
>
> Thanks.

A comprehensive introduction followed on 28 August 1999 in Indonesian. Here too it was emphasized that the intention was to build up a communication and information network between the various posts in Ambon, the Church's crisis centre in Ambon and the PPK PGI in Jakarta. The Internet, it was hoped, would enable the swift dissemination of data and the prompt checking of it by other Masariku members. Until duties had been allocated to the relevant members and the individual activities coordinated, membership was initially restricted to a small circle. A list of the ten members at this point followed. In addition to those named above a further representative of the Protestant Church of the Moluccas (Gereja Protestan Maluku, GPM) and two other Christian organizations joined, such that alongside the PGI crisis centre in Jakarta, that of the Christian University of the Moluccas (Universitas Kristen Indonesia Maluku, UKIM) and the Communication Forum of the Moluccan Christians (Forum Komunikasi Kristen Maluku, FKKM) also became involved. It was once again announced that parallel to the mailing list, part of the campaign would involve two of the members maintaining a website, which would report on the actual situation in Ambon. Neither the name nor the address of the site were given.[25] In an email on 12 September 1999 Paul explained that this campaign for the Moluccas was solely about centring attention on the endeavours and struggle of the Church and the Christian community in the Moluccan conflict and identifying supporters of the Church and the Christians in the Moluccas. He called on the members to do some brainstorming. They were to put forward ideas as to how information should be disseminated (he himself proposed text and images in VCD format), and how the campaign could arouse sympathy among and attract attention from other Christian communities. He concluded with 'May the FATHER in Heaven assist us all.'[26]

While these basic positions were still being negotiated and formalities clarified,[27] the flood of information began flowing. Chronologies of the conflict for July, first analyses and images were delivered. As previously mentioned, this was initially done under the leadership of the PPK PGI and Yayasan SAGU (Solidaritas Anak Negeri Maluku, the Moluccan Solidarity Foundation).[28] Despite the Christian orientation of Masariku, at this stage there was still talk of attacks on both sides (Christian and Muslim). No side was clearly superior to the other, and the conflict continued in the form of strike and counterstrike. This form of pursuing the conflict was typical of this stage of it, but then reports of massive Muslim attacks on Christian quarters in Ambon City arrived. The first target, on 27 July 1999,[29] was the shopping centre in the street Jl. A.Y. Patty, which mainly affected Christian Chinese. There were many victims and numerous shops, houses and transport vehicles were destroyed. The conflict then spread and other Christian districts were attacked. The military did not intervene. The thousands of attackers, according to the PPK PGI, were Muslims from Hitu, a Muslim village on the northern coast of Ambon, and the surrounding area, and wore white headbands as a symbol of Islam (20 August 1999).

The membership profile of the Masariku mailing list

Through the MML, a social space developed online that was structured by the posts and actions of the list members. By main actors assuming different roles, at the heart of the social fabric differentiation emerged on the horizontal plane. On the periphery, the clear allocation of roles and subdivision into discussants, posters and lurkers, as Stegbauer (2001) proposes, was often not possible.

Bernhard Giesen (1999: 116) assumes that a sense of community between those involved exists when the differences in status in a social relationship – for example, between political and cultural leaders and their followers, or between priests and laypersons – are consensual and the diversity of means does not become a topic of the interaction and communication. The social fabric called 'Masariku' was less about differences in status in the sense of a social hierarchy than about various roles. The communal structure was characterized by its heterogeneous composition, in which each member assumed a role of his own and for the most part was recognized and accepted as an authority in the relevant field. Mutual recognition was revealed through the type of list discourse and the stability of the MML social web, which existed for several years. Communities, Giesen continues (1999: 117), often take their cue from the idea of consensual solidarity-based support for needy members, who are, in the case of Masariku, though not directly members of the online community, its main focus of attention and assume a guiding role in the Masariku identity project. According to Giesen (1999: 117–18), collective identity projected over a long period of time by the active members of the MML through their contributions and actions is a necessary illusion of the actors, without which neither we the observers nor the actors themselves would be able to understand their social relationships. In this, the imagination, which is intended to replace the term 'illusion', which Giesen somewhat unfortunately uses, plays a decisive role. It is not about the question of whether in a strictly sociological sense the social structure of the MML was a community or group, but about imaginary communities that emerge in cyberspace and can represent an extension of small local communities.

From what we know, the Masariku egroup was made up, among others, of the founders (activists in Ambon and Jakarta), Moluccans at home and abroad, Christian organizations and Moluccan NGOs. Based on the number and type of posts, we can draw conclusions as to the whereabouts of each member. Whether, for example, he or she had firsthand access to information, whether he or she could fall back on local experiences and investigations, whether it was possible for him or her to surf for any length of time on the Internet in order to search, for example, for suitable articles in the press, and whether access to the Internet was guaranteed on a permanent basis. In some cases the various member categories mutually excluded each other. Given the precarious situation in Ambon with regard to the Internet and the difficult financial situation, the activists, who made the information available locally, did not have continuous Internet access. Furthermore, their main task was to collect data and photos locally and not through online research into the Moluccan conflict. This could be conducted, for example, by members abroad, who had Internet access at all times. Judging by the responses and comments in the MML, authentic local information was more sought after, and well-founded scholarly analyses recognized more than, for example, a large amount of forwarded press reports. According to Stegbauer (2001: 199), although purely in terms of communication history a large number of articles alone can be interpreted as an indication of centrality, it says nothing about the extent to which such an actor is involved socially and how central he is for the other members of the social space.

The number of Masariku members was relatively constant and was based far less on the different stages of the conflict than the number of posts. As with most mailing lists, the discourse was dominated by a small percentage of group members, the core population, who either posted their own contributions or forwarded information they considered to be of relevance to the Masariku Network's objectives. For most of the time the majority of members (approximately 90 per cent) were lurkers, like myself. So as not to exceed the individual capacity limit with too many incoming emails and to structure the handling of the mailing list, members, says Stegbauer, have two options: either to read news with an interesting subject heading or base their choice on well-known names, which promise high-quality, interesting articles (Stegbauer 2001: 174–75). By basing the choice on the subject heading, for example, the Masariku categories 'Report', 'Update', 'Potret', etc. could gain importance. A choice based on the name of the sender is influenced by the respective role and by familiar or supposed identities (Stegbauer 2001: 179) associated with it. However, in view of the joint cause, namely, awareness work with regard to the Moluccan conflict and the representation of the Churches and Christian communities, individual identities take a backseat. The enormous importance of the collective interests and the collective identity is revealed, among other things, by the fact that individual members seldom make themselves the subject matter or present their backgrounds in detail. Only from individual indications during the course of the list discourse can conclusions be drawn about individual identities. For this reason, the Masariku founders and their closest staff in Ambon usually signed their reports with 'Masariku Network Ambon' and those in Jakarta with 'Masariku Network', not with their individual names.

A short profile of the main, and some peripheral, actors enables us to identify the *roles* that, as opposed to individual identities, are extremely important for a functioning community structure. The profile is determined by the type of Internet presence in each case, that is, primarily the type of posts by individual members. With just a few exceptions, all the active members were of Moluccan descent.[30] Key actors, as I define them, were characterized by the frequency and quality of posts or their multiplying effects. The Masariku founders in Jakarta and Ambon belonged to the core of the list community and were key actors. The number of posts by them based exclusively on firsthand data was closely related to occurrences in the conflict. Several other members exceeded the founding members as regards the quantity, but not the authenticity, of posts. In the first ten months, from August 1999 until May 2000, only the list founders were really active. Other individual members popped up at best to register, make recommendations for new members or, for example, to respond to the offer of a video by Masariku. In June 2000, after the Laskar Jihad had arrived in the Moluccas, there was an explosion not only in the number of posts, but also of Masariku members that became active and aired their views in the MML. Never had there been so many authors at one and the same time.[31] Yet more key actors emerged during this phase. Even if from then on the mailing list was dominated by other members in terms of the frequency of posts, the founding members still knew how to attract attention, for example by means of special subject headings such as 'BREAKING NEWS', as well as the established headings, detailed local knowledge, large series of photos and of course their names and the 'Masariku Network' label.

In the short profiles I will not painstakingly list who delivered what type of contribution, as there is much overlapping, but rather illustrate what made the individual active members stand out, what differentiated them from the others, and through this what role they assumed in the communal structure.[32] To begin with, the MML's founding members featured prominently. I have described their manner of working, their type of posts and their sources above. They are the ones who made most local information available. I would classify the members in Ambon themselves as *local activists*, as the *authentic contributors* to the list who invested a lot of time in gathering information from which the other list members benefited. The Internet provided these people with an opportunity to demonstrate their expertise and gain esteem among the other members.[33] The members in Jakarta were primarily the *facilitators* of the list and the members in Ambon, took care of organizational matters and in addition functioned as *moderator,* a role which also involved a certain *mediating function,* as I will explain later on.

Teddy, Emil and the cofounder Bob assumed the role of *scholars* and *analysts,* although they were supported by other list members. In relatively few posts, the pastor Bob primarily delivered political background information and well-grounded analyses of the Moluccan conflict, and commented on reports by the Masariku Network. In hundreds of his own posts and forwarded press articles, Teddy made a considerable contribution to discussions, to educational work, in particular in a legal respect, to shedding light on the more and less immediate background to the conflict and to the search for approaches to solving the conflict. Teddy also paid particular attention to the role of Europe in Indonesia and the Moluccan conflict. Emil, a lecturer at Unpatti,[34] although working on a dissertation project on Java at the time, wrote scholarly articles of his own, in which he analysed different aspects of the conflict and looked for solutions. He posted this material on the MML for discussion.

In Robert, Masariku had among its members a *human rights activist* and devout Christian who worked in Indonesia for the Suffering Church Ministry, a Christian missionary and charitable organization based in America. In this function he was frequently in the Moluccas and Poso, in Central Sulawesi, where conflict had likewise been erupting on a regular basis for years. He got a picture of the situation for himself locally, attempted to help clarify the reasons for the conflict and pointed out human rights violations, in particular with regard to the massive attacks by fundamentalist Muslims on Christians. He then posted the resulting reports online at Masariku. Henrich forwarded calls to prayer by different Christian organizations as well as press declarations by the Jubilee Campaign U.K. and the International Christian Concern (ICC) devoted to the Moluccan conflict and the critical situation of the Christians there, thereby attempting, as a *Christian,* to offer support to the people affected in the Moluccas.

Julius, Febian and Ernst acted as *online multipliers.* Julius and Febian posted on their own websites Masariku reports, updates, and photos addressing the Moluccan conflict. Ernst forwarded Masariku articles to the mailing list of the Maluku Outreach Foundation (MOF), an NGO in California founded by Moluccans, which, among other things, had set itself the task of making the Indonesian population in the United States aware of the tragedy in the Moluccas and supporting refugees financially.[35] While Febian likewise drew attention to his website, Lawamena Victoria, directly in the MML,[36] the previously mentioned introductory emails dated 18 and 28 August 1999 made direct reference to Julius's website. Febian also translated a few of the Masariku reports into English and forwarded, like Julius, articles on the Moluccan conflict from the Indonesian and Australian press to the MML. Julius also had an integrative function, as he occasionally posted contributions on the Masariku list by other Moluccans in Australia and other countries who were in contact with relatives and friends in the Moluccas. Like Febian and Brigitte, Julius lived in Australia and was active in the Moluccan lobby there. Together they built up a Moluccan network in the country and, through their untiring commitment, ensured that in mid-2000 the Australian press finally devoted an appropriate amount of attention to human rights violations in the Moluccan conflict (Febian, 28 June 2000). The members in this category were not characterized by the very high frequency of their posts, but they were key, continuous members who played a role in the decisive expansion of the reach of Masariku, especially if we consider that Masariku itself maintained no openly accessible website.

Like Ernst, Clark, chairman of the Maluku Watch Network (MWN), a Moluccan NGO in Washington, also assumed the role of *lobbyist* for the Moluccan cause in America. Within Masariku he was a diligent poster who, in addition to MWN's own reports, also delivered reports on the Moluccan conflict by the International Crisis Group (ICG, headquartered in Brussels) and the U.S. Commission on International Religious Freedom (USCIRF). Otherwise, he concentrated on articles in the American and in some cases the Indonesian press, among other things devoted to politics in Indonesia and Indonesian policy in America. Through his work in the MWN, he likewise acted as a multiplier with regard to the reach of Masariku news.

Timo, who was highly active in 2000 and 2001, seemed to have specialized in searching for posts about the Moluccan conflict in the local (Ambon) and national press and national online news services; thus, I classify him as a *press representative*. He delivered good insight into how the topic was treated in the selected media, though this is not to be pursued further here. His posts were complemented by a wide range of press articles forwarded to the list by other members, in particular by Arno, who, from March 2001, had stood out for the mass of articles (almost five thousand in two years) and the diversity of his interests. In addition to the Moluccan conflict and the situation in Aceh and East Timor, Islam and its different forms in Indonesia and worldwide was one of the main focuses of his attention. He also addressed many topics that appeared of interest to him in connection with the Moluccas, as well as Indonesia in general, namely history, politics and business, communism, Islam, fundamentalism, democracy, human rights, Marxism, racism, nationalism and terrorism, to name just a few. To this end he made use of a wide variety of different national and international online daily newspapers and magazines, including the Islam-influenced spectrum, such as, for example, *Hidayatullah* and *Republika,* which Timo disregarded. Moreover, Arno forwarded invitations to protest and solidarity events worldwide relating to the Moluccas and Indonesia.

However, what made Arno particularly stand out was his function as a *cross-poster.* He was a member of numerous Indonesian mailing lists such as, for example, Ambon.com, Indonesia_Damai (Indonesia_Peace), Nasional, Proletar, Wanita-Muslimah (Muslim Woman) and IHRC-NZ (Indonesian Human Rights Committee), which, among other things, addressed the Moluccas, Indonesian politics, Islam, and human rights in Indonesia. By means of intensive cross-posting, he attempted to merge the various list discourses. He forwarded entire discussion threads, in which he mostly participated, to the MML, attempting to prompt and, through corresponding posts, for example, from Muslim mailing lists, provoke discussions. He did not appear to enjoy that much success, as his articles rarely triggered responses. Most members were probably overwhelmed by the sheer mass of his posts. The manner in which he dealt with the FKAWJ mailing list is of greater interest here. He often posted its emails on the MML but changed the subject heading in order to comment on and criticize it and to discredit the Laskar Jihad, which made him a genuine *provocateur* after all. He was also seen as such in, for example, the Nasional mailing list (MML 14 June and 8 July 2002).

Given the roles they played and the characteristics mentioned above, I would classify all the members mentioned thus far as key actors at the heart of the MML communal structure. The Dutchman Arie was not really at home at the heart or on the periphery. He was one of the few non-Moluccans that were active in the list to frequently air their views in the first three months of 2001. In this phase, alongside ICG analyses and appeals by Christian organizations, he primarily forwarded reports in the English-language press in Indonesia. What gave him special significance in the Moluccan issue was the fact that he, too, boasted his own website,[37] of which, under the motto 'Help Ambon!', a large proportion was devoted to the Moluccan conflict.

Most of the members on the periphery were lurkers. They did not, however, have to remain so for their entire list life. Many, for example, uploaded posts on a specific event and then disappeared silently into the background again. Members who delivered only very few posts and who played no clear role in the mailing list's social fabric also belong on the periphery. However, these members could also assume an important, relationship-engendering function, and they were in a position to contribute to the stability of the social structure, be it through their constant membership, valuable individual posts, comments or support. We could also say that they gave the list discourse additional spice, for example, short individual comments by Agus, who often added suitable quotations from the Bible, or by Hendrik, whose dialect left no doubt whatsoever that he was a child of the Moluccas. Tony, a Moluccan living in Bali and a member from the very beginning, surfaced to draw attention to a Moluccan website maintained in Ambon (LopaLopa), and then several times consecutively after the Bali bombing of October 2002. He offered those affected, their families and interested members information and help. Following a lengthy quiet period of almost two years, Rick from Ambon only became active again in March 2002, when he was embroiled in the Ambon Plaza incident, where several Christians were held by Muslims in a shopping centre in Muslim territory until they were freed by the military. Other members not (or no longer) living in the Moluccas, such as Rein or Stevie, surfaced whenever they themselves had just been there and were able to deliver up-to-date information and analyses or got such information from contacts there. Bobo, who had made New Zealand his home, was the second active, though only at times, non-Moluccan who was involved with the MML until August 2001. He was a very open member of the Apostolic Church of New Zealand, who on 16 June 2001 even posted a detailed CV on the MML and often called on people to pray. Yet he was also one of the few to upload various reports on the Muslim view of the conflict in the Moluccas (although not that of the FKAWJ), such as 'This is what the Muslim Students tell us in New Zealand' (18 December 2000).

With regard to these joint endeavours to exchange information, clarify and offer mutual support, a small group of members represented an exception to the rule. They expressed their discontent by insulting the leader of the Laskar Jihad, Ja'far Umar Thalib, and Muslims in general in regular tirades of hatred and jokes about them. These *aggressors* and supposed *buffoons* made use of what are known as flame wars. Their comments were hardly constructive and added little in terms of content to the list discourse. Even though we are basically only talking about three members who did not fit in with the typical list discourse, they nonetheless also had an influence on the image of the Masariku community, precisely because they 'stepped out of line'. It seems two of these members left the list in late 2001, whether voluntarily or not is unclear. Examples of their posts are provided in Chapter 8.

The communitization process

In addition to role distribution in the Masariku social fabric, the argumentation, interaction and communication patterns, the relation to a common homeland, sanctions, jointly planned actions, the group dynamism and the resultant networks are additional decisive elements in the communitization and identity-defining process in the MML.

Identification with the homeland and sanctions

The Moluccan conflict was the common point of reference for all MML members. It was the reason this forum was created, and it was what brought the members together. By reading and themselves posting information on the list, many Masariku members were involved personally and emotionally; it was their friends, their families, their religious communities or the village from which they originally came that were affected by the conflict and that were the subject of the posts. So on the one hand it was their common interest in this conflict that ultimately made the Masariku mailing list a network based on solidarity and an online communal social structure, while on the other it becomes evident from the list discourse just how important a common origin, a common homeland, and common friends and relatives were for building relationships among list members. A sense of identification with the homeland was aroused. Moluccans in Indonesia (the Moluccas, Java, Bali, Sulawesi, Papua) and worldwide (primarily in Australia, the United States and the Netherlands, but also in Tasmania,

Canada, the United Kingdom and Sweden) heard of the Masariku initiative and offered their cooperation and help, the impact and reach of which will become evident in the course of this chapter. The MML membership also included various Christian and human rights organizations and other interested non-Moluccan individuals. The majority of the list members, however, were Moluccans; those members who were active over a long period of time were exclusively Moluccans. Many members introduced themselves briefly, and some even attached business cards to their emails, while in the case of others their name and email address provided an indication of where they came from and where they were living at the time.[38] Revealing individual identities, however, was not necessarily the rule in the MML. As already mentioned, the list discourse needs to be followed for some time in order to be able to draw conclusions about the function, identity and backgrounds of individual key members, or make direct contact with them.

Having assembled online in the form of the MML, the members, who were spread wide and far, set about exploring their new online environment. Several were surprised to find out that they came from the same village in the Moluccas, had common relatives and friends, or even knew each other from back home. Then of course they started using the Ambonese dialect. On 21 June 2000 Febian (Australia) posted a question on the list in which he inquired about two members of the list, Elias and Teddy, whom he thought he knew from school in Ambon or the district he used to live in. That same day Merry replied: 'Febian, you used to live in Kar-Pan, didn't you? If you did, you know me, right?'[39] Elias also responded and told Febian where he was currently living, in West Papua. Stevie asked Febian if he was not the younger brother of E. K.. Stevie himself was still living in Ambon. In addition, they talked in the list about the past, common acquaintances, how they were doing and their own situation, or asked members still living in Ambon to see that their relatives were all right. Masariku was even used as a platform for mourning *(Berita Dukacita)*. The death of a Moluccan who had emigrated to California was announced in the list so as to inform the Moluccan community, in particular those who knew the deceased and his family from before (12 February 2003). Ernst thereupon not only expressed his sympathy, but also gave a eulogy for the deceased. On 5 October 2001 Franky posted on the list photos of beautiful places on the island of Ambon in which no traces of the conflict were visible. Many of the members who then surfaced expressed a longing to return to their homeland. Many list members expressed their gratitude to the founders of the list, who were the ones who made all this possible.

As is the case offline, a community can only exist over a lengthy period of time if its members obey certain rules. Not only is positive integration through common goals, common references, symbols and cases of interaction between the community members necessary, but also protection from elements in the community that could endanger its stability and effectiveness. Physical *sanctions* do not apply online. Otherwise, the sanctions imposed within the Masariku community were not so different from those that are customary offline. Depending on the seriousness of their offence, members who acted in contravention of the Masariku philosophy were either cautioned and rebuked, or excluded from the community. The list founders did not want junk mail, grave insults or excessively emotional or heated discussions. Other mailing lists such as Ambon.com served as negative examples (15 November 2002). Another measure for protecting a community is to make it secure on the outside. For this reason the list moderator was from the outset highly selective with regard to the admission of members. Even if, according to selected Yahoo! characteristics, the MML was not moderated, in such cases the moderator still plays a decisive role as a mediator and vigilante. On 21 December 2000, for example, the moderator apologized to a list member who the previous day had complained that another person was misusing the list for his business interests. The administrator assured the member that were the person to do it again he would be removed from the list.

The members also exerted a certain amount of control among themselves. One member was accused of spreading rumours and untruths, as he posted an article referring to the Muslims as the legitimate owners of Waai, from which several thousand Christians had been driven out in July 2000. The heaviest protest came from the supposed author of the article, as he had not in fact written it and had only wanted to post it for discussion. The accuser was left with no choice but to officially apologize to the accused and the Masariku community and to retract his false assertions (23–24 September 2000). In another case, Arno took to task a member who, upon the death of Agus Wattimena, one of the key figures among the fighters on the Christian side, indulged in lengthy expressions of sympathy and solidarity (23 July 2001), without even knowing the person or the background to the case. Incensed, he asked: 'Are you joking or what? Where have you been and have you been sleeping all the time and just wake and want to pray? You are acting a star in a cartoon movie' (24 July 2001).

In July 2000 several parties complained that because of too many useless articles the MML had lost effectiveness. Tony (3 July 2000) criticized that Timo was posting news and images that were of no urgency. He told him to behave like an adult and give careful consideration to which articles really were useful for the network and the brothers and sisters in Ambon. He concluded by expressing the hope: 'MAY GOD GIVE YOU THE RIGHT INSTINCT TO DO SO!!!!!!!'[40] Mark complained about having to open two hundred emails from Masariku every day, only to ascertain that approximately one hundred of them were basically the same, and called for more effectiveness (3 July 2000). Overlapping had to be avoided, but first and foremost messages that were not urgent had to be left out, as did unnecessary rumours and gossip. He asked the moderator to take action with regard to this matter and to filter out the relevant posts before they were published in the list. Two other members supported him in this. The moderator, however, dismissed the requests, as they contradicted the basic principle of Masariku. The list had already been closed to the public; only members were able to post items. At this level, however, the exchange ought to be completely open. To this, Agus, who saw precisely this freedom disappearing already, replied, evidently relieved: 'WHOOPS, I am relieved!!! Thanks again for all your hard work. May God bless you' (4 July 2000). Things were different for the moderator when a virus attack occurred (29 January 2001). He informed the list that several members' computers had already been infected and there were fears the entire MML would be affected if nothing were done. For this reason it had been decided to change the MML settings to protect it from the virus. Each and every email was now first to be directed to the moderator, who would check it for viruses before forwarding it. All those members whose computers were already infected were removed from the list. However, just how long this time-consuming intention was actually put into practice is not clear.

On 23 January 2002 Bob, who, judging by the type of his posts and the response to them, was a respected list member, posted a message on the list in which he gave a positive assessment of a team of regional politicians (Moluccans) put together by the government in Jakarta to find a solution to the Moluccan conflict. Sammy, in several tirades of abuse, immediately accused him of having betrayed the Moluccans and benefited the Javanese dominance of the Moluccas (29 January 2002). Bob initially replied only briefly that he had no time for this type of comment, as it was more like a dog's bark. However, when Sammy did not let up, resorting to further insults, Bob wrote a detailed letter to Sammy and the list, in which he pontificated on mutual respect and tolerance, which everyone on the list could and indeed should demand (5 February 2002). He added a note to the moderator in which he described the dispute with Sammy in detail. He complained that the latter had repeatedly referred to him in an offensive, provocative and insolent manner and in the process not even mentioned what he had actually wanted to say. He asked the moderator to in future ensure that this type of post was no longer published in the list. This was essential if it were to be protected from verbal anarchism and verbal violence and its productivity and effectiveness preserved. The moderator (5 February 2002) thereupon posted a letter to all members calling on them to preserve the Masariku ethics and continue conversing like sensible adults. Teddy immediately agreed in two languages (English and Indonesian): everyone was free to choose either to obey the Masariku rules and adopt an appropriate tone, or to leave the list.

Argumentation structure[41]

Even though the type and number of posts made by individual members in their various functions and roles were very different, in their basic positions, their main arguments and the basic alignment of their posts they were all nonetheless the same: to gather and disseminate information via the MML, checking it and having others confirm it or prove it false and correct it. This way, common positions could be negotiated and educational work performed in an interactive, dynamic online process. Even if it was the core members who determined the discourse, individual members on the periphery contributed important posts, too. Thus numerous threads emerged in the MML revolving around topics such as the military's involvement in the conflict, the government's incompetence, the emergence of the Laskar Jihad and the looming Islamization of the Moluccas.[42]

Masariku members were convinced that parts of the military were involved in events in the conflict, sided with the Muslims and did nothing to stop the Laskar Jihad training camps on the island of Ambon. They saw the cause of the conflict as being outside the Moluccas and assumed that those pulling the strings were to be found in the political and military elite in Jakarta. Furthermore, on a local basis, they believed that there were crooks *(preman)* from Jakarta involved. The PPK PGI (20–21 August 1999) was sure that originally the Moluccan conflict was not a religious war, but that at local and indeed national levels religion nonetheless played a decisive role. It saw the Moluccan conflict ultimately as a consequence of the *Orde Baru,* when religion had been used as a political tool. As Muslim attacks on Christian areas often occurred in several places simultaneously, one could conclude that they were part of an elaborate plan and a larger scenario. According to Bob, the Islam factor in the conflict had to be seen as ideology and as the continuation of a long history in Indonesia, where since independence there had been rivalry between the defenders of a secular state, which so far had always had the upper hand, and those of an Islamic state. For the Muslim community the conflict was part of the jihad against the dominance of the Christians *(kafir,* faithless). The PPK PGI was well aware of the fact that this stance did not reflect the mind-set of the entire Muslim community. Their fears were nonetheless genuine, in particular on account of the presence of the Laskar Jihad and its declared aim of introducing Sharia in the Moluccas, and this was expressed in numerous articles in the national press that were forwarded to the MML. In this oppressive situation Masariku members readily made comparisons with the situation of Christians threatened by Muslims in other countries, as well as in other parts of Indonesia, such as Lombok, Sulawesi, Madura, Bima and Java, and with the Jews in Israel.

In the MML numerous detailed descriptions of attacks proved the military's involvement or lack of action. On 4 April 2002 an MML member stated that only the military, through its enormous influence and the power it had enjoyed for thirty-two years under Suharto's reign, had any experience in conflict management and was at all in a position to orchestrate the type of conflict that prevailed on the Moluccas. Disputes within the military and between the military and the police, which could be traced back to the separation of the two forces, as well as the planned gradual stripping of the military's political power following Suharto's fall, were contributing to the further escalation of the situation. As well as the military, the Indonesian government was also arraigned for its inability to end the conflict and for its discriminatory policy. Neither the noncommittal visits of the president(s) and other government representatives to the Moluccas nor the civil state of emergency imposed since June 2000 had provided relief. The government was not taking any serious measures and was not in a position to enforce its own laws and protect the minorities (the Christians). It was Java-oriented, only lined the pockets of the central government and exploited the Moluccans.

There was also criticism of the fact that after Megawati had been elected the new president in 2001, the Moluccan conflict became the responsibility of the new vice president Hamzah Haz, who was well known for not opposing radical Islamic groups. This was confirmed by his visit to Ja'far Umar Thalib in prison after his arrest in May 2002, which was completely incomprehensible to Masariku and the Christian population of the Moluccas. The ban on foreign journalists visiting the Moluccas, which was imposed in January 2001, also met with major protest in the MML. The government should just continue in this vein, one of the members commented (29 January 2001), and then the population would become more and more discontent and the calls for independence ever louder. For the Christians, the fact that the government was unwilling to take steps against the Laskar Jihad, which let the Muslim militias in the Moluccas become almost untouchable, was unforgivable. Thalib's acquittal in January 2003 confirmed that his arrest had been pure theatre (30 January 2003): while a terrorist who had thousands of Christians in the Moluccas and Poso on his conscience was acquitted, a Christian leader was sentenced to three years in prison.[43]

Suggesting to the Muslims in Indonesia that the Muslim community in Ambon was in great danger and that the whole of Indonesia was in danger of Christianization, which in the opinion of MML members was totally fabricated, was part and parcel of Laskar Jihad propaganda. However, by means of, in some cases, exaggerated numbers of thousands and thousands of Laskar Jihad in the Moluccas and the announcement in large red letters of the arrival of twenty-two thousand jihad warriors from the Muslim Brotherhood's Holy Army (Laskar Jundullah Ikhwanul Muslimin, JIM) (21 April 2001, according to *Tempo Interaktif*, 17 April 2001), the Christians and Masariku members also knew how to whip up fear. According to Masariku, the Laskar Jihad were very well armed, which on the one hand was on account of their links with the military and on the other the result of the attack on the headquarters of the Mobile Police Brigade (Brimob) in Tantui, Ambon, in June 2000, when they were allegedly able to seize several hundred weapons and ammunition. The Laskar Jihad had also, they claimed, seized equipment and medication for the FKAWJ hospital in Ambon in an attack on the Catholic hospital. Although the FKAWJ constantly emphasized how eagerly the Muslims in the Moluccas had awaited the Laskar Jihad and how warmly they had been welcomed, Masariku was convinced that the Laskar Jihad came of their own accord and put the local population under pressure not to deviate from the uncompromising stance towards the Christians that they propagated. For proof, Masariku members resorted to informers of their own and local experiences, press articles, and online reports by the Laskar Jihad themselves, which Arno forwarded to the MML on a regular basis. In this way the Masariku members were confronted directly with the other side's point of view, with their accusations and arguments. Ja'far Umar Thalib's declaration of war, which was broadcast in early May 2002 by the local Laskar Jihad radio station in Ambon, SPMM, attracted enormous attention. Several Masariku members forwarded transcripts of the address, in both Indonesian and English.[44] The text combines, so to speak, all the clichés and prejudices the Laskar Jihad harbour against Christians and the West.[45] Nonetheless, the MML was not jubilant at the official disbanding of the Laskar Jihad in October 2002, as members supposed that they would escape punishment and most likely go underground.

For some Masariku members there was an obvious link between the Laskar Jihad and the Middle East. They assumed that the Laskar Jihad were being supported by the Arab world (28 and 30 November 2002), and attempted to deliver proof, such as, for example, an article in *Republika* dated 10 November 2001, which was posted on the MML the very day it was published. On 11 May 2000 the SiaR news service, on the basis of an interview with Ja'far Umar Thalib, published an article with the significant title 'THE LASKAR JIHAD REQUEST THE BLESSING OF THE MIDDLE EAST, NOT OF THE INDONESIAN PEOPLE' (14 May 2000).[46] The assistance, however, was not only of a financial nature, as warriors from the Middle East also took part in fighting in the Moluccas. According to statements by Christian witnesses, people who, judging by their appearance and the language they spoke, could have come from the Middle East often mingled with the attackers, and the Laskar Jihad in Ambon were often seen with people of this description. According to Masariku, these intruders, be they from Java or the Middle East, were a major factor in the Moluccan conflict.[47] The course of Ja'far Umar Thalib's life, who had studied in the Middle East for a long time and in 1987 took part in the jihad in Afghanistan, provided proof of this link, as did the open willingness of the Laskar Jihad, following 9/11, to send warriors to Afghanistan to support the Muslims there against the Americans. Some MML members maintained that the Laskar Jihad had links to

Osama bin Laden and that Al-Qaeda itself was behind the massacre of Christians in the Moluccas and Poso (28 September 2001; 6 October 2001; 28 April 2002).

Masariku, however, was firmly convinced that it was not the Muslims in the Moluccas as such who were pulling the strings in the conflict. For this reason it made repeated attempts to emphasize the basis unity between Christians and Muslims there: 'ONE PEOPLE ... ONE BLOOD ... ONE ORIGIN ... LONG LIVE MALUKU ...' (21 April 2001).[48] Moluccan Christians and Muslims alike were victims of a political and military elite, which exploited religion in the conflict for its own purposes. As such the Christians endeavoured to follow the situation of the Muslims as well, but given the extremely difficult conditions with regard to communication between the two sides in the conflict, they had little success. With just a few exceptions, the only data delivered were regarding victims and losses on the Christian side. Many Masariku members emphasized that not all Muslims could be lumped together and that there were different forms of Islam in Indonesia, as there were throughout the rest of the world. For this reason, very early on the PPK PGI expressly called on the Christians to take a more differentiated view of the Muslim side (26 August 1999). Another MML member invited moderate Muslims in Indonesia to raise their voice and state their opinion on the true Islam, which allowed its followers to live with others in peace so as to build the Indonesian nation together (4 January 2002). Based on these fundamental convictions the MML also attempted to reveal positive developments and reported various peace initiatives in the Moluccas such as, for example, the Christian-Muslim BakuBae movement and the large meeting of *adat* and religious leaders in Langgur. For the Christians, the question of guilt, of who exactly had started the conflict in the first place, initially seemed to be less important than ending the violence. From mid-2002, after Malino and the last terrible attacks on the Christian village of Soya di Atas near Ambon, Franky, the local activist, relied more and more on peace journalism. He increasingly reported positive developments such as the gradual establishment of contact between Christians and Muslims, the gradual emergence of cross-border actions and joint peace initiatives.

In order to pinpoint the reasons for the conflict, Masariku conducted analyses of its own and forwarded and discussed academic investigations by nonmembers, and made book recommendations.[49] As such, for example, on the occasion of a hearing of the USCIRF[50] in Washington, D.C., on 13 February 2001, lectures on the Moluccan conflict were forwarded, as were articles by Gerry van Klinken, then editor of the magazine *Inside Indonesia,* George J. Aditjondro, sociologist and anthropologist, Tamrin A. Tomagola, one of the few academics (a sociologist) in Indonesia to openly express his criticism of the government and the military with regard to the Moluccan conflict, and Smith Alhadar, who explains the background to the conflict in the Northern Moluccas. The Moluccan social scientist Emil posted articles on the Moluccan conflict he had written himself on the MML for discussion. Among other things, he wrote about the elite groups behind the conflict, the reconstruction of Unpatti, which was destroyed by Muslims and the military, the poor general level of education in the Moluccas, the problem of foreign NGOs there, possible contributions by Moluccan leaders on solving the conflict and how to implement the points resolved upon at Malino II. On various occasions in the MML Emil's essays were mentioned and supplemented, and became the basis of concrete proposals for action. The Masariku members invested much time, both online and offline, unearthing the background of the cases of enforced conversion. Other topics of discussion included the role of the military in the conflict, the situation with regard to human rights in the Moluccas, the civil state of emergency, of which most were very critical, and approaches for solving the conflict (potential of local NGOs, involvement of the local population, etc.). During the discussions some Masariku members repeatedly called on those who were committed to the Moluccan conflict in general, and the Masariku members in particular, to stick to the facts and not spread untruths just to be able to achieve something in the short term (e.g., 5 October 2001; 28 April 2002).

Group dynamism and networks

With the help of the MML, a worldwide network of information, solidarity, and action was set up that encompassed Australia, Indonesia, Europe and the United States. Information on Masariku was intended, via this network, to reach circles – such as the Moluccan diaspora, the United Nations, the European Union, the United States, Church circles and national and international Christian organizations – that were able to help Masariku end the Moluccan conflict and assist the Moluccan population, in particular the Christians, who after the arrival of Laskar Jihad were extremely threatened. The Masariku archive was the basis of the lobbying work of various organizations addressing the Moluccan conflict and enabled them to produce reports and analyses of their own. By means of enquiries and short interjections it became clear how many members whose role was actually that of lurker actively handled the information they received, using it for specific purposes.

Solidarity network

Many usually passive Masariku members abroad expressed their solidarity with the local Masariku actors, sometimes in English, sometimes in Indonesian:

> Brothers and sisters, you who have current information from Ambon, please pass this on to us. We, who are far away from Ambon, are very worried about

our friends and relatives in Ambon. May the Lord Jesus Christ help all brothers and sisters in Ambon in their struggle and protect them. (25 June 2000)[51]

Dear brothers, We are following all the actions from you step by step. We still support you. MAY GOD STILL BLESS YOU! Thanks that you still forward the messages to us. Regards. (27 June 2000)

Anton, a lecturer at Unpatti who was in Canada at the time, confirmed that in the current difficult situation solidarity was the most important thing (4 July 2000). Several members worldwide, from both the core and the periphery of the list, prayed for the Moluccans at home and for the Masariku members and stated this on the list. For its members the MML was the quickest and safest way of receiving up-to-date information about the conflict. In this way they were not reliant on the national media, which were often very slow or did not give the Moluccan conflict sufficient attention (27–28 June 2000). In addition to information that was of interest to everyone, very personal things were also exchanged via the MML. Members in the diaspora, for example, would enquire as to the whereabouts and well-being of relatives and friends living in trouble spots in the Moluccas, who had not been in touch since, were regarded as missing, or had had to flee, or they asked for details of lists of victims in order to find out whether they knew the people on them. This is how an announcement of good news, for example, would read:

Terimah kasih!!!! THANKS SOMEONE FOR TELLING MY NIECE TO CONTACT US IN HOLLAND. This afternoon at 16:00 hrs she called us in Holland telling us that they'd fled to Batu Medja. The situation is still frightening but they stay HOPEFULL, knowing that He will set them FREE. She asked me to tell everyone to keep PRAYING for that day will come soon!!!!! (28 June 2000)[52]

Febian thanked the Masariku people in Ambon and Jakarta for their hard work and the excellent collaboration between Masariku and his organization Lawamena Victoria, which also maintained a website[53] and ran an aid programme for schoolchildren in the Moluccas affected by the conflict, and offered Masariku his continued support (15 December 2000). With the subject heading 'Support News = Support Masariku' he called on all list members not just to receive information but to actively support Masariku, be it by taking measures or in material form. With its reports, photos and videos, Masariku was performing an invaluable service. All this had to be paid for, however. Other members also said they were worried about Masariku's financial situation, calling on people to pray for it and make donations. On 5 February 2001 the list moderator himself made an appeal in English and Indonesian to all members of the Masariku Network worldwide, in which he depicted its disastrous financial situation. The spread of the conflict and the action that had taken place in the context of the enforced conversions had resulted in an enormous rise in costs. Furthermore, the information and emergency call network had to be expanded in the Central Moluccas, which would also cost a lot of money. A number of members responded to this appeal, primarily from the periphery, with concrete proposals, while others decided to establish contact with one another outside the list with a view to taking action together. The moderator offered his thanks for the positive feedback and generous donations (4 March 2001).

Networking and circulation

The MML and its contacts extended Masariku's catchment area and sphere of influence enormously. Some members posted their information on the list with the express request that it be forwarded to friends it could be of use to; the list moderator also wrote in the same vein: 'Please forward to anyone who cares about Ambon' (6 October 1999). Members also exchanged more detailed contact information; the paths of some also crossed offline. Whenever members living outside the Moluccas were planning a journey there, they would make online contact beforehand with Masariku members there and get information about establishing contact with other local institutions such as the *Siwalima* editorial office and the GPM. By involving the Masariku members in their respective social, political and institutional offline context, those active among them gained access for the Masariku Network to the offline sector in the various localities, which had a multiplying effect. This occurred at the local, national and international level, some examples of which are given in the following.

The Association of the Children of the Moluccas (Ikatan Anak-Anak Maluku, IKAAMA) in East Java was one such multiplier. This moral movement of Moluccans was committed to peace in the Moluccas and to this end regularly organized events, for which Masariku provided the background information (5 September 2002). Ernst's MOF in Washington, D.C., was engaged in lobbying the Presbyterian Church and the U.S. government with regard to the Moluccas and organized the U.S. programme for the Moluccan delegation in 2002 (26 and 30 June 2000). In this context, via the list Arno gave Ernst the telephone number of a progressive pastor in New York and the address of the Interreligious Foundation for Community Organization, which has a large network of various churches and NGOs throughout the United States (20 July 2002). Febian's and Julius's actions in Australia were mentioned previously. Both received the information for their websites for the most part from Masariku. A human rights activist in the United States asked Masariku online for photos of attacks on Christian villages, in which, if possible, those Laskar Jihad warriors were supposedly seen who, it was assumed, were not Indonesian citizens (27 September 2000). She was planning to subsequently forward this proof to the organization Human Rights Watch and the U.S. Senate. The videos produced by Masariku made available via the list and requested by Masariku members throughout the world served to give an even wider audience access to information about the conflict.

In particular, Dutch (Moluccan) NGOs such as Malra70, HAIN and Den Helder voor de Molukken were effective interfaces via which, on the one hand, information was passed on, but via which, on the other hand, planned concrete aid was also given, based on this information. Den Helder voor de Molukken, for example, organized a benefit concert for the Moluccas on 28 April 2001 (28 February 2001).[54] Malra70 worked with local NGOs (e.g., Baileo and Hualopu in Ambon) and provided assistance. HAIN (Help Ambon in Nood, based in Houten near Utrecht in the Netherlands) disseminated Masariku information on its website,[55] sent investigation teams to the Moluccas, produced reports of its own, and, together with other NGOs, performed lobbying work in the Netherlands. The Netherlands-based webmaster of the Maluku WEB Portal[56] proposed to the MML moderator that, at his own cost, he set up a website on which the members could post all their news and images (6 February 2000). The global Masariku Network also benefited Masariku activists on their travels in Europe and the United States. When, for example, Franky spoke in front of the United Nations in Geneva, Paul posted an appeal on the list, asking all members living in Switzerland to contact Franky and help him when he was there.

Despite all the networking, the list moderator repeatedly emphasized that Masariku material should be treated with caution. In an email dated 5 February 2000, for example, he announced the dispatch of a Masariku video that various members had requested, and stressed to them that they should only use the videos in Masariku's interest and only forward them to people that had the same vision and could help the Masariku campaign. On 20 April 2000 he asked members to use all the photos that would be appearing shortly only within the Masariku circle. Elsewhere he called on the members to confer with the Masariku Network in Ambon or Jakarta before publishing Masariku photos (16 February 2000). Bob also addressed the problem of authorship and copyright regarding Masariku data (29 September 2000). From the list discourse it occasionally emerged that strategically important information and detailed plans of action were in some cases exchanged privately, outside the list, something that active members of the Masariku Network later confirmed to me.

The secular and religious pillars

In addition to the networks of Moluccans, Masariku was also explicitly aimed at international and Christian organizations and institutions worldwide, as it was of the opinion that given the precarious situation of the Christians in the Moluccas and indeed of the entire Moluccan people, only outside intervention could provide relief and offer a solution to the conflict. At the very least, these institutions, through corresponding declarations and letters, could exert influence on the Indonesian government to take concrete, serious measures in the Moluccan conflict.

The West

Numerous articles in the press that were included in the list expressed the interest and worry of the 'West' with regard to the Moluccan conflict. Some examples might serve to illustrate this:

> *Antara,* 27 January 2001: 'Uni Europa Delegation to Visit the Moluccas on 10 February' (Delegasi Uni Eropa ke Maluku 10 Februari, 27 January 2001)
>
> *Tempo,* 21 February 2001: 'EU Concerned about Maluku Conflicts' (21 February 2001)
>
> *Indonesian Observer,* 24 February 2001: 'World Ready to Help Refugees in North Maluku – At Least 17 European Countries Have Pledged to Assist North Maluku in Dealing with its Refugee Crisis' (27 February 2001)
>
> *The Jakarta Post,* 14 March 2001: 'Dutch to Provide More Aid' (15 March 2001)
>
> *Koridor,* 24 February 2001: 'NGO Network Formed (in Washington) to Pressure RI' (27 February 2001).

In the MML there were various articles from the national press that reported on financial aid for the Moluccas. In this the West played the major role. The United States Agency for International Development (USAID), for example, donated US$309,000 to the Moluccas, and Sweden donated US$250,000 to Moluccan refugees (2 and 22 March 2001, according to *The Jakarta Post,* 23 March 2001, and *Indonesian Observer,* 27 February 2001). As the country in which the largest Moluccan diaspora is living, the Netherlands felt particularly obliged, supporting the Moluccas to the tune of US$10.8 million (16 April 2002). As already discussed, there was also intensive collaboration between Moluccan NGOs in the Netherlands and the local population in Ambon and the surrounding area. As many Dutch Moluccans were MML members, Indonesian reports by the radio station Radio Nederland Wereldomroep (world service) about the Moluccan conflict were forwarded to the list, as were reports and photos about Moluccan events in the Netherlands such as, for example, images from Capelle of an event to mark the anniversary of the South Moluccan Republic (Republik Maluku Selatan, RMS) declaration of 25 April 1950 (25 April 2002).

Certain Masariku members had contacts in the U.S. Congress and the European and British Parliaments. On occasion, transcripts of debates in the upper and lower houses of parliament in the United Kingdom were forwarded. In a debate on 19 December 2000, for example, members of the lower house expressed their concern about the situation of the Christians in the Moluccas, who were threatened by militant Muslims, supported by the military, in the form of a violent jihad. Masariku news and reports by the CCDA were important sources for these debates. The European Parliament also gave the Moluccan conflict great attention, which on the one hand was due to the fact that Masariku information from members was also forwarded to these circles, and on the other to the fact that Franky, Masariku activist from Ambon, travelled to various EU countries, the United States and UN facilities to address the relevant institutions (see, e.g., 23 May 2002). On the basis of this information, the European Parliament passed resolutions, which Masariku members forwarded to the list. In one of these resolutions it noted, for example, that despite the Malino II agreements there had been further massacres of Christians (21 May 2002).[57] It criticized the Indonesian government for not taking sufficient measures to end the conflict, but spoke in positive terms of the arrest of Ja'far Umar Thalib. Through email actions of their own addressed to the White House, Masariku members attempted to step up the pressure on the U.S. government to take action with regard to the Moluccas (29 June 2000). Furthermore, excerpts from the U.S. State Department's human rights reports, analyses and recommendations by international aid organizations such as the ICG and UN reports on the Moluccan conflict, in particular by the UN Office for the Coordination of Humanitarian Affairs (OCHA) and the UN Resource Centre (UNRC) in Ambon, were included on the Masariku list. On a neutral basis these attempted to compile what was for them most important about the conflict, in particular with regard to humanitarian aid, and provide an unofficial compilation of local Christian and Muslim press reports.

In their concern for their Moluccan brothers and sisters, Masariku members worldwide placed special hope in the United Nations, to which they untiringly sent petitions and appeals such as the 'Stop the War in the Moluccas' petition of 20 December 2000, addressed to UN High Commissioner for Human Rights Mary Robinson and Secretary-General Kofi Annan, which were also forwarded to the MML. On occasions the petitions were also forwarded by individual members in their respective countries, for example, by fax. One of the first things a Masariku founder did in early September 1999 was to post the address of the secretary-general of the UN on the MML to whom corresponding messages could be sent. Teddy repeatedly appealed to the UN with regard to the upholding of human rights. On 28 June 2000 Ernst appealed to all list members to mobilize all forces to get the UN to go to the Moluccas. While the UN did provide humanitarian aid, it was reluctant to become directly involved in the conflict, involvement that the Indonesian government also strictly rejected. The longer the conflict went on, the more despairing and angry the Masariku members' calls to the UN became. The UN was doing far too little to protect the Christians from what were referred to as the 'Laskar butchers' (16 March 2001). There was no more time to lose, Franky warned on 21 September 2000. Why was the UN ignoring more than two thousand dead, a member complained (21 September 2000), while another, in an article written in capital letters and punctuated with several question marks, wanted to know whether the UN, like the United States, only intended to watch as Christians were slaughtered in the Moluccas and in Poso (13–14 August 2002). Reference was made in the list to the comparison the press had made between Bosnia and the Moluccas. The situation in the Moluccas was far more tragic than that in the Balkans and yet the UN still failed to intervene (19 January 2001). There was much frustration when, after the Malino II agreements, on 28 April 2002 there was yet another massacre in a Christian village. Febian said that it was now high time for the UN to take action, and that the UN had to be pestered for as long as it took for it to do something (28 April 2002). His article met with much approval in the MML.

The Christian community and the Church

In addition to the UN and European and U.S. political organizations, Masariku used local, national, and international Christian organizations and associations to address the worldwide community of Christians and Churches. These circles likewise gathered information from Masariku and the reports of the CCDA, but also supplied the MML with contributions. From the outset the list moderator and the Masariku members in Ambon posted, for example, press statements by the PPK PGI, as well as declarations and reports of action by the GPM on the list.[58] On 9 October 1999 Paul explicitly called on list members to forward these declarations, primarily to other Christian networks. On 25 June 2000 the auxiliary bishop of the diocese of Ambon and the chairman of the Synod of the Protestant Church in the Moluccas wrote a 'letter of appeal' to the president of Indonesia, which was also forwarded to the secretary-general of the UN. In it they demanded that the government take strict measures to prevent another massacre of Christians by the Laskar Jihad and avoid further escalation of the conflict through the military and the police. On 1 May 2002 a joint SOS letter from the Catholic Church and all Protestant Churches in the Moluccas was sent to the secretary-general of the UN[59] and posted on the MML, demanding that it be distributed to all human rights organizations, Churches, governments, etc. For Christian organizations at all levels, the many cases of forced conversions among Moluccan Christians was of course an important topic.

At the international level, for example, the Fellowship of Indonesian Christians in America (FICA) was a member of Masariku. This organization posted reports of its own, for example, 'Indonesian Christians Suffer Torture, Death in Brutal Jihad' on 7 April 2001, and, when nec-

essary, posted direct inquiries on the MML, for example in conjunction
with the enforced conversions on Kesui and Teor. Jubilee Campaign U.K.,
an international Christian human rights organization based in the United
Kingdom, the United States and the Netherlands and which exerts pressure primarily on national parliaments, the European Parliament and the
United Nations, was another member at this level. In this function it operated as a lobbyist for the Christians in the Moluccas. In December 1999
the Jubilee Campaign U.K. produced an analysis of the conflict, which
shortly afterwards surfaced in the MML (2 February 2000).[60] The title
alone – 'Analysis of the Sectarian Conflict in Maluku and Its Role in the
Islamicisation of Indonesia' – is an indication of its attitude towards the
conflict. According to the Jubilee Campaign U.K. it was the Islamic Indonesian military and Islamic organizations in Indonesia that pulled the
strings in the conflict, and it was their goal to change the plural principles
of the Indonesian constitution, introduce Islamic laws and turn the entire
country into an Islamic state. That said, it was not, however, the Jubilee
Campaign U.K.'s wish to condemn the Muslim community in the Moluccas in general, but rather certain of its leaders and certain Islamist generals and organizations that were using religion for their political ends. The
Jubilee Campaign U.K. was one of many recipients of Masariku videos. In
return the list moderator hoped for the Jubilee Campaign U.K.'s support
for the Masariku documentary programme (28 January 2000). Reports by
the ICC could also be found on the MML. Like the Jubilee Campaign
U.K., the ICC reported to the international community interested in
the situation of the Christians in the Moluccas, who had been attacked
by three thousand jihad warriors. In one 'Maluku Report', the ICC announced that it was working on collecting money and means to save and
resettle approximately seven thousand Christians being held hostage by
jihad warriors.[61]

Like the Jubilee Campaign U.K. and the ICC, the Barnabas Fund,
based in Wiltshire, U.K., also reported in its 'Update on the Suffering
Church' on the situation of the Christians in the Moluccas (30 April
2002).[62] The International Friends of Compassion (IFC) is an international Christian organization that was founded in 1974 under the name
Indonesia for Christ.[63] It included the Moluccas in its East Indonesia
updates, which the MWN and Arno posted on the MML. The reports
contained passages from the Bible and calls to prayer for those affected.
Furthermore, reports by the World Council of Churches Office of Communication based in Geneva, an open letter by the Christian Conference
of Asia (CCA, an association comprising 115 churches from 18 Asian
countries) to President Megawati, a Missions Insider report by Christian Aid,[64] calls from the organization Persecuted Christian Concern
(PCC) and reports by the Uniting Church in Australia all appeared on
the MML.

Action network

As the last sections revealed, many MML members endeavoured to ensure that discussion of the conflict was not too abstract, but that concrete approaches were developed and concrete action planned. Time and again individual members urged the others not to just follow the list discourse passively, but to be proactive. These actions often took the form of the (as widespread as possible) dissemination of petitions, letters and appeals by email, websites, fax, post and local networks. Apart from the Masariku actors in Ambon and Jakarta and the institutions and organizations mentioned above, individual MML members also wrote open letters, for example, to the president and vice president of Indonesia (25 December 2000). Ernst wrote a letter about the massacres of Christians in the Moluccas, who in late June 2000 were close to being wiped out by the (alleged) fifteen thousand jihad warriors, and asked all list members to send the letter by email, post or fax to the Committee for International Relations of the U.S. House of Representatives, in order to exert as much pressure as possible on the U.S. government (27 June 2000). He also offered to build up a network that the relevant GPM team could use to procure means it needed, primarily for refugee aid. On 23 June 2000 Julius called on the MML for a quick vote on the CNN website:[65] 'Should the international community intervene in the ongoing conflict in Indonesia's Moluccas islands? Yes No.' Richard appealed enthusiastically to members, encouraging them to cast their vote in order to help their brothers and sisters in the Moluccas; Julia proposed sending the appeal to as many friends, relatives and colleagues as possible (23 June 2000). Teddy forwarded the advertising campaign of the organization Cry Indonesia, which had compiled CDs comprising songs and stories recorded over the past three years in the Moluccas, which were marketed with the help of singer Cliff Richard (2 May 2002).[66] The proceeds from CD sales were intended for the Christians in East Indonesia.

The wish for people to be proactive was also the reason why information about events was often exchanged via the MML, calling on them to attend events worldwide, which, to a greater or lesser degree, had something to do with the Moluccan conflict. On 22 December 2000, for example, the list moderator appealed to readers to take part in a long march the following day in Ambon being organized by the Church as an expression of protest against the cases of forced Islamization in the Moluccan conflict. In the United States the Indonesian Human Rights Network (IHRN) called for action intended to exert pressure on the U.S. government to stop the violence by the Indonesian military in Aceh, West Papua, the Moluccas and West Timor (3 April 2001); Ernst's MOF inspired a Moluccan cultural night in California: 'A Fundraising cultural performance for the refugees in Maluku' (22 June 2000). The MOF website also had information about it. Among other things, Teddy announced a demonstration being held by the organization Vrouwen voor Vrede op de Molukken (Women for Peace in the Moluccas) on 5 November 2001, an anti-VOC demonstration in Amsterdam (2 February 2002) and a Moluccan Sovereignty Front (Front Kedaulatan Maluku, FKM) demonstration in The Hague (15 May 2002). Arno, for instance, invited readers to take part in a campaign in Amsterdam against human rights violations and the humanitarian crisis in Indonesia (15 April 2001), and a press conference being given by the human rights organization TAPAK Ambon in Jakarta (6 April 2002). He also forwarded a call by a Moluccan in New York who was planning a demonstration there to raise awareness of the Moluccan conflict and was looking for people to take part (5 November 2002). A member in the Netherlands asked readers to participate in a demonstration in The Hague on the occasion of the visit of the then Indonesian president Abdurrahman Wahid, intended to express concern about the Moluccas to him (27 January 2000). This range of activities was intended to wake up the global population and draw its attention to the Moluccan problem. Moreover, it would ensure that the feeling of solidarity in the international Moluccan Masariku community would be strengthened. The (active) members could see in this confirmation that they were fighting for the right side and that there was an international community of solidarity supporting them.

Strength in faith

A common faith and joint prayer, to which several members repeatedly called (e.g., Bobo in New Zealand, Clark in the United States, Teddy in the Netherlands, Paul in Jakarta or Franky in Ambon), were further pillars of the Masariku community and its identity project. In this way all members became part of a larger Christian community that gave them confidence and strength and promised a better future. Agus quoted encouraging passages from the Bible, for example:

> Psalm 27:1: The Lord is my light and my salvation; ... The Lord is the strength of my life; ...
>
> Psalm 9:10: The Lord also will be refuge for the oppressed, a refuge in time of trouble. (28 June 2000)

On 10 August 1999 the PGI called on all churches in Indonesia and the world to pray together and help bring an end to the Moluccan conflict being waged against humanity (30 December 1999). On 4 February 2000 SAGU forwarded a call to joint prayer for the Moluccans in the Church of St Jacob in Utrecht, the Netherlands, and the following day to a memorial service for the Moluccans in California, which was to feature background music and a film presentation. The proceeds were to go to the Moluccas. Teddy called on readers to pray for the Moluccans as part of Human

Rights Day on 10 December 2001, while Juliet regularly invited readers to attend church services in Jakarta, in particular the former pupils of the grammar school in Ambon. As a result of another attack on 23 January 2000, in which at least twenty-four Christians lost their lives, the Jubilee Campaign U.K. announced an international day of prayer and fasting for the Moluccas on 27 January 2000 and urgently asked the Christian community worldwide to attend (27 January 2000). The next day of prayer and fasting for the Moluccas was scheduled for 20 February 2000, less than a month later. The Jubilee Campaign U.K. launched the call as an urgent appeal by the worldwide community of Christian Moluccans, which was to be forwarded to as many Christians as possible and not just create awareness for a single day, but form the basis of a long-term commitment. The entire appeal featured quotations from the Bible, such as:

> 1 Corinthians 12:25–27: So that there should be no division in the body, but that its parts should have equal concern for each other. If one part suffers, every part suffers with it; if one part is honoured, every part rejoices with it. Now you are the body of Christ, and each one of you is a part of it.

As a Christian one should show solidarity with brothers and sisters who are being persecuted, and not be concerned with the reward for doing so (Galatians 6:9–10). To strengthen the reconciliatory Masariku line, Johan forwarded various Bible passages that emphasize that God is there for all people and that by trusting in God all problems can be solved. To this end, he related Christian stories that highlight how important it is to love your enemy as well, as is written in the Bible, and to aim fully for reconciliation.

Online environment

The MML online catchment area was extended both by the online networks and activities of its members and by other actors interested in the Moluccan conflict in the mailing list's online environment. Websites and mailing lists that posted and forwarded Masariku news or made it available on the Internet acted as additional multipliers and considerably enlarged the reach of the MML. In the case of the posting of Masariku contributions on publicly accessible websites, the border between the self-contained social sphere of the MML and the general public was actually broken down.[67]

The fact that in addition individual Masariku members maintained their own websites, on which they either posted Masariku articles directly or on which Masariku information was translated, processed, or analysed, has already been mentioned. Those made known by members via the MML were Febian's Lawamena Victoria website, the HAIN website,

Arie's 'Help Ambon!' website and the Jubilee Campaign U.K. website.[68] The webmaster and owner of the Maluku WEB Portal was also a member of Masariku.[69] His site made reference to the Maluku News Portal, which listed articles by the Masariku Network, though these were limited to a selection of Masariku's own articles.[70] In his capacity as secretary of the MOF, Ernst had access to its website and mailing list. The MOF website was first and foremost devoted to portraying the motives, values and goals of this NGO, which was founded in February 2000 by a number of Moluccans in California.[71] Though MOF emerged from a Christian-Moluccan prayer group, in its statutes it forwent any religious terminology and symbols. MOF worked with NGOs in Indonesia, in particular in the Moluccas, and set itself the goal of relieving the suffering of the Moluccan population and promoting the rehabilitation process in the Moluccas. To this end it gave financial support to the wounded, refugees, orphans and others in need and organized various information events. On 1 July 2000, Ernst asked people on the MML to please visit his website for English-language news about the Moluccas[72] and to click on the News button, which, however, was no longer available in 2002. The Useful Links section the MOF website also made reference to the Masariku Yahoo! group. In addition, on 27 June 2000 Ernst called on all MML members to send information relevant to the Moluccas to the MOF email address so that it could be disseminated even further. He also sent particularly urgent messages, such as an SOS from the Protestant and Catholic Churches in the Moluccas following the destruction of the UKIM on 23 June 2000, to twelve hundred email addresses worldwide (26 June 2000).

However, not only those members who publicly announced it in the list served as multipliers. It was precisely in this respect that lurkers could also play a decisive role. The other members were not necessarily aware of their connections. I know, however, of at least one lurker on the MML, namely, the Information and Documentation Centre for the Moluccans in Utrecht (Infodoc Maluku), the Netherlands, which regularly published up-to-date reports on the Moluccan conflict both on its website and in the form of an online newsletter.[73] Infodoc Maluku explicitly included Masariku posts in its reporting, though generally speaking also attempted to register other views of the conflict and for this reason also took online FKAWJ news, for example, into consideration. Other MML members made reference to new sites devoted to the Moluccan conflict in general or to a specific aspect of it, such as the FKM Europe website, that of a small group in Ambon, which, however, only provided information on the conflict very sporadically and unsystematically, and the information site for the Soya case, a Christian village that was brutally attacked on 28 April 2002.[74] The latter also posted photos from the Masariku archive on its site.

If we consider cyberspace in its entirety, a number of other websites made reference to the MML. The Masariku reports, for example, were one of the main sources for the well-known site Ambon Berdarah Online (ABO), with which Christians and Muslims were familiar and which I will come back to in Chapter 8.[75] Individual Masariku reports could also be found on a site devoted to the village Sirisori Amalatu (Saparua, Central Moluccas).[76] Masariku photos in particular were popular and were often integrated in reports about the Moluccas, such as, for example, on the site of the International Friends of Compassion.[77] Christian organizations such as Pax Christi and Passie voor Vrede, the Indonesian online news service Indopubs, and Maluku2000 made reference to Masariku's Yahoo! site.[78] On account of the Yahoo! access check, however, non-MML members had no access to Masariku news via these sites. Though other sites, such as Human Rights Without Frontiers and Christian Solidarity Worldwide, did not post any Masariku contributions, they did quote the Masariku Network as a source for their own reports.[79] Cross-posting by Masariku members meant Masariku articles were forwarded to other mailing lists such as Ambon.com and the e-bulletin EskolNet.[80] In some cases membership of Ambon.com and Masariku seemed to overlap. Arno, the most well-known MML cross-poster, was also a member of Ambon.com., and Franky was not unknown at Ambon.com either. On 4 and 5 July 1999 a thread even emerged on it devoted specifically to the question of 'Who is Franky … ?' That was too much attention for Franky – in particular because one of the posters questioned his integrity and his motives with regard to the Moluccan conflict – and he left the list.

Summary

The MML was a mailing list with only Christian, for the most part Protestant, members that endeavoured to portray the points of view of the Christians involved in the conflict. In principle it also made efforts to consider the Muslims' position; its ideal ultimate goal was the integration of the Muslims and the well-being of all Moluccans. It was hardly possible, however, to achieve this noble objective. The more intensive the conflict became, the more the Christians got into difficulties, the more one-sided the reporting in the list naturally became. The heterogeneous membership composition of Masariku produced a multilayered and many-voiced discourse that was based on events in the conflict, but that also allowed for corresponding background information, the exchange of personal matters and feelings, assistance and encouragement, as well as sanctions – a heterogeneous community, in other words, that could have also existed in the offline context, but whose reach and integrative potential were far greater than an offline context would have allowed. Despite their many voices and the different strategies and focuses of the individual list members, there was an unequivocal argumentation pattern and a common goal. The involvement of the military, the government's inability to solve the conflict and the presence of the Laskar Jihad were to be denounced. The Moluccan conflict, they claimed, was ultimately initiated by wire-pullers in the political and military elite in Jakarta. In this precarious situation the Christian Masariku members placed all their hope in the United Nations and the global Christian community.

Interaction, for example, the joint educational and analytical work, played just as great a role as imagination in the emergence of an (imagined) online Masariku community extending far beyond the original core of the founding members in Ambon and Jakarta and underpinned by three elements: the Moluccan identity, the Christian religion and the 'West'. Each member had to undergo a certain acceptance ritual and obey common rules. Troublemakers had to leave the 'room'. The list's common reference was the Moluccan conflict, its sociocultural, political and historical background, as well as the Moluccas themselves. The majority of the Masariku members originate from the Moluccas. The Internet enabled the Moluccans to reunite, regardless of where they were living, and to establish a sizeable online Moluccan community. Religion also played an important role in the communitization and imagination process. Their common faith gave the Masariku members a set of symbols, for example, prayers, verses from the Bible, the Church and joint church services, as well as the feeling of finding strength and support in a far bigger worldwide Christian community, which is guided and led by a common God. Confidence in the United Nations as the guardian of human rights all over the world was a third source of hope for Masariku members. The UN and human rights became inviolable symbols to which they clung as the situation became ever more hopeless – a symbol that, however, in view of the continuing conflict, was increasingly shaken to its foundations as the UN intervention they had hoped for failed to materialize. What remained was their Christian faith and their longing for a peaceful homeland, which lots of the members knew and loved. These were the foundation of the Masariku community and identity project, and cyberspace provided the means and the ways for their realization. It became clear that in terms of its dissemination the MML, through its specific online context, was by no means restricted just to its subscribers. If one were to comment on the influence Masariku actually had on the information policy relating to the Moluccan conflict, these extensive circles must necessarily be considered.

The Masariku online project had been running for almost four years by the time this study first went to press, during which time, through regular online communication, members acquired extensive contextual knowledge, the number of members and the core of main actors remained stable, specific roles and identities emerged and mechanisms developed to impose sanctions on members and shield them from the outside. As such, the conditions for communitization named by Stegbauer (2001: 70–72) were fulfilled.[81] Other important aspects that ensured the Masariku project was successful, such as appropriate wording, the differentiation between the 'we' group and 'the others', and the authenticity factor, will be discussed in Chapter 7 by way of comparison with the other cyberactors discussed in Chapters 5 and 6.

Notes

1. With regard to the history and development of the Internet in Indonesia, see Basuki (1998); Hill and Sen (1997); Minges (2002); and Sen and Hill (2000: 194–217).
2. Asosiasi Penyelenggara Jasa Internet Indonesia. For the association's webpage see http://www.apjii.org, which has now moved to http://www.apjii.or.id/ (status 13 January 2012).
3. These processes were analyzed by Basuki (1998) and Lim (2002, 2003).
4. These data are based on Hill and Sen (1997: 74); KOMITEL (2002); and Minges (2002); and an interview with Pandji S. Choesin, director of APJII in Jakarta, on 28 March 2002.
5. Despite the low level of Internet access in Indonesia, the rate of cybercrimes such as card fraud in Internet transactions is the second highest in the world, after Ukraine (Soekanto 2002).
6. The PDI was split into followers of Megawati and Surjadi. Supported by the government and the army, on that day Surjadi's followers attacked the PDI headquarters, which was occupied by Megawati's followers, triggering unrest throughout Jakarta and leading to the splitting off of Megawati's followers in the PDI-P (Indonesian Democratic Party – Struggle) (K. van Dijk 2011: 11).
7. See, for example, Vaudine England's article 'Terror on our Doorstep' in the *South China Morning Post* on 17 September 2001, the article 'Internet Partially Responsible For Riots in Regions' in *Koridor* on 3 November 2000, and '"Perang Saudara Ambon" – Menyebar ke Dunia Cyber' ('"Siblings" War in Ambon Spreads to Cyberspace') in IndoNews on 4 February 2000.
8. At Rp. 9,000 (approximately €1) per hour, the price was above the average price in Indonesia of Rp. 6,000 (Minges 2002: 14) and Internet connections were extremely slow. Furthermore, at times during the unrest in Ambon the Internet crashed completely, frequently for several hours, and in 1999 and 2001 did not work for several weeks. The Internet officer at the main post office in Ambon City estimated the number of Warnet visitors to be around twenty a day.
9. Students had no Internet access at the university at the time; access was only at certain institutes.
10. I would like to thank Anthon Sapulette in the 'Christian' and Ibu Gaya Eli in the 'Muslim' post office for allowing me to examine these data and helping me analyse the entries.
11. The computers and the Internet provider used by the UN were far more powerful than those of the post office, though they cost Rp. 15,000 per hour.
12. A list of Internet addresses in the Appendix provides an overview of what was available about the Moluccan conflict online before the German edition of this book first went to press. It does not, however, claim to be complete.

13. Given the more detailed description of the groups, readers will be able to form a better picture with regard to the question of representation. Whatever claims to representation Moluccan cyberactors might have, it should be noted here that the attitudes, stances, and opinions discussed in the following chapters do not necessarily represent the opinion of *all* Christians and Muslims in the Moluccas.

14. As the online communities examined only exist in the imagination of the members and initiators of the respective online projects, the description of these online processes as 'communities' (of whatever kind) with a specific collective identity is nevertheless based on my interpretations.

15. In this chapter dates in parentheses refer to articles that were posted on the Masariku mailing list on that particular date. As such the date need not always be identical to the date on which the forwarded document was written. The author is only mentioned if this is of importance for the argument, or to highlight different positions. In order to protect those involved, the names of all individual persons have been changed. For this reason it is not possible to go into details with regard to the significance of possible pseudonyms. The names of organizations were retained. Any instances where changed names are identical to those of real people are unintentional and have no implications.

16. After the number of members had sunk in this period to approximately 175, by early 2003 it had interestingly risen to over 200 again.

17. For the original of the description see Illustration 3.

18. As there was never any official introduction to the mailing list and its background, the following more or less basic and formal information had to be accessed from the list discourse, which results in jumps in the date of source material.

19. It may be of interest to those familiar with the Indonesian and international press landscape to mention a few names. At local level these are *Siwalima* and *Suara Maluku* (not, for example, the Muslim *Ambon Ekspres*); at national level, among others, *Antara*, Astaga.com, *Bali Post*, Detikcom, Forum, Gatra. com, *The Jakarta Post, Jawa Pos, Kompas,* Koridor.com, Mandiri.com, *Media Indonesia, Rakyat Merdeka,* Satunet.com, *Sinar Harapan, Suara Karya, Suara Merdeka, Suara Pembaruan, Surabaya Post, Tabloid Bangkit, Tempo Interaktif* and, in exceptional cases, *Hidayatullah* and *Republika;* and at international level, for example, Agence France-Presse, *Asiaweek, Baptist Press,* BBC, *Far Eastern Economic Review, Jerusalem Post, LA Times, National Post – Canada, New York Times, Newsweek, South China Morning Post, Sydney Morning Herald, The Age,* The Associated Press, *The Australian, The Christian Science Monitor, The Straits Times, The Washington Times, Times of Asia, Washington Post,* Workers World News Service, and *Xinhuanet.*

20. This mailing list (Ambon.com on Yahoo!) was analyzed by David Hill and Krishna Sen (2002).

21. If no other details are given, this and the following two paragraphs refer to this contribution.

22. The categories 'Masariku Report' and 'Masariku Update', etc. emerged at this time.

23. The TPG was founded by the Moluccan Protestant Church and the Ambon Diocese and recognized by all Christian churches in the Moluccas (CCDA, 26 September 2000). In 2001 the TPG was dissolved after the Protestant Church

in the Moluccas, like the Catholic Church, had set up a crisis centre of its own.

24. masariku-owner@egroups.com or http://www.egroups.com/group.masariku (now available at http://groups.yahoo.com/group/masariku/, 13 January 2012).

25. I will discuss this site in Chapter 8.

26. 'Biarlah BAPA di Sorga menyertai kita semua.'

27. In the terminology of Herbert Rauch (1983: 169), who conducted investigations of participation and achievement in large groups, this phase, in which the different roles of the founders and new members evolve, can be referred to as the structuring phase, which is followed by a cooperation phase that exploits the structure.

28. The background of SAGU was generally never mentioned online and neither was it given following an enquiry from a list member on 28 January 2000.

29. Subject heading 'Bloody 27 July in Ambon' (*27 Juli Berdarah di Ambon*).

30. Unless otherwise stated, in the following role descriptions this is the case.

31. Whereas in the first ten months a total of thirty-nine people delivered posts, with the founders accounting for 90 per cent of posts, in June and July 2000 there were one hundred and one different authors, of whom eleven, among them the founders, uploaded articles on a massive scale, and twenty-three uploaded articles on several occasions.

32. The boundaries are, of course, fluid; a member who primarily assumes the role of analyst could certainly also post calls for action and thus take on the role of activist. The allocations made here indicate the focus the persons set themselves as MML members.

33. On the free rider problem, public goods and the reciprocity principle online and different positions on it, see, for example, Donath (1999: 30–31); Kollock (1999); Kollock and Smith (1996: 116); Rafaeli and LaRose (1993); Rheingold (2000: 47); and Wellman and Gulia (1999: 177).

34. Personal details such as profession and place of residence are mentioned as long as they were entered in the online representations.

35. http://www.geocities.com/moutreach/index_files/frame.htm (no longer available in 2012).

36. http://www.geocities.com/lawamena_victoria/ (moved to http://www.geocities.ws/lawamena_victoria/, but not updated any more, 13 January 2012).

37. http://www.angelfire.com/rock/hotburrito.

38. An analysis of the address list of MML subscribers confirmed that the majority of members were Moluccan (as at August 2002). With approximately two-thirds of the email addresses it was possible to draw conclusions as to the origin and current place of residence of the users. Approximately two-thirds of them were of Moluccan, approximately 88 per cent of Indonesian origin (including those of Moluccan descent). Approximately 27 per cent of the email addresses examined were located in the Netherlands, 8 per cent in the rest of Europe, 45 per cent in Indonesia, 8 per cent in Australia, 8 per cent in the United States, and one in each of Canada, Japan, Papua New Guinea and Singapore. For information on identities in online communication and in email addresses see, for example, Donath (1999: 40). Masariku – unlike FKAWJ – does not actually grant access to its members' Yahoo! user profiles, should they have been set up. For this reason I would like to take this opportunity to

thank one of the founders of the list, who wished to remain anonymous, for the confidential provision of the subscriber email address list.

39. 'Febian, ale dolo tinggal di Kar-Pan ka? kalau batul ale kanal beta ka seng?'
40. 'SEMOGA TUHAN MEMBUKA MATA HATI ANDA!!!!!!!'
41. In the argumentation structure section the issue of presentation of the conflict by both parties, Christians and Muslims, is excluded, as that is addressed in Chapter 7. The main topics are forced conversion and the RMS.
42. As the following is about arguments that portray a sort of consensus in the list discourse, I will only state the author and the date of the individual posts in exceptional cases. The MML provides numerous instances of concrete evidence for each of the arguments.
43. This is a reference to the arrest of Alex Manuputty, the leader of the FKM.
44. The speech was also delivered by the CCDA and was available on the Ambon Berdarah Online (ABO) website in Indonesian (http://www.geocities.com/kariu67/pidatojafar080502.htm, 22 January 2003) and the Ambon Information website in English (http://www.websitesrcg.com/ambon/documents/laskar-jihad-010502.htm, 22 July 2002 and 13 January 2012).
45. See Chapter 6 for Ja'far Umar Thalib's declaration of war.
46. 'LASKAR JIHAD MINTA RESTU DARI TIMUR TENGAH, BUKAN DARI RAKYAT INDONESIA.'
47. According to Teddy, the Jamaah Tablig, for example, a fundamentalist group from Pakistan which also supported the Taliban, had been operating in Ambon since August 1999 (22 February 2003).
48. 'SATU SUKU ... SATU DARAH ... SATU GANDONG ... VIVA MALUKU ...'
49. There was a positive response, for example, to *Kerusuhan Maluku: Halmahera Berdarah* (Moluccan unrest: Bloody Halmahera), which was published by the former Christian director of Unpatti, Jan Nanere (2000), and the realization of which the Masariku Network actively supported by providing much information (16 March 2001). The book published by the former police chief of the Moluccas, General Firman Gani (2002), on the tragedy in the Moluccas, *Perjalanan Panjang Anak Bangsa Menuju Perdamaian* (The people's long path to peace), was heavily criticized, as he is alleged to have stirred up the Laskar Jihad against the Christians (9 July 2002). An MML member referred to the book *Tragedi Kebun Cengkeh* (The tragedy of Kebun Cengkeh), which was written by FKAWJ members (Syafruddin and Prasetyo 2001), as 'the untruthful propaganda of wicked people' (*Propaganda Putar Balik Orang Jahat*, 28 June 2002).
50. Here internationally recognized scholars such as Robert Hefner (2001), William Liddle (2001) and Daniel Lev (2001), as well as Moluccan representatives such as Dr. John Titaley (2001), a lecturer at a Christian university on Java, and Jusuf Ely (2001) from the Muslim side, stated their position. As a result the commission sent several missives to the U.S. president so as to exert pressure on him to take action in the Moluccan case and in particular to use his influence in this respect at a meeting with Indonesia's president Megawati Sukarnoputri (18 September 2001).
51. 'Basudara samua yang tahu informasi ambon yang terkini, tolong di format ke kami. Kita yang jauh dari ambon sangat mengkuatirkan keadaan samua

basudara di ambon. Semoga TUHAN YESUS KRISTUS selalu menjaga dan menyertai setiap perjuangan samua basudara di ambon.'

52. Moluccans in the Netherlands are referred to as Dutch Moluccans.
53. See above; immediately beneath the website's title there is a quotation from the Bible: '[O]ur love should not be just words and talk; it must be true love, which shows itself in action' (1 John 3:18).
54. http://www.denheldervoordemolukken.nl (no longer available in 2012).
55. http://www.maluku.org/hain/, discontinued on 9 October 2002.
56. http://www.maluku.org.
57. The Internet address is likewise given: http://www.parliament.the-stationery-office.co.uk/pa/cm200001/cmhansrd/cm001219/halltext/01219h03.htm#01 219h03_head0 (13 January 2012).
58. There was also occasional criticism in the MML of the Protestant Church in the Moluccas, which according to the posters was still doing too little for the Moluccan people and had to be forced to take action by email and letter bombs (24 June 2000; 30 January 2001).
59. A copy of the letter was also to be sent to the Indonesian government in Jakarta, the U.S. president, the British prime minister, the governments of the EU, the pope in Rome, the World Council of Churches in Geneva, the Association of Churches in Indonesia, the Association of Pentecostal Churches in Indonesia, the Bishops' Conference in Indonesia, the Baptist World Alliance in the United States, the International Headquarters of the Salvation Army in London, the World Alliance of Reformed Churches in Geneva and the Church of the Salvation Army in the United States.
60. http://www.jubileecampaign.demon.co.uk/church/ind5.htm (no longer available in 2012).
61. The ICC called on all its readers to donate via both its website (http://www.persecution.org) and email (11 March 2001). Among other things, the organization also reported the attack on the Christian village Soya di Atas on 28 April 2002 (1 May 2002). The ICC was quick to assume that the attackers, dressed in black, were Muslim and, without having any actual proof, to blame the attack on the Laskar Jihad. Even today the case has not yet been cleared up, but it is assumed that Christian militias were also involved.
62. http://www.barnabasfund.org.
63. http://cryindonesia.rnc.org.au (no longer available in 2012).
64. http://www.christianaid.org.
65. http://www.cnn.com/ASIANOW/southeast/.
66. http://cryindonesia.rnc.org.au (no longer available in 2012).
67. Unless otherwise stated, all the Internet sites mentioned here were still available in early 2003, rechecked in January 2012.
68. http://www.geocities.com/lawamena_victoria (see above); http://www.maluku.org/hain (discontinued on 9 October 2002); http://www.angelfire.com/rock/hotburrito; and http://www.jubileecampaign.demon.co.uk (moved to http://www.jubileecampaign.co.uk/, 13 January 2012).
69. http://www.maluku.org.
70. PosKo Zwolle-Maluku (http://www.malra.org/posko/, no longer available in 2012). Internet sites that only posted reports from Masariku Ambon and Jakarta give rise to a totally different picture of the Masariku online project.

Their authors are not concerned with the way Masariku is perceived as an on-line community, but as another source of information.

71. http://www.geocities.com/moutreach/index_files/frame.htm.
72. http://www.geocities.com/moutreach/index2.htm or www.malof.org (no long-er available in 2012).
73. http://www.midc.nl and infomaluku@midc.nl. In January 2003, however, In-fodoc Maluku had to cease its activities because the Dutch government ended its support of the project. The online archives were still available thereafter, but were obviously discontinued at one point (last checked 13 January 2012).
74. http://www.fkm-europa.nl, 15 April 2002; http://www.geocities.com/chosye, 16 February 2001; and http://www.geocities.com/pertjok/tragedi_soya.html, 5 May 2002 (no longer available in 2012).
75. ABO changed its URL on a regular basis (for more details see chapter 8), e.g., http://www.geocities.com/kesui2001/index.htm (no longer available in 2012; an archived version is available at http://www.oocities.org/batoegajah/index_mei2006.htm).
76. http://www.sirisori.demon.nl/news.html (no longer available in 2012).
77. http://cryindonesia.rnc.org.au/breaking_news.htm (no longer available in 2012).
78. http://www.paxchristi.nl/indonesialinks.html; http://www.passievoorvrede.nl/page.php?pag_id=112; http://www.indopubs.com/panel2.html; and http://www.maluku2000.org/subdomain/weblinks/weblinks.html (except for Indo-pubs, no longer available in 2012).
79. http://www.hrwf.net/newhrwf/html/england2000.html; http://www.csw.org.uk/CSWnews.asp?item=171 (no longer available in 2012).
80. http://groups.yahoo.com/group/ambon; http://www.mail-archive.com/eskol@mitra.net.id/.
81. Jordan postulates similar factors (1999: 100) for 'virtual communities', from news groups to MUDs (see also Kollock 1999: 235). Rheingold (2000: 38) confirms the importance of a core population and community builders. Fur-thermore, the definition of online communities by Bakardjieva and Feenberg (2002: 182) applies to the MML: 'By online community we mean the forma-tion of relatively stable long-term online group associations. Community involves the participatory engagement in a collective practice aimed at con-structing collective identities. As such, communities are inherently capable of self articulation and mobilization vis-à-vis society at large.'

5

The CCDA Newsletter

Online to the International Community

The online project of the Crisis Centre of the Diocese of Ambon (CCDA) is quite different in nature from the Masariku project. The structures are far simpler, there are not as many active participants and a unidirectional mode of communication was selected, which is why the project is far less diverse and dynamic than that of Masariku. In this case it is not so much the online project itself that represents a communitization process, but rather that the project calls for an imaginary community, which is to be mobilized and networked by the newsletter, in the joint interest of the 'Moluccan conflict'.

The CCDA was founded in July 1999 and from 22 June 2000 sent newsletters with up-to-date information about the Moluccan conflict via email directly from Ambon City all over the world. One person, Father Kees Böhm, who hails from the Netherlands, was responsible for writing the articles and organizing the distribution of all the online information. Unlike Masariku, he did not use a service platform, but instead sent the newsletter via a mailing list he compiled himself. He alone determined who was included on the list of subscribers.

The beginning

The online platform was initially not particularly well organized. The first reports had to be sent by fax and were only posted online later on. Panic, in the true sense of the word, characterized these initial writings; this was no wonder, as the conflict was just seeing a drastic turn against the Christians. The Laskar Jihad had arrived to defend their Muslim brothers in the Moluccas. In this phase the number of Masariku emails rocketed from 94 to 570 per month. The CCDA, of which Father Kees Böhm wanted to be seen as the representative and spokesman, no longer wanted to talk of 'riots' or a 'conflict'. What was now happening in the Moluccas was a systematic slaughtering of Christians, comparable with the Holocaust. For this reason the CCDA's information and mobilization campaign kicked off with a series of SOS letters to various recipients, beginning with the Indonesian government in Jakarta, the top brass of the Indonesian military and the Indonesian police, the U.S. embassy in Indonesia, and the United Nations. To capture this moment of panic, I quote the first CCDA report, which was initially faxed and then emailed to influential recipients, in full:

Report no. 1 – June 22, 2000
Since the situation became more and more unbearable, the Diocese of Amboina and the Diocesan Crisis Centre sent out the following 'URGENT APPEAL' to the whole civilized world:

URGENT APPEAL
from victimized Christians in the Moluccas
The unrest in the Moluccas, which has been going on for nearly one and a half year now and has claimed the lives of thousands of civilians and the destruction of thousands of houses and other facilities, originally started as a **conflict** between certain muslim and christian groups.

However since the arriving of thousands of Jihad ('Holy War') troops, equipped with standard and organic weaponry, it can no longer be looked upon as a **conflict**. It has now become a straight-away endeavour to **cleanse the Moluccas from all what is christian.** Part of the security forces apparently sympathize with these Jihad Troops. Those who do not, are outnumbered and – fearing for their lives – in many cases choose to withdraw as soon as the attacks start.

The most recent evidence of this change in the Moluccas unrest (from conflict to slaughtering) is illustrated by the following sad happenings:

In the North Moluccas
According to reports from Father Titus Rahail, parish priest of nearby Tobelo and of parson Z.Dungir, the latter of whom actually was in Duma at that moment, but managed to escape to Tobelo, on June 19th 2000, at 05.00 in the morning, the christian village of DUMA/Galela on the island of Halmahera, was attacked by at least 5.000 muslim fighters, killing 176 residents and injuring 137, including women, children and old people. Ten women and twenty children are reported to be abducted. The protestant church (together with all people who had taking refuge there) and 292 houses were burned down. The military security forces, Yonif 512/Brawijaya, reportedly withdrew before the attack was launched, except some of them who paved the way for the attacking Jihad Troops to carry out their holocaust. This sad happening, like others to follow, was hardly reported in the national newsmedia and broadcasting.

In Ambon
On June 12th 2000 several thousands of muslim fighters came down Malintang hill and attacked the villages of Galala and Hative Kecil at the out-skirts of Ambon town. About thirty houses and the catholic church were burned down. The attackers met hardly any resistance. On that occasion the local security forces were reported to have a conflict among themselves. Six persons were killed, including two Brimob policemen; 16 were injured.

On June 21st 2000 the village of Tantui, situated between Hative Kecil and Ambon town, location of Brimob Police Headquarters, was attacked. Once again the christians were more or less left to themselves. The result: the catholic church and the protestant Efrata church were burned down together with some dozens of houses and Brimob quarters. Among the five casualties was the Brimob vice-commander, Mayor Pol. Eddy Susanto. The number of casualties was restricted because the local residents could flee in time.

What to expect in the near future
Apparently the muslim forces not just want to ***dominate*** the Moluccas, but they ***don't want any christian presence in the Moluccas***. In the North Moluccas they have already succeeded in cleansing most islands from all what is christian: the islands of Ternate, Tidore, Morotai, Obi, Bacan, Sula are 100% muslim now. Only the relative small islands of Mangole and Taliabu are still untouched: muslims and christians there live in peace together.

The town of Ambon is more and more being surrounded by the Jihad Troops, who in this way will prevent any christians to escape from the great-scale slaughter they have in mind and is apt to be launched any moment now.

Conclusion
What is happening now, cannot possibly be called any more 'riots' either 'violence' or 'bloody conflict' or even 'war'. Since there is no reason at all for the latest assaults of the muslim troops on the christian civilians, it can only be called ORGANIZED COLD-BLOODED MURDERING OF INNOCENT PEOPLE, conceded by the muslims themselves by means of the loudspeakers on their mosques who call for annihilating those 'christian infidels'.

The security forces, who overwhelmingly consist of muslim troops, have to choose to be loyal either to their military oath or their religious conviction. Besides, they are being confronted now with strongly motivated Jihad fighters with equal weaponry. These factors make them more and more choosing the side of the muslim attackers, letting them do their destructive activities, in many cases even supporting them by shooting at the same target i.e. the christians.

The christians are trying to defend themselves to their last drop of blood, but are outnumbered and do not have adequate weapons. They are ready to die, but not without the world to know what has been done to them. The Indonesian Government – though undoubtedly wishing this mass murdering to end – has not the military forces that are able to put a halt to this 'Holy Murdering'.

The christians address a (possibly last) urgent appeal on the outside world, especially the United Nations' Security Council and Human Rights Commission, to come and bring about peace in the Moluccas.

Ambon, June 22, 2000

Rev. Agus Ulahaiyanan Pr.   Rev. Ancis Homenara Pr.
Chairman Crisis Centre   Chairman Justice & Peace Com.
Diocese of Amboina   Diocese of Amboina
                      Msgr. Yos Tethool MSC
                      Auxiliary Bishop of Amboina

This fax was followed by further reports about the hopeless situation of the Christians. The feeling was that the end was nigh. The banks in Ambon were closing, the flow of money had stopped. Two rice silos were still in Christian hands, but there was neither petroleum (for cooking) nor petrol available. Although a state of emergency had been declared for the Moluccas on 27 June 2000, absolutely nothing had changed as far as the situation of the Christians was concerned. According to the CCDA, only outside forces could free the Christians from this trap, which is why the United Nations had to take immediate action (5 July 2000)[1] and at least 100,000 Christians had to be evacuated without delay (7 July 2000).

The newsletter

The online newsletter quickly became a fixture and was sent to ever more interested individuals and organizations worldwide. The CCDA online project's primary objective was to give the Christians in the Moluccas a voice on the global Internet and, as in the case of Masariku, balance out the one-sided reporting in the national media.[2] So as to be able to address the international community directly, the reports were written in English. Depending on what phase the conflict was in, up to two reports were sent every day; as a rule, however, there was one report every two to four days. In the CCDA project's first year, the number of emails per month was around twenty, after which the number was mostly between five and ten, with the exception of February 2002, when there was a great deal to report about the Malino II agreements, and April and May 2002, when Ja'far Umar Thalib's famous declaration of war was transmitted by the Laskar Jihad radio station SPMM and, despite the Malino II agreements, the Christian village Soya di Atas had been attacked. As the CCDA project rose and fell with a single person, and furthermore was dependent on the technical situation regarding the Internet in Ambon, in July 2001, for example, none, and in October 2002 just two reports were sent. Given the structure and modus operandi of the Catholic crisis centre there was no alternative Internet access available, such as in Jakarta, as was the case with Masariku. By the end of February 2003, 353 CCDA reports had been sent. In order to enable his reports to be accessed by purely Indonesian-speaking readers, in April 2001 Father Böhm delivered an initial summary in Indonesian by email, and as of May 2002, at more or less regular intervals, short summaries in Indonesian of the current reports in English – eleven until February 2003 – and in January 2002 a chronology of the conflict covering the period January 1999 to December 2001. This he called 'Lintas Peristiwa Kerusuhan di Maluku' ('Chronology of the Moluccan conflict').

By August 2002, 347 individuals and organizations had subscribed to the CCDA newsletter, among them important political bodies and websites that addressed the Moluccan tragedy.[3] An evaluation of the email addresses on the subscriber list (as at August 2002) revealed that approximately one-third of the subscribers were international Christian, primarily Catholic, organizations, such as Caritas, Pax Christi, Parokinet, Secours Catholique, Misereor, Missio, International Christian Concern (ICC), Forum Komunikasi Kristen Indonesia (FKKI, or the Communication Forum of Indonesian Christians, ICCF) and Summer Institute of Linguistics (SIL). In addition, government organizations such as the Australian Foreign Ministry and the Dutch Parliament received the CCDA newsletter on a regular basis, as did the embassies of various countries, human rights organizations, UN organizations, foreign media representatives (e.g., ORF, Radio Canada, Dutch daily newspapers, the BBC and *Far Eastern Economic Review*), Moluccan organizations, especially in the Netherlands (e.g., Maluku Terbakar and Posko Zwolle), as well as a number of individuals. The majority of subscribers lived outside Indonesia. The newsletter was sent to more than two dozen states, including Vatican City, with most recipients in Europe.[4] Father Böhm endeavoured to give these international readers, in as neutral a manner as possible, a short overview of the main events, without commenting on them in any detail. The motto was 'short and sweet'; the intention was to put as many people as possible in a position to be able to, in addition to pursuing their daily activities, follow the events in the Moluccas. For this reason Father Böhm really did limit himself to events that were directly related to the Moluccan conflict.

Like the Masariku founders, Father Böhm informed his readers about the background to the newsletter relatively late, in report no. 145 on 6 March 2001. At the time the situation was comparatively calm, and as such there was time to provide information about how the online newsletter fitted into the crisis centre's framework of action as offline context.[5] The crisis centre employed five full-time and nine part-time staff members, among them several priests. The initial focus was on mediation and reconciliation, but the refugee problem took up ever more space. In collaboration with the government, local NGOs and the St Lucas Foundation (a health care organization), attempts were made to lessen the refugees' plight. As, of course, there were only limited financial resources available here as well, efforts were necessarily concentrated on Catholic refugees, although attempts were also made to help followers of other religions. The crisis centre helped evacuate refugees, provided them with accommodation (be it by housing them in existing localities or by building shelters for them), provided them with food and clothing, offered financial support and advice to schoolchildren and students and also endeavoured to help people earn their living themselves, by means of a small business, farming, fishing, etc. For its activities the crisis centre was also reliant on outside donations. The newsletter itself got hardly a mention in report no. 145, though reference was made to its impact: it provided those unable to get a picture of the situation directly with information and evoked corresponding responses. Messages of solidarity were received by email and telephone, saying that people were praying for the Christians in the Moluccas and even that financial assistance had been granted. Father Kees Böhm attributed the wide-scale acceptance of his newsletter and the positive encouragement from readers to the brevity and conciseness of the reports and its neutral language (15 December 2000). This was never inappropriate, nor was it vulgar, as was the case with the Laskar Jihad on their website, which furthermore made false allegations, for example, that all Christians were South Moluccan Republic (Republik Maluku Selatan, RMS) separatists.

As opposed to Masariku, the CCDA had employees, whose work concentrated more on humanitarian help for victims of the conflict than the procurement of information, and which was paid for by the Church. Father Böhm asked subscribers for donations for this humanitarian aid (5 October 2000). The CCDA was the body that many people and groups turned to, primarily asking for support for the distribution of food among refugees and evacuations. For a long time Cordaid, in the Netherlands, primarily financed these projects (15 July 2000). As the main source of information for his reports, Father Böhm used the daily newspapers *Suara Maluku* and *Siwalima*, which were denounced by the Muslims as Christian, and broadcasts by the local stations of the national radio RRI and the national TV station TVRI. These sources were complemented by observations by CCDA's own employees, telephone messages from priests in other Catholic parishes throughout the Moluccas and press releases by the Moluccan churches, as well as reports and analyses by the Church's team of lawyers (TPG). On various occasions Father Böhm also made reference to Masariku articles and forwarded letters and calls by the Moluccas Concerned Women's Movement (Gerakan Perempuan Peduli Maluku, GPPM) in Ambon, which looked after the needs of women and children in the conflict in particular.

Father Böhm also attempted to introduce a Muslim perspective into his reports, although for this his source material was extremely restricted. With regard to, for example, the number of victims and instances of destruction, he was only able to make well-founded statements about the Catholic side, as Masariku about the Protestant side. On 14 September 2000 Father Böhm himself admitted that he actually had scarcely any contact with the Muslim civil population of Ambon. One could only speculate about the situation 'on the other side' (3 and 14 July 2000). The CCDA seldom received confirmed data from the Indonesian Ulema Council (Majelis Ulama Indonesia, MUI) or the Al-Fatah Hospital in Ambon.[6] For this reason Father Böhm attempted to find other sources. He would use, for example, items of news from FKAWJ that did not appear in the 'Christian' media, such as an attack by Christians on a Muslim motor boat in the North Moluccas, during which the entire crew died; the report was subsequently confirmed by *Suara Maluku* (22 December 2000). The problem was that those daily newspapers that were regarded as Christian in some cases quite simply refused to give any information about the situation on the Muslim side (20 July 2000). In another case the CCDA quoted an article in *Republika*, which reported an attack on a Muslim fishing boat near Saparua, with the comment that there was no mention of this in the local Christian media (25 February 2002). According to Father Böhm, the local TVRI TV station was also an exception, which on occasion broadcast images of the situation on the Muslim side that he then integrated in his reports (3 July and 2 August 2000). The local Muslim daily *Ambon Ekspres* did not feature in the CCDA reports.

Father Böhm was of the opinion that several attacks could have been avoided had the military and the government taken nascent rumours more seriously. For this reason he included in his reporting rumours that, to him, seemed plausible or explosive. He ended one of his first reports, dated 5 July 2000, for example, with the words: 'There are wide-spread rumours that next July 7–9, the big attack on Ambon town will be launched. Often rumours have proved to be true. S.O.S.' He frequently reported the (alleged) arrival of new Laskar Jihad, though the exact circumstances and their number were often not yet known or confirmed, or a planned attack by Laskar Jihad troops. In this way Father Böhm was able to give his readers an impression of the outstanding role rumours at the local level played for the affected population. As the English reports were of scarcely any significance at the local level, it can be assumed that Father Böhm played no role in the rumours gathering strength by referring to them and disseminating them in his newsletter. Rumours did, however, repeatedly prove to be wrong. In one case, for example, the CCDA featured a report about a Christian woman who had first been raped and then murdered in a gruesome way; her body was discovered cut up into pieces. The woman's father and son had allegedly been murdered and subsequently burned (26 September 2000). One day later Father Böhm had to revise his report: the woman had neither been raped nor chopped into pieces, but shot and injured in her right shoulder. The two men were her brothers, of whom one had indeed been murdered and burned, but the other was missing, in other words, could well have also escaped (27 September 2000). In another case Father Böhm mentioned four dead in the border area of Batumerah and Mardika, a Muslim and a Christian district, respectively, of Ambon City (17 April 2002). Two days later he admitted that his statement was based on a widespread rumour, which, according to a *Siwalima* report, had in the meantime proved to be untrue. Troublemakers had started it deliberately in order to detract Muslims and Christians from cross-border interaction (19 April 2002).

The CCDA reports attempted to give readers an idea of everyday life in the conflict, in particular in Ambon City. Father Böhm very much endeavoured to respond to readers' inquiries, be it in the form of private emails or via the newsletter. Many readers, for instance, were interested in what the current situation was actually like for the people in Ambon and the Moluccas, whether they lived in fear and what the real living conditions were like. As a result, the things he reported on included the situation of the refugees and the dangers the high level of unemployment involved, the population's insecurity and mistrust of the military and the government, the situation at the few joint markets in Ambon and the basic division between the living areas for Christians and Muslims (24 November 2002), which often meant death for anyone attempting to cross the border (25 July 2000). In addition, he regularly gave practical information about things that directly affected the everyday life of the Moluccan population, for example, interruptions to international telephone lines, the limited electricity supplies to Ambon, the (un)availability of daily newspapers and TV news, air traffic in the Moluccas, the reliability of the postal service and the (un)availability of the Internet, which of course was of particular interest for Father Böhm and all subscribers.

Argumentation structure[7]

Given that the first CCDA reports were written after the arrival of the Laskar Jihad, the fear of religious cleansing and the fear of Christians being wiped out in the Moluccas were initially the main item in the CCDA argumentation structure. As of mid-2000 Father Böhm came across numerous pieces of evidence of this in the Central Moluccas and in the North Moluccas: mass attacks on Christians by Muslims, by thousands of white-clad, well-armed Islamic warriors, the support of the Muslims by certain units of the military, the destruction of entire Christian villages, the murder of Christian women and children, the destruction of churches and the expulsion of thousands of Christians. Several previously mixed areas were already 100 per cent Muslim, in particular in the North Moluccas. One area, one island after another was being conquered by the Muslims (15 and 25 July 2000). Patterns such as these came up repeatedly in the reports. The CCDA assumed that behind the Muslim attacks there was a comprehensive plan aimed at capturing, step-by-step, all strategic places in the Moluccas, gradually cutting off Christians from the outside world – electricity, telephones, the airport – and ultimately extinguishing them, without them having even the faintest hope of rescue. The legitimizing pretext for the Laskar Jihad was that they, by fighting the Christians, were at the same time fighting the RMS separatists, who wanted to secede from Indonesia – an assumption that according to the CCDA was absolutely untruthful (see, e.g., the 'Urgent Appeal' of 29 September 2000).

Even if in the reports there were apparently frequent references to *the* Muslims and *the* Christians, Father Böhm certainly had no intention of lumping all Muslims together. He assumed that Muslim activists from outside the Moluccas were the main culprits. Since the arrival of the Laskar Jihad the pattern of the conflict had changed completely. Since then it had no longer been a struggle between Christians and Muslims. The head of the crisis centre, the Reverend Agus Ulahaiyanan, subsequently categorized the Moluccan conflict as a vertical conflict and as 'organized crime'. Religion was being abused and politicized for certain people's goals (28 August 2000). Not only the Christians, but in all probability local Muslims as well, were being harried by jihad troops from outside the Moluccas and their local sympathizers (14 May 2001). This became very clear in a quotation translated by and commented on by the CCDA from an SPMM article by Ustad[8] Muhammad Attamimi, in which Muslims who dared to trade with Christians were threatened with death:

> If there is anyone amongst the moslems who still wants to talk about reconciliation: kill him [three times repeated]. We have been patient enough by now with the treason of our leaders [meant are the governor and his aides]. By not arresting Manuputty,[9] they repudiate the nation and the islam. Do not be afraid – if needed – to offer your lives. From now on there will be no business of buying and selling any more between moslems and the christian pagans [three times repeated]. No need to do transactions about vegetables and so on. If a moslem is caught doing business with a christian, kill him, for it is better to slay one moslem than that the whole moslem community is wiped out. (27 April 2001)

The fact that it was often not clear who was behind an attack was a major problem for reporting on the Moluccan conflict in general, and in particular for a solution. The reality of the conflict was by no means as simple and clearly structured as certain groups and media propagated to the outside world. The CCDA attempted to take this aspect of the 'real', often chaotic conflict situation into account in its reports. There was frequent talk of struggles and shootings, in which it was not exactly clear who was fighting whom: Christians against Muslims, security forces against insurgents, or fighting within the ranks, that is, Muslims against Muslims, Christians against Christians, the military against the police. Within the Muslim community there were said to have been altercations between groups of Muslims of different descent, for example, between the BBM Muslims and local Muslim groups, or between local jihad warriors and those from outside.[10] Within the Christian community there were, among others, quarrels between the grassroots gang of Agus Wattimena and the Coker gang. These internal struggles also resulted from time to time in houses burning down, and people being injured and even killed.

In some cases Father Böhm made quite clear that it was not always Muslims who were the attackers, but Christians as well. The destruction of the Pattimura University (Unpatti) on 5 July 2000 by Muslims and the military, for example, was preceded on 1 July by Christian attacks on Muslim quarters in Poka, the location of the university (5 July 2000). In most cases, however, the Christian attacks were acts of defence or revenge, such as the attacks by the Christian villages Noloth and Ihamahu on the Islamic village Iha (Saparua) on 23 September 2000 (25 September 2000).[11] This way the sides became entangled in a spiral of violence, from which it became increasingly difficult to escape; and as such the conflict continued, regardless of who had begun it. The cycle of strike and counterstrike had to be broken. For this reason sections of the military and a Protestant pastor called on Christian youths not to let anything or anyone provoke them into attacks and acts of violence and to refrain from acts of revenge (13 July 2000). On the other hand, according to the CCDA, it was precisely these youths the Christian community had to be thankful for, as on innumerable occasions they had defended the Christian districts and villages against Muslim attacks and protected them by their patrols.

In his report no. 41, dated 20 August 2000, Father Böhm reflected on the background to the conflict, on how it could be so violent and go on for such a long period of time, especially in the Moluccas, where the famous *pela* alliances and peace had ruled for so long, while in other parts of Indonesia hundreds of churches had already been destroyed or damaged. Father Böhm assumed that the incidents in Kupang (Timor) in late 1998, in the course of which mosques had also been destroyed, triggered rumours that now it was the Moluccans' turn, just as later on the struggles in the Moluccas triggered disturbances in other parts of Indonesia. After Kupang there were more minor incidents in the Moluccas – in Air Besar (on Ambon Island) a pig was discovered stabbed to death in the courtyard of a Butonese (Muslim) citizen, in Dobo (Aru, Southeastern Moluccas) a minor incident caused a violent clash between Christians and Muslims – and ultimately the dispute between a Christian bus driver and a Muslim passenger in Ambon City on 19 January 1999 unleashed the bloody conflict, primarily fought out between Christians and Muslims, which lasted for several years and into which, slowly but surely, all parts of the Moluccan Islands were drawn. According to Father Böhm, the conflict became a valve for pent-up frustration on the part of the Christians, in particular the Protestants, as well as on the part of Muslims.

Primarily in the Central and Southeastern Moluccas, for a long time the Protestants represented the majority of the population. However, according to Father Böhm, various factors had led to the Muslim proportion of the Moluccan population having continually increased over the past decades. On the one hand, many of the Muslims who after the 1965 communist putsch had been taken to the Moluccan prison island Buru had stayed in the Moluccas, and on the other, many Muslim transmigrants arrived, spontaneously or organized by the government. Over the course of time these Muslims, for the most part Butonese and Bugis (South Sulawesi), were no longer satisfied with the simple menial jobs (rickshaw driver, docker, etc.) the Christians were glad to give them and also began striving, extremely successfully, and in competition with the Christians, for higher positions. Furthermore, the presence of so many outsiders weakened the traditional *pela* system, causing the Christians to fear looming Islamization.

The Muslims, on the other hand, had always disputed the Christian Moluccans' loyalty to the Indonesian state. First, many of them had fought in the Dutch colonial army when it attempted to quash the anti-colonial uprisings in Indonesia between 1945 and 1949, with, in particular on Java, many Muslims feeling the brunt of the soldiers' atrocities; and second, then as now, they were meant to harbour separatist intentions, which is why the Muslims had renamed the Republic of the South Moluccas (Republik Maluku Selatan) the Christian Republic of the Moluccas (Republik Maluku Serani). Furthermore, according to Father Böhm, the Muslims in the Moluccas needed to uphold their reputation with their Muslim brothers throughout Indonesia, which is why they were not to be subjugated and beaten by the Christian minority and, in addition, be given worse positions in the fields of administration and education, as had been the case for a long time. Even if ethnicity did play a certain role, Father Böhm continued, it was nonetheless basically a religious conflict. The autochthonous Muslim Ambonese, for example, had not waited long before deciding whether to fight alongside their ethnic brothers, the Christian Ambonese, or their fellow Muslim brothers who had immigrated to the Moluccas. The Catholics had long been attempting to keep out of the conflict and assume a mediating role, but in the course of the conflict had just as much become a target for the Muslims as the Protestants. According to Father Böhm, the statement made by a Moluccan Muslim leader, Jusuf Ely, that Catholics were not involved in the conflict, was endangering Christian unity in the Moluccas (27 February 2001).[12]

Like Masariku, the CCDA assumed that certain military units were embroiled in the conflict, siding with the Muslims, supplying them with weapons and ammunition, and doing nothing against the Laskar Jihad.[13] According to I Made Yasa, who in June 2000 was appointed commander in chief of the military in the Moluccas, 'only' 5 per cent of the military were collaborating with the Muslim warriors, which, according to Father Böhm, meant that at least 350 military personnel were fighting on the side of the Muslim attackers. Furthermore, according to I Made Yasa, the Muslim jihad troops were superior to the security forces in terms of both their numbers and their weaponry (8 July 2000). The police chief of the Moluccas, Firman Gani, also admitted that his people were unable to do anything against the Laskar Jihad, as they feared the consequences in other parts of Indonesia and their presence enjoyed the support of influential people in Jakarta (1 December 2000). Moreover, the CCDA criticized the government in Jakarta and the Moluccas for not taking any serious, honest measures to end the Moluccan conflict. Not only were they doing nothing against the defectors in the military and the Laskar Jihad, but bureaucracy and corruption were also ensuring that humanitarian aid in the form of funds and foodstuffs was only reaching the refugees for whom it was intended in part, or not at all.

According to Father Böhm, the Moluccan conflict was the result of a conspiracy, the people behind which were to be found outside the Moluccas. Christians and Muslims alike were affected by the many incidents, for example, the destruction of the telephone network and Unpatti. According to the CCDA, the governor of the Moluccas was also convinced that troublemakers from outside were responsible for the ongoing conflict and called on Christians and Muslims to join forces against the common enemy. Father Böhm expressed his disappointment about the fact that although almost all the authorities talked about provocation, not a single troublemaker had yet been convicted (3 August 2000). At any rate, jihad warriors from outside the Moluccas seemed to be involved. In the Muslim attacks Christians claimed, for example, to have regularly seen non-Moluccans among the attackers, be they from Java or from outside Indonesia.[14] A foreign journalist had encountered two people from the Middle East, who had refused to engage in any form of conversation, and at the airport Governor Saleh Latuconsina had come across seven men from Afghanistan who were being picked up there by Laskar Jihad friends. Incomprehensibly, the security forces were unable to deport them (18 and 31 August 2000).

Father Böhm also played a role in increasing the panic with regard to the Moluccan Christians' situation by frequently speaking of thousands of Muslim attackers and on 15 November 2000 quoting *Siwalima,* which claimed to know that 15,219 Laskar Jihad were currently in the Moluccas. A few days later Father Böhm himself admitted that nobody knew how many Laskar Jihad were actually in the Moluccas (2 December 2000). As the FKAWJ was striving for the Sharia to be introduced in Ambon, thereby disregarding the Indonesian constitution, Father Böhm classified the Laskar Jihad as the actual separatists (5 May 2001). He repeatedly reported on local radical Islamic organizations such as the Task Force for the Enforcement of Divine Commandments and Prohibitions among Moluccan Muslims (Satgas Amar Ma'ruf Nahi Munkar Muslim Maluku, AMNM3), headed by Muhammad Attamimi, which, together with the Laskar Jihad, were fighting prostitution, sodomy, gambling and alcoholic drinks in Ambon. For detailed information about the arguments Ja'far Umar Thalib and the FKAWJ used, Father Böhm frequently allowed them to present their case themselves by quoting their Internet articles and speeches broadcast on SPMM. Like the Masariku members, he took the opportunity to make corresponding comments about the articles and referred to SPMM as an illegal, provocative radio station that spread lies, twisted facts and prolonged the conflict, and that the government should have closed down long ago (27 March 2001). The CCDA also provided its subscribers with a complete transcript of Ja'far Umar Thalib's declaration of war, which SPMM broadcast from 1–3 May (18 May 2002) and which had led to Thalib being arrested for the second time (5 May 2002). Rustam Kastor's books were discussed in the CCDA reports, which, however, contained warnings against regarding Kastor as representative of the Muslim community in the Moluccas (13 February and 7 April 2001).

Like Masariku, the CCDA attached great importance to providing its readers with information about peace efforts and joint Christian and Muslim projects for ending the conflict. It reported, for example, on the Christian-Muslim BakuBae movement, the cooperation attempt between the Protestant Church of the Moluccas (Gereja Protestan Maluku, GPM) and the MUI, initiatives by local religious leaders, workshops held by Christian and Muslim delegations from the Moluccas on Java, and on cases of Christians and Muslims helping each other when they were fleeing, Muslims saving Christians whose boat had capsized in the Bay of Ambon and Christians coming to the aid of Muslims who had strayed into Christian territory (11 December 2000; 18 January 2001; 19 February 2001; 29 March 2001; 2 April 2001; 10 November 2001). Father Böhm also reported in great detail on the major peace initiatives of Langgur and Malino II. The fact that both the Christian and the Muslim population had long since become war-weary and wanted peace was repeatedly stressed. Yet according to the CCDA, peace initiatives often failed on account of both sides' basic demands: though the Christians, Protestants and Catholics alike emphasized that it was important to act together in an open, honest dialogue with each other and avoid acts of violence, they demanded that the Laskar Jihad first leave the Moluccas and that the military maintain neutrality. The Muslims, on the other hand, insisted that the question of guilt first be clarified, that is, precisely who had started the conflict, before there could be peace (26 July 2000; 2 August 2000; 10 September 2000; 22 October 2000; 27 January 2002). Father Böhm (2001) readily recognized that there were also representatives on the Muslim side who advocated peace, but that they often had a tough time among their own ranks.

Networking

The principle objective of the CCDA was, by means of its reports, to provide the international community with information in the quickest possible manner, in other words, via the Internet, and thus build up a network of individuals and organizations that were interested in the situation in the Moluccas and could help save the Christians and resolve the conflict. The unidirectional spread of information (the newsletter) produced a star-shaped network, whose terminal nodes, at least within the framework of the CCDA Internet project, were not networked.[15] There was no evidence of an online community emerging like the one the Masariku mailing list produced. The subscribers' relationships with one another initially played no role, and their origin was just as unimportant. However, through the manner of his reporting and the selection of his subscribers, Father Böhm also appealed to his readers' imagination. He appealed for awareness of the fact that an international community, represented by institutions such as the UN, and a Christian world community, represented by the Catholic and Protestant Churches and other Christian organizations, did exist. These communities were far-flung and as such, like Benedict Anderson's national communities, needed to be firmly ensconced in people's minds. However, given their institutional anchoring in the world's various regions, they could certainly become active and exert influence on the sort of conflict being waged in the Moluccas. Given this scenario the CCDA was counting on a sense of solidarity emerging among the subscribers to the newsletter, which would motivate them to become proactive in the Moluccan matter. They could also coordinate this action with one another.

The Church

The author of the CCDA reports, Father Kees Böhm, placed value on the fact that they did not represent his personal opinion but rather the view of the Catholic Church on the Moluccan conflict. The CCDA newsletter also served as a platform for making official statements by the Catholic Church, as well as the Protestant Church, in the Moluccas accessible to international readers and for forging a link to the global Church community. The unity of the Christian community in the Moluccas was important to the authors. In a letter to the government in Jakarta and in the Moluccas, which was also included in the CCDA newsletter, for example, fifteen Moluccan church communities called on the government to take concrete measures against the terrorists behind the Moluccan conflict and make it clear that it was serious about safety in the Moluccas and ending the conflict (23 November 2001).[16] Furthermore, they organized joint days of mourning and prayer in which several thousand Christians took part, assembling along the streets in Ambon to sing religious songs. There was, however, evidence of solidarity not just within the Christian community on the Moluccas, but between the Moluccan Christians and the community of Christians outside Indonesia, as already demonstrated by the keen interest in the CCDA newsletter on the part of Christian organizations. Even the Catholic Church's governing body, the Holy See in the Vatican, was worried about the Moluccas, and in November 2000 sent an envoy to the islands of Ambon and Kei to meet the Bishop of Ambon as well as Protestant and Muslim representatives (25 November 2000).[17]

The West

Father Böhm, however, emphatically stressed that the CCDA and the Moluccan conflict also receive international attention, above and beyond the Church as an institution. Among other things, this was attributable to the CCDA's information policy, geared as it was to an international audience, as well as to delegations heading from the Moluccas to Europe to promote their cause and drum up support. In March and April 2001, for example, a Christian-Muslim delegation organized a total of twenty-two meetings, including in London with the Upper House of Parliament, the BBC, various representatives of the Foreign and Commonwealth Office and the Moluccan community in the U.K., in Geneva with various UN representatives and bodies and several U.S. institutions, and in Brussels with representatives of the European Parliament. The result was a joint appeal to the international community, that is, the UN, the European Parliament, and other governments, calling on these to provide help and to intervene in the Moluccas. Father Böhm posted the scanned document bearing the original signatures of the Muslims, Catholics, and Protestants involved (17 April 2001). The Christians, however, also sent petitions directly from Ambon to the UN, calling on the international community to ensure human rights were upheld in the Moluccas, and, especially after mid-2000, to keep the Christians from being wiped out and enable them to be evacuated. Father Böhm put all this online. Mention was made earlier on of one such impressive example.[18] In October 2000 the CCDA sent a personal letter by email to UN Secretary-General Kofi Annan, with an urgent request to take measures to end the violence in the Moluccas (10 October 2000).

Through its newsletters the CCDA offered thanks for the attention displayed by the international community and the UN, demonstrated, among other things, by the presence of various international aid organizations in the Moluccas, such as Médécins sans Frontières (MSF), Action contre la Faim (ACF) and Mercy Corps International (MCI), and of representatives of the following UN bodies: the United Nations Development Programme (UNDP), the World Food Programme (WFP), the United Nations Children's Fund (UNICEF), the World Health Organization (WHO), and the Office for the Coordination of Humanitarian Affairs (OCHA). The respective programmes took Christians and Muslims alike into consideration, but were unfortunately limited to Ambon and Ternate (Böhm 2001). The European Union also expressed its concern and sent a delegation of five ambassadors to the Moluccas. Talks with the governor and the vice governor of the Moluccas and leaders of the various security forces centred mainly on the refugee problem and the presence of the Laskar Jihad. The delegation also visited the diocese in Ambon, the MUI and representatives of the Protestant Church (13 October 2000). According to *Siwalima,* the Protestant side expressed its disappointment with the visitors, who, it claimed, were not open to information from their side and had not really listened. The delegation, on the other hand, maintained that the Christians refused any form of dialogue with the Muslims. They seemed, however, not to be interested in the background reasons for this, and the Christians were not given an opportunity to clearly present their standpoint (14 October 2000). Father Böhm was nonetheless optimistic and viewed as a good sign the fact that the EU was addressing the conflict and, through its reports, could perhaps help further clarify the circumstances of the conflict (14 October 2000).

Other countries, such as the United States, Australia and Japan, took action and sent their ambassadors to the Moluccas to get an idea of the current situation firsthand (24 October 2000; 15 November 2000; 18 November 2000). Famous personalities also stood up for the Moluccan people. In her testimony before the United States Commission on International Religious Freedom on 13 February 2001, Sidney Jones, for example, then Asia director of Human Rights Watch, called on the United Nations to help the Indonesian government draw up a security plan for the Moluccas, which would be recognized by both sides and would also include the removal of the Laskar Jihad (21 February 2001).

With regard to the significance of the West in the Moluccan conflict, the financial support of refugee and evacuation projects, first and foremost from the Netherlands, must once again be mentioned. We certainly cannot attribute all this action to the CCDA newsletter alone, but it did play an outstanding role in the communication of local information to an international audience, which will become clearer still in the description of its online environment.

Father Böhm also engaged in networking inasmuch as, where necessary, he set up contacts between subscribers and between subscribers and institutions and people to which he had access and contact. Even though public discussion was not possible directly via the CCDA email project, when asked, Father Böhm was more than willing to exchange ideas about certain topics with his readers by email, provide additional information and, as stated, set up contacts. He also gave other organizations with local operations such as GPPM and TPG a voice in cyberspace.

The online environment

The CCDA project was by no means isolated on the online level. Even if the CCDA subscribers were not networked with each other via the newsletter, Father Böhm nonetheless engaged in active online networking through the newsletter project by calling on his community of readers to pass on important appeals using the usual channels, such as websites, acquaintances, etc., and thereby ensuring that they reached an even wider audience. One of the CCDA subscribers claimed to have forwarded the reports to several thousand other email recipients (12 May 2002). Moreover, the CCDA reports were quoted and published on several well-known, publicly accessible websites that addressed the case of the Moluccas. Pointing out the large number of websites devoted to the Moluccan conflict already in existence, Father Böhm rejected the suggestion that he set up a website of his own. On 12 September 2000 he provided a list of relevant Internet addresses:

http://www.intl-crisis-group.org
http://www.infomaluku.net
http://www.angelfire.com/rock/hotburrito/index.html
http://www.go.to/ambon_menangis
http://www.geocities.com/alifuru67
http://www.egroups.com/group/masariku
http://www.maluku2000.org
http://www.maluku.org/hain
http://www.paxchristi.nl
http://www.welcome.to/lawamena
http://www.rmsfanaticz.cjb.net
http://www.websitesrcg.com/ambon
http://www.laskarjihad.or.id
http://www.egroups.com/subscribe/laskarjihad
http://www.tanahjihad.net
http://listen.to/Rustam-Kastor
http://www.reliefweb.int

With these he covered a relatively wide range of sites featuring an even wider range of authors: international and Christian organizations, Moluccans abroad, RMS supporters, the Laskar Jihad and other radical Muslims, and the UN. Information about further websites was always welcome, according to Father Böhm. Now and again other addresses were added to the list, such as, on 16 October 2000, that of Caritas (http://www.caritas.org), which also featured information about the situation in the Moluccas in French and Spanish. Father Böhm explicitly warned against the Moluccan Sovereignty Front (Front Kedaulatan Maluku, FKM) website (http://www.fkm-europa.nl); the reports were scarcely credible and tended to exaggerate (23 April 2002).

In order to emphasize the reach and the significance of the CCDA reports in the online context once again, I myself would like to make reference to some websites that likewise posted these reports, and thereby complement the list above.[19] Moluccans living in the Netherlands in particular were very active online. The Help Ambon In Nood (HAIN) site, for example, used the CCDA reports.[20] The Maluku News Portal made all English-language CCDA reports as well as the Indonesian summaries available in its own archive.[21] The site was directly linked to the Maluku WEB Portal, which described the CCDA information as very regular and reliable.[22] Maluku2000 and the Lawamena Victoria website both posted the CCDA reports.[23] A Canadian whose wife is from Ambon hosted the Ambon Information Website, which posted a lot of background information and statistics about the Moluccan region.[24] In his links section he drew attention to several sources of information about the Moluccan conflict, including the CCDA reports, without listing these, however. That said, he did recommend visitors to the site subscribe to the newsletter, which, in his opinion, was the most reliable and most unprejudiced source of information about the Moluccan conflict. LopaLopa, a Christian website directly from Ambon that referenced the CCDA reports without itself providing daily reports of its own about events in the conflict, was set up in November 2000.[25] In its links section the Dutch organization Pax Christi drew attention to the CCDA newsletter with the following remark: 'In this mailbox you can read in English the last news from the Crisis Centre of the Diocese Ambon, several times a week. Reliable actual information without sensation.'[26] Visitors to the Help Ambon! website hosted by Masariku member Arie would occasionally come across CCDA reports,[27] as they would on the site devoted to the village Sirisori Amalatu and the Den Helder voor de Molukken site.[28] As with Masariku, there were also sites that did not include reports in full but referenced them as their source of information, such as the Human Rights Without Frontiers site.[29]

Summary

When the Catholic Crisis Centre in Ambon launched its online project there was enormous fear of Christians on the Moluccas being driven out and extinguished. The last resort seemed to be intervention from outside. This explains the urgent appeals that can repeatedly be found in the CCDA newsletters. According to the CCDA, the military, together with the Laskar Jihad, had conspired against the Christians, and the government was doing nothing about it. Only the international community could offer any help to combat this general conspiracy, which is why the reports were in English. The most important facts were to be communicated in short, succinct terms to enable as broad a mass of people as possible to stay abreast of developments. So as to appear credible, a factual method of expression was used, the reports of occurrences in the conflict were as neutral as possible and attempts were made, even if relatively unsuccessfully, to take the Muslim perspective into account. The result was a plea to the international community to address the Moluccan conflict and rescue the Christians. The CCDA project was a community project, but in a completely different sense than Masariku's. No attempt was made to establish a community, but rather to join forces with existing communities, namely the international community and the worldwide Christian community, so as to make clear to the subscribers to the newsletter, and indirectly to the Christians in the Moluccas, that they were part of a large (imaginary) community based on solidarity, that could assist those currently in distress.

Notes

1. The dates in parentheses in this chapter on the CCDA online project refer to the date on which the relevant CCDA report was written and sent to the subscribers.
2. Facts were twisted and lies spread here. Christians and Church representatives scarcely had any say in these media. Were the national media to print a pro-Christian report, they would be threatened with demonstrations and acts of violence (see, e.g., 22 June 2000; 6 September 2000).
3. According to Kees Böhm (2002b), however, this was not the highest number of members, which is thought to have been approximately four hundred.
4. I would like to take this opportunity to thank Kees Böhm for the confidential provision of the address list.
5. There is an Indonesian report about the Catholic Crisis Centre in Böhm (2001: 2).
6. In a very few cases Christians had an opportunity to find out about the circumstances on the Muslim side firsthand. On 13 September 2000, for instance, a group of Christian Dutch Moluccans, accompanied by a Catholic nun from Ambon and the (Muslim) governor's wife, was able to visit a Muslim refugee camp and report on the living conditions there, which seemed to be far worse than in comparable Christian refugee camps (14 September 2000).
7. As in the MML, the subject of forced conversion plays a major role in the CCDA reports and the topic of the FKM is repeatedly mentioned. These points are also dealt with in Chapter 7. As central CCDA arguments that crop up repeatedly in the reports are discussed in this section, for reasons of clarity there are for the most part no specific references or dates given.
8. Form of address for an Islamic religious teacher.
9. The leader of the FKM movement.
10. Kees Böhm bases this on a Masariku report (4 November 2000). Whoever started these rumours, it could also have been a tactical move aimed at creating an image of an enemy split by internal disputes. It is easier to counter such an enemy than an overpowering, uniform block carried by a common ideology that sweeps people along.
11. Iha was completely destroyed in this attack and razed to the ground.
12. For those interested in a detailed analysis of the background to the conflict, on 9 September 2000 Father Böhm forwarded a lecture to be given that same day by a Manadonese priest, Reverend J. Mangkey (2000), at a Kirche in Not (Church in Need) conference in Königstein, Germany, and called on readers to contact the author directly by email for further discussion.
13. As the arguments of the CCDA and Masariku concerning the military, the government and the Laskar Jihad were very similar, I will address here only those aspects that complement those offered by Masariku.
14. Their foreign faces and their clothing, for example, their head scarves, were clear indications (e.g., 28 September 2000; 26 October 2000).
15. There were, however, plans in this direction. A reader of the CCDA reports proposed, for example, directly networking various aid organizations with one another in order to jointly tackle the Moluccan problem. The CCDA expressed interest in a project of this nature and called on its readers to state their opinion on the matter or contact the initiator directly (12 September 2000).

16. To give an impression of the diversity of the Protestant Churches in Ambon, in addition to the Diocese of Ambon, signatories included the GPM, Gereja Bethel Indonesia (GBI, Bethel Church of Indonesia), Gereja Pantekosta Tabernakel (Tabernacle Pentecostal Church), Gereja Pantekosta Pusat Surabaya (Surabaya Pentecostal Church), Gereja Suara Tebusan Maluku (Moluccan Voice of Salvation Church), Gereja Masehi Advent Hari Ketujuh (Messiah Seventh Day's Adventist Church), Gereja Tuhan di Indonesia (The Lord's Church in Indonesia), Gereja Pantekosta di Indonesia (Indonesian Pentecostal Church), Gereja Misi Injili Indonesia (Evangelical Mission Church Indonesia), Gereja Elim Tabernakel Ambon (Ambon Elim Tabernacle Church), Gereja Baptis Indonesia (Indonesian Baptist Church), Gereja Sidang Jemaat Allah (God's Community Church), Gereja Bethel Injil Sepenuh (Full-Evangelical Bethel Church) and Gereja Bala Keselamatan (Salvation Army Church).
17. The official unveiling of a large statue of Christ on a hill on the island of Kei Kecil was another reason for his visit (Böhm 2001).
18. See, too, the newsletter dated 10 July 2000 about a joint Catholic and Protestant declaration to Kofi Annan requesting not weapons but ships for an evacuation.
19. Unless otherwise stated, each of the websites mentioned here was still available in early 2003.
20. http://www.maluku.org/hain/, discontinued on 9 October 2002.
21. http://www.malra.org/posko/ (no longer available in 2012).
22. http://www.maluku.org/portal/.
23. http://www.maluku2000.org; and http://www.geocities.com/lawamena_victoria/ or http://www.geocities.com/jembong 710/ (no longer available in 2012; for the Lawamena Victoria website, see Chapter 4).
24. http://www.websitesrcg.com/ambon/links.htm.
25. http://www.geocities.com/chosye/ (no longer available in 2012).
26. http://www.paxchristi.nl/indonesialinks.html, 6 April 2003.
27. http://www.angelfire.com/rock/hotburrito/bohm/bohm6.html. In early 2003 the Hotburrito webmaster posted all the CCDA reports on his site.
28. http://www.sirisori.demon.nl/news-04.html; http://www.denheldervoorde molukken.nl (no longer available in 2012).
29. http://www.hrwf.net/newhrwf/html/england2000.html (no longer available in 2012).

6

The FKAWJ Online
Jihad in Cyberspace

Ever since the Laskar Jihad were dispatched to the Moluccas, the Forum
Komunikasi Ahlus Sunnah wal Jama'ah (FKAWJ) attracted great attention
both within Indonesia and abroad.[1] The international community's interest grew immensely following the 9/11 attacks on the World Trade Center
in New York and the bomb attack on Bali on 12 October 2002. The chaotic circumstances in Indonesia, the United States suspected, would create
ideal conditions for sheltering terrorist groups. It was insinuated that the
Laskar Jihad had connections to the Al-Qaeda network, which, it was assumed, was behind the attacks in the United States.

As opposed to the MML, visitors to the Laskar Jihad and FKAWJ websites are treated to detailed self-representation.[2] However, the depiction of
its view of the conflict and the creation of an identity image of an Islamic
community were also central to the FKAWJ online projects.

The FKAWJ and its founder

The FKAWJ goes back to a Koran school *(pesantren)* and community that
Ja'far Umar Thalib founded in 1994 in Yogyakarta, the Jama'ah Ihya'us
Sunnah, the Community of the Revival of the Sunnah – a nonpolitical
Islamic missionary movement *(dakwah)* whose objective it was to re-
Islamize society from the lowest level by implementing Islamic law, Sharia.
Wahhabism, an important revivalist movement from Saudi Arabia, exerted
a pivotal influence on it. Its leader was Muhammad ibn 'Abd al-Wahhab
(1703–1792),[3] who in turn was very much inspired by the ideas of Ahmad
ibn Taymiyyah (1263–1328), an important Medieval representative of the
Hanbalite school, one of the strictest of the four Sunni Islamic schools of
law. Worried about the political developments at the time in Indonesia (Suharto was to resign soon after in May 1998 and conditions in the country
were becoming more and more chaotic; see, e.g., Aspinall, Klinken, and
Feith 1999; K. van Dijk 2001; Forrester 1999; Manning and Diermen 2000;
Schwarz and Paris 1999), on 14 February 1998 the Jama'ah Ihya'us Sunnah

held a mass religious meeting and founded the Forum Komunikasi Ahlus Sunnah wal Jama'ah.[4] The FKAWJ warned the Muslims of the current dangers[5] and explained that the best way to protect Indonesia's Muslim community was to install an Islamic government led by a pious Muslim male.

The FKAWJ was a hierarchical organization headquartered in Yogyakarta, Java, with forty-seven branches spread throughout Indonesia (on Java, Kalimantan, the Moluccas, Bali, Bangka, Sumatra, Sulawesi and Riau). The founder and charismatic leader was Ustad Ja'far Umar Thalib, to whom general chairman Ustad Muhammad Umar as Sewed, a former pupil of Thalib, and secretary Ma'ruf Bahun were directly subordinate. First chairman Ayip Syafruddin was responsible for public relations, legal affairs, education and research and development, the second chairman for business, finance and donations, and the third chairman for social affairs, health and the military units.[6] There was a religious committee superior to the board, which, headed by Ja'far Umar Thalib, served as an advisory body and was made up of young religious scholars, many of whom had been taught by Salafy-Wahhabi teachers[7] or had studied at various universities in the Middle East. The Laskar Jihad (Jihad Troopers) – also known as Laskar Jihad Ahlus Sunnah wal Jama'ah (LJAWJ)[8] – were under the command of Thalib and formed a subdivision of the FKAWJ, which, in the context of the events in the Moluccas, emerged from what was known as the Special Forces (Pasukan Khas, Paskhas) or Sword Warriors (Pasukan Berpedang) of the FKAWJ.[9] Together with the FKAWJ the Paskhas was founded in 1998, after neither the government nor the forces responsible had been able to ensure an appropriate level of security in Indonesia. The troops' duties included protecting certain areas, facilities and major religious events (22 February 2001).[10]

Ja'far Umar Thalib's biography was published on both the mailing list (3 June 2001) and the Laskar Jihad website (http://www.laskarjihad.or.id/about/cvjafar.htm, 5 August 2001). Thalib was born on 29 December 1961 in Malang, Java; he has four wives and nine children. His father was an Islamic spiritual leader of Yemeni-Madurese descent and a war veteran, who raised Ja'far and his seven siblings in a strict military fashion and taught them Arabic. Ja'far went to school at various *pesantren* before studying at the Institute of Islamic and Arabic Studies (Lembaga Ilmu Pengetahuan Islam dan Arab, LIPIA) in Jakarta. In 1987 he went to the Maududi Institute in Lahore, Pakistan, to continue his studies, and that same year went on to Afghanistan to join the jihad against the Russian troops stationed there. In 1989 he returned to Indonesia, where he headed a Koran school in Salatiga. From 1991 to 1993 he studied under various Salafy religious scholars in the Middle East. In 1994, back in Indonesia, he founded the Ihya'us Sunnah in Yogyakarta, and four years later the FKAWJ. In early 2000 Thalib sent a reconnaissance team to Ambon, which allegedly brought back to Java proof of a religious cleansing of Muslims and South Moluccan Republic (Republik Maluku Selatan, RMS) separatism. On 30 January 2000 he announced a resolution for a jihad in the Moluccas with a three-month deadline aimed at the Indonesian government, within which the gruesome murdering of the Muslim community in the Moluccas had to stop. Given the government's inability to end the conflict, Thalib declared on 6 April 2000 that the Laskar Jihad were leaving for Ambon and would take the matter into their own hands. The events in North Halmahera in late December 1999, when hundreds of Muslims, including women, children and the elderly, are said to have been burned alive in a mosque, were the actual trigger. Terrible images were circulated on Java and the Internet,[11] which understandably caused much anger among the Muslim community and prompted the Laskar Jihad to go to the aid of their Muslim brothers in the Moluccas. They wanted to give them a voice and to this end offered them the means of the FKAWJ, including its troops and influence. In this way the Christian attackers were to be defeated and peace restored, in line with the ideas and visions of the FKAWJ.

The FKAWJ on the Internet

Shortly after deploying its troops to Ambon, the FKAWJ went online in order to disseminate news of the Moluccan conflict as well as information about the background to it and the religious basis of their mission. Administration of the Internet projects was the responsibility of the FKAWJ webmaster in Jakarta, where there was continual Internet access. The FKAWJ was therefore not dependent on the unstable Internet situation in Ambon, as was absolutely the case for the CCDA, and in part for Masariku. This might well have been one reason for the FKAWJ maintaining a very polished Internet project encompassing both a mailing list and a website, the contents of which, however, were closely linked. The FKAWJ chose a combination of what Kollock and Smith (1999: 6) refer to as a push and pull medium: emails are sent directly to the list members (push), while visitors have to retrieve information from the website themselves (pull).

LJAWJ mailing list

Like Masariku, the FKAWJ used the free Yahoo! service for its mailing list, http://groups.yahoo.com/group/laskarjihad. The LJAWJ group (laskarjihad for short) was founded on 17 May 2000 and in October 2002 had 1,447 members.[12] Indonesian was chosen as the language of use, though as of September 2000 some reports were translated into English. The official FKAWJ website had an English section of its own, though with far less content than the Indonesian section. The LJAWJ Group Settings in Yahoo! are very different from the Masariku settings: 'Open membership', 'All messages require approval', 'Only the moderator may post', 'Public archives', 'Email attachments are permitted'. On the one hand, membership of the list and the archives were open, but on the other only the moderator could post articles, making the statement 'All messages require approval' a matter of course. By choosing these options the FKAWJ, or rather, its webmaster, created a unidirectional newsletter, with which any open discussion was avoided and the authority of the FKAWJ preserved.[13]

In line with the LJAWJ's self-description on the Yahoo! site, the list was intended to deliver up-to-date information, when possible on a daily basis, about the jihad in the Moluccas and the Laskar Jihad. The latter, and the mujahideen[14] in the Moluccas, were the exclusive sources of this information.[15]

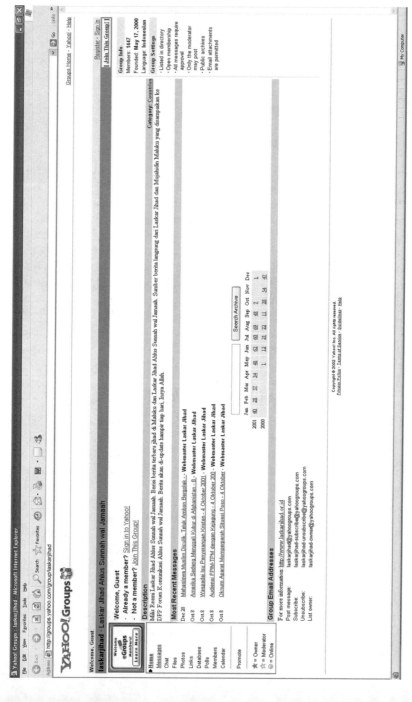

Illustration 4. Laskar Jihad – Yahoo! Groups on 22 October 2002

Even if in practical terms the members could not actively participate in the 'list discourse', an email address was given for posting messages: laskarjihad@yahoogroups.com. However, these did not appear on the list, but instead on the webmaster's monitor, who answered them individually. For more information the FKAWJ referred to its own website, http://www.laskarjihad.or.id. Until the list was discontinued on 8 October 2001 (in December 2001 one more nonstarter appeared), 629 messages had been sent; however, the Yahoo! group as such, including its members and archives, continued to exist. On 28 November 2001 it was announced in the LJAWJ website FAQ section *(Tanya Jawab)* that the list operations had been discontinued, as advertisements showing bikini-clad women had often been attached to emails sent via the Yahoo! platform. Nonetheless, even after the list had been closed, membership, which at the end of 2001 had totalled 1,351, continued to rise.

Whereas in the case of Masariku the number of messages rocketed in June and July 2000, the FKAWJ list moderator let things develop slowly (Illustration 4).[16] It was not until October/November 2000 that the number of emails gradually began to rise. Just as with the CCDA, a link between the course of the conflict and waves of messages was far less clear than with Masariku. All the list articles bore the FKAWJ letterhead (Illustration 5), and as such were considered to have the blessing of the central leadership *(dewan pimpinan pusat)*.[17]

The addresses given in Illustration 5 are of the FKAWJ headquarters in Yogyakarta, where Ja'far Umar Thalib was based, and the branch in Jakarta, which also served as the FKAWJ public relations headquarters. Until September 2000 the only address displayed was that of the FKAWJ branch in Semarang, from whence the Laskar Jihad webmaster, Arif Rahman, originally hailed.[18] In the first few months, day-to-day events and chronologies of the conflict were primarily posted. The subject heading read '24–29 May', '15 July 2000' or 'latest news' *(berita terbaru).* Gradually, however, other categories began appearing among the strictly chronological observations, and the reports on the course of the conflict were given more informative subject headings, such as 'Continuation of the worldwide Christianization strategy', 'The Christian world wants to intervene in the Moluccas', 'The Muslim university STAIN is being terrorized by Christians', or 'The Laskar Jihad get more members in Ambon'.[19] The abbreviation MHI ('Maluku Hari Ini', 'Maluku today') and the relevant date were usually inserted at the beginning of each message. Other article categories included press releases and official statements from the LJAWJ leaders, opinions on declarations by the Protestant Church of the Moluccas (Gereja Protestan Maluku, GPM), im-

---

**Dewan Pimpinan Pusat
Forum Komunikasi Ahlus Sunnah wal Jamaah**

Jl. Kaliurang Km 15 Tromol pos 08, Pakem, Sleman, Yogyakarta 55582 - Indonesia
Phone/Fax: +62-0274-895790
Jl. Cempaka Putih Tengah XXVIB No. 78 Jakarta 10510 - Indonesia
Phone/Fax: +62-021-4246417

Illustration 5. The FKAWJ letterhead

ages of destroyed Muslim and Christian facilities and of dead and wounded Muslims, maps of conquered territory, interviews with Ja'far Umar Thalib and like-minded Muslim leaders, reports from individual FKAWJ divisions, readers' letters, stories about the fate of individual martyrs in the Moluccan conflict, book recommendations, sections of the Koran, fatwas issued by respected Muslim spiritual leaders regarding current problems, calls to support the jihad in person or financially and requests to download the audio file of a speech by Ja'far Umar Thalib from the website.

In addition to the Laskar Jihad, the Muslims' team of lawyers (Tim Pengacara Muslim, TPM) in Ambon was often cited as a source in the FKAWJ reports, in a few cases the local Muslim newspaper in Ambon, *Ambon Ekspres,* national newspapers and magazines such as the Muslim daily *Republika,* and Indonesian online news services such as Detikcom. Especially in the initial phase of the online project, contacts in the North Moluccas, and here in particular contacts with the mujahideen of Abu Bakar, seemed to be of importance as a source of information. The jihad command posts in the North Moluccas worked together with the public relations department and the jihad mobilization centre of the FKAWJ (see, e.g., 25 May 2000; 4 June 2000). Some articles reporting on real incidents among Moluccans in the Netherlands revealed that there, too, the Laskar Jihad must have had informants.[20]

The Laskar Jihad would quite clearly have liked to make its news items accessible to a wider audience throughout the world and also to have them translated into other languages, but they did not have sufficient staff. There were repeated attempts via the mailing list to find Muslims willing to help translate the news into English and Arabic: 'May Allah reward your goodness with many benefits Amen.'[21] Later on an email address was set up to which applicants could write: translate@laskarjihad.or.id (8 November 2000).

Like Masariku, FKAWJ primarily made use of the Yahoo! site's archive function. Under Files (see the individual menu items in Illustration 4), only a Laskar Jihad web logo as a graphic file was made available – a changing image with the headings 'Laskar Jihad' and 'Struggle for the Defence of the Moluccan Muslims'.[22] The Links section made reference to the official Laskar Jihad website: http://laskarjihad.cbj.net/ or http://www.laskarjihad.or.id/. On occasions the polling function was also used: http://www.yahoo.com/group/laskarjihad/polls. A poll that was still open on 24 October 2002, for example, stated the following:

The Christians will lose! (*Orang Kristen Akan Kalah!*)

To which one could answer 'I agree' (*Setuju*) or 'I do not agree' (*Tak Setuju*). In October 2002 only one poll had been concluded:

Are you in agreement with the Muslims in the Moluccas making peace with the Christian side? (*Setujukah Jika Muslimin Maluku Berdamai dengan Pihak Kristen?*)

Eighteen members had taken part, two of whom were in agreement; sixteen were not.

It was possible to register with the LJAWJ mailing list via the official LJAWJ website. Those who did so were then sent a welcome email – 'Welcome to laskarjihad' – which contained a short description of the mailing list and made reference to the logging-off modalities and the official Laskar Jihad site. It was emphasized that only the list moderator could post articles and that it was at his discretion whether certain features of the Yahoo! platform were used or blocked. As a welcome gift, so to speak, those who had registered were sent another email with the Laskar Jihad web logo described above.

The LJAWJ website

In terms of content there were many parallels between the Laskar Jihad mailing list and the official website, http://www.laskarjihad.or.id, which was likewise set up in mid-2000.[23] Up-to-date news was made available both on the list and the website. The other posting categories on the list also featured on the site again. However, with the menu structure and the visual design of the site, the material was arranged in a far more comprehensible way than on the mailing list, where the various articles ended up in the subscriber's inbox and the list's archive in the order in which they were written. For this reason, exploring the site's menus and submenus was a good way of gaining an overview of, and insight into, the Laskar Jihad's Moluccan and online project (see Table 2). On the other hand, of course, the mailing list had the advantage of the subscriber being able to expect that information be provided, without himself having to actually be proactive. These were two completely different concepts, which together were of most benefit to the individual. However, the website was not only more comprehensible, but also more complete, particularly in terms of photos, audio files, fatwas, stories of the fate of martyrs, lists of donations that had been received, and the financial situation of the FKAWJ. Not all of this was forwarded to the list, which is why requests to visit the official website were often attached to list posts. In addition to the comprehensible nature of the contents, the impact of the graphic design on those visiting the site should not be underestimated. As Daniel Chandler (1998) demonstrated, depending on how it is structured, how texts and audiovisual material are combined and configured, and how elements such as links, forms, FAQs, email, etc., are used, a website can be a means of expression for a specific identity project.

Upon opening the Laskar Jihad site, it very quickly becomes clear what the outstanding elements in the organization's struggle in the Moluccas are. The site's background is dominated by the Laskar Jihad logo: two crossed sabres and, in between, an open copy of the Koran and the Islamic profession of faith, 'There is no God but Allah and Muhammad is the messenger of Allah' (*La ilaha illa Allah, Muhammad Rasul Allah*), in Arabic script (Illustration 7). On other occasions a banner, flanked by a bullet and calling for victory or martyrdom, welcomed visitors to the site (Illustration 6).

Illustration 6. Banner on the LJAWJ website

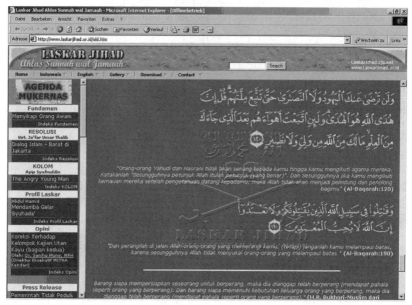

Illustration 7. LJAWJ website: Quotations from the Koran and logo

The site was basically blue in colour. 'Laskar Jihad Ahlus Sunnah wal Jamaah' appeared in large green letters at the top left. At the lower edge of the site there were, first, two quotations from the Koran in green Arabic script, of which there was also an Indonesian translation, and then the exact bank and contact details of the FKAWJ or LJAWJ. Religion, violence and finance were all very close together. The two quotations from the Koran are two verses from the second sura of the Koran, Al-Baqarah (The Cow):[24]

> 2:120: For, never will the Jews be pleased with thee, nor yet the Christians, unless thou follow their own creeds. Say: 'Behold, God's guidance is the only true guidance.' And, indeed, if thou shouldst follow their errant views after all the knowledge that has come unto thee, thou wouldst have none to protect thee from God, and none to bring thee.

> 2:190: And fight in God's cause against those who wage war against you, but do not commit aggression-for, verily, God does not love aggressors.

Every day a different Muslim who had contacted the FKAWJ by email was given an opportunity to contribute to the Message of the Day at the

upper edge of the Laskar Jihad home page. Here, thoughts about the conflict were posted and thanks for, admiration of and solidarity with the
jihad troops in the Moluccas expressed.

Via the menu structure, visitors were then introduced to the various
areas of responsibility and activity of the Laskar Jihad, online and offline
(Table 2).

The left-hand side bar of the website was divided into categories such as
resolutions passed by Ja'far Umar Thalib, a column by Ayip Syafruddin,
profiles of individual members and martyrs, more press releases, images
depicting the Christians' cruelty, maps, current topics such as statements
about and responses to the arrest of Thalib and opinions on Osama bin
Laden, the topic of Christianization and Poso, and a service section, in
which all the forms and contact details were listed again. Even though the
restructured version of the Laskar Jihad website (May 2002) was never
actually finished, it did offer a few interesting features, such as a Top 25
section – a compilation of the twenty-five most-read news items on the
LJAWJ site. In addition, the section 'Welcome to the top page for Laskar
Jihad Online!' featured lists of the most active categories, the most-read

Table 2. Menu structure of the LJAWJ website

Main menu	Submenu 1	Submenu 2
Home		
Indonesia	Laskar Jihad	Tentang Laskar Jihad
		Alamat Laskar Jihad
	Infaq	
	Berita[25]	
	Artikel	
	Pernyataan	
	Risalah Jihad	
	Tanya Jawab	
English	Laskar Jihad	About Us
		Address
	Donation	
	News	
	Article	
	Press Release	
	Question & Answer	
Gallery	Slaughtering Tragedy	
	Territorial Map	Where Is Ambon
		Muslims >< Christ April 2000
		Muslims >< Christ Feb 2001
Download	Tabligh Akbar (religious speeches at major events)	
	Wallpaper	
Contact	Send Us email	
	Infaq (donation form)	
	Jihad in Ambon (application form)	

articles, and the most frequently downloaded audio files. With regard to news items, at the time there were a lot of reports about Ja'far Umar Thalib's arrest, while the most active categories focused on topics such as Christianization, jihad and Sharia. With regard to the articles, the list of the one hundred RMS figures in particular attracted great interest, and in the Download section, in addition to the various jihad resolutions, the speeches of the Catholic politician and former general Theo Syafei, who was harshly criticized by the FKAWJ, were popular with visitors. Assuming that these lists were not manipulated, they provided an informative insight into the interests of visitors to the website.

In the finance section, the FKAWJ set great store by openness and transparency. This was also a deliberate process of demarcation from the Christians, who, it was maintained, did not reveal where they got their money from or how they used it. The website's menu item 'Infaq' contained donation forms and financial reports by the FKAWJ, listing donations received and money spent. In a fundraising proposal of October 2000 the FKAWJ once again outlined to potential donors the normative principles of their mission (Koran and Sunnah), their motives and objectives, what form their actions took and their financial resources (http://www.laskarjihad.or.id/bantu/propdppeng.htm, 5 August 2001). The LJAWJ stated that financial support came from its own members and from domestic and foreign donors, and moral and personal support came, among others, from Middle Eastern countries, in particular from major ulemas[26] in Saudi Arabia and Yemen, as well as from Islamic groups in the United States and Australia. It did not receive any money from the military or Suharto's circle, as the press of the unfaithful frequently falsely maintained (http://www.laskarjihad.or.id/service/qa/tanyajawab.htm, 24 October 2002).[27] Using the corresponding forms on the website (http://www.laskarjihad.or.id/service/forminfaq.htm, 22 October 2002) and the bank account details, which were distributed via the mailing list, visitors and subscribers were encouraged to make donations for the jihad in the Moluccas. According to the webmaster, in order to ensure transparency, every donation appeared in the list of donors on the Laskar Jihad website, though rather than their real names an alias could also be used. If the donor so wished, the FKAWJ could issue a receipt (3 July 2000). Apart from money, donations in kind such as food, medication, clothes, soap and tents were also welcome (http://www.laskarjihad.or.id/bantu/carainfaq.htm, 22 October 2002). Only with this support could the Muslim population in the Moluccas be helped and the number of Laskar Jihad in the region increased. The logistics for a single day alone cost approximately Rp 15,000,000, the webmaster stated.

Through the FKAWJ accounts, visitors to the website gained an insight into its budget. In October 2000 income and expenses totalled Rp 511,922,100 (http://www.laskarjihad.or.id/bantu/uangdppokt00.htm, 14 November 2001). The expenses comprised the cost of transferring 3,500

Laskar Jihad to the Moluccas, further costs for the troops in combat and spending on social matters, health, finance, organization, public relations, advance payments, etc. Cost estimates for upcoming campaigns were also provided (http://www.laskarjihad.or.id/bantu/prop3.htm, 14 November 2001). It was also emphasized, however, that some LJAWJ members were permanently engaged in collecting money outside the Moluccas on the street, at traffic lights, front doors and in mosques (4 June 2000). In the course of this they were repeatedly terrorized by Christians, it was stated. One of the money collectors, for example, had almost been run over, while another had been shot at with an air rifle. A priest had even threatened to kidnap an FKAWJ donor. The Laskar Jihad were also being terrorized in other ways, for example, by callers singing church hymns to them on the telephone, expressing insults and threatening to attack the FKAWJ office (29 June 2000). In order to reinforce the plea for donations and help, for example, the FKAWJ published a list of names of children who had lost their parents in the religious war on Ambon and whom the FKAWJ was now taking care of (31 October 2000; http://www.laskarjihad.or.id/about/anakasuh-des.htm, 14 November 2001). A recruitment form (Pendaftaran Laskar Jihad) was also posted on the website, which could be used to apply to be recruited into the troops (http://www.laskarjihad.or.id/service/formjihad.htm, 22 October 2002). The form, which was in English, was deliberately aimed at Muslims worldwide. There was space for contact details and a short comment, and it was preceded by the logo seen in Illustration 8.

Via the mailing list as well, those subscribers wishing to join the LJAWJ were asked to contact the FKAWJ using an email address (daftar @laskarjihad.cjb.net) set up specifically for that purpose (14 July 2000). The FKAWJ often received enquiries in the form of online readers' letters about the registration conditions and procedure. These were answered individually in the Question of the Day column or the Question and Answer section on the website (see, e.g., 1 September 2001; 11 February 2002; http://www.laskarjihad.or.id/service/qa/faqregistration.htm, 22 October 2002). Conditions for being recruited included the applicant being an adult Muslim male, of sound mind and body and willing to follow the commands of the jihad leader. Parents' consent was not necessary, as the jihad in the Moluccas had been legitimized by several fatwas issued

Illustration 8. Logo of the LJAWJ registration form

by respected ulemas. Following an interview in the FKAWJ office, applicants underwent approximately two to three weeks of physical training and were instructed in war strategies, but they were primarily instructed in the religious principles of the mission (see also 23 February 2001; 24 March 2001). Before the recruits were allowed to travel to the Moluccas they frequently had to take part in money-collecting campaigns. To a degree, the social affairs section of the FKAWJ looked after the family members of the mujahideen who were left at home. In addition to the recruits from outside the Moluccas, local Muslims also received instruction in the Laskar Jihad training camps on Ambon. From 9 to 12 March 2001, for example, nine hundred mujahideen from Ambon, Seram, Haruku and Saparua attended a four-day training course in the (Christian) village of Waai, which the previous year had been completely destroyed by Muslims. A photo of these manoeuvres shows participants dressed in military gear practising with heavy weapons (13 March 2001).

Idealization process[28]

Following and analysing the Laskar Jihad online projects for a lengthy period of time, we can observe a process in the course of which the picture of an ideal Islamic community – at least in the eyes of the FKAWJ – emerges. This was achieved through a clear method of argumentation, which knows no compromise, the deliberate use of comprehensive religious symbolism and specific online strategies.

Motives, arguments and scenarios

Shortly after the launch of the online projects, on 21 May 2000 the Laskar Jihad issued a memorandum on their website in the name of the 'leaders of Islamic communities, religious organizations, youth, student and non-government organizations in Maluku' that, in a brief, matter-of-fact manner and stating the relevant sources, listed in tabular form the reasons for the conflict in the Moluccas (http://www.laskarjihad.or.id/bantu/memoeng.htm, 10 December 2001). Having read various editions of the daily newspaper *Suara Maluku,* a letter written by the Church Lawyer's Team (TPG) and an appeal by the Christian community in the Moluccas to the UN Commission on Human Rights; following the military's discovery of RMS documents;[29] and having studied an interview with Otto Matulessy, the foreign minister of the government in exile of the RMS in the Netherlands, a letter by the RMS Board of Defence, a special report of the Indonesian embassy in The Hague, a statement by the former Christian director of the Pattimura University in Ambon (Unpatti), Dr.

Nanere, and various other sources, for which the exact date and document number were provided, the FKAWJ came to the following conclusions:

1. The riots in Maluku is planned evilly by RMS Government in its abroad headquarter (Nederland). Its aim is to proclaim their independence and establish a Christian State in Maluku. Instability of politics and economy in Indonesia is taken as their early struggle.
2. Christian church in Maluku is used as RMS's political tools.
3. Christian communities, Universities and their folks are included in its struggle.
4. Christian political elite and bureaucrat are also recruited as its colleagues.
5. Christian civil chiefs and its bureaucrat environment speak on three languages, i.e.: language of humanity, peace and law.
6. The aim of Maluku Christian Church is to control bureaucracy system in Maluku.
7. The annihilation of Moslem people in Maluku.
8. Church Master plan to seize the legal government of Indonesia in Maluku.

Ultimately, the FKAWJ concluded that the RMS and the Church sought the independence of the Moluccas and the obliteration of all Moluccan Muslims.[30] The authors then explicitly avowed their allegiance to the Indonesian state and the Indonesian constitution. The letter was then sent to the Indonesian president, the commander in chief of the Indonesian army, the governor of the Moluccas and the police and military chiefs in the Moluccas, who were called on to immediately halt the separatist movement of the Christian rebels and preserve the unity of the state: 'May Allah give us His *taufiq* [help] and *hidayah* [leadership].'

This stance was reflected in all the following reports and analyses. From the outset a specific method of argumentation seemed to have been decided on, and there was no compromising. Report no. 1 on the mailing list, emailed on 25 May 2000 and which also appeared on the website, gave details of a *tabligh akbar* in the course of which one hundred thousand Muslims had gathered in front of the Al-Fatah Mosque in Ambon to oppose the crusaders. Ja'far Umar Thalib declared that the jihad was the last option for fighting the separatists and the international conspiracy behind the Moluccan conflict. The Laskar Jihad saw proof in everything of the Christians in the Moluccas wanting to secede from Indonesia and of the international community actively helping them to do so: Christians were constantly provoking and insulting Muslims, for instance, by way of foul, coarse language and even luring Muslim refugees into a trap, and turning to the United Nations for help, parts of the military were helping them with their attacks on the Muslims, the United States was sending the Christians/RMS containers full of weapons, and much more. All this justified classifying Christians as dogs and animals, as dirty infidels, and insulting them in all manner of ways. According to the FKAWJ, without the Laskar Jihad the Moluccan Muslims would be lost. These reports of Christian cruelty, which according to the FKAWJ was even worse than the sadism demonstrated by the Indonesian Communist Party (PKI) in 1965, made a far greater impression through the accounts of Muslim eye-witnesses: 'Eyewitness statements from victims of the cruelty of the infidels in the Moluccas.'[31] Youths, women and men in the North Moluccas described how people were hacked to death or hung in front of their eyes, how women were stripped naked and raped, how their children were taken away from them, how they all feared for their lives and how ultimately the Al-Ikhlash Mosque in Togolihua, North Halmahera, had been set on fire in December 1999 and six hundred people burned alive.

The Laskar Jihad in the conflict

According to an article on the FKAWJ website in 2000, the jihad troops were united by a joint vision and a joint mission, namely, putting an end to all forms of suppression and humiliation of Muslims (http://www. laskarjihad.or.id/english/article/ljtroopers.htm, 22 October 2002). The only response and the only solution was the jihad.[32] Who was better suited to declaring this than a man who had firsthand experience of the efforts of the jihad in the desert of Afghanistan, Ja'far Umar Thalib? According to their website, based on the three main goals of the Laskar Jihad – the dissemination of the call for the oneness of God *(tawhid)*, the humanitarian mission and protection – together with the people the Laskar Jihad were fighting for Allah, for the Almighty's cause. The Laskar Jihad provided help in the humanitarian and social field on the one hand, and on the other by supporting the fight against the Christians. In numerous articles the FKAWJ repeatedly stressed that it had no political motives and had no wish to be involved in any political machinations. The LJAWJ opposed the accusation by the Christians that they had played a role in fuelling and considerably prolonging the conflict. To substantiate their arguments they posted an article entitled 'Laskar Jihad, the Accused' by Herry Mohammed on their website, which had previously been published in the Indonesian magazine *Gatra*. Mohammed primarily pointed out that the conflict in the Moluccas had already been going on for a year before the Laskar Jihad even arrived there, and as such that they could not have been either the reason for or trigger of the conflict. Rather, they had come to help the Muslims and bring the chaotic situation in Ambon, as far as jurisdiction and religious education were concerned, in line with their standards (http://www.laskarjihad.or.id/english/article/theaccused. htm, 24 May 2002). According to Ja'far Umar Thalib, the Laskar Jihad in the Moluccas were principally religious preachers who were to improve the religious life of the Muslims in Ambon, though who at the same time also had to undergo physical training, having, after all, been sent to a war region.[33]

Help in the social and religious field

From the outset the Laskar Jihad emphasized that they had come to Ambon primarily for social and missionary *(dakwah)* reasons, so as to help the Moluccan Muslims in the fields of health, education, business and religious life. In line with the organizational structure of the FKAWJ, the website had a section of its own for social affairs and health. Entitled Divisi Sosial FKAWJ, it provided an overview of the Laskar Jihad's social activities in the Moluccas (http://www.laskarjihad.or.id/about/divsosial. htm, 14 November 2001; see also 8 February 2001). These included distributing wills for the potential martyrs planning to head for Ambon and presents for the families of the volunteers, mental and religious training in the Moluccas, opening provisional schools and Koran schools, Koran readings with the population, caring for the widows and children of martyrs and orphans whose parents had died in the religious war in Ambon, reconstructing mosques, cleaning streets and positioning guards. According to the FKAWJ, there had been a strong decline in morals and manners due to the conflict, which, through their missionary activities, they wanted to restore. The primary goals were spreading faith in the oneness of God[34] and the unity of the Muslim community in the Moluccas. Were we to believe the FKAWJ, the activities of the Laskar Jihad on Ambon and the surrounding islands were very popular with the population (19 June 2000). Youngsters in particular enthusiastically emulated the Laskar Jihad role models in terms of their religious activities and clothing, which, according to the FKAWJ, was decisive for the future of the Moluccas (14 March 2001).[35]

The health sector was also of significance, and included the treatment of the sick and wounded, the administering of medication and the circumcision of Muslim children and young people. The FKAWJ health department regularly provided information about corresponding activities (see, e.g., http://www.laskarjihad.or.id/about/divkesnov2000.htm, 14 November 2001). The FKAWJ medical team (Ahlus Sunnah Wal Jama'ah Medical Team, AHMed Team) was comprised of trained general practitioners and specialists, as well as medical students from institutes in Yogya, Semarang, Solo, Surabaya and Makassar. It was responsible for all the population's medical matters, and in particular for the victims of the conflict, evacuation measures, sanitation matters and refugees' health problems. Detailed accounts were provided of donations and fund-raising activities (Rp 54,500,000 in November), and how much was spent on what: medication, medical equipment, costs of the mujahideen carers and the families they had left behind, costs of evacuating victims, etc. The first FKAWJ health station in the Moluccas was founded on 1 May 2000, and by the end of 2001 there were already twenty: fourteen on Ambon Island, three on Seram, one on Haruku, and two on Saparua. Circumcision played a central role in the FKAWJ medical team's field of activity in the Moluccas. Between July 2000 and March 2001, 1,143 Muslim boys were circumcised on Ambon Island alone (22 June 2001). This normally happened in routine mass circumcisions in individual villages. It also provided an opportunity to distribute medication to the population free of charge.

Despite this extensive social commitment, it was not only the Christian population that perceived the Laskar Jihad as a militant force. In an interview with *The Jakarta Post* on 10 November 2000, Ayip Syafruddin, the head of the FKAWJ public relations department, attempted to improve the image of the Laskar Jihad 'as a bunch of sword-carrying young men' by highlighting their humanitarian work, which was absolutely at the forefront of their mission in the Moluccas (http://www.laskarjihad. or.id/english/article/index.htm, 22 October 2002). According to Syafruddin, the Laskar Jihad had come to restore the (Muslim) community, not to complicate the conflict between Muslims and Christians, or even obliterate the Christian community, as many people had maintained.[36] The Christians and the media were responsible for this incorrect image. The Laskar Jihad had only played a partial role in it, particularly because of activities such as the training camp in Bogor, where before their deployment to the Moluccas they had undergone a sort of basic military training, and various protest events in Jakarta, at which LJAWJ members had wandered around the streets illegally armed with swords.

Campaigns of conquest

If one follows the online reports of the Laskar Jihad, the importance of military action such as the capture of Christian territory and the fight against Christian troops very quickly becomes clear. On the one hand, it was emphasized that it was always Christians who did the attacking and the Muslims were just defending themselves, but on the other, there was talk of nothing less than campaigns of conquest that resulted in the recapture by the Laskar Jihad or allied local troops of an area controlled by Christians, the occupation of Christian territory and the expulsion of Christians from Muslim territory. According to Abu Bakar, in Galela in the North Moluccas, for example, an area occupied by infidel troops *(pasukan kafir)*, that is, Christian troops, had successfully been recaptured. He proudly reported that in the process five hundred Christians and only eight jihad warriors had been killed and that the Christians' weapons had been captured (11 June 2000). Refugees, casualties and deaths on the opposing side appeared to strengthen the Laskar Jihad only in their perspective of the conflict. At long last the 'RMS Christians' were suffering what the Muslims had tolerated for months. God the Almighty *(Allah Ta'ala)* was avenging the Muslims (14 August 2000). The Christians also now had to suffer with regard to education, the Christian University of the Moluccas (Universitas Kristen Indonesia Maluku, UKIM) in Ambon having been destroyed by Muslims in a four-day campaign in June 2000, followed shortly after by the destruction of Unpatti.

The news that the daily newspaper *Siwalima* was reportedly going bankrupt triggered a sense of triumph among the Laskar Jihad. They claimed it had been a tool of the Christians/RMS, had been provocative in its reporting and constantly twisted facts. The boycott on the part of the Muslims, they claimed, had ultimately led to the bankruptcy (12 July 2000).[37] Ja'far Umar Thalib's strategy of fighting the 'RMS Christians' on all fronts and thus slowly smoking them out (24 March 2001) appeared to be working. However, not only the Moluccas and the RMS, but the whole of East Indonesia was a thorn in the side of the Laskar Jihad, as compared with the rest of Indonesia the proportion of Christians in the population was very high. They suspected, for example, that there was a secret link between the RMS and Papua, where many RMS Christians had fled during the course of the conflict. It sounded like a threat when the author of an FKAWJ article stated that the Christian inhabitants of Papua had hopefully learned from the events in Ambon, from whence the Christian RMS provocateurs had fled to Papua (30 July 2000).[38]

The chief ideologist, Rustam Kastor

Rustam Kastor, a retired brigadier general in the Indonesian military with alleged links to influential circles in the armed forces and close to Suharto in Jakarta, was frequently cited as the chief ideologist of the Laskar Jihad with regard to its method of argumentation in the Moluccan conflict. This link also became clearly evident in the Laskar Jihad online project. Various reports made reference to the fact that he was an important partner and one of *the* mujahideen figures in Ambon (http://www.laskarjihad. or.id/service/qa/tanyajawab.htm, 24 October 2002). In addition, Kastor was deputy chairman of the (Muslim) Forum of the Defenders of Justice in the Moluccas (Forum Pembela Keadilan Maluku, FPKM). In this capacity he on various occasions released press statements on the current situation in the Moluccas, which the LJAWJ published online, explaining the theory he had already proposed and propagated in several books on the Moluccan conflict. It maintained that the conflict was an initiative by militant RMS supporters in the Netherlands and the Moluccas who were working with the GPM and the Moluccan section of Megawati's (allegedly Christian) Indonesian Democratic Party – Struggle (Partai Demokrasi Indonesia – Perjuangan, PDI-P). Some of the books were even available online. According to Aditjondro (2001a: 116), Kastor's first book, *Fakta, Data dan Analisa Konspirasi Politik RMS dan Kristen Menghancurkan Ummat Islam di Ambon – Maluku* became a best seller in Indonesia.[39]

The Laskar Jihad offered it for sale online (http://www.laskarjihad.or.id/bantu/bukukastor.htm, 25 January 2001). If a donation to the FKAWJ was large enough, the donor was even sent it free of charge. It was hoped that the book would clarify the background to the Moluccan conflict and the Laskar Jihad mission once and for all (3 July 2000).

The West and the Christianization of the world

Ja'far Umar Thalib was convinced that Jews and Christians worldwide had joined forces in a global Zionist-Christian conspiracy to fight the Muslims and dominate the world. The United States, which needed a new foe following the end of the Cold War, was the main player in this scenario (Question of the Day, 11 April 2001; see also Thalib 2000). According to the FKAWJ, the United States was one of the biggest supporters of the RMS (15 July 2000). In a statement on 19 July 2000, Ja'far Umar Thalib warned the UN and the United States against becoming involved in the Moluccan conflict:[40] 'We are prepared to destroy the American troops!!! ... America has never won, apart from in *Rambo*!'[41] The United Nations was just a marionette of the United States and Israel, he claimed (22 July 2000). As such, the struggle for world dominance went hand in hand with a worldwide Christianization campaign on the part of these powers and would automatically end in the West's opposition to Islam.[42] For the West and its stooges, that is, the secularists, the elements of Islam that it could not 'tame' *(menjinakkan)* and that it classified as fundamentalist, extremist and radical Islam, represented a major threat (22 July 2002). According to Thalib, the Moluccan conflict, through which the Moluccan Muslims were to be wiped out, was part of this plan, a small piece in the large mosaic that was the global conspiracy. As in the Moluccas and in Central Sulawesi (8 August 2000), Muslims worldwide were being systematically massacred, for example, in Afghanistan, Bosnia, Chechnya, Kosovo, Palestine, Kashmir and Moro (31 August 2000), which was the reason for the show of solidarity with the persecuted Islamic world community.[43]

According to Thalib, the combat cries by the red troops *(pasukan merah)* of the RMS were a clear indication of the West's involvement in the Moluccas: 'Long live the Netherlands!' *(Hidup Belanda!)*, 'Long live Australia!', 'Long live America!', and 'Long live Israel!' were said to have been heard. At a mass demonstration on 18 July 2000, he claimed, they had even carried the Israeli flag (21 July 2000). Human rights organizations and the UN were the mouthpiece for the Christians' accusation that the jihad movement was conducting Christian cleansing.[44] The fact that this charge was totally unfounded could be seen from the number of victims alone, he said: whereas by June 2000 more than five thousand Muslims had supposedly died, only a few hundred Christians had suffered the same fate (28 June 2000). Unlike the Christians, for Muslims UN help was not decisive for victory, but rather that of God the Almighty *(Allah*

Ta'ala). For the FKAWJ, shots repelled by an invisible hand, Christian bombs that failed to explode, a lame enemy (21 July 2000), the scent of the blood of wounded and dead mujahideen, the smile on the faces of martyrs and, not least of all, the fact that the Muslims were able to inflict more and more losses on the enemy at all levels provided proof of Allah's blessing of the jihad in the Moluccas (1 August 2000).

Proof of Europe's involvement, the FKAWJ claimed, was provided by the visits to the Moluccas by delegations of the European University and both the European and British Parliaments, which, according to the LJAWJ, fuelled the conflict even more and moreover hurt the self-esteem of the Indonesian people (see, e.g., http://www.laskarjihad.or.id/artikel/bldbertindak.htm, 24 October 2002). For them, the colonialist and imperialist danger that emanated from Europe and that had already manifested itself in the appearance of the RMS became very clear (4 November 2000). For this reason, not only the Laskar Jihad, but also the Indonesian government and the military were against outside intervention, the latter seeing the danger of a forthcoming referendum on independence, as had been held in East Timor (26 June 2002). The United States, Australia, the UN and Europe, in particular the Netherlands, were supporting the Christians not just ideologically, but also in the form of medication, money and weapons, which were brought to Ambon by individuals (26 June 2000) or by foreign NGOs allegedly providing 'humanitarian aid' (4 August 2000). The Laskar Jihad were certain that Pattimura University in Ambon was where these weapons changed hands (19 July 2000). They themselves had no weapons unless, that is, the local population voluntarily supplied them in order for them to be able to guard the borders, as there were insufficient soldiers to do so. They could, of course, also capture weapons in attacks on the enemy (19 July 2000). The Laskar Jihad saw no difference between foreign (aid) organizations such as Doctors Without Borders and Action contre la Faim, which were operating in the Moluccas, and a spy network. Under the pretence of bringing aid, these foreigners were conducting all manner of investigations, they claimed, making recordings and spying on the Muslim community in order to discover its strengths and weaknesses. In the field, although they were actually doing very little for the Muslim community, they were said to be attempting to entice and dupe the Muslims (1 December 2000). Furthermore, the staff of these organizations were attempting to drive a wedge between the local Muslims and the Laskar Jihad and question Muslims about the role of the military in the conflict, which was causing further unrest (24 June 2002).

According to the FKAWJ, the Christians were using all the means at their disposal to divide the Muslims, be it through their 'divide et impera' policy – a legacy from the colonial era – or through the highly successful SST concept (secularism, syncretism, interreligious tolerance), to which the then president of Indonesia, Abdurrahman Wahid, also lent his support (31 August 2000; 17 October 2000). This meant that the Muslims who had to flee in droves from the RMS in the Moluccas, from Papua's independence movement in Irian Jaya, from the United Nations in Timor, and from Poso and Pontianak were receiving scarcely any help from their Muslim brothers and sisters in Indonesia. Moreover, the Christians were exploiting the principle of religious freedom anchored in the constitution and, under the pretence of wanting to resurrect the tradition of *pela gandong,* were continually cheating the Muslims. All this was happening in the name of human rights and humanity (1 November 2000). According to the FKAWJ, the Bible was virtually encouraging Christians to kill Muslims. Several quotations from the Bible were quoted as evidence (23 October 2000):[45]

> Matthew 10:34: Do not suppose that I have come to bring peace to the earth. I did not come to bring peace, but a sword.
>
> Luke 12:49 and 51: I have come to bring fire on the earth, and how I wish it were already kindled ... Do you think I came to bring peace on earth? No, I tell you, but division.
>
> Joshua 6:21: They devoted the city to the Lord and destroyed with the sword every living thing in it – men and women, young and old, cattle, sheep, and donkeys.

Like Rustam Kastor, the Laskar Jihad were of the opinion that the Moluccan conflict was both a secessionist and a religious war (1 August 2000), with the RMS being the decisive link. The members of the RMS were all Christians and had contacts and connections throughout the world, people who were supporting them in their fight for independence. The RMS was using the Christians, which was why the conflict was being fought between Christians and Muslims and why not only were people being killed, but religious symbols were also being destroyed and insulted (mosques, the Prophet Mohammed, etc.). The Laskar Jihad were accordingly attempting to legitimize their mission in the Moluccas.

The FKAWJ maintained that media were important war strategies for the Christians (4 June 2000). Using electronic (TV, radio, Internet) as well as conventional media (magazines, newspapers, books, seminars, etc.), they were constantly twisting facts, thereby destroying the image of Muslims and Islam at the local (*Siwalima, Suara Maluku,* etc.), national (*Jawa Pos, Kompas, Suara Merdeka,* SiaR mailing list, online news services, etc.) and international levels (BBC, CNN, Christian websites, etc.). They were thus attempting to divert attention from the despicable behaviour of the RMS Christians and make the Muslim community, the Laskar Jihad and those close to Suharto scapegoats *(kambing hitam)* for all the crimes in the Moluccas (9 August 2000). Moreover, these media reported attacks on Muslims and about Muslims who had been forced to convert only scarcely, if at all. As such, Muslim citizens and groups in the Moluccas repeatedly launched protest campaigns against the reporting in the daily newspapers *Siwalima* and *Suara Maluku* and against the national TV (TVRI) and radio (RRI) stations, demanding that the government take appropriate measures (11 September 2000; 15 September 2000; 17 October 2000; 24 October 2000; 19 May 2002; http://www.laskarjihad.or.id/, 26 January 2002).

At the national level, the FKAWJ public relations department directed, for example, a protest letter to the editorial desk of Indonesian online magazine *Tempo Interaktif,* explaining that the report of an attack on the village of Galala near Ambon was far removed from what had actually happened. The FKAWJ version of the incident then followed, and a request that the editorial desk dismiss the relevant correspondent and in future be more careful about checking its material before publishing it (13 October 2000; http://www.laskarjihad.or.id/press/fkawj-protes-tempo.htm, 24 October 2002). On 19 May 2002 the magazine was once again accused of slander on account of an article about the arrest of Ja'far Umar Thalib, which FKAWJ members picked to pieces sentence by sentence and corrected (19 May 2002). In some cases the FKAWJ also levelled concrete criticism on an international level. Radio Nederland, for example, reported a bloodbath among Christians on Kesui, an island east of Seram in the Central Moluccas, in which the Laskar Jihad were meant to have been embroiled. They maintained, however, that they had never been on the island and accused the radio station of disseminating Christian propaganda and that of the TPG (6 December 2000; http://www.laskarjihad.or.id/press/ned5122000.htm, 24 October 2002; in English: http://www.laskarjihad.or.id/english/press/eprenedh.htm, 20 August 2001). Likewise, it attacked an article in the *Los Angeles Times* that reported on the life of a Christian as a Muslim slave, the sole objective of which, they claimed, was to discredit Muslims and the Laskar Jihad.[46]

The military and the government

The Laskar Jihad were frequently accused of being in league with the military and of being financed by certain generals (see, e.g., Aditjondro 2001a, 2001b). The FKAWJ rejected this accusation in a press statement on 25 January 2002. The LJAWJ, it said, had been established for purely religious, not political or military, reasons and had received neither US$9.3 million from generals in the Indonesian military, as certain media maintained, nor any other money from military circles. If that had been the case, the Laskar Jihad would certainly not have made the effort of collecting money on the streets and in mosques (http://www.laskarjihad.or.id/press/fkawj-25jan2002.htm, 24 October 2002). Rather, they said, there were units in the military that supported the Christians, the United Battalion (Batalyon Gabungan, Yongab), which was characterized by its brutality and arrogance towards Muslims, being the most prominent.[47] The reason for this was the high proportion of Christians in the unit (17 June 2001). The 'enmity' between the Muslims and the United Battalion reached a peak in the Hotel Wijaya II case in January 2001 and culminated in the Yongab attack on the LJAWJ polyclinic in Ambon in June 2001. With the help of eyewitnesses who were involved, the FKAWJ compiled a 'Chronology of the Yongab Brutality in Ambon':[48] From 20–22 January 2001, in a brutal Yongab raid in the border area between Batumerah and Mardika and the subsequent storming of the Hotel Wijaya II, fifteen innocent Muslims had died (17 March 2001)[49] and four police officers had been beaten. Contrary to what the Yongab maintained, the hotel had not been the headquarters of radical Muslims and manipulators in the Moluccan conflict. In this context the Laskar Jihad immediately took six eyewitness reports from victims and on 8 February 2001 posted them on the mailing list. The Hotel Wijaya II case triggered huge protests among the Muslim population. They demanded an investigation into the violation of human rights on the part of the Yongab. According to I Made Yasa, who, being a Hindu from Bali, the government had deliberately appointed military commander, the Yongab had behaved correctly and not violated human rights (24 January 2001).[50]

As if that were not enough, on 14 June 2001 the Yongab attacked the LJAWJ polyclinic in Ambon. This was where the Laskar Jihad medical team had treated the Muslim population and provided free medication. According to the FKAWJ, the attack on the clinic was a crime against humanity. The military had not only beaten and killed patients and doctors in a sadistic manner, but had also generally insulted Islam and Muslims. They had torn a copy of the Koran to shreds and slandered and mocked Islam (18 June 2001). To the great satisfaction of the Laskar Jihad, however, the clinic was able to be reopened just a few days later (20 June 2001). Although those affected were questioned by the national human rights commission (4 July and 22 August 2001), according to the TPM this case of the 'bloody Wednesday' (*Kamis berdarah*) was not sufficiently investigated either (24 August 2001). In response to a reader's letter of 9 July 2001, the Laskar Jihad stated that the very same day they had taken revenge on the Yongab by attacking the lorries in which the Yongab had been taking hostages from the clinic and allegedly killing twenty-two and wounding several Yongab members in the process (26 July 2001).[51] On 17 June 2001, on the Laskar Jihad radio station SPMM, Ja'far Umar Thalib issued a death sentence (*fatwa mati*) against I Made Yasa, the person most responsible for the anti-Muslim acts of violence by the Yongab, the reach of which increased enormously by being posted on the Internet (18 June 2001; http://www.laskarjihad.or.id/berita/jun2001/mhi010618b.htm, 5 August 2001). Throughout Indonesia Muslims expressed their solidarity with the victims of the Yongab brutality, for example, in the shape of a demonstration by several Islamic mass organizations in Bandung, West Java, which issued a declaration on the 'murderer of the Islamic community'

(*Pembantai Umat Islam*) and in the name of all the Muslims of West Java condemned I Made Yasa (24 July 2001).

Despite all this, however, the FKAWJ emphasized that the Yongab represented an exception in the Indonesian military. In principle, the Muslims did not reject the presence of the military and the police. On the contrary, the FKAWJ was convinced that it was impossible to imagine the Muslim community in Indonesia without the military. They had fought shoulder to shoulder for the sovereignty of the Indonesian people, be it against the colonial rulers or other disruptive powers. It went without saying that on account of the cases depicted they were worried about the neutrality of the military and demanded a neutral replacement for the Yongab, yet regardless of this the presence of the security forces was indispensable, in particular to protect the Muslim side from the RMS Christians and to prevent the conflict from spreading even further (5 December 2000). The Laskar Jihad correspondingly mourned (Muslim) soldiers who were victims of the Christians. Through their death, Muslim self-esteem was also automatically damaged (26 May and 4 July 2001).

The relationship of the Laskar Jihad to the Indonesian government as the representative of the Indonesian state was ambivalent. They criticized the government's inability to protect the Muslims in the Moluccas, to eliminate the RMS and the Moluccan Sovereignty Front (Front Kedaulatan Maluku, FKM) and to end the conflict. They had come to the Moluccas for precisely that reason.[52] Measures in which the government was involved, such as the various investigation teams, the civil state of emergency, peace movements and Thalib's arrest in May 2002, really only served to divert attention from its lack of success in dealing with the separatist RMS, they claimed (5 and 11 May 2002). On 25 April 2001 the RMS/FKM had still been able to fly its flag unpunished (29 October 2001). Were the government to expel the Laskar Jihad from the Moluccas, which it was being pressured to do from various sides, it would make the Laskar Jihad the scapegoat in the Moluccan conflict and give its blessing, so to speak, to the Islamic community in the Moluccas being butchered yet further (12 May 2002).

On the other hand, the Laskar Jihad emphasized their pronounced national consciousness. Their declared objective in the Moluccas was to preserve the unity of the Indonesian state. As an expression of their nationalist stance and their support of the government in its fight against the RMS, the Laskar Jihad were deliberately cooperative when it came to certain matters. By way of example, at the request of the vice president Hamzah Haz, together with other organizations in Ambon close to the LJAWJ, they staged an official handover of weapons by Muslims to the government. In return, however, the government was expected to at long last take action against the RMS (19 May 2002). There was a second handing-over ceremony on 11 June 2002 on the occasion of Hamzah Haz's visit to Ambon; once again, hundreds of various types of weapons were surrendered. Although, according to the FKAWJ, the Muslims had been the victims of the 'Bloody Idul Fitri' (*Idul Fitri Berdarah*) on 19 January 1999, they had initially handed over their weapons voluntarily (11 June 2002). The FKAWJ and the local Friendship Forum of the Islamic Community in the Moluccas (Forum Silaturahmi Umat Islam Maluku, FSUIM), which played a decisive role in organizing the handover, hoped that it would help them shake off their antipeace and hardliner image (12 June 2002).[53] The Christians were accused of not cooperating with the central government and continually refusing to surrender their weapons. This made it clear that they had no intention of ending their uprising against the government and the conflict with the Islamic community (19 July 2000). The Muslims' show of handing over weapons certainly made an impact. Hamzah Haz left the Moluccas saying, 'I never again want to hear anything about a bloodbath against the Islamic community.'[54] According to Husni Putuhena, the FSUIM speaker, and Muhammad Attamimi, the leader of the Task Force for the Enforcement of Divine Commandments and Prohibitions among Moluccan Muslims (Satgas Amar Ma'ruf Nahi Munkar Muslim Maluku, AMNM3), the appeal to the military to remain neutral had to be dropped. It was clear who the military's enemy was: the separatist RMS (11 and 13 June 2002).

Solution to the conflict

As opposed to the Christian cyberactors, to the very last the Laskar Jihad set no store by the various attempts at reconciliation and peace such as the BakuBae movement and the Malino II agreements, as until then the Christians had broken every single promise of peace (12 July 2000). The only people to benefit at all from these movements were private individuals who operated under the guise of NGOs, launching reconstruction and reconciliation projects (24 December 2000). Husni Putuhena, who was also the Moluccan coordinator for the TPM, referred to the independent national investigation team put in place by the government (Tim Penyelidik Independen Nasional) as nothing but a waste of money, as the culprits were already known (22 June 2002). The secretary of the FSUIM, Abdul Wahab Lumaela, assumed that the team had only been established on the back of pressure from the European Parliament (7 July 2002). Nor was there any point, according to a lecturer at the State Islamic University (Sekolah Tinggi Agama Islam Negeri, STAIN) in Ambon, in looking for a peaceful solution in cultural factors such as *pela*. These initiatives only served to divert attention from the actual problem and further expose the Islamic community to threat by the separatists (27 July 2002).

According to the FKAWJ, the only people who could conclude an agreement with the Christians were the mujahideen who were fighting in the Moluccas, and not people who just claimed to represent the Islamic community in the Moluccas. The FKAWJ saw itself confirmed in this when the car of Jusuf Ely, who as the alleged representative of the Muslims was part of the BakuBae movement, was blown up. The only real solution lay in the elimination of the RMS/FKM and admittance on the part of the Christians that they were the cause of the conflict on 19 January 1999. They had to apologize to the Muslims and then, of course, be held accountable (21 July 2000).[55] Before that there could be no dialogue, nor could Christians be allowed to return to their villages (14 November 2000; 8 October 2001; 15 August 2002). As the Christians could not be trusted, war, not reconciliation, was the only way to end the Moluccan conflict, or, in the words of Ustad Attamimi, '[w]ar to end war'.[56] The war against the infidels was a command by God to the faithful, each and every one. The Muslims would have to continue the jihad for as long as it took for the Muslim community to no longer be slandered and for Islam to structure life in Moluccan society. In this the unity of the Muslims was decisive and manifested itself in the following four elements: faith, the Koran, the Hadith and the mosque, which was not divided like the Christian churches (29 October 2001; see also 6 September 2000; 2 July 2001).

Religious pillars

For the LJAWJ the Moluccan mission was a religious project. Accordingly, in its online representations relating to the Moluccan conflict and the manner in which the FKAWJ portrayed itself, there was a focus on Islamic concepts and principles that legitimized its approach in the Moluccas.

Principles of the jihad

So as to underpin its line of reasoning and its interpretation of the jihad, as well as to confirm its image of an idealized Muslim community, the FKAWJ included on its website a section containing treatises on jihad in general (*Risalah Jihad*) and religious judgements (*Fatwas*) relating to the Moluccan conflict in particular (http://www.laskarjihad.or.id/berita/jun2001/mhi010618b.htm, 5 August 2001).[57] In addition to the FKAWJ's own scholars, respected clerics were also given a voice, such as Sheikh Abu Bakr Jabir Al Jazairi, a professor at the Islamic University in Medina and a famous teacher at the An-Nabawi Mosque (http://www.kusza.edu.my/~hakim/Islam/Masalah/smokingl.html, 28 February 2003), and Sheikh Abdullah bin Abdulaziz bin Baz (died 1999), who was Grand Mufti of Saudi Arabia, chairman of the Committee of the Highest Ulemas, chairman of the Department of Scholarly Research and the Ifta (Islamic Foundation) (http://www.saudiembassy.net/press_release/statements/99-ST-0513-Baz-death.htm, 28 February 2003), and also the former teacher of Ja'far Umar Thalib (Hasan 2002). For bin Baz the jihad on God's path (*Jihad fi sabilillah*) is the most important religious duty of each and every Muslim. It would bring the faithful victory, subjugate the infidels and hypocrites, accelerate the spread of the Islamic mission in our world and lead from darkness to light *(zhulumat ilann ur)*.[58] Bin Baz also quoted verses from the Koran, which illustrated his interpretation of the jihad:[59]

> 2:193: Hence, fight against them until there is no more oppression and all worship is devoted to God alone.

> 9:5: And so, when the sacred months are over, slay those who ascribe divinity to aught beside God wherever you may come upon them, and take them captive, and besiege them, and lie in wait for them at every conceivable place! Yet if they repent, and take to prayer, and render the purifying dues, let them go their way: for, behold, God is much forgiving, a dispenser of grace.

> 9:29: [And] fight against those who – despite having been vouchsafed revelation [aforetime] – do not [truly] believe either in God or the Last Day, and do not consider forbidden that which God and His Apostle have forbidden, and do not follow the religion of truth [which God has enjoined upon them] till they [agree to] pay the exemption tax with a willing hand, after having been humbled [in war].

According to a hadith bin Baz referenced, Jews, Christians and followers of Parsism could be attacked for as long as it took for them to convert to Islam. Women, children and the elderly were to be spared, as long as they did not take part in the war (http://www.laskarjihad.or.id/risalah/binbazz2.htm, 14 November 2001).[60]

The Sunnah, the exemplary practice of the prophet Mohammed *(Sunnah Qunut Nazilah)*, was the basis of the FKAWJ philosophy (http://www.laskarjihad.or.id/risalah/qunut.htm, 24 November 2002). Every good deed performed and every measure taken by the FKAWJ had to be based on the Koran or the Sunnah, as did the jihad. In response to a reader's letter, the FKAWJ emphasized once again that it had no political motives and had neither gone to the Moluccas at the request of a few generals, nor was it being paid by the old regime of the *Orde Baru*. The sole basis was the Koran and the Sunnah, which was why it had also contacted those ulemas who were experts in the field of Islamic law and the Hadith in order to have the legitimacy of the jihad in the Moluccas examined and confirmed. As, given the slaughter in the Moluccas, the academically trained Muslims in Indonesia had remained silent, it had turned to well-known, experienced ulemas in the Middle East (24 September 2000): Sheikh Abdul mukhsin Al-abbad (Medina), Sheikh Ahmad An-Najmi (Jizan region, Saudi Arabia), Sheikh Muqbil bin Hadi Al-Wadi'i (Yemen), Sheikh Rabi' bin Hadi Al-Madkholi (Mecca), Sheikh Shalih As-Suhaimi (Medina), Sheikh Wahid Al-Jabiri (Medina) and Sheikh Muhammad bin Hadi Al-Madkhali (Medina). It had procured their judgements on the jihad in the Moluccas either by telephone or by personal visit (9 October 2000; http://www.laskarjihad.or.id/risalah/fatwa2.htm, 14 November 2001).

All the fatwas agreed that it was the duty of all Muslims to go to the Moluccas and defend their Muslim brothers and sisters, but under certain conditions: the Muslims needed to be strong enough, the infidels had to have begun the hostilities, a war between Muslims had to be ruled out and the jihad had to be conducted in the name of the Sunnah and must not be politically motivated. On 26 December 2000 Sheikh Muqbil bin Hadi Al-Wadi'i[61] from Yemen, one of the most important former teachers of Ja'far Umar Thalib, issued another fatwa. He pointed out that on the Moluccas more than five thousand Muslims – men, women and children – had already been killed, and more than one hundred mosques and one thousand residential buildings destroyed, and called on all Muslims in and outside Indonesia to conduct a *Jihad fi sabilillah* and drive out the enemy. This time even the Sheikh's contact details, including his telephone and fax numbers, were provided (http://www.laskarjihad.or.id/laskar/syaikhmuqbil.htm, 4 March 2001). The original of the fatwa was scanned and stored in the image section of the LJAWJ website (http://www.laskarjihad.or.id/picture/syaikhmuqbil.gif, 25 October 2002). By publishing these fatwas on the Internet the judgement requested by a small group became a general message to a far wider audience.[62]

Sharia

The aim of the FKAWJ was to introduce Sharia in the Moluccas and throughout Indonesia so as to create an Islamic state. According to the FKAWJ, basic principles of Islamic law had until then been ignored at both the local and national level. It criticized in particular the government. Abdurrahman Wahid, the first democratically elected president of Indonesia, had stood up too much for the infidels (i.e., the Christians) and initiated dialogue between the various religions in Indonesia, thereby totally neglecting the Muslim community, which indeed made up the majority of the country. Then, in 2001, Megawati Sukarnoputri came to power, which was a big thorn in the side of the FKAWJ, as a woman governing a predominantly Muslim country violates Sharia principles. It was an insult to the Islamic community. Megawati's election was a result of the democratization process, which was an expression of the infidels' culture (Question of the Day, 5 August 2001). It was not possible for the FKAWJ to work together with a female president for religious reasons. Thus, it cooperated with the vice president Hamzah Haz, who assumed a mediating role and had to register the wishes and hopes of the Islamic community (9 August 2001).[63]

On 10 March 2001 in the Al-Fatah Mosque, the main mosque in Ambon, the Laskar Jihad declared Sharia to be the applicable law for Ambon. The news was spread via pamphlets and the radio (Mohammad, Bakri and Rahman 2001).[64] According to the FKAWJ, only the introduction of Sharia could fill the legal vacuum in the Moluccas and create a way out of the chaotic conflict situation (21 March 2001). As a first step in implementing Sharia in the Moluccas, Islamic rules such as bans on gambling, prostitution and the sale of alcohol were to be applied more strictly in Muslim areas (26 August 2001). In order to eradicate this evil, Ja'far Umar Thalib himself set up a Team for the Destruction of Wickedness (Tim Pemberantasan Kemaksiatan, TPK), which worked closely with local organizations and jihad stations (3 March 2001). Here, the AMNM3, led by Ustad Muhammad Attamimi and represented by Ustad Luqman Ba'abduh, an LJAWJ member, was particularly prominent (28 March 2001). In numerous FKAWJ reports there was talk of raids and cleansing missions in Ambon and surrounding villages, in the course of which an (alleged) brothel had been closed, containers full of alcohol destroyed in the docks, the corresponding trading points shut down in cooperation with the military or the local population and some of the operators handed over to the police. Allegedly, the Muslim population visibly supported these activities. The old market *(pasar lama)* in Ambon, for example, where there was prostitution and gambling and alcoholic drinks were consumed, was seemingly burned down on the spur of the moment by the Muslim masses (2 August 2000).

For the Laskar Jihad, introducing Sharia also meant implementing what are known as the *hadd* punishments (chopping off a hand for theft, stoning for adultery, etc.). So as to set an example, the first judgement was passed on 27 March 2001, with the LJAWJ member Abdullah from Ahuru (Ambon City) stoned for adultery. In a ceremonial speech, Ja'far Umar Thalib announced the enforcement (30 March 2001, translated by the author):

Assalamu'alaikum Warahmatullahi Wabarakaatuh

Dear honoured attendees, today we shall enforce Allah's punishment, the stoning of our brother Abdullah, who is married, has a child, and is a member of the LJAWJ.

My Muslim brothers and sisters, Allah Subhanallahu Wa Ta'ala commands us to uphold this punishment.

Thalib also explained that applying the *hadd* punishments (including stoning) had the blessing of Sheikh Muqbil bin Hadi Al-Wadi'i and was in accordance with the Koran and the Hadith: while sura 2, verse 2 demanded one hundred lashes of the whip for an adulterer, the Hadith called for an adulterer who was already married to be stoned. In this particular case the culprit had also admitted his offence and decided voluntarily to be stoned. Ja'far even posted the corresponding dialogue between himself and Abdullah online (30 March 2001). According to the FKAWJ, the stoning was legal, as the Indonesian constitution allowed every religion to enforce its own laws (14 June 2001; 23 March 2002).[65] As an indication that the Muslim community in Ambon was behind Thalib's decision, thirty-one personalities and chairmen of Moluccan Muslim organizations, mosques and jihad stations issued a declaration stating that the stoning was in line with the national law and the religious duty of Muslims, which was why it had the full support of the Islamic community in Ambon.[66] The FKAWJ posted a scanned copy of this declaration, together with all the signatures of those involved, on its mailing list (19 May 2001) and its website: 'Joint Declaration by the Islamic Community in Ambon.'[67] On 24 May 2001 the FKAWJ announced that the Friendly Association of Islamic Media (*Suara Hidayatullah, Sabili, Ummi, Media Dakwah,* etc.) intended to bestow the Syariah Award on the stoned Sharia hero Abdullah. The award would be presented by the secretary of the Islamic Propagation Council of Indonesia (DDII), Hussein Umar, to the FKAWJ as a representative of Abdullah's family. The editor in chief of the magazine *Suara Hidayatullah* emphasized that the stoning was a high point in the fight for the people's rescue by enforcing the Sharia (24 May 2001). Nevertheless, the stoning was the reason for Ja'far Umar Thalib's first arrest in early May 2001.[68]

Martyrdom

Initially the Laskar Jihad repeatedly stressed that there had not been as many casualties on their side as the Christians always maintained. This was just a tactic, they claimed, to weaken Muslims' spirit, and in particular that of the Laskar Jihad, and unsettle their families. By way of example, during the first four months the Laskar Jihad had been operating, there had been nine dead and twenty wounded in their ranks, as opposed to the two hundred claimed (25 August 2000). Nonetheless, the martyrs' cult played an outstanding role in the online activities of the Laskar Jihad, similarly to on the websites of other jihad groups (see, e.g., Anti-Defamation League 2002; Bunt 2000: 97). In some cases individual deaths were announced via the mailing list (see, e.g., 4 June 2000; 19 July 2000). The motto was 'Vanquish or die a martyr.'[69] If one of the mujahideen were to die in battle against the infidels, he would have died for God and would be a martyr *(syahid).* This was in line with the Prophet's ideal:[70]

> A person who has gone to Heaven has no desire to return to Earth ..., except a martyr, who hopes to return to Earth and be killed ten times again on account of the honour he enjoys in heaven because of it. (Hadith according to Bukhari Muslim)

The Laskar Jihad had not gone to the Moluccas for selfish reasons, but to sacrifice themselves for their Muslim brothers and sisters in the name of God (24 September 2000). To this end they had left their wives and children at home, given up their work and in some cases sold their possessions so as to be able to pay for the journey to Ambon and support their families. They were often diligent students – in many cases from science faculties – from humble backgrounds, who were given leave from their studies to go to Ambon for the jihad. There, the Laskar Jihad only received food twice a day (2 March 2001). To underscore this, the life stories of martyrs were published: 'The Path of a Mujahideen: The Martyr Ibnu Hajar' or 'The Steadfastness of a Young Mujahideen',[71] an article about Ismail who, at the age of just sixteen, gave his life in the jihad as proof of his devotion to God. A special section was set up on the website for these tales, entitled Indeks Profil Laskar. According to the descriptions the typical martyr was young, courageous and came from a humble background, had a close relationship with his parents and had a religious upbringing. In view of the tragedy on the Moluccas these young people had, on the spur of the moment and with great enthusiasm, decided to help their Muslim brothers and sisters there and join the FKAWJ for the jihad, and were prepared to die as martyrs. In death they had a content expression on their faces and left their parents with the knowledge that their son had died for God and the unity of the Indonesian state and had defended his religion and country to the very end (25 October 2000; see also 27 October 2000; 4 February 2001; 16 February 2001). The Koran promises martyrs an eternal life with God (4 September 2001):[72]

> 3:169: But do not think of those that have been slain in God's cause as dead. Nay, they are alive! With their Sustainer have they their sustenance.

Muslim unity

According to the philosophy of the FKAWJ, the unity of all the faithful was a prerequisite for the Muslims being able to win the fight against the infidels, for the Indonesian state. The whole Islamic community corresponded to a human body: if one part of the body were injured or threatened, the entire body felt ill and it had to unite all its strength to fight and defeat the illness or threat. For this reason the Laskar Jihad had to come to the aid of the Moluccan Muslims, who were being threatened by separatists and Christians (4 August 2000; 6 May 2001). From numerous FKAWJ articles it became clear that this unity was the result of a common faith and its foundations, a joint goal, joint events, such as the major religious meetings at the Al-Fatah Mosque in Ambon, and the numerous declarations of solidarity. Through the FKAWJ thousands of Muslims from Timor, the Moluccas, Bali, Nusa Tenggara Timur, Sulawesi, Kalimantan, Sumatra and Java had gone to Ambon to 'help their brothers and sisters in the Moluccas with their time, their thoughts, their strength and their assets' (18 August 2000) and thus to fulfil what the Laskar Jihad called the holy duty (3 October 2000). In particular the Muslims in Ambon had to ensure that the Christians there, with their provocative announcements, did not drive a wedge between the Islamic community, but rather that unity was preserved (6 November 2000).[73] If one follows the FKAWJ reports, the Laskar Jihad enjoyed wide, across-the-board support from the local Muslim population and local organizations. They had been welcomed, were permanently being called on to help and local Muslims were resisting the demand by certain circles (the Christians and the local government) that they leave the Moluccas (28 July 2000; 18 August 2000; 30–31 October 2000). The Laskar Jihad had already become part of the population; people felt themselves to be brothers and sisters, a community. The Laskar Jihad were often excused from paying the fare on public transport and offered food by the people; there were even women who voluntarily washed their clothes (1 March 2001).

In Ambon City the Laskar Jihad worked with local Muslim figures and organizations such as Muhammad Attamimi's AMNM3 and Husni Putuhena's FSUIM. As far as the conflict and its causes were concerned, all these organizations and figures pursued the same line of argument. Figures like Ustad Ali Fauzi, the chairman of the DDII in the Moluccas, the retired brigadier general Rustam Kastor and Abu Bakar Al-Banjiri, the leader of the mujahideen in the North Moluccas, were even present at the large assembly in Senayan Stadium in Jakarta on 6 April 2000, when the jihad resolution for the Moluccas was officially announced (4 January 2001). The active Indonesian Council of Islamic Religious Scholars (Majelis Ulama Indonesia, MUI) unit in the Moluccas also supported the presence of the Laskar Jihad. The temporary chairman of the MUI, Abdul Wahab Polpoke, however, was increasingly criticized for the reconciliatory course he was pursuing with regard to the Christians, demonstrated, among other things, in his support of the Malino II agreements (15 May 2002). As is also evident from the FKAWJ reports, anyone who failed to keep in line with the hardliner organizations with close ties to the FKAWJ was attacked. The house of Jusuf Ely, who played an active role in the BakuBae movement, was set on fire, as was that of Thamrin Ely, the head of the Muslim delegation to the Malino II peace negotiations (15 May 2002).[74]

In the FKAWJ Internet articles, less central Muslim personalities who very much championed the struggle of the Laskar Jihad also had their say. Jumu Tuani, for example, the assistant of the Jihad Command Centre in the Moluccas (Pusat Komando Jihad Maluku), was present in several media at the same time. He was quoted in the Internet articles and himself provided articles for the Laskar Jihad magazine and the radio station SPMM. As such, the FKAWJ also became a mouthpiece for his ideas, which were primarily restricted to his hate of the RMS and their alleged followers. For the Laskar Jihad, Jumu's statements may well have been particularly conclusive and authentic, as until the outbreak of the troubles he had lived in what was now the entirely Christian district of Kudamati, where Alex Manuputty, Berthy Loupatty and, until his death, Agus Wattimena also lived (e.g., 18 May 2002; 2 June 2002; 29 June 2002; *Tabloid Laskar Jihad,* edition 20, 22 May 2002, announced on the FKAWJ website). For the Laskar Jihad, Alex Manuputty as the leader of the separatist FKM, and the grass rootsleader Agus Wattimena, whom in numerous articles they referred to as 'Panglima Laskar Kristus', the 'military commander of the Christian troops', were the personification of evil.

In the North Moluccas it was the local mujahideen in particular, led by Abu Bakar Al-Banjiri, with whom the Laskar Jihad cooperated, and from whom they received necessary information about the jihad in the North Moluccas (19 July 2000; http://www.laskarjihad.or.id/laskar/wawanabu. htm, 26 January 2001). On 16 February 2000 the MUI representative office in the North Moluccas issued a power of attorney appointing the FKAWJ coordinator of aid and relief efforts for the Muslims in the Moluccas (http://www.laskarjihad.or.id/bantu/mandat.htm, 14 November 2001). The FKAWJ also received support in the shape of protest letters to the government and the military (in particular in conjunction with the Yongab cases), letters of recommendation and official declarations from the Islamic Defenders Front of the Moluccas (Front Pembela Islam Maluku, FPIM) (http://www.laskarjihad.or.id/press/pernyfpim.htm, 24 October 2002), the Association of Islamic Students in Ambon and Makassar (Ikatan Pelajar Mahasiswa Islam Ambon – Makassar, IKPMIA) (http://www.laskarjihad. or.id/press/ipkima010126.htm, 24 October 2002), the DDII[75] and the Indonesian Commitee for Solidarity with the Islamic World (Komite Indonesia untuk Solidaritas Dunia Islam, KISDI) (19 January 2001). Ja'far Umar Thalib's first arrest in May 2001 (like the second in May 2002) triggered an enormous wave of protest not just in local and national Muslim circles. There was allegedly also an outcry among the Muslim population in the United States, which praised Thalib on account of his achievements in Afghanistan and in the fight for the Moluccan Muslims, not to mention the introduction of Sharia in Ambon, and which demanded his release by the Indonesian government (13–14 May 2001; 16 July 2002; http://www. laskarjihad.or.id/english/article/ljl-arrest3.htm, 14 November 2001).

In addition to the forms, readers' letters were one of the interactive elements on the LJAWJ website. They gave visitors to the site and subscribers to the list an opportunity to respond directly to articles and current events, make contact with the FKAWJ and get feedback on specific questions. Since, according to the webmaster in an email dated 3 December 2000, the intention was to make necessary information available to the public, any questions directed at the Laskar Jihad would be answered.[76] For the FKAWJ the letters and the replies to them were an instrument to propagate and strengthen their philosophy still further by stating their stance on important issues such as the recruitment of the Laskar Jihad, their relationship with Al-Qaeda, the role of the United States and the RMS, the signs of the increasing Islamization (in the interest of the FKAWJ) of the Muslims in Ambon, etc.; visibly dealing with criticism, misgivings and rumours; and, not least of all, making the messages of solidarity that were so frequently expressed available to a wider audience. In his letter dated 25 May 2001, Robby, a 'reader' from Jakarta, answered his question of whether peace was possible in the Moluccas himself, thus confirming the Laskar Jihad's approach:

> Allahu Akbar!!! Allahu Akbar!!! Allahu Akbar!!!
>
> I am very pleased and happy about the willingness of the members of the Laskar Jihad to leave their families, their work and their in some cases very pleasant lives to defend our Muslim brothers and sisters in Ambon, who are being suppressed by the Christian troops.
>
> I am very annoyed about the reporting on the part of the Christians, which constantly twists facts and maintains that it was the Islamic community that first attacked the Christians. And, as far as I have gathered, they have great fear of the Laskar Jihad, as with the latter's arrival their ambitions of wiping out the Muslims have been stopped.
>
> I would just like to advise the Laskar Jihad and the other troops there not to be merciful with the Christian troops, who, now that they are in a fix, are re-questing peace. PLEASE DO NOT BE!!! as I am sure that they will cause a bloodbath among the Muslims as soon as they have regained their strength and the Laskar Jihad have left the Moluccas. ('Question of the Day', 7 June 2001, translation by the author)

The 'readers' could also turn to the Laskar Jihad with their worries, as in the Question of the Day on 23 March 2001 (abridged and translated version):

> ALLAHU AKBAR......
>
> I am a Muslim ... and I come originally from Ambon ... I am at a loss ... what will happen if the government cannot solve the AMBON problem ... I am afraid that Ambon will suffer the same fate as East Timor ... which was successfully Christianized and was separated from Indonesia ...
>
> What I do know is that on 25 April 2001 these infidels are going to dare to openly raise the RMS flag ... and if things have already gone that far I am convinced that the well-being of the Muslim community in Ambon is in danger, and I would like to ask which stance the LJAWJ is going to adopt, if this actually occurs??????
>
> I am very satisfied with the Laskar Jihad, I still remember the first day of the troubles, 19 January 1999, which is known as the IDUL FITRI BERDARAH (Bloody Idul Fitri) ... Then we, the Muslim community, were at a loss ... we saw the attacks by the BAD infidels, who completely turned the Muslim settlements upside down ... But, thanks to GOD the Greatest, GOD the Almighty sent the LJAWJ.

This way the FKAWJ was able to give the people solace, saying the Muslims would be victorious, as they were fighting a war in the name of God, who was on their side, a fact that was underscored with numerous verses from the Koran.

Generally speaking, it was possible to lend enormous weight via the Internet to the image of a Muslim unity by bringing together different voices at all manner of levels, which declared their solidarity and offered all forms of support. The charismatic leader of the Laskar Jihad, Ja'far Umar Thalib, was another important unifying factor in circles close to the FKAWJ. Not only his philosophy and interpretation of Islamic sources were made public via the Internet, but also his speeches in the form of audio files.[77] The overarching categories were jihad resolutions he had announced at various mass meetings, speeches about the rebellions in various parts of East Indonesia, articles about the topic of Christianization in Indonesia, and the success of the mujahideen. The jihad resolutions, for example, included the speech Thalib held on 6 April 2000 in Senayan Stadium in Jakarta, shortly before the Laskar Jihad set off in the direction of the Moluccas. The commentary read as follows: 'On 6 April 2000 the Islamic community entered the ring to wage war on the crusaders and the Communist Party of Indonesia.'[78] Two other speeches about the jihad were primarily about criticism of Abdurrahman Wahid. These audio documents added an important authentic element to and strengthened the manner of argumentation of the Laskar Jihad. The Internet extended the reach of the Laskar Jihad leader's voice. It became a mouthpiece with which his speeches were transported directly into the homes of the Internet users involved. They got the impression that they were actually there in person and being addressed by Thalib himself; Muslims could feel themselves part of a larger imagined Muslim community that, thanks to the Internet, was growing ever stronger. The speeches transported not only the actual content and Thalib's forceful, loud voice, but also captured the mood at the respective event. One could hear background noises, voices, people cheering and 'Allah, Allah, Allahu Akbar'.

Limits to Muslim unity

Despite all the solidarity with the 'suppressed' Muslims in Indonesia and the rest of the world, the FKAWJ resisted Western terminology, which rashly and unilaterally classified the Laskar Jihad as fundamentalist, militant, aggressive, destructive and uncompromising and tarred it with the same brush as organizations and associations with whose philosophy the FKAWJ could not identify.[79] In this way, for example, the FKAWJ officially distanced itself from the occurrences during Christmas 2000, the so-called Bloody Christmas *(Natal Berdarah),* when churches were destroyed throughout Indonesia. Bloody Christmas was about political manoeuvres and power struggles, which the FKAWJ did not want to have anything to do with (25–27 December 2000). After 9/11 there were increasing rumours that Indonesia was the training camp for terrorist and fundamentalist Islamic groups. The U.S. government implied that Osama bin Laden's Al-Qaeda network, which it supposed was behind the 9/11 attacks, could possibly have relocated to Indonesia, and was exerting enormous pressure on the Indonesian government to adopt strict measures to counter corresponding terrorist and radical Islamic organizations in the country. Since then the FKAWJ and its followers had been confronted with the accusation that it had links to Osama bin Laden and Al-Qaeda, and having a common cause or being financed by bin Laden.

An official statement on 12 December 2001 by A. M. Hendropriyono, the head of the national intelligence agency, stating that Al-Qaeda was operating in Poso and maintained a training camp and links to extremist Islamic groups in Indonesia caused a great stir. It was enthusiastically taken up by the international press and interpreted to mean that the Laskar Jihad were cooperating with the Al-Qaeda network.[80] A few days later, however, Hendropriyono retracted his statement in front of journalists in Jakarta. He emphasized that the Laskar Jihad had no contact with the Al-Qaeda network and that the latter was operating neither in Poso nor anywhere else in Indonesia (16 December 2001; http://www.laskarjihad. or.id/english/news/des2001/engdes0116.htm, 25 September 2002).

In principle, Thalib applauded the attack on the World Trade Center in New York and the obvious impotence of the United States. He saw it as the answer from God the Most Holy and Almighty *(Allah Subhanahu wa Ta'ala)* to America's arrogant stance (15 September 2001). In an interview with MetroTV, Thalib also said that by attacking Afghanistan the United States had clearly declared its enmity towards Islam and as such had manoeuvred itself into a dangerous position (8 October 2001). That said, in numerous articles and official statements in English and Indonesian to the national and international press, the FKAWJ strictly denied having any links to those allegedly behind 9/11, bin Laden and Al-Qaeda (19 December 2001; 1 January 2002; http://www.laskarjihad.or.id/english/press/ fkawj-011219.htm; http://www.laskarjihad.or.id/english/press/fkawj-020 101.htm; http://www.laskarjihad.or.id/fkawj-01sep22.htm, 22 October 2002). Moreover, as early as January 2002 the FKAWJ denied any link to Jemaah Islamiyah (http://www.laskarjihad.or.id/press/fkawj-26jan2002. htm, 22 October 2002), who was assumed to be behind the October 2002 bomb attacks on Bali.

According to Thalib, any suggestion that the Laskar Jihad had links to Osama bin Laden was nothing if not absurd, because their interpretation of Islam differed immensely from that of bin Laden and his followers. As the activities of the Laskar Jihad were always in line with the Koran and the Sunnah, and the FKAWJ was also advised by various well-respected ulemas, the Laskar Jihad were not even in a position to engage in terrorist or anarchist activities. In the 16 September 2001 edition of the Indonesian magazine *Panji,* Thalib explained that the incompatibility of his ideas and those of bin Laden had come to light as early as their first meeting in Peshawar, Pakistan, in 1987. At the time, bin Laden was still a jet-setter with no academic knowledge of his religion. Moreover, he was a follower of the *khawarij*, an Islamic group that had splintered off from Ahlus Sunnah Wal Jama'ah, to which the Laskar Jihad belonged. The attacks by aircraft, like all other suicide attacks, were not compatible with Sharia, Thalib claimed (30 September 2001). Anti-Americanism was the linking element between bin Laden and Thalib: 'Death to America!!!' (*Mampuslah Amerika !!!*) was the title of a post on 30 September 2001 in which the hope was expressed that the greatest nation of terrorists on Earth, the United States, would learn from the 9/11 attacks.[81]

Ja'far Umar Thalib's declaration of war

As previously stated in the chapters on the Christian cyberactors, Ja'far Umar Thalib's declaration of war, which was broadcast from 1–3 May 2002 on the radio station SPMM in Ambon, provides a good overall view of all the lines of argument of the Laskar Jihad, and the accusations it made in connection with the Moluccan conflict. Masariku, the CCDA, and various websites devoted to the Moluccan conflict played a part, online, in the further dissemination of this aggressive speech. Its background was outlined in an *Asia Times Online* article on 24 August 2002: as early as 26 April 2002 Thalib gave an address to several thousand Muslims in the Al-Fatah Mosque in Ambon, in which he openly demanded war against the Christians and called on all Muslims to be prepared. Two days later the village of Soya, in the vicinity of Ambon City, was attacked and several Christians killed in a barbaric way, which, given Thalib's inflammatory speech, many sides immediately attributed to the Laskar Jihad. In early May, the SPMM then broadcast said declaration of war (*maklumat perang)*, whereupon, on 4 May, Thalib was arrested for a second time.[82] In the declaration Thalib addressed his beloved, venerated Muslims, called on them to remain united, to wage war in the name of God and to die as martyrs and underscored this duty with quotations from the Koran. He accused the government of having ignored all ultimatums to put an end to the conflict, accused the Church of having a common cause with the RMS and demanded of his brothers in faith that they defend the integrity of the Indonesian state. He warned the governor, as well as the military and police chiefs in the Moluccas, of Allah's revenge, and he addressed the United States, the international community of churches, the Zionist crusaders and all Christians and Jews when he announced that the Moluccas would become a second Afghanistan. He closed with the words: 'Until we meet on the battlefield. Allahu Akbar.'[83] Here are a few excerpts from the declaration of war:[84]

> Assalaamu'alaikum warah matullallahu wabarakatuh
>
> My beloved Muslim community whom I love and honor. Leaders of Islam, priests of mosques, society leaders and all of the Muslim community, wherever you may be when you hear the call which I am declaring.

We give thanks to Allah Subhaanahu wa Ta'ala who has chosen us as His army. The army of God has the responsibility to go to war, even as God commanded [2:216][85] ... Allah has reminded us [4:75]: And why should ye not fight in the cause of Allah and of those who, being weak, are ill-treated (and oppressed)? Men, women and children, whose cry is: 'Our Lord! Rescue us from this town, whose people are oppressors; and raise for us from Thee one who will protect; and raise for us from Thee one who will help!' ... And what laws in this world are able to prohibit the religious obligation expressed in the command of God,[86] [8:72] if they seek your aid in religion, it is your duty to help them. Therefore I stress, all laws and regulations which are in contradiction to the word of God are null and void.

Muslims, whom I love and honor. For these reasons, we have found evil and treachery in the Government of the Province of Maluku which has since been given the title as Civil Emergency authority. For more than three years Muslims have been toyed with and mocked by various deceptions, wicked intrigues and evil stratagems put forward by the Government of the Province of Maluku together with the church, which has become the command headquarters of the RMS movement. The Government of the Province of Maluku, led by Saleh Latuconsina[87] and the churches, led by inhuman criminals, the ministers who devour illicit property, have consulted together to carry out wicked designs against the Muslim people, that is, to evict them from Maluku and then proclaim the establishment of the RMS state of which they dream. We have endeavored to lobby against the evil which has disseminated. We have lobbied the central government, the defense forces, the army and the police, both those in the Army and in the Police headquarters and those in the Government of the Province of Maluku. These efforts we have been carrying on for over three years. Nevertheless all of this has not helped the situation of the Muslims ...

Muslim people whom I love and I honor, all of that [the Laskar Jihad mission in the Moluccas] was carried out in the process of conducting our rights and responsibilities to defend ourselves as citizens of the state of Indonesia. More than that, all of it was conducted in the process of carrying out religious responsibilities, that is to defend the national unity of the Unity State of the Indonesian Republic. But all the ultimatums we gave were ignored by the Civil Emergency authority. They were the ones who specifically permitted and allowed the anniversary celebrations of the RMS throughout all of Maluku ...

Woe to you, Saleh Latuconsina! If you hear my voice then listen to my final piece of advice. Be afraid of Allah knowing that the Church leaders, both national and international, cannot protect you from Allah's curse, damnation and wrath when you oppress the Muslim faithful ...[88]

Then I want to give some advice to you, Commander of the Army, Mr Mustopo. Fear Allah and His curses! ... To the Chief of Police Sunarko, take warning!!! Fear Allah!!! ... Woe to the servants of God. You will be defeated if you come against the greatness of Allah. You will be destroyed if you are determined to come against the power of God. Do not trust too much in the physical power you possess ... If you boast in your tens of thousands of soldiers and police, remember that Allah has an army whose members are uncountable. The angels of Allah are always watching you ... What tanks and special force troops of the military would you use to oppose Allah's angels? ...[89]

Muslims whom I love and honour. Continue to prepare all forms of resistance against the efforts of the Civil Emergency Authority who wants to manipulate our defense forces to come into conflict with us. Let us prepare everything. Prepare the bombs which we have. Prepare the ammunition which we are ready to vomit forth from the barrels of the weapons we possess. And we swear by Allah! By Allah! By Allah! If there is even one Muslim killed by the defense forces, Kudamati and Passo will become seas of fire. By Allah, we declare it! We do not want to be faced with emissaries who are paid to come into conflict with us ...[90]

Woe!!!!! We are determined that we do not want to come into conflict with the Army and the Police. But, when they attack us with the excuse that they are sweeping or whatever other reason,[91] we will fight against them to the last drop of blood. We will also continue our resistance to Kudamati, Passo and until we free Maluku from the filthy hands of the RMS. That is our determination. Do not play around with these tigers of Allah. We will not retreat from this principle!

Therefore, I have ordered every Jihad soldier in the Ahlussunnah Wal Jama'ah to write out their wills and prepare themselves to welcome their fate as martyrs. Get out all your weapons. Because of the busyness of this war, I am forced to announce to the Muslims that the activities of the SDIP, TKIP and TPQ (schools) are for the present on holiday in order to prepare themselves to get ready for this civil war. And to the medical forces, may they prepare themselves for all possibilities to be ready to serve those who are wounded in the battle.

To the Muslims I counsel that they unite their ranks and prepare themselves in facing the opposition of the people towards the betrayal of the state and the nation. We all serve Allah, reject all forms of sweeping and the like. We are prepared to confront tanks and the like. We are even ready to face fighter planes and helicopters. We do not care. All of this is a warning to the world.

You listen to this. Woe to the pawns of America. You listen to this. Woe to the pawns of the World Church Council. You listen to this. Woe to the pawns of the Zionist Crusaders. You listen to this. Woe to the Jews and the Christians. We the Muslim people invite the army of America to prove their strength here in Maluku. Let us fight to the bitter end. Let us prove for the umpteenth time that the Muslim people cannot be defeated by the physical strength which is always boasted about.

The events of the second Afghanistan will take place in Maluku when you are determined to carry out your threats. Woe to America. Now you! Woe to America who is now suffering various defeats, various awesome beatings in Afghanistan. Let us meet like men on the battlefield. We will pass down to our grandchildren the spirit of battle because we have been raised up by God as His armies. And we hope Allah includes us among His servants who receive of His mercy and His servants who uphold the honor of His religion ... Until we meet on the battlefield! Allahu Akbar!!!

Wassalaamu'alaikum wr.wb!

The online environment

The online environment of the Laskar Jihad Internet project, that is, the sites with links to the Laskar Jihad website and the sites referred to on the LJAWJ website, give an indication of both the project's reach and the impact of what it presented. Links referring to the LJAWJ site considerably extended its sphere of influence, because as a result there were usually more visitors to the site and it gained in popularity in the Internet search engines, which are based on a site's link structures.[92] In the first year the FKAWJ site still had a link frame that referenced those sites that addressed the Muslims in the Moluccas and Rustam Kastor's books, as well as other Muslim and jihad websites (http://www.laskarjihad.or.id/linkframe.htm). Without comment the link frame was removed from the site in mid-2001. Nonetheless, it is interesting for us to follow these old paths and see in which circles the Laskar Jihad moved online. The link frame referenced the following sites, on each of which the webmaster commented in one or two lines:[93]

Salafy-Net	http://www.salafy.net/
Rustam Kastor	http://listen.to/Rustam-Kastor
Muslim Cyber Book	http://listen.to/mcb
Al-Buynan.net	http://www.al-bunyan.net
Listen to Ambon	http://scroll.to/ambon
Suara Ambon Online	http://www.come.to/suaraambon
MER-C	http://come.to/mer-c
Qoqaz Malaysia	http://www.qoqaz.com.my
Mujahideen	http://www.jihadtimes.com/
Lashkar-e-Taiba	http://www.dawacenter.com/
Ayoh Jihad	http://qital.tripod.com/
Tanah Jihad Indonesia	http://www.tanahjihad.net/indonesia/front.htm

These sites were very different in design. Some focused more on text, while others worked a lot with images; many used clear symbols such as Arabic characters and verses from the Koran as symbols of the fight and the jihad, and crossed swords, red image bars from which blood dripped down, a sea of flames as a border or bombs with long fuse cords as a reference to the time bomb that the Moluccas were. The first link on the FKAWJ's Jihad homepage section referenced the site of the FKAWJ's Salafy network, which, as opposed to the Laskar Jihad website, was mainly devoted to purely religious treatises. Nevertheless, the Laskar Jihad logo also appeared on the Salafy site. Right underneath was a quotation alluding to sura 2, verse 120 of the Koran: 'And never will the Jews and Christians approve of you until you follow their religion'.

The next link in the FKAWJ link frame made reference to the site http://listen.to/Rustam-Kastor, which, featuring edges in flames, made two

 Homepage Salafy Online 2000

Illustration 9. Banner of the FKAWJ's Salafy website[94]

books by Kastor available online, including the best seller *Konspirasi Politik RMS dan Kristen Menghancurkan Ummat Islam di Ambon – Maluku* and corresponding reviews. There was also a reference to Al-Bunyan.net, a site which in April 2003 was being revised, but which otherwise championed the strengthening of Muslim solidarity and reported on the jihad in East Indonesia. While I was conducting my online research the Listen to Ambon site was no longer available. Featuring bloody edges, Suara Ambon Online promised to report the experiences of the Muslims in Ambon, while MER-C was the Indonesian Medical Emergency Rescue Committee, which, among other places, also operated in Ambon and clearly took a Muslim stance. The official Qoqaz website posted news from jihad regions worldwide, as did Ayoh Jihad, which also featured various links to sites on the jihad in the Moluccas.[95]

In its own words, Tanah Jihad Indonesia (Jihad Region Indonesia) was devoted to the brothers and sisters in the Moluccas and was maintained solely by Muslims in Indonesia, but was only available until 2001. The site used verses from the Koran to champion the combatant jihad and stated that what Samuel Huntington had predicted was actually taking place.[96] The links to the online books and the Lashkar-e-Taiba were removed from the list of links as early as April 2001; there was obviously no desire to be tarred with the same brush as the jihad warriors in Kashmir.[97]

The bulk of these sites were also linked with one another. The first impression one got was that they all represented a jihad concept that corresponded with the LJAWJ: the call for an armed fight against the infidels. This strengthened the picture outsiders got of the alleged unity of the (fundamentalist) Muslims.

With regard to the websites that made reference to that of the FKAWJ,[98] we must distinguish between those which, by all appearances at least, represented a similar concept of the jihad to the Laskar Jihad, those that mentioned the FKAWJ site more or less neutrally as a source of further information, and those that were absolutely against the site. Sites featuring a link to the Laskar Jihad website included, for example, those of Indonesian Muslim organizations such as the Indonesian Muslim Students' Action Group (Kesatuan Aksi Mahasiswa Muslim Indonesia, KAMMI) in Malang and Jember, the District Board of the Muhammadiyah Youth (Pemuda Muhammadiyah) in Surabaya and the Indonesian Islamic magazine *Hidayatullah*.[99] We can suppose these institutions approved the FKAWJ website, and the same applies to the Indonesian Sharia Consultation Centre (Pusat Konsultasi Syariah), which on its online Sharia site made reference to the Internet presence of the LJAWJ, and IslamicWorld. net, which maintained a 'Jihad site for Muslim's who love Allah and Jihad', featuring links to jihad regions worldwide, such as Afghanistan, Bosnia, Palestine, Kashmir, Chechnya, Ambon and Aceh.[100]

Whereas the abovementioned sites by no means addressed only the Moluccas, there were some that devoted themselves almost exclusively to the topic, such as http://connect.to/maluku/ (21 April 2001), which referenced both the Laskar Jihad site and one that invited visitors to 'Come and Save Moslems'.[101] It called for a jihad in the Moluccas and made reference to 'The Official Website of Maluku Tragedy',[102] which, however, was discontinued in 2002–3. Once the FKAWJ site had been set up, 'Come and Save Moslems' gave up its reporting of current events. It initially posted one of the FKAWJ bulletins[103] and some FKAWJ news items from June 2000, but was then frozen.

This linear consensus was broken if Christian or Jewish sites made reference to the Laskar Jihad project. Nonetheless, Pax Christi in the Netherlands, for example, included the link without comment in its Religious Movements section.[104] The site http://www.israel.com posted the link in its directory of Islamic organizations, stating that this was a Muslim jihad organization in Indonesia that was involved in the jihad in the Moluccas and only had a few articles in English.[105] The Jewish Watch Dog (JWD) site adopted a far harsher tone: 'Jews need a watchdog and we've taken on the job. The JWD is alerting the world to the anti-Jewish/anti-Israeli propaganda on the Internet';[106] and, among others, referenced the LJAWJ site. Links to the Laskar Jihad site could, however, also be found on far more neutral territory, such as in the Moluccan section of the Australian National Library's website directory, and in the regular reports of the Information and Documentation Centre for the Moluccas in the Netherlands.[107] Other Internet projects such as the CCDA newsletter and the Masariku mailing list, Muslim contributions on the Web, for example, on Islam Net[108] and online newspapers and magazines, had no explicit link to the LJAWJ site, but did provide additional background information and reports about the Laskar Jihad, and also quoted or processed the information made available through the FKAWJ online presentations.

In October 2002 the FKAWJ announced it was disbanding. While the Yahoo! archives of the FKAWJ mailing list are still in existence and accessible, the site was removed from the Internet. All links to it suddenly led nowhere. In its last days in October 2002 the website featured a press release of 16 October 2002 in white letters on a green background. It was a comment on the disbanding of the FKAWJ and the LJAWJ: the founding council of the FKAWJ had convened from 30 September to 2 October 2002 and a special team of the founding council had met from 3 to 5 October 2002 in Yogyakarta, and both had jointly decided to disband. It was noted that the founding and the activities of the FKAWJ were based on the Koran, Sunnah and the fatwas of the ulemas of the Ahlus Sunnah wal Jama'ah. In the meantime, however, there had been various incidents that the FKAWJ could not morally accept; it had been unable and too weak to consistently introduce Sharia.[109] It was now afraid of stooping even lower morally and neglecting the mission of the Ahlus Sunnah Wal Jama'ah. The decision to disband was based on the advice of the ulemas and had nothing to do with political influence from outside or anything else. It was now asking the Indonesian government to take care of the Muslims.[110]

The question now arose of whether the discontinuance of the Laskar Jihad website would render insignificant the FKAWJ online projects and the image they propagated of an ideal (and imagined) Islamic community. For various reasons I assume that was not the case. Firstly, despite the dissolution of the organization behind it, the mailing list still existed, and even after the list's activities ceased, the number of members continued to rise for months.[111] Secondly, various sites had serious doubts as to whether the Laskar Jihad had actually disbanded and not gone underground. Press reports and those of various human rights organizations on the Laskar Jihad having relocated from the Moluccas to Papua were a clear indication of this. Thirdly, the FKAWJ online project was not an isolated project. In parts the online context remained in place, was still linked with the shadows cast by the FKAWJ and still active. And fourthly, this was a project that has, or will have, numerous parallel projects. Over the past few years many radical Islamic groups have emerged in Indonesia. The Islamist 'scene' in particular is well-known for the fact that it makes avid use of modern media, and in recent years the Internet in particular, as strategic means for its objectives. The results of the investigation of the FKAWJ online projects can provide valuable findings for the analysis of comparable cases and serve as a basis for comparison.

Summary

The FKAWJ and the Laskar Jihad presented themselves and the Moluccan conflict online by means of a mailing list and a website that was updated on a daily basis. With these they provided information about the course of the conflict and the basis of their mission in the Moluccas. The FKAWJ online project was unmistakably religious in character, and saw the Moluccan conflict as part of the struggle against the worldwide dominance of the Jews and Christians. On the one hand, the Laskar Jihad wanted to help their brothers in faith in the Moluccas in humanitarian and social matters. This was emphasized again and again in their online reports. On the other, they were out to overcome this dominance, which in the Moluccas was allegedly evident in a conspiracy between the Protestant Church and the separatist RMS movement, which was supported financially, ideologically and in terms of weapons by Europe, the United States, the UN and Christians worldwide. The Indonesian government had unfortunately proved incapable of helping the Muslims in the Moluccas against the Christian aggressors and initiators of the Moluccan conflict. On account of the close links between the RMS and the Christians and the consequent Christianization of the Moluccas, the war in the Moluccas, according to the Laskar Jihad, was both secessionist and religious in character. Images of destroyed enemy facilities, numbers of victims and maps illustrating territory that had been captured were posted online as proof of the success of the Laskar Jihad in the Moluccas. The ultimate goal was to spread Islam still further and introduce Sharia in the Moluccas and throughout the whole of Indonesia.

Given the means of communication it selected, a publicly accessible website and a readily accessible mailing list, the FKAWJ had created a high degree of openness, which, however, was severely curtailed by the strict interpretation of the liberties it offered, in particular as far as the interactive aspect was concerned. In this way, a multidirectional mailing list became a unidirectional newsletter. Initially, perhaps, the website gave the impression of being interactive, thereby allowing visitors a certain say. Readers' letters, email contact addresses, the Question of the Day and Message of the Day, online forms and fan articles (wallpaper, logo, etc.) were responsible for this. However, these were manipulated in such a way that they became a part of the uncompromising, monotone line of argumentation of the Laskar Jihad, which did not allow any negotiation of points of view. Religion and nationalism were the cornerstones of the FKAWJ identity presented online. What the FKAWJ had in mind was an undiluted unified state of Indonesia, in which the population lived according to Islamic law. Religious symbols such as faith in one God, the Sunnah, the Koran, Sharia, martyrdom and the unity of Muslims played an important role in the Internet presentations. The good relationship between the local population and the Laskar Jihad, as well as the excellent collaboration with local Muslim organizations, was repeatedly stressed.[112] Furthermore, the Laskar Jihad received declarations of solidarity from national and international bodies. So as to further legitimize their activities, the FKAWJ included fatwas pertaining to the Moluccan conflict issued by respected ulemas in the Middle East in their online presentations, as well as treatises by Muslim authorities on the jihad and related topics.

The Laskar Jihad wanted to appear credible in their reporting on the Moluccan conflict. The impression of authenticity was created first and foremost by the fact the information about the conflict was firsthand, that is, it came directly from the Laskar Jihad in the field. It was strengthened by images and audio files, printed interviews with Ja'far Umar Thalib, and eyewitness reports and scanned documents, not to mention readers' letters. They exhausted the multimedia potential the Internet offered. It must have left a strong impression on visitors, who were able to follow Thalib's speeches, read news items, view images of torched Muslims and mosques, make email contact with the people behind the website and fill out donation and registration forms online all at the same time. They were closely confronted with the ideas and expectations of the FKAWJ. However, as the principles and the authorities that determined the discourse in the FKAWJ online projects were already defined, visitors were not involved in the construction process of the images and identities presented, or exploited through readers' letters. In only this way could visitors be offered a picture of a purely Islamic identity that united all Muslims. Correspondingly, Noorhaidi Hasan (2002) argued in relation to the offline sphere that in times of crisis, in which all other identities appeared to be becoming insignificant, the FKAWJ had risen to become a central identity authority by presenting strict guidelines and a coherent picture of Islam.

There is an idealization and enlargement process underway in cyberspace. The online Laskar Jihad projects were able to create an ideal picture of an Islamic community and heighten the reach and sphere of influence of the FKAWJ, from its philosophy in general to Ja'far Umar Thalib's speeches in particular. As such, in its own opinion, the FKAWJ came a significant step closer to its goal of uniting all Muslims. The fatwas issued by the ulemas in the Middle East, through which, according to Hasan (2002), the holy war in the Moluccas had clearly become part of the international jihad movement, and which called for the participation of the Muslim community *(ummah)*, were just a part of the extensive FKAWJ online project.

Notes

1. A few examples of articles in the national and international press that provided background information on the Laskar Jihad and their leader Ja'far Umar Thalib are: BBC World News (2000); Dhume (2001); Fealy (2001); Handoko (2001); Rahmanto and Yusniar (2001); Vatikiotis (2002); Wahyuni (2000a, 2000b); and various articles in *Tempo* (20 February 2000, 23 February 2000 and 5 March 2000), *Jurnal Islam* (11–17 May 2001) and *Xpos* (no. 12, 10–16 April 2000). In an academic context, George J. Aditjondro (2000c), Noorhaidi Hasan (2002) and Kirsten Schulze (2002) were among those who commented
2. The following portrayal of the Laskar Jihad is complemented by information provided by Hasan (2002).
3. Wahhab, Muhammad ibn 'Abd al-, *Encyclopaedia Britannica 2003*, http://www.britannica.com/eb/article?eu=77848, 21 April 2003 and 13 January 2012.
4. Hasan (2002: 146n2) warns against confusing the term 'Ahlus Sunnah Wal Jama'ah' with the eponymous doctrine *ahl al-sunnah wa al-jama'ah* developed by the Nahdlatul Ulama (NU), the largest Muslim organization in Indonesia. For NU followers this doctrine simply meant Sunni Islam, which follows one of the four orthodox schools of law. According to Hasan, the NU

leader, Hasyim Muzadi, had questioned the use of this term by the Laskar Jihad and emphasized that the NU doctrine should not be confused with that of the Laskar Jihad.

5. There was more substance to this suspicion after Suharto's fall. According to Adam Schwarz (1999: 347–48), under Habibie, the interim president after Suharto, rumours increasingly spread of a Christian-Zionist putsch or a demonic Communist alliance, which intended seriously harming the largest Muslim country on earth.

6. Organizational structure of the FKAWJ as of May 2001 (http://64.177.60.231/fkawj/struktur.htm, 19 September 2001).

7. Followers of the teachings of Salafy or Salafi are followers of a form of Islam that is geared to the way of life of the Prophet and his companions.

8. FKAWJ and LJAWJ are used almost synonymously in connection with the Moluccan conflict, though of course outside the Moluccas there is far more behind the FKAWJ than the LJAWJ.

9. Hasan (2002) classifies the Laskar Jihad as a paramilitary civil group.

10. In this chapter, dates in parentheses (and those not in parentheses in the footnotes) with no mention of an Internet address refer to articles on the FKAWJ mailing list written or posted on the list on that day. If the date is after the list was discontinued on 8 October 2001, it refers to an article from that particular day on the FKAWJ website. Many of the FKAWJ Internet posts appeared both on its mailing list and website. Under normal circumstances I will refer to one of the two sources only.

11. For example, on 'The Official Website of Maluku Tragedy' (http://www.maluku.org, February 2000) and the website of the magazine *Hidayatullah* (http://www.hidayatullah.com/maluku.htm, February 2000).

12. Of these 1,447 members, 321 provided personal information in their Yahoo! profile. Fifty (16 per cent) of them had stated their real (?) name, 51 (16 per cent) their place of residence or the country, 43 (13 per cent) their age, 47 (15 per cent) their civil status, 311 (97 per cent) their sex, 41 (13 per cent) their profession and 53 (17 per cent) other information about hobbies, their own websites and email, other interests and 'cool links'. Of the 51 who stated their place of residence, 36 (71 per cent) lived in Indonesia. In terms of the age structure, the majority (80 per cent) was between 23 and 33, and as such representative of the majority of Internet users worldwide. Of the 47 who listed their civil status, roughly half were married. Of the 311 who listed their sex, 94 per cent were male. Approximately a quarter of the 41 who provided information about what they did were students, approximately a third worked in information technology and about an eighth worked in teaching.

13. These would have been in danger in mailing lists and news groups on which all members could post: 'Responses will be received from, recalling Francis Robinson's phrase, "any Ahmad, Mahmud or Muhammad" on the Internet and this represents a further decline in the authority of the ulama' (Mandaville 2001: 168).

14. In the LJAWJ reports the Laskar Jihad were also often referred to by the term 'mujahideen', which generally means warriors who defend their religion, Islam. Of course, other jihad warriors in the Moluccas also fell into this category, both local and from elsewhere.

15. For the original of the description, see Illustration 4.

16. The arrival of the Laskar Jihad was indeed of help to the Muslims, and the Christians had to fight for their survival.

17. Yet another indication that in connection with the Moluccan mission of the FKAWJ and LJAWJ, there was scarcely any difference between the terms 'LJAWJ', which dominated the website header and was the name of the Yahoo! group, and 'FKAWJ', which appeared in front of the individual posts, and that they were actually used synonymously.

18. Over the course of time the physical and Internet addresses changed. Likewise, in September the email address of the group's newsletter and mailing list changed from berita-laskar-jihad@egroups.com to laskarjihad@egroups.com and the website's address from http://laskarjihad.cjb.net to http://www.laskarjihad.or.id (1 September 2000).

19. 'Ulasan Strategi Kristenisasi di Dunia' (2 November 2000), 'Dunia Kristen Ingin Intervensi Maluku' (4 November 2000), 'Muslimin Kompleks STAIN Diteror Kristen' (9 November 2000) and 'Laskar Jihad Tambah Anggota di Ambon' (14 November 2000).

20. See, for example, the articles 'Around 600 RMS Christians have already moved to the Netherlands' (Sekitar 600 Kristen RMS Telah Pindah ke Belanda, 6 September 2000) and 'RMS youths almost burn down two mosques in the Netherlands' (Dua Masjid di Belanda Nyaris Dibakar Pemuda RMS, 9 November 2000).

21. 'Semoga Allah membalas kebaikan Anda dengan pahala yang berlipat ganda Amiin' (24 September 2000).

22. 'Perjuangan Membela Muslimin Maluku' (http://www.yahoo.com/group/laskarjihad/files).

23. With regard to its look, but primarily to the programming behind it, in May 2002 the LJAWJ website was restructured, though as far as the menu structure was concerned it in principle remained the same. The new site was never really completed; even at the very end not all the image and audio files had been integrated that had long since been available via the old website. Unless otherwise stated, from now on I refer to the 'old' website, which was still accessible via the 'new' site. In the case of content-related references, the date indicates which of the versions is meant.

24. Translation by Muhammad Asad, available at http://www.islamicity.com/quransearch/ (7 October 2011).

25. All MHI reports are archived here.

26. Islamic religious scholar (ulama in Arabic).

27. Of the eighty donors (of in total Rp 81,649,642) announced online in a list for the year 2000, sixty-one were from Indonesia, eight from Japan, five from Australia, five from Malaysia and one from Europe (http://www.laskarjihad.or.id/bantu/donatur2000.htm, 14 November 2001). For the year 2001 there were eighty-eight names (who donated a total of Rp 38,582,696), of which seventy-three gave Indonesia as their home, eight Japan, two the United States, two Singapore and one each Korea, Kuwait and France (http://www.laskarjihad.or.id/bantu/donatur2001.htm, 22 October 2002). According to Ayip Syafruddin, the FKAWJ received financial support from various countries, including Saudi Arabia and the United States. Such support took the form of donations from individuals, not organizations. Laskar Jihad members abroad and the Internet were very helpful in this respect. The financial support from abroad,

however, only covered approximately 10 per cent of the FKAWJ's spending (*Republika,* 10 November 2001, forwarded the same day to the MML). In October 2002, Rp 8,880 was the equivalent of one euro.

28. As many articles appeared on both the website and the mailing list, unless otherwise explicitly stated the following chapters refer to the Laskar Jihad Internet project itself and not exclusively to one of the two modes of presentation.

29. Reference was made here to a daily newspaper in Surabaya, *Surya,* dated 7 February 2000.

30. The FKAWJ and the LJAWJ used the terms 'RMS' and 'Christians' practically synonymously. They did not distinguish between Christians who actually sympathized with the RMS and those who did not. The Churches of the Moluccas and the Dutch government issued statements in which they officially distanced themselves from the RMS and the FKM, which were clearly not recognized by the Laskar Jihad.

31. 'Kesaksian Korban Kekejaman Kaum Kafir di Maluku' (14 February 2002). The eyewitnesses' statements were taken by the FKAWJ from Kastor (2000c).

32. Here, too, allusions to the communist putsch of 30 September 1965 in Indonesia and the PKI behind it (see, e.g., Hefner 2000a: 16) were made at regular intervals. According to the FKAWJ, then, as now, the Muslims were the target, and were thus forced to declare holy war on the rebels (see, e.g., 16 September 2000; 29 January 2001; 8 July 2001).

33. Interview with *The Jakarta Post,* 15 May 2000.

34. An article dated 5 August 2000 reported on how the Ambonese Muslim population was gradually moving away from polytheism *(syirik)* and the associated customs and was professing the oneness of God *(tawhid).* The fact that the Muslims no longer took amulets, symbols, and objects to which certain powers were attributed with them into battle against the Christians, but rather turned to the greatness of Allah, as the Prophet had taught, was noted in a positive light.

35. According to Hasan (2002), as supporters of a Wahhabi form of Islam, the Laskar Jihad preferred to wear traditional clothing, that is, long white shirts, white trousers and corresponding headgear, and to grow their beards.

36. Ja'far Umar Thalib also emphasized this at a DDII press conference on 18 July 2000 in Jakarta. There could be no obliteration of the Christians, because Sharia forbade killing women and children (19 July 2000).

37. The newspaper in fact continued to be published.

38. According to a report by the CCDA (3 January 2001), Ja'far Umar Thalib had visited Sorong in Papua as early as the beginning of 2001. As of mid-2002 there were increasing indications that despite having allegedly disbanded in October 2002, the Laskar Jihad were becoming more and more active in Papua. This was reported, for example, by the Indonesian Human Rights Committee (MML, 2 June 2002), the Barnabas Fund, which referenced reports by human rights groups in Papua (MML, 11 March 2003), Watch Indonesia in its Human Rights Report (MML, 18 April 2003) and the *South China Morning Post* of 19 February 2003 (MML, 20 February 2003).

39. Facts, Dates and Analyses Referring to the Conspiracy Policy of the RMS and Christians with Regard to the Destruction of the Islamic Community in Ambon – Moluccas, published by Wihdah Press in Yogyakarta in 2000. Two other books by Kastor were also available online: *Suara Maluku Membantah, Rus-*

tam Kastor Menjawab (translated as Suara Maluku Protests, Rustam Kastor Answers) at http://listen.to/Rustam-Kastor and *Damai Sekarang atau Perang Berlanjut* (translated as Peace Now or Permanent War) in the Ambon section of Islam Net Indonesia (http://media.isnet.org/ambon/Kastor/index.html).

40. Proof of intentions to this end were provided, for example, by the pressure being exerted on the Indonesian government by the U.S. embassy in Jakarta to stop the violence in the Moluccas and expel certain extremists from the Moluccas (15 July 2000), the visit by the U.S. Consulate-General, Robert S. Pollard, to the Moluccas (29 June 2001) and the presence of three thousand U.S. troops in the southern Philippines who were allegedly waiting to be transferred to the Moluccas (26 May 2002).

41. 'Kami siap membantai Pasukan Amerika!!! ... Amerika tak pernah menang, kecuali di film Rambo!'

42. The fear of the possible Christianization of Indonesia has a long history; see, for example, Becker (1996: 135–37); Boland (1971: 225–31); Djaelani (1999); Feillard (2000a, 2000b); Hefner (2000a: 107); Rasjidi (1976); Schuhmann (1981: 60); Wawer (1974: 218–19); and http://www.laskarjihad.or.id/artikel/fakta-krist.htm (5 August 2001). According to the Laskar Jihad, confirmation of this looming Christianization was provided in speeches by the former general and Catholic Theo Syafei in 1998, in which he emphasized the significance of the Christian community in the history and development of Indonesia and thereby, according to the FKAWJ, slandered the Islamic community. Entitled 'Theo Syafei's Slander' (*Hujatan Theo Syafei*), the original of the speeches could be downloaded from the newly structured FKAWJ website. For responses to Syafei's speeches by other Muslim organizations, see Kees van Dijk (2001: 380–81); Hasan (2002: 161); and Sumargono (2000).

43. See, for example, the press statement of October 2000 on the bloodbath carried out by the Zionist Israeli soldiers on the Muslims in Palestine (http://www.laskarjihad.or.id/press/press-fkawj-palestine.htm, 24 October 2002).

44. Post from the year 2000 (http://www.laskarjihad.or.id/english/article/ljtroopers.htm, 22 October 2002).

45. New International Version, http://www.biblegateway.com/versions/New-International-Version-NIV-Bible/ (13 January 2012).

46. Answer to a reader's letter of 18 March 2001 (http://www.laskarjihad.or.id/english/qa/eqa0103/eqa010323.htm, 24 October 2002).

47. The Yongab was made up of a unit each from the Navy, the Special Forces Command Unit (Komando Pasukan Khusus, Kopassus) and the Air Force.

48. 'Kronologis Kebrutalan Batalyon Gabungan di Ambon' (23 January 2001).

49. The CCDA reported that according to the MUI, ten Muslims died (23 January 2001).

50. Christian cyberactors likewise addressed the Hotel Wijaya II case. According to CCDA reports, on 21 January 2001, during clashes between Muslims and the military, the Muslim attackers increasingly encircled the naval base and the Yongab. The attackers' central command was in the Hotel Wijaya II nearby, from which a shot at Yongab soldiers had allegedly also been fired. In a raid on the hotel early in the morning of 22 January 2001, the Yongab had encountered a number of well-armed military and policemen, including three very high-ranking police officers and one military officer. Forty people, among them twenty-nine military and policemen, were arrested. The incident was

a huge scandal, and two teams from Jakarta were sent to investigate it. Like I Made Yasa, however, the supreme commander of the Indonesian military, General Widodo, ascertained that the military units had behaved absolutely correctly (CCDA, 22–23 January 2001; 27 January 2001).

51. It is unclear whether this actually relates to the truth. What is certain is that the Laskar Jihad were primarily concerned with saving face – whether they had indeed killed the military personnel or not.

52. The Laskar Jihad became a deciding factor in the conflict, which became clear, among others, after, in September 2000, Ja'far Umar Thalib had been invited by the governor of the Moluccas to a meeting in which he asked him to ensure that the Laskar Jihad worked together with authorities in the civil state of emergency to find a solution to the conflict (16 September 2000).

53. According to a Laskar Jihad report, it was the FSUIM itself that had invited the vice president to Ambon (2 June 2002). In connection with the Malino II agreements, the FSUIM was also known as 'the Group of Eleven' (*Kelompok Sebelas*), which opposed the peace negotiations. One reason more for the Christians to have very mixed feelings about Hamzah Haz's visit (see also 10 February 2002).

54. 'Saya tidak ingin mendengar lagi umat Islam yang dibantai di kemudian hari' (11 June 2002).

55. See in this context a press statement by Rustam Kastor, as chairman of the FPKM (19 January 2001; 25 January 2001; http://www.laskarjihad.or.id/press/fpkm-perkrms.htm, 14 November 2001).

56. 'Perang Untuk Menyelesaikan Perang' (29 October 2001). Accordingly, Putuhena and Tawainella (2001) wrote a book entitled *Perang untuk Damai di Maluku* (War for peace in the Moluccas).

57. These explanations and treatises were occasionally posted on the mailing list (e.g., on 18 June 2001).

58. Post from the year 2000 (http://www.laskarjihad.or.id/risalah/binbazz1.htm, 14 November 2001).

59. Translation by Muhammad Asad, available at http://www.islamicity.com/quransearch/ (7 October 2011). In his explanations bin Baz makes no reference to 'reconciliatory' verses such as 2:256, 49:13, and 5:48, which address religious freedom, humanity itself and the difference between these peoples as God's will.

60. Interestingly, bin Baz had a website of his own at http://www.ibnbaz.org.sa/ or http://www.binbaz.org.sa/ (accessed on 24 March 2003; 13 January 2012).

61. There also used to be a website on Muqbil bin Hadi Al-Wadi'i (http://www.sunna.com.ye/), to which the Bengali Islam site – 'An invitation to Islam in the Bengali language' – made reference in the link section (http://www.banglaislam.com/links.htm, 14 March 2003).

62. See also Messick (1996). Messick's investigations are based on the radio muftis in Yemen and the change in the reach of their personal fatwas, which through the medium were suddenly acquiring a public rather than private character.

63. This has repeatedly become clear in this and previous chapters. Furthermore, on 8 August 2001, for example, Thalib visited Hamzah Haz to discuss the Moluccan conflict and the RMS problem with him (9 August 2001), and Hamzah Haz gave the opening speech on the occasion of the FKAWJ National Labour Conference (Musyawarah Kerja Nasional, Mukernas) on 13 May 2002.

64. In an interview with the Indonesian magazine *Forum* (no. 7, 14 May 2001), Ja'far Umar Thalib stated that the MUI Board in the Moluccas had already made this decision on 4 January 2001. At a large religious meeting on 8 January in the Al-Fatah Mosque, the decision was then read out and accepted by the Muslim citizens.

65. On 3 June 2001 the FKAWJ posted a detailed treatise on the principles of stoning in the Koran and the Hadith entitled, 'Is It True that the Punishment of Stoning Has Been Debated Ever Since the Age of Umar bin Khattab?' (*Benarkah Hukum Rajam Telah Diperdebatkan Sejak Zaman Umar bin Khattab?*).

66. In the 2 May 2001 edition of the Indonesian magazine *Gatra*, Mohammad, Bakri and Rahman (2001) reported on the case of stoning, relying primarily on statements by Thalib at a press conference organized by the Laskar Jihad (Media Indonesia Online, 10 May 2001). According to Mohammad, Bakri and Rahman (2001), several leading representatives of Islam in Indonesia condemned this approach. Other articles about stoning and Sharia in general were to be found, for example, in the Indonesian magazine *Tempo* (16 May 2001; 20 May 2001), *FORUM KEADILAN* (no. 7, 20 May 2001) and *Jurnal Islam* (no. 42, 11–17 May 2001).

67. 'Pernyataan Bersama Umat Islam Ambon' (http://www.laskarjihad.or.id/press/images/pro-rajam1.htm to pro-rajam3.htm, 18 May 2001).

68. The FKAWJ itself complained primarily about the illegal character of the arrest, as at the time it was made the requisite documents had not yet been available (8 May 2001).

69. 'Menang atau Syahid' (Question of the Day, 27 July 2001).

70. 'Seseorang yang masuk surga tidak menginginkan kembali ke dunia ..., kecuali orang yang mati syahid, ia mengharapkan kembali ke dunia kemudian terbunuh sebanyak sepuluh kali, karena kemuliaan yang didapatinya (di dalam surga)' (Hadis disepakati Bukhari Muslim) (25 August 2000).

71. 'Perjalanan Seorang Mujahid: Syahidnya Ibnu Hajar' (25 October 2000) and 'Keteguhan Hati Mujahid Muda' (4 January 2001).

72. Translation by Muhammad Asad, available at http://www.islamicity.com/quransearch/ (7 October 2011).

73. The Christians were said to be spreading, for example, rumours that the Laskar Jihad were making life difficult for the Muslims in the Moluccas and living at their expense, whereas in fact the opposite was the case (25 August 2000; see also http://www.laskarjihad.or.id/english/article/ljarrival.htm, 22 October 2002; http://www.laskarjihad.or.id/about/kegiatan.htm, 24 October 2002).

74. Stones were also thrown at the house of the MUI secretary Malik Selang. See also CCDA (30 April 2001) and Böhm (2001).

75. The scanned letter was available at http://www.laskarjihad.or.id/images/reko_ddii.jpg (14 November 2001).

76. In the Tanya Jawab section of the website, frequently asked questions were answered and there was an index of readers' letters and the Question of the Day.

77. Download section of the website: http://www.laskarjihad.or.id/downloadframe.htm (26 January 2001). In some cases the audio files were also sent to the members of the LJAWJ Yahoo! group by email, or these were told in an email to download them from the website (e.g., 31 October 2000).

79. See in this context the post by Reza Indragiri Amriel, a lecturer at one of Indonesia's State Islamic Institutes (Institut Agama Negeri Islam, IAIN), on 16 April 2001.
80. See, for example, *The Washington Times* (13 December 2001), the BBC (12 December 2001) and *Asia Times Online* (18 December 2001).
81. It should be noted, however, that anti-Americanism in Indonesia is generally widespread, though it of course is not always this extreme (see, e.g., Hefner 2000a: 104).
82. According to the FKAWJ, the arrest was part of a conspiracy engineered by the United States that aimed at doing away with all Islamic movements in Indonesia. All the accusations made against Thalib, that he was provocative and in his speeches had insulted the president, were unfounded, as the only thing the Laskar Jihad were interested in was fighting separatism (in other words, the RMS), which was in Indonesia's national interest. For this reason the arrest was totally counterproductive (http://www.laskarjihad.or.id/english/press/fkawj-04may2002.htm, 23 May 2002).
83. 'Sampai jumpa di medan tempur. Allahu Akbar.'
84. Translation by Jeff Hammond (International Friends of Compassion, IFC), which was disseminated by, among others, Masariku on 21 May 2002. I checked the translation against the original.
85. In the original there was no information given about the suras and verses from the Koran; this was added by the translator.
86. For reasons of comprehension the IFC translation of the last sentence was amended slightly.
87. Saleh Latuconsina himself is a Muslim. Until the autumn of 2002 he was governor of the Moluccas and also the person responsible for the civil state of emergency.
88. In a slightly amended form, this paragraph was taken from the BBC translation (CCDA, 18 May 2002), as it appeared in the Indonesian original, but not in the IFC translation.
89. I myself translated the last sentence from the Indonesian.
90. This was an allusion to government delegations, fact-finding teams and peace initiatives.
91. An allusion to the Hotel Wijaya II case and similar raids.
92. Unless otherwise stated, the websites mentioned here were still available in early 2003.
93. None of these websites was available any more by January 2012.
94. After the FKAWJ had gone online the Salafy site was hardly updated at all. However, after the FKAWJ was disbanded, the site was active again and changed its layout. The Laskar Jihad logo was removed, as was the above-mentioned quotation from the Koran.
95. Ayoh Jihad was no longer available from April 2003 at the latest.
96. In 1993, military strategist and advisor to the U.S. government Samuel Huntington published an essay, and in 1996 a book entitled *The Clash of Civilizations,* in which he outlined his ideas with regard to the world order following the end of the Cold War. In his opinion, in the next century cultural and religious convictions would determine global policy. One of his main points was that Islam was willing to go as far as bloodshed and, in the era that had just begun, embodied the West's enemy.
97. Neither site was available any longer from April 2003 at the latest.

98. Unfortunately the link search of search engines such as Google did not produce any particularly reliable results, as they checked similarities between sites rather than an actual link. For this reason, search results had to be checked for actual links. Apart from that, further Internet research was indispensable for gaining an idea of the online environment of the FKAWJ site.

99. http://kammimalang.tripod.com/utama.html, accessed on 20 January 2003; http://www.kammi-jember.org/links.htm, 29 January 2003; http://www.pemuda-muhammadiyah.com/link.htm, 29 January 2003; and http://www.hidayatullah.com/info/link.htm, 28 February 2003.

100. http://www.syariahonline.com/index.htm, 14 March 2001, and http://www.islamic-world.net/youth/jihadambon&aceh.htm, 20 January 2003.

101. http://www.geocities.com/nur_zayani/c_index.html (no longer available in 2012).

102. http://www.malu.ku.org/ (no longer available in 2012).

103. http://www.geocities.com/nur_zayani/buletin1.html (no longer available in 2012).

104. http://www.paxchristi.nl/indonesialinks.html, 14 March 2002.

105. http://www.israel.com/directory/People_of_the_Book/Islam/Organizations, 17 March 2003.

106. http://www.mish-mash.ca/jwd-na_isps.html, 21 June 2002 (no longer available in 2003).

107. http://www.nla.gov.au/asian/indo/indsites.html, 20 January 2003, and http://www.midc.nl or http://www.infomaluku.net (no longer available by 2012).

108. http://media.isnet.org.

109. According to Ja'far Umar Thalib, many members had become too involved in the political affairs of certain Muslims; they had also posed for photos and had given interviews to female journalists (http://www.geocities.com/soija2002/laksamana181002.htm, 20 October 2002).

110. According to other information on the Internet, Thalib was again contenting himself with running the Community of the Ihya'us Sunnah Islamic Boarding School (http://www.geocities.com/soija2002/laksamana181002.htm, 20 October 2002).

111. It was of course highly probable that there were some among the subscribers who were more interested in the matter itself than agreeing with the philosophy of the Laskar Jihad, as was the case, for example, with myself. Unfortunately, however, the FKAWJ did not conduct statistical surveys of membership of the mailing list (personal email from the FKAWJ webmaster, 7 November 2002). In this context I can only make reference to endnote 12 (this chapter).

112. There are good grounds for suspecting that this was also meant to hide the fact that there were disagreements as far as the relationship between the Laskar Jihad as outsiders and the local population in the Moluccas was concerned.

7

Textual and Visual Argumentation in Moluccan Cyberspace

In portrayals of Moluccan cyberspace there is a predominance of certain themes in the conflict, for which Christian and Muslim cyberactors presented different arguments. To be convincing and appear authentic, they resorted to typical patterns for the presentation and conduct of religious, ideological and ethnic conflicts offline in the structure of their argumentation, and they used the potential of the Internet to integrate a wide range of sources and visually underpin their points of view and arguments.[1]

Patterns of integration and exclusion in the Moluccan cyberdiscourse

> In war you must hate somebody or love somebody, you must have a position or you cannot stand what goes on.
> Susan D. Moeller, *Shooting War*

In a conflict or war fought between two parties, all those involved have to have a position, that is, they must support one of the two sides. Depending on the scale and scope of the conflict, and what type it is, this leads to a dichotomy in society and the breakdown of the participants' world – be it their village, region, country, the entire world or other social categories – into 'us' and 'them'. The others are usually denounced and are seen as evil, cruel and inhumane, whereas the 'we group' is regarded as humane, just and fair. In the Moluccan conflict this dichotomy was also underpinned by the use of religious and historical symbols.

Authenticity

Whether the parties to the conflict are portraying themselves, describing the conflict or denouncing their opponents, they at all times attempt to be authentic, that is, credible and 'genuine', so as to convince their members and their audience of their position. With regard to the reports and portrayals of the Moluccan cyberactors, the greatest proof of authenticity was firsthand information, which reached the homes of the list subscribers and website visitors from the scene of the action, from the battlefield, as it were. Unlike, for example, the national and international press, there were no third parties to change or even 'falsify' this information. The Moluccan cyberactors underscored this authentic impression through eyewitness reports and accounts of the fate of individuals. Furthermore, visual arguments relating to the consequences of the violent conflict were an important tool in providing authenticity.

Photographs in particular played a significant role in the presentations of the conflict and the impact they had. Siegfried Frey (1999) wrote about the power of images and the influence on the observer of visualization in the media. Images are classified as far closer to reality than texts, and thus strengthen the authenticity of the reporting (see also, e.g., Butler 1995: 118–23) or, as one MML member remarked, 'ONE PHOTO SPEAKS MORE THAN A THOUSAND WORDS!' (12 February 2001). These seemingly authentic representations veil the high degree of constructedness and the strong dependence on context of the interpretations of the images (Devereaux 1995: 1). According to Susan D. Moeller (1989: 9), war photography has never been objective. In a conflict, each side shows just part of the reality, that is, the images that underscore their argumentation and promote their cause. The images can serve to arouse emotions and give observers the impression that they are actually involved in the conflict and the suffering of the people portrayed (see, e.g., Carruthers 2000: 194; Hudson and Stanier 1998: 315; Moeller 1989: 4). Pictures and films such as these dominate the collective image of a war (Hüppauf 1995: 99) and construct the reality of the conflict for the observer. In connection with TV news, Peter Michael Spangenberg (2001: 219) speaks of an insurmountable belief in the reality of TV images, which has caused reality to become standardized. The counterinsurgency expert Richard Clutterbuck even maintained that in a conflict the camera was a weapon anyone could use (Carruthers 2000: 194).[2]

The Moluccan cyberactors primarily showed images of the situation on their side of the conflict, mainly of victims, refugees and refugee camps, destroyed houses and religious buildings, and graffiti, but in some cases also of attacks by the enemy and of their weapons, and, on the side of the Christians, also of joint religious services and evacuation missions. The images of the wounded and dead during the first few months, when for the most part traditional weapons such as machetes and bows and arrows were in use, were particularly gruesome. Masariku and the FKAWJ mostly used just a few words or lines to comment on the individual images. One seldom knew who took them, or when and under what circumstances.[3] Thus, there was a very high danger of the observer being manipulated. For the Laskar Jihad, their visual arguments were proof of their achievements in the struggle against the threat of Christianization in the Moluccas (territorial conquests, images of destroyed Christian buildings, etc.) and a demonstration of the inhumanity and the power of their enemies (see, e.g., FKAWJ, 12 November 2000; 3–4 December 2000). For Masariku, images and videos served as campaign material they intended to disseminate via the Masariku network and the mailing list to drum up financial, moral and legal support worldwide and to deliver proof of the suffering of their brothers in faith in the Moluccas, the brutality of radical Muslims and the involvement of the military (see in particular the MML posts of 17 October 1999; 21 October 1999; 27 January 2000). Subscribers and governmental, nongovernmental and Christian organizations worldwide took notice of the services offered by Masariku and had video recordings of the conflict sent to them; in this way the images made it to various regions of Indonesia, Europe and the United States. The recipients used the images in their own campaigns and disseminated them even farther.

In the case of Masariku, attempts were made to move its public awareness work forward by means of the images. When, for example, the Masariku team in Ambon posted on the list a picture of the city after the bomb attack on 3 March 2002, a list member noticed a person in the photo dressed in camouflage climbing over a wall to get away from the scene of the incident. The member put a circle around the person, posted the picture on the list again on 21 April 2002 and asked the photographers if it could not be enlarged, as this person might have been able to provide information about the culprits (Illustration 10).

Thanks to the achievements of computer technology, the cyberactors also provided visual arguments of a different kind: scanned documents,

Illustration 10. Masariku awareness work (MML, 21 April 2002)

signatures and sketches from the scenes of the action, through which the Internet user became even more involved in events occurring at the local level. Masariku and, to a far lesser extent, the CCDA scanned, for example, letters and faxes on various occasions from the Churches in the Moluccas and posted them on their list so as to extend their reach and give them greater impact. On 16 July 2000, for instance, an SOS letter from the TPG was posted on the MML that was addressed to the United Nations, friendly governments, international human rights organizations, the Pope, church leaders worldwide and the International Red Cross. Attached was a sketch of a map of the village of Passo, on which arrows and lines indicated from where exactly the Muslims had attacked which parts of the village. All this was accompanied by the poster's call to forward the letter to all those who were worried about the ever more menacing situation of the Christians in the Moluccas. In another case the pages of a diary that had been smuggled from Lata-Lata, a Christian village on the island of Bacan, North Moluccas, were photographed. In it one of the inhabitants of the village described how in February 2000 thousands of jihad warriors had attacked the village and its inhabitants and forced them to convert to Islam (MML, 23 March 2001). For the Masariku team this diary was an important piece of evidence and had to be handled carefully (MML, 17 March 2001).

On the Muslim side, too, important information was scanned and made accessible to visitors to the FKAWJ sites. This included the declaration by various Muslim organizations and figures regarding the stoning case in the Moluccas, a declaration about the recognition of a unitary Indonesian state, a letter of recommendation from the DDII for the LJAWJ mission and the original fatwa issued by Sheikh Muqbil bin Hadi Al-Wadi'i for the jihad in the Moluccas. In each case the primary objective was to present the original signatures and, with regard to the last case, give the fatwa more weight by providing the handwritten Arabic original as well. As opposed to the FKAWJ, the Masariku team in Ambon from time to time attempted to record peace efforts and anything that could unite Christian and Muslim Moluccans, in written posts as well as visually. By way of example, photos of the wonderful countryside on the island of Ambon, the beaches and the sea (MML, 5 October 2001), pictures of Christian-Muslim reconciliation events and processions through Ambon City (e.g., in February 2002) and drawings of Ambonese children who longed for nothing more than peace and to be able to play with their old friends again, regardless of what religion they were (MML, 24 July 2002), were among those disseminated via the list.

Dichotomization

Differentiation from others is a prerequisite for the emergence of a collective identity. Only through this differentiation can one's own identity be successfully explicated, which in a conflict situation is particularly exigent.

Here, clear positions need to be adopted, and only by showing solidarity with and identifying with one's own side can victory be achieved over the others. This very fact, however, intensifies and prolongs the conflict. In some circumstances, fabricated differences are made primordial and essential, and violent conflict the only possibility at all of communicating with the enemy. In the case of the Moluccas, these mechanisms are transported from the local level into cyberspace by the cyberactors' reporting.

After the outbreak of the Moluccan conflict, a dichotomy along religious lines emerged in Moluccan society. Over the course of time, various terms became established to classify and differentiate between the Christians and the Muslims, which were just as much adopted by the Moluccan cyberactors as by the local population. According to Susan Zickmund (1997: 192), such labels are not only pejorative in character, but also an expression of essential identities. In the Moluccan conflict the two sides were associated with specific colours. Red was the colour of the Christians (*kelompok merah,* red group), green or white that of the Muslims, though white predominated (*kelompok putih,* white group). In attacks, the individual warriors frequently identified themselves by means of corresponding headbands. According to Nils Bubandt (2001: 238), in a global Muslim orthodoxy white indicates prayer, purity, martyrdom and death, while in many Moluccan communities red stands for war and magic and as such is a symbol of something autochthonous and warlike. Red is also associated with Megawati's secular party PDI-P, the Moluccan section of which the FKAWJ regarded as a Christian party. Green symbolizes Islamic parties such as the PPP (Partai Persatuan Pembangunan, United Development Party) and the PBB (Partai Bulan Bintang, Crescent and Star Party), white the Islam of the Middle East (Klinken 2001: 20).[4]

The parties in the conflict were also referred to by two boy's names, Obet and Acang. After the first few weeks of the conflict the national TV channel broadcast a clip about two Ambonese boys that was intended to promote harmonization. Robert and Hassan, the names of the two boys of different faiths, became the nicknames Obet and Acang.[5] In the space of just a few months, Obet (for the Christians) and Acang (for the Muslims) emerged as (self-)representative names for both groups.[6] This achieved the exact opposite of what was actually intended. For the FKAWJ the Acang were the local Muslim warriors, as opposed to the Laskar Jihad from elsewhere (FKAWJ, 27 November 2000). Otherwise, both sides used these colour and name labels for all Muslims and all Christians without differentiating between them. Everybody knew who was meant when there was any mention of *pasukan putih* and *pasukan merah,* the white and the red warriors, or Acang and Obet.

Those Christian actors represented in cyberspace, however, were also intent on a more neutral depiction, thereby attempting to break out of the dichotomy in Moluccan society. These efforts involved, for example, referring to attackers as a group of troublemakers (*kelompok perusuh*) or 'snipers', without assigning them to any particular religion. Whereas in the case of the Moluccas the FKAWJ put all Christians in one (RMS) basket – in one article only the Catholics were credited with being opposed to the FKM movement (10 March 2001) – the CCDA and Masariku saw the Muslims in a more differentiated way. Their criticism was primarily levelled at the invaders and agitators from elsewhere, in particular the Laskar Jihad, as well as local organizations and individuals with close ties to them.[7] According to one of the founders of Masariku (28 January 2000), the elite from the worlds of politics, the military and business were exploiting religion and intensifying the conflict with ideological issues such as those of the RMS. The Laskar Jihad and their allies were radical Muslims intent on spreading terror and were not representative of the Muslim population of the Moluccas. Over the course of time the term 'terror' appeared more and more frequently on the MML, an expression of their perception that it was just a small group of people that was provoking and terrorizing the Moluccan population. Nonetheless, in descriptions of Muslim attacks Masariku often referred without differentiation to 'the white group' (*kelompok putih*), 'the Muslim group' (*kelompok Muslim*), 'the Muslim side' (*pihak Muslim*), 'the Muslim masses' (*massa Muslim*) and 'the white horde' (*gerombolan putih*), who during attacks wore white or green headbands or were clothed in white garments.

For the FKAWJ and its Laskar Jihad, all Christians were RMS supporters; this is why they were referred to as the 'Christian RMS masses' (*massa Nasrani RMS*) or as 'RMS Christians' (*kristen RMS*). The Laskar Jihad frequently used far clearer language, to lend expression to their hate of the RMS Christians. They referred to them as bugs (*kutu busuk*) who were impure because they ate pork and dogs and had dirty hands (*tangan-tangan najis* or *tangan-tangan kotor*). In the eyes of the LJAWJ, the RMS Christians were not actually humans, which was why on occasion the Indonesian counting word for animals (*ekor*) was used for their dead and wounded. When naming the opponent, the emphasis was always placed on their religion, such that the Christian warriors, for example, were referred to as the 'red Christian warriors' (*pasukan merah Nasrani*), instead of just *pasukan merah*. In other articles they differentiated between the 'jihad warriors' (*pasukan Jihad*) and the 'troop of infidels' (*pasukan Kafir*), with Christian and infidel amounting to one and the same thing for the FKAWJ, which often mentioned them both in the same breath: 'the Christian infidels' (*kafir Kristen*). Naturally, the accusation of infidel was extremely provocative for the very devout Ambonese Christians. For the Laskar Jihad, the conflict in the Moluccas was both a war of secession and a religious war (*perang agama*), terminology that the Christians tried to avoid.[8] The FKAWJ spoke of an international Christian conspiracy, the objective of which was a worldwide crusade (*perang salib*). Through the use of religious terminology, the identities involved in the conflict were essentialized and the associated value systems reified,[9] which, according to Gerd Baumann (1999: 71) essentialized the conflict itself.

All the parties in Moluccan cyberspace attempted to portray the guilty ones – be they the RMS Christians or the Laskar Jihad and their allies – as evil, cruel and inhuman and set them apart from their own group. They accused their enemies of murdering in a sadistic, barbaric way, cruelly torturing and mutilating their victims, treating prisoners in a humiliating way and raping women. They even claimed people were being burned and buried alive. Neither side shied away from detailed descriptions and photographs of the condition the dead and wounded were in. There was talk of massacres and bloodbaths, of crimes against humanity. Each side accused the other of being responsible for there being no end to the conflict, or for having started it. For the FKAWJ and Masariku in particular it was clear that their own people would only ever defend, but never attack, unless in revenge for an attack by their opponent. Both sides were sure that the other wanted them eliminated in order to rule the Moluccas and, ultimately, the whole of Indonesia. The government, the security forces and the press were accused of taking the side of 'the others'. On the one hand, both the Christians and the Muslims often maintained that the other side was better armed, and as such superior, while on the other, both sides claimed to know of internal conflicts in the ranks of the other in order to create the impression of a weakened opponent and to make the opponent believe it, too.

Both sides highlighted the fact that the opponent did not stop at killing women and children, even deploying them to fight on the front lines.[10] Masariku made strategic use of images of these Christian child warriors in its Internet presentations.[11] In the pictures entitled 'Reflection Pictures From Maluku', which were posted on the MML without further comment on 2 February 2001 as no. 33 in the 'Potret-Maluku' series, the children were wearing blue uniforms and carrying small Bibles around their neck or in their hands, boys and girls clearly listening attentively and with a serious look to someone outside of the camera's view (Illustration 11). The headings for the pictures expressed what the photos stood for: the sad story of a generation that had grown up in wartime and had no other choice but to accept the relevant rules and either fight as well or be killed. If you looked into the eyes of these children, which is what the next headline encouraged you to do, you were directly confronted with their hopeless and inhuman situation.

As in other wars, many innocent children became victims, either by having to actively take part in the fighting by themselves or by having their parents wounded or killed. The Moluccan conflict also resulted in a large number of orphans. Under the title 'SAYING SORRY FOR THEM' (16 October 2001), the Masariku team in Ambon compiled several photos of small, sad-looking children and in the captions to the pictures encour-

Illustration 11. Christian child warriors in the Moluccan conflict (MML, 2 February 2001)

aged people to 'Save their future in Jesus' name and you begin to change the world'.

So as to demonstrate the Christians' inhumanity, the Laskar Jihad showed pictures of their polyclinic in Ambon, which in June 2001 had been attacked by the (allegedly predominantly Christian) United Battalion (Yongab) and partially destroyed. This denied the patients medical care and hope of recovery. As proof of the brutality of the Yongab, the Laskar Jihad showed several photos of their weapons (22 June 2001).

Yet the Laskar Jihad also proudly presented photos on the Internet of the Christian university in Ambon, which had been destroyed by the mujahideen (FKAWJ, 3 December 2000), and maps of conquered territory (see Illustration 16).

History

Referencing real historical circumstances to underscore their own method of argumentation was another effective means in the effort to appear authentic. According to Mark Juergensmeyer (2000), warring parties deliberately attempt to associate current events with history in order to increase the scale and importance of the conflict and to morally justify the violence. Depending on what the conflicting parties aim to achieve, history is interpreted and viewed highly selectively. The FKAWJ went far back in history in its accusations. It made reference to the crusades, the colonial era and the accompanying Christianization of the Moluccas and developed a conspiracy theory adapted to the Moluccan conflict (the RMS and Christians worldwide against the Muslims in the Moluccas), which was closely linked to the Jewish-Christian conspiracy theory that is widespread in the Muslim world. The conflict was deliberately anchored in history. History was exploited and in some cases reconstructed in order to make credible the hopeless situation of the Muslims in the Moluccas, who were being suppressed and persecuted, and give it more weight. As a result, the current events were not a new occurrence, but rather the continuation of a long Christian tradition that had begun first with the Portuguese and then, in 1599, with Dutch troops arriving in Ambon with all their European missionaries – in one hand a sword, in the other the Bible – to enforce their rule and their faith on the Moluccan population. Only with Allah's help had the Muslims ultimately succeeded in driving the Christian European warriors out of the Moluccas (FKAWJ, 17 February 2001).

Masariku and the CCDA did not go as far back with their historical references. They preferred to refer to more recent history, since Indonesia's independence, and to the developments of the last ten to twenty years. So as to be able to correct the Laskar Jihad's portrayal, the events of 1950, when the independence of the Republic of the South Moluccas (RMS) was proclaimed, were important. Furthermore, the first constitution and the state philosophy of Indonesia, the *Pancasila*, played a major role in the context of the discussions about an Islamic state and the introduction of Sharia, with which, on account of the presence of the Laskar Jihad in the Moluccas, the Christians were constantly being confronted. In any case, it became clear that the processes and values in Moluccan cyberspace were in no way detached from history and local links; indeed, as Manuel Castells maintains (see Chapter 1), it was quite the contrary.

Thomas Matulessy was one such historical topic in Moluccan cyberspace. Under the name Pattimura he became a national hero in Indonesia, having, in 1817, led an uprising against Dutch colonial power on Saparua. Together with other Muslims, the FKAWJ forwarded the proposition that Pattimura had been a Muslim[12] and that present-day Muslims were continuing his fight against suppression by the West and the Christians. It would have been impossible, they claimed, for a Christian to attack his brothers in faith, the Dutch, and furthermore, the Moluccan Christians had always been loyal to the Dutch. Thus, the 1817 uprising was a conflict between Dutch colonial power and the Muslim community in the Moluccas. However, various press and members' articles posted by Masariku repeatedly emphasized that Pattimura had quite clearly been a Christian, given the historical facts and his Christian name.[13] As the Muslims were also aware of this, they modified his name to Ahmad Lussy, thereby deliberately falsifying the history of the Moluccas (MML, 30 August 2002). According to the FKAWJ (17 and 20 February 2001), Pattimura's full name was Ahmad Anakotta Paria Pakalessy, who called himself Haulessy, alias Haulussy. An article in the Muslim magazine *Hidayatullah* forwarded to the MML on 22 September 2002 considered his being renamed Thomas Matulessy an example of how Moluccan history had been de-Islamized.[14]

The destruction in July 2000 of Pattimura University (Unpatti) in Ambon, the main university of the Moluccas, represented correction of a somewhat different nature. Referencing Rustam Kastor, the FKAWJ referred to Unpatti as the intellectual centre of the RMS Christians. This was allegedly where the RMS cadre was trained and the links to the Netherlands maintained. For this reason the FKAWJ was very happy to have destroyed the university facilities and the surrounding accommodations of the RMS Christians in Poka and Rumah Tiga and to have caused the RMS damage worth several billion rupiah. They had killed thirty Christians, wounded hundreds and forced thousands to flee. Lecturers at Unpatti had always discriminated against Muslim students, if they had been accepted in the first place, which was why its closure was justified and its destruction an historic event that the descendants of the Moluccan Muslims would remember for a long time to come (FKAWJ, 8–14 July 2000; 8 July 2001).[15] For the Christians the destruction of Unpatti was one of the peaks of the Moluccan conflict and a clear sign that the annihilation of the Christian community in the Moluccas was imminent. It was proof of the fact that behind the Moluccan conflict there was a major political and ideological conspiracy, of which even the Indonesian president was no longer in control (MML, 5 July 2000). Various threads appeared in which contributors appeared extremely worried about the current situation and the many refugees, but were also giving thought to the reconstruction of Unpatti, where several MML members had themselves studied or taught (MML, 4 July 2000; 24–31 October 2001).

The arguments surrounding the case of the Christian village Waai, which had been completely destroyed shortly after the university, took a similar form to the debate about Unpatti. Whereas the Muslims justified the conquest of the village with their historical claim to it, the Christians saw in the destruction of the relatively large village further proof of the Muslims' obliteration strategy. For the FKAWJ, it was a case of correcting history and reconquering the land that had been taken from the Muslims by the Christians, who reached the Moluccas far later than Islam did.[16] According to the Christians, at least seventeen people died in the attack (CCDA, 8 July 2000), with no consideration shown to women and children, the elderly or the sick. The entire population of the village, more than five thousand people, were forced to flee, with many dying of hunger and illness during the flight (CCDA, 2–8 August 2000). Thank God, the FKAWJ maintained, that Waai, which had been lost to the Christians in 1670, officially reverted to Islam on 31 August 2000. Together with military and civil authorities – including rajas of the Muslim villages bordering on Waai, namely, Liang,[17] Tulehu, Tial and Tengah-Tengah – Ja'far Umar Thalib resolved to rebuild Waai Islam and construct a mosque on precisely the same spot where one had stood in the sixteenth century (FKAWJ, 20 September 2000; 6 October 2000).[18] It goes without saying that within Masariku the news of the planned reconstruction of Waai as an Islamic village sparked considerable dismay and debate. The question was asked whether Waai was actually Muslim property, and what could be done. One MML member was of the opinion that it was wrong to speak

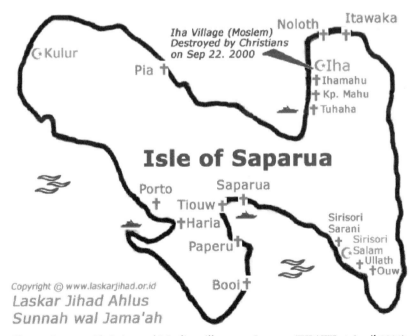

Illustration 12. Christian and Muslim villages on Saparua (FKAWJ, 4 April 2001)

of Christian or Muslim property. Only outsiders could argue like that, such as Thalib, who had no idea of Ambonese culture. What was important was that the village belonged to the Ambonese, regardless of whether they were Christian or Muslim. And ultimately it had been Islam, not Christianity, that had first subjugated Waai and its inhabitants, who lived according to Ambonese *adat* (22 September 2000).[19]

The FKAWJ saw another historical link when, on 22–23 September 2000, Iha, one of the three Muslim villages on the island of Saparua, was attacked by (allegedly) tens of thousands of RMS followers and completely destroyed. As Iha was encircled by Christian villages, the only thing the inhabitants could do was flee by sea (FKAWJ, 25 September 2000). By way of illustration the FKAWJ provided a map of Saparua, together with an eyewitness statement by an LJAWJ member, who had come to the aid of the Muslims in Iha (see Illustration 12).

The destruction of Iha was an enormous loss: alongside Hitu on Ambon and Huamoal on Seram, it was the oldest Islamic kingdom of the Moluccas and its inhabitants were the original population; they had not moved there from other villages or areas on Saparua.[20] Until the arrival of the Dutch East India Company (VOC), large parts of the island of Saparua had been owned by Iha. The VOC had then divided up the land between the subjugated villages. From a VOC file from 1651 the FKAWJ listed all the areas that had been taken away from Iha and followed it with a detailed description of developments in the seventeenth century, in which Iha had allegedly been repeatedly attacked by the VOC. Time and again the inhabitants had had to flee, as they did in 2000, in a *hijrah* to the island of Seram.[21] The Muslims, however, were not going to just ignore this ignominy, as Ja'far Umar Thalib stated in an FKAWJ report of 25 September 2000:[22]

> **The Christians will suffer far greater revenge** than the Muslims ... The wealth of the village of Iha was not given to the infidels for free, they will be made to pay for it immediately.

From a Christian point of view, the destruction of Iha was primarily an act of revenge for the complete destruction of the Christian village of Sirisori Kristen on 21 September 2000[23] and several other Christian houses and churches on Saparua (MML, 24 September 2000). Although only three of the seventeen villages on Saparua were Muslim, here too the Christians feared religious cleansing, as both the military and the police seemed to be supporting the Muslims (MML, 24 September 2000).

Religious symbolism

Regardless of whether the cyberactors talked of a religious war or not, religion played a major role in their Internet presentations. In particular in connection with world religions, religious symbolism was used to create the link to an overarching community of faith, with shared fundamental values and ideas. Religious events at the local level could evince internal solidarity and differentiate one's own community from others. No one at the local level in the Moluccas doubted the importance of having a religion, as all areas of everyday life were separated along religious lines. Crossing these lines was often fatal. Even though the consequences were not fatal in cyberspace, here too the religious boundaries were observed. With regard to the religious symbols used in cyberprojects, a distinction must be made between two levels. On the one hand, religious symbols were used to engender solidarity in one's own online community or the extended community one was ideally trying to appeal to. This level was already discussed in the chapters on individual cyberactors and the structure of their projects. On the other, the violation and destruction of religious symbols and their use in the offline struggle was adopted in cyberspace.

Destroying and insulting key religious symbols

During the course of the Moluccan conflict, several hundred mosques and churches were damaged, desecrated or destroyed.[24] The destruction of a single religious building was an insult not only to all Christians and Muslims at the local level, but to Christianity and Islam in general. In the Moluccan conflict, rumours of the setting alight or destruction of churches or mosques often triggered new waves of violence (Human Rights Watch 1999).[25] It was these suspicions that, on 19 January 1999, also turned a minor incident into a long, bloody conflict between Christians and Muslims. In the conflict, places of worship often became gathering points before a renewed attack or meeting points for the local population to demonstrate unity. The argumentation of the FKAWJ in particular made it clear that other buildings as well were attributed religious significance in the conflict, for example, Unpatti. According to the cyberactors' reports, the attackers were often not satisfied with the mere destruction of religious buildings, but also desecrated them by daubing insults on the walls left standing[26] or, as a CCDA report (4 November 2000) states, by Muslims indulging in abnormal sexual practices in the ruins of a church. The news of this caused such outrage that a message was immediately sent to the governor of the Moluccas, the Pope, the United Nations and various other people and bodies.

An MML report on an attack on the village of Waemulang on the island of Buru contained a whole repertoire of insulting graffiti the village was said to have been covered with after the attack (1 December 2001). Examples include:

> There is no unkempt God apart from Jesus. (Tiada Tuhan yang gondrong selain Yesus.)

Christians have the face of a thief. (*Orang Kristen muka pancuri.*)
Jesus has the face of a thief. (*Yesus muka pancuri.*)
Jesus is the child of a pig/a dog. (*Yesus anak babi/anjing.*)

One MML eyewitness report (18 March 2001) listed the ways in
which Muslims insulted Christians while forcing them to convert to Islam: saying that Christianity was a religion of infidels and unclean, that
Christians stank and believed in three Gods, that they honoured Jesus as
God, although he was not one, that the New Testament had been written
by someone from Ambon and that all Christian priests called on their
parishes to kill Muslims. In the various cyberactors' reports, numerous
pictures provided proof of these insults. On 4 December 2000 under the
title 'Christians do not want peace' (*Kristen Tidak Ingin Berdamai*), the
FKAWJ showed in its mailing list photos of a mosque that had allegedly
been burned down by Christian RMS militia.[27] A crucifix was positioned
on the roof of the mosque and the remains of the walls covered in graffiti
(Illustration 13). Each picture had a heading and was briefly commented
on by the Laskar Jihad. Here are a few examples:

Salib di Atap Masjid Crucifix on the roof of the mosque	*Penghinaan Terhadap Rasulullah* Insults directed at the Prophet

A mosque that was burned down by Christians, where the minaret has been replaced by a crucifix. The Christians destroyed more than 200 mosques in this way, whereas a total of only 24 churches were destroyed.	Mosques burned down and destroyed by Christians are always daubed in filthy language that insults the Prophet. As a sign of their love of the Prophet, the mujahideen already eliminated them in this graffito.

Yesus Penyelamat
Jesus the saviour

Islam Muka Lon . . .
Islam has the face of a wh ... (ore)

The red warriors always write confused slogans in which they consider Jesus to be the child of God. Actually, though, God the Holiest said: 'It is not conceivable that God should have taken unto Himself a son: limitless is He in His glory!' (Maria:35)[28]

Their hate of the Islamic community will never fade, as God spoke in Sura 2 (The Cow), verse 120: 'For, never will the Jews be pleased with thee, nor yet the Christians, unless thou follow their own creeds ...'

Tak Ada Damai
There is no peace

Graffito: 'The soldiers of the crucifix will murder Islam until it is finished.' That is a promise made by the Christians, who will continue killing the Islamic community in Ambon (Muslim cleansing). The Christians have no wish whatever for peace. That has been proven, as more than 300 promises of peace made by the Christians have already been broken again. Thank God the Laskar Jihad will endeavour to halt their evil plans.

Illustration 13. Graffiti insulting Islam (FKAWJ, 4 December 2000)

Masariku displayed pictures of graffiti in which Muslims insulted Jesus and Christianity, such as the photos posted on 16 February 2000 documenting the unrest in Halmahera (Illustration 14):

In December 1999 the conflict reached new heights, and so did the use of religious symbolism, on both the Muslim and Christian sides. On 26 December 1999 the large Silo Church in the centre of Ambon was burned down to its foundations; this had been the bulwark of the Christians in the Moluccan conflict against the Muslims, whose activities were coordinated in the large Al-Fatah Mosque only approximately one hundred metres away. On the one hand, this represented the destruction of an outstanding ancient symbol of the Protestant Christians, and on the other, Christmas, one of the holiest Christian celebrations, had been dishonoured. Masariku immediately informed its subscribers of the incident online by means of a press release: 'Silo Church on fire' (*Gereja Silo Terbakar*). According to the Muslims, almost at the same time in Togolihua, a village in Tobelo District (North Moluccas), Christians had set fire to a mosque into which hundreds of Muslim women and children had fled and who had now been burned alive. This tragedy had a huge emotional impact on the

Jesus has lice

Jesus is a dog – Jesus is barbaric

Jesus is an infidel

Jesus is a drunkard

Illustration 14. Graffiti insulting Christianity (MML, 16 February 2000)

Muslim community in Indonesia and led to the call for a jihad to save the Moluccan Muslims.

On the Christian side, the destruction of the Silo Church determined Internet discourse for some time. Masariku provided a detailed chronology of the events on the evening of 26 December until the morning of 27 December 1999 (MML, 26–28 December 1999).[29] According to Christian depictions, although the military was present and even had two tanks available, it had failed to intervene to halt the Muslim masses. Rather, it acted against the Christians, who were trying to save their church. The Christians were shocked. In a chain reaction, further mosques, churches and residential buildings on Ambon and the surrounding islands were destroyed in retaliation (MML, 27–29 December 2000). From a Christian point of view, the heroes of 26 December 1999 were those people who had been killed (ten) or wounded (forty-eight) defending one of the most important Christian symbols in the Moluccas.[30] A list of the victims was posted on the MML. One of those injured was a Masariku member who had been shot trying to photograph and film the events surrounding the Silo Church (MML, 28 December 1999). The Silo tragedy attracted international attention; CNN and the BBC reported on it (MML, 29 December 1999). Via the mailing list, the Masariku team in Ambon provided photos of the turmoil and the military's tanks and videos of events related to the burning of the Silo Church (MML, 23–27 January 2000).[31] The images of a Sunday service held in the ruins of the burned-down church are also particularly striking (Illustration 15).

The images are an expression both of the incredible suffering of the Christian community and the terrible humiliation the Church was subjected to, and the solidarity of the community of Churches, which as a result was strengthened in its faith and social cohesion. In response to the pictures, on 6 February 2000, for example, an MML member commented that although the church might have been burned down, the Body of Christ and community of God could never be touched, and would always exist.

In late December 1999 the FKAWJ turned to concentrate entirely on events in the North Moluccas. They claimed (16 March 2001) that the massive attacks on Muslim villages likewise began at Christmas 1999 and peaked in the attack on the village of Togolihua on 28 December 1999,[32] where about eight hundred Muslims were executed. To underscore the cruelty of the Christian attackers, the FKAWJ posted reports by people who had actually been there (see Chapter 6). For the Muslim community, the events in the Tobelo region and the burning down of the Togolihua village mosque became a (negative) key event in the Moluccan conflict, and in their reports the Laskar Jihad, who at the time were not yet in the Moluccas, repeatedly referred to it. The Christians scarcely reported on the fate of the Muslims in the North Moluccas: the CCDA not at all, and

Illustration 15. Service in the burned-down Silo Church (MML, 1–2 February 2000)

while Masariku made attempts to, on account of limited transportation, communications and funds, they had hardly any access to relevant data (MML, 27 December 1999; 1 January 2000). In a post intent on clarifying the events in Tobelo, Masariku vehemently rejected the accusations that had been spread in both electronic and print media that the Christians had begun the series of attacks in the North Moluccas. Nor was it true that the Tobelo Christians had slaughtered children, raped women and burned hundreds of Muslims to death. So as to add emphasis, these sections were written in uppercase letters. What had actually happened was described in both Indonesian and English (MML, 7 January 2000). The article finished with the following appeal:

> We deeply regret the news reports issued by the media which place the Christian community of Tobelo in a bad light, without trying to get the facts straight.

The report of children being slaughtered and women being raped is simply not true! Please report objectively without any partiality. We were only acting in self defense and fighting for our faith and convictions. We refuse to be trampled upon by any one group or party in this Pancasila based state. We appeal to the leadership of this nation to immediately settle the present chaos.

The Muslims, on the other hand, complained that there was scarcely any reporting in the media on the fate of their brothers in faith in North Halmahera. The Christians made the same accusations when, a few months later, at 5 AM on 19 June 2000, to be precise, more than five thousand mujahideen led by Abu Bakar allegedly attacked the Christian village of Duma in Galela District (North Halmahera), killing 176 people and wounding 137, including women, children and the elderly (CCDA, 22 June 2000). As far as the FKAWJ was concerned, this was merely justified revenge for the Christians' atrocities; it proudly listed how many Christians had already been killed, injured or driven out, and how many churches destroyed.[33]

Religious symbols as a means of differentiation in battle

During the actual fighting, Christians and Muslims alike attempted to denote themselves by means of certain symbols closely related to their particular denomination. Reference has already been made to colour symbolism. The Muslim fighters, in particular the Laskar Jihad, often wore white garments associated with the Muslim heartland in the Middle East. During attacks on Christian villages and city districts their (combat) cry 'Allahu Akbar!' ('God is great!'), known throughout the world, was meant to create unity among the warriors and forge a link to God. For the Christians, these elements became the characteristic features of their enemies, symbols of a struggle in the name of religion (MML, 26 August 1999), which is why they received great attention in Christian reporting in cyberspace.[34]

On the Christian side, certain hymns appeared to play a role in mental preparation for a fight. There were several mentions in CCDA reports, for example, of the song 'Laskar Kristus Maju' ('Forward Christian Soldiers'), which Christian youths would sing on their forays through the city. Kees Böhm criticized this as clear provocation of the Muslims. On one occasion, armed Christian youths had entered Muslim territory in procession. They had allegedly sung this song and had been led by a female priest, who had also been wearing a crucifix. Because the procession had not been registered the military intervened, and people were killed and wounded. The churches dissociated themselves from this 'unapproved act' and criticized the fact that there had been no previous announcement that this was a peace march and there were plans for an official handing over of weapons to the supreme military commander (CCDA, 6–7 December 2000). Of course, acts of this nature triggered protest on the Muslim side. Muslims also criticized, for example, the three days of prayer that fifteen

Christian churches had announced in November 2001, and during which all public life, at least on the Christian side, stood still. No Christian civil servant went to work. The Muslims accused the Christians of disrupting economic life in Ambon and Moluccan society itself, and called on the governor to instigate measures to stop such days of prayer from happening (FKAWJ, 23 November 2001). What was not mentioned, however, was the fact that leading Muslims, first and foremost Muhammad Attamimi, had threatened Muslims with death if they traded with Christians, which certainly did not help economic development in the Moluccas. The ban was repeatedly announced via the Laskar Jihad website and on the Laskar Jihad's SPMM radio (see, e.g., CCDA, 2 May 2001).

If one follows the descriptions in cyberspace, it becomes apparent that times of attack in the Moluccan conflict were related to those the faithful normally devoted to their religion and religious community, for example, joint church services or prayers at the mosque. Each side accused the other of deliberately choosing this particular time so as not only to injure the people physically, but also their religious sentiments and what was holy to them. The Muslims complained that precisely for this reason the Christians had begun the conflict on Idul Fitri, for Muslims the end of the month of fasting. The Muslims renamed the day 'Bloody Idul Fitri' (*Idul Fitri Berdarah*). According to the FKAWJ (21 November 2000), they had learned their lesson from this and ever since the month of fasting had been prepared for a Christian attack. The Christians, in turn, maintained that the Muslims had deliberately initiated this in order to be able to pin the blame on them. The Muslims had repeatedly adopted this strategy, that is, scheduled attacks on Muslim holy days, so as to avoid any accusations of guilt from the outset (see, e.g., CCDA, 26 October 2000). According to the Muslims, the Christians essentially attacked at times when they had assembled in the mosque for one of the five obligatory daily prayer sessions, regardless of whether at dawn (*waktu subuh*) or in the evening (*sholat maghrib*). In several cases, merely disturbing a church service or prayers in the mosque in some way or other was sufficient to trigger a fresh wave of violence.

Christians throughout the Moluccas, as emerged from numerous MML and CCDA reports, were often attacked at the time of Sunday services. The attacks occurred when the Christians were already seated in church or on their way there, and as such were in no position to defend themselves. Nor did the Muslims refrain from attacking on important Christian feast days such as Christmas or Thanksgiving. Since the outbreak of the conflict the Christians feared that every Christmas would be bloody (*Hari Natal Berdarah*), as the Laskar Jihad announced every year on their website in order to take revenge for 'Bloody Idul Fitri'. Their motto was, for instance, 'Let's turn off the candles in December', candles being a symbol of Christianity and Christmas in Ambon (MML, 29 November 2000).

On Christmas 1999, for example, Muslims instigated a bloodbath among Christians on the island of Buru in which more than fifty people died (MML, 26 December 2000). The Laskar Jihad (26 December 2000), on the other hand, maintained that Christmas was not even holy for Christians, as they themselves provoked the attacks on these days.

The Bible and the Koran also played their part in the fighting. The child soldiers illustrated above (see Illustration 11), for example, held small Bibles during the fighting, which gave them the feeling that they were closer to God (MML, 5 February 2001). The 'homemade Laskar' *(Laskar Rakitan),* who, according to FKAWJ, though not real warriors, still emulated the Laskar Jihad in terms of clothing and religious behaviour, consequently wore a small booklet with the first sura of the Koran (FKAWJ, 14 March 2001). The Christians and the Christian military units were also accused of repeatedly tearing up and stamping on copies of the Koran during fighting, thereby insulting Islam.

Selected issues

The discourse in Moluccan cyberspace was determined on the one hand by the features just described and by the characters of the individual actors, and on the other by a number of issues that had emerged over the course of time. The accusation of separatism and that of religious cleansing are two issues that played a central role in the Moluccan cyberactors' presentation of the conflict and were decisive factors in these groups' identity formation both offline and online. It is appropriate to first devote a short section to 'truth' and selection in the reporting in general.

'Truth' and selection

> Perception Management targets the human dimension in politics
> and conflict in a way that kinetic weapons cannot.
> Douglas H. Dearth, 'Shaping the "Information Space"'

An investigation of Moluccan cyberspace is not about uncovering the truth about the conflict in the Moluccas. As Senator Hiram Johnson remarked in 1917, truth is the first victim in war, and, according to Phillip Knightley (1975), war correspondents and the media play a decisive role in this. Reports can be falsified or exaggerated, images staged or doctored and material in general censored. In particular if the reporters' own country (in the case of the Moluccas, the cyberactors' religious community) is involved, the reports can scarcely be objective. Reporters need not necessarily invent news, but on account of their sources, their organizations and the other structures they are embedded in, they produce news and 'invent' reality (Carruthers 2000: 17).[35] According to Anthony Smith (1978: 135), all reporting consists of describing events in a certain context for people who live in a different context. This automatically involves selection and presenting only part of the 'truth'. Even with firsthand reporting, as in the case of Moluccan cyberspace, there is selection in terms of which events and news are worth being disseminated on the Internet, how they are presented and how they are commented on, if at all. By selecting information, reporters can have a pivotal influence on the emotions, opinions and behaviour of their audience and its perception of an event, in our case the Moluccan conflict (see Collins 2000: 191; Williamson 2000: 177).

Through the widespread use and reach of the Internet, the Moluccan cyberactors became key figures in the perception management of the audiences interested in the Moluccan conflict. This without doubt also represented a question of power (see, e.g., Butler 1995: 165; Slevin 2000: 89). The Moluccan cyberactors enjoyed the privilege of having access to the Internet and deciding which news items were presented to their national and international audiences. Given the many different communication channels the Internet offers, however, the public can also participate in this negotiating process, as was the case with the Masariku mailing list. As opposed to mass media, this interaction became a decisive element in the success of the cyberproject. If one follows the discourse in Moluccan cyberspace, it is possible to portray what Niklas Luhmann (1996) referred to as the various constructions of reality. According to constructivist theories, reality is always constructed, as no one has access to real projects such as these that is independent of epistemology, and thus no one can know what is actually real and true. According to Luhmann (1996: 17–20), the only thing one could do is observe how people, organizations, the media, etc., construct realities and then compare these equal versions. Adopting this approach, I will attempt to sketch the various versions of reality presented by the Moluccan cyberactors with regard to the issues selected. Such issues become part of common knowledge and, according to Nancy Baym (1995: 20), are a prerequisite for an increasing awareness of solidarity within computer-mediated groups. They give online communities permanence (Slevin 2000: 94).

Separatism

The Muslims, that is, the FKAWJ, insinuated that the RMS and FKM[36] were using religion to mobilize all Christians in the Moluccas to join their war of secession and separate the Moluccas from the unitary state of Indonesia. The Christians, on the other hand – the CCDA and Masariku – accused the Laskar Jihad and its affiliated local groups of wanting to introduce Sharia and Islamize the Moluccas, a fear that became very tangible through corresponding cleansing campaigns (alcohol, prostitution, etc.), the destruction of entire Christian villages and the forced conversion of thousands of Christians. These Muslims were the actual separatists, as they were depriving the Christians of their right to practice their religion and thus breaking away from the *Pancasila* state philosophy and ignoring national law (CCDA, 1 December 2000).[37] Correspondingly, they were referred to as a 'religious separatist group' *(kelompok separatis agama),* as 'Islamic separatists' *(kaum separatis Islam)* or quite simply as 'separatists' (MML, 15 December 1999; 25 September 2000; CCDA, 1 December 2000).[38]

In the eyes of the FKAWJ, by adopting Christianity and separatism the RMS/FKM became the number one enemy of the Muslims, who saw themselves as having to defend the unity of their country and their religion. Kathleen Turner (2002) rightly supposes that the Laskar Jihad deliberately presented the Christian enemy as a separatist movement, which was undermining the Indonesian state and therefore illegal. This provided them with the justification to assume the position of the defendants of national unity, become involved in the conflict and demand support from the army, which had never before become embroiled in a SARA conflict. Or, in Juergensmeyer's (2000: 183) somewhat exaggerated words, you often have to invent your enemies in order to justify a conflict. In any case, the Laskar Jihad were hoping that, as in 1950 and the years that followed, the government and the military would fight the RMS and thus support the Laskar Jihad against the Christians. The anti-RMS/FKM propaganda was not unsuccessful. In April 2001 the governor of the Moluccas banned all FKM activities, which in particular included a ban on flying the RMS flag on 25 April, the day the RMS declared independence in 1950 (MML, 16 April 2001, according to *The Jakarta Post* and *Kompas).*[39] Around 25 April 2002 the curfew was extended and the military chief of the Moluccas declared that anyone who even attempted to hoist the RMS flag would be given just one warning before being shot (CCDA, 23 April 2002). On 10 April 2002 the governor of the Moluccas, who was also responsible for the civil state of emergency, banned not only the local media from reporting on RMS activities, as in the previous year, but foreign journalists as well (MML, 23 April 2002), which was very reminiscent of the repressive Suharto era. Furthermore, foreigners were banned from entering the region, regardless of whether they were journalists, NGOs or tourists, for more than a year.

The FKAWJ on the issue of RMS/FKM[40]

At the very beginning of the conflict, the Muslims were convinced that it was the RMS that had initiated it and were intent on using it for their own purposes, namely, the independence of the Republic of the South Moluccas. In order to better understand this line of argumentation I will include a short excursus here on the background to the origin of the RMS in 1950. As the former colonial rulers of Indonesia, the Dutch were accused of having shown preference to the Christian Ambonese and having treated them better than the Muslims with regard to the offices they held and the education they received. The Christians belonged, as it were, to a higher class, known as the Christian class *(Pankat Serani)*, which had collaborated with the Dutch. According to the FKAWJ, no notice had been taken of Muslim interests. At the time, *Agama Ambon*, the Ambonese religion, was seen as Protestantism, indicating that this was, so to speak, the original religion of the Ambonese (although Islam had reached the Moluccas before Christianity). Furthermore, it had primarily been Christian Ambonese who had effectively volunteered for the Dutch colonial army, and whom many Muslims saw as being simply renegades and traitors. After Indonesian independence, many Christians in the Moluccas feared having to live as a minority in the Muslim country without the support of the Dutch (see, e.g., Chauvel 1980, 1990: 39–70; Cooley 1961: 122–26, 383–99, 548; Kraemer 1927: 77, 1958: 13–20; Steijlen 1996: 35; Wertheim 1956: 147, 199).[41]

When, immediately following the departure of the Dutch, Sukarno dissolved the federal system negotiated and the unitary state of Indonesia was declared, Dr. Christian Soumokil, the Ambonese justice minister in the former state of East Indonesia (Negara Indonesia Timur, NIT), and his allies decided to declare an independent Republic of the South Moluccas, hoping for the loyalty and help of the Dutch who, however, never fulfilled their promises. Shortly afterwards, the RMS was disbanded by the Indonesian military. According to Richard Chauvel (1980: 74–77), though Muslims were also involved in the RMS proclamation, the majority of RMS activists had been Christians and little attention had been paid to the interests of the Muslims (see also Cooley 1961: 371–72). There were cases in which the Christian guerrillas attacked Muslim villages they suspected of collaborating with the Indonesians. According to Dieter Bartels (1977: 222–25, 2000: 6–7), there were, however, also instances of Christian soldiers preventing attacks on allied Muslim villages. According to Bartels, it was when they saw the political and economic advantages for themselves under Suharto's *Orde Baru* that the younger generation of Ambonese Muslims began seeing the RMS as a Christian construct. The RMS was then sarcastically called the Christian Moluccan Republic (Republik Maluku Serani).

In the opinion of the Muslims, following the end of colonial rule the Christians in the Moluccas had continued the colonization of the region and the suppression of the Muslims, which was evident in bureaucracy and in education (see, for example, Unpatti). The current Moluccan conflict was the final attempt to Christianize the Moluccas and separate them from Indonesia. The Laskar Jihad did not tire of repeatedly emphasizing this in their reports.[42] According to the FKAWJ (14 February 2001), one day before the outbreak of the conflict RMS flags had already been raised and loud cries of 'Hidup RMS' ('Long live the RMS') heard in various parts of Ambon. For the FKAWJ, the raising of the blue, white, green and red striped RMS flag seemed to be a central element of the RMS movement. Correspondingly, the Laskar Jihad reported any opportunity that was used to raise one of these flags and often seemed to be far better informed than the Christian side, which was allegedly meant to be responsible for the initiative. On Indonesian Independence Day (17 August) in 2001, RMS flags were demonstratively burned in front of two mosques in Ambon and the red and white Indonesian national flag raised to express the Muslims' loyalty to the Indonesian state (18 August 2001). The following year, some five thousand Muslims staged a long march in Ambon towards the Al-Fatah Mosque carrying a giant national flag allegedly measuring 150 by 7 meters and shouting anti-RMS slogans (18 August 2002).

Alex Manuputty provided the ultimate evidence of the Christians' separatist aims for the FKAWJ when, on 18 December 2000, in the guise of the FKM he proclaimed the RMS a second time, even quoting the original declaration text of 1950. Manuputty took the opportunity, they claimed, to arrogantly put the FKM on the same level as the independence movements in Papua (OPM) and Aceh (GAM) and the PLO (25 December 2000). According to the FKAWJ the FKM had close links with the Protestant Church of the Moluccas (*Gereja Protestan Maluku, GPM*). This was particularly clear from the perseverance with which the Church's team of lawyers (TPG), and especially Semmy Waileruny, who was also involved in the ceremony on 18 December, defended the head of the FKM, Alex Manuputty, after his first arrest (19 January 2001). In a headline dated 20 February 2001, the FKAWJ summarized its arguments in a sort of equation: 'The Church is behind the RMS, the RMS behind the Church' (*Gereja Dibalik RMS, RMS Dibalik Gereja*). Just like the RMS, the TPG also had to be incapacitated (26 July 2000); this was the key to the conflict being solved (20 January 2001). For this reason the FKAWJ repeatedly wrote letters of protest against declarations and letters by the TPG and then published them online.[43]

In May 2002 the Laskar Jihad posted a list of one hundred RMS activists (*Daftar 100 Aktor Intelektual RMS*) on their website, who, according to the FPIM, operated as designers, intellectual actors, facilitators, inspirers, provocateurs and driving forces of the Moluccan conflict. The list primarily featured Protestant pastors, members of the Protestant Churches and the TPG, the former auxiliary bishop of Ambon and the priest who had founded the Catholic Crisis Centre.[44] According to FKAWJ statistics the list met with enormous interest on the part of website visitors. The Laskar Jihad provided further 'clear' evidence of the Christians' anti-Indonesian stance in their mailing list on 17 February 2001, namely, a scanned declaration of the recognition of the Indonesian unitary state, signed by numerous Muslims. In the column intended for representatives of the Christians, however, the signatures were missing. That same day the article was forwarded to the Masariku mailing list, as one of the members had asked whether there was actually any truth behind this contention.

According to one of the founders of the list it was an expression of an RMS phobia. The Muslims had surprisingly presented the declaration to the Christian delegation at a Christian-Muslim event devoted to the Moluccan conflict on Bali, without this having been agreed to with either the Christians or the organizers and before there had been a chance to discuss any other, far more fundamental points. This was why the Christian delegates had not signed it, which was confirmed by the organizer, the Indonesian National Human Rights Committee.

The neo-RMS, which was how the FKAWJ also referred to the FKM, was using not only the Church network, they claimed, but also Western countries, in particular the Netherlands and the international community, which, through corresponding propaganda and provocation, it was attempting to win over to its separatist mission. The FKM and Alex Manuputty were paving the way, so to speak, for a global conspiracy of RMS Christians (3 May 2002). In so doing the FKM was deliberately exploiting religious sentiment and whipping up hatred of the Islamic community in countries such as the United States, Australia, the Netherlands and other European countries. According to the FKAWJ, the fact that both the Catholic and the Protestant Churches (26 May 2001) and the FKM had turned to the United Nations, urging it to intervene in the Moluccan conflict, was further evidence that the FKM and the Christians did not see themselves as part of the Indonesian people (14 February 2001). By building up an international lobby, the FKM was selling off the Indonesian people (4 March 2001). All they were concerned with was the Moluccan people *(Bangsa Maluku)*, and not Indonesian unity. According to the FKAWJ, the Muslims were not regarded as part of the Moluccan people. Rather, it was quite evident that through independence the Christians were attempting to restore the supremacy they had enjoyed owing to their denomination under Dutch colonial rule, asking the Netherlands, their former ruler and sponsor, for help in this respect (10 March 2001).

The Netherlands were seen, so to speak, as the root of the evil, as since the arrival of Moluccans in the 1950s the RMS had always been able to pursue its activities there, unlike in the Moluccas, and even formed a government in exile (12 November 2000). Now, the FKAWJ claimed, their followers were exerting enormous influence on the Ambonese and instigating a joint conspiracy against the Muslims.[45] It accused RMS youths in the Netherlands of drug dealing in order to be able to buy weapons for the fight in the Moluccas, and said that RMS demonstrations were regularly being held to put pressure on the Dutch government. Moreover, RMS youths in the Netherlands had tried to set fire to two mosques in Reederkerk and Waalwijk, catastrophes that the Moluccan Muslim population had, however, been able to avert (2 July 2000; 9 November 2000; 12 November 2000). During the conflict various Dutch Moluccans had come to the Moluccas, made 'unpleasant' videos and broadcast them on Dutch

TV to discredit Indonesia, provoke the Dutch and spread propaganda for the RMS (12 November 2000).

The Laskar Jihad made it clear that they were not alone in their opinion, and that they enjoyed enormous support from the national and the Moluccan Muslim community (Umat Islam Maluku, UIM) and their organizations, with which they formed a joint front against the RMS rebels.[46] The secretary of the Muhammadiyah branch in the Moluccan Province assumed that following its suppression in 1950, the RMS movement had until today continued to exist as an underground movement *(gerakan clandestine)* and now, on 19 January 1999, had resurfaced (20 June 2002). Correspondingly, the Laskar Jihad also referred to the RMS as a guerrilla movement (18 February 2001; 5 September 2001). Since the outbreak of the Moluccan conflict the RMS had, however, been openly canvassing for new members and support by means of flyers that were being distributed in particular in Christian residential districts in the city of Ambon (23 October 2001) or among refugees, whose unfortunate circumstances the RMS groups were exploiting (5 April 2001).

The CCDA and Masariku on the issue of RMS/FKM

The Christian cyberactors officially distanced themselves from the RMS and the FKM just as much as the Protestant and Catholic Churches in the Moluccas, as well as the Dutch government. To place even more emphasis on this, in 2001 the GPM disbanded the TPG, which on account of the dual role of Semmy Waileruny as the lawyer of both the Church and FKM had very much come under fire from the Muslims, and replaced it with an official Protestant Crisis Centre, similar to the CCDA (CCDA, 28 April 2001). According to a CCDA report (11 January 2001), influential figures, including Protestant and Catholic church leaders, had even attempted to deter Alex Manuputty from making the FKM declaration on 18 December 2000. Christians, too, the CCDA continued, became nervous in the run-up to 25 April every year, and hoped that no RMS flags would be raised, causing further trouble. Masariku and the CCDA documented every 25 April in detail in words and pictures.[47]

Quite in contrast to the Muslims, the Christians addressed the history of the FKM and attempted to give their audience at least an idea of the FKM/RMS perspective by allowing members a say in various posts. One Masariku member, for example, forwarded to the list an exclusive interview by the newspaper *Siwalima* with Alex Manuputty (19 April 2001), another an essay by Manuputty (2001) entitled 'Republik yang Hilang' (Lost republic; 11 September 2001), tracing the history of the RMS and revealing the motivation of the FKM. Others again provided the FKM declaration on the Malino II agreements and the subsequent events, which, according to the FKM, clearly indicated that the peace agreement had failed and the government still did not know how to protect the Moluccan people's human rights, as well as the extremely detailed petition for the abandonment of the case against Alex Manuputty, compiled by his lawyers after he had been arrested for the second time (MML, 28/17 September 2002).

According to the CCDA (25 April 2001), the RMS movement in the Moluccas had been dead since the early 1960s, and the Dutch Moluccans' hopes of receiving support from the Dutch government with regard to the RMS had also been disappointed. Furthermore, the RMS had never been bound to any one religion, even if in the 1950s the majority of its followers were Christians fearful of a Muslim-dominated republic of Indonesia, and was restricted to Ambon and the surrounding islands. And even if, as the CCDA maintained on 15 December 2000, there were separatists at work in the Moluccan conflict, this was not a matter for the Laskar Jihad, but for the Indonesian government. As the latter was clearly not in a position to put a stop to the atrocities in the Moluccas, Alex Manuputty had seen himself with no other choice but to found the FKM in order to enforce human rights with international help (CCDA, 28 April 2001). His motivations become very clear in the following excerpts from the declaration on the founding of the FKM dated 18 December 2000, which a Masariku member forwarded to the list:

The unanimous Declaration of the Moluccan People, Voices of the Islands,

When in the course of human Events, it becomes necessary for one people to dissolve the Political Bands which have connected them with another, and to assume among Powers of the Earth, the separate and equal station to which the Laws of Nature and of Nature's God entitle them, a decent Respect to the opinions of Mankind requires that they should declare the causes which impel them to the Separation. We hold these Truths to be self-evident, that all men are created equal, that they are endowed by their Creator with Certain unalienable Rights, that among these are Life, Liberty and the Pursuit of Happiness. That to secure these Rights, Government are instituted among Men, deriving their just Powers from the consent of the Governed, that whenever any Form of Government becomes destructive of these Ends, it is the right of the People to alter or abolish it, and to institute new Government, laying its Foundation on such Principles, and organizing its Power in such Form, as to them shall seem most likely to effect their Safety and Happiness.

The History and tract record of the present government of the Republic of Indonesia is a record of repeated abuses, injuries and usurpations, all having in direct object the establishment of an absolute Tyranny over the Moluccan people. To prove this, let the Facts be submitted to a candid world.

** The Human tragedy that occurs in the Moluccan islands in the past two years was the result of a collaboration and conspiracy organized by the Indonesian government by using the Indonesian Army and the Jihad vigilantes as a means to fossilize the Moluccan people …

** The government of Indonesia, from the perspective of documented agreements and its original constitution (not to mention agreements made to the UN), has no claims to the Moluccas. It nonetheless invaded and has occupied the area against the wish of the people since the early 1950s. Since that time, Indonesia has carried out overt strategies to undermine the economic, social and cultural bases of Moluccan society ...

We, therefore, the Moluccan Sovereignty Front (Front Kedaulatan Maluku-FKM), the Representative of the Moluccan People, appealing to the Supreme Judge of the world for the rectitude of our intentions, do, in the Name, and by Authority of the good People of the Moluccas, solemnly publish and declare, That these United Moluccas are, and of Right ought to be Free and Independent States, that they are Absolved from all Allegiance to the Republic of Indonesia, and that all political connection between them and the Republic of Indonesia, is and ought to be totally dissolved.

In a letter to the Indonesian president dated 18 January 2001, the FKM governing board emphasized that the FKM should not be equated with the RMS, but that as a neutral body its intention was to liaise between the RMS and the Indonesian government. The FKM wanted to make it clear to the government that the 1950 RMS independence declaration had been legal (CCDA, 27 March 2001).[48] The CCDA and Masariku reports attempted to make clear what Alex Manuputty and his FKM were actually about: in principle he, too, like the Laskar Jihad, was resisting colonization from outside, which, following the departure of the Europeans and the Japanese, had been continued not by the Christians, but by the Indonesian government (CCDA, 26 April 2001). For this reason Alex Manuputty's arrest in January 2001 triggered protest among the Christians, as no action had yet been taken against Ja'far Umar Thalib, who was still able to deliver provocative speeches (CCDA and MML, 13 January 2001). According to CCDA reports, when on 30 April 2001 Manuputty, his arrest having been deferred in January, gave himself up to the police, Christian FKM sympathizers marched through Ambon's streets holding banners high with slogans such as:

When will they stop to oppress us, the Alifuru[49] people?

Non-Alifuru, get out of the Moluccas! (30 April 2001; 1 May 2001)

Manuputty's followers were not addressing a specific religious group, but the indigenous population of the Moluccas, Christians and Muslims alike.[50]

The Waisarissa case was another example of how repressive the government was in its treatment of the FKM, and prompted discussion among all cyberactors. In August 2001 various Christian and Muslim *adat* leaders invited representatives from Seram, Ambon and the Lease Islands to an *adat* meeting in Waisarissa, West Seram, in an attempt to help end the conflict. As those invited included Alex Manuputty, the military declared the *adat* meeting to be a conspiratorial FKM meeting and intervened. Forty-seven participants, allegedly all FKM members, were beaten by soldiers and detained for two days. Journalists from the daily newspapers *Siwalima* and

Suara Maluku were also roughed up by the military. As a result, there was enormous protest on the part of the Christians, as well as from the Alliance of Independent Journalists (Aliansi Jurnalis Independen, AJI) (Böhm 2001). With regard to the two journalists in particular, this was a clear case of a violation of human rights (MML, 12 September 2001). As far as the FKAWJ was concerned (5–8 September 2001), however, the military intervention was absolutely justified, as this was a meeting intended to strengthen the power of the RMS on Seram.

According to a post by Joshua Latupatti,[51] the RMS was a Muslim strategic weapon for discrediting the Christians in the Moluccas. During a raid on the Al-Fatah Mosque in Ambon, fifty RMS flags had even been discovered that were intended for distribution in Christian areas. Generals such as Feisal Tanjung, Suaidi Marasabessy and Hendropriyono were nonetheless convinced that the Christians in Ambon were separatists and the RMS a purely Christian matter (MML, 17 January 2000). Masariku demanded that the military provide unequivocal proof if they continued accusing the Christians of being RMS supporters (MML, 14 September 1999). Furthermore, there were certainly members of the military, for example, I Made Yasa, who was military chief in the Moluccas in 2000, who confirmed that there was no RMS in Ambon (MML, 30 June 2000). According to various Masariku members, there were increasing signs that the military and the government were making the RMS and the FKM a scapegoat for the Moluccan conflict, with the two groups being seen as the cause of the conflict and serving as a pretence for fighting the Christians and covering up the real causes of the conflict (MML, 22 April 2002; 24 April 2002). Yet, on the contrary, for many Moluccan youths the RMS was simply the last refuge for giving expression to all the injustice that had occurred in the Moluccas (MML, 8 May 2002). The Christian cyberactors seemed convinced that the RMS and the FKM did not have a large following.

For the CCDA, the FKM was not a solution to the Moluccan conflict; if anything, it complicated the situation. In Kees Böhm's view, the majority of the population of the South Moluccas was of the opinion that they were better off as part of the Indonesian state than independent (CCDA, 27 March 2001). In various threads MML members discussed the extent to which independence could be a solution to the conflict at all, and there were differing opinions on the subject. Most members seemed convinced that Alex Manuputty had chosen the time for his declaration badly; if anything, it had provided their opponent with even more arguments and heightened and prolonged the conflict. Whereas one could accept the FKM idea as a sort of shock therapy to demonstrate to the Indonesian government that at long last it had to do something and take care of the Moluccan people, at the same time people were afraid that through his activities Alex Manuputty could endanger the Moluccas and that this could lead to an avalanche of destruction, as in the case of East Timor. Only a few members really considered independence as a (final) option, as the government had been proved incapable of ending the Moluccan conflict. Those members, however, felt that any decision must be that of a majority of the Moluccan population and that the whole idea must be based on a joint vision and a transparent programme, which was certainly not so in the case of the FKM. One member attempted to draw the discussion to a close, referring to the FKM as an insignificant group because it enjoyed no support among the people and had no negotiating power and no resources. However, one of the founders of the list warned against making any hasty conclusions, saying that in-depth analyses were necessary. In any case, it became clear that positions were being negotiated here, whereas on the part of the FKAWJ an uncompromising judgement was continually repeated.

Religious cleansing

Among both Christian and Muslim cyberactors the predominant opinion was that in each case their brothers in faith were being wiped out and the Moluccas were going to be Christianized or Islamized (Christian and Muslim cleansing). Both sides often spoke of thousands of attackers, who in most cases swarmed into a Christian or Muslim village from several directions at once, giving the inhabitants no real chance of survival apart from fleeing to the forest or the mountains. Whereas the FKAWJ in its Internet articles explicitly emphasized its Islamization intentions, in the Christian cyberpresentations there were no indications that the Christians were intending to capture the Moluccas and Christianize them. According to the FKAWJ, however, on account of their separatist ambitions all Christians had to be driven out of the Moluccas. As proof of the success of the Laskar Jihad, the website featured maps of Ambon Island showing exactly which areas were in Christian and which in Muslim hands. A comparison of the map from May 2000 with that from February 2001 shows which villages had already been conquered by the Muslims since the arrival of the Laskar Jihad (Illustration 16).

Christian and Muslim cyberactors alike could link their argumentation to theoretical debates, thereby giving their fears greater weight. For the Christians, the global discussion of continuing Islamic fundamentalism and radical Islamic terrorist networks were of significance, which for them were directly linked to the problem of the Laskar Jihad in the Moluccas and in Indonesia in general. In their posts some Masariku members directly referenced these debates. The FKAWJ used the Christian and Jewish world conspiracy theory, which had its followers in many parts of the Islamic world and in Indonesia as well (see, e.g., Bruinessen 1994; Hefner 2001).[52] By utilizing these much farther-reaching, overarching categories, the cyberactors' descriptions and actions gained importance and support, which in turn strengthened their identity projects.

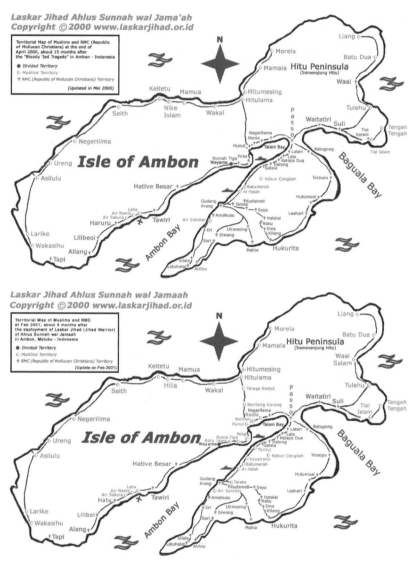

Illustration 16. Maps depicting Laskar Jihad conquests, May 2000 and February 2001

The CCDA and Masariku on the issue of forced conversion

For the Christians, it was clear that the Islamization of the Moluccas was looming or indeed already in progress. In his speeches in the mosques of Ambon and on the Laskar Jihad's radio station SPMM, Ja'far Umar Thalib repeatedly openly called on the Muslims to put an end to the Christians in the Moluccas. The Muslims' conversion drives, in which hundreds if not thousands of Christians were forced to convert to Islam, were clear proof of this. The Christians involved were offered a choice of either dying or converting to Islam. They were humiliated and referred to as pork and dog eaters, which is why they had to be purified in a ritual; they were co-erced into wearing other clothes and changing their names; men, women and children were circumcised and had to recite the Islamic profession of faith and listen to readings of the Koran. Previously Christian women were forced to marry in Islamic fashion, and the recently converted were forced to erect a mosque in their village.[53]

From the beginning of 2000, Masariku and the CCDA repeatedly re-ported forced conversions among Christians throughout the Moluccas. According to a TPG report, by the end of 2000 at least 5,948 Christians had been forced to convert to Islam, with the island of Bacan in the North Moluccas, northern Buru, the Bula district in northeastern Seram, Tehoru and surrounding villages in southern Seram, and Kesui and Teor, small islands in southeastern Seram, primarily being affected (CCDA, 14 De-cember 2000). The wave of forced conversions continued in 2001 in the Bula district on Seram and on Halmahera, among others.[54] In this con-text the Christian cyberactors and the Churches repeatedly appealed to the Indonesian government and the military. However, in view of their lack of action, they primarily turned to the various foreign embassies in Jakarta, the United Nations and human rights organizations such as Am-nesty International, church leaders worldwide, and the Pope in Rome. It was not until the incidents in Teor and Kesui, however, that these cases of massive human rights violations actually became an issue in national and international news. As a result, Christian and human rights organizations worldwide began to address the problem and championed the setting up of an international lobby.

In November and December 2000 the CCDA devoted many of its re-ports to the Kesui-Teor case:[55] between 23 and 26 November 2000 four Christian villages (Utta, Karlomin, Wunin, Tansoa) on the small island of Kesui in eastern Seram were unexpectedly attacked by two thousand to three thousand Muslim fighters. Several Christians were killed (the ex-act figure is difficult to ascertain) and large parts of the villages, includ-ing their churches, burned down. Only a few Christians managed to flee. Between six hundred and seven hundred were detained by Muslims in several local mosques and forced to convert to Islam. According to the CCDA, the attack was surprising in that the islands had not previously been involved in the conflict and the interreligious relations there had al-ways been very good, as both religious groups had the same ethnic roots. From 1 December 2000 the Christian villages on the neighbouring island of Teor were attacked. Two evacuation commissions dispatched by the government were unable to get any of the Christian inhabitants to safety, on account of the inability and the insensitivity of the teams deployed. The delegates allowed themselves to be deceived by the local Muslims, or, because they feared for their lives and the families they had left behind in the village, those converted Christians who were asked did not dare talk about forced conversion, saying they had voluntarily converted to Islam. In both cases there was seemingly no need for evacuation. Only in another evacuation campaign on 23 January 2001, which was personally headed by the governor of the Moluccas, Saleh Latuconsina, could the Christians (729 in total) be moved out (CCDA, 30 January 2001). On 23 December 2000 a church service was held in Ambon especially for the refugees from Kesui and Teor, attended by Church leaders, priests and Christians of all denominations. The event was photographed by Masariku and posted on the list (MML, 24 January 2001). The Catholic Church in Ambon organized a ceremony of its own for the Catholic refugees from Kesui, at which the converted were officially welcomed back into the Church (CCDA, 18 January 2001).

Masariku was just as critical as the CCDA of the Kesui case and the government's 'efforts' to solve it. An analysis conducted by the Masariku team in Ambon of 'Forced Conversions as an Outcome of Violence in Maluku' (7 April 2001) was published in Indonesian[56] and English, so as to reach as wide an audience as possible. The failed government attempts revealed yet again that it was no longer in a position to protect a minority in its country. When a large part of the Christians had been evacuated from the island the government declared the case solved. For the Masariku team, the fact that the case did not go to court and the violation of human rights was pursued no further was unforgivable. Even the national human rights committee, which had sent a team to Kesui, was not given an opportunity to report its results. Furthermore, it was clear that military and police forces had been involved in forced conversions. There was no other solution, they claimed, than for the international community to exert pressure on the outsiders who were currently in the Moluccas and responsible for the continuation of the conflict (in other words, the Laskar Jihad) and force them to leave. For the author of the report, the forced conversions had a political dimension, as they effectively whipped up the emotions of the masses, thereby helping prolong the conflict. To illustrate the Kesui-Teor case geographically, on 25 January 2001 the Masariku network in Ambon posted on the list a specially made map of the two islands showing which areas were Islamic, which Christian, and which Christian villages had been Islamized.

The Christians' accusations were underscored by eyewitness statements and photographs. In words and pictures these made quite clear to list subscribers what it meant to be forced to convert. The case of Berthy, a sixteen-year-old boy from Liliama in eastern Seram, was depicted in a particularly vivid way (MML, 7 April 2001). Berthy had been the victim of a forced conversion and had told the Masariku team in detail about the hardships of fleeing, his discovery by his pursuers, his return to the village and, ultimately, the conversion process, to which he and his fellow sufferers had been subjected by the Muslims in the neighbouring village and soldiers from the Indonesian military. The eyewitness account was again provided in Indonesian and English. The background to the email was filled with a portrait photograph of Berthy showing a pleasant boy with whom, given his fate, one automatically sympathized. However, the observer was also confronted with a close-up photograph of Berthy's circumcised genitals. In other cases as well Masariku presented comparable intimate online images and video recordings (available for order), which visually underpinned the cruelty and inhumanity of the situation. Berthy's firsthand account gave detailed insight into the various conversion rituals (heavily abridged version):

> Afterwards the (Muslim) village authorities came to visit the houses where the Christian villagers of Liliama were staying to force them to change religions by signing a statement to the effect that they had turned from Christianity to Islam. Because they were pressured by the village authorities who were flanked by soldiers of the 611th unit of the TNI Army, the Christian villagers of Liliama were forced to submit to the wishes of the village authorities and TNI Army personnel. There were in total around 300 people in the Christian village of Liliama, but as many as 80 of them were forced to become Moslem, whereas the rest of the villagers had escaped. On 15 January 2000 the Christians of Liliama village were ordered to clean up by taking a bath in the river, so that they would be purified from the filthy dogs and pigs that they had eaten previously. After taking a bath the Christians were brought before the imam of the Polim village, then taught to say the sahadat (Moslem creed), and a lock of hair was cut as a token that they had become Moslems, and then they were given a (Moslem) head cap.

> On 20 January 2000 they would hold a mass circumcision ceremony. The circumcision would be done in groups, each one consisting of 5 to 6 people for the men (the men were circumcised on 20 January 2000, and the women on 21 January 2000). My (Berthy speaking) circumcision was done without any medical preparation. I was ordered to unzip my trousers and my penis was cut, then I cannot tell what happened next, because I lost consciousness. After I regained consciousness I felt such pain in my penis and blood kept flowing. The soldiers of 611th unit of the TNI Army administered bethadine (yodium). Afterwards they put on some bandage and added some more bethadine, then I was given some ampicillin tablets to swallow. Three days later we were ordered to take a bath in the sea so that the wound would heal quickly, so they said. I suffered for 2 weeks.

> After we had taken a bath in the sea the Christians who had been islamized were given some new clothes and a sarong, then we were welcomed with 'qasidah' dancing and escorted to the mosque to celebrate the occasion and enjoying a meal together. The Mojim (religious leader) said, 'You have now returned to the right path and abandoned the wayward road.' Afterwards the villagers who had married the Christian way had to undergo another marriage ceremony according to Islam.

The CCDA provided no self-recorded eyewitness accounts, but did, for instance, summarize an interview in the newspaper *Siwalima* in which a woman described her fate in connection with the forced Islamization on Kesui (11 December 2000). Corresponding eyewitness accounts by Christians would hardly have been conceivable in the national press. The international press, however, was more than willing to publish them. Several of those articles were forwarded by Masariku, such as 'A War Only God Sees' in the *Seattle Times* on 26 March 2001, articles by Lindsay Murdoch in *The Age* dated 27 January 2001, and 'Nightmare of Life as a Muslim Slave' by Richard C. Paddock in the *Los Angeles Times* on 13 March 2001.

The FKAWJ on the issue of forced conversion[57]

According to the FKAWJ (19 December 2000), all these reports of hundreds of Christians having been forced to convert were a lie and were only serving to win over the international community for the Christians and discredit the Laskar Jihad and the Muslims. The Christians had not been forced, but had voluntarily converted to Islam after they had come to see the depravity of their own religion. A Christian village on Kesui, for example, had decided to convert to Islam after the Protestant pastor had fled, leaving his parish members, encircled and being attacked by Muslims, to fend for themselves. The Muslim attack had merely been in response to an attack by RMS Christians on the Muslims of Kesui.[58] Furthermore, they claimed, the government's evacuation measures had revealed that none of the newly converted had wanted to leave the island.[59] According to the FKAWJ (6 December 2000), the Laskar Jihad themselves had never been in Kesui, which is why it issued a press release contradicting a report on Dutch radio in which it rejected any guilt and accused the radio station of working with the RMS. For the Laskar Jihad, the fact that Islam had reached the Moluccas before Christianity and that the former colonial rulers of Indonesia were Christians justified almost anything, and certainly it justified the reconquering of allegedly former Islamic areas (including Kesui, for example).[60] If attacked, the local population could either convert to Islam, be killed or flee.

If the Muslims failed to defend themselves and win back their territory, they said, the Christians would either kill them or drive them out, enabling them to establish a Christian RMS state (19 December 2000). The FKAWJ interpreted the Churches' offer for former Christians who had converted to Islam to be able to return to their parishes more as a threat to those concerned than an invitation, which would only be successful on the back of intimidation on the part of the pastors (20 December 2000). As in the rest of Indonesia, the Christians in the Moluccas were also applying other methods to gradually annihilate the Muslims. In Muslim areas, for example, churches were being built and Muslim girls impregnated by Christian men in order to marry them. At the same time, the women would convert to Christianity (13 August 2002; 11 September 2002). As opposed to the Muslims, even before the Kesui case the Christians had for years forced thousands, if not millions, of Muslims in Indonesia to convert to Christianity (19 December 2000). During the Moluccan conflict many Muslims, in particular in Tobelo in the North Moluccas, had been forced to convert.[61] The FKAWJ (16 March 2001) reported, for example, on a small group of Muslims who had allegedly been held hostage by Christians for more than a year in the village of Paca, Tobelo.[62] One of them managed to escape, and through his constant tears was able to tell the FKAWJ reporters about his fate. Following the same pattern as in the Masariku reports, the FKAWJ witness talked about his experiences of forced conversion. The Muslims were initially attacked during prayers and then forced to eat pork, convert to Christianity and sing Christian hymns. The witness originally came from the village of Togolihua where, in December 1999, several hundred Muslim women had been burned alive in a mosque. He had had to look on as his wife had been brutally murdered and dismembered by Christians.

Other than in FKAWJ presentations, the forced conversion of Muslims is scarcely an issue. Sidney Jones from Human Rights Watch, however, pointed out that in December 1999 there had been forced conversions among Muslims, in particular in the North Moluccas, and that the Christians bore guilt in this respect as well (MML, 24 February 2001, according to the *Baptist Press*, 21 February 2001). The Indonesian sociologist Tamrin Tomagola also made corresponding insinuations at the U.S. embassies in Jakarta and Brussels, without, however, providing any proof; no such proof has yet been presented by an independent body. This situation was further exacerbated by the fact that at a meeting of a Moluccan delegation with representatives of the United Nations in Geneva on 4 April 2000, Jusuf Ely maintained that he had never heard anything about instances of forced conversion to Christianity in the Moluccas, which he, as the 'leader of all the Muslim communities living in the province',[63] ought to know (MML, 17 April 2001). In April 2001 a discussion thread on the MML also explored the accusation of Christianization, though here again there was no real proof of enforced Christianization. One member with an information network in Halmahera, for example, was only aware of voluntary conversions in an extended family. Masariku members in Ambon even dispatched an investigation team of their own to the north. Here too, however, it emerged that Muslims had only converted to Christianity in one village in North Halmahera, but that they had not been forced to do so. The Muslims in question had fled from their villages to the forest and at some point in the Christian village of Togasa asked for protection and, a few days later, to be christened (MML, 1 July 2001). According to an MML member, if there had actually been cases of forced Christianization, he failed to understand how the national media, whose reporting was for the most part pro-Muslim, had missed news of this nature. Furthermore, the issue of Christianization had only come to light after the cases of enforced Islamization had received so much attention, and there was no information available about the current whereabouts of those people who had been subjected to forced Christianization. An international investigation team would have to look into the case and provide unequivocal proof, or all the accusations would have to be dropped (MML, 24 April 2001).

Summary

The textual and visual argumentation in Moluccan cyberspace was dominated by certain discourse characteristics and issues, by means of which the individual cyberactors aimed to convince members and their audience of their perspective on the conflict and drum up support. The integration and exclusion mechanisms determining the lines of conflict at the local level were transmitted into cyberspace and expanded strategically. Because they transmitted firsthand information directly from source to the Internet and thus into the homes of their subscribers and the visitors to their websites, all the cyberactors claimed to deliver authentic reporting. This authenticity was underscored by eyewitness reports and visual argumentation elements in the shape of photographs, which captured the consequences of the conflict on the respective side, and scanned documents that were of importance to the cyberactors' line of argumentation. Images served as evidence and campaign material. For the observer they depicted reality; for the poster they were a pivotal means for manipulating the observer and winning him over. As at the local level, in Moluccan cyberspace too there was typically a dichotomization into groups of 'us' and 'them', which were given corresponding attributes best expressed by a 'me and the monster model'. In the Moluccan case both the Christian and the Muslim side were also characterized by different labels, such as the colours red and white, the boys' names Obet and Acang and, for the FKAWJ, by jihad versus the RMS Christians. Each side emphasized that it was always the other that attacked first, and that it was simply defending itself.

By anchoring the conflict in history, the FKAWJ in particular attempted to increase its scale and significance and morally justify the use of violence. According to the FKAWJ, the causes of the conflict were to be found in the colonial era, when Christianity was introduced to the Moluccas and the local Muslims were suppressed. The injustice of the past now had to be rectified and the history of the Moluccas corrected. Even though not all Moluccan cyberactors were convinced that the Moluccan conflict was religious in nature, religious symbolism, both at the local level and in cyberspace, was of fundamental importance when it came to distinguishing between one's own group and the 'enemy'. Images of places of worship that had been destroyed were posted on the Internet, as was graffiti that insulted key religious figures. Religious attributes played a major role in the description of attacks, be they the attackers' clothing, their battle cries and songs or the times of the attacks, which often took place at prayer time or on religious holidays. The use of this religious symbolism extended the conflict's reach, as suddenly not just individuals were being attacked, but entire religious communities, whose followers lived throughout the Moluccas and indeed worldwide.

The conflict discourse was also dominated by a number of issues the cyberactors used to construct a reality that had a decisive influence on the image of the conflict portrayed to the outside world. Central issues included the accusation of separatism and religious cleansing. Whereas the Muslims accused the Christians of wanting to secede from the Indonesian state in the form of the RMS/FKM, the Christians claimed that the radical Muslims were the real separatists, as they intended introducing Sharia and as such breaking with the Indonesian constitution. Each side accused the other of aiming to achieve its goal by Christianization or Islamization of the Moluccan population. The cases of forced conversions, which the Christian cyberactors documented by means of eyewitness accounts, images and SOS messages to the international community, were a key argument in this respect. The FKAWJ claimed that Islamization was desirable and indeed in progress, as was proven by corresponding maps of the conquered territory. It did, however, maintain that all the Christians had converted to Islam voluntarily, whereas the Christians had forced hundreds, if not thousands, of Muslims to convert.

Notes

1. As these are patterns that recurred on a regular basis in the relevant portrayals and discourses of Masariku, the CCDA and the FKAWJ, in parts I will refrain in this chapter from making reference to specific list and website posts. When referring to the mailing lists/newsletters of the three cyberactors, in addition to the date the relevant abbreviation will be provided: FKAWJ, MML or CCDA.
2. However, when we are not dealing with the usual media environment, as was the case with the Moluccan cyberactors, then for reasons of infrastructure and finance it is certainly a privilege and by no means a matter of course to have access to this weapon.
3. Digital photographs posted by Masariku, with the time showing, were an exception. The CCDA did not post any photographs online.
4. For the significance of the colour red in the Moluccan context see also Penonton (1977: 241) and Pollmann and Seleky (1979: 211), and in the context of the North Moluccas see the Halmahera Report no. 2 by Masariku of 2 January 2000.
5. According to Kees Böhm, Obet was not derived from Robert. Rather, Obet was a Biblical figure, the son of Boaz and Naomi, the grandfather of King David, or so it goes at the end of the Book of Ruth in the Bible (personal email, 21 February 2003).

6. See Böhm (2002a: 4) and Bubandt (2001: 238). Böhm heard a Christian mother saying to her cheeky child, 'Behave yourself or I'll take you to the Acangs!' (CCDA, 5 February 2001).

7. In press articles posted by MML, the Laskar Jihad and troublemakers in general in the Moluccas were often referred to as the 'Troublemakers' Movement' (Gerakan Pengacau Keamanan, GPK).

8. With regard to this topic the MML published a survey of the population that the BakuBae movement had conducted in 2002 together with an NGO and in which 1,400 Christians and Muslims took part. Whereas a clear majority of Christians (73.3 per cent) was of the opinion that a political elite was behind the Moluccan conflict, many Muslims (34.2 per cent) placed the guilt on the separatist RMS or referred to the Moluccan conflict as a religious conflict (17.8 per cent). The Muslims who supposed several factors (including the RMS and/or religion) were behind the Moluccan conflict (29.8 per cent) were not taken into account here. Only 7.2 per cent of the Christians characterized the conflict as religious, and none of them saw the RMS as a factor (MML, 21 May 2002). As the Institut Studi Arus Informasi (2000b) demonstrated, in the Muslim-oriented national press the Moluccan conflict was also far more frequently referred to as a religious war than in the more Christian-oriented and more neutral daily newspapers.

9. See also Peter van der Veer (1994) for the Hindu-Muslim conflict in India.

10. According to the Masariku network (26 January 2000), the Muslims were abusing their women and taking them along to motivate the attacking troops. On the issue of child warriors in the Moluccas, Masariku forwarded various articles from the international press such as the *Los Angeles Times* and the *South China Morning Post* of 13 March 2001, *The Toronto Star* of 25 March 2001 and *The Australian* of 22 April 2002. The CCDA commented on and corrected the article in the *Los Angeles Times* that had been quoted on several websites. Though the Catholic Church had taken in a few children and youngsters whose parents had died in the conflict and who had in some cases been actively involved in belligerent and violent clashes, it was not true that the priests had prayed for the youths and given them holy water to drink after they had set houses alight and killed people (CCDA, 17 March 2001).

11. In this they were following the general trend in the media that deliberately used pictures of child soldiers to attract the attention of readers or viewers (see, e.g., Atkinson 1999: 212; Beer 2000: 186).

12. Abdul Gafur, former minister of sport and youth under Suharto, who himself came from the North Moluccas, had already put this forward in 1995 (Aditjondro 2001a: 110).

13. According to Masariku, the 'lies' of the Muslims could clearly be refuted, as the Pattimura uprising was well documented. In May and August 2002 a member forwarded several references to relevant literature.

14. See the original article at http://www.hidayatullah.com/2002/08/sejarah.shtml.

15. Even the Christian side admitted that with regard to the students and lecturers at Unpatti the Christians were in the majority, though for different reasons. The Muslim lawyer Ridwan Hasan, for example, confirmed that Muslims normally had little motivation to embark on a university degree. Muslim Unpatti graduates preferred to return to their villages or enter commerce and business.

The CCDA was also of this opinion (17 February 2001). There was no indication that Unpatti had been an RMS cadre training ground.

16. In his 1886 work *De Sluik- en Kroesharige Rassen Tusschen Selebes en Papua*, Johan Gerard Friedrich Riedel (1886: 59) actually pointed out that when the first Protestant minister had arrived in 1615, Waai had been Muslim. Only later, under duress and the threat of punishment, had they converted to Christianity.

17. Here too the fronts had long been marked out. In the collections on Indonesian *adat* law published by the Royal Netherlands Institute of Southeast Asian and Caribbean Studies (KITLV), Liang was already referred to as the archenemy of Waai, the main bone of contention being land disputes (KITLV 1925: 403, 1933: 436).

18. According to the CCDA, the governor of the Moluccas forbade the establishment of an Islamic Waai (16 October 2000). Issues such as this indicate very clearly how the Christian cyberactors in particular referred to and responded very strongly to what the FKAWJ presented on the Internet.

19. Although the Laskar Jihad seemingly never began building the mosque, after the destruction of Waai they did for a long time maintain a local recruits' training camp there without being bothered by the military (FKAWJ, 13 March 2001).

20. Whereas Iha had indeed previously been a powerful realm, a large majority of its clans, according to the history of the village as recorded by Dieter Bartels, had come from outside the Moluccas, though before the colonial era. In an interview with the village leader of Iha in 1975, the latter even claimed to be able to trace his ancestors back to Arabia (personal email from Dieter Bartels, 12 September 2003).

21. On 3 February 2002 an MML member forwarded this FKAWJ article to the MML, referring to it in the subject heading as 'War propaganda from the disreputable warriors' (*Propaganda perang Laskar Jahat*).

22. '**Orang kristen akan mendapatkan balasan yang lebih dahsyat** dari kaum muslimin . . . Kekayaan desa Iha tidak digratiskan untuk kafirin, harus dibayar segera' (bold in the original).

23. According to the FKAWJ this was, however, only a response to the attacks by Christian villages on the village Sirisori Islam (24 September 2000).

24. Parallel to the destruction of places of worship, key religious figures were also murdered. The Christian side in particular repeatedly reported priests who had been killed by Muslims so as to send a signal to the Christian community. As far as the Laskar Jihad was concerned, these deaths were justified, as most priests were allegedly acting as troublemakers in the conflict.

25. According to Nils Bubandt (2001), in the Indonesian context the reasons for this are to be found in the *Orde Baru*. Lots of churches and mosques were built during this period. A genuine competition developed, in which a person whose place of worship was bigger and more magnificent enjoyed greater status. Churches and mosques became sources of religious identity, which were sanctioned by the state and had to be strictly guarded.

26. The problem here, of course, is that one can never say with any degree of certainty who actually daubed the insults.

27. The mailing list also makes reference to further photos on the website at http://www.laskarjihad.or.id/picture/masjidambon.htm.

28. Sura translation here and in the next caption (verse 2:120) by Muhammad Asad, available at http://www.islamicity.com/quransearch/ (7 October 2011).
29. According to the MML the trigger was a traffic accident in which a car driven by a Christian injured a Muslim youth. There were violent clashes between Christians and Muslims, which peaked with the bombardment and burning down of the Silo Church when Christians were in it celebrating Christmas. See also Böhm (2002a: 11).
30. According to a report in the local newspaper *Siwalima*, twenty-eight people on the Muslim side died (MML, 28 December 1999).
31. A picture of the church in flames was available at http://www.geocities.com/ambon67/noframe/links.htm (picture source: Masariku network).
32. One FKAWJ report has the date as 27 December, another 29 December; a Masariku report gives the date as 28 December.
33. FKAWJ conflict chronology of the Moluccas and the North Moluccas, 1998–2001 (http://www.laskarjihad.or.id/, 26 January 2002).
34. For the Christians these elements sometimes also provided proof of the fact that the Moluccan Muslims and the Laskar Jihad were being supported by Muslims from outside Indonesia. The Arabic characters often seen on the robes of the jihad warriors were also an indication of this (Masariku Testimony no. 6, 18 March 2001).
35. Carruthers makes reference here to Michael Parenti's phrase *Inventing Reality* in his eponymous 1993 book (New York: St. Martin's Press).
36. For the Laskar Jihad, both movements were in principle the same.
37. In the course of the conflict, Ja'far Umar Thalib as the leader of the LJAWJ and Alex Manuputty as that of the FKM were both arrested twice, although only Manuputty was accused of separatist activities, while Thalib was charged with criminal activities and deemed to be a troublemaker.
38. In the case of the Christians, their fear of Islamization and 'Islamic separatism' was also based on the transmigration and Islamization policy of the Indonesian government.
39. In principle, precautionary measures against the RMS were nothing new in the Moluccas. Even during the *Orde Baru*, every year ahead of 25 April the police issued warnings and almost every year a Christian was arrested as a preventative measure to avoid the RMS flag being raised (personal conversation with Dr. I. J. W. Hendriks, chairman of the GPM Synod, in Ambon on 21 March 2002). If flags had after all been raised, according to Hendriks and other Christian and Muslim informants, this had occurred less out of ideological conviction and more because the Dutch Moluccans had given financial support for precisely this to happen. Despite all of this, in October 1999, for the first time since the RMS had gone into exile almost fifty years before, the transitional president who succeeded Suharto, B. J. Habibie, officially welcomed a delegation of the RMS government in exile in the Netherlands, which many RMS supporters in exile interpreted as a positive sign (Radio Nederland Wereldomroep, MML, 18 October 1999).
40. Unless otherwise stated, the dates in parentheses in this section refer to corresponding contributions on the LJAWJ website or their mailing list.
41. On the history of the RMS in general see, for example, Bosscher and Waaldijk (1985); Chauvel (1990); Kaam (1977); Manusama (1952, 1999); Parker (1996); Penonton (1977); Pollmann and Seleky (1979); and Steijlen (1996).

42. For this reason the posts cited in this chapter are only to be seen as examples. Numerous others could also have been provided, but for reasons of clarity were not.

43. Such as that written on 30 September 2000 (http://www.laskarjihad.or.id/ press/fkawj-30sep2000.htm, 24 October 2002).

44. The list also featured members of the Moluccan regional parliament (DPRD Maluku), the mayor of Ambon, the head of the PDI-P Maluku, various senior employees and lecturers of Unpatti, TVRI staff, editors and photographers at *Siwalima* and *Suara Maluku*, a *Jakarta Post* journalist, Agus Wattimena (the now deceased leader of the Laskar Kristus), Berthy Loupatty (the leader of the Coker gang), RMS members and Moluccan provincial police officers. The governor of the Moluccas was accused of covering for the RMS/FKM (2 June 2002).

45. Husni Putuhena, the head of the FPIM, even reported to the FKAWJ a visit by the president of the RMS government in exile, Tutuhatunewa, to Ambon (19 August 2001), something that was not, however, confirmed by any other side.

46. On 11 January 2001 the FKAWJ reported a joint request on the part of UIM to those responsible for declaring the civil state of emergency to undertake measures against the RMS. It involved nineteen Muslim village leaders, fifteen jihad stations on Ambon Island and thirty Islamic organizations, including MUI Maluku, NU, Muhammadiyah, ICMI, Partai Islam, FPI, Majelis Dakwah Indonesia (Islamic Missionary Association of Indonesia) and various student and youth associations such as KAMMI (Indonesian Muslim Students' Action Front), HMI (Muslim Students' Association) and Pemuda Muhammadiyah (Muhammadiyah Youth).

47. With such strict security measures having been enforced in 2002, RMS followers had to be particularly inventive if they wished to raise their flag. Masariku documented 25 April 2002 in a total of four reports. In addition to pictures of protesting Muslim masses, it showed images of the most original ideas to, despite the ban, 'raise' RMS flags, such as several balloons sporting the colours of the RMS flag, to which flags were attached.

48. The FKAWJ (31 January and 15 April 2001) also seemed to have knowledge of these FKM letters to the Indonesian government and saw proof in this that the RMS was not dead, but presented a genuine threat.

49. The Alifuru people are the indigenous people of Seram Island, which Central Moluccans also refer to as the mother island, as all life is meant to have come from it and it was from there that people settled on the other islands.

50. Nonetheless, at the FKM declaration on 18 December 2000 and at corresponding ceremonies such as flag raising, only Christians and in some cases even pastors of the Protestant Church were present, from whom, however, the GPM distanced itself. Yet Alex Manuputty maintained that as on the Christian side, there was also support for the FKM/RMS on the Muslim side (personal conversation, 4 March 2002). Only by means of a thorough investigation could one judge whether it was true that no Muslims supported the FKM/RMS, or whether, given the current situation, they did not dare admit to doing so; and, a very important point, how many followers there actually were among the Christians. Everything pointed to there being very few.

51. Latupatti was one of the main sources of the Christian Ambon Berdarah Online website (see Chapter 8). His articles were occasionally forwarded to the MML.

52. Among other things, Hefner pointed out that following the storming of Megawati's PDI-P headquarters in July 1996, ultraconservative Muslim organizations in Indonesia such as KISDI had been enjoying increasing support from the former regime and their propaganda measures against the democracy movement, with which the NU and Muslim leaders such as Abdurrahman Wahid had joined forces, had in some cases escalated into violence. In addition, they were also beginning to refer to Western and human rights organizations' reports on East Timor as Christian and Jewish attempts to discredit the Muslims in Indonesia.

53. See, for example, Masariku Report no. 131 of 7 April 2001, which includes statements by those affected, as do Masariku Testimony no. 5 of 18 March 2001 and CCDA reports of 29 November 2000, 5 December 2000, 9 December 2000, 14 December 2000, 16 December 2000, 13 January 2001, 22 January 2001, 12 March 2001 and 25 April 2001.

54. Masariku's investigations into the Bula case became an eight-part report (Masariku Report no. 136 I–VIII, 15–16 June 2001). See also CCDA reports of 13 January 2001, 25 April 2001, and 13 June 2001 and the MML Report of 1 July 2001.

55. For a summary of the events on Kesui and Teor in November and December 2000 see CCDA report no. 118, dated 29 December 2000.

56. 'Peralihan Agama Secara Paksa Sebagai Dampak Kerusuhan Maluku'.

57. Unless otherwise stated, the dates in parentheses in this section refer to corresponding posts on the LJAWJ website and its mailing list.

58. The CCDA (15 December 2000) did wonder, however, why the Christian minority on Kesui would launch an attack on its ethnic brothers, and pointed out that the majority of Christians on Kesui were not Protestants but Catholics, on whom a Protestant pastor fleeing would have made little impression.

59. These FKAWJ reports were written prior to the governor's successful evacuation mission (12 December 2000; 19 December 2000).

60. On the Christian mission in Kesui see Schreurs (1992: 95–98).

61. See, for example, the Message of the Day on 31 March 2001 (http://www.laskarjihad.or.id/, 1 April 2001).

62. A few days before, the article 'Nightmare of Life as a Muslim Slave' had appeared in the *Los Angeles Times* (see above).

63. Many Muslims in the Moluccas would certainly contradict this.

8

Cyberstrategies

'Holy War On the Web' was the title of an article in the 15 October 2001 edition of *Newsweek*, in which author Melinda Liu accused the radical and militant Laskar Jihad of using the Internet for the purpose of jihad. A Masariku member forwarded it (prior to publication) to the MML without comment on 13 October 2001. Christian and Muslim cyberactors alike were well aware that the Internet played a strategic role in the Moluccan conflict. It has already been pointed out in various places that the Moluccan cyberprojects were not isolated from one another, but indeed referenced each other. Both Masariku and the CCDA made frequent references to the media, including the Internet, that the Laskar Jihad used to spread their anti-Christian propaganda – unchecked by the state and the military. The FKAWJ accused the Christians of bringing the Muslims in Ambon and the Laskar Jihad into disrepute so as to achieve their goal in the Moluccas by means of biased reporting in the mass media and electronic media, and in particular on the Internet.

A few exceptions aside, at the local level the groups of people the cyberactors claimed to represent did not communicate beyond religious borders, be it because a direct exchange was simply not possible due to the current critical situation or because one or both of the sides was or were not prepared to do so. Via the Internet, both parties – Christians and Muslims – theoretically had an opportunity, unhindered and via email, chat rooms, etc., to exchange opinions and interact unobserved. Yet even in cyberspace the parties to the conflict did not communicate directly with each other. The cyberactors used other opportunities the Internet offered as a medium to make reference to and attack one another. Via the Internet, the cyberactors familiarized themselves with the 'opposing side's' perspective on the conflict and its interpretation of individual events. Regular access to its information was a prerequisite. For a long time the author of the CCDA reports subscribed to the LJAWJ mailing list, while various Masariku members regularly visited the Laskar Jihad website or were subscribers to its mailing list. The Christian cyberactors were also networked. The MML subscribed to the CCDA newsletter and the CCDA was a member of the MML. Even though the FKAWJ did not subscribe to the Christian articles, it sourced its information from the Moluccan Christian ABO website, which primarily posted information from the CCDA and Masariku.

Just as at the local level a strike was followed by a counterstrike and an act of violence was repaid with another, on the Internet, too, there was an action and reaction pattern in the opposing parties' posts on current events. The other side's statements and arguments were addressed, criticized and refuted, members of 'the others' and their online and offline activities were commented on and denounced. In this way the discourse on the Moluccan conflict was given another component, one that played no less a role in negotiating and defining the different positions and identities than, for example, textual and visual argumentation. The cyberactors not only commented on and documented the events occurring in the conflict in the Moluccas, but also the behaviour of other cyberactors on the Internet. They knew about their opponent not only at the local level, but also in cyberspace. The conflict was thus not only transferred to cyberspace, but was also continued there in a manner that was only possible online. A new level in the conflict emerged, which, though it fed on events at the offline level, could develop a momentum of its own, given the self-reference of the cyberdiscourse described previously. The fact that at the online level the opponent could be attacked verbally and, to a certain extent, physically as well, without really being exposed to any danger, was decisive. The way the conflict was portrayed on the Internet and described and analysed in the last three chapters would never have been possible in the national media – the coarse language of the Laskar Jihad, for example, or certain Christian eyewitness statements about the conflict. In their online confrontations, however, the cyberactors also used certain Internet-specific strategies, the likes of which we already encountered in Chapter 1. Flame wars and cross-posting were of pivotal importance here, although physical attacks on the cyberactors' websites, cyberwar, also played a role.

Cyberwar

Physical attacks in cyberspace include, for example, shutting down a website by manipulating the provider, virus attacks on a mailing list and email bombs. Masariku members and the CCDA accused the Laskar Jihad and other Muslims of infecting their mailing lists and email addresses by means of emails containing viruses and bombarding them with pornographic and other spam mail,[1] causing themselves and their subscribers great difficulties (personal email, 20 and 23 November 2002). The viruses could cause unforeseeable damage and downloading email bombs would not only take a very long time but also incur unnecessary costs. No one, however, could provide watertight evidence that it was indeed the Laskar Jihad or Muslims in general that were behind the unwanted emails. One Masariku member recommended filtering off some email addresses, which in his opinion the 'cursed warriors' *(Laskar Jahanam)* were behind (MML, 7 June 2001). Another was firmly convinced that Al-Qaeda was behind a certain email address and under the subject heading 'VIRUS TERRORIST IN OUR WEB' warned the other members about opening corresponding attachments. This terrorist was sending emails to the MML and was using Western names as pseudonyms so as to deceive the members about the 'fatal danger' (MML, 6 January 2002). When large numbers of MML members complained about having received viruses via list posts, the moderator removed Muslim subscribers from the address list, making the MML a purely Christian project. According to the moderator, however, those Christians were also removed from the list who indulged in incessant torrents of hatred against the Muslims, such as the head of the FKM representative office in the United States (personal conversation, 11 February 2002).

The Laskar Jihad continually had to fight for survival online. The Christians in particular regarded their website as provocative (CCDA, 13 December 2000) and for this reason it was in permanent danger of being 'attacked'. An article in the 8 February 2002 edition of the *Tabloid Laskar Jihad* describes the 'ordeal' of the Laskar Jihad website: it had been established to counterbalance Christian presentations of the conflict on the Internet, such as the mailing list Ambon.com and the ABO site, which were comprised of, they said, nothing more than a 'heap of foul words that insulted Islam'. For Muslims abroad, the Laskar Jihad website was the main source of information about their Muslim brothers' struggle in Ambon and Poso. For this reason, attempts were being made to translate more into English and Arabic, though there were not enough people to do so. Since the Laskar Jihad had gone online a major debate had erupted, for instance, on the mailing list of the IDNIC (Indonesia Network Information Center).[2] Here there were calls for the domain laskarjihad.or.id. to be terminated. When the IDNIC did not succumb to the pressure, the Christians hassled Indosite.com, on whose server the FKAWJ website was. This time they were successful and the site was shut down. According to the FKAWJ webmaster, this was triggered by an interview in *Jurnal Islam* in December 2000 in which Thalib had announced a bloody Christmas (personal conversation, 13 February 2002). Subsequently, Indosite.com saw other religions endangered, something the provider did not want to encourage. According to the webmaster, the fact that the Muslims only intended to defend themselves in response to planned Christian attacks in December and not actively take the initiative had not been taken into account. First and foremost, he had not understood that although the website had been banned, the other Laskar Jihad media had not.

According to the author of the abovementioned *Tabloid* article, this was probably the only Indonesian website that had ever been shut down for SARA reasons.[3] The site was subsequently moved to a server in the

United States, enabling 'the Laskar Jihad, thank God, to continue existing in cyberspace *(dunia maya)*'. It had even been enjoying enormous success: the website was registering approximately 24,000 hits a day and the LJAWJ mailing list already had 1,300 members. The editors of the online presentations had received a lot of feedback from home and abroad – from threats to support. They had also had to struggle with spam and pornographic emails, of which they got dozens, sometimes hundreds, a day. The Laskar Jihad had taken on a tough assignment in fighting the Christians online as well, yet this was part and parcel of the *Jihad fi sabilillah* (jihad on God's path). The war in cyberspace was well planned and thought through by the Laskar Jihad. Yet the eyes, brain and hands used for the jihad in cyberspace would be useless without God's help.[4] In 2001 the Christians had also allegedly aimed their attacks at the FKAWJ's religious online project, the Salafy site, which without reason had been removed from a free web server. According to the FKAWJ the explanation could be found in the Koran: 'And the Jews will not be pleased with you, nor the Christians, until you adopt their religion' (http://www.salafy.net, 10 October 2001, alluding to sura 2, verse 120 of the Koran).

The LJAWJ website had moved to the HostRocket server in the United States, from which, however, it was removed on 5 September 2002 because the Laskar Jihad were accused of having terrorist links. The same thing then happened at BurstNET (U.S.), as it was assumed that the Laskar Jihad was associated with Al-Qaeda (personal email from the FKAWJ webmaster, 26 September 2002).[5] According to the FKAWJ, here too Christians and Jews were responsible, having posted protests, for instance, on the Maluku WEB Portal, allegedly a Christian RMS militia website, and on the website of the Jewish Federation of South Illinois (http://www.maluku.org or http://www.simokyfed.com/mt/haganah/, 20 October 2002).[6] Above all, the Laskar Jihad (9 September 2002) criticized the fact that nothing was being done against provocative and insulting Christian websites such as ABO. In this context, it is interesting that the FKAWJ website was blocked by the Saudi Arabian government (http://cyber.law.harvard.edu/filtering/saudiarabia/sa-O.html, 17 October 2002), in the very country where a large number of the fatwas legitimizing the jihad in the Moluccas were issued. According to the FKAWJ webmaster, though they had heard that people in Saudi Arabia had no access to their website, they could not explain why the Saudi government treated it like a pornography site (personal email, 22 October 2002).

Flame war

> The way in which power is exercised is through the process of 'flaming', where the errant voices are 'burnt out' and subdued and quieted.
> Ananda Mitra, 'Virtual Commonality'

'Flame war' is a term generally used to describe verbal battles conducted by members in an online forum, be it a mailing list, news group or chat room. In Moluccan cyberspace, however, these so-called flames were aimed less at members of one's own online group and more at the portrayals posted by other cyberactors and actors at the local level. The choice of words of the Laskar Jihad provided typical examples. The Christians were referred to as infidels, RMS supporters, colonialists, liars, bugs, pigs and dogs. The Laskar Jihad stopped at nothing to express their hatred of the RMS and the Christians. As the Laskar Jihad repeated time and again, the Moluccas had to be cleansed of this 'filth' once and for all. As flaming was an integral part of the LJAWJ website, many of these points have been addressed in previous chapters. The vocabulary chosen by the Christians, on the other hand, was far less blunt and insulting. The CCDA reports never used strong language to characterize the Muslims. In principle, this was also true of the MML, though there were exceptions among Masariku members who expressed their displeasure by means of sudden emotional outbursts, metaphors and jokes. Because these really were exceptions, unlike with the FKAWJ project, it makes sense here to present a few examples away from the Masariku argument context. Even if these examples were not the rule at Masariku, perhaps precisely because of their intensity they still influence the image of the mailing list received by a passive member and give it a Muslim-critical feel, however much many of its members endeavoured to ensure balanced reporting.

In 2000 several radical Muslims warned that that year's Christmas would be a bloody one, as the Muslims intended to take revenge. In December 2000 an interview with Ja'far Umar Thalib in the Indonesian magazine *Tempo Interaktif* was published online and forwarded to the MML. In it Thalib emphasized his standard accusations against the Christians and concluded with a very pessimistic forecast with regard to the peace process in the Moluccas. The mood was bound to be explosive, in particular because in 2000 Christmas and Idul Fitri almost coincided. At this, one Masariku member lost his temper, verily shouting on the list (18 December 2000):[7]

HEY ... YOU DOG ...!!!!

WHY DID YOU GO THERE ...???

YOU CAME TO STIR UP TROUBLE, THEN SAY ALL SORTS OF THINGS.

HEY ... ANIMAL ...!

LEAVE OUR LAND QUICKLY.

On 17 October 2001 the same person posted a picture with the heading 'Anti-Jihad-Rocket over Kabul', in which Afghanistan was shown being bombarded with pigs converted into rockets, but also, by way of contrast, on 15 October 2001 had posted images with Christian motifs and 'I love you, Jesus Christ' titles. Under the subject heading 'haram ... haram ... haram ...'[8] another member poked fun at a letter by a Muslim youth to a Muslim authority, in which he enquired whether it was consistent with Islamic law to eat in the house of a Muslim who ate pork and drank alcohol. According to the Masariku member (MML, 17 October 2001), if Muslims were so afraid of being defiled, they should not be allowed to buy mobile phones, TVs, radios, refrigerators and other Western, Japanese and Chinese products, as they could never know if the production workers had washed their hands after eating food banned for Muslims *(haram)* before going back to work. In another email the member went even further; in cyberspace the war of words knew no boundaries. In his opinion, the best solution to the Laskar Jihad problem would be to kill their charismatic leader, Ja'far Umar Thalib. On 16 July 2001 he put forward this proposal on the MML, calling on the courageous to get in touch with him as soon as possible with regard to this matter. On 15 October 2001, however, he announced that the plot to murder Thalib had failed. His team's operation 'Jihad eats shit' *(Jihat makan tahi)* had been unsuccessful, as they had attempted to kill Thalib by shooting him in the head and chest. As opposed to normal people, however, his brain and heart were in his rear and his knees, and so he survived the attack.[9]

Yet another MML member sought to use humour to express his criticism of Muslims. On one occasion, for example, he forwarded a story by Ayesha Ahmed that compared Muslims with children: 'Have you ever noticed how much is common between beliefs and thinking of little children and grown up Muslims' (19 August 2002). The author of the story also asked readers to consider the following:

> Children believe everything in their storybooks without a question; Muslims believe everything in their religious books without a question ... Children dream of visiting Disneyland one day, and when this dream comes true it is the happiest time of their lives; Muslims dream of visiting Mecca one day, and when this dream comes true, it is the happiest time of their lives ... When in Disneyland, children wear Disney character T-shirts and Mickey Mouse caps and very excitedly follow big crowds to different points of fascination; when in Mecca Muslims wear special clothes, shave their heads/wear hijab and very excitedly follow big crowds to different points of fascination ... Children pretend to beat the imaginary monster with a real stick; Muslims pretend to beat the imaginary Satan by throwing real stones ... Children believe that all the good kids will be rewarded with candy and all the bad kids will be punished by spanking; Muslims believe that all the Muslims will be rewarded with houries and all the non-Muslims will be punished with hellfire. (MML, 19 August 2002)

The member concluded by saying that children eventually grew up, but Muslims never did.

The other MML members hardly responded to this kind of contribution, at least not online, so if the posters had intended to provoke, in the inner MML community they had missed their target.

Cross-posting

The strategic use of cross-posting can fulfil several functions. By posting articles by their opponents on their website, cyberactors are in a position to comment on them, criticize them and even change them and discredit their authors while sitting comfortably at home or in their offices. They can also provoke the members of their own online community and spark debate. According to Watson (1997: 119), corresponding posts by the enemy, which all members see as a threat, help strengthen the communal spirit. Cross-posting and forwarding articles also enables communication across several lists and forums and an extension of a discourse's reach. Cross-posting was a speciality of some MML members. It was in this way, for example, that innumerable LJAWJ online posts reached the MML. One consequence was that the MML members were kept abreast of the Laskar Jihad's reporting and argumentation. One of the most diligent cross-posters also took the opportunity to provoke other members and comment on the posts that were forwarded. For the most part he forwarded the content of the posts unchanged, but did alter the subject heading. In this way he criticized either the Laskar Jihad themselves or the content of the post, thereby in principle underscoring the general line of argumentation of the Masariku community, which is why many of the members probably did not consider it necessary to respond to these cross-postings. According to Christine Hine (2000: 125), it is standard practice in news groups not to send a separate message to signal agreement. This prevented forums from being flooded with posts that in principle stated nothing more than 'me too'. Certain FKAWJ posts, however, did spark discussions on the MML, for example, in connection with the declaration on the recognition of the Indonesian unitary state, which the Christians, as opposed to the Muslims, had not signed, or the discussion on the death of the Christian grassroots leader Agus Wattimena (March 2001).

As an expression of general criticism of the Laskar Jihad, the above MML member changed the subject heading of his FKAWJ cross-postings to 'Malicious warrior' *(Laskar Jahat)* or 'Cursed warrior' *(Laskar Jahanam)*, to 'Provocation' *(Provokasi)* or 'Propaganda of the malicious warriors' *(Propaganda Laskar Jahat)*. According to him, the eyewitness accounts of Muslim hostages were just as much propaganda as the reports of alleged RMS attacks on the Indonesian military and the readers' letters the FKAWJ published on its website. He referred to the response by the FKAWJ public relations department to a reader's letter with the question 'God is peace not war. Why does Laskarjihad Murder?' as 'The voice of Satan':

We at Laskarjihad reject the term 'murder', as we are not out to murder anyone. We have only defended ourselves and our Ambonese brothers when necessary. The only people that have commited murder in Ambon are the Christians. Please don't forget that the war in Ambon started because more than 3,000 Muslims were murdered by the Christians. This is what started to war. Regarding your slogan, 'God is peace not murder.' You should read the bible before you make such empty comments. While there are mentions of peace in the bible, there are also countless wars mentioned in the bible. Therefore, your slogan, 'God is peace not murder,' only shows that you do not understand the history of your own religion. Consider the following verses from the bible, the book you claim to believe in: Joshua 8:8, 11:38. (FKAWJ, 26 March 2001)[10]

The changed subject headings meant that in just a few words, posts were brought down to a common denominator in terms of content, interpreted or rejected as being nonsense. By way of example, the MML poster headed a post in which Thalib called on the Muslim community to fight the Christians for as long as it took for the defamation of the Muslims in the Moluccas to be brought to an end with the words 'Jihad threat' (*Ancaman Jihad*) (13 September 2000). He dismissed as a 'Confused report' (*Berita Ngawur*) the FKAWJ theories on a Church and RMS conspiracy in Ambon (13 March 2001). Reports that the goal of the RMS was to advance a global Christianization mission were a new version of the *Arabian Nights* fairy tale, he continued (*Versi baru Cerita dongeng seribu satu malam*, 30 May 2002). Another MML member forwarded parts of the download section of the FKAWJ website with a directory of Thalib's speeches on Christianization and the conflicts in East Indonesia, referring to them in the subject heading as 'DEFAMATION & LIE' (*FITNAH & KEBOHONGAN*, 26 May 2002). Various other MML members posted on the list parts of the FKAWJ website or list articles, which in addition to daily news and readers' letters offered background information, without comment or with a neutral heading, and let them speak for themselves. These included, for example, a list of donations to the FKAWJ, the address list of its branches throughout Indonesia and the table of contents of a Laskar Jihad bulletin (ninth edition), which among other things addressed the arrogance of the Christian minority in Indonesia and the supremacy of the Christians in the Moluccas (MML, 31 December 2000; 4 August 2001; 8 September 2001). In just a few cases MML members commented in detail on the forwarded LJAWJ posts, although in terms of content these commentaries differed little from the debates that have already been addressed.

Obtaining proof of one's own line of argumentation or receiving indications of how the Laskar Jihad would subsequently proceed in Indonesia's Islamization process provided additional motivation to 'spy' on the enemy and extract certain posts. By way of example, LJAWJ posts were forwarded to the MML that clearly revealed that Muslim military units were collaborating with the Laskar Jihad, with the latter emphasizing that it was necessary to defend the unity of the state together with the Indonesian military. The report about a visit by Thalib to the Lesser Sunda Islands (Nusa Tenggara Barat, NTB) gave cause to suppose that this was the next target of the 'cursed warriors', as the poster claimed in the subject heading (MML, 4 August 2001). The Laskar Jihad's statements on Megawati's election as president (MML, 26 August 2001), as discussed in the chapter on the FKAWJ, were proof of the fact that the Laskar Jihad were by no means as faithful to the state and the government as they claimed to be.

In some cases the CCDA translated excerpts from FKAWJ posts or summarized them in English. This kept readers abreast of the Laskar Jihad's activities, goals and war philosophy, and the CCDA took the opportunity to respond to the depictions and correct 'misinformation'. It was wrong, for example, that on 6 January 2001 RMS posters and flags had been put up on roads and residential buildings in all Christian areas. Because in Ambon no Muslim would dare venture into a Christian area, the question arose as to who sent this 'nonsense' to Yogyakarta (CCDA, 11 January 2001). The CCDA almost despaired of the FKAWJ's never-ending separatist accusations against the Christians. Regardless of what happened, they were always given the blame, and if nothing happened something was invented. The Laskar Jihad, for instance, reported a heavy exchange of fire between the military and RMS dissidents after the burial of Agus Wattimena, which according to the CCDA was pure fabrication: 'We just want to ask: when will this unholy twisting of facts by this Communication Forum stop? For in fact that afternoon not any shot was fired except firing in the air in honour of a hero' (CCDA, 24 March 2001). Whereas in its reports the FKAWJ repeatedly made reference to individual Masariku members and the CCDA, only in two cases did it forward posts by the MML directly to its list (2 October 2000),[11] which was wholly in line with the doctrinaire philosophy of the Laskar Jihad. The posts in question were both letters by the Church's team of lawyers in Ambon (TPG), which were vehemently contradicted using the standard arguments of the FKAWJ.

Further strategies[12]

In addition to flame wars and cross-posting, the Moluccan cyberactors used a number of strategies to underscore their own positions and criticize and defame the other side. Underscoring their own position was about appearing authentic: the online platform integrated textual, visual and audio documentation, which was supplemented by further authentic documents such as important declarations and letters that had been scanned in. So as to illustrate the huge support of the local population, all Moluccan cyberactors included local figures and organizations in their reports. By also posting articles about other conflicts in Poso, Israel and

Palestine, and Afghanistan, they also linked the Moluccan conflict with these trouble spots and elevated it to a higher level, involving the defence of fundamental values, be they of the Christians and Jews or the Muslims, regardless of where they lived. All these different posts could be brought together on the Internet, such that the local level was directly transferred to the global, and vice versa. The local level was extended further still by links to other websites and mailing lists. If there were links between people and groups with similar interests, large networks, even imaginary online communities, could emerge, which extended far beyond the original Moluccan cyberspace. When evaluating links, however, it should be noted that these were an expression of a very wide range of relationships, as became clear in the discussion of the Moluccan cyberactors' online environments.

Manipulating websites provided another opportunity for attacking an opponent online. Here I would like to present the Ambon Berdarah Online website (Bloody Ambon Online, ABO) in greater detail, which was not actually part of Moluccan cyberspace as defined by myself, as the site's Moluccan webmaster lived in Australia. I wish to consider ABO here for several reasons. Firstly, along with the Ambon.com mailing list, in the context of the Moluccan conflict Muslims saw the site as *the* Christian Internet presence (see above). Secondly, from the outset the initiator of ABO had been an active member of the MML. Thirdly, as far as local information was concerned, the site relied primarily on the Masariku network and the CCDA. A mysterious informant by the name of Joshua Latupatti was another important source for the ABO, who appeared to be in Ambon, but whose real identity was only known to the ABO webmaster.[13] His posts were sometimes forwarded to the MML. Like Latupatti, the webmaster wished to remain anonymous so as not to endanger himself and his family (personal email, 12 September 2002). By posting a great deal of Masariku news, analyses and images, the well-visited, freely accessible ABO site made these available to a wider audience, thereby extending their reach enormously.[14]

ABO was clearly a Christian-oriented project. In August 1999 the ABO webmaster decided to go online in order to balance out the portrayals on Muslim websites such as Suara Ambon (Voice of Ambon)[15] and in the national press, which predominantly denounced the Christians, thus expressing support for his brothers and sisters in the Moluccan Islands. On the left-hand side of the ABO website, right next to the page heading, there was a cross, and in Joshua Latupatti's articles in particular the Muslim enemy was described in very clear language (Illustration 17). He referred to the Laskar Jihad as lice (*kutu*), idiots (*idiot*), wicked (*jahad*), stupid (*dungu*), robbers (*jarah*) and poisonous vipers (*ular beludak*), with a low character (*rendah budipekerti*); he claimed that with their treatment of the FKM/RMS issue, they took people for fools and only wanted to distract attention from the true causes of the conflict.[16]

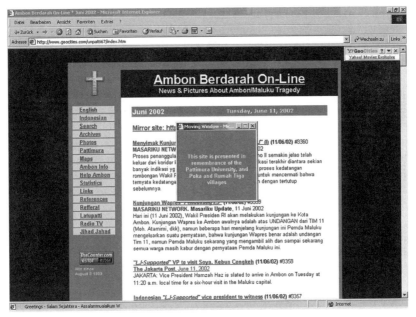

Illustration 17. Ambon Berdarah Online (11 June 2002)

If one clicked on the menu item 'Help Ambon', a window popped up that did not ask for financial support, as could perhaps have been expected, but, in English and Indonesian, for prayers: 'Help Ambonese by Praying for them in the name of Jesus Christ – *Berdoalah di dalam Nama Yesus Kristus bagi saudara-saudara kita di Maluku.*' The link menu was dominated by an image of the burning Silo Church in Ambon. On account of the quotas imposed by the free home page provider (http://www.geocities.com),[17] the Internet address had to be changed frequently (personal email from the webmaster, 16 September 2002). The webmaster made strategic use of this, selecting for addresses the names of localities in the Moluccas where the Christians had suffered great casualties. For instance, the address http://www.geocities.com/unpatti67/index.htm made reference to the destruction of Pattimura University (Unpatti) and the murder and expulsion of many Christians from this area. With the change of address, the words appearing in a red window that popped up upon opening the ABO site also changed (see Illustration 17, 'Moving Window'). In connection with the attack on the Christian village of Soya in late April 2002, the address changed to http://www.geocities.com/soija2002. The red window again provided an explanation of this: 'This site is dedicated to Soija (or Soya) Village and its people who suffered from a bloody attack by Laskar Jihad.'[18] When the address changed to http://www.geocities.com/waai67/index.htm, the site drew visitors' attention to the destroyed Christian village of Waai: 'This site is dedicated to the lost Waai Village – still occupied by the Oppressor Laskar Jihad –, the people of Waai – living in the refugee camp –, and the pastor Diana Akyiwen.' When the address changed to http://www.geocities.com/kesui2001/index.htm, the site made reference to the islands of Kesui and Teor, where hundreds of Christians had been forced to convert to Islam.

Posts on the ABO site were written partly in Indonesian, partly in English – a great advantage for an international audience. An English translation was also provided for images depicting graffiti in Indonesian. Several other Masariku images were accompanied by short descriptions – partly in English, partly in Indonesian – which were often missing even on the MML. Admittedly, this meant that it was easier to sway the observer in a specific direction. At the bottom of the website visitors were requested to send their comments to its webmaster (alifuru67@yahoogroups.com). However, I never received an answer to any of the emails I sent to this address.[19] According to the webmaster, emails had initially been answered, regardless of whom they were from and the sender's motives. Yet this was highly time-consuming, and many of the emails had been hateful and contained threats (personal email, 13 September 2002). This had been the start of a 'cyberwar', as the webmaster put it, in which the others ('they') had tried to destroy their ('our') mailing list (MML) and website (ABO) by means of viruses, junk mail and pornographic emails, etc. After a while they hardly answered any emails addressed to alifuru67. In addition to the email address at the bottom of the site, there was a reference to who was behind the site: 'This site is maintained by the Real Ambonese.' In his email of 13 September 2002, the webmaster explained what was meant by 'real Ambonese', with clear criticism of those who claimed to represent the Moluccan people or, as he put it, the Ambonese:

> Both of us were born, grew up, studied (from primary to university) and worked in Ambon. So, we know Ambon better than those who claim Ambonese (1) because of the ancestor but in fact had never lived in Ambon, (2) because they lived Ambon after their parent 'moved' to Ambon but in fact had never accepted/understood local traditions and customs and (3) because they only studied in particular at the Pattimura University in Ambon. My point is that as long as you have heart for Ambon you are also a real Ambonese.

Let us return to the strategy of the manipulation of websites. In late 2001 the ABO webmaster launched an interesting coup by adding to the menu the item *Jihad Jahad* (Wicked Jihad), a play on words. It was a link to a manipulated FKAWJ website, which the author had entitled *Jihad Jahad*:[20]

> You are visiting the official site of Laskar Jahad: 'Jahad in Ambon': *www.LaskarPlastik.or.id*

The site's layout was very similar to the official LJAWJ site, with strategic changes to a few menus and special contents. The webmaster describes the motive behind this:

It's our idea to let others know this evil organisation exists and is real and is responsible for all the trouble in Indonesia. We also consider ourselves the Laskar Jihad (and alike) Watch. We are carefully watching the activities of LJ in Indonesia in particular in Ambon, Poso, Papua. (personal email, 16 September 2002)

The menu item About Jahad on this site provided information from G. J. Aditjondro about the sociological and financial background to the Laskar Jihad and their links to political parties, Rustam Kastor, the military and the police. The Gallery section of the LJAWJ site, which exclusively showed pictures of Muslim victims, was renamed Pictures, where now Christian victims were displayed under the heading Pictures of our Victims, and under Our Achievements, images of graffiti insulting Christianity were shown. The historical images under the menu item Muslim RMS were intended to serve as evidence that in the 1950s Muslims had also been involved in the RMS movement, not just Christians. The images show Muslim RMS activists in the Netherlands holding banners calling for support from Christians in the Netherlands.

The ABO had been a thorn in the side of the Laskar Jihad from the outset, although the Laskar Jihad did not specifically respond to this caricature of their website. In addition to the content, they were most annoyed by the fact that the ABO webmaster did not openly reveal his identity. In a letter to the FKAWJ (19 March 2001), one Muslim visitor complained about the anonymity of the 'Christians' Homepage (OBET = Robert), Ambon Berdarah Online'. This was a clear indication, he wrote, of the author's bad, dishonest intentions, whereas the Laskar Jihad openly admitted their identity online, providing names, addresses and further contact details.

It becomes clear here that in Moluccan cyberspace, too, the anonymity that the Internet offers everyone who wishes it could become a problem, be it for Internet research or individuals or groups who felt attacked by this anonymity. Yet for provocative actors on the Net – who use flame wars or cross-posting – or for sites like ABO, which adopt a clear position in a conflict, this anonymity was advantageous.

On the Internet, however, it is possible to not just remain anonymous, but also to use a pseudonym or a different name, and to pretend to be someone else so as to make the 'original' look ridiculous, harm him or wreak havoc in his name. For a short time a certain Osama bin Laden surfaced on the MML, who, as opposed to what we would have expected, was very indignant about the incapability of the Indonesian government and the cruelty of the jihad militias involved in the Moluccan conflict. Behind the pseudonym was the email address of one Abdul Kafir (unbelieving Abdul), whose aim appeared to be to criticize jihad Muslims in general and poke fun at them (see, e.g., MML, 19 October 2001). According to the MML moderator, other Internet users adopted pseudonyms and false names in order to be included on the list so as to be able to disseminate provocative articles and even viruses (personal meeting, 11 February 2002).

The following case is a good example of how different Internet users use the same identity online while pursuing completely divergent goals. Both Masariku and the FKAWJ issued warnings about an email address that was very similar to that of the LJAWJ (laskar-jihad@yahoogroups. com instead of the original laskarjihad@yahoogroups.com), behind which there was clearly a quite different group or person. Without apparently having anything to do with it, one MML member was included in the laskar-jihad mailing list. He claimed this was related to his criticism of the Laskar Jihad, which was why he did not now know whether he had become a member of a 'normal' mailing list or been included on the Laskar Jihad blacklist (MML, 16 May 2001). Nor did other members of the group seem to be perfectly clear about the motives of the list's founders. In posts forwarded to the MML, one person, for example, who likewise was behind the Laskar Jihad label and used the email address laskar_j@hotmail. com, speculated that infidels, Christians or Jews were behind it and that the list was a fake. Another advised Muslims to leave the list quickly. In its Yahoo! group description, however, the founder of laskar-jihad maintained that this was the official LJAWJ mailing list (*Milis Resmi Laskar Jihad Ahlus Sunnah wal Jama'ah*). That, of course, triggered a wave of protest from the FKAWJ, which via email (27 November 2000) and on its website explicitly warned against this false Laskar Jihad mailing list. Behind it were swindlers and liars, frauds and infidels, who were out to put the jihad and the Laskar Jihad in a bad light. They were probably even in cahoots with the RMS Christians. Moreover, the only thing members were sent via the list was spam (FKAWJ, 28 May 2001).[21] To some extent, the situation on the offline level also reflected this. In its online portrayals the FKAWJ complained on several occasions that the name 'Laskar Jihad' was also being misused offline by private persons and organizations, either for private benefit, to defame the name of the LJAWJ or accuse it of things it had not done in order to harm it (see, e.g., FKAWJ, 27 November 2000; 14 March 2001).

Hitherto we have considered the Internet primarily as a tool that enabled those parties involved to stake out their positions and set them apart from others, extend their struggle to encompass the online sphere and essentialize identities. However, I do not wish to neglect to draw attention to a trend that had been becoming increasingly evident on the Masariku mailing list since mid-2002. It illustrated that the Internet could not only be a weapon, but also an instrument for peace in the conflict. From the outset, Masariku members (like the CCDA) also included news of peace efforts and initiatives in their reporting and evaluated them in a positive light, even taking part in them. They repeatedly emphasized that the majority of the Moluccan population – Christians and Muslims alike – were tired of war and wanted peace, whereas the FKAWJ was only ever interested in confrontation. Since mid-2002 one of the Masariku founders had quite deliberately dedicated himself to peace journalism and had fashioned his articles on the list accordingly. Opposition, cruelty, traumatic experiences and corresponding images were no longer the focal point of his reporting, but rather the description of the slow attempts to come together at the lowest level made by the parties to the conflict (at the market, in the street, joint sporting activities, etc.). He emphasized things the Moluccans had in common and their common heritage – their common origins and common traditions, the beautiful countryside of their common home. He reported on the first trips made by the Masariku team into Muslim territory, the friendly reception there, the reunion with old Muslim friends from whom, on account of the conflict, they had been separated for a long time, and on joint prayers. The intention was to send out a positive signal and demonstrate that peace was possible. For this reason, he also criticized those who were attempting to prolong the conflict still further, and strongly condemned the bomb attacks and raids following the Malino II agreements.

Summary

The Moluccan cyberactors did not use the opportunities the Internet offers to communicate directly with one another, but rather pursued specific online strategies to make reference to one another and also to attack one another online. The discourse on the Moluccan conflict conducted in cyberspace developed a momentum all its own. This was due to the fact that the cyberactors perceived themselves and knew one another as such and, on account of the importance they accorded their online presentations, not only referred to one another's activities at the local level, but also quite specifically to their online presence and the shape this took. Through their online reporting the Moluccan cyberactors expanded the local conflict to encompass the Internet, using other means to continue it there. The strategies were by no means restricted to cyberwar, that is, physical attacks on websites and mailing lists. Rather, the following were typical of the Moluccan conflict waged online: (1) flame wars (online wars of words) in all variations; (2) cross-posting strategies, used to promote solidarity among one's own ranks as well as to criticize and defame the opponent; (3) the inclusion of material from local and international sources and the use of links to corresponding online presentations to lend a larger dimension to one's own conflict; and (4) the manipulation of websites and online identities. The potential of the Internet as an instrument for peace, that is, a space where the opposing parties could exchange views undisturbed and negotiate joint peace, was not, however, exploited. After three years of conflict, just one of the people active in Moluccan cyberspace had consciously dedicated himself to peace journalism.

Notes

1. Spam emails are those that are sent unsolicited to several Internet users or news groups at the same time (for advertising purposes or the like).
2. IDNIC is responsible, for example, for domain registration in Indonesia (see http://www.idnic.net.id).
3. See also the 6 December 2000 post on the LJAWJ list, in which the webmaster provided several alternative URLs for the website: http://www.laskarjihad.cjb.net; http://server.as.gs/~laskar; http://www.laskarjihad.com; http://www.laskarjihad.net; or http://www.laskarjihad.org.
4. *Tabloid Laskar Jihad*, issue 16, 8 February 2002: 12–3.
5. The webmaster drew my attention to an article in the *Scranton Times Tribune* of 15 September 2002 entitled 'Terrorists' Websites Hosted by City Firm – A Scranton Internet Company Has Found Itself Under the Microscope of at Least Two Political Groups for Hosting Radical Islamic Web Sites' (http://www.zwire.com/site/news.cfm?newsid=5375642&BRD=2185&PAG=461&dept, 20 October 2002).
6. The Federation's website displayed a Star of David and called itself 'Haganah – an online self-defence force'; it had vowed to fight jihad websites such as those of Al-Qaeda (known online as Al Neda) and the LJAWJ.
7. 'HEY ... ANJING ...!!!! KAMU DATANG KE SANA BUAT NGAPAIN ...??? DATANG BIKIN RUSUH, LALU BICARA MACAM-MACAM. HEY ... BINATANG ...!!!!! CEPAT KELUAR DARI KATONG PUNG TANAH.'
8. *Haram* refers to things banned for Muslims, such as certain foods.
9. Whereas Ja'far Umar Thalib announced the death sentence he had passed by religious decree on the brigadier general I Made Yasa not only on the Internet but also on the local radio station SPMM, this anonymous MML member would never have dared address his requests to any other audience than that of the MML.
10. The original quoted the said verses from the Bible.
11. A Masariku member presumably posted these articles beforehand on a freely accessible website, as it is highly unlikely that an LJAWJ member was a subscriber to the MML.
12. The choice of communication method, the open or closed nature of mailing lists, the use of a moderator, the selection and publication of readers' letters, etc., as discussed in previous chapters, should also be mentioned here as specific Internet strategies used by the Moluccan cyberactors.
13. For one of his analyses of the conflict see, for example, Latupatti (1999).
14. According to the webmaster, the site had on average one hundred visitors a day, and between March and May 2002 as many as approximately three hundred daily (personal email, 16 September 2002). Actually, almost anybody who was interested in the Moluccan conflict and had Internet access appeared to know of the site.
15. http://come.to/suaraambon (no longer available in 2012).
16. http://www.geocities.com/waai67/joshua21032002.htm (no longer available in 2012).
17. The provider has now been closed, 13 January 2012.

18. Actually, for a long time there was no proof of who was behind this attack. In addition to the Laskar Jihad, Berthy Loupatty, the leader of the Christian Coker gang, which was alleged to have been incited and supported by the military's Special Forces Command (Kopassus), was also suspected (see, for example, *The Jakarta Post,* 2 May 2002; *TEMPO Interaktif,* 17 May 2002; Detikcom, 7 January 2003; *Kompas,* 20 January 2003).

19. During my time in the field in Jakarta and Ambon I found out, through Masariku, who was behind ABO. Only after the webmaster had identified me as a Masariku member and learned of my contacts with his Masariku friends in Indonesia was he willing to talk to me.

20. http://www.geocities.com/unpatti67/jahad_evil.htm.

21. Indeed, in the archive (http://groups.yahoo.com/group/laskar-jihad/messages/, 19 May 2003), there were only a few threads to be found devoted to Islamic topics. The majority are advertising mails or mails containing just a few words, which were then reproduced and sent to members.

9

Cyberactors Online and Offline

In this chapter we retreat somewhat from cyberspace and take a look at the three cyberactors in their offline environment, how they came to be and their activities. Moreover, we get to know individual members of the communities and groups present in Moluccan cyberspace, their motives and their expectations with regard to use of the Internet. Examples are intended to illustrate how, via these actors, the online and offline levels are very closely linked, how online and offline activities complement each other and how they impact on each other. As opposed to the previous chapters, this chapter is not based on a 'collective' of the presentations in Moluccan cyberspace in the shape of mailing lists, newsletters, and websites, but on private email exchange and personal face-to-face interviews with major individual actors in Moluccan cyberspace, as well as local observations.

Regarding membership and the archives, the FKAWJ online project was very open, though in terms of content and concept doctrinaire. This stance also became very clear offline, though here there was no trace whatever of the openness practised on the Internet. Being given an appointment with the FKAWJ public relations department was not a matter of course. In Jakarta, people were weary of the continual accusations in connection with 9/11, and in the Moluccas there were fears that the Laskar Jihad could be unnecessarily distracted and diverted from the right path by a visit from outside.[1] In discussions the FKAWJ members were very cautious and in principle repeated what they propagated on the Internet and via their other media. The Christians behaved quite differently. The MML was a closed project to which only those who had registered and, where possible, recommended guests were admitted. The Masariku founders feared being robbed, exploited or attacked by intruders verbally or by means of viruses and mail bombs. This closed set-up was made publicly accessible via websites that also posted Masariku articles. Face-to-face, however, as within the MML social structure, the Masariku members turned out to be very open and willing to discuss issues. The same applies to the author of the CCDA report.[2]

The Masariku network

In comparison with the other two Moluccan cyberactors, Masariku had the greatest diversity in terms of contributions and members. Correspondingly, there was enormous variety both online and offline. The different motives of individual active Masariku members, their commitment offline and their views on identity and community in the MML are of interest here. This is also a good opportunity to expand on how Masariku came into being in the first place, why the initiators planned to use the Internet for their project and how they rated its importance and impact.

Masariku – the story of a 'bird of fate'[3]

The founders of Masariku deliberately chose the name for their mailing list. In one of the local Moluccan languages, 'Masariku' means a small bird that delivers messages – a bird of fate, so to speak. Masariku was established by a group of friends, all of whom hailed from the Moluccas and the majority of whom, under the auspices of the Crisis Management Centre run by the Indonesian Communion of Protestant Churches (Pusat Penanggulangan Krisis Persekutuan Gereja Indonesia, PPK PGI) in Jakarta, had been committed to putting an end to the Moluccan conflict even before the Masariku network was founded.[4] Via landlines and mobile phones, the PPK PGI received information from the current flash points and issued statements to the national and international press. However, according to Paul, later the MML moderator, the centre kept too many of its reports and too much information for its own agenda only, which is why he decided with his Moluccan friends to found an organization that was independent of the Church, the Moluccans Solidarity Foundation (Solidaritas Anak Negeri Maluku; SAGU).[5] This, however, very quickly proved to be too ineffective and too political. In their search for an ideal instrument to disseminate information, they hit on the idea of using the Internet, and founded Masariku. As Teddy, an early Masariku member, put it, they endeavoured 'to maintain a continuing flow of constant information from Ambon to the World', which was not always easy, as working for Masariku was voluntary and unpaid. Whenever there was no fresh information from Ambon, this was often because their friends there lacked the money to pay their telephone bills or Internet connections (personal email from Teddy, 25 January 2002).

The advantage the Internet still had, however, was that, in comparison with print media, the dissemination costs could be kept low and few staff were necessary. SAGU was never officially disbanded and in the first phase of the Masariku online project many reports were still posted on the MML under the name SAGU, without, however, the background to SAGU being explained. So ultimately it was always the same people who were behind these projects, and it was merely the strategies they used in their endeavours to transmit information about the Moluccan conflict to the outside world and disseminate it nationally and internationally that changed. In Ambon the Masariku project was presented in the office of the mayor and at UKIM, which until its destruction had maintained a crisis centre of its own. So as to avoid old mistakes and guarantee effectiveness, the Masariku founders decided to remain independent and not strive for the status of an NGO. As such they dissociated themselves from the hundreds of NGOs that had been established in Ambon during the course of the conflict or had settled there from elsewhere, of which several were trying to profit from the conflict. Masariku was not concerned with fighting for money, but for their homeland, the Moluccan Islands. For this reason the information was not to be sold, either. What is more, it stressed that it wished to remain independent of the Church, its politics and finances. The MML was intended to be an alternative voice for the Christians, outside the Church. The disadvantage was that as a 'loose network' Masariku had scarcely any prospect of financial support.[6] Franky decided not to use the name Masariku for offline Masariku network activities so as not to risk being pigeonholed every time it embarked on something. Furthermore, as an independent body, Masariku offline also hoped to have access to the existing NGOs and so receive additional information. The result was that at the local level many people knew the Masariku staff, but not by the name 'Masariku', which for most people not directly involved in the activities of the Masariku network meant the eponymous military battalion 733, which was stationed in the Moluccas.

As Masariku was established among a circle of friends, so to speak, many things that for outsiders would no doubt have been of interest, such as the background to the project's establishment and the (offline) identities of its founders, were not explained in the MML and only became clear if one followed the list discourse for several months or had made personal contact with active members. The duties the Masariku project involved were divided up according to where the individual founding members lived and their skills: Franky (Ambon) was responsible for the 'field', the local information network, and for corresponding reports and maps. Paul (Jakarta) was appointed list moderator and editor of the posts (written and pictorial) from Ambon. He also played a part in acquiring means for equipping the Ambon team (with cameras, filming equipment, computers, etc.). Fanny, a Moluccan likewise living in Jakarta but who scarcely featured on the MML, was responsible for finances. Richard (Jakarta) was the second list moderator and responsible for the technical part of the project, such as computers, Internet access and the initial online connection. He was initially supported by Ron (Ambon). Though Timo, likewise a Jakarta-based Ambonese, was not a founding member, he was one of the few members to have been given a specific duty from the list moderator, namely, searching local and national media for interesting material and posting it on the list; this explained his preference for press articles.[7] As a result the Masariku core was divided into a team in Ambon, comprising Franky and his voluntary local staff, and a Jakarta team, the so-called facilitators.

However, it was not just the situation within the PPK PGI in Jakarta that led to Masariku being founded, but also the local situation in the Moluccas. There was no central body that felt responsible for both gathering information about the conflict and disseminating it effectively. In principle, there was no lack of a facility to do so. In January 1999 the Catholic and Protestant Churches had founded the Church Lawyers' Team (TPG), which was intended to gather information and data about the conflict and use it in its work. A month later the Protestant Church of the Moluccas (Gereja Protestan Maluku, GPM) in Ambon set up a communications centre (BANKOM), which was supported financially by the Netherlands. It was meant to collect, via radio, data from throughout the Moluccas on people who had been killed or wounded, as well as buildings and churches that had been destroyed, and to discuss defence strategies.[8] In August 2001 the Maranatha Church/GPM Crisis Centre was founded and the TPG was disbanded. Among other things, the Crisis Centre, which the active Masariku members in Ambon regularly visited, was the place people went to register the dead, wounded and refugees. However, none of these facilities managed to disseminate the information on a large scale at the national and international levels.[9] For this reason Masariku, and later the CCDA as well, assumed the task of building up an information network. There was just as buoyant an exchange of data between TPG and Masariku as there was between the Crisis Centre and Masariku. Although Masariku deliberately attempted to distance itself from the Church, the close links between them cannot be missed.

The local team estimated the number of MML members in Ambon to be approximately ten. Only three of them, however, were really active (Franky and two BANKOM staff members), while another two sporadically delivered information (other voluntary Masariku helpers were not MML members). Via BANKOM, the Masariku team in Ambon had access to a radio network in which all the Protestant Churches throughout the Moluccas were integrated. This was an incredible advantage, as many villages and islands in the Moluccas still had no telephone. The range of the antennae for mobile phones in Ambon was also very restricted and most were destroyed during the conflict. No other organization on either the Christian or Muslim side could avail itself of such an intricate, synchronous communication network.[10] The three active local members were entitled to directly post Masariku reports on the Yahoo! list, in some cases using their personal email address, and in others the group address (masariku@yahoogroups.com). The group identity was the focal point here. If there were any problems with Yahoo!, the news was forwarded via Hotmail to Paul in Jakarta, who then posted it on the Yahoo! MML. If at times there was no Internet access at all, as was repeatedly the case during the conflict in Ambon, the information was forward via fax or telephone, which incurred high costs, or even by using members of the military who often travelled back and forth between Ambon and Jakarta, to integrate them in the process.

As the local active Masariku members could not be at all the flash points at the same time, through liaison officers and friends Franky received additional information via telephone and help from students, primarily members of the Christian Student Movement of Indonesia (Gerakan Mahasiswa Kristen Indonesia, GMKI). However, none of these students had any training as reporters or photographers, which was why the background to and contents of photos and recordings were often not questioned, and in some cases not even documented, nor eyewitness accounts seen in a critical light. The students were keen to demonstrate how bad the Christians' situation was.[11] The photos posted on the MML were frequently taken from videos that were made in the Moluccas and then sent to Jakarta. The problem with this was that no one in Jakarta knew any details about the individual shots and for this reason inadequate commentary was frequently all that was possible.[12] There were insufficient funds for professional staff and often even for film and photo material. Masariku itself owned a computer, three or four cameras and three cassette recorders, which of course was never enough. Moreover, repair costs were constantly incurred. Through the GPM Crisis Centre they had another computer at their disposal. Over the course of time the number of voluntary helpers at Masariku shrank from approximately twenty to a handful of students. This was because initially the level of idealism and motivation was still very high, but as time went on students had to return to their studies and move on, or were tempted away by NGOs that were able to pay them more, or at least something, for their work. Thanks to these former staff members, however, Masariku had better access to the relevant NGOs. On account of staff and financial restrictions, Masariku did not make use of any further Yahoo! options, such as chat, and apart from the very sparse Yahoo! platform did not maintain a website of its own. Such sparseness was thus not a strategic move to appear serious, as Miller (2000: 17) would perhaps have seen it.

According to the list's founders, another problem Masariku constantly struggled with was the theft of information and data, which was made far easier in cyberspace than in other media: copy and paste, and that's it. Numerous organizations, international human rights and Christian organizations as well as local NGOs, benefited from Masariku data and used them in their reporting and analyses. Even though this multiplier effect is of course desirable, the Masariku staff expected their work to at least be acknowledged by Masariku being quoted as the source. Yet that was not always the case. Data were often simply stolen. There were cases in which their material was reproduced and then even sold without, however, Masariku being referred to, let alone sharing in the profit (although it did not wish to, as it would contradict its philosophy). Other organizations had confirmed they would support Masariku with its projects, but never did. All this was, of course, all the more annoying considering that all Masariku members worked on a voluntary basis and without pay, on top of their normal jobs.

At the local level the issue of collaboration between Christians and Muslims was a tricky one. Ideally, Masariku sought to build up an extensive information network that also embraced the Muslim side. In personal discussions with Masariku members, they were convinced that radical Muslims were in a minority that was not representative of the local Muslims in the Moluccas, but nonetheless had enormous influence. Like Kees Böhm from the CCDA, Paul believed that most local Muslims were afraid of radical Muslims and the Laskar Jihad. According to Richard, as the Laskar Jihad claimed to give all Moluccan Muslims a voice, the local Muslims no longer dared to raise theirs. Young people in particular were influenced by the Laskar Jihad through their media, clothing and behaviour in religious matters. Given the precarious situation, any collaboration between Christians and Muslims with regard to procuring and exchanging information was extremely difficult, if not impossible. Though Franky, for example, emphasized the fact that he had good contacts with the Muslim side and was a member of the Christian-Muslim BakuBae movement, he did not seem to have any success in building up a regular exchange of ideas either. As soon as it became known that a Muslim had handed over reports or photos of the situation on the Muslim side to Christians, he could no longer be sure of his life. If contact was established, the parties concentrated on more urgent matters such as social and economic affairs. According to Franky, however, the fact that Masariku had set itself the task of creating a counterbalance to Muslim reporting, and as such had to emphasize the Christian point of view, certainly played a role as well. Once again he pointed out that from the outset Masariku had had a few Muslim members who then, on account of their behaviour online (insults, viruses, etc.), were excluded.

Significance and impact of Internet use[13]

Central questions:[14]
What was the purpose of Masariku online?

Whom do you think Masariku is representative of?

What do you think is the influence on the conflict itself of mailing lists like Masariku?

The founders of the Masariku network opted for the Internet because it was the most effective medium for quickly making information accessible to as wide a global audience as possible, extending local campaigns to the outside world and drumming up support. The Internet made it possible to integrate a wide range of institutions and organizations, Moluccans and other interested parties at home and abroad and directly confront them with the Moluccan conflict at the local level. Moreover, the Moluccan Internet presentations fed websites worldwide that addressed the tragedy in the Moluccas. Ambon Berdarah Online (ABO), for example, existed before Masariku. It was via the mailing list of former pupils of the Christian secondary school in Ambon (XSMANSA at Yahoo!), which was maintained by Moluccans in Jakarta and through which some of the early MML members were already in contact online before Masariku, that ABO webmaster Julius asked his Moluccan friends Richard, Paul, Franky and Yoppy in Jakarta and Ambon to help him procure information for his website. He initially received data from the PPK PGI and Franky, and then from Masariku, through which, on top of this, he had access to other sources, such as the CCDA reports, which were also forwarded to the MML. Here again it was emphasized that the Christians' use of the Internet was a necessary response to the reporting in the national media[15] and to Muslim websites, large numbers of which had been set up after the outbreak of violence in Ambon. As opposed to other media in Indonesia, the Internet was not filtered, and for this reason it was the only genuine provider of information for all those involved. For fear of the consequences and acts of revenge by radical Islamic organizations, even the Indonesian daily newspaper *Kompas,* for example, which was not normally considered to be pro-Muslim, did not dare to include Christian points of view on the Moluccan conflict in its reporting. Online, however, the Christians were able, freely and without danger, to post counterstatements to the Muslim perspective. Given the background to the Masariku network's establishment and corresponding declarations of intention, it became very clear that the MML was seen as the representative of the Christians in the Moluccas.

In order to build up the Masariku network and win over a global public for its cause, first of all Moluccan students at universities throughout the world were contacted and international church contacts activated. They were provided with information from the Moluccas and in return asked to support humanitarian aid for conflict victims. These initial contacts served as multipliers, to make Masariku known, and led people to apply for MML membership who were eager to know what was really happening in the Moluccas and who wanted to help. The Internet became a tool with which to exert international pressure on the Indonesian government to finally put an end to the violence in the Moluccas and bring about peace, which primarily meant driving the Laskar Jihad off the islands. Over the course of time more and more responses were received from members outside the Moluccas. According to Richard, an information network became a strategic network. More and more MML members contacted the Masariku teams in Ambon and Jakarta directly, many of them just to get additional information, but a few in order to plan direct action to help solve the conflict.

From the outset, Franky's goal was to provide balanced information about the conflict and, by means of this information, build up solidarity and advocacy networks for the Moluccan case. International Christian aid organizations and churches such as the Uniting Church in Australia and the Baptist Mission in America relied on Masariku information. Yet Masariku was, among other things, also a reference source for debates in the British Parliament and the U.S. Congress, as Masariku members or their liaison officers had contact with some of their members.[16] The Masariku members were certainly familiar with, and indeed welcomed, the online Masariku environment, which was discussed in Chapter 4, as it helped disseminate information still further. On the other hand, the Internet was also a source of information from other organizations such as the CCDA and the Suffering Church. Franky referred to the Masariku project as a sort of 'supporting system'. He saw the MML as wielding the greatest influence with regard to the problem of refugees; several international organizations had launched projects in the Moluccas as a result of information from Masariku. According to human rights activist Robert, the mailing list had won over international supporters and attracted the attention of the international community and churches worldwide regarding human rights violations in the Moluccas, to which the Indonesian government shut its eyes. Julius, an MML member and the ABO webmaster, did not wish to think about what would have happened to Ambon had it not been for the Internet:

> Can you image what would happen to Ambon if the cyberworld were never invented and the information technology were not existent? We are independent and have only one motivation i.e. to bring peace and harmony back to Maluku by international pressure. To us, Indonesian government has done little to restore order. We don't care whether Maluku remains within the Republic of Indonesia or whatever as long as humanity comes first irrespective of your beliefs. (personal email, 13 September 2002)

Franky and Robert agreed that although the MML had no direct influence on the conflict, it did trigger action and responses from certain international organizations, be it the Church, NGOs or government organizations, which in turn impacted on the conflict. According to Bob, what the MML was attempting to achieve, namely, support for the Moluccan population and intervention in the Moluccan conflict, did not occur through the list, but through other channels.[17] As a project the Masariku mailing list had an outward focus. There was no intention of integrating the local level by also forwarding the information disseminated by Masariku to the local population. According to Paul this was, firstly, too dangerous, and secondly, the simple folk preferred to take notice of rumours or relied on their own sources.

According to Julius, another of the mailing list's great achievements was keeping Moluccans living abroad or in other parts of Indonesia who still had family and friends in the Moluccas abreast of the situation there and, Franky maintained, making edited news available, on the basis of which they could check their own information. Moluccans abroad often used the list to try to get in touch with family members with whom they had lost contact during the conflict. Furthermore, many active MML members were of the opinion that the different types of information and the extensive background information made available on various issues relating to the Moluccan conflict widened the perspective of the list members.[18] Only one of the active MML members explicitly mentioned that Internet presentations did not only have positive effects, as they contributed to what I refer to as the essentialization of identities: 'World knows instantly (advantage) but this also has contributed to growing hatred (disadvantage??)' (personal email from Julius, 16 September 2002).

Individual members, their motives and their offline activities

Central questions:
Why are you interested in the Moluccan conflict?

What was your motivation in joining the Masariku mailing list?

Do you take part in any other activities (on- or offline) concerning the Moluccan conflict?

Who was 'behind' the different MML roles, who were the people involved with the mailing list, what were their personal motives for joining the MML and how were their MML activities related to what they did offline? Franky and Yoppy were two of the *local activists* in Ambon. Both studied in Jakarta, Franky theology and Yoppy law, before returning to their home, the Moluccas, Franky in 1997 and Yoppy in early 1999, shortly before the outbreak of the conflict. Franky became a pastor on his home island of Saparua and a lecturer at the Christian University in Ambon (Universitas Kristen Indonesia Maluku, UKIM); Yoppy could not find a job. Since the conflict erupted both had invested most of their time in awareness work on the Moluccan conflict, aid for refugees, peace efforts and, in particular for Franky, setting up the Masariku information and solidarity network. Both were directly affected by events in the conflict; the areas where they lived were attacked and their houses destroyed. Masariku, however, was by no means the first and only result of Franky's commitment during the conflict. In addition to his activities for the PPK PGI, SAGU and ABO, shortly after the conflict broke out he had already formed a team with Alex Manuputty and others that took care of the Christian community in the Moluccas (Tim Peduli Layak Umat Kristen Maluku) and intended to exert pressure on the Indonesian government.

Even at the time, however, Franky had warned against including the word 'Kristen' in the title. The group was later renamed Nunusaku,[19] although still only Christians were involved. Following the destruction of the Silo Church in late December 1999, Team 20 (ten Christians and ten Muslims) was founded. Alongside Alex and Franky, it now also included members of the military and the police, which according to Franky was a prerequisite for being able to get something done. Yet the security forces did not support the group's aims and it did not achieve its desired goals, causing enormous frustration.

Subsequently, Alex Manuputty founded the purely Christian Nunusaku for Human Rights, which, like the previous groups, was intended to serve as a corrective for the government. When he started increasingly focusing on the issue of independence, seeing recognition of the 1950 independence of the Republic of the South Moluccas as the only solution to the conflict, Franky and Alex went their separate ways. Alex went to the United States and the Netherlands, where he founded the FKM, announcing this publicly on 18 December 2000 in the city of Ambon. He took the opportunity to have the 1950 declaration of independence of the RMS read out, thus making the FKM a political issue. As far as Franky was concerned, this was not the right time for activities of this nature, and not the right way out of the conflict. With the FKM Alex was only playing into the hands of his opponents: the military, the police, the Laskar Jihad and the Indonesian government. The FKM was regarded as a welcome counterweight to the Laskar Jihad. Franky preferred to be active in the Masariku network, became a member of the BakuBae movement and was part of the Christian delegation to the peace negotiations at Malino II. In 2001 he became secretary of the new crisis centre set up by the Protestant (Maranatha) Church. In his efforts to drum up international support for ending the Moluccan conflict he frequently travelled to Europe and the United States, sometimes alone, sometimes as a member of Christian-Muslim delegations, where he visited government organizations and parliaments, human rights organizations and UN institutions, etc. He also had excellent contacts with the international church community. He visited these institutions as a representative of the Moluccan Protestant Church, not of the Masariku network.[20]

The *facilitators* and *moderators* of Masariku, Paul and Richard, had likewise left Ambon to study, Paul to study theology in Jakarta and Richard to study engineering in Ujung Pandang. Afterwards, both settled permanently in Jakarta, where Paul worked in the car business and Richard was a manager at a consulting firm. Since the outbreak of the conflict they had very much been committed to the Moluccan cause, initially as part of the PGI and through SAGU, and then with Masariku. In addition to its Internet activities, the Masariku team in Jakarta had also set itself the task of contacting influential people – members of the government and parliament of Indonesia and other countries, Indonesian military officers, church and human rights organizations – to discuss information about the conflict and urge them to wield their influence to help the Moluccan people. Of the *scholars* and *analysts,* Emil was the only one on the list to 'come out' as a lecturer at Pattimura University in Ambon (Unpatti) (although he was currently working on Java). Bob, likewise previously a member of staff at the PPK PGI and a former secretary-general of the GMKI in Jakarta, had been an MML member from the first hour and was currently the head of a politically oriented Christian youth organization in Jakarta. He too hailed from Saparua, grew up in the city of Ambon and studied theology there. Having spent two years as a pastor in a village on Seram, he moved to Jakarta, studied philosophy and from then on was active in Christian youth movements. Bob emphasized that in the Moluccan conflict a distinction had to be made between various levels of information. Masariku members in Ambon provided local information, but the government and the military also had their own points of view. Having access to political circles and information in Jakarta, he tried to include these aspects in the MML.

Teddy also had the almost typical background of the Masariku actors. Having finished secondary school he left Ambon to study in Jakarta, where he decided to take up postgraduate studies in law in the Netherlands, returning to Java in August 2002. From the outset he too had been involved in humanitarian aid for those affected by the Moluccan conflict. He placed great importance on the MML founders' wish to build up a database for studies of the conflict. He saw this as a unique chance to avoid another 'dark episode' in Indonesian history:

> There are many dark-side and dark-time in Indonesia's history that still dark until now. Such situation will not contribute anything for people. By preparing and collecting information as much as we can, hopefully we can contribute something for the history of our country ... I'm part of new generation in Maluku. In some extent, we're in different position from older generation. But this conflict, created youngest generation that live in their worst experience of life. Only by provide as much information, they will able to learn about their history. (personal email, 11 December 2001)

Not all the Moluccans involved with the Masariku project stayed in Indonesia after their school and university education. Febian and Julius, for example, emigrated to Australia.[21] Both maintained Christian-oriented websites devoted to the Moluccan conflict, ABO and Tawamena Victoria, with ABO in particular based on Masariku information, and as such served as *online multipliers* in the dissemination of the Christian perspective on the Moluccan conflict. We already became familiar with Julius as the 'true Ambonese', having been born and brought up in Ambon, and having gone to school and then university there. He formulated his motivation for becoming active online, as both a member of Masariku and the ABO webmaster, as follows:

Anyway, as we are real Ambonese, we've been very concerned with atrocities in our homeland. Neither Indonesian government nor other Indonesian institutions have exercised good will to stop the violence. As far as we are concerned, they are biased. The only way we thought we were able to help was to publicise the true. In 1999, both of us then launched Ambon Berdarah Online.[22] We've been working for no-body but for the Moluccan. We don't accept any funds but encourage others to raise funds or to donate thru crisis centres and other organisations as appeared on the website. To keep Ambon Berdarah Online alive and online, we use free-web provider. We never stop publicising unless the true peace has been established in our homeland; those who are responsible for the atrocities are brought to justice and homeland is Laskar-Jihad free and is free of other TNI-supported, TNI-backed up militia. (personal email, 12 September 2002)

Like Ernst, a Moluccan in the United States, Julius engaged in *lobby work* in Australia. He supported various peace demonstrations, organized appeals to the United Nations with friends and gave lectures in church circles on the Moluccan conflict, attempting in this way to exert pressure on the Australian media and government to give more attention to the conflict in the Moluccas. Clark, who lived in America, but whose mother came from Saparua, was secretary of the Maluku Watch Network (MWN) and, in this function, also championed the cause propagated by Masariku offline. MWN primarily lobbied the U.S. government and Christian coalitions, and organized demonstrations. Information the MWN received from Masariku was forwarded to friends as well as national and international NGOs. Alongside the MML, the churches in Ambon, Australian sources and the press in Jakarta were other sources for the MWN. The MWN was not only firm in its rejection of terrorists and jihad warriors operating in the Moluccas and in Poso,[23] but also of all forms of separatism. Its only goal was a peaceful solution to the Moluccan conflict, which had to be brought about by working together with moderate Muslims.

The diligent *cross-poster* and *agent provocateur* Arno was likewise born in Ambon, where he still had relatives. For a long time he had been living in Sweden, but like Clark visited the Moluccas during the conflict. Arno had been addressing the problem of injustice in Indonesia, such as the East Timor and Aceh cases, long before the outbreak of the Moluccan conflict, but also had several other interests, which he expressed in the wide range of his posts. From the very first day of the Moluccan conflict he had actively fought the false propaganda of fundamentalist Muslim groups in Indonesia, and for this reason had become a member of Masariku. He too attempted to fulfil his mission as a Masariku member:

Yes, I choose the subject which I consider is important for better understanding of the problem from broad perspective. My opinion is that each contribution should have an educative aspect to readers. (personal email, 25 January 2002)

He was disappointed by the fact that with his numerous cross-posts and by posting provocative discourses from other mailing lists such as Proletar and Ambon.com he was unable to be more effective in challenging MML members and stimulating even more discussions. With his posts he wanted on the one hand to be provocative and on the other to demonstrate that many other people – Christians and Muslims – were fighting Islamic fundamentalism. Arno was quite clearly not just a man of words, but also was active offline. Above and beyond the Moluccan case he was particularly involved with the independence movements in Aceh and Papua as well as the United States' oppression of Cuba.

Arie, a Dutchman, operated on the periphery of the MML social structure. Arie's interest in the Moluccan conflict stemmed from the fact that he had a large circle of Moluccan friends in the Netherlands and had lived with a Moluccan family for a long time. As such, he was concerned about the fate of the Moluccan diaspora in his home country, which was traumatized by the tragedy taking place in their country of origin, where they all still had friends or relatives:

> That is the reason that I am very interested in what happens in Maluku. This nightmare, which already goes on for 3 years, is not only a nightmare for people in Maluku. Their family here in Holland are traumatised by it as well. Traumatised because of all the things their family is going through, but also traumatised by the fact that the rest of the world doesn't care.
>
> We have been, and will continue to do so, asking the world's attention to a possible extermination of some 2 million people and have to see how everybody is indifferent to that. It hurts to see that there is a worldwide outrage against those that committed that vicious crime on September 11 in New York, but at the same time ignore our cry for help for something that is by far worse.
>
> In New York there were 'only' a few buildings destroyed – in Maluku complete villages have been whiped off of the face of this earth.
>
> In New York there are somewhere about 1,000 people to be mourned – in Maluku there are tens of thousands murdered (most often in a very brutal way).
>
> In New York (and the rest of America) they live in fear for 3 months now – in Maluku fear is part of everyday life for 3 years already.
>
> In New York some people lost their house and/or job – there are more than half a million displaced Moluccans.
>
> In New York the people who lost their house are being taken care of – displaced Moluccans are trying to survive under deplorable circumstances. (personal email, 12 December 2001)

Arie championed the Moluccan cause by posting the latest news about the Moluccan conflict on his personal website.[24] For him, the Internet was the perfect medium for reaching the world. When the news was well received and he was getting more and more feedback from visitors, he began providing background information on his site, as well as addresses and suggestions for how to get involved. Furthermore, he compiled a newsletter of his own in three languages, which he sent to subscribers throughout the world. Via his website he made contact with people and organizations in and outside the Moluccas, including members of the MML, who asked him to help with their projects. In addition to his online activities he organized demonstrations, forums and discussion rounds on the Moluccan conflict.

In addition to the key actors in the MML, there were numerous other members on the *periphery* who only contributed to the list very sporadically, such as Rick from Ambon, who had studied with Richard in Ujung Pandang, Tony, Franky's brother, who had grown up in the Moluccas, studied economics in Jakarta and then worked there and on Bali, Johan from Saparua, the joke teller, who now lived in Jakarta, and Henrich, a believing Christian, who came from the island Haruku and now worked in Sulawesi. One other member in Ambon was also of interest who, though not active online in the MML, in his function as a police officer provided the Masariku team with information from police and military circles. It goes without saying that he had a moral conflict with this and as such wished to remain anonymous.

One of the passive MML members, Buce, serves as an example of the fact that despite their silence, online *lurkers,* who were often accused of being freeloaders, could become multipliers.[25] Buce's parents hailed from the Southeastern Moluccas and went to the Netherlands in 1951 during the decolonization process. He still had lots of relatives in the Moluccas, about whom he was very worried. Buce worked for the Dutch Refugee Council and was a board member of a Moluccan organization for sustainable development, Titane, which worked to help the Moluccans in Indonesia. To this end he organized events and seminars, which naturally enough also addressed the current situation in the Moluccas. Titane[26] in turn worked with Novib, a member of Oxfam, Baileo, a Moluccan NGO in Ambon, and the Indonesian human rights organization for Ambon, TAPAK, in Jakarta. In January 2001, on behalf of the Dutch Moluccans, Buce was in the Moluccas with a delegation of nine people. He was convinced that mailing lists were important sources of information for Dutch Moluccans as well, as in the long term phoning was too expensive. It is also interesting that one of Buce's nephews was involved with Maluku WEB Portal, which had an extremely wide range of information about the Moluccan conflict.[27] Another lurker in the MML was, for instance, the Moluccan Information and Documentation Center in Utrecht, which integrated information from Masariku in its online newsletter on the Moluccan conflict, thereby extending its reach.[28] It should also be noted that in the crucial stages of the conflict, members who otherwise followed the list discourse passively raised their voice. Franky spoke in this context of 'reactive members', who became active if the conflict escalated.

Regardless of where they lived, Bob also divided up the MML members into active and passive members, but extended yet further the passive members category I have been using thus far. In his opinion, it embraced more than just MML members who received information via the list – be it to keep up to date with developments or to use it as a journalist, church member, embassy employee or NGO staff member – but never themselves posted comments on the list. Rather, nonmembers should also be included in this category who, for example, received Masariku information via acquainted MML members and used it for corresponding offline and online activities and in this way, if indirectly, helped the Masariku project. This extended reach was important inasmuch as it represented confirmation by other central Masariku members of the importance of MML members' offline contacts with regard to the efficacy of the Masariku network and as such the interplay between the online and offline levels. Franky stressed that several nonmembers received and indeed worked with the Masariku information. These observations will be very relevant in the discussion on the Masariku 'metanetwork'.

What most certainly became clear here was the evidence of the influence and impact of the Masariku online presence, primarily in members' offline and online activities, which served as multipliers and represented a global mouthpiece for Masariku's concerns. In connection with the Moluccan conflict, all the main MML actors were also active offline, be it by gathering data and conducting evacuation programmes on a local basis, lobbying abroad, forwarding and processing information, organizing events and requesting humanitarian and financial aid, writing academic analyses or being politically active. Their activities were complemented by the commitment of temporarily active or passive members on the periphery, as well as other 'passive members' who in this respect did not necessarily have any direct link with the MML.

Community and identity[29]

Central questions:
Would you call the Masariku mailing list an online community (please consider whether members exchange more than just information, whether they share emotions, whether they share common interests and values, common oppositions, common goals and whether they interact with each other)?

Do you think Masariku is providing an identity for its members?

Given my long-term participation in the MML, I came to the conclusion that an imaginary community had emerged within its framework that on the one hand was created and shaped by very specific common points of reference and interests and strengthened by close offline relationships in various local contexts, and on the other was backed by the idea of an international (Christian) community and corresponding symbolism. This insight has already been confirmed in this chapter by the descriptions of the background to the emergence and the building up of the Masariku network, as well as several statements from MML members. The above questions show my interest in the extent to which these ideas, which of course were not discussed explicitly in the list discourse, corresponded to the personal feelings of individual members. Whereas I had reached my own conclusions by means of my own observations and analyses during several years of field research in the social domain of the MML, to conclude my studies I now asked the members themselves relatively specific questions.[30] As I restricted myself here to questioning the key MML members, these statements are not necessarily representative of all MML members.[31]

For all active members it was clear that they had committed themselves to a common cause and were now fighting for it. The MML was a community of common interests that exchanged information, examined and commented on it, and ideally planned specific activities and drew up approaches for solving the conflict. Each member actually agreeing with each individual post on the list was not the decisive factor. According to Teddy, local information was just as important as background information delivered by other active MML members elsewhere. It was often this information that enabled members to form opinions and was also important for local members. Reference was made here to the requisite combination of a micro and a macro perspective, without which it was impossible to understand the Moluccan conflict. Ideally, all members contributed as much as they could to achieve their joint goal.[32] According to Julius, the MML provided its subscribers with an opportunity to exchange information, and provided the Masariku team in Ambon an opportunity to send a cry of help to the outside world. For various members the MML represented the conflict's victims, those who wanted peace and not independence, those persecuted by Muslim fundamentalists, politicians and members of the military and police, and, not least of all, the Christians in the Moluccas. Like Franky, Richard also longed for the day when Masariku would represent the new generation of the Moluccan people, which would define itself not by religion, but its common homeland, the Moluccas. In the current situation, however, Masariku felt obliged to give the Christians in the Moluccas a voice, which they were denied in reporting in the national media, thereby creating solidarity among all Christians worldwide:

> Masariku mailing list is the communication media used especially for showing the condition of the churches and Christians in Indonesia which are being pressed, tortured and abandoned by the goverment. Through this media, the christians can straighten the unrevealed fact/made up news by the goverment and jihad. This media is also used for communicating the Christian in all parts of the world to pray for the condition happening to the Christians. (personal email from Robert, 28 August 2002)

The important things were what was associated with the list and what was ultimately achieved, and in this the MML differed from a community determined solely by a joint current interest. Solicitude and solidarity, a Moluccan identity and the profession of the same faith, Christianity, as well as action against and resistance to the passivity of the Indonesian government and the involvement of the military were what the MML was primarily associated with. According to Bob, Masariku thus became the expression of what at least the active members of the MML could identify with in their current situation, even if they were not Ambonese. The MML provided an identity; on that point all the members questioned agreed. As far as Teddy was concerned, however, after the second year of the conflict the community character of the MML increasingly dwindled, as the number of those who merely wanted information about the Moluccan conflict grew while the active members stagnated and the list's focus expanded. Teddy had a strict interpretation of the term community, which embraced only the active list members, in contrast to Bob's far broader definition.

Purely theoretically, membership of the MML did not involve any obligations when one was accepted. According to Bob, however, practically every member felt obliged 'to share the truth and objective information about Moluccas riot as well as solidarity to the helpless'. For Arno the MML represented an online community with common interests and values. As the information exchanged via the MML was often confidential, Masariku was from the outset highly selective with regard to its members, preferably relying on recommendations from friends and other contacts. Members who misbehaved, that is, who flooded the list with insults, hate tirades and junk mail, were removed from the subscribers' list so that the community could pursue its goals again undisturbed. In the same way, some MML members disassociated themselves from mailing lists such as Ambon.com, where practices of this nature were normal and not punished. Furthermore, Ambon.com accommodated pro-FKM members and all its subscribers resided outside the Moluccas, which is why it was unable to deliver firsthand information. Here too it became clear that demarcation and alienation were important strategies in the identity-finding process.

Thus there were numerous indications in the statements by individual MML members that within the MML a community had emerged that gave its members an identity. Bob's following statement provided confirmation of the conclusion I drew from my online investigations:

> I can say that this is a real community in the sense of interacting in some level, in the sense of making endeavour to working together based on common concern that develop through on-line net, in the sense of sharing with awareness and respect of differences the members have, in the sense of member's obligation to respect the rule and conditions and in the sense of the same goal. I think that is real community; on-line community, eventhough I aware that the kind

of interaction is quite different with what people always experienced in their daily life (offline interaction). For example, we never know exactly if people always use their real name and address or not. (personal email, 13 March 2003)

The CCDA

The Crisis Centre of the Diocese of Ambon (CCDA) was an initiative launched by the Catholic Church, and its secretary and later head, Kees Böhm, expressly emphasized that the reports on the Moluccan conflict did not reflect his personal opinion but were the voice of the CCDA. The CCDA online newsletters were part of the Crisis Centre's strategies for ending the Moluccan conflict and finding support for its victims. I shall now consider the embedding of this newsletter in an offline context shaped by the stance of the Catholics in the conflict and the offline commitment of the CCDA.[33]

The Catholics in the conflict

The CCDA also held supporters of the former Suharto regime, Muslim fundamentalists and the Indonesian military, which was at least 85 per cent Muslim, responsible for the Moluccan conflict. Though the police forces in the Moluccas, many of whom were Christians, occasionally took the Christians' side, they never took part in attacks on Muslims. Members of the military, however, had often been sighted among those attacking a Christian village or Christian facilities. The Christians' fate seemed to be in the hands of the Christian militia alone:

> During those fearful 18 months (June 1999 – December 2000) our fate lay in fact in the hands of the spontaneously arisen christian militia – led by the late Agus Wattimena – with their home-made rifles and primitive grenades. Many sacrificed their lives to maintain a christian stronghold in the city of Ambon. However, they could not prevent that farther off lying sites were totally cleansed of christians. (Böhm 2002b)

According to Kees Böhm, in the last few years before the conflict, religion had become ever more important for the Moluccan population, which was why it could now become the decisive element in the conflict. Even before the outbreak of the violence, houses of worship on both the Muslim and Christian sides had been the only places where people met regularly. If there was a problem, the people were more likely to have gone to religious leaders than to traditional leaders, who in previous times would have settled arguments. Kees Böhm was convinced that there were also certain imams and Protestant pastors *(pendeta)* who were involved in the conflict and fuelling it.

According to the CCDA, at least in the beginning the Catholics assumed a special position in the conflict. They attempted to keep a distance and to play the role of mediator between Protestants and Muslims. The fact that the Catholics were in some cases closer to the Muslims than Protestants was advantageous here:

> In a certain way they had a tradition of 'closeness' to the muslims in a shared preoecumenical – pre-Second-World-War – stance against the protestants of Ambon, that were looked upon as arrogant and dominating. (Böhm 2002b)

Moreover, according to the CCDA, almost 90 per cent of the Catholics in the Central Moluccas and the North Moluccas originally came from the Southern Moluccas or the island of Flores, which was why they did not feel as affected by the clashes between groups of the local population as they would have been had their own families been involved. If they were attacked nonetheless, they had hardly any means of defending themselves, preferring to flee, which was why the number of dead among the Catholics was relatively low.[34] Their houses and property were nonetheless looted and destroyed.

Catholic leaders appealed to their communities not to counter hate with hate, to defend themselves but not actively go to war, and instead to support reconciliation. By way of example Kees Böhm mentioned the Kei Islands in the Southeastern Moluccas, where the conflict, which had reached the islands by March 1999, had been ended very quickly as a result of the mediating role played by the Catholics and *adat*, which in this part of the Moluccas was still very strong:

> I may illustrate this with what happened in the Kei Islands during the unrest there, lasting from 30 March to 3 May 1999 (a little over one month). The Kei Islands lie at a distance of about 500 km south-east of Ambon. They have a mixed population of muslims, protestants and catholics, each of these consisting of about one-third of the local population. There was a sudden explosion of violence, bringing destruction and bloodshed to a large number of muslim villages and protestant villages. We went there twice in order to ensure that the catholics would not involve themselves in this violence. Together with the local parish priests and the local Church Councils we made a firm stance, meanwhile making use of the good relationship of the catholics with both muslims and protestants to bring the conflicting parties together. And indeed, these reconciliation efforts, mainly based on the traditional culture of ethnic brotherhood, yielded success in the whole Kei archipelago. (Böhm 2002b)

However, when the Catholics were also attacked by jihad troops, local Muslims and members of the military, primarily in the North Moluccas and on the islands of Seram and Buru (Central Moluccas), the Catholic priests were left with no choice but to join their communities and flee to the forests or other islands. According to Böhm, hundreds of Catholics had been forced to convert to Islam and been circumcised.

The Crisis Centre and its newsletter

The Crisis Centre, which was founded on 1 July 1999, aimed to address the consequences of the Moluccan conflict and offer assistance to those people who had been affected by the violence and had lost everything when they fled. As opposed to Masariku, the CCDA was firmly integrated in Church structures, which was why it had access to the Catholic Church's network as far as financing and infrastructure were concerned. Nonetheless, it was still reliant on outside support, in particular with regard to aid for refugees, which it received from various national and foreign organizations and private individuals.[35] For the first two years, Father Agus Ulahaiyanan headed the CCDA. In a personal conversation (5 March 2002), he stated that it was not until the year 2000, in view of all the urgent matters, that the CCDA became really aware of the importance of information. The reporting in the national media had spread a very one-sided picture of the conflict, which had to be balanced out. There was a need for objective and impartial information, especially when it came to presenting the conflict to the outside world. Father Böhm, who had come to the Moluccas from the Netherlands more than thirty-five years before and had stayed, was elected secretary of the Crisis Centre, firstly because he was almost always present in Ambon and secondly because he could speak and write English. A decision was made to disseminate via the Internet short, succinct reports about the conflict and the reconciliation efforts. These reports were to be based on information from the Catholic Church's communication network throughout the Moluccas (via mobile phones, landlines and fax)[36] and the personal network of Father Agus, who claimed to have contacts with all social classes and several important groups and people on both the Christian and Muslim sides, and in particular with the government as well.

However, as with Masariku, it also seemed to be the case that the CCDA preferred to use existing connections to Muslims to jointly solve the everyday problems caused by the conflict than to receive information via these channels from 'the other side', which could then be included in the reporting. According to Father Agus, especially after the Malino II agreements it had become difficult to make contact with the Laskar Jihad; even contact between radical and moderate Muslims had subsequently become problematic. Father Böhm and Father Agus both rejected the Muslims' accusation that with the local daily newspapers *Siwalima* and *Suara Maluku*, the TVRI and the RRI the CCDA was using Christian sources. According to them, both *Siwalima* and *Suara Maluku* endeavoured to be neutral, even though unfortunately they did not report everything. They were in any case more objective than the Muslim daily newspaper *Ambon Ekspres,* which for reasons relating to organization and time did not feature in the reports. Though the TV station TVRI was run almost exclusively by Christians, because its main office was located in a Christian district, it nevertheless attempted to portray the Muslim side as well and was in no way pro-Christian and anti-Muslim. The fact that representatives of the military very frequently commented on the current situation in the Moluccas was a clear indication of this.

Kees Böhm soon assumed sole responsibility for the CCDA reports and also, as of mid-2001, was head of the CCDA. Yet Father Agus was not entirely satisfied with Father Böhm's reports, which seemed to him to be too short and omitted important information, though in comparison with Masariku they were more neutral. Though the latter provided more facts it also added its own opinion, which made the reporting tendentious. Kees Böhm accused the MML of burdening its subscribers with too many emails. With regard to the CCDA, the Masariku list moderator criticized the fact that in comparison with the Masariku network Kees Böhm did not have a good information network (personal conversation, 11 February 2002). Father Agus was in any case convinced that with their different portrayals of the conflict they were all out for recognition and prestige (personal conversation, 5 March 2002). In addition to the online reports the CCDA attempted to circulate information by giving journalists interviews, arranging meetings with representatives of regional, national and foreign organizations and providing a point of contact for international visitors looking for information about the conflict or wanting to provide help. According to Father Agus, the CCDA's information policy was primarily aimed at targets abroad, hoping that in this way the 'real truth' about the conflict could be discovered, something that was not possible in Indonesia itself.

The Indonesian summaries of incidents in the conflict, which as of April 2001 were sent via the newsletter, were essentially written for the Diocese of Ambon's monthly journal *Warkat Pastoral* (Pastor's news) and distributed to the Catholic churches in and around Ambon in the form of brochures (approximately ten copies per church). The CCDA was officially disbanded in 2002 when the situation had calmed down. The remaining activities relating to the consequences of the conflict were divided up among the usual commissions of the diocese's parish centre. Kees Böhm, however, continued to send out email newsletters on the current situation.[37] Böhm did not claim to provide his subscribers with an identity, though he did believe that most people saw the CCDA reports as the mouthpiece of the Catholic Church in the Moluccas: 'that this is the voice of that little non-combat Catholic Church that not just wants to come off safely and unharmed, but feels responsible that the strife must end and justice be done' (personal email, 23 November 2002).

Offline activities and their impact

As with Masariku, behind the CCDA online project there were a number of offline activities at the local, national and international levels. At the local level it attempted, for example, to provide the government with information, was involved with and initiated reconciliation events in the Moluccas, such as the large peace meeting in Langgur in March 2001, and helped refugees. Fifty Protestant families from Ahuru had found refuge for almost two years in the diocese's parish centre in the city centre of Ambon alone, the school complex of the Maria Mediatrix order had taken in refugees from the island of Buru and initially the diocese's Gonzalo Veloso training centre had opened its doors to over one thousand refugees, for whom barracks were then built behind the centre, where they also had an opportunity to farm the land.

To draw the attention of people in Indonesia and indeed worldwide to the tragedy in the Moluccas, representatives of the diocese of Ambon sent the CCDA reports and innumerable declarations and appeals, online and offline, to the Indonesian government, the United Nations, foreign governments and international Christian and human rights organizations, and undertook national and international journeys. The Bishop of Ambon Msgr. P.C. Mandagi MSC (Missionaires du Sacré Coeur), for example, repeatedly met representatives of the Indonesian government, envoys of the United Nations and ambassadors of various countries in Jakarta. He always emphasized how important it was to maintain moral law in the Moluccas, where basic human rights were being seriously violated (Böhm 2002a: 8). According to Kees Böhm, one of the objectives of these journeys was to spread information about what was actually happening in the Moluccas and to denounce the Indonesian government for its inability to take effective action:

> Indonesia wants to become a 'great Nation' ... Indonesia is begging for international acknowledgement ... in all fields ... So one way to end the conflict in the Moluccas should be: making the nation ashamed of allowing its citizens to butcher one another – even degrading to head-hunting – like it is taking place in the Moluccas. (Böhm 2002b)

However, as the Moluccan church representatives were not concerned about the Christians as such, but about ending the conflict and human rights violations,[38] they were on occasion accompanied on their missions to Europe by representatives of the Moluccan Muslim community. As an interreligious team they were not specifically championing the Christian cause, nor requesting support with regard to Moluccan independence, but rather any possible form of help relating to the conflict: help for the Indonesian government in finding a solution to the conflict, help with the repatriation of the troublemakers in the Moluccan conflict to their home territories, help through humanitarian aid and help via the deployment of an independent delegation of the U.N. Commission on Human Rights and a team to keep an eye on the Indonesian government and the seriousness of its efforts to end the conflict.

As Kees Böhm explained in his exposé on the Moluccan conflict (2002b), the efforts of the diocese of Ambon and its Crisis Centre were not unsuccessful. As a result of the Crisis Centre's daily reports on the Internet, which began with the 'Urgent Appeal from victimized Christians in the Moluccas' on 22 June 2000, the Moluccan conflict became a topic worldwide and the CCDA received corresponding feedback. According to Kees Böhm, the balanced, credible CCDA reports had opened the eyes of his readers, who had until then mostly received incorrect and misleading information about the Moluccan conflict. The reports had engendered an intensive email exchange between many different people (politicians, church leaders, journalists, students, etc.). Some one hundred subscribers had responded once or on a regular basis to the CCDA reports and contacted the Crisis Centre. In addition to mails purely concerned with information exchange, the CCDA received through these channels much solace and the promise that prayers would be said for the Moluccan people. In some cases Böhm even served as a kind of contact person who was to search for subscribers' relatives and deliver news to specific people, or put individual subscribers with similar interests in contact with one another. On occasion people also asked him to pass on money, letters and even outboard motors and generators. Thus the subscribers also 'exploited' the Internet for their own purposes.

The Crisis Centre built up a particularly good relationship with the Dutch ambassador in Jakarta, Baron Schelto van Heemstra. He could be contacted at any time on his private telephone and he visited the Moluccas three times during the conflict. Contacts with the Vatican were also very good. Pope John Paul II took the opportunity several times to call on Christians worldwide to pray for the victims of and those affected by the Moluccan conflict, for peace in the region and for genuine reconciliation. Nor were the visits by representatives of the Catholic Church in the Moluccas to important people in Jakarta, Geneva and elsewhere in Europe without consequence:

> It may have helped the government in Jakarta to come to a better understanding of the nature of the conflict, of the lack of serious endeavours to end the conflict by those responsible in the Moluccas. It directed the attention of Ambassadors and Governments of foreign countries and of the United Nations – especially the United Nations Commission for Human Rights and the United Nations HCR (High Commissioner for Refugees) in Geneva – to the suffering of the common people in the Moluccas. This led to certain statements and pressure on the Indonesian Government to enhance its efforts in dealing with the conflict. It probably contributed also to their willingness to provide funds to the Indonesian government and certain NGOs, in addition to the rutine help of various international bodies that had already come to the Moluccas in order to provide humanitarian aid, like the ACF (Action contre la Faim), MSF (Médécins sans frontières), MCI (Mercy Corps International), UNICEF (United Nations Children's Fund), WHO (World Health Organisation) and OCHA (UN Office for the Coordination of Humanitarian Affairs). (Böhm 2002b)

The FKAWJ

Though the FKAWJ headquarters were in Yogyakarta, as Ja'far Umar Thalib's Koran school was close by, the public relations department, and as such the official point of contact for all interested nonmembers, was in the Jakarta branch of the FKAWJ.[39] The financing commission and the legal department, for example, were also located here, as this way they were physically closer to the Indonesian government and making contact was less problematic. The premises were on the road named Jl. Cempaka Putih Tengah in Jakarta, in a bungalow in the middle of an overgrown garden. On the patio there was a wooden table, a sort of reception, where visitors had to produce identification, state the reason for their visit and enter their name in a guest book. In the 'reception room' a thick curtain separated a seat from the rest of the room, where visitors (at least the female ones) could sit down. FKAWJ members were not allowed to conduct a face-to-face conversation with a woman.[40] On the walls there were maps and pictures that were familiar from the FKAWJ online projects: maps of conquered territory on Ambon Island, pictures of the destroyed Muslim village of Iha, images of the Laskar Jihad medical centre in Ambon and various cover pages of the Laskar Jihad magazine.

The FKAWJ and the local context

In total the FKAWJ had some ten thousand members, of whom approximately three thousand were operating in the Moluccas and, based on a rotation principle, were replaced every few months. Many of the FKAWJ members were students.[41] Eko Raharjo, a student of technical sciences and head of the FKAWJ public relations department, had just returned from an eight-month stint in Ambon when I met him on Cempaka Putih. His explanations of the aims and mission of the Laskar Jihad in the Moluccas reflected what could be termed part of the Laskar Jihad doctrine. Eko primarily emphasized the social and religious character of their Moluccan mission and stressed that it was not the Laskar Jihad who had caused the Moluccan conflict, as they had only gone to Ambon more than a year after it had begun in order to help their Muslim brothers.[42] In addition to spreading and implementing the religious visions of the FKAWJ, they also intended to ensure that the manipulators behind the conflict were brought to justice, which the Indonesian government had proved incapable of. Whereas the online presentations only stressed the harmonious relationship between the Laskar Jihad and the local population in the Moluccas, in our conversations in Jakarta Eko Raharjo and Arif Rahman to some extent also revealed other perspectives. The police, for example, would never dare to take action against an LJAWJ member, as they feared the anger of the Muslims. Nor, after a while, did all the local Muslims in the Moluccas welcome and support the Laskar Jihad.[43]

Among Muslims in Ambon the social aspect of the Laskar Jihad mission was nonetheless often at the forefront, something that my conversations with various Muslim representatives, the heads of jihad stations and students revealed. The fact that critics of the Laskar Jihad did not have an easy time in Ambon and had to fear revenge should be taken into account.[44] According to a journalist from *Ambon Ekspres,* approximately 80 per cent of the Laskar Jihad who had come to the Moluccas were students; they lived a relatively secluded life and were very active religiously (personal conversation, 17 February 2002). The radical slogans of the Laskar Jihad such as 'War without end' *(perang terus)* were pure politics, to lend expression to the dissatisfaction with the government. Several informants were convinced that it was local Muslims who were playing the decisive role in the attacks and that the Laskar Jihad were scarcely in the field, that is, involved in the fighting. It was only because the local Muslims wore similar clothing to the Laskar Jihad that the Christians assumed the latter were involved in it. Arif Rahman did admit, however, that the FKAWJ certainly had military units in the Moluccas.

Reference has already been made to the Laskar Jihad's close collaboration with and ideological links to several radical Islamic organizations at the local level. While I was in the country, even the MUI office in Ambon, whose temporary head Polpoke and former secretary Malik Selang championed reconciliation among Christians and Muslims, seemed to be dominated by FKAWJ sympathizers, such as the deputy head of the MUI public relations department and assistant at the jihad command centre in the Moluccas, Jumu Tuani, who regularly gave lectures on the FKAWJ radio station SPMM and was quoted on the FKAWJ website on several occasions. In addition to their typical 'Laskar Jihad slogans', the inscription on a panel in the MUI office reduced the line of argumentation of the Laskar Jihad and their followers, who regarded the Moluccan conflict as the result of a conspiracy between the RMS, the GPM and the PDI-P in the Moluccas, to the simple diagram seen in Illustration 18.

In a personal conversation with me, Jumu confirmed all the suspicions of the Laskar Jihad, even providing 'unequivocal' evidence such as letters from the RMS presidium, an organization that for some time had been supporting the RMS underground, bearing an original stamp (of which he even owned a specimen). He declined, however, to hand over this valuable evidence. The letters always referred to certain pastors, but never

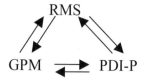

Illustration 18. Conflict diagram by Rustam Kastor, the Laskar Jihad & Co.[45]

to imams, which proved that the RMS was a purely Christian affair. The circles in which Jumu moved had just as little respect as the FKAWJ for the Association for the Coordination of Muslims in the Moluccas (Badan Immarat Muslim Maluku, BIMM), the central organ set up in 2001 by the government for the Moluccan Muslims. According to Eko Raharjo, the BIMM took just as little notice of the needs of the local population as the Malino II peace negotiations, from whose supporters he resolutely disassociated himself.

The tactical use of the Internet

Arif Rahman, a medical student and the FKAWJ webmaster, had long since been a faithful follower of Ja'far Umar Thalib's teachings and, even before the FKAWJ was founded, attended his seminars in Semarang and Yogyakarta. He was responsible for organizing and designing the website and the mailing list, and for answering emails addressed to the FKAWJ. After late 2001 he had an assistant, as he was no longer able to handle the constantly increasing number of news items and the corresponding website updates alone. The use of the Internet was a strategic move in the holy war in the Moluccas. In an article entitled 'Laskar Jihad *Online:* Jihad in cyberspace' (Laskar Jihad *Online*: Berjihad di Dunia Maya) in the *Tabloid Laskar Jihad* of 8 February 2002 (12–13), the outstanding role the Internet assumed in the jihad in the Moluccas became evident: in the author's opinion, the war against the infidels *(orang kafir)* could be waged in three ways: by physical force, in the economy, and by forming opinion. For this reason the FKAWJ published a tabloid and, since June 2000, had maintained a website that was updated daily (http://www.laskarjihad.or.id/). As opposed to other mass media, whose reporting was often even detrimental to the Muslims, the forum reported clashes between the Christians and Muslims directly from the scene. The author of the article continued, saying that only through the FKAWJ Internet presentations did certain incidents come to light in the first place. The stoning case, for example, like the attack on the Laskar Jihad polyclinic in Ambon, only hit the headlines in the mass media after they had appeared as exclusive news on the Laskar Jihad website.

One of the website's main objectives, according to that article, was to provide people with explanations.[46] Via the Internet, press releases and protest letters could immediately be made available to the broad masses. Furthermore, the website's Download section enabled visitors to listen to speeches by the Laskar Jihad commander in chief at various mass events *(tabligh akbar)* if they had not been able to attend. According to Arif Rahman, the Laskar Jihad Internet presentations gave those Moluccan Muslims who had no computer and scarcely any access to the Internet a voice in cyberspace. In an attempt to secure their support, Indonesian Muslims at home and abroad were the main target group. Indonesians abroad were as a rule educated and for that reason very critical, which was why they intended to provide them with as detailed information as possible, to legitimize the activities of the FKAWJ. Even though Ja'far Umar Thalib actually had nothing to do with the online presentations of his forum, according to Eko Raharjo he was involved at a higher level; after all, he was the one who decided what was to appear on the Internet, and what not. Arif Rahman, for example, was against publishing the stoning case, for fear of criticism. Thalib, however, decided that the matter, which ultimately led to him being arrested for the first time, should be made public, as in particular the statements about the case issued by local Muslim organizations revealed just how much support the Laskar Jihad had in Ambon.

The FKAWJ set great store by the fact that its news items came from local sources. They were provided by ten to fifteen (nonprofessional) reporters dispatched to command posts on Ambon and the surrounding islands.[47] They collected information that was then forwarded to the headquarters in Ambon, from where it was sent to Jakarta by email or fax, if no Internet was available. The reporters' main sources of information were local Muslims and FKAWJ members. According to Eko Raharjo, Rustam Kastor was the major FKAWJ source regarding the situation of the Christians in the Moluccas. Kastor was a native Moluccan and former general in the Indonesian military, which was why he knew his way around, including in Christian areas. He had a pronounced military sense, and according to Eko this was the reason for his being able to make predictions with regard to the Christian-Jewish conspiracy. It was decisive that FKAWJ people shared the same Islamic goals as Kastor *(aspirasi Islam)*.[48] Otherwise, the FKAWJ had no access to primary sources in Christian areas, apart from in an attack. They nevertheless knew all about people like Alex Manuputty, his followers and their motives. Eko Raharjo also stated that the Alifuru principle was pure rhetoric, as given their suppression and discrimination by the Christians in the Moluccas and in view of Manuputty's separatist intentions, it was inconceivable for Muslims to make common cause with Christians.

According to Arif Rahman, the FKAWJ online projects were a total success. On average the website had between 1,500 and 2,500 hits a day and by the end of 2001 the mailing list already had more than 1,300 subscribers. It was set up in addition to the website because numerous firms did not allow their employees to surf on the Internet, meaning that they had no access to the FKAWJ website but were able to receive emails. Whereas the FKAWJ site and list posted news about the Moluccan conflict on a daily basis, Christian online projects such as ABO only spread hatred of Islam.[49] Arif also maintained that what appeared on such websites and lists had no news value. According to him, the FKAWJ logo (crossed sabres and the Koran) was a decisive element of the website, as it was an expression of the forum's philosophy: the depiction of the Koran meant that all the activities of the FKAWJ related to the Koran, and that of the sabres meant that the Koran's message had to be followed, which was the reason for their having gone to Ambon. The webmaster deliberately selected the verses from the Koran that were shown on the site. They best related to the situation in Ambon and provided the reason for their mission there: the Christians on the Moluccas had attacked the Muslims first, in order to spread their faith (2:120), which is why it was the duty of all Muslims to help their brothers in faith there (2:190).[50]

The LJAWJ received the photos posted on the website, which dated from the beginning of the Moluccan conflict when the Laskar Jihad still had no local presence, from local Muslims and organizations and thus had to rely on their comments. The more recent images came from the members themselves, who documented exactly what was taken, when, and where. The FKAWJ made mistakes nonetheless. On one picture, for example, which shows an insulting graffito, '*Islam puki*',[51] the date is given as the year 1994. Though Arif admitted this was a mistake, he highlighted that this still did not change the slogan's basic message. With the first photos attempts had been made to protect the identity of the people shown by covering their faces with black bars to make them unrecognizable, but this practice was quickly dropped.

According to Arif, the English translations of the FKAWJ articles were an attempt to address the international community and answer their questions, such as why the Laskar Jihad had gone to the Moluccas and what activities they were involved in there, or which direction of Islam they supported. The few translations the FKAWJ provided sufficed for these basic questions. At this level it was not about continually providing the public with news, but about clarifying fundamental matters and tracing the major lines of thought. They did of course attempt to inform this public of important individual incidents as well. On the one hand, the FKAWJ webmaster planned to make the website more dynamic and more interactive for visitors, but on the other this interaction had to be continually controlled and edited, which would cost a considerable amount of time. For this reason the only way for visitors to make an appearance on the FKAWJ site itself (apart from on the list of donors) was readers' letters, which, however, according to Ekos, were subjected to a strict selection process depending on whether they supported the FKAWJ cause or not. Every day, from ten to fifteen readers' letters Arif selected one and published it on the website and mailing list, together with a reply from employees in the FKAWJ public relations department. Support was also forthcoming via the website for the financing of and recruitment to the Laskar Jihad. Those interested could fill out online registration forms and request information. However, before actually being accepted as members and deployed, applicants first had to present themselves in person in one of the main FKAWJ offices. According to Arif, every day two to three applicants filled out the form, approximately 70 per cent from Java and approximately 5 per cent from abroad.[52]

Primarily on the back of enquiries from visitors to the site, Arif had included a link section in the FKAWJ website that referred to other Muslim sites that addressed the Moluccan conflict or the jihad worldwide. In mid-2001 the link frame was removed without comment, as Western visitors had maintained that the online links meant genuine FKAWJ connections with the organizations or movements behind the sites. According to Arif, however, this assertion was incorrect.[53] So as to avoid similar accusations in the future, he removed the links. As already explained, a link need not necessarily indicate conformity. Indeed, we should not be blind to the fact that there were possibly fundamental differences in the religious philosophy and ideology of the individuals behind the sites, in their political views and specific ideas on how the jihad was to be conducted. The links on the FKAWJ site were quite different in nature. Arif accused those who had set up http://www.tanahjihad.net and http://www.qoqaz.net, for example, of having links to Osama bin Laden, with which the FKAWJ could not identify.[54] According to Arif, however, the site http://www.al-bunyan. net was primarily devoted to social and medical projects that supported the Muslims in the Moluccas. The links to the jihad in other parts of the world had been included to provide information, not as an expression of the FKAWJ's ideological approval of these projects. The FKAWJ disassociated itself offline and online from groups such as Hamas and the Taliban, which was why links to their websites were never included on the FKAWJ site, something the LJAWJ was accused of in the *Newsweek* article mentioned (note 53). As every mujahideen group had different ideas on Islam and jihad, Arif was also against the idea, propagated in that article, of a global jihad to which the Laskar Jihad had created a link through its website.

In May 2002 Arif Rahman decided to give the FKAWJ website a complete makeover. Although as far as the outward appearance was concerned not much was to change, the intention was to transform the static site into a dynamic one. This, however, referred not to the opportunities open to the site's visitors, but to its programmers. Instead of HTML, the programming language used was PHP. Thanks to the MySQL database, the innumerable news items could be organized far more simply and dynamically. Theoretically, any LJAWJ reporter could now update the database with his news, which in practical terms, however, never occurred, as the news from Ambon had to be checked and edited before being published. Nonetheless, the administration of the online project in particular became far simpler and more manageable. Arif considered himself obliged to take this step so as not to lag behind other professional news services such as CNN.com, Foxnews.com and LAtimes.com. His next goal was to finally set up an English and Arabic version of the website. This came to nothing. As with the mailing list in the autumn of 2001, in October 2002, on account of the official disbanding of the FKAWJ, all website activities were discontinued. As opposed to the mailing list, whose archives are still available through Yahoo! Groups,[55] in late October 2002 the FKAWJ site was removed from the Internet completely. For Arif Rahman it was important to emphasize that the decision to disband the FKAWJ had been taken before the devastating bomb attack on Bali on 12 October 2002.

The Laskar Jihad media

For the Laskar Jihad, the media played a pivotal role in the information policy relating to the Moluccan conflict. They became weapons in the struggle against the Christians, the intention being to correct and fight their false reporting. As not everyone had access to the Internet, the FKAWJ also used other media to be able to reach as large a section of the population as possible. It published magazines, such as the *Tabloid Laskar Jihad* already mentioned on several occasions,[56] flyers,[57] brochures (e.g., Thalib 2000) and books,[58] and set up its own radio station, SPMM (105.5 FM), in Ambon. The station's predecessor was the Echo of the Muslim Voice (Gema Suara Muslim, GSM), the first radio station of the Islamic community in Ambon, which the head of the FKAWJ information department, Abdul Hadi, had founded on 21 August 2000 (FKAWJ, 12 September 2000). The Muslims in Ambon now had another effective weapon: 'Ambonese Muslims speed up attacks by air' (*Muslimin Ambon Gencarkan Serangan Lewat Udara*). The station was intended to objectively inform Muslims about all the occurrences in Ambon and thus support the Muslim population in its struggle. It could also broadcast Friday speeches in the Al-Fatah Mosque and Ja'far Umar Thalib's addresses live, as well as call on the entire Islamic community to take part in the jihad against the RMS militias intent on destroying the unity of the Indonesian state. Criticism was soon voiced on the Christian side that the broadcasts were very provocative, did not promote peace and that the station did not have an official licence. According to the LJAWJ, the Christians only felt attacked because their supremacy was being threatened. Whereas they already owned four private radio stations, they were unwilling to grant the Muslims even one. The Christians' complaint, submitted to the governor of the Moluccas, was ultimately unsuccessful (see also FKAWJ, 13 September 2000).

The FKAWJ radio station, the Voice of the Moluccan Muslims' Struggle (Suara Perjuangan Muslimin Maluku, SPMM) was the successor to the GSM in Ambon. The broadcasts were managed by the Laskar Jihad, with local Muslims regularly submitting material. According to Eko Raharjo, this was the only reason the SPMM broadcasts were so radical and led, for example, to trade between Muslims and Christians being forbidden, as they expressed precisely the mood of the Muslim grassroots, which no other medium did. According to the FKAWJ, the SPMM broadcasts led to positive results in several areas: in their mission, in health education and in the dissemination of current information, be it at the local, national or international level. They provided an opportunity to counter the TVRI and RRI, as well as the Christian daily newspapers *Siwalima* and *Suara Maluku* (FKAWJ, 9 April 2001). According to the Christians, the reporting was now even more provocative and aggressive. In a Yongab raid on the Muslim district of Kebun Cengkeh in June 2001, part of the SPMM radio station was destroyed. According to the FKAWJ, the members of the Yongab were the 'dogs of the RMS' *(para anjing RMS)*, which had commissioned this particular military unit to destroy the SPMM studio and deprive the Muslims in Ambon of their voice. Although the damage totalled tens of millions of rupiahs, as stated by the Laskar Jihad, SPMM was able to start broadcasting again within the space of just a few days, thanks to the participation of the local population in the reconstruction work. For the FKAWJ this was a clear indication that the people stood behind the SPMM (FKAWJ, 20 June 2001).

Thus, the messages and speeches of the Laskar Jihad and Ja'far Umar Thalib were disseminated on a multimedia basis: via the radio, the Internet, the *Tabloid Laskar Jihad*, which was sold in the mosque in Ambon and other central places, and flyers, which they attached to building walls, mosques and jihad stations. All media were part of a major strategy and directly linked with one another. Either the articles overlapped or the various media referenced each other. On the Internet, for example, there were reports about SPMM and references to the *Tabloid Laskar Jihad.* On occasions a speech given by Ja'far Umar Thalib in the mosque in Ambon and broadcast on SPMM was also published on the Internet, either as an audio file or a written article.[59] If one clicked on the FKAWJ website a pop-up window appeared with the cover page and the table of contents of the current edition of the *Tabloid.* The magazine was listed as a source in a great many online articles, such as the profiles of individual LJAWJ members. According to Arif, when the website was redesigned in May 2002 there was even a plan to make all the editions of the *Tabloid* available online. In turn, the magazine featured advertising for all FKAWJ websites: the official Laskar Jihad website, that of its medical team and that of the Laskar Jihad financing commission,[60] which in turn had close contacts with the bulletin Nusroh, which featured excerpts from the *Tabloid,* the website and the financial reports (see, for example, *Tabloid Laskar Jihad,* issue 17, 15–29 March 2002). As already mentioned, the edition of 8 February 2002 featured an article on the importance of the Internet for the jihad in the Moluccas. The website also advertised the FKAWJ books, such as the book by Syafruddin and Prasetyo referred to above, which was also presented at a book fair in Jakarta in June 2002 (FKAWJ, 28 June 2002). With this multimedia approach, by means of news, appeals, and their religious programme, the Laskar Jihad reached a broad spectrum of very different classes in the population, from the simple man on the street to intellectuals at their desk.

Summary

From offline and individual-related online research it became clear that all active actors in Moluccan cyberspace were men (women appeared only sporadically in the MML). Most of them had a university degree and, with the exception of the author of the CCDA report, were in their mid-twenties to mid-thirties, thus corresponding with international statistical surveys of Internet users. In contrast to the statistical mean, however, many of them did not live in a Western country, but in Indonesia, a developing nation. In terms of their level of education, commitment and manner none of them was ultimately representative of the population in the Moluccas, though all claimed to represent either the Christian or Muslim Moluccan population. The Moluccan cyberactors used the Internet consciously and strategically in an attempt to disseminate credible local information quickly and to drum up financial and moral support at both the national and the international level, in religious and worldly circles. For them, the largely unfiltered and unmonitored Internet was of inestimable value, without which their information policy would be impossible to imagine.

The Masariku network emerged from a circle of friends who had been active in Church organizations since the outbreak of the Moluccan conflict, but which, thanks to the Internet, had since expanded far beyond them. On the one hand, the Masariku founders deliberately distanced themselves from the Church, but on the other, given the links in terms of staff and infrastructure, an actual split was not possible. As online, on the offline level duties and roles were distributed among the Masariku members in line with their abilities and opportunities. From the outset, the CCDA and the LJAWJ operated as representatives of a religious institution. Whereas the CCDA at least strove for neutrality, the LJAWJ took an unequivocal stance. Much of the information received by Masariku and the FKAWJ came from lay reporters; those working for Masariku did so on a voluntary basis, whereas with regard to the FKAWJ they were part of a strictly organized structure. Both online and offline, the FKAWJ endeavoured to represent and implement its organizational doctrine uncompromisingly.

Whereas the CCDA and the FKAWJ were more concerned with using the Internet to appeal to a specific imagined, and in the case of the FKAWJ, idealized community and, by means of certain identification patterns, integrate it, with the MML the direct involvement of several affected parties made identity and a communal spirit much more concrete. The different aspirations and ideals with which the members each joined the list did not alter that fact. Masariku was the expression of an identity, the basis of a closer and extended (imagined) Masariku community.

The FKAWJ repeatedly emphasized its close contacts with the local population, probably because it was the only one of the groups to have come from outside the Moluccas and as such initially had to bridge the distance to the local people. In order to reach as wide a spectrum of the population as possible, the FKAWJ operated not just in cyberspace, but opened up further media channels in the form of magazines, radio stations and flyers.

Masariku and the CCDA became active both nationally and internationally through petitions, appeals, interreligious meetings, talks and discussions, and trips, primarily to Europe. All those active in Moluccan cyberspace were also active offline with regard to the Moluccan conflict. Cyberspace merely made another channel available through which they could expand their activities. The online and offline levels were both part of the same strategic plan and were only able to be fully effective in combination – with regard to Masariku, the CCDA or the FKAWJ.

Notes

1. Personal conversation with the head of the FKAWJ public relations department on 11 February 2002.
2. I am well aware of the fact that my own religion (Christian) and my origin played a role in this. Regardless of their religion, however, the treatment of women by the Laskar Jihad was problematic. By way of example, an Indonesian female friend was not allowed to talk to an FKAWJ member face-to-face, even though she was a devout Muslim and as always wore a headscarf; face-to-face contact was only permitted at 'Reception'. According to my Muslim interlocutors, in the Moluccas the Laskar Jihad were generally very reserved with regard to the local population and they were forbidden to have any contact with women they did not know (religious instruction and the joint reading of the Koran being an exception).
3. The following is based on personal conversations with the founding members and other active members of the Masariku network in Jakarta and Ambon in February and March 2002.
4. The PPK PGI had been founded as a result of the increasing number of attacks on churches from 1995 to 1996.
5. At the beginning, SAGU even supposedly had one or two Muslim members of staff.
6. Online, however, Masariku certainly did endeavour to procure financial support.
7. See Chapter 4.
8. I would like to thank Victor Joseph for this information about the TPG and BANKOM.
9. According to Tonny Pariella, the head of the Crisis Centre, the problem was that they had information, but no dissemination network. Those interested had to pick up the information themselves. At local level these were so-called representatives, less so the common inhabitants. Only the middle class had access to the Internet, and as such to Masariku online. In these circles, however,

print copies of Masariku reports were certainly in circulation and Internet content became a discussion topic (personal conversation, 16 March 2002).

10. Personal conversation with BANKOM staff members in February 2002.

11. However, it was not just the students who were looking for suitable motifs; Franky also sought to achieve something specific with the photos. By way of example, he deliberately posted on the list the picture of the child warriors wearing blue uniforms and holding the Bible and a wooden sword (see Illustration 11 in Chapter 7). Though only a few of the child warriors actually wore these blue uniforms, they were an expression of an identification process he had ascertained among these children. Franky wanted the picture to make a strong impression and draw attention to the children's situation (personal conversation, 23 February 2002).

12. According to Bob, an early list member, names of victims displayed in photos, and thus any indication of their religion, were deliberately omitted. Victims were victims, regardless of their religion.

13. The following descriptions refer to my email exchange with active key MML members between late 2001 and early 2003 and to personal conversations in Jakarta and Ambon in February and March 2002. Whereas I also made contact offline with members in Ambon and Jakarta, I corresponded with Moluccans living throughout Indonesia and abroad via email.

14. These are questions I asked active MML members in this or a slightly modified form face-to-face or by email once initial contact had been made or after we had already been corresponding online or offline for a certain period of time. Any ambiguities with regard to the questions were clarified with the individual discussion partners. Some of the conversations were held in English, some in Indonesian.

15. The situation was aggravated by the fact that from late 1998 lots of new Muslim media had sprung up in Indonesia and now represented a mouthpiece for Muslim points of view in the Moluccan conflict (personal conversation with Bob, 12 February 2002).

16. MML members or their contacts to the relevant bodies had to translate the Masariku reports, which were primarily written in Indonesian. This was the case at least in the United States, the Netherlands, Australia and the United Kingdom.

17. Richard also argued, for example, that forming and cooperating in groups online could be far more effective, but that in the case of Masariku resulting contact and interaction would take place offline and online. As confirmed by other members, final decisions with regard to concrete action and strategies in the conflict were often made in private cyberspace or offline.

18. The fact that there were also opposing opinions and that other members complained about the unnecessary abundance of emails was discussed in Chapter 4.

19. Nunusaku is the name of a sacred mountain, *Gunung Nunusaku,* on the mother island (*Nusa Ina*) of Seram, where the Ambonese believe they have their roots (Bartels 1994: 29).

20. The offline commitment of *human rights activist* Robert, who was likewise of Moluccan origin, was already referred to in Chapter 4.

21. Correspondence with Julius took place via email as of August 2002. In an earlier email Febian, for his part, had said that he was prepared to take part in a 'conversation', but never replied to my subsequent enquiries.

22. He declined to reveal the identity of the coauthor so as to protect him.

23. In Sulawesi the MWN worked with the local Poso Watch Network.

24. http://www.angelfire.com/rock/hotburrito.

25. Contact was made by email in November 2002 after I had posted a general request on the MML for the passive members to get in touch with me. The response was extremely weak, but in view of the way other enquiries that were not directly related to the list interest were dealt with, this was certainly standard procedure.

26. http://www.Titane.org (no longer available in 2012).

27. http://www.malra.org/posko (no longer available in 2012).

28. Among the lurkers there were of course also a number of people who indeed only wanted to receive information without processing or forwarding it on a large scale. I propose, however, that they too had a certain multiplier effect as they, like myself, are sure to have passed on what they read to relatives, friends, colleagues, etc., or discussed it with them.

29. The following views are based on my email exchange with the relevant persons between mid-2002 and early 2003.

30. I am well aware of the abstract nature of the questions, but for the reasons given (an emic view of the MML as a community) I wanted to conduct this experiment and in fact received several very interesting thoughts and statements in reply.

31. The views in this section are in no way intended to be a basis for comparison with the analyses in Chapter 4, but rather to add a few interesting aspects to them.

32. Unfortunately, according to Richard, not all MML members invested in interactive communication. Many only benefited, but did not actually contribute anything themselves. This was another reference to the free rider problem typical of many other mailing lists and news groups on the Internet.

33. As information was already provided about this in the online depictions of the CCDA, this section will be relatively short. Unless otherwise stated, the following depictions refer to Kees Böhm's *Exposé on Various Aspects of the Conflict in the Moluccas* (2002b) and my personal conversations with him in February and March 2002.

34. According to CCDA statistics, by early 2002 there had been 143 deaths in the Catholic community in the Moluccas.

35. The main donors included Cordaid (The Hague, the Netherlands), Caritas Indonesia, various Vatican organizations, Missio-Aachen and Misereor-Aachen (Germany), Trident Seafoods (Seattle, U.S.), the Missionaries of the Sacred Heart (MSC, Tilburg, the Netherlands), the Protestant Church of the Moluccas in the Netherlands, the Catholic Relief Services in Jakarta, the Dutch Embassy and the Bishops' Conference in Jakarta, and Petrokhimia (Gresik, Java). Together they raised some 450,000 euros. Others sent donations directly to Catholic initiatives in Ambon such as the Rinamakana Foundation and the Movement of Concerned Moluccan Women (GPPM), to which women of other denominations belonged as well.

36. On account of their being fewer in number, the Catholics' network in the Moluccas was less well established than that of the Protestants. Throughout the Moluccas, the Catholics accounted for approximately 5 per cent of the population.

37. In mid-2003 Böhm offered for sale, via the newsletter, a bound version of his collection of reports, which had grown to a work comprising three hundred pages: *Brief Chronicle of the Unrest in the Moluccas 1999–2003.*

38. However, it was primarily Christians as a religious minority who were affected by these violations of human rights in the form of, for example, forced conversions, for which the radical Islamic jihad troops from outside the Moluccas were said to be responsible.

39. Unless otherwise stated, I refer in the following depictions to my personal conversations with Eko Raharjo (public relations, FKAWJ) and Arif Rahman (FKAWJ webmaster) on 11 and 13 February 2002 and my email exchange with the latter between August 2001 and late 2002. Matters of general interest regarding the FKAWJ, its organizational structure, philosophy, objectives and motives were discussed in Chapter 6, as the FKAWJ was also prepared to provide detailed information on these points online.

40. On occasions Arif Rahman nonetheless came to my side of the curtain so as to explain various things to me in more detail with his laptop. On Ambon as well I was later able to have a face-to-face conversation with another LJAWJ member. According to Kirsten Schulze, who had conducted interviews with FKAWJ members one year previously, at that time the rules were not yet adhered to so strictly. I would like to thank her for this information. Arif Rahman repeatedly pointed out to me that since 9/11 the security regulations had become much stronger and as such the treatment of visitors far more restrictive.

41. According to the FKAWJ webmaster, between a third and half of the members now had a bachelor's degree, while the remainder had completed secondary education. According to Hasan (2002), all the members of the FKAWJ board and advisory committee, in his opinion the leading actors in the movement, were graduates, whereas the mass of the movement was composed of people with low incomes, university students, minor civil servants and the unemployed.

42. As proof of this, Arif Rahman had already sent me by email (4 February 2002) an article from the 26 December 2001 edition of the *International Herald Tribune,* in which its author, Diarmid O'Sullivan, a member of the research group the Indonesia Project in the Brussels-based International Crisis Group, argued as follows: 'It would be a mistake to assume that Laskar Jihad erupted bloodily into a harmonious landscape, and that curbing its activities will resolve the tensions that brought it into being. In both the Moluccas and Poso, Laskar Jihad arrived more than a year after fighting started … The press focuses on mass murder and destruction of property by Laskar Jihad. In fact, mass murder and house burnings have been used against civilians by all sides in the half-dozen major communal wars since the fall of the former strongman Suharto in 1998.' O'Sullivan also commented that the conflict, which had just begun to quiet down in the Moluccas before the Laskar Jihad arrived, had flared up again as a result of their military capabilities and motivation, which, however, Rahman did not go into.

43. This approximately corresponded with what Christians had observed, like Sister Brigitta in Ambon, one of the leading members of the interreligious Movement of Concerned Moluccan Women (Gerakan Perempuan Peduli Maluku, GPPM), which was very much committed to helping the victims of the conflict. According to her, the local Muslims had initially been glad about

the arrival of the Laskar Jihad and their help in social and religious matters. However, when they realized that on top of this they were also taking part in the fighting, they withdrew their support for the Laskar Jihad, something, however, they were unable to show openly.

44. Any judgement as to how the broad population perceived the Laskar Jihad would have needed a lengthy field study in Muslim territory, which, in view of the situation, was not possible. Furthermore, the questions could possibly have embarrassed the local Muslim population, and even put them in danger.

45. As early as 28 January 1999 the RMS was an important topic at a press conference organized by Yusuf Rahimi, a leader of the Ambonese Muslim community in Jakarta, and the radical Islamic Indonesian Committee for Solidarity with the Islamic World (Komite Indonesia untuk Solidaritas Dunia Islam, KISDI) (Human Rights Watch 1999: 9). The retired lieutenant general A. M. Hendropriyono propagated still further the theory of the close connections between the Church, Christians and the RMS at a public meeting with the governor of the Moluccas, religious and other leaders, and students and youths in Ambon. Faisal Tanjung, another retired general, underscored Hendropriyono's accusation (Aditjondro 2001b). The fact that a good job was being done in propagating this conspiracy was very clearly revealed during my research trip to the city of Ambon. Even moderate Muslims willing to compromise and discuss matters with regard to joint peace initiatives with the Christians always seemed to revert to this model as an explanation of the conflict.

46. According to Arif Rahman, ever since the conflict had started more and more people had been coming to the FKAWJ centres and enquiring about the situation in Ambon. Information was also frequently provided by telephone and fax. However, as this involved a considerable amount of time and high telephone bills, the decision was taken to set up an Internet presence, where members and outsiders could glean information. For the webmaster, however, this meant that he now spent five to six hours a day, voluntarily and unpaid, updating the website and answering emails. Given the amount of time and effort involved, the FKAWJ did not use Yahoo! options such as chat, as this would have had to be moderated and controlled.

47. Personal conversation with Arif Rahman, Eko Raharjo and Abdul Hadi, head of the FKAWJ public relations department in Ambon.

48. According to a female Muslim activist in Ambon who took part in various initiatives aimed at bringing Christians and Muslims closer together, Rustam Kastor represented a problem. As a former general he still received his pension from the government. Thus, one was not really able to criticize him. He could be judged privately, but not officially – the government itself had to do that. Kastor's books were widely read in Ambon, though how they were received depended on the readers' level of education.

49. Among the Muslims, ABO and the Ambon.com mailing list were far better known than, for example, Masariku, because apart from the articles taken from public websites, access to Masariku was restricted.

50. Arif once again emphasized here that the mission had also been authorized by the fatwas issued by respected Islamic figures. They were not fighting against Christians in general, which was why the FKAWJ, for example, was not involved in the anti-Christian disturbances on Java.

51. *Puki* is a vulgar expression for the female genitals.

52. According to the former head of the FKAWJ communication department, Hardi Ibn Harun, the Laskar Jihad had members in Yemen, Saudi Arabia, France and the United States. Those directly involved in the mission in the Moluccas came primarily from Yemen. It was not a case, however, of hundreds of foreign warriors, as one Western diplomat in Jakarta had maintained (Liu 2001). On 11 June 2003 the daily newspaper *The Australian* reported on a small Laskar Jihad network in Sydney, which had recruited comrades in arms for the LJAWJ in Australia as well.

53. The article in the magazine *Newsweek* of 15 October 2001 (Liu 2001) was decisive here; see also the article by Andrew Marshall in the 10 March 2002 edition of the *New York Times*, 'The Threat of Jaffar'.

54. During my conversations with FKAWJ members in Jakarta und Ambon, without my having broached or made allusions to the topic, they emphasized several times that they had no links to Al-Qaeda and Osama bin Laden and were not supported financially by him. According to Arif Rahman, the FKAWJ did not believe the Al-Qaeda accusations that the Saudi Arabian government was unbelieving, just as they did not support the kidnappings and suicide attacks practised by Al-Qaeda followers.

55. According to Arif Rahman, they wanted to prevent someone else using the list to spread false information about the Laskar Jihad.

56. The *Tabloid* appeared every two weeks and had a print run of seventy thousand to one hundred thousand; five thousand copies were sent each time to Ambon, where according to Arif and Eko it was primarily read by the local population. Even prior to publication of the *Tabloid* the FKAWJ, and previously Ihya'us Sunnah, issued a magazine entitled *Salafy*, which initially only addressed religious topics, but which in the critical political situation and on the back of the founding of the FKAWJ in 1998 also increasingly began commenting on political topics, for example, in the discussion about Megawati as a female presidential candidate (DPP Forum Komunikasi Ahlus Sunnah Wal Jama'ah 2000–1; Ponpes Ihya'us Sunnah 1995–99).

57. For example, *Bel@* (Berita Laskar) was a daily regional newsletter with Laskar news from Ambon and Poso. It had a print run of approximately one thousand according to Eko and five thousand to ten thousand according to Arif, and was distributed not only in the city of Ambon but also in the villages on the islands of Ambon, Haruku and Saparua.

58. For example, Syafruddin and Prasetyo (2001) and Thalib (2001). Syafruddin and Prasetyo were members of the FKAWJ board (in the public relations or information departments). Thalib's book was meant to contain information about what was actually going on in Ambon and who the real culprits were (FKAWJ, 19 March 2001).

59. See, for example, the death sentence Thalib issued against the (former) military commander of the Moluccas, I Made Yasa (18 June 2001; http://www.laskarjihad.or.id/berita/jun2001/mhi010618b.htm, 5 August 2001).

60. http://www.laskarjihad.or.id/; http://www.ahmed.or.id; or http://www.zisonline.com (no longer available in 2012). ZIS stood for *Zakat, Infaq and Shadaqah* (obligatory charity, donations and voluntary charity).

10

Cyberidentities at War

Summary, Conclusion, Perspectives

This summary of the results relating to the issues of identity and community in Moluccan cyberspace is intended to be a basis for making conclusions with regard to the impact of the use of the Internet in the Moluccan
conflict and for formulating findings and research perspectives that go beyond the case of the Moluccas.

Communitization, networking and idealization – these three terms
could be the keywords used to characterize the Moluccan cyberspace
projects and differentiate them from one another. The individual words
do not exclusively stand for one particular project; rather, they represent
different facets of all three projects, but lend expression to one of the relevant main characteristics: (1) The Masariku project used the Internet's
interactive potential to conduct online awareness work, promote the communitization of the list members and, building on this, develop a comprehensive network; (2) by means of a large subscriber base and supplying
corresponding websites, the CCDA project built up as broad-based a network as possible; and (3) the FKAWJ project created an online picture of
an idealized Islamic community that was faithful to the state. All three
used the medium of the Internet strategically for their goals and purposes,
as it enabled them to report current events, which on account of their
speed, detailed nature, persistence and stance differed in quality from the
national media (Hill and Sen 1997). As far as the identity patterns involved
in the conflict were concerned, even the Internet – where Christians and
Muslims could theoretically, without danger, unobserved and, if desired,
even anonymously, have met – was unable to build interreligious bridges.
By forming up along religious lines the cyberactors, like the local population, resorted to the only identities that, following the developments in
the Moluccas in recent years and decades and given the tense conditions,
still seemed to be able to mobilize people and promote solidarity: Christian and Muslim. The Internet even made it possible to expand and ideal-

ize existing communities, which at the local level were by no means as homogeneous and united.

Identity, representativeness and authenticity

In cyberspace Masariku, the CCDA and the FKAWJ portrayed their view of the Moluccan conflict, attempting in this way to establish solidarity and drum up as much support as possible for their mission in the Moluccas. To this end, various conflict realities and identities were constructed in the hope of acquiring as many followers as possible. Expressed in Manuel Castells's logic (2001b: 8–11, 357), the cyberactors attempted to establish 'resistance identities' against the dominant 'others', by whom they thought they were being suppressed and even in danger of being obliterated. In order to achieve their goals the cyberactors each employed different strategies. According to Miller and Slater (2000: 192), the Internet does not exist absolutely, but in each case in the specific way it is used, which they refer to as 'the dynamics of mediation' (ibid.: 14). The choice and setup of the mode of communication were the first strategic steps and were geared either to encouraging discussion and an exchange of ideas among members, thereby enabling a negotiation process (Masariku mailing list), or to making information available in a unidirectional (and authoritarian) manner, so as to deliver short news items directly from the scene of action to as many people as possible with as little administration as possible and without any 'background noise' and unnecessary ballast (CCDA newsletter), or so as to indoctrinate readers and visitors (FKAWJ website and mailing list).

Furthermore, purely practical aspects such as the amount of time and staff required also influenced the setup of the individual modes, which was why Masariku, for example, did without a professional website and open archives and, like the FKAWJ, did not maintain a chat forum. The range of strategies used included a specific line of textual and visual argumentation based on current events in the Moluccas, and in the case of the FKAWJ also extended to audio. Such strategies were geared towards integration and exclusion, in each case demarcating the 'we' group from the others, and revolved around selected topics. Internet-specific strategies, such as cyberwars, flame wars, cross-posting, the integration of different sources, file types, levels, etc., and the linking and manipulation of websites and email addresses, were also utilized. If one considers the offline context of these cyberprojects and actors, it becomes evident that the Internet was embedded in a far larger plan of action, initiated at the offline level. The Internet was an additional weapon, an additional strategic tool in the conflict, and was only effective and of significance because it was embedded in the offline context.

The Moluccan cyberactors derived their symbol and value systems from this offline context, which featured in their Internet presentations. Here the local offline context played just as much a role as the national and international. The local context accounted primarily for historical and cultural arguments and symbols, such as the heroic figure of Pattimura, the colonial era and the role of *adat* in finding a solution to the conflict. Masariku in Ambon, the CCDA and the Laskar Jihad operated at the local level and in this way played their role in the conflict and finding a solution to it; it was from here that they sent firsthand information directly to the rest of the world. The national context was important primarily for the LJAWJ, whose activities were geared entirely to preserving the unity of the Indonesian state. At the international and transnational levels the world religions involved, Islam and Christianity, played a role, as did human rights. Without these offline links the cyberprojects would never have received such a warm response and been so readily accepted, as was reflected in the number of their members and their online environments, nor would it have been possible to create or develop collective identities and communities.[1] Theoretically, having a voice on the Internet by no means meant one was also heard. By integrating their online and offline activities, the Moluccan cyberactors nonetheless succeeded in this. The Internet enabled not only all these symbols and elements to be combined on a single platform and become part of integrated identity constructs, but also enabled the local level to be directly transferred to the global by the reporting of actors involved in the conflict.

On the one hand, Moluccan cyberspace enabled old hierarchies, such as the government bureaucracy and censorship in Indonesia's national media, to be circumvented. On the other, however, new hierarchies and authorities based on other principles were created (see, e.g., Jordan 1999), or offline authorities taken over, whose reach was extended still further by the Internet.[2] This had to do with the particular type of list discourse, in the course of which certain roles and authorities emerged, as with Masariku, or the authority with regard to definition and information that the FKAWJ assumed by choosing a unidirectional mode of communication, but one which anybody could view. Hierarchies also emerged through the Internet inasmuch as by no means everyone had access to it (see also Hill and Sen 2002: 20). In Indonesia, and in the Moluccas in particular, that was still an extremely small, privileged class. In this respect the question necessarily arises as to whom these people represented, or could represent. The Zapatista movement's Internet presence is often cited as a classic example of how the medium enabled a local group of insurgents in the depths of the Mexican forest to communicate with the world and Mexican society and attract their attention (Castells 2001b: 79). In this context Oliver Froehling (1997: 302) urgently warns against exaggerated enthusiasm – 'self-congratulatory technology fetishization' – as it was not the

Zapatista movement in Chiapas itself that had controlled these Internet campaigns, but rather groups (churches, human rights groups, left-wing political groups) for which the Zapatista movement's uprising had been the unifying, motivating element. Nonetheless, according to Froehling (1997), the Internet had given the local uprising a new dimension and re-configured the political landscape (see also Warf and Grimes 1997: 270). The reach and visibility of these events were increased and ensured that within just a few days human rights organizations were calling for letters of protest to the U.S. and Mexican governments and for donations and appealing for voluntary human rights' observers.[3]

The Moluccan cyberactors were actually voices coming directly from the scene of the fighting and members of the groups involved in the lo-cal clashes: the Laskar Jihad, the Protestants and the Catholics. Nonethe-less, here too one must take a close look at who was claiming to represent whom. With the MML, its Masariku founders intended to give the Chris-tians in the Moluccas a voice. However, the fact became very clear that given their background and commitment during the conflict, the MML members were not really representative of the local Moluccan population. Nonetheless, the Masariku staff in the Moluccas were very close to the population, first because they were a part of it, second via their trips to the various areas affected, and not least of all through their activities within the Church. As a pastor, Franky had a great deal of close contact with the local population. Though Kees Böhm from the CCDA hailed from the Netherlands, he had been working as a priest in the Moluccas for more than thirty-five years. However, he deliberately referred less to the local population, whose statements, in his opinion, were influenced too much by their own traumatic experiences and therefore not objective, preferring to rely instead on the local media, whose journalists at least had a certain professional neutrality. The FKAWJ claimed to represent and give a voice to the Moluccan Muslims. Yet even the Laskar Jihad stationed in the Mo-luccas came almost exclusively from outside the Moluccas. The common religion was their only link to the local population, though the FKAWJ interpretation of Islamic sources was far removed from what everyday Islamic life was actually like for most of the Moluccan Muslim population before the Laskar Jihad had arrived. Even if numerous Muslims there were initially relieved by their presence, the Laskar Jihad could scarcely be seen as representative of the Moluccan Muslim population. Even so, at the local level many Muslims seemed to have adopted their line of argumentation.

The three groups' Internet projects deliberately targeted the outside world from the Moluccas.[4] Although in Moluccan cyberspace democracy did not take the form of equal participation or the befitting representation of all groups of the population, previously unheard voices were nonethe-less carried to distant ears, which played a pivotal role in the emergence of solidarity groups, which in turn were able to benefit the local population (see also Dahlberg 2000). As a tool, the Internet is suited to searching for people of the same persuasion across continental, social and political boundaries and influencing, even manipulating, the opinion of a broad-based, widely scattered audience and mobilizing at least some of it for certain purposes. Masariku and the CCDA concentrated primarily on countries abroad, from which they expected support and assistance. The FKAWJ deliberately attempted to disseminate its messages through several channels, using different media, including at the local level, in order to be able to reach all Muslims, local, national, and international and win them over to its cause. Independent of their representative role, these three groups controlled Moluccan cyberspace. They determined what was portrayed there and how, and as such had a decisive influence on the image of the Moluccan conflict and the parties involved in the outside world. Even if the discourse in cyberspace, as in other public domains, was dominated by the elite, leading figures and outstanding leaders, as Piliang (2000: 116) argues, it was only the performances of the Moluccan cyberactors that led to the Moluccan conflict entering the global arena and its dynamics being presented to a wide audience worldwide. Each of the Moluccan cyberactors carved out a space on the Internet in which to spread their view of the conflict and integrate people throughout Indonesia and the world.

The Moluccan cyberactors demonstrated their representativeness and concern by delivering proof of authenticity. First of all, the cyberactors considered their portrayals credible and authentic, as they got their information directly from the source. In Moluccan cyberspace this impression of authenticity was strengthened by the type of elements we were familiarized with in the chapter on cybertheory – that which Christine Hine (2000: 143) referred to as the 'performance of authenticity': the portrayal of their embeddedness in the local context and the reference to certain places, a range of aesthetic and discursive strategies, the exaggerated expression of feelings, the topicality and immediacy of information and posts on the one hand and on the other their archiving, the presentation of facts as common context knowledge, of details, witnesses' statements, visual material, information pertaining to sources and links and the publication of readers' letters, questionnaires and forms. For the website and list designers the imagined public played a decisive role (Hine 2000: 136–41) in whom information was intended to appeal to and who was intended to be won over – Indonesian Muslims, Moluccans in Indonesia and the diaspora, Christians and Muslims worldwide or the international community. An aura of authenticity was to be created for that group so that they could identify with those affected in the Moluccas. This made it possible for people not involved locally in the conflict to experience it more directly than was possible via other media, amounting to more than purely an 'illusion of participation' (Froehling 1997: 304), at least for that part of the audience that itself hailed from the Moluccas or intervened directly in the course of the conflict. The individual identities behind the

Moluccan cyberactors took a backseat here. Anonymity and authenticity were not therefore necessarily mutually exclusive; what counted was the collective identity of those who were to be represented (optimized self-presentation) and acceptance by the desired audience (idealized perception).

Expansion of communities and identities

As I outlined in the last few chapters, through the three Moluccan cyberprojects communities, or ideas of them, emerged that, like the associated identity projects, differed greatly from one another in terms of their manner and composition. In the discussion on cybertheory it became clear that existing communities on the Internet are imagined communities, the members of which do not all need to know or even interact with one another, but who have committed themselves to a common goal and common values, ensure that these are adhered to in their community and create a common identity. The Internet enabled the Moluccan cyberactors to expand and idealize existing communities and identities. Miller and Slater differentiated between two modes of using the Internet for identity-related purposes:

> This dynamic of objectification between identity and the Internet can be thought of in two interrelated ways: In one case, which we have dubbed expansive realization, the Internet is viewed as a means through which one can enact – often in highly idealized form – a version of oneself or culture that is regarded as old or even originary but can finally be realized: through these new means, one can become what one thinks one really is (even if one never was). What might be characteristic of the Internet is that this 'realization' is indeed 'expansive': through the global inter-connections offered by the Internet, a Trinidadian may feel able to act as the Hindu he or she 'really is' (but could not be within the confines of Trinidad) by participating in worldwide Hindu networks that can be integrated into their everyday local reality. In the second case, which we might call expansive potential, the encounter with the expansive connections and possibilities of the Internet may allow one to envisage a quite novel vision of what one could be, a vision that is often projected as a feature of the Internet itself (for example, transcendence of mundane identities) ... In some cases this was a state that had been realized but then lost; in other cases it was projected but never yet attained. (2000: 10–11)

Regarding the Moluccas, the Masariku and the CCDA project can be assigned to the first category, and the FKAWJ project to the second, though the boundaries between them were fluid. Inasmuch as they were able to evade all form of censorship online, the Moluccan cyberactors could be themselves on the Internet.[5] There it was possible for them to express their point of view and their identity, which would not have been as feasible in other media or offline.

Via the Internet and the list members' offline networks, Masariku succeeded in integrating part of the Moluccan diaspora, Christian organizations and church communities worldwide, European government organizations and UN human rights institutions into its network. Through the Masariku mailing list a community emerged that was not, however, only imagined. Many of the members, in particular the founders and very first members, had already known each other offline for some time, which was an important factor in the emergence of a communal spirit in the online community (see also Baym 1998; Rheingold 1993; WZB – Projektgruppe Kulturraum Internet 1996). The expansion of this small community into the global Masariku network transferred the community to the sphere of imagination of its worldwide members. The imagined community was strengthened and fed through the offline context and the individual members' offline communities and networks, which at the same time were the determining factors of their identity (Illustration 19). In connection with the Moluccan conflict, in particular the Moluccans in the diaspora and their activities – a good example of Appadurai's 'ethno and mediascapes'[6] – were of great importance.[7] The largest Moluccan community outside the Moluccas lives in the Netherlands.[8] Even if the Dutch Moluccans were for the most part also able to avail themselves of personal contacts in the Moluccas, obtaining information via the Internet played an important role for them, which became evident both from the fact that many Dutch Moluccans were members of the MML and from the numerous websites that Dutch Moluccans dedicated to the Moluccan conflict and which often featured Masariku and/or CCDA reports. As such, on the Internet there was no limit to the extent to which Masariku members could be Moluccans, Christians and at the same time world citizens; they were part of a worldwide Moluccan, Christian/Church and human rights network. During the conflict the Masariku members in the Moluccas and Indonesia had no opportunity to live out these identities.

Building up a community of its own through online interaction was not one of the CCDA project's objectives. Rather, from the outset it deliberately addressed established communities – primarily Christian and international, represented through the Church, Christian organizations, charitable and human rights organizations, the UN and European governments – and with the newsletter attempted to integrate them and win them over to the common cause in the Moluccas (Illustration 19). Like a radial network, the CCDA made information available from the centre, but played only a very limited role in networking the terminal nodes. Nonetheless, for the CCDA, too, the Internet was an important factor in establishing links with those communities with which it had shared values, which in the opinion of the Christians were currently being suppressed and destroyed at the local level, and thus in creating an imagined community at the same time. All subscribers and all those to whom the numerous appeals and letters from the CCDA were directed could consider them-

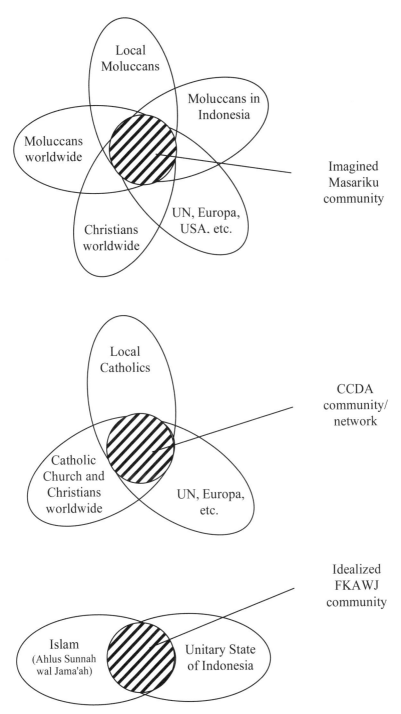

Illustration 19. Identity levels in Moluccan cyberspace[9]

selves part of this community. The CCDA, however, did not provide its members with the means to lend expression to a communal spirit, relying instead on the strength of its reports to connect people.

Owing to the discursive practices in the MML and the strong interaction between the online section of Masariku and the offline integration of individual members, an imagined community emerged that was characterized by common interests, the exchange of information, interaction, joint prayer, feelings, consternation, solidarity, potential for action, inclusion and exclusion mechanisms and in some cases by the common origin of the members. The FKAWJ project involved a totally different type of imagination and community. The Laskar Jihad also lived out their religiousness on the Internet. Their focus of attention was Indonesian Muslims at home and abroad. The aim of the FKAWJ, however, was not to build on an interpretation of Islam shared by a large proportion of the Indonesian population;[10] rather, they intended to convert Indonesian Muslims to the ideas of Ja'far Umar Thalib and several Islamic scholars in the Middle East. With its online presentations, the FKAWJ attempted to win over as many Muslims as possible for the Laskar Jihad mission in the Moluccas and in Indonesia in general, thereby creating a Muslim unity that was based on the doctrinaire ideas of the FKAWJ and that supported their brothers in faith in the Moluccas. However, since, readers' letters aside, there was no exchange between the FKAWJ and its list members and website visitors, as opposed to the MML, the extent to which a community of this nature was actually established cannot be ascertained. This gave the FKAWJ an opportunity, with the help of its view of the conflict and its interpretations of Islamic sources, to establish an image of an idealized Islamic community and to appeal to it.[11] The Internet provided the 'expansive potential' for the FKAWJ to return to the lost ideal situation in the time of the Prophet and to project it into the present time and link it to a specific locality via the Internet (and via the other FKAWJ media and activities). In this way, depending on visitor frequency and motivation, imagined communities could certainly emerge, whose members did not all need to have an interactive relationship with one another. Nils Zurawski (2000: 215) determined that, among other things, a reference to ethnicity and local cultural identities on the Internet served to provide 'historical' roots for orientation in a global context. Accordingly, in times of difficult identity crises in Indonesia, the FKAWJ online project attempted to make religious and national roots available on the Internet for Indonesian Muslims worldwide (see Illustration 19).

Religion became the determining factor at the local level and in Moluccan cyberspace. The division in Moluccan society, like the online reporting by those directly involved in the conflict, ran along religious lines, and the main cyberactors were active members of their religious communities. As outlined in Chapter 3, religion in particular can be an ideal source of identity in a conflict, one that takes the focus off all the differences in a particular religious community as opposed to another, but which at the same time harbours the danger of essentializing identities. Religion offers many symbols, which attract people emotionally and spiritually and help strengthen their (religious) identity. It allows the parties in a conflict to connect to larger-scale communities and becomes a strategy for drumming up moral and material support. At the height of the conflict, religion, whether instrumentalized by the various groups involved in the Moluccan conflict or not, became the primordial component that determined coexistence, fighting and reporting. In this respect the depictions of the conflict on the Internet could certainly have had a negative feedback effect on the course of the conflict, as the cyberactors made use of religious symbolism, turning, among other things, to Christian and Muslim communities, thus strengthening the impression of a religious war in the Moluccas and contributing to the essentialization of identities. The Internet as an environment in which to construct and reveal identities and religion as a source of identity seemed to be ideal partners in a conflict in which other identities had lost significance and influence.

One final point I would like to mention in this context is the archives, which can play a decisive role in the success of an online community project. All Masariku and FKAWJ mailing list posts, visual and textual, were archived on their Yahoo! Groups sites; the FKAWJ additionally provided a text, image and audio archive on its website. The CCDA made all its reports available via a number of (other) websites.[12] These archives fulfilled two essential functions. Firstly, they traced the discourse or monologue, in the course of which the relevant identities were negotiated, developed and presented. They made important information and identity symbols available to members and visitors and enabled newcomers to undergo a sort of enculturation process with regard to the relevant community, whenever and wherever they so wanted. The fact that the Internet, and as such the archives, were available around the clock, worldwide, was also of importance here. Secondly, archiving the posts and regular reporting meant that history was written online, so to speak, in our case the history of the cyberactors and their communities and an excerpt from the history of the Moluccas – naturally enough from the perspective of the relevant cyberactors. For all members the archives were a record of their common past and represented their social and cultural or, in the words of Maurice Halbwachs (1985), their collective memory.

According to Heike Behrend (1993), every party to a conflict provides reports, photographs, records, lists of victims, etc., in order to reveal the truth and present their version of history. Thus in the course of the Moluccan conflict, too, each side developed a selective historical memory (Sidney Jones 2001). For years the events in the Moluccan conflict were recorded in the Moluccan cyberactors' list and site archives and influenced the members' interpretation of recent Moluccan history. According to Allen and Seaton (1999a: 4), the media assume an important role in the construction of history. It was the explicit goal of Masariku to set up a database for investigations and analyses of the Moluccan conflict that could become a basis for writing Moluccan history from the Christian viewpoint. As in the writing of history, individual events and news items take on meaning only through context, in our case the events in the Moluccan conflict that were recorded in the archives. According to Ananda Mitra (1997: 60), in order to be able to interpret individual news items, the user must be able to fall back on a memory that encompasses earlier news items. Judith Donath (1999: 55) maintains that it is also important that the social and historical context for which the archived posts were written be taken into account, too.

The impact of Internet use in the conflict

It is difficult to ascertain the extent to which the Moluccan cyberactors' use of the Internet actually influenced the course of the conflict. In general, questions of this nature can never be answered unequivocally. This applies not only to the reporting of the Moluccan conflict on the Internet, but to reporting in the media in general. Anthony Smith commented on the problem as follows:

> In trying to discover a precise or even meaningful connection between the media and smoking, or violence or hygiene or drugtaking or the increasing incidence of sunspots, we are at the outset nearly always involved in a methodological error: we are trying to build discussion about human values around a mathematical metaphor. To study the influence of something on something else one is, implicitly, promising to find a numerical answer to a question which cannot have a fair answer at all; we want to be able to say that a mysterious factor X in television programmes causes the viewers to behave in certain ways; we half-consciously hope we will isolate the virus of violence from the totality of media content, and thereby cure society of a hitherto undiagnosed disease … Yet at this inference we have set ourselves one of those quasi-scientific problems; we are to talk about the connection between community conflict and the media. A law of uncertainty supervenes in all attempts to examine connections between social phenomena. (1978: 129–30)

Although scholars assume that the mass media exert a decisive influence on conflicts (see, in particular, Allen and Seaton 1999b), it is almost impossible to determine the type and scope of this influence. One cannot say that a conflict would have taken a different course, and which, if the reporting in the media had been different (Halliday 1999: 145). As such, it is even harder to estimate the influence of the Internet on the Moluccan conflict, as the Moluccan cyberactors were also very active offline, which makes a separate investigation of the two levels – offline and online – and their impact in each case extremely difficult. According to Nils Zurawski

(2000: 186), what is at least certain is that technology, in our case the Internet, also has an influence on the people and groups not directly involved in it, as these have no possibility of influencing the consequences of the images and depictions disseminated about them. In the Moluccan conflict there were, however, indications of how Internet presentations directly impacted the conflict. By way of example, as a result of the FKAWJ depictions, Muslims in and outside Indonesia decided to sign up for the jihad in the Moluccas; Masariku and the CCDA received direct feedback from some of their subscribers, and not just online, but also in the form of activities at the local level in the Moluccas.

Ultimately, the effect the Internet had and the manner in which it was used by the Moluccan cyberactors in the context of the Moluccan conflict can only be clearly ascertained by means of the integration and simultaneous observation of the online and offline spheres. In the previous chapter I already began expanding the picture of the online sphere I had gained from the long-term observation of the three cyberprojects to include concrete results from private cyberspace and my offline research. This is now to be continued at an abstract level. This involves an analysis of the networks created online and offline, and it is important to take all online and offline contexts into consideration. The very open term network seems more suitable than community, as the structure of the entire network created through the Moluccan cyberactors' various online and offline activities is to be revealed here, regardless of social formation. According to Stegbauer (2001: 90), the term network can also include communication that goes beyond the actual social space. However, I have no intention here of carrying out the type of network analysis conducted by Stegbauer. I do not seek to determine the concentration of relationships for use as a benchmark in judging the structure of the social space (Stegbauer 2001: 92), but rather to reveal the interconnectedness of the Moluccan cyberpresentations with other mailing lists, websites, etc., as well as how individual members were integrated in their respective offline context and offline contacts. Through these processes, the Moluccan conflict as such evaded isolation and local exclusivity and was given a global stage on which it became the subject matter of discussions and the object of concrete action planning.

Multipliers, weak ties and the metanetwork

In the deterritorialized space of the Internet it is possible to combine local references and global processes, which can thus influence each other, as Nils Zurawski (2000: 170) stated in his remarks on globality and locality. In Moluccan cyberspace we have on the one hand the reports about events in the Moluccan conflict with specific local and temporal references, and on the other direct reference to, appeals to, or reports from supraregional communities (Christian, Muslim, Western, etc.). Offline, the Moluccan cyberactors and their allies were active locally, nationally and internationally, though in this case 'local' refers to the respective member's place of residence, be it in the Moluccas, Indonesia, Australia, Europe or the United States. Thanks to the many active MML members, each of whom acted as a multiplier online and/or offline, not to mention the (apparently) passive members, Masariku in particular was able to establish an all-embracing network extending far beyond list members. John B. Thompson's (1995: 87–118) 'arenas of circulation' are very helpful in determining the reach of such networks, as are Mark S. Granovetter's (1973) explanations of what are known as 'weak ties'.

James Slevin applied Thompson's analyses of the mass media to the Internet and differentiated between the following circulation levels involved in the use of the Internet:

> First, there are the arenas of circulation involving primary regions of internet use, for instance the structured contexts of mediated interaction and mediated quasi-interaction between internet users situated in separate locales. This primary arena of circulation concerns all the action and interaction online. Second, there are the arenas of circulation involving the secondary region of internet use, such as the structured contexts of face-to-face interaction between internet users sharing the same locale. Third, there are the arenas of circulation involving the peripheral regions of internet use, for example the structured contexts of face-to-face interaction between internet users and non-internet users. (2000: 81)

With regard to the Moluccan case, on the first level we find the members of the Masariku, CCDA and FKAWJ online projects. However, the online multipliers of these three groups, who posted their news and analyses on their websites, disseminated them via their own mailing lists or processed them further in their own reports (extended mediatization; see J. Thompson [1995: 110]) must also be included here. The second level consists of members of the three online projects who lived in the same place where, above and beyond the list discourse, they also communicated face-to-face and potentially discussed certain news items and activities. On the third level we essentially find all members of the Moluccan online projects who exchanged ideas face-to-face with nonmembers, be it in the office of the Catholic or the Protestant crisis centres in Ambon City, at one of the FKAWJ jihad stations on Ambon Island, in one of the numerous FKAWJ offices throughout Indonesia or in the offline context or network of other members worldwide. This is where we also find the numerous members of staff of the three groups with no access to the Internet, who nonetheless played a role in the procurement of information and material and accordingly could act as multipliers. Slevin (2000: 85) argues that these different circulation levels enable new forms of human associations and social organizations.

To illustrate this citing Moluccan cyberspace as an example, I must once again refer back to and address points that some Internet researchers consider particularly problematic in relation to the use of the term community in cyberspace, namely, the noncommitment of online groups and the weakness of ties. With regard to communities on the Internet, there is far more frequently talk of communities of interest, in which factual interest takes precedence over personal interest, than there is of communities of values. Jan van Dijk (1999) and Steven G. Jones (1997) assume that these communities of interest are very unstable and short-lived. Two things are often overlooked here: firstly, which interests are shared and what is exchanged in addition to pure information, and secondly, the importance for social networks of what are known as weak ties. A common interest as a community-building factor – depending of course on the subject of interest – is frequently underestimated. If a mailing list's Internet presentations are, for example, about a current conflict in which the members themselves or their relatives are involved, emotions and spatial and temporal references to the offline sphere automatically also come into play, through which social links are strengthened, new ones come into being and robust communities can emerge (see also Watson 1997: 124). Another example is the Kava Bowl (KB), an Internet platform for inhabitants of Tonga worldwide, whose common origin, culture and history represent their common interests (Morton 1999: 244), which also involve personal matters and values. Helen Morton (1999: 249) sees the main function of KB as establishing social networks and offering other aspects of a community, such as the exchange of experiences and the giving and receiving of advice and support.

Other authors, such as Wellman and Gulia (1999: 172–73), insist as well that not just information but also values and worries are shared online, emotional support is exchanged and a feeling of solidarity created. This became particularly clear in the MML. Wellman and Gulia are of the opinion that the emergence of strong, intimate links is certainly possible on the Internet. In particular, they emphasize the fact that electronic mail is not tied to a specific location, enabling users to maintain contact over long periods of time despite geographic mobility (ibid.: 178–81). Ultimately, they point out, the Internet promotes far more informal yet helpful weak communal links, which, however, only operate in very special areas (ibid.: 181). That said, some authors point out precisely the positive aspect of this state of affairs. Castells (2001c: 388), for example, is convinced that weak bonds are far more suitable than strong ones for bringing together people who are strangers to one another, with different social backgrounds, in an egalitarian interaction pattern, as there are no indications of the status and situation of individuals. According to Wellman and Gulia (1999: 176), only these weak ties can explain the positive finding that in cyberspace there is far greater willingness to communicate with and help strangers than in real life: 'Cyberlinks between people become social links between groups that otherwise would be socially and physically dispersed' (ibid.: 188). The two authors maintain that in general, weak bonds account for the majority of informal links between people, regardless of whether offline or online (ibid.: 183). Other experts claim that online communities are not genuine communities, but confuse the idealized community myth with reality. Community ties are already geographically scattered, sparse, heavily dependent on telecommunications (telephone and fax) and highly specialized in terms of content. According to Wellman and Gulia, investigating the changes in the size, composition and structure of Internet communities is of greater interest (ibid.: 186–87).

The debate about weak ties goes back to Mark S. Granovetter, who highlighted the difference between strong and weak ties. On the basis of group sociological findings, Granovetter (1973) assumes that the circle of friends and acquaintances of people with strong ties to one another overlaps far more than if their relationship is based on weak ties. He is convinced that strong ties tend to bond people with similar personal and social attributes, whereas weak ties tend to bring together people with different characteristics. Consequently, on the one hand weak ties can offer access to resources and information that lie outside the opportunities provided by someone's close circle, and on the other a far larger circle of people can be reached and a larger social distance overcome.[13] Weak ties extend the group horizon and are in a position to bond smaller groups and communities both with one another and with larger, more amorphous social groups. In this way a wide range of levels can be linked. According to Granovetter, strong ties, in contrast, are characterized by a higher motivation potential for mutual support.

Both strong and weak ties played a role in the Moluccan cyberprojects. The circle of founders of the MML, for example, and (Moluccan) circles of friends abroad, who through the MML had 'weak' or 'strong' associations with the Masariku network, revealed strong ties. Behind the Laskar Jihad cyberpresentations there was an organization, the FKAWJ, whose members in the individual branches and schools in each case had close ties with one another. Via weak ties, the MML linked various people and organizations worldwide: Moluccans at home and abroad, NGOs, Christian organizations, the Churches, and European and UN organizations, behind which there were, in turn, other networks. This might be the case as well with the CCDA and the FKAWJ, though this was far less apparent than with Masariku, as none of the list members stated anything 'in public'. Based on the Moluccan cyberactors and their Internet connections, a 'metanetwork' came into being that embraced all these networks and subnetworks, which in some way were in contact with the Moluccan cyberactors, helping the globalization of what were originally local networks. Every member was the potential starting point for a new network, as was every friend or acquaintance of the members, those who were sympathetic to the cyberactors' cause or other people who came into contact with Masariku, CCDA and FKAWJ posts and members. One should bear this enormous potential in mind in the investigation of online projects and their impact. Statements of various members of the three online projects gave an indication of this in the previous chapter. It was the Internet that made all this possible. It enabled the Moluccan cyberactors to extend their struggle far beyond the local level and to lend unreserved expression to their criticism of the 'enemy', the Indonesian government, the Indonesian military and other interest groups that were involved. Given the increasing expansion of the Internet's infrastructure and its constantly increasing number of users, the local actors were able to make their cause the subject of interest of a wide circle of different people.

Only when one considers this metanetwork does the full reach of the Moluccan cyberprojects become clear (Illustration 20). They were about far more than just an online extension of existing communities, which Virnoche and Marx (1997: 87) refer to as 'virtual extension'. The metanetwork embraced the online and offline levels and represented not only an information network, but also an activity network. Activities related to the Moluccan conflict were planned and conducted abroad (demonstrations, lobbying, etc.), in Indonesia (assemblies, meetings with influential people, the Laskar Jihad's recruitment campaigns, etc.) or in the Moluccas themselves (the sending of delegations, peace initiatives, humanitarian aid, financial support, etc.). The cyberactors likewise used local, national and international symbols for their identity and community structures on the Internet.

The Internet was the decisive factor, on the one hand for the wide-scale extension of the local communities, but primarily for the stability and effectiveness of the links that emerged. According to a founder of the MML, the solidarity and advocacy network that Masariku built up worldwide could only come into being through the Internet-based information net-

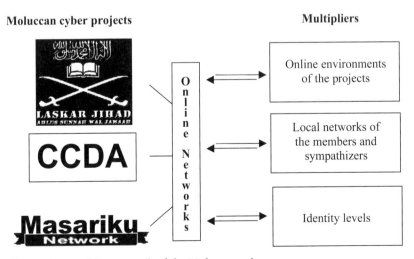

Illustration 20. Metanetwork of the Moluccan cyberactors

work. Only the Internet enabled effective communication in which, in particular in the case of Masariku, members worldwide could participate. Moreover, at the local level and in the subdivisions of these comprehensive networks, face-to-face contacts, telephone contacts and the dissemination of information through other media most certainly played a role, though these were not the subject of my investigations.

The Internet as a factor in the conflict

Even if it is not easy to gauge the direct influence and impact of the Moluccan cyberprojects on the Moluccan conflict at the local level, they are highly visible in a national and international context. For an analysis of the Moluccan conflict in general, the processes described, which had their origins in the Moluccas and in one way or another impacted on them, must most definitely be taken into consideration. Only in this way is it possible to fully understand the momentum of the conflict and how it became embedded in a local, national and international context. We need to grasp the global dimension of the conflict, in which the Internet was a pivotal component. The descriptions in Moluccan cyberspace thus themselves become a factor in the conflict.

Though the Internet played no role in the democratization of the conditions in the Moluccas, as we saw above it did give a few actors a voice and ensured that detailed information about and analyses of the Moluccan conflict, about which one would have learned far less through other media, became public. With the Internet it was possible to create a counterpublic to the national media, a sort of alternative public sphere. Also, it was only via the Internet (as part of the MML) that Moluccans and other interested parties worldwide could play an active part in negotiating positions in the conflict, not to mention the worldwide networking, which was initiated and moved significantly forward at least by the Christian cyberprojects. What was decisive was the fact that the Internet enabled influential authorities in Indonesia, the government and the military to be circumvented. Even after the Suharto era, the mass media (print, TV, radio) did not offer an opportunity of this nature. Their contents were still strictly controlled, not by the Indonesian government, but by influential (e.g., Islamic) groups. The Internet brought together a wide range of voices in the conflict on one platform, which gave more points of view and diversity to the presentation of local events. Local rumours and flyers as well as reports and analyses from local activists were displayed on the global stage of the Internet in the same social sphere as articles about the topic in renowned newspapers and magazines, the opinions of international organizations and the calls of Moluccan and religious associations worldwide. In cyberspace the local discourse could link up with similar discourses being conducted worldwide, which somehow or other were posted on the Internet (in Moluccan cyberspace, for example, these were conflicts between Christians and Muslims in other parts of the world), thus revealing its integration in a larger, global dimension.

Seen from a purely statistical point of view, the broad masses in Indonesia, on account of the relatively low percentage of Internet access in the country (approximately 2 per cent in 2002), were not yet in a position to be a part of all this. However, as became evident in the explanations relating to the Internet in Indonesia (Chapter 4), that number says nothing about the real influence of the Internet in the country. The percentage that actually had access to Internet news was far larger. This was due on the one hand to joint-use Internet accounts and on the other to the traditional informal networks, via which the news from the Internet cafés was swiftly disseminated. Not without reason were the Internet cafés named after the traditional kiosks and snack stands *(Warung)*, that is *Warnet = Warung Internet* (Lim 2003). Here, J. Thompson's (1995) and Slevin's (2000) 'arenas of circulation' come into play again. In this way, directly or indirectly, many people in Indonesia, as indeed worldwide, had access to documents about Moluccan cyberprojects they would otherwise have been unable to view or listen to (letters to the government, the Pope and the press, statements by local organizations, articles in the local daily press, recordings made by local radio stations, etc.), and, through texts, images and sound, became closely familiar with the points of view of representatives of influential parties to the conflict (Laskar Jihad, Catholics, Protestants). It was not just the broad public that characterized and qualified Internet presentations, but also and above all the diversity of the sources and intensity of the reporting.

It remains to be seen how long the imagined communities and identities in Moluccan cyberspace will survive (for some indications, see the epilogue). There were many who saw the Malino II agreements in February 2002 as the official end of the Moluccan conflict, even though afterwards villages and in particular individuals were still ambushed and victims of bomb attacks. The civil state of emergency was only lifted in September 2003, more than eighteen months after Malino II. The FKAWJ online project had already been discontinued, as the organization as such was disbanded in October 2002; its Yahoo! Groups archive is, however, still available. Though the CCDA was officially dissolved when the conflict began to calm down, the regular reports on the situation in the Moluccas were still being sent some time after. As of June 2003, the MML continued to exist, the Moluccans abroad were also still active (at least online) and the Masariku team in Ambon was still sending its updates, even if the intervals between them were longer.[14] They primarily addressed the mutual, very slow process of rapprochement between Christians and Muslims, as well as the consequences of the years of violent conflict and depraved morals, which could only be improved step-by-step. *Ambon Manise* (Sweet Ambon), which was how prior to the conflict the Ambonese had advertised Ambon and expressed their love of their homeland, was elevated to a motto again so as to give greater prominence to what the people had in common rather than their differences. Like the Moluccas themselves, the Moluccan cyberactors were in a state of upheaval, at a point of transition from conflict to peace. Insofar as they still existed, they had to realign themselves and redefine their goals. If the MML was to be used in the future as well, it remained to be seen which would be the community-defining elements – whether it, for example, would become a communal forum for Moluccan Christians and Muslims, as was the list founders' dream, whether it would still create a bridge to their homeland for many Moluccans abroad or whether it would be used to maintain links between Moluccans in the diaspora. At any rate, it became clear that with regard to the Moluccan conflict, as in many other cases, the Internet was an ambivalent thing. It played a role, on the one hand, in the essentialization of identities and as such, possibly, of the conflict, and on the other in the establishment of solidarity networks and the mobilization of aid measures for the conflict's victims.

Further findings and research perspectives

The intensive anthropological investigation of Moluccan cyberspace as a factor in the complex machinery of the Moluccan conflict could well be a source of new findings, in particular for anthropological research into conflict and identity, as well as social scientific Internet research in general. Furthermore, the methods with which anthropological research can be conducted on the Internet were advanced, and fundamental conditions for anthropological Internet research were formulated in the context of these investigations.

Research into conflict, identity and Internet

In the previous chapters it became clear in which diverse, in some cases subtle, ways the Internet is able to become a tool, indeed a weapon, in a conflict, whose repertoire goes far beyond cyberwars and flame wars, hitherto the focus of attention. For local groups, such as those that played a role in the Moluccan conflict, as well as for all kinds of international organizations – from human rights organizations to terrorist associations – the Internet has become an important means of exchanging ideas and getting organized, quickly, in an integrative way, and at least still, to a certain extent, unobserved, as security services are unable to cope that quickly with the rapidly growing Internet population and technological progress. This study reveals which aspects have to be taken into consideration if the role of the Internet in a conflict, whose actors have gone online, is to be analysed: the choice of the mode of communication, the setup and design of a list or website, the role of the webmaster, the authors and members, the contents of the Internet presentations and their sources, the symbols and language used, the structure and development of the discourse, the reference to people and groups at offline and online levels, links and the online environment, the manipulation of websites and email addresses, and of course cyberwars, flame wars and cross-posting. Creative and content-related aspects need to be encompassed just as much as the dynamics of an online presentation. The analysis of the reporting, self-portrayals and portrayals by others of the online actors can be of great importance when it comes to understanding their perspective of the conflict and their offline activities, which is also a prerequisite for being able to formulate meaningful solutions.

The way the Moluccan cyberactors designed their online presence – in particular, the reports and images of the immediate battlefield and eyewitness reports, as well as, for example, the design of the FKAWJ website itself (logo, banner, etc.) – indicates that the Internet can play a role in a further medialization of conflicts, albeit different in terms of quality as we became familiar with in the mass media reporting on the Gulf War in 1991 and the Iraq War in 2003.[15] In the latter, the U.S. administration made what is known as embedded journalism the norm. The journalist was to report as an integrative part of the troops directly from the front line, on the one hand providing viewers with images of the greatest possible authenticity, while on the other sparking fears that objective reporting was no longer possible. The Indonesian government promptly adopted and indeed intensified this principle with regard to reporting on the Aceh initiative by the Indonesian military in May 2003 against the rebels of the Aceh Independence Movement (GAM): 'The reporters must wear an army uniform, they are required to report favourably about the missions, GAM members may not be quoted.'[16]

The Internet enables a different, more in-depth kind of embedded reporting in a conflict, as it enables not only journalists and other middlemen to reach a wide audience with their reports, but also the locals, who are directly involved in the action, and not for professional reasons. These people are possibly even more interested than the embedded journalists in providing a certain perspective of the conflict; they frequently have no opportunity of revealing another perspective, because they have no access to information from the other side. As such, the ambivalence of the Internet is continued here as well: on the one hand, the Internet offers detailed local information, which enables users to participate in the events in the conflict down to the street combat level, but which on the other is to be treated with caution and which must certainly be categorized in an offline and online conflict context. Furthermore, it must also be taken into consideration that the spread of a conflict to the Internet makes it less controllable than if it were just reported in the mass media. The presence of the Moluccan conflict on the Internet is certainly a clear indication that in the future we will also have to take this level into account as a potential factor in conflict analysis.

In Moluccan cyberspace a merging of the issues of conflict, religion and identity occurred. It became clear how the Internet could be used to construct identity and the role religion could play in this. The reporting in Moluccan cyberspace ran along religious lines, and the actors availed themselves of corresponding symbols. The Laskar Jihad online project deserves first mention here; the intention was to reflect an idealized Islamic community by using Islamic sources (the Koran, Sunnah, Sharia) to evaluate the situation in the Moluccas as interpreted by the FKAWJ and by issuing a corresponding code of conduct. This confirms investigations of the relationship between fundamentalist currents and the achievements of the Modern Age, expressed on the one hand in rejection, and on the other in the exploitation of cutting-edge technology, in particular electronic media (see, e.g., Appleby 2000: 88; Bielefeldt and Heitmeyer 1998: 15; Cigdem 1998: 96). Here, fundamentalists opted to beat the secular Modern Age with its own weapons (Appleby 2000: 90). The use of the Internet by fundamentalist groups advanced the 'process of making religion visible', which, according to Ahmet Cigdem (1998), the fundamentalists sought to do.[17]

Moluccan cyberspace also revealed quite clearly that identity projects of a very different nature could be planned and conducted on the Internet, and not just within the framework of fantastical role playing or as the self-representation of an individual person, but also as collective identities, which were either developed and negotiated in an online community, as was the case with the MML, or presented as the ideal image of a community by an authoritarian and influential body (FKAWJ). Here the Internet offers all manner of freedoms, including the freedom of uncompromising, unilateral identity portrayal, which has no intention of an honest exchange with its audience. Through my online research it became clear that the online constructs in Moluccan cyberspace referred very heavily to the cyberactors' offline contexts, which encompassed the local, national and even international levels. Despite great imagination, the concrete offline context was still of the utmost importance. The Internet enabled these different levels to be integrated and a unique identity to be created that was adapted to the needs of the various parties in the conflict. It is interesting that on the one hand in Moluccan cyberspace traditional elements were used in textual argumentation, which were characterized primarily by exclusion and inclusion mechanisms and the differentiation between 'us' and 'the others', and on the other Internet-specific strategies such as flame wars, cross-posting, commented links and archives. By also integrating text, audio and image documents, thereby appealing to several senses at one and the same time, the identity projects on the Internet could be made far more convincing and be structured more convincingly than in other media.

With regard to the analysis of mailing lists as a social sphere, I advocate Stegbauer's (2001) model, which differentiates between key actors, discussants, posters and lurkers, even if one can argue about the names given to the various roles and their characteristics. Stegbauer simply undertook a basic structuring, which, depending on the respective case, has to be refined. The allocation of roles that emerged for me given my long-term membership of the MML can serve as a schema, which, in this or a modified form, can be applied to other forums. The roles in the social structure of the MML are not the fantastic spawn of the active list members, but rather, in line with their abilities and opportunities, emerged in the online and offline sphere. No matter what issue is being addressed in a mailing list, in many online communities there will always be roles such as that of the activist, arbitrator, moderator, troublemaker, joker or lurker. Depending on the subject and objective of the mailing list, the range of roles will extend in a certain direction. These roles are a prerequisite for the formation of a stable, functioning community structure online, one condition being, however, that they continue to exist for a relatively long period of time and are confirmed and accepted by the other members.

In order to be able to comment on the impact and efficacy of the Internet in a case such as the Moluccan conflict, the offline level must also be included. This means, on the one hand, familiarizing oneself with the background literature about the events, places, people, organizations, etc., that are the subject of the online investigations, and viewing the results in relation to the online depictions. On the other, it is a good idea to complement online research with offline field research, not in order to verify or disprove the depictions on the Internet, but so as to be able to better classify them as a factor in the conflict context and get to know the cyberactors' social environment – how they were embedded in the local context and the conditions under which the Internet posts were produced. In addition to this embedding in the offline context, the embedding of an online identity project in its online environment cannot be disregarded. What is meant here is the linking structure between websites, the integration of mailing lists in other mailing lists and the direct or indirect exchange between different Internet projects, be it by means of cross-posting, manipulation of an opponent's websites or reference to participants of another online project. These analyses can provide valuable information about how the cyberactors investigated are portrayed by themselves and others.

Recognition of the fact that researching social spheres on the Internet can only produce meaningful results if one follows the list discourse for a lengthy period of time is also crucial. The time required is determined by factors I mentioned in Chapter 2. If one follows a list discourse for long enough and during that period the members remain relatively stable, as was the case with the MML, the identities and motives of individual members also become clear, even if they do not reveal their true, or offline, identity. Given long-term participation in online projects, it is possible to understand their identity policy and identify communitization processes. Lengthy participation is also recommended in order to be able to recognize, analyse and classify the various (conflict) strategies used in and around the online area investigated. As such, the anthropological field research premise also applies to the new field that is cyberspace: in order to become familiar with an internal perspective of the people and groups being studied, long-term participation is indispensable, which, however, is no longer based on the annual cycle of a local population, but on the rhythm of cyberspace, its users and their specific offline context.

Research perspectives

Given the different nature of the three cyberprojects investigated, different research perspectives emerged in each case. With regard to the Christians, the integration of the online and offline levels produced far more than just a combination of the online and offline projects of Masariku and the CCDA, as the metanetwork clearly revealed. The members of the MML actively conducted both online and offline networking, through which far-reaching solidarity and action networks were built up. For this reason, in the case of Masariku in particular a comparison with a social movement[18] is warranted. Though the Christians assumed that the social, political and cultural change in the Moluccas in recent years and decades had been one of the factors responsible for the outbreak of the conflict, Masariku first wanted to restore things to how they were before the outbreak of the conflict, in other words, the peaceful coexistence of Christians and Muslims. Although this contradicts the notion of a social movement geared to initiating social upheaval, definitions as offered by, among others, Mario Diani – a sociologist who has worked on social movements and collective identity both offline and online (Diani 1992, 2000) – suggest a comparison. For Diani (1992: 17), social movements are an analytical concept, which he describes as follows:

> Social movements are defined as networks of informal interactions between a plurality of individuals, groups and/or organizations, engaged in political or cultural conflicts, on the basis of shared collective identities. (ibid.: 1)

According to Diani (ibid.: 17), this results in three basic components of social movements, namely, networks of informal activities between a number of actors, collective identity and conflict-ridden issues to which the collective activities are geared (the type of conflict would, of course, have to be defined more closely here).

> Such networks promote the circulation of essential resources for action (information, expertise, material resources) as well as of broader systems of meaning. Thus, networks contribute both to creating the preconditions for mobilisation … and to providing the proper setting for the elaboration of specific world-views and life-styles. (ibid.: 7–8)

Through the metanetwork 'Masariku', a large number of different individuals, communities and organizations were linked that could clearly identify with the collective identity negotiated in the MML and wanted to be engaged in the matter of the Moluccan conflict. Via the network, information, experiences and material resources were exchanged just as much as systems of values and meaning. The MML and other Masariku activities (e.g., the trips to Europe undertaken by a list founder) mobilized members and others sympathetic to the cause to become involved, online or offline, in the Moluccan conflict. This mobilization factor is characteristic of social movements.

Mobilization in the context of the Masariku projects took a similar course to that identified by Katja Cronauer (2001: 10) in her study of mailing lists that had been established by two protest movements against the globalization agenda of an APEC (Asia-Pacific Economic Cooperation) summit in Canada, and against an EU and a G7/G8 summit in Germany. According to her, the online activities of social movements involve posting items on the mailing list (e.g., forwarding online information, uploading and forwarding newspaper articles, involvement in discussions and announcing group activities[19]), setting up online facilities (e.g., websites and other mailing lists) to support the goals and activities of a group, forwarding and disseminating information from the mailing list (in our case the MML) to, for example, other mailing lists or individuals, or initiating or participating in email campaigns. Offline activities encompass, among other things, taking part in letter or telephone campaigns, events and group meetings and assuming responsibility for certain duties, such as planning a meeting or an event. The Internet offers groups of social activists an opportunity to extend their reach enormously (among other reasons, because the Internet reduces transaction costs considerably), expand their networks, increase their visibility, form opinions and conduct strategic planning (Cronauer 2001: 14). Alongside mobilizing people and resources and organizing activities, the creation of a collective identity is important (see Diani 1992; Melucci 1995). We also come across all these elements and corresponding announcements in the MML and the associated social space online and offline. So as to learn more about the functionality, capacity to act, efficacy and actual reach of the metanetwork presented and its subnetworks, it would be worthwhile and interesting to examine these patterns of mobilization and action more closely. They could well provide valuable information about the impact and efficacy of the use of the Internet by social movements.

Moreover, the results of this study suggest there should be a more detailed investigation of the Moluccan diaspora, parts of which, in connection with the Moluccan conflict, have come together and organized themselves via the MML. How important is the Internet in general for Moluccans abroad, their links to one another and to their home country? In this respect, how important is the Internet in comparison with other modes of communication such as the telephone and letters, and has this changed over the course of time or is indeed still changing? When it comes to the links between the diaspora and the country of origin and their mutual influence on one another, the Internet will play an ever greater role in corresponding research. Here, Appadurai's (1996) 'ethnoscape' and 'mediascape' models could well be helpful. The Internet is an important part of mediascapes and at the same time a significant tool of ethnoscapes.

Research perspectives are somewhat different if we consider Moluccan cyberspace from the Muslim side. From the outset one is bound to a very narrow point of view, as from the Moluccas themselves the only voice to be heard via the Internet was that of the radical Islamic Laskar Jihad. Though the Laskar Jihad was intent on establishing an Islamic state in Indonesia, in other words bringing about social change, its members certainly did not want to achieve this by negotiating a position in a collective movement together with the members of their mailing list and visitors to their website.[20] Their views, to which as many Indonesian Muslims as possible were to be won over, were based on what for them were the sacrosanct basic principles of Islam.

The preservation of Indonesia as a unitary state was another pillar of the FKAWJ identity project. Could the Internet serve to establish a uniform identity in the widely dispersed islands that make up Indonesia, something the rulers in Jakarta had been striving for since Indonesia gained independence? Could it play a role in building up and expanding an imagined Muslim community in Indonesia? The extent to which the Internet, the number of whose users has grown rapidly in Indonesia in recent years, actually succeeded in becoming a sort of mediator in such matters would certainly merit closer investigation.

As the FKAWJ disbanded in October 2002, other stable Internet projects conducted by Indonesian Muslims must be selected for corresponding analyses, the identity constructs of which differ of course from those of the Laskar Jihad. This research could start, for example, from the investigations conducted by Gary Bunt (2000) on the topic of Cyber Islamic Environments and the creation of idealized perceptions of Muslim identity in cyberspace, as well as other works discussed in Chapter 2. Compared to the Christian projects, it is far more difficult to ascertain from the online presentations of the Laskar Jihad the actual reach of its online network. From their reporting it is clear that they had close ties with the mujahideen in the North Moluccas and with various radical Muslim organizations and individuals in the Central Moluccas, as indeed throughout Indonesia in general. What is far less clear is the importance of the Internet with regard to their links and contacts abroad, with the exception, for example, of foreign warriors who were recruited for the jihad in the Moluccas on the back of Internet portrayals, messages of solidarity from American Muslims and the previously mentioned donation lists.[21]

In general, the research into Moluccan cyberspace hitherto could be complemented by a perception analysis. This would need to be conducted on a major scale and to investigate the way Moluccan cyberprojects were perceived both by their direct members and visitors as well as people who came into contact with the Moluccan cyberpresentations via other Internet projects. This would provide an indication of the importance the Moluccan cyberprojects and identities actually had for these people, how they rated the authenticity of the projects and where they saw their significance for the Moluccan conflict, thus finding further answers to the question of the role of the Internet in the Moluccan conflict. It would also be meaningful to conduct corresponding comparative studies, so as to apply the findings of this study on a broader basis.

The Internet and peace

In conclusion I would like to mention an issue in which from the outset I had placed great hopes, namely, the use of the Internet as an instrument of peace. During the conflict, peace-seeking Christians and Muslims could theoretically have met in cyberspace to bypass the essentialization of their faiths, initiate an interreligious, or rather a Moluccan, dialogue and find a peaceful solution to the Moluccan conflict together. Even though from the beginning the Christian side had been keen on integrative approaches, there was no Christian-Muslim exchange on the Internet. The main reason for this 'failure' was the fact that moderate Moluccan Muslims had no voice on the Internet, be this because they had no access to it, or because they did not dare raise their voice because the FKAWJ already claimed to represent them. The FKAWJ fundamentally rejected all dialogue, online and offline, as long as the Christians failed to admit their guilt. In order to be able to contact those Muslims who were open to peace online, the Christians would have first had to establish contact offline and coordinate a corresponding procedure. For this the situation proved in most cases to be too dangerous, or the Muslim contacts did not dare to forward information to the Christian side.

Without active communication between the two sides (online or offline), no peace could come about. According to Craig Calhoun, merely creating a public domain for each identity group, as the Moluccan cyberactors did, without observing and promoting interaction between them throughout the entire public domain, does not mean progress. Democracy is only possible if exchange takes place beyond the boundaries of these different public domains (Calhoun 1995: 242). Things did not get that far in Moluccan cyberspace. Essentially, individual Masariku members' approaches did move in this direction, in particular in the months following the Malino II agreements, by their emphasizing what all Moluccans had in common rather than repeatedly focusing on the polarization of society, describing joint peace initiatives and slow attempts at rapprochement between the parties to the conflict and concentrating on the humanitarian aspect instead of the dehumanization of the opponent. It was not primarily about identifying the perpetrators and winners of the conflict, but instead about tackling the problem of the conflict together and questioning the sense behind it.[22] For this reason, Internet research in the future should also investigate how in a conflict the Internet can be used as an instrument of peace to overcome existing boundaries and promote a balanced dialogue. This represents an additional huge potential that the Internet offers. Whether the Internet has already successfully played this role in other cases should be examined, so as to be able to apply the findings to the Moluccan conflict and other conflicts and construct a common identity on the Internet from the 'cyberidentities at war' that brings peace.

Gandong Song

Below is a common song in the Moluccas, which prior to the conflict was often sung in association with the *pela* alliances, and during the conflict was a sign of reconciliation.

> Sibling, come sibling,
> come here soon!
> I want to tell you,
> we both have the same mother.
> The life of siblings is so sweet.
> You feel what I feel,
> we are from a single womb.
>
> Oh, my sibling
> let me bear,
> I bear only you.
> We are both one womb,
> one heart and one soul.
>
> *Gandong la mari gandong*
> *mari jua ale yo*
> *beta mau bilang ale*
> *katong dua satu gandong*
> *hidup ade deng kaka sungguh manis lawang nge*
> *ale rasa beta rasa*
> *katong dua satu gandong*
>
> *gandonge sio gandonge*
> *mari beta gendong*
> *beta gendong ale jua*
> *katong dua cuma satu gandonge*
> *satu hati satu jantonge*

Notes

1. Werner Gephart (1999: 235–36) also sees the reference to 'constituted forms of community', from which members of a group, an association and complex social systems draw their identity, as a prerequisite for the emergence of imagined communities.

2. Ja'far Umar Thalib, for example, was an authority both offline and online; although he did not contribute directly to the online discourse, he was a topic of it.

3. The population of Trinidad at home and worldwide examined by Miller and Slater (2000), for which the Internet is, so to speak, a natural platform to lend expression to their values and the core of their Trinidadian identity on a global stage, represents another extreme.

4. The language problem was 'solved' in different ways. Whereas the CCDA wrote its reports in English from the outset, in the MML and in the case of the FKAWJ the majority of the posts were in Indonesian. Particularly important information was translated into English. With regard to Masariku, in the offline sphere too MML members in various countries produced translations in the relevant language and forwarded them to key platforms.

5. Apart from the attacks on the relevant online presentations described in Chapter 8, which, however, never led to one of the projects actually discontinuing.

6. Mediascapes refer both to the distribution of electronic potential in order to produce and disseminate information (mass media) as well as to the images of the world created by these media (Appadurai 1996: 35).

7. Benedict Anderson (1992: 11) and Arjun Appadurai (1996: 196) correspondingly point out the significance of the electronic connection of the Indian diaspora to movements in their country of origin. By way of example, they quote an Indian businessman in Canada who supported the Khalistan movement, and the influence of the Indian diaspora on the violence following the destruction of the Babri Mosque in Ayodhya, India, on 6 December 1992.

8. According to Wim Manuhutu, then director of the Moluks Historisch Museum in Utrecht, the Moluccan community in the Netherlands certainly played a role in the Moluccan conflict, at least as far as the representation of the conflict and corresponding propaganda was concerned (personal email, 20 February 2001); see also Manuhutu (2000b); Patty (2000); Smeets (2000); and Steijlen (2001). With regard to the situation of the Moluccan community in the Netherlands see, among others, Bartels (1990); Benda-Beckmann and Benda-Beckmann (1993); Bosscher and Waaldijk (1985); Hoek (1994); Huwaë (2001); Manuhutu and Smeets (1991); Patty (2000); Penonton (1977); Pollmann and Seleky (1979); Rinsampessy (1992); Smeets (1977, 1992, 1996, 2001); Steijlen (1991, 1996); and Strijbosch (1985, 1988, 1992).

9. The extent of the intersection between circles says nothing about the 'identity proportions'. It is merely intended to show which identity patterns and which symbols play a part in the imagined or idealized communities of the Moluccan cyberactors.

10. What is meant here is not that there was an Indonesia-wide unitary interpretation of Islamic sources and that the population lived uniformly according to them, but that a large proportion of Indonesian Muslims could if anything be

considered moderate, as opposed to radical Islamic groups such as the Laskar Jihad, who represented a minority in Indonesia. Through their offline and online performances, the Laskar Jihad nonetheless became known throughout the world. As Peter Mandaville argues (2001: 169), the Internet '(allows) the more marginalized sects of Islam ... to appear as "mainstream" as any Sunnī site'.

11. The lack of interaction and the presentational character of websites prompted Steven Rubio (1996) to refer to communities constituted via the World Wide Web – as opposed to mailing lists – at best as the simulation of a community. I have replaced the word 'simulation' with 'idealization', which in this context seemed more meaningful and suitable.

12. The CCDA used this multiplier effect far more systematically than Masariku.

13. Granovetter (1973: 1366n10) defines 'the "social distance" between two individuals in a network as the number of lines in the shortest path from one to another'.

14. For an update see the epilogue.

15. On the subject of the medialization of conflicts, we learn on a Tübingen University website devoted to the special research field 'War Experience', project section D (Medialization of War Experience): 'War has increasingly become an event that is communicated by the media; mediatized communication processes have had a decisive influence on warfare and the portrayal of the experience of war to contemporaries and subsequent generations' (http://www.uni-tuebingen.de/SFB437/phase2/p2_TDlb.htm, 8 July 2003).

16. *Jungle World* 30, 16 July 2003 (watchindonesia@snafu.de, 18 July 2003).

17. 'This process of making religion visible not only means constructing religion as a discourse, which is then introduced to economic, social and in particular political and public circles; at the same time it also means that religion is transformed into an imperative and constructive force in individuals' social and political worlds. In this context fundamentalism forms the, in a political respect, more dominant dimension in the process of the de-privatization of religion' (Cigdem 1998: 93).

18. There is already a whole series of publications on the topic of social movements on the Internet, of which the following are just a few examples: Diani (2000); Loader and Keeble (2002); Nip (2002); and Sassi (2000). Furthermore, Brian Loader has (co-)edited various books on this and similar topics. I seek here to present a perspective but by no means an introduction to this topic.

19. With regard to the Masariku metanetwork, these activities never related to the entire group, but always to subgroups or networks.

20. The hierarchical structure of the FKAWJ and its strict doctrine contradict the very concept of social movements (Diani 1992: 14).

21. According to Kirsten Schulze, the Laskar Jihad did indeed have international connections. As they belong in the nationalist Islamic category, she maintains (2002: 61), these connections if anything provided a sort of framework concept for the FKAWJ and its philosophy. It provided an insight into the forces driving the Laskar Jihad, such as fear of globalization, the political and cultural hegemony of the West and the worry about moral decay caused by materialism, secularism and individualism.

22. For further perspectives on peace journalism see, for example, Botes (1998); Eriyanto and Qodari (2000); and Galtung (1998).

Epilogue

So the joke goes that Mubarak dies and meets Nasser and Sadat in
the afterlife. They ask him, 'were you poisoned or shot?' Mubarak
shrugs and answers 'Facebook!'
　　　　　Annabelle Sreberny, 'A Social Media Evolution?'

In the late 1990s and early 2000s *Cyberidentities at War* and ethnographic
field research in cyberspace were still pioneering work. There was not much
literature to fall back on and not much advice on how to proceed methodologically. A decade later, the situation is different in some respects, yet in
others a great deal still needs to be done, as I seek to show in this epilogue.
The above quotation refers to the role of the Internet in the so-called Arab
Spring, an 'insurrectionary wave that started in Tunis in December [2010]
and is still unfolding across the Maghreb and Middle East' (Sreberny 2011).
Interestingly, in the end, European countries such as Spain jumped on the
bandwagon and staged massive protests against their governments. In all
those revolutions and protests, the Internet figured prominently as a means
to express peoples' frustrations to their own governments and the world,
acted as a mobilizing force and enabled people to coordinate movements
and actions. Debate on the role of the Internet and other new media in current sociopolitical developments and events is more important than ever.[1]

　　With this epilogue I wish to give the reader an idea of how the events
and theoretical and methodological issues discussed in this volume have
developed. Naturally, such a brief epilogue cannot and does not seek to do
justice to the wealth of new publications and the various topics on which
research has advanced in this field of study since the German version of
the book went to press in 2004; it has to remain selective and precursory,
particularly as this is a highly interdisciplinary field of study and much
of the research done is anchored in the various disciplines. I nonetheless
want to provide at least an idea of the direction in which the various matters are heading, to make it easier for the interested reader to continue. I
will first provide a brief update on what happened to the Moluccan cyberactors and the media scene in the Moluccas and what progress was made
with regards to other conflict analyses (or rather, a list of new references
for those interested in reading more than a discussion of those publications). Next I will attempt to provide more general insights into theoreti-

cal and methodological developments in cyberanthropology and will then focus on more recent research conducted in two particular areas that are of interest in terms of this book's subject matter, that is, conflict and religion online.

What happened to the Moluccan cyberactors?

Although mass violence in the Moluccas ended in 2003–4, it will still take the Moluccans a long time to completely recover from it. However, in most places people have found their way back to a daily routine that also involves interreligious communication and interaction, sometimes based on common ancestry or shared *adat*, sometimes on more practical thoughts such as economic relations or interreligious communication at the workplace or in the education sector. As indicated in the book, the Laskar Jihad website was discontinued in October 2002 owing to the dissolution of the FKAWJ. Its Yahoo! mailing list is still available today, but no more posts were made after late 2001. The Masariku mailing list exists to this day and is still active with hundreds of posts each month, but was taken over by one of its members who uses it as a more general news forum that only partly touches upon issues discussed during the conflict. Father Böhm delivered regular reports on the postconflict situation in the Moluccas via the newsletter of the Catholic Crisis Centre until May 2006. With a last report in December 2006 he bade his subscribers farewell and officially ended the newsletter.

As I have shown in the book, the Internet was part of a larger media landscape that impacted on the conflict and, as my more recent visits to the Moluccas demonstrate, also impacted on the peace process. Whereas media acted as influential warmongers in times of conflict, they are now actively used to promote peace and foster the integration of Moluccan society. The Maluku Media Centre (MMC) played a major role in this turnaround. The MMC was set up in early 2001 by local journalists with the help of the Indonesian Association of Independent Journalists (Aliansi Jurnalis Independen, AJI) and became an independent forum in 2004. Its members not only translated their newly acquired knowledge about peace journalism into their own everyday work, but also offered training courses for media representatives (newspaper, radio, TV) throughout the Moluccan Province.[2] Today, major Moluccan dailies such as *Siwalima* and *Ambon Ekspres* are online and other online news portals have emerged, such as balagu.com. Important peace initiatives such as the MMC (http://www.malukumediacentre.org/), the Moluccan wide raja council (http://latupatimaluku.blogspot.com/) and the Moluccan Interfaith Council (http://maluku-interfaith.blogspot.com/) launched their own websites. Most of them, however, are updated only irregularly, if at all (partly owing to funding problems).

Many more academic analyses of the conflict were published in the years after it had officially ended (see, e.g., Bertrand 2004; Coppel 2006; Klinken 2007; Pannell 2003; Pieris 2004; Trijono 2004). Some of them focused on certain aspects or a certain dimension of the conflict, such as its local roots (K. von Benda-Beckmann 2004), conflict entrepreneurs (Vermonte 2006), its last episode in 2004 (International Crisis Group 2004), religion and history (Wattimanela 2003), the war of ideologies (Turner 2006), *pela* as peace- or troublemaker (Hohe and Remijsen 2003), the role of the military (Azca 2004), the fate of migrant refugees during and after the conflict (Palmer 2004), displacement (Sidel 2008), land and migration issues (Adam 2009), and past and former bureaucracy policies (Tomagola et al. 2008). Others focus more explicitly on the conflict dynamics in certain areas, such as the Central Moluccas (Yanuarti et al. 2003), the North Moluccas (Armaiyn 2006; Duncan 2005; Wilson 2005; Yanuarti et al. 2004), Banda (Winn 2003) or the Southeast Moluccas (Kaartinen 2007; Thorburn 2005, 2008). We even find popular scientific accounts such as Lingsma's *Het Verdriet van Ambon: Een geschiedenis van de Molukken* (2008; The grief of Ambon: A story from the Moluccas) and Vatikiotis's novel *The Spice Garden* (2004). In various articles and contributions to edited volumes I myself tried to introduce this book's issues in a more condensed way or to examine certain aspects of them in more detail (see Bräuchler 2003, 2004a, 2004b, 2004c, 2006a, 2006b, 2006c, 2007b, 2009b, 2010a). Over the past few years I have been researching the peace process in the Moluccas. In more recent publications I aim to give an impression of the transitions Moluccan society is undergoing: (1) the transformation from conflict to peace and (2) the transformations triggered by the decentralization process in Indonesia and increasing self-determination at the local level, legalized and promoted by new laws passed in 1999 and 2004 (implementation still ongoing) (see, e.g., Bräuchler 2007a, 2009a, 2009c, 2010b, 2011a). The revival of tradition plays an outstanding role in both processes, as a means for peace (to build interreligious bridges) and to return to local political structures.

Ideological and methodological change in cyberanthropology

At the outset I would like to state that, despite all the changes and developments that have occurred over the last few years, this book is still highly relevant for various reasons: (1) although online modes of communication are constantly changing and expanding and social networks (such as Facebook), blogs and Twitter have become extremely popular, websites and email are still very much in demand – a point that is often forgotten in the face of the 'social network' hype; (2) although anthropologists have produced a great deal in recent years to make up for their delayed start in

Internet research, many researchers have still not consistently transferred long-term participant observation to the online space; and (3) although much has been written on conflict and the Internet, very different perceptions exist of what online conflict actually is and what the notion of it comprises – in both intradisciplinary and interdisciplinary terms. To my knowledge there is still no ethnographic study based on long-term participant observation of sites and places where (religious) offline conflict has been extended and transferred to cyberspace and continued there with other means, the offline and online levels being intimately interrelated and mutually influential. Moreover, most of the book's findings are relevant in terms of other modes of communication due to characteristics inherent to the medium of the Internet.

Having said this, of course a lot has happened in the field of cyber-anthropology since Escobar's (1994) early 'Welcome to Cyberia: Notes on the Anthropology of Cyberculture' and Mizrach's (1995) CyberAnthropology website (see also Budka and Kremser 2004). The term 'cyberanthropology' itself has even been questioned by various media scholars.[3] The need to academically engage more with media and new media in order to grasp social and cultural developments and dynamics is reflected in the increasing number of universities worldwide offering media anthropology master's programmes and working groups such as the one led by Michael Wesch (Kansas State University) on digital ethnography (http://mediatedcultures.net/ksudigg/) (Wali 2010) and the master's programme in digital anthropology introduced by Daniel Miller and Lane DeNicola at University College London in 2009 (http://www.ucl. ac.uk/anthropology/digital-anthropology/).[4]

Around the turn of the century debate was still raging on the relationship between the 'real' and the 'virtual', the 'offline' and the 'online'. On the one hand it seems to be common sense nowadays among those conducting research on and about the Internet that the online and the offline are closely interlinked and cannot be analysed in isolation. The debate nonetheless flares up time and again, triggered by studies such as Tom Boellstorff's *Coming of Age in Second Life* (2008), one of the few studies based on long-term ethnographic online research (June 2004–January 2007), on the culture of *a free 3-D virtual world 'where* users can socialize, connect and create using free voice and text chat' (http://secondlife.com/, 18 June 2011). Promoting an analytical separation of the offline and online spheres, Boellstorff conducted his fieldwork entirely within Second Life, arguing that 'there do exist distinct cultures in virtual worlds, even though they draw from actual-world culture. This is why researching them "in their own terms" is now one viable methodological strategy' (Boellstorff 2008: 18). As Boellstorff (ibid.: 61) explains: 'For instance, if during my research I was talking to a woman, I was not concerned to determine if she was "really" a man in the actual world … Most Second Life residents meeting this woman would not know the answers to such questions, so for my ethnographic purposes it was important that I not know either.'[5] Alex Golub, who conducted an ethnographic study of knowledge production in the multiplayer online role-playing game World of Warcraft, used his data to criticize Boellstorff for exactly that, for bracketing out Second Lifers' 'actual world lives', but also for excluding 'from his study the websites, blogs, and other online sites where Second Lifers interact' (Golub 2010: 24). According to Golub (ibid.: 25), 'such a claim reinscribes assumptions of boundedness which the anthropological critique of locality and colonialism have long sought to destabilize.'[6]

Christine Hine focused in her early pioneering work on the online sphere, giving the offline context only a marginal space in her ethnography (Hine 2000). In her later studies on e-science, however, she promotes the combination of online and offline research and visiting 'a diverse array of online and offline sites … [o]ver a period of three years' to obtain 'a holistic understanding of the disciplinary scene' (Hine 2007).[7] I agree with Garcia et al. (2009: 56) that there might be some social phenomena that justify conducting research exclusively online – and Boellstorff's study is probably a case in point given his particular research question. But in most cases the isolationist view of the online would rather distort the close interrelationship between the online and the offline in users' experiences, where the Internet is just one more means to communicate and as much part of reality as any other mode of communication. Social change more generally – be it ordinary or revolutionary – I would argue, can only be grasped if we integrate offline and online research and, as Leander and McKim (2003) point out, strategically adapt our 'ethnography across online and offline space' (see also Kozinets 2010: 55). In line with Burrell (2009), I would like to promote our field as 'a heterogeneous network' (ibid.: 182) 'that incorporates physical, virtual, and imagined spaces' (ibid.: 181) and thus opt against the notion of a 'conventionally bounded field site' (ibid.: 185). As we are dealing with anthropological research, it should still be the human aspect that is the focus of our attention, not the media. Moreover, as Kozinets (2010: 12) emphasizes, 'there is not a lot that is particularly unique about much of what goes on in the online environment. Culture exists, and always has, in a continuous state of flux whose transformations have been driven by our inventions, which we simultaneously shape and drive.'

As anthropology has increasingly opened up to the field of Internet studies, at least some long-term ethnographic studies have been produced. These include Jonathan Marshall's (2007a) *Living on Cybermind: Categories, Communication, and Control,* based on more than a decade of participant observation in a mailing list devoted to 'the philosophy and psychology of cyberspace,'[8] and Tom Boellstorff's (2008) *Coming of Age in Second Life* mentioned above. Whereas Boellstorff consciously gives the offline context the backseat, Marshall explores 'the ways people use and "live on" an Internet mailing list' and 'the influence of external social factors, social categories and the way that communication is structured, on self identity presentation, co-operation, community and conflict on-line' (Marshall 2007b).[9] Just as some of the terms popular in Internet research (such as 'community') have been discussed and questioned (see, for example, Guimarães 2005; Marshall 2007a; Postill 2008), there is ongoing debate regarding what to call ethnographies resulting from Internet research such as virtual ethnography, online ethnography, webography, digital ethnography and cyberanthropology. However, as Kozinets (2010: 5) complains, such debate has so far produced no 'specific, procedural guidelines to take a researcher through the steps necessary to conduct an ethnography of an online community or culture and to present their work'. Interestingly, it is often nonanthropologists who try to systematize methodology for online research, such as Hine (a sociologist) in her edited volume on *Virtual Methods* (2005b) or Kozinets (a professor of marketing) in his *Netnography: Doing Ethnographic Research Online* (2010). Maybe this is because anthropologists are used to creatively adapting their methodological toolbox to constantly changing situations and challenging new contexts and settings, and thus don't feel such an urgent need to standardize and formalize it.[10]

With his expertise in consumer and marketing research, Kozinets seeks to provide a guide for social science researchers who 'must follow people's social activities and encounters onto the Internet and through other technologically-mediated communications' in order to understand society going digital (Kozinets 2010: 1). What he calls *netnography* is 'a specialized form of ethnography adapted to the unique computer-mediated contingencies of today's social worlds' (ibid.: 1), in brief, 'participant observational research based in online fieldwork' (ibid.: 60; see also Masten and Plowman 2003). According to Kozinets, '[t]he way that technology and culture interact is a complex dance, an interweaving and intertwining' (ibid.: 22). He sees netnography as a natural and organic part of every future ethnography next to 'participant-observation … interviews, descriptive statistics, archival data collection, extended historical case analysis, videography, projective techniques such as collages, semiotic analysis, and a range of other techniques' (ibid.: 60). Whereas I consider this divide between ethnography and netnography artificial, since the latter can, as I see it, include all methods Kozinets lists under ethnography, his account nonetheless provides some helpful notes on how to organize online fieldwork for beginners.[11]

Online conflict and social movements on the rise

I would roughly differentiate between two kinds of conflict on the Internet that I dealt with in the research underlying this book. One is social conflicts in online networks and environments such as mailing lists and virtual worlds. In *Living on Cybermind,* Johnathan Marshall (2007a) conducted extensive research on such conflicts developing in the social space created by the mailing list Cybermind: invasion, dissent, convulsion, spamming, trolling, disruption, flaming, concerns with authenticity, disputes, gender and race and so forth (see also Marshall 2004, 2007c). However, in this epilogue I wish to focus on the second type of conflict, which is not a mere online phenomenon, but originates in an offline sociopolitical setting, of which the Internet has now become an integral part. Most prominent in public discourse is the use of the Internet by terrorist and extremist groups such as right-wing or, in particular after 9/11, Islamic extremists who use the Internet for psychological warfare, publicity and propaganda, data mining, fund-raising, recruitment and mobilization, networking, providing, gathering and sharing information, planning, and coordination (see, e.g., Conway 2006, 2008; Hoffman 2006; Ramsay 2008; Weimann 2004). Focusing more on the technical side of the Internet, a great deal has been published on hacktivism, such as Jordan and Taylor's edited volume *Hacktivism and Cyberwars: Rebels with a Cause?* (2004). Their unique contribution, as Kleinknecht (2005: 585) puts it, lies in 'illustrating how hacktivism developed within and out of the anti-globalization movement to take on a significant role in the current state of information-based activism'. Another strand of research focusing on the technical side of the Internet is that on 'cybercrime', which, according to Turrini and Ghosh (2010: 9), 'has been committed when the attacker has successfully wrestled away and extended some form of unauthorized control over the "computing process"'.

What I am most interested in is how conflicts that have been initiated offline (partly even before the rise of the World Wide Web) are extended into cyberspace, where they are continued with other means, where they are '(re)presented' and discussed, thus enormously extending their reach, and the kind of people who are involved and how they get involved. There are many ways in which actors in conflicts make use of the Internet and in which the Internet influences or shapes the way such conflicts are fought. They range from the deliberate dissemination of misinformation about a conflict to win over people's hearts and minds (and maybe their votes), exemplified by the 'social production of misinformation in the United States' preceding the Iraq war in 2003 (Arsenault and Castells 2006), to conflict actors themselves moving online, thus expanding the conflict directly into cyberspace. One prominent example is the Israeli-Palestinian conflict,[12] in which both the state and the military as well as nonstate actors or grassroots movements use the various online media to fight one another and to present their own narrative and version of current and past events, thus altering 'the nature of the Arab-Israeli conflict and the Israeli occupation of Palestinian lands' (Kuntsman and Stein 2010). Strategies range from hacking other actors' websites and disabling their computer networks to using blogs, Twitter, Facebook, YouTube and even Wikipedia (see also Armin

2009; Byers 2008). Another example is the Moluccan conflict. Although the transfer of contemporary warfare into cyberspace does get attention and is researched, as mentioned above there is to my knowledge no ethnographic research other than this book that follows a particular conflict for an extended period of time. The field is still dominated by political scientists and international relations scholars who focus on state security and so-called cybersecurity (see, e.g., Karatzogianni 2009; Latham 2003).

What has become known as the 'first war in cyberspace', in April–May 2007 (Landler and Markoff 2007), were the waves of so-called denial-of-service attacks[13] that 'brought down the Websites of the Estonian President, Parliament, a series of government agencies, the news media, [and] the two largest banks' (Hansen and Nissenbaum 2009: 1168). What triggered these cyberattacks was 'Estonian authorities' decision to remove a memorial commemorating the Soviet sacrifices during World War II from a park in the center of Tallinn to a military graveyard farther afield. This act was constituted by a significant proportion of the ethnic Russian minority as a threat to their cultural and political status and led to major demonstrations (ibid.: 1169). In response to the cyberattacks, the Estonian government blocked all international Web traffic, 'effectively shutting off the "most wired country in Europe" from the rest of the world' (Richards 2009). Although these cyberattacks in Estonia were unprecedented in their effectiveness and success, it is somewhat misleading to declare them to be 'the first war in cyberspace', since they had many predecessors and a long history, not only in Estonia but worldwide.[14] In the late 1990s Arquilla and Ronfeldt (1998: 1) realized that 'prevailing hopes for the peace-enhancing tendencies of interconnectivity must be tempered by a realization that the information revolution augurs a new epoch of conflict, in which new modes of armed combat and social upheaval emerge' (see also Gardner 2009: 21) – especially warning against the 'new vitality that is enfusing transnational terrorist and criminal organizations, as well as ethnonationalist and revolutionary groups' (Arquilla and Ronfeldt 1998: 2). Their focus was on conflicts between state and nonstate actors, as in the majority of this kind of security studies.

There have been numerous efforts to categorize conflicts on and around the Internet. To start with, in 1993 Arquilla and Ronfeldt distinguished between '"netwar" – societal-level ideational conflicts waged in part through internetted modes of communication – and "cyberwar" at the military level', both of them, in the end, being about knowledge, about 'who knows what, when, where, and why' and how to strategically use this knowledge (Arquilla and Ronfeldt 1993: 27).[15] Karatzogianni introduced another classification in her book *The Politics of Cyberconflict* (2006).[16] Aiming to analyse how the Internet has affected politics and political conflict, she identified a 'duality of cyberconflict' (ibid.: 198) and differentiated between sociopolitical cyberconflicts that 'seem to rely heavily on decentralized networks and indicate the use of rhizomatic structure' (ibid.:

196) and ethnoreligious cyberconflicts that 'primarily include hacking enemy sites and creating sites for propaganda and mobilization purposes' (ibid.: 197). According to Karatzogianni, the former use the Internet as an empowering resource, to recruit and mobilize support (financially and personally) and to influence public opinion, whereas the latter use it to enforce hierarchies and as a weapon. As I have argued in more detail in 'Religious Conflicts in Cyberage' (Bräuchler 2007b), the Moluccan case attests to the ambivalent nature of the Internet but also illustrates that online conflicts are not easy to categorize, as Karatzogianni suggests. More generally, this epilogue can be considered a call for more anthropological studies that help to deconstruct such simplistic categorizations and the often very state-centric conceptions of security and warfare in the interdisciplinary field of conflict and Internet studies.

A more recent volume edited by Karatzogianni, *Cyber Conflict and Global Politics* (2009), sheds light on the broad variety of so-called cyberconflicts. It includes essays that provide interesting insights into the strategic use of the Internet and its various modes of communication by various actors: by the military and soldiers to, for example, 'sustain a more network-based approach to warfare, utilizing psychological and information warfare and "winning the hearts and minds of the population"' (Karatzogianni 2009: 2); by Al-Qaeda and militant jihadism to recruit and train its followers and evade security services; by peace groups for mobilization purposes; by antigovernment dissidents to open up alternative public spheres; and in the Israeli-Palestinian, Indian-Pakistani and Sri Lankan (cyber)conflicts (in each case, both sides compete for control of the Web, through, for example, propaganda, hacking, defamation, etc.). Further chapters in that volume cover the above-mentioned 'first cyberwar' between Russian and Estonian computer hackers, cyberespionage and information warfare by the Chinese, the contradictory coverage of wars and conflicts by mainstream media and Internet tools such as blogs struggling over perceptions, issues of global security, Web activism and hacktivism, and propaganda. The book thus also bridges the gap between Internet-related studies on conflict and social movements/activism.

There is no real lack of literature on how social movements and political activists make use of the Internet (see, for e.g., Cammaerts and Audenhove 2003; Carty 2010; Castells 2007; Dartnell 2009; Deibert 2002; Hands 2010; Jordan and Taylor 2004; Marmura 2008; McCaughey and Ayers 2003; Meikle 2002; Postill 2008; Stein 2009; see also information available on John Postill's blog, http://johnpostill.wordpress.com/2010/05/11/materials-on-internet-esp-social-media-and-activism/, 11 May 2010). Prominent recent examples include studies on the Arab Spring mentioned above and WikiLeaks articles. In its founding mission of 2007, the latter's primary interest was outlined as 'exposing oppressive regimes in Asia, the former Soviet bloc, sub-Saharan Africa and the Middle East' and providing 'assistance to people of all regions who wish to reveal unethical behaviour in their governments and corporations' (*The Economist* 2010). The leftist Alistair Davidson (2010) describes it as 'a key part of the free culture movement's assault on the bastions of privatised information'. In 2010 and 2011, WikiLeaks made global headlines by publishing classified U.S. military documents and videos about the wars in Iraq and Afghanistan and the Guantanamo Bay detention centre online (http://en.wikipedia.org/wiki/ Wiki_leaks, 22 June 2011). As indicated above, there is much debate on the extent to which the Internet really supports, expands or even enables social revolutions. As the Moluccan conflict showed, the Internet (including digital activism) is a double-edged sword – and that has not changed to this day. Taking the case of the 2009 postpresidential election protests in Iran, Coleman (2010: 493) affirmatively underlines that 'social media tools can simultaneously support grass-roots political mobilizations as well as government surveillance and human rights violations'. Also seeking to dampen the enthusiasm with the omnipotent Internet, Dartnell (2009: 75) argues that 'web activists *do* have an impact, but do not overthrow states or necessarily even redirect public policies'. Moreover, although Internet access has grown considerably throughout the world in recent years, we still have to take 'the digital divide' into account (see also Meikle 2002: 175). However, after revolutions and wars have come to an end, who wants to be the one to definitively determine what role the Internet or the media in general played in the process? Again, long-term anthropological studies that do not only focus on the media but also on the broader sociocultural and political context they are embedded in could help to find answers to this most difficult of questions.

Religion conquers cyberspace

Finally, I would like to briefly address how research on Internet-related religious phenomena has developed, especially given the predominant focus on terrorism and radicalism online, which is often linked to a stereotypical image of a fundamentalist Islam allegedly spreading worldwide. On 22 June 2011 'religion' delivered 810,000,000 hits on google.com! It is obvious that the Internet is not used only by extremists, but also by a broad range of people transferring religious matters to cyberspace as well as seeking religious information and revelation online. This trend is reflected in the publication of a number of edited volumes (the majority by sociologists of religion) such as *Religion on the Internet: Research Prospects and Promises* (Hadden and Cowan 2000), *Religion and Media* (Vries and Weber 2001), *Religion Online: Finding Faith on the Internet* (Dawson and Cowan 2004) and *Religion and Cyberspace* (Hojsgaard and Warburg 2005). Together with a flood of more recent studies, they try to grapple with how established offline religions make use of the Internet, how they are transformed by it, and what kind of new religious forms and new religious movements evolve on the Internet. Heidi Campbell provides a very helpful overview and survey of research on religion and the Internet and how that has changed in kind and in focus since the 1990s in her publications (see in particular Campbell 2010a) and on her blog 'When Religion Meets New Media' (http://religionmeetsnewmedia. blogspot.com/).[17] According to Campbell (2010a), earlier works were often 'highly descriptive and focused on identifying and defining the latest religious practices online' (ibid.: 236) or 'overly utopian or dystopian in their views; the Internet was seen as either building religious solidarity or potentially destroying traditional religiosity' (ibid.: 234). A second wave of publications 'moved towards a "more realistic perspective" by seeking to more concretely define and compare different forms of online religious phenomena' (ibid.: 234). A key question has been how online and offline religious communities are connected (ibid.: 239). At present, according to Campbell, research is moving to 'more collaborative, longitudinal, and interdisciplinary explorations of religion online', where 'we can expect to see a sharper turn towards theoretical and interpretive scholarship' (ibid.: 235).[18]

Following this trend and the enormous rise of 'religion online' and 'online religion',[19] various other publication and research projects were set up. The University of Heidelberg, for example, in its interdisciplinary Collaborative Research Center (Sonderforschungsbereich, SFB 619) on 'Ritual Dynamics,' organized a subproject with a focus on 'Between Online Religion and Religion Online: Constellations for Ritual Transfer on the Internet' (http://www.ritualdynamik.de/ritualdynamik_en/organisation/projektbereichC/c_2.php?navanchor=1110049). In her new book *When Religion Meets New Media*, Campbell (2010b) illustrates with case studies from Christianity, Judaism and Islam how media use is negotiated through the filter of the social life of the group and how users adapt their use of new media to 'ancient laws' and religious traditions. Focusing on one particular religion, Gary Bunt continues to update us with new developments in the field of the Internet and Islam. In his latest book, *iMuslims: Rewiring the House of Islam,* Bunt (2009: 1) explores how transformations in Islamic societies 'play out in diverse cyberislamic environments and how they are responding to shifts in technology and society' – on the one hand continuing a tradition of online presentation of classical Islamic knowledge, and on the other hand going beyond that and exposing Muslims to radical and new influences. In a 2007 special issue of the *Journal of Computer-Mediated Communication* (volume 12, issue 3) on 'Cross-Cultural Perspectives on Religion and Computer-Mediated Communication', edited by Charles Ess, contributors investigate how religious traditions are 'adapting to and adopting CMC technologies to their own requirements and values' (Ess 2007). In another special issue on 'What Is a Medium? Theologies, Technologies and Aspirations', edited by Patrick Eisenlohr for *Social Anthropology* in February 2011 (volume 19, issue 1), contributors go one step further and reflect on 'the tendency of media to disappear in the act of mediation' as 'the very condition of their functioning', which would seemingly contradict predominant 'media constructionism and generativism' (Eisenlohr 2011: 44).[20] As these new developments illustrate, media have turned from an objectified tool into an inherent part of religious practices. These latest findings in research on religion and the Internet especially lend, again and more generally, expression to the fact that media practices[21] have become an integral part of daily life – be it conflict, activism or religion – to an extent that they can no longer (if they ever could) be regarded as separate from their sociocultural and sociopolitical context and vice versa.

As I have sought to indicate in this epilogue, a great deal has been achieved in cyberanthropology and related fields in recent years. Cyberanthropological studies can make essential and revolutionary contributions to this highly interdisciplinary field of Internet studies. At the same time, things are moving quickly, and technological change is fast-paced. We have to try to keep up. That said, we should not make our findings as short-lived as some Internet facilities are, but rather aim for broader research questions and also engage in more conceptual work that retains its relevance for a longer period. It is this course I attempted to follow with *Cyberidentities at War*.

Notes

1. However, the degree to which the media were responsible for the revolts is very much debated. See, for example, 'The Tunisia and Egypt Uprising' thread on the mailing list of the EASA Media Anthropology Network (4 February 2011; 7–10 February 2011; 13 February 2011). For a very critical stance on the Internet's revolutionary potential, see Evgeny Morozov (2011c), some of whose writings are available online at http://www.evgenymorozov.com/writings.html (27 June 2011). Acknowledging 'the democratic gains the internet has helped to achieve', Morozov warns against 'the real danger ... that authoritarian states in the Middle East and elsewhere will now develop more cunning strategies to tame the web' (2011b), turning the Internet into a 'tool of repression' (Morozov 2011a) rather than liberation. For a critical perspective see also Hindman (2009) and Murphy (2011).
2. For a more detailed description of the transformation of the Moluccan media scene from war to peace, see Bräuchler (2011b).
3. See, for example, the thread 'What Ever Happened to Cyberanthropology?' on the mailing list of the EASA Media Anthropology Network, 5–6 October 2010. For a review and preview of Internet studies by one of the first sociologists studying the Internet and how people communicate online, see Wellman (2010). The different phases and developments in research into CMC until 2005 are described by Hine (2005a).

4. For an overview of ethnographic approaches to digital media, see Coleman (2010).
5. For a continuation of the online-offline debate, see also the 'Cyborganic Paper – Ethnography and Theory' thread on the EASA Media Anthropology Network list, 26 June–3 July 2010.
6. Lehdonvirta (2010) also problematizes the dichotomous real-virtual model for research on 'massively-multiplayer online games and virtual environments (MOO)', because it contradicts the overlapping of our social worlds. For further critique, see John Postill's 'Review Notes on Boellstorff's (2008) Second Life Ethnography, July 20, 2009' (http://johnpostill.wordpress.com/2009/07/20/review-notes-on-boellstorffs-2008-second-life-ethnography/, 23 August 2010).
7. For more on e-science in connection with e-research and laboratory studies, see Beaulieu (2010) and Beaulieu and Wouters (2009).
8. For reviews of Marshall's book, see Kossoudji (2010) and Sondheim (2009).
9. For those interested in a more analytical exploration of their online field, there are now many more software tools available – both ready-to-hand such as Goggle's TouchGraph browser and more specialist approaches (Hine 2007) – for mapping and visualizing online worlds through the analysis of hyperlinks or for analysing online data by old and new Internet media (see, e.g., Hansen, Shneiderman and Smith, 2010). See also the thread 'Ethnographic Methods for Virtual Places' on the mailing list of the EASA Media Anthropology Network, 10–12 March 2010.
10. For other attempts to grasp online ethnographic research methodologically, from defining the field to obtaining access to the field, from data collection (textual, visual, sound) to participant observation, interviewing and field notes, and research ethics, see, for example, Beaulieu (2004) and Garcia et al. (2009). Another collection on qualitative Internet research was edited by Markham and Baym (2008). For reviews see Beaulieu (2009); Breindl (2009); Tateo (2009).
11. One needs to keep in mind that Kozinets's work is, at certain points, clearly led by marketing considerations, for example, when it comes to the effectiveness and the length of research (see, e.g., Kozinets 2010: 56). This makes one doubt whether participant observation as the central tool for ethnographic research was really grasped in its totality. In the entire study, Kozinets does not really elaborate on that main ethnographic method seemingly underlying netnography and ethnography (for a very superficial depiction see Kozinets [2010: 58–59]).
12. I would like to thank Tim Stevens for drawing my attention to this particular case and for providing me with some of the references.
13. As Richards (2009) explains, by way of various methods 'denial-of-service attacks block the access of legitimate users, rendering the entire site or network unavailable'.
14. Moreover, as Tim Stevens (personal communication, June 2011) remarked, the terminology used is misleading, as the Estonian example does not really qualify as war.
15. More broadly, Rawnsley (2009: 79) defines 'cyberwar' as 'computer-based information warfare'.
16. For a review of the book, see Robinson (2008).

17. Another helpful bibliography of the use of the Internet for religious purposes was compiled by Meritxell Ramírez-Ollé in Catalan (2010).
18. For possible future issues and research topics see Campbell (2010a: 243–45).
19. Christopher Helland (2000: 207) differentiates between *religion-online*, 'an organized attempt to utilize traditional forms of communication to present religion based upon a vertical conception of control, status and authority' (that is, established offline hierarchies), and *online-religion*, which 'offers participants a form of religious liminality outside of traditional religious structures' through online interaction and multidirectional communication, something that is avoided in the mostly unidirectional *religion-online* sites.
20. See especially Birgit Meyer's (2011: 37) essay in the special issue.
21. For more detailed accounts on *Theorising Media and Practice* see Bräuchler and Postill (2010).

Websites on the Moluccan Conflict

I cannot exclude the possibility that the websites or links to information pages on the Moluccan conflict given below are no longer accessible; but unless marked otherwise, the sites stated below were still accessible in April 2003. Sites that are already offline can possibly be found in the Internet archive at http://www.archive.org. In line with the subject of this study, I distinguish initially between websites on the Moluccan conflict that are clearly Christian and those that are clearly Muslim, and between those that exclusively/primarily focus on the Moluccan conflict and those that only dedicate part of the site or individual articles to it. The sites differ greatly in terms of the quality and quantity of the information provided on the Moluccan conflict. The list below contains key examples of the different perspectives on and presentations of the conflict (1999–2003) and does not claim to be exhaustive. One could no doubt find other sites, and many of the sites are linked to and refer to one another.

Muslim websites exclusively or primarily dedicated to the Moluccan conflict

AHMed Team
http://www.ahmed.or.id/
Ahlus Sunnah Wal Jama'ah Medical Team (Java, Ambon, Poso)

Al-Bunyan
http://www.al-bunyan.net
News on the jihad in East Indonesia (Muslim solidarity)

Bukti-bukti nyata tragedi berdarah di Ambon manise
http://members.tripod.com/sabiluna/ambon/ambon.html
'Concrete evidence of the bloody tragedy in sweet Ambon' (images)

Laskar Jihad
http://www.laskarjihad.or.id (no longer accessible)

Laskar Jihad Yahoo! Groups (mailing list)
http://groups.yahoo.com/group/laskarjihad (inactive, archive still accessible)

Listen to Ambon
http://scroll.to/ambon (no longer accessible) or http://listen.to/ambon (no longer accessible)

Maluku
http://connect.to/maluku/
Links to 'Save Moslem', Laskar Jihad and MER-C sites

MER-C
http://come.to/mer-c
Medical Emergency Rescue Committee: 'Ambon Berdarah' section (Bloody
    Ambon)

Rustam Kastor
http://listen.to/Rustam-Kastor
Books on the Moluccan conflict, including reviews

Save Moslem
http://www.geocities.com/nur_zayani/c index.html (no longer available in 2012)
'Come and save Moslem!!' and 'Jihad's calling Us!!': images, eyewitness accounts
    and narratives from Ambon

Suara Ambon Online
http://come.to/suaraambon
'Voice of Ambon online'

Tanah Jihad Indonesia
http://www.tanahjihad.net/Indonesia (no longer accessible)
'Jihad Region Indonesia: This site is dedicated to our brothers and sisters in
    Maluku provided exclusively by brothers of Muslims of Indonesia'

The Muslims Cleansing: Ambon & Poso Berdarah
http://www.webs88.com/~zulfank/Riot/index-ambon.html (no longer accessible)
'It's time to call for Jihad'

The Official Website of Maluku Tragedy
http://www.malu.ku.org/ (no longer accessible)

Muslim websites that are dedicated, among other things, to the Moluccan conflict

Al-Irsyad Al-Islamiyyah
http://www.alirsyad-alislamy.or.id/index.htm
Islamic organization in Jakarta
→ Series of articles on the bloody tragedy in Ambon (accessed 25 May 2002)

Al-Madeena
http://www.al-madeena.com/
'The Journal of Islamic Knowledge and Fraternal Unity'
→ Ambon Tragedy (http://www.al-madeena.com/ambon.html)
→ Muslim Life in Maluku (http://www.al-madeena.com/MuslimWorld/indo/
    maluku.html)
→ Ambon Pictures (http://www.al-madeena.com/victims.html)

Al-Sofwah
http://www.alsofwah.or.id/html/berita.html
Yayasan Islam (Islamic foundation) Ahlus Sunnah Wal Jama'ah

Ayoh Jihad
http://qital.tripod.com/ (no longer accessible)
Links to jihad websites worldwide and in several languages, including Kashmir, Bosnia, the Philippines, the Moluccas

Gema Khadijah
http://www.gemakhadijah.cjb.net/
Muslim women's organization in Indonesia
→ Ambon Tragedy – Genocide of Muslim Ummah (http://www.geocities.com/gemakhadijah/ambon.htm)

Islamic World
http://www.islamic-world.net/
'Jihad site for Muslims who love Allah and Jihad': links to jihad websites worldwide (Afghanistan, Ambon and Aceh, Bosnia, Palestine, Kashmir, Chechnya, etc.)

Komite Indonesia untuk Solidaritas Dunia Islam (KISDI)
http://www.kisdi.com/
'Indonesian Committee for Solidarity with the Islamic World'
→ Ambon section (http://www.kisdi.com/ambon/, no longer accessible)

Media Isnet
http://media.isnet.org/
→ Tragedi Ambon (http://media.isnet.org/ambon/)

Pusat Konsultasi Syariah
http://www.syariahonline.com/index.htm
'Consultation Centre Sharia': Sharia online page

Ummah.com
http://www.ummah.net
'The Muslim Directory Online'
→ Supporters of Sharia – Jihad in Indonesia (http://www.ummah.net/sos/Indonesia.htm, no longer accessible)

Christian websites exclusively or primarily dedicated to the Moluccan conflict (maintained by Moluccans inside and outside Indonesia)

Ambon Berdarah Online
http://www.geocities.com/ambon67
'Bloody Ambon Online': changing addresses (depending on where in the Moluccas Christians were being threatened ambon67 was replaced by maluku67, arumbaikole, nualu67, baguala67, waai67, kariu67, unpatti67, soija2002, kesui2001, batu-capeu, nusaniwe, amahoesoe)
Mirror page: http://go.to/alifuru67
→ http://www.fortunecity.com/tatooine/leiber/275/amahoesoe/index.htm
Website footer: 'Thank You for Your Visit To Read The Truth About Ambon/Maluku Tragedy'
Webmaster: a Moluccan in Australia

Lawamena Victoria
http://www.geocities.com/lawamena_victoria/ or http://www.geocities.com/
    jembong_710/
Webmaster: a Moluccan in Australia

Masariku
http://groups.yahoo.com/group/masariku
Yahoo! Groups mailing list/website
Founded by Moluccans in Jakarta and Ambon

Tragedi Soya
http://www.geocities.com/pertjok/tragedi_soya.html
Images of the attack on the Christian village of Soya
Webmaster: Moluccans in the Netherlands (homepage: http://www.geocities
    .com/alvinJea/home)

Christian websites that are dedicated, among other things, to the Moluccan conflict

Fellowship of Indonesian Christians in America (FICA)
http://www.fica.org/
Church and human rights persecution in Indonesia
→ Ambon (http://www.fica.org/hr/Ambon.html)

International Christian Concern (ICC)
http://www.persecution.org/
→ Country Report Indonesia (http://www.persecution.org/Countries/indonesia.
    html)

Indonesian Christian Webwatch (ICW)
http://www.sabda.org/icw/archives/00-064.htm_
→ Reference to Maluku-Net (mailing list)

International Friends of Compassion
http://cryindonesia.rnc.org.au/
International Christian organization, founded in Indonesia

Jubilee Campaign
http://www.jubileecampaign.demon.co.uk
International Christian organization

Passie vor Vrede
http://www.passievoorvrede.nl
Christian organization in the Netherlands

Pax Christi
http://www.paxchristi.nl
Christian organization in the Netherlands
→ Indonesia links: websites and online media relating to Indonesia and the
    Moluccas

Websites by Moluccans in the Netherlands (unless already mentioned), exclusively or primarily dedicated to the Moluccan conflict

HAIN (Help Ambon in Nood)
http://www.maluku.org/hain/ (discontinued on 9 October 2002)
Moluccan foundation in the Netherlands

Infodoc Maluku
http://www.midc.nl or http://www.infomaluku.net
Information and Documentation Centre for the Moluccans in Utrecht, Netherlands (as of January 2003 no longer updated, as the Dutch government terminated financial support for the project)

Maluku News Portal
http://www.malra.org/posko/
PosKo Zwolle-Maluku: information and documentation centre in Zwolle, Netherlands, that cooperates with several (Moluccan) organizations

Maluku WEB portal
http://www.maluku.org

Maluku2000
http://www.maluku2000.org/
Moluccan foundation in the Netherlands

Websites by Moluccans worldwide (unless already mentioned) dedicated, among other things, to the Moluccan conflict

AmbonNet
http://groups.yahoo.com/group/ambon
Yahoo! Groups mailing list/website

Djangan Lupa Maluku
http://www.maluku.net/dlmforum/dlmforum.cgi
'Don't forget the Moluccas!': discussion forum by and above all for Moluccans living in the Netherlands

FKM Amerika
http://www.nunusaku.net

FKM Europa
http://www.fkm-europa.nl

Lima Service-Site
http://home.wanadoo.nl/lima5/
FKM and Maluku news service

LopaLopa – Voice from Maluku
http://www.geocities.com/chosye/
NGO in Ambon

Maluku Media Centre
http://www.malukumediacentre.net/web/index.php
Christian-Muslim media centre in Ambon: Journalists for Peace in the Moluccas
(AJI initiative)

Maluku Outreach Foundation
http://www.geocities.com/moutreach/index_files/frame.htm
Moluccan NGO in the United States

Moluccas Interactive
http://groups.yahoo.com/group/moluccas
Yahoo! Groups mailing list/website (no public access)

Sirisori Amalatu
http://www.sirisori.demon.nl/news.html
Webmaster: Dutch Moluccan from the village of Sirisori Amalatu, Saparua

Other websites

Ambon Information Website
http://www.websitesrcg.com/ambon
Background information on the Moluccan conflict and data on the Moluccas in
general
Webmaster: a Canadian married to a woman from Ambon

Discrimination Against Minority in Indonesia
http://www.geocities.com/~budis1/index2.html
→ Religious riots in Maluku province (Ambon, Haruku and Saparua Island)

Hotburrito
http://www.angelfire.com/rock/hotburrito
'Help Ambon!'
Webmaster: Dutch and MML member

Human Rights Watch (HRW)
http://www.hrw.org/asia/indonesia.php
→ Reports on the situation in Indonesia and the Moluccas

International Crisis Group (ICG)
http://www.intl-crisis-group.org
→ Reports on the situation in Indonesia and the Moluccas

Maluku-Net (mailing list)
http://www.cenderawasih.net

Program on Humanitarian Policy and Conflict Research
http://www.preventconflict.org
President and fellows of Harvard College
→ Map of the conflict in the Moluccas (http://www.preventconflict.org/portal/
main/maps_maluku_resources.php)

Bibliography

The date given behind an Internet address refers to the date I accessed it and need not correspond to the date when the document in question was made.

Adam, Jeroen. 2009. *Communal Violence, Forced Migration and Social Change on the Island of Ambon, Indonesia.* Unpublished Ph.D. diss., Ghent University.

Adams, Paul C., and Barney Warf. 1997. 'Introduction: Cyberspace and Geographical Space'. *The Geographical Review* 87, no. 2 (April): 139–45.

Aditjondro, George Junus. 2000a. 'Die Molukken sind das Schlachtfeld der Eliten'. *Jungle World* 29. http://www.munindo.brd.de/george/george_moluken_schlachfeld.html (6 March 2001).

———. 2000b. 'Maluku: While Elephants Fight, the People of Maluku Die'. *Asia Pacific Network,* 27 January. http://www.asiapac.org.fj/cafepacific/resources/aspac/maluku.html (13 December 2000).

———. 2000c. 'Notes on the Jihad Forces in Maluku'. July. http://www.malra.org/posko/malra.php3?oid=234885 (3 October 2000).

———. 2000d. 'Playing Political Football with Moluccan Lives'. 15 July. http://www.indopubs.com/archives/0126.html (9 October 2000).

———. 2000e. 'The Tragedy of Maluku'. Lecture and seminar at the Institute of Aboriginal Studies and Research at Macquarie University, Sydney, 2 May. http://www.infomaluku.net/res/views/000503GA.htm (13 December 2000).

———. 2001a. 'Guns, Pamphlets and Handie-Talkies: How the Military Exploited Local Ethno-religious Tensions in Maluku to Preserve Their Political and Economic Privileges'. In *Violence in Indonesia,* ed. Ingrid Wessel and Georgia Wimhofer, pp. 100–128. Hamburg: Abera-Verlag.

———. 2001b. 'Orang-Orang Jakarta Di Balik Tragedi Maluku' [People in Jakarta are behind the tragedy in the Moluccas]. 8 June. http://groups.yahoo.com/group/ambon/ (15 June 2001).

Ahmad, Kasman Hi., and Herman Oesman, eds. 2000. *Damai yang Terkoyak: Catatan Kelam dari Bumi Halmahera* [Peace destroyed: Somber notes from Halmahera]. Ternate, Moluccas: Madani Press.

Ajawaila, Jacob W. 2000. 'Orang Ambon dan Perubahan Kebudayaan' [Ambonese and cultural change]. *Antropologi Indonesia* XXIV, no. 61:16–25.

Alhadar, Smith. 2000. 'The Forgotten War in North Maluku'. *Inside Indonesia* 63 (July–September). http://www.insideindonesia.org/edit63/alhadar.htm (9 October 2000).

Al-Jakartaty, Erwin H. 2000. *Tragedi Bumi Seribu Pulau: Mengkritisi Kebijakan Pemerintah dan Solusi Penyelesaian Konflik* [Tragedy in the country of one thousand islands: Critique of the government concept and the solution to end the conflict]. Jakarta: Gubuk Kajian Mutiara Nasional.

Allen, Tim. 1999. 'Perceiving Contemporary Wars'. In *The Media of Conflict: War Reporting and Representations of Ethnic Violence*, ed. Tim Allen and Jean Seaton, pp. 11–42. London: Zed Books.

Allen, Tim, and Jean Seaton. 1999a. 'Introduction'. In *The Media of Conflict: War Reporting and Representations of Ethnic Violence*, ed. Tim Allen and Jean Seaton, pp. 1–7. London: Zed Books.

——, eds. 1999b. *The Media of Conflict: War Reporting and Representations of Ethnic Violence*. London: Zed Books.

Alqadrie, Syarif Ibrahim. 1999. 'Konflik Etnis di Ambon dan Sambas: Suatu Tinjauan Sosiologis' [Ethnic conflict in Ambon and Sambas: A sociological view]. *Antropologi Indonesia* XXlll, 58:36–57.

Anderson, Benedict. 1992. 'Long-Distance Nationalism. World Capitalism and the Rise of Identity Politics'. *The Wertheim Lecture 1992*. Amsterdam: CASA – Centre for Asian Studies.

——. 1998. *Die Erfindung der Nation: Zur Karriere eines folgenreichen Konzepts*. [Imagined communities: Reflections on the origin and spread of nationalism]. Extended ed. Berlin: Ullstein.

Anderson, Benedict, Takashi Shiraishi and James T. Siegel. 1999. 'Current Data on the Indonesian Military Elite: January 1, 1998 – January 31'. *Indonesia* 67 (April): 134–62.

Anderson, Jon W. 1996. 'Middle East Diasporas on the Internet'. The Internet Global Summit (INET) Conference, Transforming our Society Now, Montreal, Canada, 24–28 June 1996. http://www.isoc.org/isoc/whatis/conferences/inet/96/proceedings/e8/e8_2.htm (29 June 2002).

——. 1997. 'Globalizing Politics and Religion in the Muslim World'. *Journal of Electronic Publishing* 3, no. 1 (September). http://www.press.umich.edu/jep/archive/Anderson.html (29 June 2002).

——. 1999. 'The Internet and Islam's New Interpreters'. In *New Media in the Muslim World. The Emerging Public Sphere*, ed. Dale F. Eickelman and Jon W. Anderson, pp. 41–56. Bloomington: Indiana University Press.

Anti-Defamation League. 2002. 'Jihad Online: Islamic Terrorists and the Internet'. http://www.adl.org/internet/jihad_online.pdf (20 October 2002).

Appadurai, Arjun. 1991. 'Global Ethnoscapes: Notes and Queries for a Transnational Anthropology'. In *Recapturing Anthropology: Working in the Present*, ed. Richard G. Fox, pp. 191–210. Santa Fe, NM: School of American Research Press.

——. 1996. *Modernity at Large: Cultural Dimensions of Globalization*. Minneapolis: University of Minnesota Press.

——. 1998. 'Globale ethnische Räume'. In *Perspektiven der Weltgesellschaft*, ed. Ulrich Beck, pp. 11–40. Frankfurt: Suhrkamp.

Appleby, R. Scott. 2000. *The Ambivalence of the Sacred: Religion, Violence, and Reconciliation*. New York: Rowman & Littlefield.

Argyle, Katie. 1996. 'Life after Death'. In *Cultures of Internet: Virtual Spaces, Real Histories, Living Bodies*, ed. Rob Shields, pp. 133–42. London: SAGE Publications.

Armaiyn, Thaib. 2006. 'A Governor's Perspective on North Maluku Conflict'. *The Jakarta Post,* 13 March: 6.

Armin, Jart. 2009. 'Battle for Gaza Fought on the Web, Too'. *internet evolution.* http://www.internetevolution.com/author.asp?section_id=717&doc_id=169872 (4 January 2011).

Arquilla, John, and David Ronfeldt. 1993. 'Cyberwar is Coming!' *Journal Comparative Strategy* 12, no. 2:141–65. http://gopher.well.sf.ca.us:70/0/Military/cyberwar (11 September 2001).

———. 1998. 'Preparing for Information-Age Conflict: Part 1 (Conceptual and Organizational Dimensions)'. *Information, Communication & Society* 1, no. 1:1–22.

Arsenault, Amelia, and Manuel Castells. 2006. 'Conquering the Minds, Conquering Iraq: The Social Production of Misinformation in the United States – A Case Study'. *Information, Communication & Society* 9, no. 3:284–307.

Aspinall, Edward, Gerry van Klinken and Herb Feith, eds. 1999. *The Last Days of President Suharto.* Australia: Monash Asia Institute.

Assmann, Jan. 1999. *Das kulturelle Gedächtnis: Schrift, Erinnerung und politische Identität in frühen Hochkulturen.* 2nd. ed. Munich: Beck.

Ata, Abe Wade. 1988. 'Introduction'. In *Religion and Ethnic Identity: An Australian Study,* ed. Abe Wade Ata, pp. 1–8. Richmond, Australia: Spectrum Publications.

Atkinson, Philippa. 1999. 'Deconstructing Media Mythologies of Ethnic War in Liberia'. In *The Media of Conflict: War Reporting and Representations of Ethnic Violence,* ed. Tim Allen and Jean Seaton, pp. 192–218. London: Zed Books.

Awwas, Irfan Suryahardi. 2000. *Bencana Kaum Muslim di Indonesia 1980–2000* [The Misfortune of the Muslims in Indonesia from 1980–2000]. Yogyakarta, Indonesia: Wihdah Press.

———. 2001. *Risalah Kongres Mujahidin I dan Penegakan Syari'ah Islam* [Minutes of the first mujahideen congress and strengthening the Sharia]. Yogyakarta, Indonesia: Wihdah Press.

Azca, Muhammad Najib. 2004. 'From Military to Militia: National and Local Contexts of the Security Forces Partisanship in the Communal Conflict in Ambon, Indonesia'. Paper presented to the Fourth EUROSEAS Conference, Paris, 1–4 September.

Badan Pusat Statistik Propinsi Maluku. 2000. *Penduduk Propinsi Maluku dan Maluku Utara 2000* [Population statistics of the provinces of the Moluccas and North Moluccas 2000]. Ambon: Central Committee for Statistics on the Moluccan Province.

Bahl, Anke. 1997. *Zwischen On- und Offline. Identität und Selbstdarstellung im Internet.* Munich: KoPäd Verlag.

Bakardjieva, Maria, and Andrew Feenberg. 2002. 'Community Technology and Democratic Rationalization'. *Information Society* 18, no. 3 (May–June): 181–92.

Barlow, John Perry. 1996. 'The Declaration of the Independence of Cyberspace'. http://www.eff.org/~barlow/Declaration-Final.html (11 September 2001) or http://www.eff.org/Publications/John_Perry_Barlow/barlow_0296.declaration (27 September 2001).

Barry, John A. 1991. *Technobabble.* Cambridge, MA: MIT Press.

Bartels, Dieter. 1977. *Guarding the Invisible Mountain: Intervillage Alliances, Religious Syncretism and Ethnic Identity among Ambonese Christians and Moslems in the Moluccas.* Ithaca, NY: Cornell University.

———. 1990. *Ambon is op Schiphol.* Leiden, the Netherlands: Centrum voor Onderzoek van Maatschappelijke Tegenstellingen/Faculteit der Sociale Wetenschappen Rijksuniversiteit Leiden.

———. 1994. *In de Schaduw van de Berg Nunusaku: Een Cultuur-historische Verhandeling over de Bevolking van de Midden-Molukken.* Utrecht, the Netherlands: Landelijk Steunpunt Educatie Molukkers (LSEM).

———. 2000. 'Your God Is No Longer Mine: Moslem-Christian Fratricide in the Central Moluccas (Indonesia) after a Half-Millennium of Tolerant Co-Existence and Ethnic Unity'. http://www.indopubs.com/archives/0401.html (9 October 2000).

Barth, Fredrik. 1969. 'Introduction'. In *Ethnic Groups and Boundaries. The Social Organization of Culture Difference,* ed. Fredrik Barth, pp. 9–38. Bergen, Norway: Universitetsforlaget.

Barth, Thomas. 1997. 'Cyberspace, Neoliberalismus und inverser Panoptismus'. 3 July. http://swiki.hfbk.uni-hamburg.de:8080/technoterroristen/3 (11 September 2001).

Basuki, Tedjabayu. 1998. 'Indonesia: The Web as a Weapon'. *Development Dialogue* 2:96–103.

Baudrillard, Jean. 2001. 'The Precession of Simulacra'. In *Media and Cultural Studies: KeyWorks,* ed. Meenakshi Gigi Durham and Douglas M. Kellner, pp. 521–49. Oxford: Blackwell Publishers.

Baumann, Gerd. 1999. *The Multicultural Riddle: Rethinking National, Ethnic and Religious Identities.* New York: Routledge.

Baym, Nancy K. 1995. 'The Performance of Humor in Computer-Mediated Communication'. *Journal of Computer-Mediated Communication* 1, no. 2. http://www.ascusc.org/jcmc/vol1/issue2/baym.html (19 June 2002).

———. 1998. 'The Emergence of On-Line Community'. In *Cybersociety 2.0: Revisiting Computer-Mediated Communication and Community,* ed. Steven G. Jones, pp. 35–68. London: SAGE Publications.

BBC World News. 1999a. 'US Cyber Terrorism Plea'. *BBC News Online: Americas.* 22 January. http://news2.thdo.bbc.co.uk/hi/english/world/americas/newsid_260000/260855.stm (27 November 2001).

———. 1999b. 'Virtual Country "Nuked" on Net'. *BBC News Online: Science/Technology.* 26 January. http://news2.thdo.bbc.co.uk/hi/english/sci/tech/newsid_263000/263169.stm (27 November 2001).

———. 2000. 'Who Are the Lashkar Jihad?' *BBC News Online: Asia-Pacific.* 20 June. http://news6.thdo.bbc.co.uk/hi/english/world/asia-pacific/newsid_770000/770263.htm (18 February 2001).

Beaulieu, Anne. 2004. 'Mediating Ethnography: Objectivity and the Making of Ethnographies of the Internet'. *Social Epistemology* 18, nos. 2–3 (April–September): 139–63.

———. 2009. 'Review 1: Annette N. Markham & Nancy K. Baym, "Internet Inquiry: Conversations about Methods". Thousand Oaks, CA: SAGE. 2008'. *Resource Center for Cyberculture Studies – Book Reviews.* http://rccs.usfca.edu/bookinfo.asp?BookID=425&ReviewID=601 (5 October 2010).

———. 2010. 'From Co-location to Co-presence: Shifts in the Use of Ethnography for the Study of Knowledge'. *Social Studies of Science* 20, no. 10:1–18.

Beaulieu, Anne, and Paul Wouters. 2009. 'e-Research as Intervention'. In *E-Research Transformations in Scholarly Practice,* ed. N. Jankowski, pp. 54–69. New York: Routledge.

Becker, Dieter. 1996. *Die Kirchen und der Pancasila-Staat. Indonesische Christen zwischen Konsens und Konflikt.* Erlangen, Germany: Verlag der Ev.-Luth. Mission Erlangen.

Beer, John M. 2000. 'Perception Management and "Media Operations"'. In *Cyberwar 3.0: Human Factors in Information Operations and Future Conflict,* ed. Alan D. Campen and Douglas H. Dearth, pp. 185–90. Fairfax, VA: AFCEA International Press.

Behrend, Heike. 1993. *Alice und die Geister: Krieg im Norden Ugandas.* Munich: Trickster Verlag.

Bell, David. 2001. *An Introduction to Cybercultures.* London: Routledge.

Benda-Beckmann, Franz von. 1990. 'Ambonese Adat as Jurisprudence of Insurgency and Oppression'. *Law & Anthropology. Internationales Jahrbuch für Rechtsanthropologie* 5: 25–42.

———. 1999. 'Multiple Legal Constructions of Socio-economic Spaces: Resource Management and Conflict in the Central Moluccas'. In *Frontiers and Borderlands. Anthropological Perspectives,* ed. Michael Rösler and Tobias Wendl, pp. 131–58. Frankfurt: Peter Lang Verlag.

Benda-Beckmann, Franz von, and Keebet von Benda-Beckmann. 1993. 'Eine turbulente Geschichte im Verhältnis zwischen Religion und Volksrecht: die Molukker in Indonesien und den Niederlanden'. In *Sprache, Symbole und Symbolverwendungen in Ethnologie, Kulturanthropologie, Religion und Recht,* ed. Werner Krawietz, Leopold Pospisil and Sabine Steinbrich, pp. 141–58. Berlin: Duncker & Humblot.

Benda-Beckmann, Keebet von. 2004. 'Law, Violence and Peace Making on the Island of Ambon'. In *Healing the Wounds: Essays on the Reconstruction of Societies after War,* ed. M.-C. Foblets and T. v. Trotha, pp. 221–39. Oxford: HART Publishing.

Beniger, James R. 1987. 'Personalization of Mass Media and the Growth of Pseudo-Community'. *Communication Research* 14, no. 3 (June): 352–71.

Benthall, Jonathan. 1995. *Disaster, Relief and the Media.* London: LB Tauris.

Bertrand, Jacques. 2004. *Nationalism and Ethnic Conflict in Indonesia.* Cambridge: Cambridge University Press.

Bielefeldt, Heiner, and Wilhelm Heitmeyer. 1998. 'Einleitung: Politisierte Religion in der Moderne'. In *Politisierte Religion,* ed. Heiner Bielefeldt and Wilhelm Heitmeyer, pp. 11–33. Frankfurt: Suhrkamp.

Böhm, Kees J. 2001. 'Lintas Peristiwa Kerusuhan Di Maluku [Chronology of the Moluccan conflict]: Period 15 January 1999 – 13 April 2001'. CCDA newsletter online, 14 April 2001. Ambon. Crisis Centre Diocese of Amboina.

———. 2002a. 'Brief Chronicle of the Unrest in the Moluccas 1999–2002'. Ambon. Crisis Centre Diocese of Amboina.

———. 2002b. 'Exposé on Various Aspects of the Conflict in the Moluccas'. Ambon. Crisis Centre Diocese of Amboina. Unpublished manuscript.

Boellstorff, Tom. 2008. *Coming of Age in Second Life: An Anthropologist Explores the Virtually Human.* Princeton, NJ: Princeton University Press.

Boland, B. J. 1971. *The Struggle of Islam in Modern Indonesia.* Verhandelingen van het Koninklijk Instituut voor Taal-, Land- en Volkenkunde 59. The Hague: Martinus Nijhoff.

Bölsche, Jochen. 2001. 'Propaganda: Der Dschihad im Internet'. *Der Spiegel,* 24 September. http://www.spiegel.de/spiegel/0,1518,158901,00.html (1 October 2001).

Bosscher, Doeko, and Berteke Waaldijk. 1985. 'Ambon – Eer & Schuld. Politiek en Pressie rond de Republiek Zuid-Molukken'. Weesp, the Netherlands: Van Holkema & Warendorf.

Botes, Jannie. 1998. 'Dialogue of the Deaf'. *Track Two* 7, no. 4 (December). http://ccrweb.ccr.uct.ac.za/two/7_4/p04_dialogue_of_deaf.html (15 January 2002).

Bräuchler, Birgit. 2003. 'Cyberidentities at War: Religion, Identity, and the Internet in the Moluccan Conflict'. *Indonesia* 75 (April): 123–51.

——. 2004a. 'Islamic Radicalism Online: The Moluccan Mission of the Laskar Jihad in Cyberspace'. *The Australian Journal of Anthropology* 15, no. 3:267–85.

——. 2004b. 'Moluccan Cyberactors'. *Antropologi Indonesia* XXVIII, no. 73: 40–57.

——. 2004c. 'Public Sphere and Identity Politics in the Moluccan Cyberspace'. 'Electronic Networks and Politics', ed. Nicholas W. Jankowski, special issue, *Electronic Journal of Communication* 14, no. 3–4.

——. 2006a. 'Constructed Identities Online: The Performance of the Moluccan Crisis on the Internet'. In *New Hybridities: Societies and Cultures in Transition,* ed. F. Heidemann and A. D. Toro, pp. 161–77. Hildesheim, Germany: Olms.

——. 2006b. 'Konfliktfaktor Internet: Der Molukkenkonflikt geht online'. In *Strand Bar Internet: Neue Orte der Globalisierung,* ed. J. Reuter, C. Neudorfer and C. Antweiler, pp. 84–91. Berlin: LIT.

——. 2006c. 'La mondialisation des conflits locaux: Usages stratégiques d'Internet dans le conflit des Moluques'. 'Les nouvelles figures de la guerre', special issue, *Revue des Sciences Sociales* 35:84–91.

——. 2007a. 'Ein Comeback der Tradition? Die Revitalisierung von Adat in Ostindonesien' [A comeback of tradition? The revitalisation of adat in Eastern Indonesia]. 'Die Revitalisierung von Tradition' [The revitalisation of tradition], ed. Birgit Bräuchler and Thomas Widlok, special issue, *Zeitschrift für Ethnologie* 132:37–57.

——. 2007b. 'Religious Conflicts in Cyberage'. *Citizenship Studies* 11, no. 4 (September): 329–47.

——. 2009a. 'Cultural Solutions to Religious Conflicts? The Revival of Tradition in the Moluccas, Eastern Indonesia'. *Asian Journal of Social Sciences* 37, no. 6:872–91.

——. 2009b. 'Der Molukkenkonflikt im Internet: Globale Dimension eines lokalen Konflikts'. In *Konflikte – Mächte – Identitäten: Beiträge zur Sozialanthtropologie Südostasiens,* ed. M. Slama, pp. 87–116. Vienna: ÖAW-Verlag.

——. 2009c. 'Mobilising Culture and Tradition for Peace: Reconciliation in the Moluccas'. In *Reconciling Indonesia: Grassroots Agency for Peace,* ed. B. Bräuchler, pp. 97–118. London: Routledge.

——. 2010a. 'Religions Online: Christian and Muslim (Re)presentations in the Moluccan Conflict'. In *Christianity in Indonesia,* ed. S. Schröter, pp. 203–24. Berlin: LIT.

———. 2010b. 'The Revival Dilemma: Reflections on Human Rights, Self-Determination and Legal Pluralism in Eastern Indonesia'. *Journal of Legal Pluralism and Unofficial Law* 62:1–42.

———. 2011a. 'Kings on Stage: Local Leadership in the Post-Suharto Moluccas'. *Asian Journal of Social Sciences* 39, no. 2:196–218.

———. 2011b. 'The Transformation of the Media Scene: From War to Peace in the Moluccas, Eastern Indonesia'. In *Politics and the Media in 21st Century Indonesia*, ed. K. Sen and D. T. Hill, pp. 119–40. London: Routledge.

Bräuchler, Birgit, and John Postill, eds. 2010. *Theorising Media and Practice.* New York: Berghahn Books.

Bredekamp, Horst. 2001. 'Leviathan und Internet'. In *Schnittstelle: Medien und Kulturwissenschaft*, ed. Georg Stanitzek and Wilhelm Vosskamp, pp. 223–31. Cologne: DuMont.

Breindl, Yana. 2009. 'Review 2: Annette N. Markham & Nancy K. Baym, "Internet Inquiry: Conversations about Methods". Thousand Oaks, CA: SAGE. 2008'. *Resource Center for Cyberculture Studies – Book Reviews.* http://rccs.usfca.edu/bookinfo.asp?BookID=425&ReviewID=602 (5 October 2010).

Bresler, Andreas. 2001. 'Nordamerikanische Indianer im Internet unter besonderer Berücksichtigung von virtuellen Gemeinschaften und der Bildung von Netzwerken'. Unpublished M.A. thesis, Philosophische Georg-August-Universität Göttingen.

Breslow, Harris. 1997. 'Civil Society, Political Economy, and the Internet'. In *Virtual Culture. Identity and Communication in Cybersociety*, ed. Steven G. Jones, pp. 236–57. London: SAGE Publications.

Bruinessen, Martin van. 1994. 'Yahudi Sebagai Simbol dalam Wacana Pemikiran Islam Indonesia Masa Kini' [The Jews as a symbol in Islamic discourse in Indonesia today]. *Spiritualitas Baru: Agama dan Aspirasi Rakyat* Seri Dian II Tahun I: 253–68.

———. 1996. 'Islamic State or State Islam? Fifty Years of State-Islam Relations in Indonesia'. In *Indonesien am Ende des 20. Jahrhunderts. Analysen zu 50 Jahren unabhängiger Entwicklung*, ed. Ingrid Wessel, pp. 19–34. Hamburg: Abera Verlag.

Bubandt, Nils. 2001. 'Malukan Apocalypse: Themes in the Dynamics of Violence in Eastern Indonesia'. In *Violence in Indonesia*, ed. Ingrid Wessel and Georgia Wimhöfer, pp. 228–53. Hamburg: Abera-Verlag.

Budka, Philipp, and Manfred Kremser. 2004. 'CyberAnthropology – Anthropology of CyberCulture'. In *Contemporary Issues in Socio-cultural Anthropology: Perspectives and Research Activities from Austria*, ed. S. Khittel, B. Plankensteiner and M. Six-Hohenbalken, pp. 213–226. Vienna: Löcker.

Bunt, Gary R. 2000. *Virtually Islamic: Computer-mediated Communication and Cyber Islamic Environments.* Cardiff, UK: University of Wales Press.

———. 2009. *iMuslims: Rewiring the House of Islam.* London: Hurst & Company.

Burrell, Jenna. 2009. 'The Field Site as a Network: A Strategy for Locating Ethnographic Research'. *Field Methods* 21, no. 2 (May): 181–99.

Butler, David. 1995. *The Trouble with Reporting Northern Ireland: The British State, the Broadcast Media and Nonfictional Representation of the Conflict.* Aldershot, UK: Avebury.

Byers, David. 2008. 'Gaza: Secondary War Being Fought on the Internet'. *Times Online*, 31 December, http://technology.timesonline.co.uk/tol/news/tech_and_web/article5424671.ece (4 January 2011).

Calhoun, Craig. 1995. *Critical Social Theory: Culture, History, and the Challenge of Difference*. Oxford: Blackwell Publishers.

Cammaerts, Bart, and Leo van Audenhove. 2003. 'ICT-Usage among Transnational Social Movements in the Networked Society: To Organise, to Mediate and to Influence'. http://www.lse.ac.uk/collections/EMTEL/reports/cammaerts_2003_emtel.pdf (17 December 2003).

Campbell, Heidi. 2010a. 'Internet and Religion'. In *The Handbook of Internet Studies*, ed. R. Burnett, M. Consalvo and C. Ess, pp. 232–50. Malden, MA: Wiley-Blackwell.

———. 2010b. *When Religion Meets New Media*. London: Routledge.

Campen, Alan D., and Douglas H. Dearth, eds. 2000. *Cyberwar 3.0: Human Factors in Information Operations and Future Conflict*. Fairfax, VA: AFCEA International Press.

Carruthers, Susan L. 2000. *The Media at War: Communication and Conflict in the Twentieth Century*. New York: St. Martin's Press.

Carty, Victoria. 2010. *Wired and Mobilizing: Social Movements, New Technology, and Electoral Politics*. London: Routledge.

Castells, Manuel. 2000. *End of Millennium: The Information Age: Economy, Society and Culture III*. 2nd ed. Oxford: Blackwell Publishers.

———. 2001a. *The Internet Galaxy: Reflections on the Internet, Business, and Society*. New York: Oxford University Press.

———. 2001b. *The Power of Identity: The Information Age: Economy, Society and Culture II*. New ed. Oxford: Blackwell Publishers.

———. 2001c. *The Rise of the Network Society: The Information Age: Economy, Society and Culture I*. 2nd ed. Oxford: Blackwell Publishers.

———. 2007. 'Communication, Power and Counter-power in the Network Society'. *International Journal of Communication* 1:238–66.

Chandler, Daniel. 1998. 'Personal Home Pages and the Construction of Identities on the Web'. http://www.aber.ac.uk/media/Documents/short/webident.html (15 August 2001).

Chauvel, Richard. 1980. 'Ambon's Other Half: Some Preliminary Observations on Ambonese Moslem Society and History'. *Review of Indonesian and Malaysian Affairs* 14, no. 1:40–80.

———. 1990. *Nationalists, Soldiers and Separatists: The Ambonese Islands from Colonialism to Revolt, 1880–1950*. Verhandelingen van het Koninklijk Instituut voor Taal-, Land- en Volkenkunde 143. Leiden, the Netherlands: KITLV Press.

Chew, Amy. 2000. 'Fight for Maluku'. *Asiaweek* 26, no. 42 (27 October). http://www.cnn.com/ASIANOW/asiaweek/magazine/2000/1027/is.indonesia.html (22 October 2000).

Cigdem, Ahmet. 1998. 'Religiöser Fundamentalismus als Entprivatisierung der Religion'. In *Politisierte Religion*, ed. Heiner Bielefeldt and Wilhelm Heitmeyer, pp. 91–108. Frankfurt: Suhrkamp.

Cisler, Steve, ed. 1998. 'The Internet and Indigenous Groups'. Special issue, *Cultural Survival Quarterly* 4, no. 21.

Cohen, Anthony P. 1985. *The Symbolic Construction of Community*. Chichester, UK: Ellis Horwood.

Cohen, Margot. 2000. 'Spite Islands'. *Far Eastern Economic Review,* 20 January. http://www.feer.com/_0001_20/p16indonesia.html (8 October 2000).

Coleman, E. Gabriella. 2010. 'Ethnographic Approaches to Digital Media'. *Annual Review of Anthropology* 30:487–505.

Collins, Steven. 2000. 'Perception Conflict in the "Modern" Balkan Wars'. In *Cyberwar 3.0: Human Factors in Information Operations and Future Conflict,* ed. Alan D. Campen and Douglas H. Dearth, pp. 191–201. Fairfax, VA: AFCEA International Press.

Conway, Maura. 2006. 'Terrorist "Use" of the Internet and Fighting Back'. *Information & Security* 19:9–30.

———. 2008. 'Media, Fear and the Hyperreal: The Construction of Cyberterrorism as the Ultimate Threat to Critical Infrastructures'. *Working Paper in International Studies 5,* Dublin. Centre for International Studies, Dublin City University. http://doras.dcu.ie/2142/1/2008-5.pdf (27 June 2011).

Cooley, Frank L. 1961. 'Altar and Throne in Central Moluccan Societies: A Study of the Relationship between the Institutions of Religion and the Institutions of Local Society Undergoing Rapid Social Change.' Ph.D. diss., Yale University.

Coppel, Charles A., ed. 2006. *Violent Conflicts in Indonesia: Analysis, Representation, Resolution.* London: Routledge.

Coronel, Sheila S. 1998. 'The Information Crisis'. *Development Dialogue* 2:7–21.

Costigan, James T. 1999. 'Introduction'. In *Doing Internet Research: Critical Issues and Methods for Examining the Net,* ed. Steven G. Jones, pp. xvii–xxiv. London: SAGE Publications.

Cronauer, Katja. 2001. 'Activism and the Internet: Uses of Electronic Mailing Lists by Social Activists'. http://www.ssrc.org/programs/itic/publications/civsocandgov/cronaueracademic.pdf (8 June 2003).

Dahlberg, Lincoln. 2000. 'Democratic Participation through the Internet: A Brief Survey'. *M/C Reviews,* 12 April. http://www.uq.edu.au/mc/reviews/features/politics/participation.html (13 June 2002).

———. 2001. 'Computer-Mediated Communication and The Public Sphere: A Critical Analysis'. *Journal of Computer-Mediated Communication 7,* no. 1 (October). http://www.ascusc.org/jcmc/vol7/issue1/dahlberg.html (19 May 2002).

Dartnell, Michael. 2009. 'Web Activism as an Element of Global Security'. In *Cyber Conflict and Global Politics,* ed. A. Karatzogianni, pp. 61–78. New York: Routledge.

Das, Veena. 1990. 'Introduction'. In *Mirrors of Violence: Communities, Riots and Survivors in South Asia,* ed. Veena Das, pp. 1–36. New Delhi: Oxford University Press.

Davidson, Alistair. 2010. 'Wikileaks, Karl Marx and You'. *Links – International Journal of Socialist Renewal,* 23 December. http://links.org.au/node/2094 (22 June 2011).

Dawson, Lorne L., and Douglas E. Cowan, eds. 2004. *Religion Online: Finding Faith on the Internet.* New York: Routledge.

Dearth, Douglas H. 2000. 'Shaping the "Information Space": Perception Management in Peace, Crisis and War'. In *Cyberwar 3.0: Human Factors in Information Operations and Future Conflict,* ed. Alan D. Campen and Douglas H. Dearth, pp. 153–63. Fairfax, VA: AFCEA International Press.

Deibert, Ronald J. 2002. 'Civil Society Activism on the World Wide Web: The Case of the Anti-MAI Lobby'. In *Street Protests and Fantasy Parks: Globalization, Culture, and the State,* ed. D. R. Cameron and J. G. Stein, pp. 88–108. Vancouver: UBC Press.

Dery, Mark. 1993. 'Flame Wars'. *South Atlantic Quarterly* 92, no. 4 (Fall): 559–68.

Devereaux, Leslie. 1995. 'An Introductory Essay'. In *Fields of Vision: Essays in Film Studies, Visual Anthropology, and Photography,* ed. Leslie Devereaux and Roger Hillman, pp. 1–18. Berkeley: University of California Press.

Dhume, Sadanand. 2001. 'Islam's Holy Warriors'. *Far Eastern Economic Review,* 26 April.

Diani, Mario. 1992. 'The Concept of Social Movement'. *Sociological Review* 40, no. 1:1–25.

———. 2000. 'Social Movement Networks Virtual and Real'. *Information, Communication & Society* 3, no. 3:386–401.

Dijk, Jan van. 1999. *The Network Society: Social Aspects of New Media.* London: SAGE Publications.

Dijk, Kees van. 2001. *A Country in Despair, Indonesia between 1997 and 2000.* Verhandelingen van het Koninklijk Instituut voor Taal-, Land- en Volkenkunde 186. Leiden, the Netherlands: KITLV Press.

Dijk, Teun A. van. 1997. 'The Study of Discourse'. In *Discourse as Structure and Process, Discourse Studies: A Multidisciplinary Introduction,* vol. 1, ed. Teun A. van Dijk. pp. 1–34. London: SAGE Publications.

Djaelani, Abdul Qadir. 1999. *Perang Sabil versus Perang Salib: Umat Islam Melawan Penjajah Kristen Portugis dan Belanda* [Holy war versus crusade: Islamic society resists the Christian colonial powers from Portugal and the Netherlands]. Jakarta: Yayasan Pengkajian Islam Madinah Al-Munawwarah.

Donaghy, Keola. 1998. ''Olelo Hawai'i: A Rich Oral History, a Bright Digital Future'. 'The Internet and Indigenous Groups', ed. Steve Cisler, special issue, *Cultural Survival Quarterly* 4, no. 21. http://www.cs.org/publications/CSQ/csqinternet.html#Donaghy (3 July 2002).

Donath, Judith S. 1999. 'Identity and Deception in the Virtual Community'. In *Communities in Cyberspace,* ed. Marc A. Smith and Peter Kollock, pp. 29–59. London: Routledge.

Doring, Nicola. 2002. 'Personal Home Pages on the Web: A Review of Research'. *Journal of Computer-Mediated Communication* 7, no. 3 (April). http://www.ascusc.org/jcmc/vol7/issue3/doering.html (19 May 2002).

DPP Forum Komunikasi Ahlus Sunnah Wal Jama'ah. 2000–1. SALAFY (Upaya Meniti Jejak Generasi Salafus Shalih) [Endeavour to Follow the Devout Path of the Time of Mohammed]. Various editions.

Duncan, Christopher R. 2005. 'The Other Maluku: Chronologies of Conflict in North Maluku'. *Indonesia* 80 (October): 53–80.

Durham, Meenakshi Gigi, and Douglas M. Kellner. 2001. 'Introduction' to Parts I–V. In *Media and Cultural Studies: KeyWorks,* ed. Meenakshi Gigi Durham and Douglas M. Kellner, pp. 33–38, 111–120, 219–24, 387–92, 513–20. Oxford: Blackwell Publishers.

Eickelman, Dale F. 1999. 'Communication and Control in the Middle East: Publication and Its Discontents'. In *New Media in the Muslim World: The*

Emerging Public Sphere, ed. Dale F. Eickelman and Jon W. Anderson, pp. 29–40. Bloomington: Indiana University Press.

Eickelman, Dale F., and Jon W. Anderson, eds. 1999a. *New Media in the Muslim World: The Emerging Public Sphere.* Bloomington: Indiana University Press.

——. 1999b. 'Redefining Muslim Publics'. In *New Media in the Muslim World The Emerging Public Sphere*, ed. Dale F. Eickelman and Jon W. Anderson, pp. 1–18. Bloomington: Indiana University Press.

Eisenlohr, Patrick. 2011. 'The Anthropology of Media and the Question of Ethnic and Religious Pluralism'. 'What Is a Medium? Theologies, Technologies and Aspirations', ed. Patrick Eisenlohr, special issue, *Social Anthropology* 19, no. 1 (February): 40–55.

Elkins, David J. 1997. 'Globalization, Telecommunication, and Virtual Ethnic Communities'. *International Political Science Review* 18, no. 2:139–52.

Elwert, Georg. 1989. 'Nationalismus und Ethnizität: Über die Bildung von Wir-Gruppen'. *Kölner Zeitschrift für Soziologie und Sozialpsychologie* 41:440–64.

Ely, Jusuf. 2001. 'Executive Summary of Moluccas Conflict'. U.S. Commission on International Religious Freedom, Washington, D.C., 13 February.

Erickson, Thomas. 1996. 'The World Wide Web as Social Hypertext'. http://www.pliant.org/personal/Tom_Erickson/SocialHypertext.html (22 August 2001).

Eriksen, Thomas Hylland. 1991. 'The Cultural Contexts of Ethnic Differences'. *Man* 26, no. 1 (March): 127–44.

Eriyanto, Oleh. 2003. *Media dan Konflik Ambon* [The media and the Ambon conflict]. Jakarta: Kantor Berita Radio 68H, Majalah Pantau dan Media Development Loan Fund.

Eriyanto, Oleh, and Muhammad Qodari. 2000. 'Mempertimbangkan Jurnalisme Damai' [Deliberations on peace joumalism]. *Pantau* 9:41–48.

Escobar, Arturo. 1994. 'Welcome to Cyberia: Notes on the Anthropology of Cyberculture'. *Current Anthropology* 35, no. 3 (June): 211–32.

Ess, Charles. 2007. 'Cross-Cultural Perspectives on Religion and Computer-Mediated Communication'. *Journal of Computer-Mediated Communication* 12, no. 3. http://jcmc.indiana.edu/vol12/issue3/ess.html (2 February 2011).

Fabian, Johannes. 2002. 'Virtual Archives and Ethnographic Writing'. *Current Anthropology* 43, no. 5 (December): 775–86.

Faruk. 2001. 'Cybersastra: Penjelajahan Awal terhadap Sastra di Internet' [Cyber-literature: First research on the topic of literature in the Internet]. VA/AVMI International Symposium on Media Cultures in Indonesia [Budaya Media di Indonesia], CNWS Universiteit Leiden, Leiden, the Netherlands, 2–7 April.

Fealy, Greg. 2001. 'Inside the Laskar Jihad: An Interview with the Leader of a New, Radical and Militant Sect'. *Inside Indonesia* 65 (January–March): 28–29.

Feillard, Andrée. 2000a. 'Religious Factor in Recent Clashes I'. *The Jakarta Post,* 25 May.

——. 2000b. 'Religious Factor in Recent Clashes II'. *The Jakarta Post,* 26 May.

Fellowship of Indonesian Christians in America. 1999. 'Ambon: Unreported Facts'. 9 April. http://www.fica.org/hr/ambon/enAmbonUnreportedFacts. html (8 January 2000).

Fernback, Jan. 1997. 'The Individual within the Collective: Virtual Ideology and the Realization of Collective Principles'. In *Virtual Culture. Identity and*

Communication in Cybersociety, ed. Steven G. Jones, pp. 36–54. London: SAGE Publications.

——. 1999. 'There Is a There There: Notes Toward a Definition of Cybercommunity'. In *Doing Internet Research: Critical Issues and Methods for Examining the Net,* ed. Steven G. Jones, pp. 203–20. London: SAGE Publications.

Fischermann, Thomas. 2001. 'Hacker im Heiligen Krieg: Die USA fürchten die nächste Terrorgeneration: Angreifer aus dem Cyberspace'. *DIE ZEIT* (11 October): 29–30.

Forrester, Geoff, ed. 1999. *Post-Soeharto Indonesia: Renewal or Chaos?* Singapore: Institute of Southeast Asian Studies.

Foster, Derek. 1997. 'Community and Identity in the Electronic Village'. In *Internet Culture,* ed. David Porter, pp. 23–37. New York: Routledge.

Franco, V., H. Piirto, H.-Y. Hu, and B. V. Lewenstein. 1995. 'Anatomy of a Flame: Conflict and Community Building on the Internet'. *IEEE Technology and Society Magazine* 14, no. 2 (Summer): 12–21.

Frey, Siegfried. 1999. *Die Macht des Bildes: Der Einfluß der nonverbalen Kommunikation auf Kultur und Politik.* Bern, Switzerland: Hans Huber Verlag.

Froehling, Oliver. 1997. 'The Cyberspace "War of Ink and Internet" in Ciapas, Mexico'. *Geographical Review* 87, no. 2 (April): 291–302.

Gabrial, Albert. 1998. 'Assyrians: "3.000 Years of History, Yet the Internet is Our Only Home"'. 'The Internet and Indigenous Groups', ed. Steve Cisler, special issue, *Cultural Survival Quarterly* 4, no. 21. http://www.cs.org/publications/CSQ/csqinternet.html#Gabrial (3 July 2002).

Galtung, Johan. 1998. 'High Road, Low Road'. *Track Two* 7, no. 4 (December). http://ccrweb.ccr.uct.ac.za/two/7_4/p07_highroad_lowroad.html (15 January 2002).

Gani, Firman. 2002. *Perjalanan Panjang Anak Bangsa Menuju Perdamaian* [The people's long path to peace]. Jakarta: Lembaga Humaniora.

Garcia, Angela Cora, Alecea I. Standlee, Jennifer Bechkoff and Yan Cui. 2009. 'Ethnographic Approaches to the Internet and Computer-Mediated Communication'. *Journal of Contemporary Ethnography* 38, no. 1 (February): 52–84.

Gardner, Hall. 2009. 'War and the Media Paradox'. In *Cyber Conflict and Global Politics,* ed. A. Karatzogianni, pp. 13–30. New York: Routledge.

Geertz, Clifford. 1993. *The Interpretation of Cultures.* London: Fontana Press.

Gephart, Werner. 1999. 'Zur Bedeutung der Religionen für die Identitätsbildung'. In *Religion und Identität: Im Horizont des Pluralisms,* ed. Werner Gephart and Hans Waldenfels, pp. 233–66. Frankfurt: Suhrkamp.

Gephart, Werner, and Hans Waldenfels, eds. 1999. *Religion und Identität: Im Horizont des Pluralismus.* Frankfurt: Suhrkamp.

Gibson, William. 1984. *Neuromancer.* New York: Ace Books.

Giddens, Anthony. 1991. *Modernity and Self-Identity.* Palo Alto, CA: Stanford University Press.

Giesen, Bernhard. 1999. *Kollektive Identität.* Frankfurt: Suhrkamp.

Ginsburg, Faye. 1995. 'Mediating Culture: Indigenous Media, Ethnographic Film, and the Production of Identity'. In *Fields of Vision: Essays in Film Studies, Visual Anthropology, and Photography,* ed. Leslie Devereaux and Roger Hillman, pp. 256–91. Berkeley: University of California Press.

Goffman, Erving. 1969. *Wir alle spielen Theater: Die Selbstdarstellung im Alltag.* München: R. Piper & Co.

Golub, Alex. 2010. 'Being in the World (of Warcraft): Raiding, Realism, and Knowledge Production in a Massively Multiplayer Online Game'. *Anthropological Quarterly* 83, no. 1 (Winter): 17–45.

Goonasekera, Anura, and Youichi Ito, eds. 1999. *Mass Media and Cultural Identity.* London: Pluto Press.

Gosman, Martin, and Hans Bakker. 1991. 'Inleiding'. In *Heilige Oorlogen: Een Onderzoek naar Historische en Hedendaagse Vormen van Collectief Religieus Geweld,* ed. Martin Gosman and Hans Bakker, pp. 9–17. Kampen, the Netherlands: Kok Agora.

Granovetter, Mark S. 1973. 'The Strength of Weak Ties'. *American Journal of Sociology* 78, no. 6 (May): 1360–80.

Graphics & Visualization & Usability Center. 1998. 'Web User Survey'. October. http://www.gvu.gatech.edu/user_surveys/ (22 July 2002).

Guimarães, Mário J. L. 2005. 'Doing Anthropology in Cyberspace: Fieldwork Boundaries and Social Environments'. In *Virtual Methods: Issues in Social Research on the Internet,* ed. C. Hine, pp. 141–56. Oxford: Berg.

Gurak, Laura J. 1999. 'The Promise and the Peril of Social Action in Cyberspace: *Ethos,* Delivery, and the Protests over Marketplace and the Clipper Chip'. In *Communities in Cyberspace,* ed. Marc A. Smith and Peter Kollock, pp. 243–63. London: Routledge.

Habermas, Jürgen. 2001. 'The Public Sphere: An Encyclopedia Article'. In *Media and Cultural Studies: KeyWorks,* ed. Meenakshi Gigi Durham and Douglas M. Kellner, pp. 102–7. Oxford: Blackwell Publishers.

Habiboe, Ron R. F. 2000. 'Godsdiensttwist op de Ambonse Eilanden'. *Allerwegen* 31, no. 37:3–10.

Hadden, Jeffrey K., and Douglas E. Cowan, eds. 2000. *Religion on the Internet: Research Prospects and Promises.* Religion and the Social Order 8. New York: JAI.

Hakken, David. 1999. *Cyborgs@Cyberspace? An Ethnographer Looks to the Future.* New York: Routledge.

Halbwachs, Maurice. 1985. *Das kollektive Gedächtnis.* Frankfurt: Fischer Wissenschaft.

Hall, Stuart. 1992. 'Our Mongrel Selves'. *New Statesman & Society* 5, no. 207 (June): 6–8.

———. 1994. 'Cultural Identity and Diaspora'. In *Colonial Discourse and Post-Colonial Theory,* ed. Patrick Williams and Laura Chrisman, pp. 392–403. New York: Columbia University Press.

Halliday, Fred. 1999. 'Manipulation and Limits: Media Coverage of the Gulf War, 1990–91'. In *The Media of Conflict: War Reporting and Representations of Ethnic Violence,* ed. Tim Allen and Jean Seaton, pp. 127–46. London: Zed Books.

Hamelink, Cees J. 2000. *The Ethics of Cyberspace.* London: SAGE Publications.

HAMKA (Haji Abdul Malik Karim Amrullah). 1976. 'Das Verhältnis zwischen Religion und Staat im Islam'. In *Indonesiens verantwortliche Gesellschaft,* ed. Rolf Italiaander, pp. 122–46. Erlangen, Germany: Verlag der Ev.-Luth. Mission.

Handoko, Dipo. 2001. 'Laskar di Hukum Darurat' [Laskar under a state of emergency]. *GATRA* 7, no. 26 (19 May): 27.

Hands, Joss. 2010. *@ Is For Activism.* London: Pluto Press.

Hansen, Derek, Ben Shneiderman and Marc Smith, eds. 2010. *Analyzing Social Media Networks with NodeXL*. New York: Morgan Kaufmann.

Hansen, Lene and Helen Nissenbaum. 2009. 'Digital Disaster, Cyber Security, and the Copenhagen School'. *International Studies Quarterly* 53:1155–75.

Hartmann, Frank. 1997. 'Under Construction: Architektur, Virtualität und Cyberspace'. Gastvortrag an der Akademie für bildende Künste Wien, April. http://mailbox.univie.ac.et/Frank.Hartmann/Essays/Architektur.htm (27 September 2001).

———. 1998. 'Annäherung an eine Metapher'. In *Informationsgesellschaft: Sozialwissenschaftliche Aspekte*, ed. Frank Hartmann, 9–22. Schriftenreihe. Vol. 3. Vienna: Forum Sozialforschung.

Hasan, Noorhaidi. 2002. 'Faith and Politics: The Rise of the Laskar Jihad in the Era of Transition in Indonesia'. *Indonesia* 73 (April): 145–69.

Hasenclever, Andreas, and Volker Rittberger. 1999. 'The Impact of Faith: Does Religion Make a Difference in Political Conflict?' *Tübinger Arbeitspapiere zur Internationalen Politik und Friedensforschung* 35, http://www.uni-tuebingen. de/uni/spi/ab2menue.htm (17 February 2001).

Hashim, Ismail Yahya. 2001. 'Intifada dalam Ruang Siber' [Intifada in cyberspace]. *Dewan Masyarakat* 39, no. 4:54–55.

Heckmann, Friedrich. 1997. 'Ethnos – eine imaginierte oder reale Gruppe? Über Ethnizität als soziale Kategorie'. In *Kollektive Identität in Krisen: Ethnizität in Region, Nation, Europa*, ed. Robert Hettlage, Petra Deger and Susanne Wagner, pp. 46–55. Opladen, Germany: Westdeutscher Verlag.

Hefner, Robert W. 1997. 'Print Islam: Mass Media and Ideological Rivalries Among Indonesian Muslims'. *Indonesia* 64 (October): 77–103.

———. 1999. 'Islam and Nation in the Post-Suharto Era'. In *The Politics of Post-Suharto Indonesia*, ed. Adam Schwarz and Jonathan Paris, pp. 40–72. New York: Council on Foreign Relations Press.

———. 2000a. *Civil Islam: Muslims and Democratization in Indonesia*. Princeton, NJ: Princeton University Press.

———. 2000b. 'Soeharto's Maluku Legacy'. *Wall Street Journal*, 16 August. http:// www.indopubs.com/archives/0287.html (8 October 2000).

———. 2001. 'Muslim-Christian Violence in Maluku: The Role of the National Politics'. U.S. Commission on International Religious Freedom, Washington, D.C., 13 February.

Helland, Christopher. 2000. 'Online-Religion/Religion-Online and Virtual Communitas'. In *Religion on the Internet: Research Prospects and Promises*, ed. J. K. Hadden and D. E. Cowan, pp. 205–23. Religion and the Social Order 8. New York: JAI.

Helmers, Sabine, Ute Hoffmann and Jeanette Hofmann. 1996. 'Netzkultur und Netzwerkorganisation: Das Projekt "Interaktionsraum Internet"'. WZB Discussion Paper FS II 96-103. Wissenschaftszentrum Berlin 1996. http:// duplox.wz-berlin.de/texte/dp103/ (27 September 2001).

Hicks, Clinton R. 1998. 'Places in the 'Net: Experiencing Cyberspace'. *Cultural Dynamics* 10, no. 1:49–70.

Hill, David T. 2002. 'East Timor and the Internet: Global Political Leverage in/on Indonesia'. *Indonesia* 73 (April): 25–51.

Hill, David T., and Krishna Sen. 1997. 'Wiring the Warung to Global Gateways: The Internet in Indonesia'. *Indonesia* 63 (April): 67–89.

———. 2002. 'Netizens in Combat: Conflict on the Internet in Indonesia'. *Asian Studies Review* 26, no. 2 (June): 165–87.

Hindman, Matthew Scott. 2009. *The Myth of Digital Democracy.* Princeton, NJ: Princeton University Press.

Hine, Christine. 2000. *Virtual Ethnography.* London: SAGE Publications.

———. 2001. 'Virtual Ethnography' (2000) reviewed – author response. *Resource Center for Cyberculture Studies – Book Reviews,* June. http://www.com. washington.edu/rccs/bookinfo.asp?authorID=32&BookID=109 (29 October 2002).

———. 2005a. 'Virtual Methods and the Sociology of Cyber-Social-Scientific Knowledge'. In *Virtual Methods: Issues in Social Research on the Internet,* ed. C. Hine, pp. 1–12. Oxford: Berg.

———. 2007. 'Connective Ethnography for the Exploration of e-Science'. *Journal of Computer-Mediated Communication* 12, no. 2, http://jcmc.indiana. edu/ vol12/issue2/hine.html (28 June 2010).

Hine, Christine, ed. 2005b. *Virtual Methods: Issues in Social Research on the Internet.* Oxford: Berg.

Hitchcock, Michael. 1996. *Islam and Identity in Eastern Indonesia.* Hull, U.K.: The University of Hull Press.

Hobsbawm, Eric, and Terence Ranger, eds. 1983. *The Invention of Traditions.* London: Cambridge University Press.

Hoek, Antje van der. 1994. *Religie in Ballingschap. Institutionalisering en Leiderschap onder Christelijke en Islamitische Molukkers in Nederland.* Amsterdam: VU-Uitgeverij.

Hoffman, Bruce. 2006. 'The Use of the Internet by Islamic Extremists'. Testimony presented to the House Permanent Select Committee on Intelligence, 4 May. *RAND.* http://www.rand.org (5 May 2011).

Hoffmann, Ute. 1998. 'Identität und Sozialität in der Netzwelt'. *Spektrum der Wissenschaft. Dossier: Die Welt im Internet* 1, no. 98:96–97. http://duplox.wz-berlin.de/texte/ident/ (2 October 2001).

Hofmann, Jeanette. 1998. '"Let A Thousand Proposals Bloom" – Mailinglisten als Forschungsquelle'. In *Online Research,* B. Batinic, L. Graef, A. Werner and W. Bandilla. Göttingen, Germany: Hogrefe. http://duplox.wz-berlin. de/texte/gortex/ (2 October 2001).

Hohe, Tanja, and Bert Remijsen. 2003. 'Peacemaker for Religious Conflicts? The Value of Pela Relationships in Ambon'. In *Hinduism in Modern Indonesia: Hindu Dharma Indonesia Between Local, National, and Global Interests,* ed. M. Ramstedt, pp. 126–43. London: Routledge.

Hojsgaard, Morten T., and Margit Warburg, eds. 2005. *Religion and Cyberspace.* London: Routledge.

Houben, Vincent. 2000a. 'Communal Conflict in Post-Suharto Indonesia: The Case of Ambon'. In *Ethnic Minorities and Nationalism in Southeast Asia,* ed. Thomas Engelbert and Andreas Schneider, pp. 39–47. Festschrift, dedicated to Hans Dieter Kubitscheck. Frankfurt: Peter Lang Verlag.

———. 2000b. 'The Other from Within: The Violence of Reformasi'. Workshop on Violence in Indonesia: Its Historical Roots and Contemporary Manifestations, Universiteit Leiden, Leiden, the Netherlands, 13–15 December.

Hudson, Miles, and John Stanier. 1998. *War and the Media.* New York: New York University Press.

Human Rights Watch. 1999. 'Report on Violence in Ambon'. *A Human Rights Watch Report* 11, no. 1(C) (March).

Huntington, Samuel P. 1993. 'The Clash of Civilizations?' *Foreign Affairs* 72, no. 3 (Summer): 22–49.

———. 1996. *The Clash of Civilizations.* New York: Simon & Schuster.

Hüppauf, Bernd. 1995. 'Modernism and the Photographic Representation of War and Destruction'. In *Fields of Vision: Essays in Film Studies, Visual Anthropology, and Photography,* ed. Leslie Devereaux and Roger Hillman, pp. 94–126. Berkeley: University of California Press.

Husaini, H. Adian. 2000. *Gereja-Gereja dibakar: Membedah Akar Konflik SARA di Indonesia* [Churches set on fire: Operating at the root of the SARA conflict in Indonesia]. Jakarta: DEA Press.

Huwaë, Sylvia. 1995. 'Divided Opinions about Adatpela: A Study of Pela Tamilou-Siri-Sori-Hutumuri'. *Cakalele* 6:77–92.

———. 2001. *Het Pelaschap Leeft Voort: De Rol en Betekenis van het Pelaschap in Molukse Gezinnen.* Nijmegen, the Netherlands: Muhabbat.

Indonesian Christian Communication Forum. 2001. 'Actual News Up Date.' 31 January. fkki@mitra.net.id (8 March 2001).

Institut Studi Arus Informasi. 2000a. *Luka Maluku: Militer Terlibat* [Injured Moluccas: The military is involved]. Jakarta.

———. 2000b. 'Petaka Maluku' [Disaster in the Moluccas]. *Pantau* 9.

International Christian Concern. 2001. 'The Untold Tragedies of Maluku: The Findings of International Christian Concern Following a Fact-finding Trip to Indonesia in February 2001'. 9 March. http://www.persecution.org/news/PR_2001/press2001-03-09.html (30 March 2001).

International Crisis Group. 2000a. 'Indonesia: Overcoming Murder and Chaos in Maluku'. Asia Report No. 10, 19 December. Jakarta/Brussels.

———. 2000b. 'Indonesia's Maluku Crisis: The Issues'. Indonesia Briefing Paper, 19 July. Jakarta/Brussels.

———. 2002. 'Indonesia: The Search for Peace in Maluku'. Asia Report No. 31, 8 February. Jakarta/Brussels.

———. 2004. 'Indonesia: Violence erupts again in Ambon'. Asia Briefing, 17 May. Jakarta/Brussels.

International Telecommunications Union. 2001. 'Internet Indicators – World'. http://www.itu.int/ITU-D/ict/statistics/at-glance/Internet99.pdf (20 August 2001).

———. 2002. Internet Indicators – World. http://www.itu.int/ITU-D/ict/statistics/at_glance/Internet01.pdf (12 November 2002).

Interrogate the Internet. 1996. 'Contradictions in Cyberspace: Collective Response'. In *Cultures of Internet: Virtual Spaces, Real Histories, Living Bodies,* ed. Rob Shields, pp. 125–32. London: SAGE Publications.

Jaffe, J. Michael, Young-Eum Lee, Li-Ning Huang and Hayg Oshagan. 1995. 'Gender, Pseudonyms, and CMC: Masking Identities and Baring Souls'. Forty-fifth Annual Conference of the International Communication Association, Albuquerque, New Mexico, U.S., May. http://research.haifa.ac.il/~jmjaffe/genderpseudocmc (22 August 2001).

Jaffrelot, Christophe. 1996. 'Gewalttätige Zusammenstöße zwischen Hindus und Moslems'. In *Religion-Macht-Gewalt. Religiöser ‚Fundamentalismus' und Hindu-Moslem-Konflikte in Südasien,* ed. Christian Weiss, Tom Weichert,

Evelin Hust and Harald Fischer-Tine, pp. 99–125. Frankfurt: IKO – Verlag für Interkulturelle Kommunikation.

Jaiz, H. Hartono Ahmad. 1999. *Ambon Bersimbah Darah: Ekspresi Ketakutan Ekstremis Nasrani* [Ambon Is Sullied by Blood: Expression of Fear of Radical Christians]. Jakarta: Dea Press.

Jenkins, Richard. 1994. 'Rethinking Ethnicity: Identity, Categorization and Power'. *Ethnic and Racial Studies* 17, no. 2:197–223.

Jones, Sidney. 2001. 'U.S. Policy Options on Indonesia'. U.S. Commission on International Religious Freedom, Washington, D.C., 13 February. http://www.hrw.org (21 February 2001).

Jones, Steven G. 1997. 'The Internet and Its Social Landscape'. In *Virtual Culture: Identity and Communication in Cybersociety*, ed. Steven G. Jones, pp. 7–35. London: SAGE Publications.

———. 1998a. 'Information, Internet and Community: Notes Toward an Understanding of Community in the Information Age'. In *Cybersociety 2.0: Revisiting Computer-Mediated Communication and Community*, ed. Steven G. Jones, pp. 1–34. London: SAGE Publications.

———. 1998b. 'Introduction'. In *Cybersociety 2.0: Revisiting Computer-Mediated Communication and Community*, ed. Steven G. Jones, pp. xi–xvii. London: SAGE Publications.

———. 1999. 'Preface'. In *Doing Internet Research: Critical Issues and Methods for Examining the Net*, ed. Steven G. Jones, pp. ix–xiv. London: SAGE Publications.

Jordan, Tim. 1999. *Cyberpower: The Culture and Politics of Cyberspace and the Internet*. London: Routledge.

———. 2001. 'Language and Libertarianism: The Politics of Cyberculture and the Culture of Cyberpolitics'. *Sociological Review* 49, no. 1 (February): 1–15.

Jordan, Tim, and Paul A. Taylor. 2004. *Hacktivism and Cyberwars: Rebels with a Cause?* London: Routledge.

Joseph, Victor. 2000. 'De Media en de Molukken: Geruchten, Feiten en Evenwichtige Berichtgeving'. In *De Molukken in Crisis*, ed. Victor Joseph, Wim Manuhutu and Henk Smeets, pp. 13–17. Lelystad, the Netherlands: Actuele Onderwerpen.

Joseph, Victor, Wim Manuhutu and Henk Smeets, eds. 2000. *De Molukken in Crisis*. Lelystad, the Netherlands: Actuele Onderwerpen.

Jubilee Campaign U.K. 1999. 'Analysis of the Sectarian Conflict in Maluku and Its Role in the Islamisation of Indonesia'. December. http://www.jubileecampaign. co.uk/world/ind5.htm (16 December 2000).

Juergensmeyer, Mark. 2000. *Terror in the Mind of God: The Global Rise of Religious Violence*. Berkeley: University of California Press.

Jürgenmeyer, Clemens. 1998. 'Hindu, Hindusthan, Hindutva. Die Politik des Hindunationalismus im heutigen Indien'. *Der Bürger im Staat. INDIEN* 48, no. 1:46–53.

Kaam, Ben van. 1977. *Ambon door de Eeuwen*. Baarn, the Netherlands: Uitgeverij in den Toren.

Kaartinen, Timo. 2007. 'How Civility Constitutes Its Publics'. 'Civility and Social Relations in South and Southeast Asia', special issue. *Suomen Antropologi: Journal of the Finnish Anthropological Society* 32, no. 3 (Autumn): 39–49.

Kakar, Sudhir. 1997. *Die Gewalt der Frommen: zur Psychologie religiöser und ethnischer Konflikte.* Munich: Beck.

Karatzogianni, Athina. 2006. *The Politics of Cyberconflict.* London: Routledge.

——, ed. 2009. *Cyber Conflict and Global Politics.* New York: Routledge.

Karetzky, Stephen, and Norman Frankel, eds. 1989. *The Media's Coverage of the Arab-Israeli Conflict.* New York: Shapolsky Publishers.

Kartodirdjo, Sartono. 1972. 'Agrarian Radicalism in Java: Its Setting and Development'. In *Culture and Politics in Indonesia,* ed. Claire Holt, Benedict Anderson and James T. Siegel, pp. 71–125. Ithaca, NY: Cornell University Press.

Kastor, Rustam. 2000a. *Badai Pembalasan Laskar Mujahidin Ambon – Maluku* [Storm of reprisal by the mujahideen warriors in Ambon – Maluku]. Yogyakarta, Indonesia: Wihdah Press.

——. 2000b. *Damai Sekarang atau Perang Berlanjut* [Peace now or permanent war]. Ambon.

——. 2000c. *Fakta, Data dan Analisa Konspirasi Politik RMS dan Kristen Menghancurkan Ummat Islam di Ambon – Maluku* [Facts, data, and analyses on the conspiracy politics by the RMS and Christians to destroy the Islamic community in Ambon – Moluccas]. Yogyakarta, Indonesia: Wihdah Press.

——. 2000d. *Suara Maluku Membantah, Rustam Kastor Menjawab: Polemik Buku* Konspirasi Politik RMS dan Kristen Menghancurkan Ummat Islam di Ambon – Maluku [Suara Maluku protests, Rustam Kastor responds: Polemic against the book *Conspiracy Politics by the RMS and Christians to destroy the Islamic community in Ambon – Moluccas*]. Yogyakarta, Indonesia: Wihdah Press.

Keen, David. 1999. '"Who's it Between?" "Ethnic War" and Rational Violence'. In *The Media of Conflict: War Reporting and Representations of Ethnic Violence,* ed. Tim Allen and Jean Seaton, pp. 81–101. London: Zed Books.

Kellner, Douglas M., and Meenakshi Gigi Durham. 2001. 'Adventures in Media and Cultural Studies: Introducing the KeyWorks'. In *Media and Cultural Studies: KeyWorks,* ed. Meenakshi Gigi Durham and Douglas M. Kellner, pp. 1–29. Oxford: Blackwell Publishers.

Kendall, Lori. 1999. 'Recontextualizing "Cyberspace": Methodological Considerations for On-Line Research'. In *Doing Internet Research: Critical Issues and Methods for Examining the Net,* ed. Steven G. Jones, pp. 57–74. London: SAGE Publications.

Kiesler, Sara, Jane Siegel and Timothy W. McGuire. 1984. 'Social Psychological Aspects of Computer-Mediated Communication'. *American Psychologist* 39, no. 10 (October): 1123–34.

KITLV. 1925. *Adatrechtbundels XXIV: Groote Oost.* The Hague: Martinus Nijhoff.

——. 1933. *Adatrechtbundels XXXVI: Borneo, Zuid-Selebes, Ambon enz.* The Hague: Martinus Nijhoff.

Kleinknecht, Steven. 2005. 'Book Review: Tim Jordan and Paul A. Taylor, "Hacktivism and Cyberwars: Rebels with a Cause?" London: Routledge, 2004'. *New Media & Society* 7, no. 4:584–86.

Klinken, Gerry van. 1999. 'What Caused the Ambon Violence?' *Inside Indonesia* 60 (October–December). http://www.insideindonesia.org/edit60/ambon.htm (9 October 2000).

——. 2001. 'The Maluku Wars: Bringing Society Back In'. *Indonesia* 71 (April): 1–26.

———. 2007. *Communal Violence and Democratization in Indonesia: Small Town Wars.* London: Routledge.

Knightley, Phillip. 1975. *The First Casualty: The War Correspondent as Hero, Propagandist, and Myth Maker from the Crimea to Vietnam.* London: André Deutsch.

Kolko, Beth, and Elizabeth Reid. 1998. 'Dissolution and Fragmentation: Problems in On-Line Communities'. In *Cybersociety 2.0: Revisiting Computer-Mediated Communication and Community,* ed. Steven G. Jones, pp. 212–29. London: SAGE Publications.

Kollock, Peter. 1999. 'The Economies of Online Cooperation: Gifts and Public Goods in Cyberspace'. In *Communities in Cyberspace,* ed. Marc A. Smith and Peter Kollock, pp. 220–39. London: Routledge.

Kollock, Peter, and Marc A. Smith. 1996. 'Managing the Virtual Commons: Cooperation and Conflict in Computer Communities'. In *Computer-Mediated Communication: Linguistic, Social and Cross-Cultural Perspectives,* ed. Susan C. Herring, pp. 109–28. Amsterdam: John Benjamins.

———. 1999. 'Communities in Cyberspace'. In *Communities in Cyberspace,* ed. Marc A. Smith and Peter Kollock, pp. 3–25. London: Routledge.

KOMITEL. 2002. 'Indonesian Internet User and Broadband Entering 2002'. *Koperasi Komunitas Telematika,* 12 November. http://www.geocities.com/komitel2002/ (12 November 2002).

Korenman, Joan, and Nancy Wyatt. 1996. 'Group Dynamics in an E-Mail Forum'. In *Computer-Mediated Communication: Linguistic, Social and Cross-Cultural Perspectives,* ed. Susan C. Herring, pp. 226–42. Amsterdam: John Benjamins.

Kossoudji, Sherrie. 2010. 'Review Essay: Jonathan Paul Marshall, Living on Cybermind: Categories, Communication and Control. New York: Peter Lang, 2007. *Qualitative Social Work* 9: 291–94.

Kozinets, Robert V. 2010. *Netnography: Doing Ethnographic Research Online.* London: SAGE.

Kraemer, Hendrik. 1927. 'Mededelingen over den Islam op Ambon en Haroekoe'. *Djawa* 7, no. 2:77–88.

———. 1958. 'Report on Amboina and the Minahassa'. In *From Missionfield to Independent Church. Report on a Decisive Decade in the Growth of Indigenous Churches in Indonesia,* ed. Hendrik Kraemer, pp. 11–42. The Hague: Boekencentrum.

Kremser, Manfred. 1999. 'CyberAnthropology und die neuen Räume des Wissens'. *Mitteilungen der Anthropologischen Gesellschaft in Wien* 129:275–90.

Kress, Gunther, Regina Leite-García and Theo van Leeuwen. 1997. 'Discourse Semiotics'. In *Discourse as Structure and Process, Discourse Studies: A Multidisciplinary Introduction,* vol. 1, ed. Teun A. van Dijk, pp. 257–91. London: SAGE Publications.

Kreuzer, Peter. 2000. 'Politik der Gewalt – Gewalt in der Politik: Indonesien'. HSFK-Report 4/2000. Peace Research Institute Frankfurt.

Kuntsman, Adi and Rebecca L. Stein. 2010. 'Another War Zone: Social Media in the Israeli-Palestinian Conflict'. *Middle East Report Online,* http://reliefweb.int/sites/reliefweb.int/files/resources/849D4BB7DAD95F6549257798000F9F16-Full_Report.pdf (27 September 2010).

Laksono, P. M. 2002. 'We Are All One: How Custom Overcame Religious Rivalry in Southeast Maluku'. *Inside Indonesia* 70 (April–June): 7–8.

Landler, Mark, and John Markoff. 2007. 'In Estonia, What May Be the First War in Cyberspace'. *New York Times*, 28 May. http://www.nytimes.com/2007/05/28/business/worldbusiness/28iht-cyberwar.4.5901141.html?pagewanted=2 (21 June 2011).

Latham, Robert, ed. 2003. *Bombs and Bandwith: The Emerging Relationship Between Information Technology and Security.* New York: The New Press.

Latupatti, Joshua. 1999. 'Let's Be Frank About Ambon'. *Indonesia Daily News Online*, 31 March. http://www.hamline.edu/apakabar/basisdata/1999/03/31/0030.html (31 March 1999).

Leander, Kevin M., and Kelly K. McKim. 2003. 'Tracing the Everyday "Sitings" of Adolescents on the Internet: A Strategic Adaptation of Ethnography Across Online and Offline Spaces'. *Education, Communication & Information* 3, no. 2 (July): 211–40.

Lee, Juliet. 1997. 'The Changing Face of the Village in Ambon'. *Cakalele* 8:59–77.

Leemhuis, Fred. 1991. 'De Djihad in de Vroege Islam'. In *Heilige Oorlogen: Een Onderzoek naar Historische en Hedendaagse Vormen van Collectief Religieus Geweld,* ed. Martin Gosman and Hans Bakker, pp. 52–65. Kampen, the Netherlands: Kok Agora.

Legge, J. D. 1964. *Indonesia.* Englewood Cliffs, NJ: Prentice-Hall.

Lehdonvirta, Vili. 2010. 'Virtual Worlds Don't Exist: Questioning the Dichotomous Approach in MMO Studies'. *International Journal of Computer Game Research* 10, no. 1 (April). http://gamestudies.org/1001/articles/lehdonvirta (27 June 2011).

Lev, Daniel. 2001. 'Testimony about the Maluku Conflict'. U.S. Commission on International Religious Freedom, Washington, D.C., 13 February.

Lévy, Pierre. 1996. 'Cyberkultur'. http://www.heise.de/tp/deutsch/inhalt/co/2044/ (27 September 2001).

Liddle, R. William. 1999. 'Indonesia's Unexpected Failure of Leadership'. In *The Politics of Post-Suharto Indonesia,* ed. Adam Schwarz and Jonathan Paris, pp. 16–39. New York: Council on Foreign Relations Press.

———. 2001. 'Indonesian Political Developments and their Implications for the United States, with Special Reference to the Maluku Crisis'. U.S. Commission on International Religious Freedom, Washington, D.C., 13 February.

Liem Soei Liong. 2000. 'It's the Military, Stupid!' International Workshop on Violence in Indonesia: Its Historical Roots and its Contemporary Manifestations, Universiteit Leiden, Leiden, the Netherlands, 13–15 December, http://www.indopubs.com/archives/0214.html (7 January 2001).

Lim, Merlyna. 2002. 'CyberCivic Space in Indonesia: From Panopticum to Pandemonium?' *International Development and Planning Review* 24, no. 4:383–400.

———. 2003. 'The Internet, Social Network and Reform in Indonesia'. In *Contesting Media Power: Alternative Media in a Networked World,* ed. Nick Couldry and James Curran, chap. 17. Lanham, MD: Rowman & Littlefield.

Lingsma, Tjitske. 2008. *Het Verdriet van Ambon: Een geschiedenis van de Molukken.* Amsterdam: Balans.

Liu, Melinda. 2001. 'Holy War On the Web'. *Newsweek,* 15 October.

Loader, Brian D., and Leigh Keeble. 2002. 'Shaping Online Welfare Cultures: Social Movements, Identification, and the Internet'. AoIR International Conference on Internet Research 3.0, Maastricht, the Netherlands, 13–16 October.

Lockard, Joseph. 1997. 'Progressive Politics, Electronic Individualism and the Myth of Virtual Community'. In *Internet Culture*, ed. David Porter, pp. 219–31. New York: Routledge.

Lokollo, J. E. 1997. *Seri Budaya Pela-Gandong dari Pulau Ambon* [Pela-Gandong culture on the island of Ambon]. Ambon: Lembaga Kebudayaan Daerah Maluku.

——. 1999. 'Kerusuhan di Maluku: Beberapa Masalah dan Kaitannya dengan Ketahanan Nasional' [Moluccan unrest: Some problems and the links to National Resistance Force]. *Antropologi Indonesia* XXIII, no. 58:88–93.

Luhmann, Niklas. 1996. *Die Realität der Massenmedien*. Extended 2nd ed. Opladen, Germany: Westdeutscher Verlag.

Luwarso, Lukas. 1998. 'The Liberation of the Indonesian Press'. *Development Dialogue* 2:85–95.

Mach, Zdzislaw. 1993. *Symbols, Conflict, and Identity: Essays in Political Anthropology*. New York: State University of New York Press.

Mandaville, Peter. 2001. *Transnational Muslim Politics: Reimagining the Umma*. London: Routledge.

Mangkey, J. 2000. 'The Church in Indonesia: Facing New Challenges towards a New Indonesia'. Annual Conference of Kirche in Not, Königstein, Germany, 19 September.

Mann, Richard. 2000. 'Bitterness in the Spice Islands'. In *A Nation Reborn*, ed. Richard Mann, pp. 191–203. Jakarta: Gateway Books.

Manning, Chris, and Peter van Diermen, eds. 2000. *Indonesia in Transition: Social Aspects of Reformasi and Crisis*. Singapore: Institute of Southeast Asian Studies.

Manuhutu, Wim. 2000a. 'Een Jaar Geweld op de Molukken: Een Terugblik'. In *Maluku Manis, Maluku Menangis: De Molukken in Crisis: Een Poging tot de Verklaring van de Geweldsexplosie op de Molukken*, ed. Wim Manuhutu, Johan Meuleman, Nico Schulte Nordholt and Jacques Willemse, pp. 7–18. Utrecht, the Netherlands: Moluks Historisch Museum/Moluccan Information and Documentation Center.

——. 2000b. 'Molukkers in Nederland en het Geweld op Ambon'. *Allerwegen* 31, no. 37:37–42.

Manuhutu, Wim, Johan Meuleman, Nico Schulte Nordholt and Jacques Willemse, eds. 2000. *Maluku Manis, Maluku Menangis: De Molukken in Crisis: Een Poging tot de Verklaring van de Geweldsexplosie op de Molukken*. Utrecht, the Netherlands: Moluks Historisch Museum/Moluccan Information and Documentation Center.

Manuhutu, Wim, and Henk Smeets, eds. 1991. *Tijdelijk Verblijf. De Opvang van Molukkers in Nederland, 1951*. Amsterdam: De Bataafsche Leeuw.

Manuputty, Alex H. 2001. *Republik yang Hilang* [The lost republic]. Ambon.

Manusama, J. A. 1952. *Om Recht en Vrijheid: De Strijd om de Onafhankelijkheid der Zuid-Molukken*. Utrecht, the Netherlands: Drukkerij Libertas.

——. 1999. *Eigenlijk Moest Ik Niet Veel Hebben van de Politiek: Herinneringen aan Mijn Leven in de Oost 1919–1953*. The Hague: Bintang Design & Communicatie.

Marcus, David L. 1999. 'Indonesia Revolt was Net Driven'. In *The Last Days of President Suharto*, ed. Edward Aspinall, Gerry van Klinken and Herb Feith, 73–75. Clayton, Vic.: Monash Asia Institute.

Marcus, George E. 1994. 'After the Critique of Ethnography: Faith, Hope, and Charity, but the Greatest of These is Charity'. In *Assessing Cultural Anthropology*, ed. Robert Borofsky, pp. 40–54. New York: McGraw-Hill.

Markham, Annette, and Nancy K. Baym, eds. 2008. *Internet Inquiry: Conversations about Methods*. Thousand Oaks, CA: SAGE.

Marmura, Stephen. 2008. 'A Net Advantage? The Internet, Grassroots Activism and American Middle-Eastern Policy'. *New Media Society* 10:247–71.

Marshall, Johnathan. 2001. 'Cyber-Space, or Cyber-Topos: The Creation of Online Space'. 'Computer-Mediated Communication in Australian Anthropology and Sociology', ed. Helen Morton, special issue. *Social Analysis* 45, no. 1:81–102.

———. 2004. 'Governance, Structure and Existence: Authenticity, Rhetoric, Race and Gender on an Internet Mailing List.' Paper presented to the Australian Electronic Governance Conference, Centre for Public Policy, University of Melbourne, Melbourne, Australia, 14–15 April.

———. 2007a. *Living on Cybermind: Categories, Communication, and Control*. New York: Peter Lang.

———. 2007b. 'Book description: Living on Cybermind: Categories, Communication, and Control'. New York: Peter Lang. http://uts.academia.edu/jonmarshall/Books/116350/Living_on_Cybermind_Categories_Communication_and_Control._NY_Peter_Lang (2 February 2011).

———. 2007c. 'The Mobilisation of Race and Gender on an Internet Mailing List, V1.0'. *Transforming Cultures eJournal* 2, no. 2:52–85. http://epress.lib.uts.edu.au/ojs/index.php/TfC/article/view/638/569 (15 August 2010).

Masten, Davis, and Tim M. P. Plowman. 2003. 'Digital Ethnography: The Next Wave in Understanding the Consumer Experience'. *Design Management Journal* 14, no. 2:75–81.

McCaughey, Martha, and Michael D. Ayers, eds. 2003. *Cyberactivism: Online Activism in Theory and Practice*. New York: Routledge.

McCawley, Tom. 2000. 'Reporter's Notebook: In the Middle of a War Zone'. *Asiaweek* 26, no. 2 (21 January). http://www.asiaweek.com/asiaweek/magazine/2000/0121/nat.indon.notebook.html (5 March 2001).

McLaughlin, Margaret L., Kerry K. Osborne and Nicole B. Ellison. 1997. 'Virtual Community in a Telepresence Environment'. In *Virtual Culture: Identity and Communication in Cybersociety*, ed. Steven G. Jones, pp. 145–68. London: SAGE Publications.

McLuhan, Marshall. 1964. *Understanding Media: The Extensions of Man*. New York: Signet.

———. 2001. 'The Medium is the Message'. In *Media and Cultural Studies: KeyWorks*, ed. Meenakshi Gigi Durham and Douglas M. Kellner, pp. 129–38. Oxford: Blackwell Publishers.

Mearns, David. 1996. 'Class, Status and Habitus in Ambon'. In *Remaking Maluku: Social Transformation in Eastern Indonesia*, ed. David Mearns and Chris Healey, pp. 95–105. Darwin, Australia: Northern Territory University.

———. 1999. 'Urban Kampongs in Ambon: Whose Domain? Whose Desa?' *The Australian Journal of Anthropology* 10, no. 1:15–33.

Meikle, Graham. 2002. *Future Active: Media Activism and the Internet*. New York: Routledge.

Mele, Christopher. 1999. 'Cyberspace and Disadvantaged Communities: The Internet as a Tool for Collective Action'. In *Communities in Cyberspace*, ed. Marc A. Smith and Peter Kollock, pp. 290–310. London: Routledge.

Melucci, Alberto. 1995. 'The Process of Collective Identity'. In *Social Movements and Culture*, ed. Hank Johnston and Bert Klandermans, pp. 41–63. Social Movements, Protest, and Contention 4. Minneapolis: University of Minnesota Press.

Messick, Brinkley. 1996. 'Media Muftis: Radio Fatwas in Yemen'. In *Islamic Legal Interpretation: Muftis and Their Fatwas*, ed. Muhammad Khalid Masud, Brinkley Messick and David S. Powers, pp. 310–20. Cambridge, MA: Harvard University Press.

Meuleman, Johan H. 2001. 'From New Order to National Disintegration: The Religious Factor between Reality, Manipulation, and Rationalization'. Third EUROSEAS Conference, London, 6–8 September.

Meyer, Birgit. 2011. 'Mediation and Immediacy: Sensational Forms, Semiotic Ideologies and the Question of the Medium'. 'What Is a Medium? Theologies, Technologies and Aspirations', ed. Patrick Eisenlohr, special issue. *Social Anthropology* 19, no. 1 (February): 23–39.

Meyrowitz, Joshua. 1997. 'Shifting Worlds of Strangers: Medium Theory and Changes in "Them" Versus "Us"'. *Sociological Inquiry* 67, no. 1 (February): 59–71.

———. 1998. 'Das generalisierte Anderswo'. In *Perspektiven der Weltgesellschaft*, ed. Ulrich Beck, pp. 176–91. Frankfurt: Suhrkamp.

Miller, Daniel. 2000. 'The Fame of Trinis: Websites as Traps'. *Journal of Material Culture* 5, no. 1:5–24.

Miller, Daniel, and Don Slater. 2000. *The Internet – An Ethnographic Approach*. Oxford: Berg.

Miller, Hugh. 1995. 'The Presentation of Self in Electronic Life: Goffman on the Internet'. Embodied Knowledge and Virtual Space Conference, Goldsmiths' College, University of London, London, U.K., June. http://www.ntu.ac.uk/soc/psych/miller/goffman.htm (22 August 2001).

Miller, Hugh, and Russell Mather. 1998. 'The Presentation of Self in WWW Home Pages'. IRISS Annual Conference, Bristol, U.K., March. http://www.ntu.ac.uk/soc/psych/miller/millmath.htm (22 August 2001).

Minges, Michael. 2002. 'Kretek Internet: Indonesia Case Study'. *International Telecommunication Union* (March). http://www.itu.int/ITU-D/ict/cs/indonesia/material/IDN%20CS.pdf (28 March 2002).

Mitra, Ananda. 1997. 'Virtual Commonality: Looking for India on the Internet'. In *Virtual Culture: Identity and Communication in Cybersociety*, ed. Steven G. Jones, pp. 55–79. London: SAGE Publications.

Mitra, Ananda, and Elisia Cohen. 1999. 'Analyzing the Web: Directions and Challenges'. In *Doing Internet Research: Critical Issues and Methods for Examining the Net*, ed. Steven G. Jones, pp. 179–202. London: SAGE Publications.

Mizrach, Steve. 1995. 'The CyberAnthropology Page'. http://www.fiu.edu/~mizrachs/CyberAnthropology.html (27 September 2001).

Moeller, Susan D. 1989. *Shooting War: Photography and the American Experience of Combat*. New York: Basic Books.

Mohammad, Herry, Kholis Bahtiar Bakri and Mujib Rahman. 2001. 'Eksekusi Rajam Untuk Penzina di Ambon' [Stoning for adultery in Ambon]. *GATRA*, no. 24 (2 May). http://www.gatra.com/artikel.php?id=5980 (12 May 2001).

Moreau, Ron. 2000. 'An Island Holy War: The Muslim Battle Cry in the Moluccas: "We Can Beat the Christians"'. *Newsweek*, 30 July. http://www.msnbc.com/news/439431.asp (31 July 2000).

Morley, David, and Kevin Robins. 1995. *Spaces of Identity: Global Media, Electronic Landscapes and Cultural Boundaries*. London: Routledge.

Morozov, Evgeny. 2011a. 'The Dark Side of Internet for Egyptian and Tunisian Protesters'. *Globe and Mail*, 28 January. http://www.theglobeandmail.com/news/world/africa-mideast/the-dark-side-of-internet-for-egyptian-and-tunisian-protesters/article1887170/print/ (27 June 2011).

———. 2011b. 'Internet Alone Cannot Free the Middle East'. *Financial Times*, 27 March. http://www.ft.com/cms/s/0/6f6f0c3c-58bc-11e0-9b8a-00144feab49a.html (27 June 2011).

———. 2011c. *The Net Delusion: The Dark Side of Internet Freedom*. New York: PublicAffairs.

Morton, Helen. 1999. 'Islanders in Space: Tongans Online'. In *Small Worlds, Global Lives: Islands and Migrations*, ed. Russell King and John Connell, pp. 235–53. London: Pinter.

———, ed. 2001a. 'Computer-Mediated Communication in Australian Anthropology and Sociology'. Special issue. *Social Analysis* 45, no. 1.

———. 2001b. 'I is for Identity: What's in a Name?' 'Computer-Mediated Communication in Australian Anthropology and Sociology', ed. Helen Morton, special issue. *Social Analysis* 45, no. 1:67–80.

———. 2001c. 'Introduction'. 'Computer-Mediated Communication in Australian Anthropology and Sociology', ed. Helen Morton, special issue. *Social Analysis* 45, no. 1:3–11.

Murphy, Emma C. 2011. 'The Arab State and (Absent) Civility in New Communicative Spaces'. *Third World Quarterly* 32, no. 5:959–80.

Nanere, Jan. 2000. *Kerusuhan Maluku: Halmahera Berdarah* [Moluccan unrest: Bloody Halmahera]. Ambon: BIMASPELA (Yayasan Bina Masyarakat Sejahtera dan Pelestarian Alam).

Nelson, Diane M. 1996. 'Maya Hackers and the Cyberspatialized Nation-State: Modernity, Ethnostalgia, and a Lizard Queen in Guatemala'. *Cultural Anthropology* 11, no. 3:287–308.

Nguyen, Dan Thu, and Jon Alexander. 1996. 'The Coming of Cyberspacetime and the End of the Polity'. In *Cultures of Internet: Virtual Spaces, Real Histories, Living Bodies,* ed. Rob Shields, pp. 99–124. London: SAGE Publications.

Nip, Joyce Y. M. 2002. 'The Queer Sisters and Its Electronic Bulletin Board: A Study of the Internet for Social Movement Mobilization'. AoIR International Conference on Internet Research 3.0, Maastricht, the Netherlands, 13–16 October.

Nirahua, Daniel. 2003. 'No More Shame to Drive Becak'. *Maluku Media Centre*, 5 August. http://www.malukumediacentre.net/web/index.php?fuseaction=news.view&newsid=080820031327201&type=1&lang=EN (10 August 2003).

Norris, Pippa. 2000a. 'Information Poverty in the Emerging Internet Age'. In *Digital Divide*, ed. Pippa Norris, chap. 1. Cambridge, MA: Harvard University. http://www.ksg.harvard.edu/iip/governance/digitalch1.pdf (20 August 2001).

———. 2000b. 'The Worldwide Digital Divide: Information Poverty, the Internet and Development'. Annual Meeting of the Political Studies Association of the U.K., London School of Economics and Political Science, 10–13 April. http://www.ksg.harvard.edu/iip/governance/psa2000dig.pdf (20 August 2001). Cambridge, MA: Harvard University.

Olalquiaga, Celeste. 2001. 'Prologue from Megalopolis'. In *Media and Cultural Studies: KeyWorks,* ed. Meenakshi Gigi Durham and Douglas M. Kellner, pp. 588–97. Oxford: Blackwell Publishers.

Onggo, Bob Julius. 2001. 'Terorisme, Siberterorisme, Bioterorisme, dan Ekoterorisme' [Terrorism, cyberterrorism, bioterrorism and ecoterrorism]. *Kompas,* 24 September. http://www.kompas.com (24 September 2001).

Orywal, Erwin. 1996. 'Krieg als Konfliktaustragungsstrategie – Zur Plausibilität von Kriegsursachentheorien aus kognitionsethnologischer Sicht'. *Zeitschrift für Ethnologie* 121, no. 1:1–48.

Paccagnella, Luciano. 1997. 'Getting the Seats of Your Pants Dirty: Strategies for Ethnographic Research on Virtual Communities'. *Journal of Computer-Mediated Communication* 3, no. 1. http://www.ascusc.org/jcmc/vol3/issue1/paccagnella.html (19 May 2002).

Palmer, Blair. 2004. 'Memories of Migration: Butonese Migrants Returning to Buton after the Maluku Conflicts 1999–2002'. *Antropologi Indonesia* Special Volume: 87–99. http://www.jai.or.id/jurnal/2004/sv/08bp_sv04.pdf (28 January 2006).

Pannell, Sandra, ed. 2003. *A State of Emergency: Violence, Society and the State in Eastern Indonesia.* Darwin, Australia: Northern Territory University Press.

Parker, Karen. 1996. 'Republik Maluku: The Case of Self-Determination'. United Nations Commission on Human Rights, Geneva, March. http://www.indopubs.com/darchives/0214.html (7 January 2001).

Pattiselanno, J. Th. F. 1999. 'Tradisi Uli, Pela dan Gandong pada Masyarakat Seram, Ambon dan Uliase' [Uli-, Pela- and Gandong tradition in societies in Seram, Ambon and Uliase]. *Antropologi Indonesia* XXIII, no. 58:58–70.

Patty, E. S. 2000. 'De Gevolgen van de Onlusten voor de Molukse Gemeenschap in Nederland'. *Allerwegen* 31, no. 37:43–48.

Pelly, Usman. 1999. 'Akar Kerusuhan Etnis di Indonesia' [Root of ethnic unrest in Indonesia]. *Antropologi Indonesia* XXIII, no. 58:27–35.

Penonton, Bung. 1977. *De Zuidmolukse Republiek: Schets voor een Beschrijving van de Nieuwste Geschiedenis van het Zuidmolukse Volk.* Amsterdam: Buijten & Schipperheijn.

Peters, Ruud. 1991. 'Djihad Tussen Wettig Gezag en Revolutie, de Heilige Oorlog in de Hedendaagse Islam'. In *Heilige Oorlogen: Een Onderzoek naar Historische en Hedendaagse Vormen van Collectief Religieus Geweld,* ed. Martin Gosman and Hans Bakker, pp. 176–91. Kampen, the Netherlands: Kok Agora.

Pieris, John. 2004. *Tragedi Maluku: Sebuah Krisis Peradaban – Analisis Kritis Aspek Politik, Ekonomi, Sosial-Budaya dan Keamanan.* Jakarta: Yayasan Obor Indonesia.

Piliang, Yasraf Amir. 2000. '"Public Sphere" dan "Cyber-democracy": Media Internet Sebagai Kekuatan Alternatif' ['Public sphere' and 'cyberdemocracy': The medium of the Internet as an alternative force]. *Demokrasi & HAM* 1, no. 2 (September–November): 101–23.

Pollmann, Tessel, and Juan Seleky. 1979. *Istori-Istori Maluku: Het Verhaal van de Molukkers.* Amsterdam: Uitgeverij De Arbeiderspers.

Polly, Jean Armour. 1998. 'Standing Stones in Cyberspace: The Oneida Indian Nation's Territory on the Web'. 'The Internet and Indigenous Groups', ed. Steve Cisler, special issue, *Cultural Survival Quarterly* 4, no. 21. http://www. cs.org/publications/CSQ/csqinternet.html#Polly (3 July 2002).

Ponpes Ihya'us Sunnah. 1995–99. *SALAFY (Upaya Meniti Jejak Generasi Salafus Shalih)* [Endeavour to follow the devout path of the time of Mohammed]. Various editions.

Porter, David. 1997. 'Introduction'. In *Internet Culture*, ed. David Porter, pp. xi–xviii. New York: Routledge.

Poster, Mark. 1997. 'Cyberdemocracy: Internet and the Public Sphere'. In *Internet Culture*, ed. David Porter, pp. 201–17. New York: Routledge.

———. 1998. 'Virtual Ethnicity: Tribal Identity in an Age of Global Communication'. In *Cybersociety 2.0: Revisiting Computer-Mediated Communication and Community*, ed. Steven G. Jones, pp. 184–211. London: SAGE Publications.

———. 2001. 'Postmodern Virtualities'. In *Media and Cultural Studies: Key-Works*, ed. Meenakshi Gigi Durham and Douglas M. Kellner, pp. 611–25. Oxford: Blackwell Publishers.

Postill, John. 2008. 'Localizing the Internet beyond Communities and Networks'. *New Media & Society* 10, no. 3:413–31.

Press Freedom Alert. 2000. 'Journalists Receive Death Threats in the Moluccas'. http://www.rsf.fr (30 June 2000).

Progress and Freedom Foundation. 1994. 'Cyberspace and the American Dream: A Magna Charta for the Knowledge Age'. 22 August. http://www.hartford-hwp.com/archives/45/062.html (11 September 2001).

Putuhena, M. Husni. 1999. *Buku Putih: Tragedi Kemanusiaan dalam Kerusuhan di Maluku* [Whitebook: Humanitarian tragedy in the Moluccan unrests]. Ambon: Lembaga Eksistensi Muslim Maluku (LEMM).

———. 2001. *Mengungkap Misteri Konflik di Maluku* [Revealing the secret of the Moluccan conflict]. Ambon: Pengurus Besar Front Pembela Islam Maluku.

Putuhena, M. Husni, and M. Nour Tawainella. 2001. *Perang untuk Damai di Maluku* [War for peace in the Moluccas]. Ambon: Pengurus Besar Front Pembela Islam Maluku.

Qodari, Muhammad. 2000. 'Minim Pemberitaan versi Kristen' [Hardly any reports from the Christian perspective]. *Pantau* 9:3–12.

Rachmat, Agus W. 2001. 'Interreligious Conflict and Reconciliation in Indonesia'. March. http://www.paxchristi.nl/indointerreligious.html (20 March 2001).

Rafaeli, Sheizaf, and Robert J. LaRose. 1993. 'Electronic Bulletin Boards and "Public Goods" Explanation of Collaborative Mass Media'. *Communication Research* 20, no. 2:277–97.

Rahmanto, Wahid, and Lutfi Yusniar, 2001. 'Ja'far Umar Thalib: Pelopor Jihad ke Ambon' [Ja'far Umar Thalib: Jihad vanguard to Ambon]. *Forum Keadilan* 7 (20 May): 34–37.

Ramage, Douglas E. 1995. *Politics in Indonesia: Democracy, Islam and the Ideology of Tolerance.* London: Routledge.

Ramírez-Ollé, Meritxell. 2010. 'Un clic per arribar a Déu: Un estudi bibliogràfic de l'ús religiós d'internet'. http://digithum.uoc.edu/ojs/index.php/digithum/article/view/n12-ramirez (26 January 2011).

Ramsay, Gilbert. 2008. 'Conceptualising Online Terrorism'. *Perspectives on Terrorism* 2, no. 7. http://www.terrorismanalysts.com/pt/index.php/pot/article/view/41/html (27 June 2011).

Rasjidi, Muhammad. 1976. 'The Role of Christian Missions – The Indonesian Experience'. *International Review of Mission* 65, no. 257 (January): 427–38.

Rauch, Herbert. 1983. 'Partizipation und Leistung in Großgruppen-Sitzungen'. *Kölner Zeitschrift für Soziologie und Sozialpsychologie* 25 (special issue): 256–74.

Rawnsley, Gary D. 2009. 'The Laws of the Playground: Information Warfare and Propaganda across the Taiwan Strait'. In *Cyber Conflict and Global Politics*, ed. A. Karatzogianni, pp. 79–94. New York: Routledge.

Reid, Elizabeth. 1991. 'Electropolis: Communication and Community on Internet Relay Chat'. M.A. thesis, Department of History, University of Melbourne. http://www.aluluei.com/ (19 June 2002).

Rheingold, Howard. 1993. *The Virtual Community: Homesteading on the Electronic Frontier.* Electronic ed. http://www.rheingold.com/vc/book (22 August 2001).

———. 2000. *The Virtual Community: Homesteading on the Electronic Frontier.* Rev. ed. Cambridge, MA: MIT Press..

Richards, Jason. 2009. 'Denial-of-Service: The Estonian Cyberwar and Its Implications for U.S. National Security'. *International Affairs Review*, 4 April. http://www.iar-gwu.org/node/65 (21 June 2011).

Riedel, Johan Gerard Friedrich. 1886. *De Sluik- en Kroesharige Rassen Tusschen Selebes en Papua.* The Hague: Martinus Nijhoff.

Rinsampessy, Elias. 1992. *Saudara Bersaudara: Molukse Identiteit in Processen van Cultuurverandering.* Assen, the Netherlands: Van Gorcum.

Robbins, James S. 2002. 'The Jihad Online: Mouse Clicking your Way to Martyrdom'. *National Review Online*, 30 July. http://www.nationalreview.com/robbins/robbins073002.asp (29 October 2002).

Robertson, Roland. 1998. 'Glokalisierung: Homogenität und Heterogenität in Raum und Zeit'. In *Perspektiven der Weltgesellschaft*, ed. Ulrich Beck, 192–220. Frankfurt: Suhrkamp.

Robinson, Andrew. 2008. 'Review 1: Athina Karatzogianni, "The Politics of Cyberconflict". New York: Routledge, 2006'. *Resource Center for Cyberculture Studies – Book Reviews.* http://rccs.usfca.edu/bookinfo.asp?BookID=385&ReviewID=531 (5 October 2010).

Rogers, Everett M., and Sheena Malhotra. 2000. 'Computers as Communication: The Rise of Digital Democracy'. In *Digital Democracy*, ed. Kenneth L. Hacker and Jan van Dijk, pp. 10–29. London: SAGE Publications.

Rosaldo, Renato. 1989. *Culture and Truth: The Remaking of Social Analysis.* Boston: Beacon Press.

Rubio, Steven. 1996. 'Home Page'. *Bad Subjects* 24. http://eserver.org/bs/24/rubio.html (10 June 2002).

Rutledge, Paul. 1985. *The Role of Religion in Ethnic Self-Identity.* New York: University Press of America.

Sala Waku Foundation. 1999. 'An Overview of the Conflict in Maluku and the Processes Needed for Its Solution'. Ambon. http://www.geocities.com/ alifuru67/1999/salawaku0712a.htm (16 December 2000).

Salampessy, Zairin, and Thamrin Husain, eds. 2001. *Ketika Semerbak Cengkih Tergusur Asap Mesiu: Tragedi Kemanusiaan Maluku di Balik Konspirasi Militer, Kapitalis Birokrat, dan Kepentingan Elit Politik* [When the scent of cloves was blown away by gunpowder: Humanitarian tragedy in the Moluccas behind a conspiracy by the military, bureauractic capitalists and the interests of the political elite]. Jakarta: TAPAK Ambon.

Sandbothe, Mike. 1996. 'Interactivity – Hypertextuality – Transversality. A Media-Philosophical Analysis of the Internet'. http://www.uni-jena.de/ms/ tele/e_top.html (22 August 2001).

Sassi, Sinikka. 2000. 'The Controversies of the Internet and the Revitalization of Local Political Life'. In *Digital Democracy*, ed. Kenneth L. Hacker and Jan van Dijk, pp. 90–104. London: SAGE Publications.

Schiller, Anne. 1997. 'Religion and Identity in Central Kalimantan: The Case of the Ngaju Dayaks'. In *Indigenous Peoples and the State: Politics, Land, and Ethnicity in the Malayan Peninsula and Borneo*, ed. Robert L. Winzeler, pp. 180–200. Southeast Asia Studies 46. New Haven, CT: Yale University Press.

Schlee, Günther. 2002. 'Introduction. Approaches to "Identity" and "Hatred": Some Somali and Other Perspectives'. In *Imagined Differences: Hatred and the Construction of Identity*, ed. Günther Schlee, pp. 3–32. Hamburg: LIT.

Schlee, Günther, and Karin Werner. 1996. 'Inklusion und Exklusion: Die Dynamik von Grenzziehungen im Spannungsfeld von Markt, Staat und Ethnizität'. In *Inklusion und Exklusion: Die Dynamik von Grenzziehungen im Spannungsfeld von Markt, Staat und Ethnizität*, ed. Günther Schlee and Karin Werner, pp. 9–36. Cologne: Koppe.

Schlesinger, Philip. 1980. 'Between Sociology and Journalism'. In *The Sociology of Journalism and the Press*, ed. Harry Christian, 241–370. Sociological Review Monograph 29. Keele, UK: University of Keele.

Schreurs, P. G. H. 1992. *Terug in het Erfgoed van Franciscus Xaverius: Het Herstel van de Katholieke Missie in Maluku, 1886–1960*. Tilburg, the Netherlands: Uitgave Missiehuis MSC.

Schuhmann, Olaf. 1981. 'Herausforderung der Kirchen durch den Islam: Beispiel Indonesien'. *Ökumenische Rundschau* 30:55–70.

Schulte Nordholt, Nico. 2000a. 'De Molukken als Oefenterrein van een Jakartaans Machtsspel'. *Allerwegen* 31, no. 37:24–36.

———. 2000b. 'De Molukken als Oefenterrein voor de Machtsstrijd in Jakarta'. In *Maluku Manis, Maluku Menangis: De Molukken in Crisis: Een Poging tot de Verklaring van de Geweldsexplosie op de Molukken*, ed. Wim Manuhutu, Johan Meuleman, Nico Schulte Nordholt and Jacques Willemse, pp. 33–44. Utrecht, the Netherlands: Moluks Historisch Museum/Moluccan Information and Documentation Center.

Schulze, Kirsten E. 2002. 'Laskar Jihad and the Conflict in Ambon'. *Brown Journal of World Affairs* 9, no. 1:57–69.

Schwara, Stefan A. 1999. 'Ethnologie im Zeichen von Globalisierung und Cyberspace'. *Mitteilungen der Anthropologischen Gesellschaft in Wien* 129:259–73.

Schwarz, Adam. 1999. *A Nation in Waiting: Indonesia's Search for Stability*. St Leonards, Australia: Allen & Unwin.

Schwarz, Adam, and Jonathan Paris, eds. 1999. *The Politics of Post-Suharto Indonesia.* New York: Council on Foreign Relations Press.

Schwimmer, Brian. 1996. 'Anthropology on the Internet: A Review and Evaluation of Networked Resources'. *Current Anthropology* 37, no. 3 (June): 561–68.

Seaton, Jean. 1999. 'The New "Ethnic" Wars and the Media'. In *The Media of Conflict: War Reporting and Representations of Ethnic Violence,* ed. Tim Allen and Jean Seaton, pp. 43–63. London: Zed Books.

Sen, Krishna, and David T. Hill. 2000. *Media, Culture and Politics in Indonesia.* Oxford: Oxford University Press.

Shaw, Martin. 1998. 'Die Repräsentation ferner Konflikte und die globale Zivilgesellschaft'. In *Perspektiven der Weltgesellschaft,* ed. Ulrich Beck, pp. 221–55. Frankfurt: Suhrkamp.

Shenk, David. 1997. *Data Smog: Surviving the Information Glut.* New York: HarperEdge.

Shields, Rob. 1996. 'Introduction: Virtual Spaces, Real Histories, Living Bodies'. In *Cultures of Internet: Virtual Spaces, Real Histories, Living Bodies,* ed. Rob Shields, pp. 1–10. London: SAGE Publications.

Sidel, John T. 2008. 'The Manifold Meanings of Displacement: Explaining Inter-religious Violence in Indonesia, 1999–2001'. In *Conflict, Violence, and Displacement in Indonesia,* ed. E.-L. E. Hedman. Studies on Southeast Asia 45, pp. 29–59. Ithaca, NY: Cornell.

Sihbudi, Riza, Awani Irewati, Ikrar Nusa Bhakti, Moch. Nurhasim, Syamsuddin Haris, and Tri Ratnawati. 2001. *Bara Dalam Sekam: Identifikasi Akar Masalah dan Solusi atas Konflik-Konflik Lokal di Aceh, Maluku, Papua, dan Riau* [Latent Danger: Identifying the Roots of Problems and Solutions for the Local Conflicts in Aceh, Maluku, Papua and Riau]. Jakarta: Mizan.

Sinansari Ecip, S. 1999. *Menyulut Ambon: Kronologi Merambatnya Berbagai Kerusuhan Lintas Wilayah di Indonesia* [Ambon Ablaze: Chronology of the Spread of Some Flashpoints in Indonesia]. Bandung, Indonesia: Mizan.

Singh, R. R. P. 1990. *Hindu-Muslim Relations in Contemporary India.* New Delhi: Wisdom Publ.

Slevin, James. 2000. *The Internet and Society.* Cambridge: Polity Press.

Smeets, Henk. 1977. *Lunetten, Kroniek van een Failliet Beleid.* Vught, Netherlands: Lunetten-Stichting/Stichting Derhalve.

———. 1992. *Moluccans in the Netherlands.* Utrecht, the Netherlands: Moluks Historisch Museum.

———. 1996. *Molukkers in Vught.* Vught, Netherlands: Boekhandel Brabant.

———. 2000. 'Machteloos, Ver Weg, Maar Niet Wanhopig'. In *De Molukken in Crisis,* ed. Victor Joseph, Wim Manuhutu and Henk Smeets, pp. 18–21. Lelystad, the Netherlands: Actuele Onderwerpen.

———. 2001. *Een Kwestie van Organisatie: Organisatie van het Molukkersbeleid en Molukse Zelforganisatie.* Utrecht, the Netherlands: Moluks Historisch Museum.

Smith, Anthony. 1978. *The Politics of Information: Problems of Policy in Modern Media.* London: Macmillan.

Smith, Anthony D. 1998. *Nationalism and Modernism: A Critical Survey of Recent Theories of Nations and Nationalism.* London: Routledge.

Sobchack, Vivian. 1993. 'New Age Mutant Ninja Hackers: Reading Mondo 2000'. *South Atlantic Quarterly* 92, no. 4 (Fall): 569–84.

Soekanto, Winahyo. 2002. 'Fighting Cyber Crimes'. *The Jakarta Post,* 21 June.

Sofos, Spyros A. 1999. 'Culture, Media and the Politics of Disintegration and Ethnic Division in Former Yugoslavia'. In *The Media of Conflict: War Reporting and Representations of Ethnic Violence,* ed. Tim Allen and Jean Seaton, pp. 162–74. London: Zed Books.

Sofsky, Wolfgang. 1996. *Traktat über die Gewalt.* Frankfurt: S. Fischer.

Sondheim, Alan. 2009. 'Review 1: Jonathan Paul Marshall, "Living on Cybermind: Categories, Communications, and Control". New York: Peter Lang, 2007'. *Resource Center for Cyberculture Studies – Book Reviews.* http://rccs. usfca.edu/bookinfo.asp?reviewID=568&BookID=410 (2 February 2011).

Southeast Asian Press Alliance. 2002. 'Fiery Reporters: Ambon and Aceh Special'. *ALERT Magazine* 3, no. 1 (January).

Spangenberg, Peter Michael. 2001. 'Elektronisches Sehen – Das Beispiel des Fernsehens: Über die technische, gesellschaftliche und psychische Organisation der Sichtbarkeit'. In *Schnittstelle: Medien und Kulturwissenschaft,* ed. Georg Stanitzek and Wilhelm Vosskamp, pp. 207–22. Cologne: DuMont.

Sproull, Lee, and Sara Kiesler. 1986. 'Reducing Social Context Cues: Electronic Mail in Organizational Communication'. *Management Science* 32, no. 11 (November): 1492–512.

Spyer, Patricia. 2002. 'Fire without Smoke and Other Phantoms of Ambon's Violence: Media Effects, Agency, and the Work of Imagination'. *Indonesia* 74 (October): 21–36.

Sreberny, Annabelle. 2011. 'A Social Media Evolution?' *OECD Insights Blog.* http://oecdinsights.org/2011/03/28/a-social-media-revolution/ (12 May 2011).

Stegbauer, Christian. 2000. 'Die Rolle der Lurker in Mailinglisten'. In *Globalisierung und Wissensorganisation: Neue Aspekte für Wissen, Wissenschaft und Informationssysteme,* ed. H. Peter Ohly, Gerhard Rahmstorf and Alexander Sigel, pp. 119–29. Würzburg, Germany: Ergon Verlag.

———. 2001. *Grenzen virtueller Gemeinschaft: Strukturen internetbasierter Kommunikationsforen.* Wiesbaden, Germany: Westdeutscher Verlag.

Steijlen, Fridus. 1991. 'An Unexplored History: Nationalism Among Moluccans in the Netherlands, 1951–1990'. *Cakalele* 2, no. 1:25–42.

———. 1996. *RMS: van Ideaal tot Symbool: Moluks Nationalisme in Nederland, 1951–1994.* Amsterdam: Het Spinhuis.

———. 2001. Door een Digitale Zenuwbaan Verbonden: Molukkers, de *Kerusuhan* op de Molukken en Vaste Denkschema's. Unpublished manuscript.

Stein, Laura. 2009. 'Social Movement Web Use in Theory and Practice: A Content Analysis of US Movement Websites'. *New Media & Society* 11, no. 5:749–71.

Strijbosch, Fons. 1985. 'The Concept of Pela and Its Social Significance in the Community of Moluccan Immigrants in the Netherlands'. *Journal of Legal Pluralism and Unofficial Law* 23:177–208.

———. 1988. 'Informal Social Security among Moluccan Immigrants in the Netherlands'. In *Between Kinship and the State: Social Security and Law in Developing Countries,* ed. F. von Benda-Beckmann, K. von Benda-Beckmann, E. Casino, F. Hirtz, G. R. Woodman and H. F. Zacher, pp. 169–85. Dordrecht, the Netherlands: Foris Publications.

———. 1992. 'Self-redress and Feud among Moluccans in the Netherlands'. *Journal of Legal Pluralism and Unofficial Law* 32:47–64.

Sumargono, Ahmad. 2000. 'I Am A Fundamentalist – An Ideological Reflection on the Challenges Facing the Muslims of Indonesia'. http://www.kisdi.com/ Kajian/Fundamentalis.htm (18 December 2000).

Syafruddin, Ayip, and Eko Prasetyo. 2001. *Tragedi Kebun Cengkeh: Fakta Pembantaian Paramedis, Pasien & Warga Sipil Ambon* [The Kebun-Cengkeh tragedy: Facts on the bloodbath among medical auxiliaries, patients and civilians in Ambon]. Jakarta: Jihad Press.

Tahalele, Paul. 1998. 'The Church and Human Rights in Indonesia'. *Indonesia Christian Communication Forum*, 30 September. http://www.fica.org/hr/ ChurchPersecution/nov516.pdf (17 February 2001).

Tambiah, Stanley J. 1989. 'Ethnic Conflict in the World Today'. *American Ethnologist* 16, nos. 1–2:335–49.

———. 1996. *Leveling Crowds: Ethnonationalist Conflicts and Collective Violence in South Asia*. Berkeley: University of California Press.

TAPOL (The Indonesia Human Rights Campaign). 1999. 'Huge Death Toll in Maluku Riots'. *Tapol Bulletin Online* 151 (March). http://www.gn.apc. org/tapol/151nHuge.htm (17 February 2001).

Tateo, Luca. 2009. 'Review 1: Annette N. Markham & Nancy K. Baym, "Internet Inquiry: Conversations about Methods". Thousand Oaks, CA: SAGE. 2008'. *Resource Center for Cyberculture Studies – Book Reviews.* http://rccs.usfca.edu/bookinfo.asp?BookID=425&ReviewID=604 (5 October 2010).

Taylor, Paul Michael. 2001. 'Underlying Sources of a Complex, Multilayered, Historic Conflict. Testimony on Religious-Freedom Violations in the Moluccas, Indonesia'. U.S. Commission on International Religious Freedom, Washington, D.C., 13 February.

Tepper, Michele. 1997. 'Usenet Communities and the Cultural Politics of Information'. In *Internet Culture,* ed. David Porter, pp. 39–54. New York: Routledge.

Tesoro, Jose Manuel. 1999. 'A Battle Being Fought. Believe It or Not, the Military – Yes, the Military – Is Reforming'. *Asiaweek* 25, no. 40 (8 October).

Thalib, Ja'far Umar. 2000. *Buku Petunjuk dan Latar Belakang Pengirim Laskar Jihad ke Maluku* [Book with references and background to the deployment of the Laskar Jihad to the Moluccas]. Malang, Indonesia: Forum Komunikasi Ahlus Sunnah Wal Jama'ah.

———. 2001. *Laskar Jihad Ahlus Sunnah Wal Jamaah Mempelopori Perlawanan Terhadap Kedurjanaan Hegemoni Salibis-Zionis Internasional di Indonesia* [LJAWJ paves the way for the struggle against the crimes of the international Zionist/Christian hegemony in Indonesia]. Jakarta: Jihad Press.

Thiedeke, Udo. 2000. 'Virtuelle Gruppen: Begriff und Charakteristik'. In *Virtuelle Gruppen,* ed. Udo Thiedeke, pp. 23–73. Wiesbaden, Germany: Westdeutscher Verlag.

Thompson, John B. 1995. *The Media and Modernity: A Social Theory of the Media.* Palo Alto, CA: Stanford University Press.

Thompson, Kevin C. 2001. 'Watching the Stormfront: White Nationalists and the Building of Community in Cyberspace'. 'Computer-Mediated Communication in Australian Anthropology and Sociology', ed. Helen Morton, special issue. *Social Analysis* 45, no. 1:32–52.

Thorburn, Craig C. 2005. *Musibah: Governance, Intercommunal Violence and Reinventing Tradition in the Kei Islands, Southeast Maluku*. Working Paper 125. Victoria, Australia: Monash University Press.

———. 2008. 'Adat Law, Conflict and Reconciliation: The Kei Islands, Southeast Maluku'. In *Indonesia: Law and Society*, ed. T. Lindsey, pp. 115–43. Sydney: Federation Press.

Tim Penyusun Al-Mukmin. 1999. *Tragedi Ambon* [The Ambon tragedy]. Jakarta: Yayasan al-Mukmin.

Tinnemans, Will. 2001. 'Familiemoord op de Molukken: "Dood aan Pongky"'. *Het Volkskrant Magazine* (3 February): 21–28.

Titaley, John A. 2001. 'Religious Freedom in Indonesia: A Loosing Opportunity for Humanity'. U.S. Commission on International Religious Freedom, Washington, D.C., 13 February.

Tomagola, Tamrin Amal. 2000. 'TNI/AD Otak & Dalang di Maluku' [The Indonesian military/army is the head and the puppetmaster in the Moluccas]. *Kathulistiwa Magazine*. http://www.geocities.com/ambon67/noframe/tamal1010y2k.htm (10 October 2000).

———. 2001a. 'Ambon Terbakar' [Burning Ambon]. In *Ketika Semerbak Cengkih Tergusur Asap Mesiu: Tragedi Kemanusiaan Maluku di Balik Konspirasi Militer, Kapitalis Birokrat, dan Kepentingan Elit Politik*, ed. Zairin Salampessy and Thamrin Husain, pp. 18–23. Jakarta: TAPAK Ambon.

———. 2001b. 'Akar Kekerasan Komunal' [The roots of communal violence]. In *Ketika Semerbak Cengkih Tergusur Asap Mesiu: Tragedi Kemanusiaan Maluku di Balik Konspirasi Militer, Kapitalis Birokrat, dan Kepentingan Elit Politik*, ed. Zairin Salampessy and Thamrin Husain, pp. 53–56. Jakarta: TAPAK Ambon.

———. 2001c. 'Halmahera Berdarah' [Bloody Halmahera]. In *Ketika Semerbak Cengkih Tergusur Asap Mesiu: Tragedi Kemanusiaan Maluku di Balik Konspirasi Militer, Kapitalis Birokrat, dan Kepentingan Elit Politik*, ed. Zairin Salampessy and Thamrin Husain, pp. 75–92. Jakarta: TAPAK Ambon.

———. 2001d. 'Maluku: Tiada Hari Tanpa Darurat' [Maluku: No day passes without an incident]. In *Ketika Semerbak Cengkih Tergusur Asap Mesiu: Tragedi Kemanusiaan Maluku di Balik Konspirasi Militer, Kapitalis Birokrat, dan Kepentingan Elit Politik*, ed. Zairin Salampessy and Thamrin Husain, pp. 102–5. Jakarta: TAPAK Ambon.

———. 2001e. 'Selamatkan Ambon' [Save Ambon]. In *Ketika Semerbak Cengkih Tergusur Asap Mesiu: Tragedi Kemanusiaan Maluku di Balik Konspirasi Militer, Kapitalis Birokrat, dan Kepentingan Elit Politik*, ed. Zairin Salampessy and Thamrin Husain, pp. 106–9. Jakarta: TAPAK Ambon.

Tomagola, Tamrin Amal, Cornelis Lay, Lies Marantika, Ricky Palijama, Rosa Pentury and Yusup Madubun. 2008. *Format Ulang Birokrasi Kota Ambon*. Ed. Eddy O.S. Hiariej. Makassar, Indonesia: Ininnawa.

Trijono, Lambang, ed. 2004. *The Making of Ethnic and Religious Conflicts in Southeast Asia: Cases and Resolutions*. Yogyakarta, Indonesia: CSPS Books.

Trotha, Trutz von. 1997. 'Zur Soziologie der Gewalt'. In *Soziologie der Gewalt*, ed. Trutz von Trotha, pp. 9–56. *Kölner Zeitschrift für Soziologie und Sozialpsychologie*, special issue. Opladen, Germany: Westdeutscher Verlag.

Tuasikal, Umar. 2000. Quo Vadis Modus Vivendi Antar Umat Beragama di Ambon [*Quo vadis modus vivendi between the religious communities in Ambon*]. Jakarta: Himpunan Keluarga Muslimin Maluku (HIKMMA).

Turkle, Sherry. 1995. *Life on the Screen: Identity in the Age of the Internet.* New York: Simon & Schuster.

———. 1997. 'Multiple Subjectivity and Virtual Community at the End of the Freudian Century'. *Social Inquiry* 61, no. 1 (February): 72–84.

Turner, Kathleen. 2002. 'Utopian Visions and Kinship Divisions: Ideological Perceptions of Ethnic Conflict in Ambon'. *Harvard Asia Quarterly* 6, no. 3 (Summer). http://www.fas.harvard.edu/~asiactr/haq/200203/turner.pdf (27 December 2002).

———. 2006. *Competing Myths of Nationalist Identity: Ideological Perceptions of Conflict in Ambon, Indonesia.* Unpublished PhD diss., Murdoch University.

Turrini, Elliot, and Sumit Ghosh. 2010. 'A Pragmatic, Experimental Definition of Computer Crimes'. In *Cybercrimes: A Multidisciplinary Analysis,* ed. S. Ghosh and E. Turrini, pp. 3–23. Berlin: Springer.

Uncapher, Willard. 1999. 'Electronic Homesteading on the Rural Frontier: Big Sky Telegraph and Its Community'. In *Communities in Cyberspace,* ed. Marc A. Smith and Peter Kollock, pp. 264–89. London: Routledge.

Valacich, Joseph S., David Paranka, Joey F. George and J. F. Jr. Nunamaker. 1993. 'Communication Concurrency and the New Media'. *Communication Research* 20, no. 2:249–76.

Vatikiotis, Michael. 2002. 'A Tale of Two Madrassas'. *Far Eastern Economic Review,* 27 June. http://www.feer.com/articles/2002/0206_27/p058current.html (24 June 2002).

Vatikiotis, Michael. 2004. *The Spice Garden.* Jakarta: Equinox Publishing.

Veer, Peter van der. 1994. *Religious Nationalism: Hindus and Muslims in India.* Berkeley: University of California Press.

Vermonte, Philips Jusario. 2006. 'Religious Conflicts in Maluku: The Role of Conflict Entrepreneurs'. *Indonesian Quarterly* 34, no. 3:241–54.

Virnoche, Mary E., and Gary T. Marx. 1997. '"Only Connect" – E.M. Forster in an Age of Electronic Communication: Computer-Mediated Association and Community Networks'. *Sociological Inquiry* 67, no. 1 (February): 85–100.

Vries, Hent de, and Samuel Weber, eds. 2001. *Religion and Media.* Palo Alto, CA: Stanford University Press.

Wahyuni, Sri. 2000a. 'Forum Aims to Protect Interests of Islam'. *The Jakarta Post,* 15 May.

———. 2000b. 'Jihad Force Is No One's Political Tool: Commander Ja'far'. *The Jakarta Post,* 15 May.

Waldmann, Peter. 1995. 'Gesellschaften im Bürgerkrieg'. *Zeitschrift für Politik* 42, no. 4:343–82.

Wali, Alaka. 2010. 'Ethnography for the Digital Age: http://www.YouTube/. Digital Ethnography (Michael Wesch)'. *American Anthropologist* 112, no. 1 (March): 147–48.

Walther, Joseph B. 1996. 'Computer-Mediated Communication: Impersonal, Interpersonal, and Hyperpersonal Interaction'. *Communication Research* 23, no. 1 (February): 3–43.

Warf, Barney, and John Grimes. 1997. 'Counterhegemonic Discourses and the Internet'. *Geographical Review* 87, no. 2 (April): 259–74.

Watch Indonesia. 1999. 'Wird Ambon zum Bosnien Indonesiens? Indonesien-Information Nr. 1/1999'. Berlin. http://home.snafu.de/watchin/II_1_99/Ambon.htm (9 October 2000).

Watson, Nessim. 1997. 'Why We Argue About Virtual Community: A Case Study of the Phish.Net Fan Community'. In *Virtual Culture: Identity and Communication in Cybersociety*, ed. Steven G. Jones, pp. 102–32. London: SAGE Publications.

Wattimanela, Daniel. 2003. *Perjumpaan Islam dan Kristen di Maluku Tengah: Suatu Pendekatan Sosiologi Historis.* Unpublished M.A. thesis, Universitas Kristen Satya Wacana.

Watzlawik, Paul, Janet H. Beavin and Don D. Jackson. 1969. *Menschliche Kommunikation: Formen, Störungen, Paradoxien.* Bern, Switzerland: Huber.

Wawer, Wendelin. 1974. *Muslime und Christen in der Republik Indonesia.* Beiträge zur Südostasienforschung 7. Heidelberg, Germany: Südasien-Institut, Universität Heidelberg.

Weber, Max. 1976. *Wirtschaft und Gesellschaft: Grundriß der verstehenden Soziologie.* 5th, rev. ed. Tübingen, Germany: Mohr.

Weimann, Gabriel. 2004. 'www.terror.net: How Modern Terrorism Uses the Internet'. *United States Institute of Peace. Special Report 116.* http://www.usip.org/pubs/specialreports/sr116.pdf (4 August 2004).

Weiss, Christian, Tom Weichert, Evelin Hust and Harald Fischer-Tine, eds. 1996. *Religion-Macht-Gewalt. Religiöser 'Fundamentalismus' und Hindu-Moslem-Konflikte in Südasien.* Frankfurt: IKO – Verlag für Interkulturelle Kommunikation.

Wellman, Barry. 2010. 'Studying the Internet through the Ages'. In *The Handbook of Internet Studies*, ed. R. Burnett, M. Consalvo and C. Ess, pp. 17–23. Malden, MA: Wiley-Blackwell.

——, ed. 1999. *Networks in the Global Village: Life in Contemporary Communities.* Boulder, Colorado: Westview Press.

Wellman, Barry, and Milena Gulia. 1999. 'Virtual Communities as Communities: Net Surfers Don't Ride Alone'. In *Communities in Cyberspace*, ed. Marc A. Smith and Peter Kollock, pp. 167–94. London: Routledge.

Wellman, Barry, and Caroline Haythornthwaite, eds. 2002. *The Internet in Everyday Life.* Oxford: Blackwell Publishers.

Wellman, Barry, and Stephanie Potter. 1999. 'The Elements of Personal Communities'. In *Networks in the Global Village: Life in Contemporary Communities*, ed. Barry Wellman, pp. 49–82. Boulder, Colorado: Westview Press.

Wertheim, Willem Frederik. 1956. *Indonesian Society in Transition: A Study of Social Change.* The Hague: Van Hoeve.

Whittle, David B. 1997. *Cyberspace: The Human Dimension.* New York: W. H. Freeman and Company.

Wilbur, Shawn P. 1997. 'An Archeology of Cyberspaces: Virtuality, Community, Identity'. In *Internet Culture*, ed. David Porter, pp. 5–22. New York: Routledge.

Williamson, Charles A. 2000. 'Perception Management and Conflict Transition: Shaping the Information Environment in Peace, Crisis and Conflict'. In *Cyberwar 3.0: Human Factors in Information Operations and Future Conflict,* ed. Alan D. Campen and Douglas H. Dearth, pp. 177–84. Fairfax, VA: AFCEA International Press.

Wilson, Chris. 2005. 'The Ethnic Origins of Religious Conflict in North Maluku Province, Indonesia, 1999–2000'. *Indonesia* 79 (April): 69–91.

Wilson, Samuel M., and Leighton C. Peterson. 2002. 'The Anthropology of On-line Communities'. *Annual Review of Anthropology* 31:449–67.

Winn, Phillip. 2000. 'Banda Burns'. *Inside Indonesia* 61 (January–March). http://www.insideindonesia.org/edit60/winn1.htm (9 October 2000).

——. 2003. 'Sovereign Violence, Moral Authority and the Maluku Cakalele'. In *A State of Emergency: Violence, Society and the State in Eastern Indonesia*, ed. S. Pannell, pp. 49–76. Darwin, Australia: Northern Territory University Press.

WZB – Projektgruppe Kulturraum Internet. 1996. 'Die Gemeinde des Internet. Organisationsethnologie und Technikgeneseforschung'. *WZB-Mitteilungen* 71 (March): 8–10.

Yanuarti, Sri, Yusuf, Josephine Rosa Marieta and Mardyanto Wahyu Triatmoko. 2003. *Konflik di Maluku Tengah: Penyebab, Karakteristik, dan Penyelesaian Jangka Panjang.* Jakarta: Lembaga Ilmu Pengetahuan Indonesia (LIPI).

Yanuarti, Sri, Yusuf, Josephine Rosa Marieta and Mardyanto Wahyu Tryatmoko. 2004. *Konflik Maluku Utara: Penyebab, Karakteristik, dan Penyelesaian Jangka Panjang.* Jakarta: Puslit. Kemasyarakatan dan Kebudayaan-LIPI.

Yavuz, M. Hakan. 1999. 'Media Identities for Alevis and Kurds in Turkey'. In *New Media in the Muslim World: The Emerging Public Sphere*, ed. Dale F. Eickelman and Jon W. Anderson, pp. 180–200. Bloomington: Indiana University Press.

Zickmund, Susan. 1997. 'Approaching the Radical Other: The Discursive Culture of Cyberhate'. In *Virtual Culture: Identity and Communication in Cybersociety*, ed. Steven G. Jones, pp. 185–205. London: SAGE Publications.

Zurawski, Nils. 2000. *Virtuelle Ethnizität: Studien zu Identität, Kultur und Internet.* Soziologie und Anthropologie 11. Frankfurt: Peter Lang Verlag.

——. 2001a. 'Book of the Month: Christine Hine, *Virtual Ethnography.* London, Thousand Oaks & New Delhi: SAGE Publications, 2000 (Review)'. *Resource Center for Cyberculture Studies.* http://www.com.washington.edu/rccs/books/hine/hine2.html (28 May 2002).

——. 2001b. '"Virtual Ethnography" (2000) reviewed – Review 2'. *Resource Center for Cyberculture Studies – Book Reviews,* June. http://www.com.washington.edu/rccs/bookinfo.asp?ReviewID=126&BookID=109 (29 October 2002).

Below is a list of online newspapers, magazines and news services consulted; it only includes those from which articles were taken that were not linked/provided by one of the mailing lists or websites studied.

Asia Times Online	http://www.atimes.com
BBC	http://www.bbc.co.uk
Detikcom	http://www.detik.com
Far Eastern Economic Review	http://www.feer.com
Gatra	http://www.gatra.com

Inside Indonesia	http://www.insideindonesia.org
Kompas	http://www.kompas.co.id
Koridor	http://www.koridorNews.com
Manado Pos	http://www.mdopost.net
Media Indonesia Ondine	http://www.mediaindo.co.id
New York Times	http://www.nytimes.com
Newsweek	http://www.newsweek.com or
	http://www.msnbc.com/news/NW-front_Front.asp
Republika	http://www.republika.co.id
Satunet	http://www.satunet.com
SiaR News Service	siar@minihub.org
South China Morning Post	http://www.scmp.com
Tempo Interaktif	http://www.tempo.co.id or
	http://www.tempointeraktif.com
The Australian	http://www.theaustralian.news.com.au
The Jakarta Post	http://www.thejakartapost.com
The Straights Times	http://straitstimes.asia1.com
The Washington Times	http://washingtontimes.com

Index